Walking in
ITALY

Sandra Bardwell
Stefano Cavedoni
Emily Coles
Helen Fairbairn
Gareth McCormack
Nick Tapp

D1042782

LONELY PLANET PUBLICATIONS
Melbourne • Oakland • London • Paris

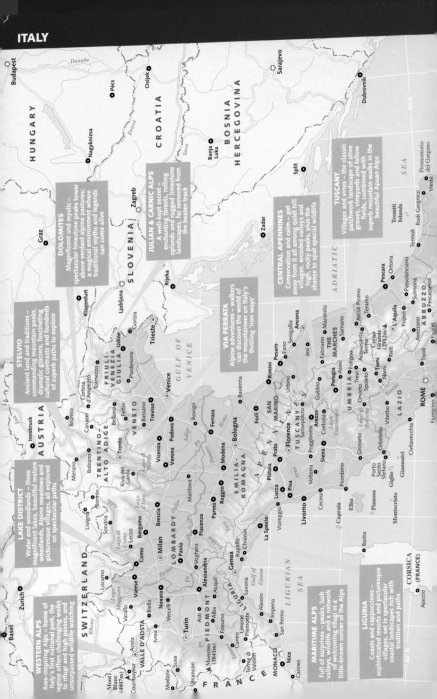

ITALY

SICILY

Intoxicating isles – active volcanoes,
quiet hideaways, remote retreats and remote
islands; drink in the stunning scenery
and explore seldom walked paths

CAMPANIA

Crater to coast – explore Italy's
most famous volcano, breathtaking
paths beneath white limestone
cliffs, colourful citrus groves and
timeless villages perched high
above the blue Mediterranean

SARDINIA

Remote and rugged – isolated
sandy coves, undisturbed
Mediterranean coastline and flora,
and some of the most remote
mountainous areas in Italy

ELEVATION

3000m
2000m
1000m
500m
0

IONIAN
SEA

TYRRHENIAN
SEA

MEDITERRANEAN SEA

GULF OF
TARANTO

AEOLIAN ISLANDS
Filicudi Salina Panarea
Alicudi Lipari
Volcano

EGADI ISLANDS
Levanzo
Marettimo
Favignana Marsala
Mazara
del Vallo

PELAGIE
ISLANDS
Linosa

TUNISIA

ALGERIA

Annaba
Banzart
Tunis
Sousse

Lecce
Otranto
Brindisi
Gallipoli
Taranto
Alberobello
Bari
Barletta
Molfetta
Trani
Altamura
Matera
Lido di
Metaponto
Spinazzola
Melfi
Troia
Benevento
Avellino
Caserta
Naples
Sorrento Amalfi
Ischia Capri
Salerno
Agropoli
Pisciotta
Maratea
Castrovillari
Rossano
Crotone
Cosenza
Catanzaro
Capo Rizzuto
Paola
Locri
Reggio di
Calabria
Tropea
Messina
Taormina
Palmi
Catania
Adrano
Mt Etna
(3350m)
Siracusa
Noto
Leonforte
Enna
Caltagirone
Ragusa
Modica
Comiso
Gela
Licata
Agrigento
Sciacca
Castelvetrano
Caltanissetta
Cefalù
Corleone
Palermo
Trapani
Valletta
MALTA
Pantelleria

PUGLIA
BASILICATA
CAMPANIA
CALABRIA
SICILY
LAZIO

Gaeta
Gulf of
Gaeta
Terracina
Anzio
Ponza
Ventotene
Palmarola

Gulf of
Salerno

Gulf of
Squillace

Mt Vesuvius
(1277m)

SARDINIA
Maddalena
Caprera
Palau
Arzachena
Goffo
Aranci
Olbia
Siniscola
Porto
Torres
Asinara
Sassari
Ozieri
Oschiri
Nuoro
Dorgali
Arbatax
Alghero
Bosa
Macomèr
Oristano
Abbus
Iglesias
Buggerru
Carbonia
Sant'Antioco
San Pietro
Pula
Teulada
Villasimius
Muravera
Sanluri
Cagliari
Lago
Omodeo

0   40   80km
0   20   40mi
1:4,500,000

Walking in Italy
2nd edition – January 2003
First published – June 1998

Published by
Lonely Planet Publications Pty Ltd ABN 36 005 607 983
90 Maribyrnong St, Footscray, Victoria 3011, Australia

Lonely Planet offices
Australia Locked Bag 1, Footscray, Victoria 3011
USA 150 Linden St, Oakland, CA 94607
UK 10a Spring Place, London NW5 3BH
France 1 rue du Dahomey, 75011 Paris

Photographs
All of the images in this guide are available for licensing from
Lonely Planet Images.
w www.lonelyplanetimages.com

Main front cover photograph
Lago Rosset near Rifugio Savoia in Parco Nazionale del Gran Paradiso,
the heart of the Western Alps and the oldest national park in Italy
(Sandra Bardwell)

Small front cover photograph
Foce di Giovo, the main weakness in the Cresta Garnerone ridge
connecting Pizzo d'Uccello with Monte Grondìlice, Apuan Alps
(Damien Simonis)

ISBN 1740592441

Printed by Craft Print International Ltd, Singapore

Contents

TRAVEL FACTS

LANGUAGE

GLOSSARY

INDEX

METRIC CONVERSION

The Walks *continued*	Duration	Difficulty	Best Time
Julian & Carnic Alps			
Fusine-Mangart Loop	3–4 hours	moderate	June–Sept
Slovenian Two-Step	4–5½ hours	moderate	June–Sept
Jôf Fuart	2 days	moderate	June–Sept
Monte Carnizza	3–4 hours	moderate	June–Sept
Monte Osternig	3–3½ hours	easy–moderate	June–Sept
Tuscany			
Chianti Classico	3 days	easy	April–Oct
Medieval Hills	3 days	easy	April–Oct
Pizzo d'Uccello	3 days	moderate	June–Sept
Procinto, Forato & Pania della Croce	2 days	moderate	June–Sept
Central Apennines			
La Gola dell'Infernaccio	3 hours	easy	May–Oct
Sibillini Traverse	4½–6 hours	moderate–demanding	June–Oct
Monte Vettore	4–4½ hours	moderate–demanding	June–Oct
Cascata del Volpara	3½–4½ hours	moderate	June–Oct
Corno Grande	5–6 hours	moderate–demanding	June–Oct
Monte Acquaviva	5½–6½ hours	moderate	June–Oct
Rocca Ridge	6–7 hours	moderate	June–Oct
Campania			
Vesuvius & Valle del Gigante	3½ hours	easy–moderate	Sept–June
Vesuvius' Crater	2 hours	easy–moderate	Sept–June
Sentiero degli Dei	5½–6 hours	moderate	Sept–May
Capo Muro	6½–7 hours	demanding	Sept–May
Valle delle Ferriere	4½–5 hours	moderate	Sept–May
Punta Penna	3–3½ hours	easy–moderate	Sept–May
Punta Campanella	4–4½ hours	moderate	Sept–May
Sicily			
Mt Etna Circuit	3 days	easy–moderate	Apr–Oct
Vulcano's Gran Cratere	2½–3 hours	easy	Apr–Oct
Nebrodi Lake Circuit	4–4½ hours	easy–moderate	Apr–Oct
Sardinia			
Tiscali-Gorropu	3 days	easy	Mar–June
Golfo di Orosei	4 days	moderate	Mar–June

The Maps

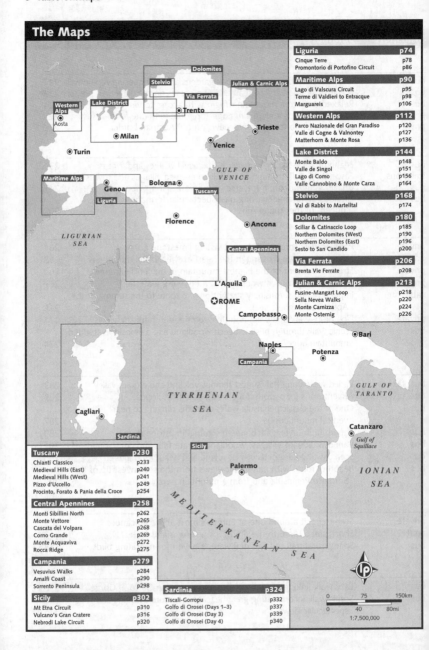

0   75   150km
0   40   80mi
1:7,500,000

The Authors

Sandra Bardwell

After graduating with a thesis on the history of national parks in Victoria (Australia), Sandra worked as an archivist and then as a historian for the National Parks Service. She has been a dedicated walker since joining a bushwalking club in the early 1960s, and became well known through a Melbourne newspaper column and as the author of several guidebooks on the subject. Since 1989 Sandra and her husband Hal have lived in the Highlands of Scotland, in a village near Loch Ness. For several years she worked as a monument warden for Historic Scotland, until Lonely Planet took over her life. She has walked extensively in Australia and Britain, and for Lonely Planet in Ireland, France, Scotland and, even more extensively, in Australia. Now, researching this book, Sandra has rekindled her love affair with Italy's mountains, valleys, coasts and people.

Stefano Cavedoni

For many years Stefano has been many different things contemporaneously. A recent creative collaboration with his old rock band, Skiantos, resulted in a final, definitive CD of new songs, which has already been tagged to become a cult item. A collection of his humoristic poetry was published in November 2001. But the mountains and forests continue to be his passion. He researched and wrote the walks for the Dolomites and Sardinia chapters, as well as the Chianti Classico and Medieval Hills walks in the Tuscany chapter and the Vesuvius walks in the Campania chapter. Stefano has also worked on Lonely Planet's *Italy*, *Mediterranean Europe*, *Western Europe* and *Rome* guides.

Emily Coles

Distantly related to George Mallory, Emily comes from a family of enthusiastic walkers who had her pounding trails and scaling summits before she was old enough to know any better. With a travel bent firmly entrenched after a childhood spent flitting between Australia and Europe, she juggled the long, slow haul towards an arts degree with regular doses of travel – a passion that eventually landed her a job as an editor, then author, for Lonely Planet. Along the way, a long-term commitment to green politics led to a brief stint in a tree platform defending a native Australian old-growth forest and a job scavenging recyclable material from a Canberra tip. Having researched *Walking in Italy* with her daughter, Portia, already more than a twinkle in the eye, Emily's latest challenge has been to scale the heady heights (and sleepless nights) of parenthood.

Helen Fairbairn

Helen is a writer specialising in adventure travel. Born in Suffolk, England, she now resides in Northern Ireland. Several years abroad, an MA in International Development and her current work all feed an ongoing interest in the wider impact of travel. A dedicated outdoor enthusiast, Helen is most at home in wild, mountainous places. This is her fourth walking guide for Lonely Planet.

Gareth McCormack

Gareth is a writer and photographer based in Ireland, and a contributor to several outdoor and adventure travel magazines. He has travelled and climbed extensively in Asia, Australia, New Zealand and North America. Other titles he has coauthored for Lonely Planet include *Walking in Ireland*, *Walking in France*, *Walking in Scotland*, *Walking in Australia* and *Hiking in the Rocky Mountains*.

Nick Tapp

Having first picked up a rucksack while at university, some time last century, Nick was instantly converted. The career in medicine never eventuated but the outdoor habit stuck, and he has since walked, skied and/or climbed in Australia, New Zealand, Nepal, North and South America, Britain and Italy. His first job in publishing, with Australia's *Wild* and *Rock* magazines, began in the packing room and ended in the editor's chair. His next job, at Lonely Planet, took him to dizzy heights as publisher of outdoor activity guides. Now he is a freelance editor and writer. He lives in Melbourne, and these days usually gets out into the hills at toddler pace or with son Oliver on his back. New daughter Amy, who was conceived during the weeks when *Walking in Italy* was being hammered into shape on the laptop, is next in line for the backpack.

FROM THE AUTHORS

Sandra Bardwell Staff at the Positano, Aosta and Valtournenche tourist offices and the Parco Nazionale dello Stelvio at Bormio were especially helpful; a special *grazie* to Mathilde Zuytwegdt at Menaggio for her friendly advice. Anne and friends were great company at Vettica House; Hans and his wife saved me a midnight march by finding a detour when a crucial bridge disappeared in floodwaters. Thanks to Emily and Quentin for the company and encouraging advice – and for the introduction to Amaretto. Sally Webb's assistance was much appreciated. The LP team in Melbourne – Nick, Lindsay, Sally, Glenn, Jennifer and Marg – and my fellow authors were, as ever, great to work with. Hal's support and guidance were, as always, profoundly appreciated.

Stefano Cavedoni I would like to thank the following friends, tourist organisations and staff for their valuable assistance: Paul and Laura Loss, Arine, Dafne Canevaro, 'Ianez' Saverio Bessone, Gioia Milani and her hospitable friends, and my Sardinian friends Roberto and Anna Pisano, 'Murena', Antonio, Salvatore, Tonino, Franco, Michele and Quinto. Thank you to ESIT Sardinia, in particular Mario Pinna and Marco Grippo, the Corpo Forestale dello Stato di Caserta, the Ente Parco del Vesuvio (Carlo Bifulco e Riccardo Rossi), and special thanks to Luigi Guido for his strategic help in the difficult Vesuvius area. I am greatly indebted to the very efficient and extremely supportive organisations of Alto Adige, in particular Alto Adige Marketing

(Utta Radakovich), Consorzio Turistico Alta Badia (Christian Pizzinini), Consorzio Turistico Rosengarten-Latemar (Klaudia De Chiusole and 'Natz' Obkircher), Consorzio Turistico Val Gardena, Associazione Turistica Sciliar Castelrotto and the guides working with Stefan Paungger, the Consorzio Turistico Alta Pusteria, and the Associazione Turistica San Vigilio di Marebbe (Emma Frontul). A special big thanks to Nick Tapp and Sandra Bardwell, whose help, as always, has been invaluable. Thanks for the very special help from Helen and my daughter, Virginia, who, just as she began to appreciate walking with me for many days in the Dolomites, was confronted with an astonishing reddish sunset. Turning to me, she said with amazement: 'Dad, what a wonderful light up here!' And the imprinting was done!

Emily Coles A big thank you to Sandra for sharing her hard-earned trekking wisdom over Avernas on our first day in Rome. Helen provided some very welcome company in the 'wilds' of Liguria, while the patient staff in visitor centres smoothed out many of the bumps along the research trail. In Sicily, Ugo Esposito left his huskies barking in their traces to answer some rushed queries, and Michele offered a very welcome rest from work in his magnificent *rifugio*. The staff of the Cesarò park office were infectious in their enthusiasm for the Nebrodi mountains, giving up valuable weekend time to look at walk itineraries. A last special word to Portia for her patience on the steep and bumpy trails, and to Quentin for taking on the role of unflagging pack mule and interpreter – *bravo!*

Helen Fairbairn & Gareth McCormack Thanks first of all to the staff at Lonely Planet who helped out with queries and planning for this book; in particular Nick Tapp, Lindsay Brown and Sally Dillon. Thanks also to Sandra Bardwell for prompt and efficient advice and direction (as ever), and to all the Italian national park and visitor centre staff who struggled bravely with our Italian. Finally, big thanks to Katie, John and the fish for a most restful week in Pinford End at the end of it all.

Nick Tapp I'm indebted to the *gestori* and staff of several *rifugi* – Garelli, Genova-Figari, Soria-Ellena, Federici-Marchesini al Pagarì and Corsi – for much help and encouragement. Particular thanks, this time, to Piero Marchisio at Rifugio Genova for the brief loan of the *grolla* pot; to Aladar and Anandadattar Pittavino at Rifugio Pagarì for ideas and inspiration; and to Alberto Magro at Rifugio Corsi for the *ferrata* gear. Thanks also to the many walkers who supplied encouragement and good company, especially Elisabetta, Marco and Federico from Pagarì, and Livio and Carmen for a grand day out on Jôf Fuart. Thanks again to Helen, Stefano and Virginia in Rome; to Sandra for her good sense and unflagging enthusiasm; to Susan Keogh and the rest of the outdoor activities team, who kept the wheels turning; and, finally, to Ely and Oliver – *grazie!* (Next time, Amy.)

This Book

Scaling precarious *vie ferrate*, exploring spectacular coastal paths, circumnavigating explosive volcanic cauldrons and savouring aromatic espresso, the dedicated team of authors responsible for this edition of *Walking in Italy* has left no stone unturned. Coordinating author Sandra Bardwell wrote the introductory, Western Alps, Lake District and Stelvio chapters, as well as the Amalfi section in the Campania chapter. Stefano Cavedoni took on the Dolomites and Sardinia chapters, and wrote the Chianti section in Tuscany and the Vesuvius walks in the Campania chapter. Emily Coles tackled Liguria and Sicily, and wrote the Apuan Alps section in the Tuscany chapter. Helen Fairbairn and Gareth McCormack wrote the Central Apennines and Via Ferrata chapters. And Nick Tapp put together the Maritime Alps and Julian & Carnic Alps chapters. Some material from the 5th edition of *Italy* was used in this book.

From the Publisher

Back at LP's Melbourne base, indulging in the occasional cappuccino, was an equally dedicated team. Editing responsibilities were taken on by Jennifer Garrett, Marg Toohey, Nick Tapp, Ilana Sharp, Janet Brunckhorst, Sally Dillon, Kerryn Burgess, Bruce Evans and Lara Morcombe. Cartographic work was done by Jarrad Needham, Eoin Dunlevy, Sonya Brooke, Jody Whiteoak, Helen Rowley, Karen Fry, Chris Klep and Andrew Smith. The colour pages and layout design were handled by Sonya Brooke. The language chapter was polished by Quentin Frayne. Climate charts were compiled by Csanad Csutoros. The wildlife chapter was checked by David Andrew. Some walks were 'roadtested' by Tony Wheeler. Images were assembled by the LPI team. The project was managed by Glenn van der Knijff. And the entire process was overseen by Lindsay Brown and Andrew Bain.

Thanks

Many thanks to the travellers who used the last edition and wrote to us with helpful hints, advice and interesting anecdotes:

John Arwe, Fraiman family, Warren & Diana Garrett, Carolyn Girvin, Christine Haida, Davide Hanau, Ina Hotzsch, Raymond Kennel, Kathleen Liparini, Lia Marcote, Chris Mattison, Dan Minor, Kenith Sobel, Igor Tavella, Anna Trotman, Susanne & Stefan Urthaler.

Walk Descriptions

This book contains 56 walk descriptions ranging from day trips to seven-day walks, plus suggestions for side trips and alternative routes. Each walk description has a brief introduction outlining the natural and cultural features you may encounter, plus information to help you plan your walk – transport options, level of difficulty, time frame and any permits required.

Day walks are often circular and are located in areas of uncommon beauty. Multi-day walks include information on camp sites, *rifugi* (mountain huts), hostels or other accommodation and where you can obtain water and supplies.

Times & Distances

These are provided only as a guide. Times are based on actual walking time and do not include stops for snacks, taking photographs, rests or side trips. Be sure to factor these in when planning your walk. Distances are provided but should be read in conjunction with altitudes. Significant elevation changes can make a greater difference to your walking time than lateral distance.

In most cases, the daily stages are flexible and can be varied. It is important to recognise that short stages are sometimes recommended in order to acclimatise in mountain areas or because there are interesting features to explore en route.

Level of Difficulty

Grading systems are always arbitrary. However, having an indication of the grade may help you choose between walks. Our authors use the following grading guidelines:

Easy – a walk on flat terrain or with minor elevation changes usually over short distances on well-travelled routes with no navigational difficulties.
Moderate – a walk with challenging terrain, often involving longer distances and steep climbs.
Demanding – a walk with long daily distances and difficult terrain with significant elevation changes; may involve challenging route-finding and high-altitude or glacier travel.

True Left & True Right

The terms 'true left' and 'true right', used to describe the bank of a stream or river, sometimes throw readers. The 'true left bank' simply means the left bank as you look downstream.

Maps

Our maps are based on the best available references, often combined with GPS data collected in the field. They are intended to show the general route of the walk and should be used in conjunction with maps suggested in the walk description.

Maps may contain ridge lines in addition to major watercourses depending on the available information. These features build a three-dimensional picture of the terrain, allowing you to determine when the trail climbs and descends. Altitudes of major peaks and passes complete the picture by providing the actual extent of the elevation changes.

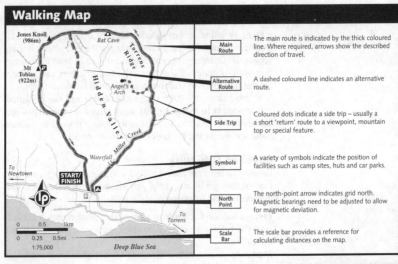

Walking Map

Main Route	The main route is indicated by the thick coloured line. Where required, arrows show the described direction of travel.
Alternative Route	A dashed coloured line indicates an alternative route.
Side Trip	Coloured dots indicate a side trip – usually a short 'return' route to a viewpoint, mountain top or special feature.
Symbols	A variety of symbols indicate the position of facilities such as camp sites, huts and car parks.
North Point	The north-point arrow indicates grid north. Magnetic bearings need to be adjusted to allow for magnetic deviation.
Scale Bar	The scale bar provides a reference for calculating distances on the map.

Walk Profiles

Graphing the elevation against the hours of walking offers an idea of a walk's steepness and how long it climbs or descends. The scale is consistent throughout the book so you can compare different routes.

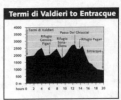

Termi di Valdieri to Entracque

Route Finding

While accurate, our maps are not perfect. Inaccuracies in altitudes are commonly caused by air-temperature anomalies. Natural features such as river confluences and mountain peaks are in their true position, but sometimes the location of villages and trails is not always so. This may be because a village is spread over a hillside, or the size of the map does not allow for detail of the trail's twists and turns. However, by using several basic route-finding techniques, you will have few problems following our descriptions:

14

1. Be aware of whether the trail should be climbing or descending.
2. Check the north-point arrow on the map and determine the general direction of the trail.
3. Time your progress over a known distance and calculate the speed at which you travel in the given terrain. You can then determine with reasonable accuracy how far you have travelled.
4. Watch the path – look for boot prints and other signs of previous passage.

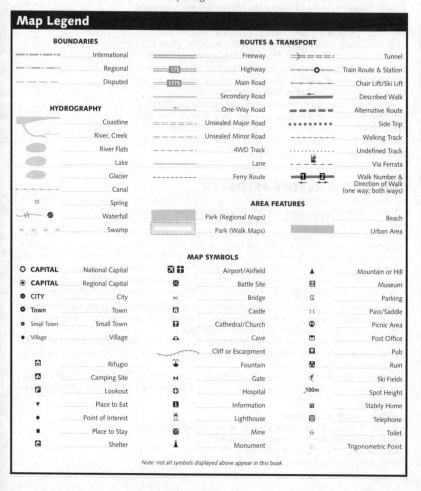

Map Legend

BOUNDARIES

International
Regional
Disputed

HYDROGRAPHY

Coastline
River, Creek
River Flats
Lake
Glacier
Canal
Spring
Waterfall
Swamp

ROUTES & TRANSPORT

Freeway
Highway
Main Road
Secondary Road
One-Way Road
Unsealed Major Road
Unsealed Minor Road
4WD Track
Lane
Ferry Route

Tunnel
Train Route & Station
Chair Lift/Ski Lift
Described Walk
Alternative Route
Side Trip
Walking Track
Undefined Track
Via Ferrata
Walk Number & Direction of Walk (one way; both ways)

AREA FEATURES

Park (Regional Maps)
Park (Walk Maps)
Beach
Urban Area

MAP SYMBOLS

CAPITAL .... National Capital
CAPITAL .... Regional Capital
CITY .... City
Town .... Town
Small Town .... Small Town
Village .... Village

Rifugio
Camping Site
Lookout
Place to Eat
Point of Interest
Place to Stay
Shelter

Airport/Airfield
Battle Site
Bridge
Castle
Cathedral/Church
Cave
Cliff or Escarpment
Fountain
Gate
Hospital
Information
Lighthouse
Mine
Monument

Mountain or Hill
Museum
Parking
Pass/Saddle
Picnic Area
Post Office
Pub
Ruin
Ski Fields
100m .... Spot Height
Stately Home
Telephone
Toilet
Trigonometric Point

Note: not all symbols displayed above appear in this book

Foreword

ABOUT LONELY PLANET GUIDEBOOKS

The story begins with a classic travel adventure: Tony and Maureen Wheeler's 1972 journey across Europe and Asia to Australia. Useful information about the overland trail did not exist at that time, so Tony and Maureen published the first Lonely Planet guidebook to meet a growing need.

From a kitchen table, then from a tiny office in Melbourne (Australia), Lonely Planet has become the largest independent travel publisher in the world, an international company with offices in Melbourne, Oakland (USA), London (UK) and Paris (France).

Today Lonely Planet guidebooks cover the globe. There is an ever-growing list of books and there's information in a variety of forms and media. Some things haven't changed. The main aim is still to help make it possible for adventurous travelers to get out there – to explore and better understand the world.

At Lonely Planet we believe travelers can make a positive contribution to the countries they visit – if they respect their host communities and spend their money wisely. Since 1986 a percentage of the income from each book has been donated to aid projects and human rights campaigns.

UPDATES & READER FEEDBACK

Things change – prices go up, schedules change, good places go bad and bad places go bankrupt. Nothing stays the same. So, if you find things better or worse, recently opened or long-since closed, please tell us and help make the next edition even more accurate and useful.

Lonely Planet thoroughly updates each guidebook as often as possible – usually every two years, although for some destinations the gap can be longer. Between editions, up-to-date information is available in our free, quarterly *Planet Talk* newsletter and monthly email bulletin *Comet*. The *Upgrades* section of our website (W www.lonelyplanet.com) is also regularly updated by Lonely Planet authors, and the site's *Scoop* section covers news and current affairs relevant to travelers. Lastly, the *Thorn Tree* bulletin board and *Postcards* section carry unverified, but fascinating, reports from travelers.

Tell us about it! We genuinely value your feedback. A well-traveled team at Lonely Planet reads and acknowledges every email and letter we receive and ensures that every morsel of information finds its way to the relevant authors, editors and cartographers.

Everyone who writes to us will find their name listed in the next edition of the appropriate guidebook, and will receive the latest issue of *Comet* or *Planet Talk*. The very best contributions will be rewarded with a free guidebook.

We may edit, reproduce and incorporate your comments in Lonely Planet products such as guidebooks, websites and digital products, so let us know if you don't want your comments reproduced or your name acknowledged.

How to contact Lonely Planet:
Online: e talk2us@lonelyplanet.com.au, W www.lonelyplanet.com
Australia: Locked Bag 1, Footscray, Victoria 3011
UK: 10a Spring Place, London NW5 3BH
USA: 150 Linden St, Oakland, CA 94607

Introduction

Italy offers a truly dazzling array of walks for everyone, from high-level mountain treks to comfortable rambles through tranquil, scenic countryside – in fact, enough to keep you busy for a lifetime or two. The key to getting the most out of this guide is to use it as an introduction; choose from the selection of walks considered to be among the best in their respective areas. None require special mountaineering skills or equipment, except the exciting *vie ferrate* (iron ways).

There are high-level walks in the little-known and relatively remote Maritime, Julian and Carnic Alps, around the magnificent Valle d'Aosta in the Western Alps, and in the famous and spectacular Dolomites. At lower altitudes, explore wooded valleys, long ridges and rugged peaks in the Lake District and Central Apennines. Ramble past olive groves, vineyards and ancient churches in Tuscany's gentle Chianti hills, and discover the enchanting Cinque Terre villages along the Ligurian coast. Ancient paths and stairways of the Amalfi Coast and Sorrento Peninsula offer insights into traditional ways of life; while Sardinia can challenge your skills with adventurous explorations of wild and remote mountainous country. For something really different scale some of Europe's most active volcanoes, including Vesuvius, near Naples, and Mt Etna, looming majestically over the eastern coast of Sicily. To get the adrenalin flowing, tackle the *vie ferrate* in the spectacularly rugged Brenta mountains.

Long-distance paths are many and varied, from numerous high-level routes providing challenging walks of several days to seriously

17

long routes from one side of the country to the other. Italy also has many large national parks, where protection of magnificently wild landscapes harmonises with preservation of traditional ways of life, especially summer grazing in alpine pastures and sympathetic harvesting of woodlands.

Although wildlife viewing isn't one of the great highlights of walking in Italy, you can expect to see plenty of ibex, chamois and marmots throughout the Alps, and perhaps catch sight of a lammergeier (bearded vulture) or golden eagle. Everywhere brilliantly colourful displays of wildflowers, from tiny, delicate plants emerging miraculously from receding snowdrifts to the vibrant hues of lilies, poppies and roses, last from early spring until autumn.

The extended walks described in this guide comprise suggested stages with accommodation in *rifugi* (mountain huts), hotels, guesthouses or camping grounds at the end of each day. The day walks are based at villages or small towns with a similar range of accommodation.

There are also recommendations for places where you can enjoy an evening meal, usually in a trattoria or restaurant offering typical local cooking. *Par excellence* Italy is the place where you can combine first-class walking with fine food; there is a wondrous array of regional cuisines and fresh produce. Not to mention the vast variety of wines and, of course, superb coffee in all its guises, the essential start to every Italian day.

Walking is hugely popular among Italians, and people from many countries share their enthusiasm, so it's very rare not to meet fellow walkers during the day. Evenings spent at *rifugi* are usually extremely sociable, and differences in language and background count for nought in the sharing of experiences and enthusiasm, stimulated by glasses of vino, grappa – and more vino.

Facts about Italy

HISTORY

Italy's history is a patchwork of powerful empires and domination by foreign powers; from the fall of the Roman Empire in AD 476 until the foundation of the Kingdom of Italy in 1861, the country was never a unified entity. Since then Italy has developed into one of the leading powers in Western Europe. The following timeline pinpoints some landmark events in Italian history. Lonely Planet's *Italy* guide includes a more detailed history – or see Books (p55) for further reading suggestions.

c. 70,000 BC – Palaeolithic period; people living on the Italian peninsula

c. 4000 BC – Neolithic people establish settlements

c. 1800 BC – Bronze Age; several Italic tribes colonise the peninsula

1300 BC – Etruscan people migrate to the Italian peninsula

900 BC – Greek settlements established in the south and on Sicily (Sicilia)

753 BC – traditional date for foundation of Rome (Roma) by Romulus

800–700 BC – peak of Etruscan civilisation, based on large city-states

509 BC – foundation of the Roman Republic

312 BC – construction of the Via Appia (Appian Way) started

218 BC – Rome consolidates what are now the frontiers of Italy

91 BC – Rome grants citizenship to Etruscan and Italic peoples

48 BC – Julius Caesar becomes consul and dictator

44 BC – Julius Caesar murdered

AD 98–117 – Roman Empire reaches its zenith

313 – Roman Empire officially recognises Christian religion

452 – Attila the Hun invades Italy

488–526 – relative peace under Ostrogothic emperor Theodoric

c. 568 – Lombard invasion of Italy

754 – Papal States established by the Franks

831 – Muslim Arabs settle in Sicily

962 – Saxon King Otto I founds Holy Roman Empire

1091 – Normans conquer Sicily

1130 – Norman Roger II crowned king of Sicily and southern Italy

1220 – Norman rule gives way to Germanic influence when Frederick II crowned Holy Roman Emperor

1268 – control of Sicily passes to France

12th–14th centuries – northern city-states evolve and regional divisions begin to take shape

1282 – Spanish take over Sicily, dividing the south between Spain and France in Naples (Napoli)

1347–48 – the Black Death kills more than one third of Italy's population

15th century – dawn of the Renaissance, period of exceptional creativity and accomplishments in political, cultural and social life

1527 – Rome sacked by Charles V

16th century – the Counter-Reformation: the Roman Catholic Church's response to the Protestant Reformation

1582 – Gregorian calendar introduced, fixing 1 January as first day of the year

1714 – control of Italy passes from Spain to Austria

18th century – the Enlightenment sweeps away the barbarism of the Counter-Reformation; towards the end of the century, serious attempts to climb the major peaks in the Alps; the Grand Tour, undertaken by privileged and adventurous British and other travellers through Europe, familiarises many with Italy's culture and geography

1796 – Napoleon invades Italy

1804 – Napoleon establishes the Kingdom of Italy with himself on the throne

1815 – Italy's monarchs reinstated and the country's boundaries largely restored after Napoleon's defeat

1830 – Mazzini founds a nationalist movement and later leads several abortive uprisings

1848 – Italian unification movement gains momentum when Garibaldi returns to Italy from South America

1855 – highest Monte Rosa peak (Punta Dufour, 4634m) climbed from the Swiss side

1860 – Garibaldi and his Expedition of One Thousand take Naples and Sicily

1861 – Kingdom of Italy declared and Vittorio Emanuele II proclaimed king; Italy's first parliament convened

1863 – Club Alpino Italiano (CAI; Italian Alpine Club) founded

1865 – summit of the Matterhorn (Il Cervino) reached, firstly from Switzerland, then from Italy

1866 – Venice (Venezia) wrested from Austria for the Kingdom

1870 – Rome declared capital of Italy; Pope later stripped of remaining secular powers

1894 – Catholics given right to vote (backlash against socialism); male suffrage completed (but women denied the vote)

1914 – WWI breaks out in Europe

1915 – Italy enters the war as an ally of France, Britain and Russia

1919 – Italy gains Trieste and South Tyrol (Südtirol), now Alto Adige; Trentino restored to Italy; Mussolini founds the Fascist Party

1921 – Fascist Party wins 35 of the 135 parliamentary seats

1922 – first national park declared

1924 – Fascist Party wins elections with 64% of the vote; world's first Fascist regime

1925 – opposition parties expelled from parliament; two-thirds of electorate disenfranchised

1929 – Catholicism declared the sole religion of Italy and Vatican an independent state

1940 – Italy enters WWII as an ally of Germany

1943 – Mussolini arrested; king and parliament take control and sign armistice with Allies and declare war on Germany; Mussolini rescued; puppet Republic of Salò declared

1944–45 – Italian Resistance fights German troops in the north

1945 – Mussolini and his mistress captured and shot by partisans; Italy liberated

1946 – monarchy abolished and republic established; newly formed Democrazia Cristiana (Christian Democrats) wins elections

Rifugi – A Potted History

Rifugi (mountain huts) have long been an essential feature of walking and climbing in Italy's mountain areas, as inseparable from the experience as the paths and routes that link them.

Their origins are quite prosaic – the provision of shelter for people engaged in both worldly and spiritual pursuits. Capanna Vincent, built in 1785 on the southern fall of Monte Rosa for workers at a nearby gold mine, is generally regarded as the progenitor of *rifugi*. Also on Monte Rosa, a *ricovero* (basic shelter) was erected 65 years later at Colle Indren for parties of scientific observers.

During the 18th century, possibly even earlier, *ospizi* (hospices or inns) sprang up at some of the passes on the high-level routes into Italy from the north, including Grand San Bernardo and Simplon (Sempione); a few eventually became *rifugi*.

Meanwhile, adventurers had begun to tackle the highest alpine peaks and so the pastime of mountaineering was born. A concerted campaign to conquer Monte Rosa's several summits began in the late 18th century. The Rock of Discovery fell to seven Gressoney men in 1778; Punta Dufour, the highest at 4634m, was climbed from Switzerland in 1855. In between these two achievements all the other summits had been conquered by local, German and British climbers.

The Matterhorn (Il Cervino), Monte Rosa's awesome neighbour, was the scene of perhaps the most famous – or notorious – first ascent in the Alps. Englishman Edward Whymper and a party of six started from Zermatt in Switzerland on 13 July 1865 and reached the summit via the Hörnli ridge the following afternoon. However, four men fell to their deaths during the descent, an incident which attracted widespread publicity. Two days later Italians Jean-Antoine Carrel and Jean-Baptiste Bich completed the ascent from Breuil at the head of Valtournenche. Two years later Félicité Carrel became the first woman to reach the top.

These feats were soon followed by a spate of *rifugio* construction with several on or near Monte Rosa and one on Mont Blanc (Monte Bianco). The first *rifugio* in the Dolomites was opened in 1877 near Marmolada. In 1891 the Turin section of the CAI acquired a stone building at Colle del Teodulo (3317m), a historic Swiss-Italian crossing between the Matterhorn and Monte Rosa, which became Rifugio del Teodulo.

In the Gran Paradiso area of Valle d'Aosta, hunting lodges built under royal authority from the 1860s were transformed into *rifugi* after the area was declared a national park; these include Savoia, Sella and Vittorio Emanuele.

By 1900 about 100 *rifugi* were dotted about the mountains. Now, over a century later, the CAI owns and manages several hundred *rifugi*, and many more are privately owned, all providing accommodation, complete with heating and running water, that would surely bemuse the pioneers.

1950 – Cassa per il Mezzogiorno founded to fund massive development projects in the south

1958 – European Economic Community founded with Italy as a member; beginning of the Economic Miracle with significant industrial expansion and drop in unemployment to mid-1960s

1968 – student uprising and the formation of revolutionary groups

1970s – left- and right-wing terrorists active

1970 – regional governments established; divorce legalised

1980 – right-wing extremists held responsible for explosion in Bologna killing 84 people

1992 – Tangentopoli – a massive corruption scandal – breaks, eventually implicating many prominent politicians and business-people

1993 – Sicilian godfather, Salvatore Riina, arrested after 24 years on the run; Mafia bombs in Milan, Florence and Rome, killing several people and damaging historic monuments

1994 – right-wing coalition government voted in; Silvio Berlusconi appointed prime minister

1995 – Berlusconi's government collapses

1996 – centre-left government elected; Romano Prodi becomes prime minister

1997 – disastrous earthquake in Assisi, severely damaging many priceless artistic works and religious buildings

1998 – Italy joins European monetary union

2000 – major nation-wide celebrations for Jubilee Year (Holy Year), with vast sums spent on museums and heritage sites; disastrous floods in the north cost many lives, homes and businesses

2001 – Berlusconi elected again, forming Italy's 59th government since 1946; violence at Genoa during World Trade Organisation meeting

2002 – euro replaces lira as Italy's currency

GEOGRAPHY

The instantly recognisable boot-shaped profile of Italy embraces an area of 301,245 sq km. The country is lapped by four seas: the Adriatic to the east, the Ionian along the south coast, the Tyrrhenian between Sardinia (Sardegna) and France's Corsica, and the Ligurian washing the northwestern coast. All four seas are part of the larger Mediterranean Sea.

Italy is distinctly mountainous – 35% of its territory lies above 702m, in two major ranges, the Alps and the Apennines (Appennini). Rising from the Gulf of Genoa in the west and tapering down towards the Adriatic Sea in the east, the Alps comprise three groups of mountains: the Western Alps, between Genoa and Valle d'Aosta; the Central Alps reaching east to the Alto Adige, and the Eastern Alps, which include the Dolomites (Dolomiti) and the Julian and Carnic Alps (Alpi Giulie e Carniche).

The highest mountain entirely within Italy is Gran Paradiso (4061m) in Valle d'Aosta; though higher, both Mont Blanc (4807m) and Monte Rosa (4634m) straddle Italy's borders with France and Switzerland respectively. The Apennines are Italy's 1220km-long backbone, extending from Liguria south to the tip of Calabria, with an extension in Sicily; they bulge out to a width of 195km in the central Apennines from narrow northern and southern tips. The highest peak is Corno Grande (2914m) in Abruzzo's Gran Sasso d'Italia group. Several smaller mountain ranges extend east and west from the Apennines; these include the Apuan Alps (Alpi Apuane) in northwest Tuscany, the volcanoes in the south, and the limestone uplands on the Amalfi Coast-Sorrento Peninsula.

Sardinia has its own mountain ranges in the island's southwest and central east; the highest peak is Punta La Marmora (1834m) in the Gennargentu massif. Sicily is even more mountainous – 83% of the island in fact; its three ranges include Europe's highest active volcano, Mt Etna (3350m).

The densely settled Po valley (Pianura Padana) is Italy's largest area of lowlands; other lowland areas are the Tavogliere di Puglia and the Pianura Campania around Vesuvius. The Po itself, Italy's longest river at 650km, flows into the Adriatic through a broad delta south of Venice; the mouth of the Fiume Adige, the next longest river (412km), is just north of the delta.

The coastline is varied (although notably short on sandy beaches) from the coastal cliffs of Liguria, and the rugged Amalfi Coast and Sorrento Peninsula, to the level profile of the Adriatic. Most of Italy's islands lie in the Tyrrhenian Sea: Sicily and the scattered Aeolian Islands (Isole Eolie) off its north coast; a small group near Naples including Capri; Sardinia; and the handful between Corsica and the coast, notably Elba.

The Tremiti Islands are the exception, situated off the east coast in the Adriatic Sea.

Italy has around 1500 lakes, the majority of which are small and high in the mountains. The largest are the glacier-carved Lago di Garda (with an area of 370 sq km), followed by Lago Maggiore (212 sq km) and Lago di Como (146 sq km).

GEOLOGY

A useful starting point for Italy's complex geological history is the era during which the area now occupied by the peninsula was covered by the vast Tethys Sea, between

The Restless Planet

The fact that geological processes are going on all the time is strikingly evident in Italy – the earth has been restive for several million years along a fault line extending from eastern Sicily, along the Apennines and into the northeastern Alps, roughly matching the collision zone of the continental plates.

In this region there are four active volcanoes: Stromboli and Vulcano (Aeolian Islands), Vesuvius (near Naples) and Etna (Sicily). The Phlegraean Fields (Campi Flegrei) and Monte Epomeo on the island of Ischia (near Naples) have volcanic histories but are now generally quiet, apart from bubbling hot springs and outpourings of gas and steam.

Few volcanoes anywhere in the world are more active than Stromboli and Etna; the latter's most recent big eruption was in July–August 2001 when a stream of lava on its southern flank seriously threatened the popular mountain resort of Rifugio Sapienza.

Earthquakes are a hazardous and, at times, disastrous fact of life in the central and southern Apennines and on Sicily. The 20th century's worst happened in 1908 when Messina and Reggio di Calabria were destroyed in a quake measuring seven on the Richter scale. In September 1997 an earthquake affected Umbria and the Marches in the central Apennines, killing 10 people and causing part of the vaulted ceiling of the Basilica di San Francesco d'Assisi, in Assisi, to collapse, destroying priceless frescoes.

245 and 60 million years ago. An even more ancient mountain mass, standing where the Alps are today, was ground down by erosion and the resulting debris transported south into the sea. There it was transformed into layers of limestone, sandstone, clay and shale; the extensive coral reefs from which the Dolomites emerged also originated at that time (see the boxed text 'Coral Reefs at 3000m', p182).

Around 40 million years ago the massive European and African continental plates collided, pushing up the edges of the plates and, with them, the layers of rock on the sea bed. This prolonged, cataclysmic event marked the real emergence of the Alps and, later, the Apennines. The strata were wrapped around the levelled remnant of the ancient mountain mass and pushed up to Himalayan heights; these ranges were subsequently worn down to their present elevations. The Apennines, comprising many rock types but predominantly limestone and sandstone, finally took shape only about 1.6 million years ago. In the meantime, the Tethys Sea had largely dried up when the Strait of Gibraltar closed; when it reopened about two million years ago the Mediterranean basin was flooded and the present shape of the Italian peninsula was settled – but the action within it was still far from finished.

During a succession of ice ages, spanning more than a million years, glaciers blanketed the mountains, resulting in the landscape seen today (see the boxed text 'Signs of a Glacial Past', p33). Outstanding examples of moraine lakes are Lago di Garda and its neighbours. In places, ice trapped in the valleys overflowed across mountain ridges, cutting deep incisions, which later became high passes. Numerous glaciers survive in the mountains, notably along the borders with France, Switzerland and Austria, in the Ortler Range in Parco Nazionale dello Stelvio and in Parco Nazionale del Gran Paradiso. However, the glaciers are presently retreating, possibly partly as a result of climate change.

[Continued on page 32]

WATCHING WILDLIFE

Italy has a diverse but not outstandingly rich natural heritage: around 500 species of bird, 90 mammals and 5560 plant species. A great array of protective legislation and the many protected areas have come to the country relatively late – too late, perhaps, to compensate for the impacts of land clearance and drainage, and the predations of hunters on habitats and species.

National and natural parks and natural reserves are the best places to go to see wildlife, and several parks and reserves are featured in this book.

This section provides brief descriptions of the species you are most likely to see on the walks described. Some books, which will help with identification in the field, are listed under Natural History (p55).

FAUNA
Mammals
Sure-footed **chamois** (camoscio) are superb climbers; if disturbed they can ascend 1000m in an enviable 15 minutes. They can leap across wide gaps with amazing ease and their tough, flexible hooves also enable them to cross snow slopes without sinking in. Resembling a cross between a goat and an antelope, their horns are short and slightly hooked at the ends, their head is white with broad, black stripes and their summer coat is reddish-brown with a black stripe along the spine. Chamois reach an overall height of 130cm. They feed on lichen, grass, herbs and pine needles. They are quite common and are almost certain to be seen in the mountains, although more likely earlier in the morning and towards evening.

Red deer (cervo) range up to 2800m in forests and alpine meadows. In the absence of their natural predators (bears, wolves and lynx) and despite the activities of hunters, the number of red deer in Italy has increased. Very impressive animals, adult males stand up to 1.5m tall. Their summer coat is reddish-brown, which develops only slowly during spring from the grey-brown winter mantle. Their impressive antlers are shed during spring.

The **roe deer** (capriolo) is not difficult to spot in open forests in the mountains. Adults stand to 90cm tall and have a red-brown coat with a yellowish-white spot under the tail during summer. Their antlers are straight or very slightly curved with a few points towards the top. The species is protected, so is safe during the hunting season.

You're likely to see the **red fox** (volpe) almost anywhere except high in the mountains. With their sleek, dog-like profile, pointed ears and long dark bushy tail and rich red-brown coat, they're easy to recognize bounding away to shelter. They prefer to hunt at night, for carrion, small rodents, and even insects and fruit.

Red deer

23

Once relentlessly hunted for the supposed medicinal properties of its flesh and large ridged horns, the **ibex** *(stambecco)* was almost extinct in Italy by the early 19th century. A major purpose in setting aside Parco Nazionale del Gran Paradiso in 1922 was the protection and revival of the ibex. There are now about 6000 of these wild goats in the park and several groups elsewhere in the Alps (see the boxed text 'Italy's First National Park', p114). Less timid and more curious than chamois, ibex are fairly readily seen in the mountains. Their fur is grey or brown, they stand to 90cm tall and their horns are almost as long, making them look top-heavy. During summer they stay well above the limit of tree growth, on warmer south-facing slopes, feeding on herbs, grass and lichens. They usually live in small herds and take up vantage points from which they can survey their surroundings; it's not difficult to get quite close if you move quietly and slowly.

The **marmot's** *(marmotta)* shrill whistle is a characteristic sound of the high valleys and mountain slopes up to 2700m. They live in small colonies and build extensive burrow systems; as soon as the lookout sounds the alarm the slopes suddenly become alive as the entire colony scurries into burrow entrances. After a long winter hibernation in their sealed-off burrows, they emerge slim and agile, but as summer progresses they put on weight and slow down, so are easier to observe. Resembling a very large squirrel, their fur is grey-brown and lighter on the underside, and their rounded head has a characteristically flat forehead. In the past marmots were prized as food in remote mountain areas.

Marmot

The shy **red squirrel** *(scoiattolo)*, a protected species, rarely leaves the trees in which it lives, feeding on pine or beech nuts. Red squirrels are known to raid birds' nests for eggs and will strip tree bark to reach the sap to supplement their diets. During autumn they bury a store of nuts to last through winter as they do not hibernate. Their fur is greyish-red to almost black. The red squirrel is quite common in coniferous forests up to an altitude of 1800m.

Reptiles

The **adder** *(marasso)* and **common viper** *(vipera comune)* are the only poisonous snakes found in the Alps, but are dangerous only if disturbed. Fatalities are extremely unusual as a result of an adder bite; the viper venom is more potent. Very versatile, they can live in rocky ground or marshes, in valleys and up to 3000m. Both measure between 40cm and 100cm in length. The adder is dark brown to black with a zigzag pattern along its back. The viper varies in colouring from light grey to reddish brown with a row of dark crossbands along the length of its body. They feed on frogs, lizards and small insects.

The attractive **green lizard** *(ramarro)* is a common sight in woodlands, on rocky ground, in stone walls, and along the margins of paths and tracks. Growing to 40cm in length, it is bright green or yellow-green with a faint black stipple pattern and a white patch on the throat. It's most likely to be seen in sunny spots in the morning and evening.

Birds

Though not particularly easy to spot, the small, sparrow-like **Alpine accentor** is seen in the mountains, usually in open, rocky areas. It has a greyish head, dark brown streaks on its back, reddish stripes on the side and a distinctive row of white dots on its wings.

The pitch-black **Alpine chough** *(gracchio)*, with its long tail, yellow beak and red feet, is found at very high altitudes. It's very acrobatic in flight and has great fun soaring on updrafts around peaks and crags. A hardy opportunist, it will swoop around *rifugi* (mountain huts) in search of food scraps, but normally feeds on worms, insects or berries.

The magnificent **golden eagle** *(aquila reale)* has a wingspan exceeding 2m, which it holds in a V-shape during its awesome gliding and soaring displays high in mountainous areas – the Alps and Sardinia. It dives with wings folded to catch small rodents, marmots or carrion, including animals trapped in snowdrifts or injured in falls. It is generally dark brown if seen from below, with white wing patches. It prefers areas with steep cliffs and ravines, which provide ideal nesting sites. Once harshly persecuted in the lowlands, it took refuge in the mountains and is now fully protected.

With a wing span up to 2.8m and a body length exceeding 1m, the **lammergeier** *(gipeto barbuto)* is Europe's largest raptor. It was mercilessly hunted as a supposed predator of sheep and, in Italy, became extinct early in the 20th century. It has been successfully reintroduced to Parco Nazionale del Gran Paradiso; between 1978 and 1995, 60 pairs were released in the park and the survival rate appears to be strong. The lammergeier, like all vultures, is a scavenger and finds plenty to eat during the winter when animals are killed by avalanches or in falls. Its diet consists mainly of bones, which it drops from a great height to smash against rocks, swallowing the fragments whole. Living in strongly-bonded pairs, it generally nests on exposed cliff ledges. A lammergeier will vigorously defend its large territory (up to 80 sq km) against intruding birds and territorial fights are common. In flight its wings and tail droop slightly, and the head is usually turned downwards. It is generally slate-black in colour, with a darker stripe across the eyes, and buff-coloured head and underparts. The head is completely feathered (unlike other vultures) and it has a bristly tuft of feathers under the chin.

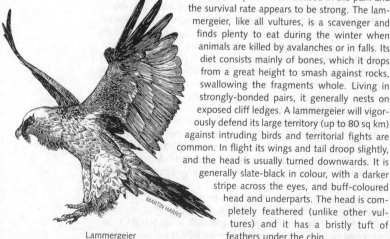

Lammergeier

The **ptarmigan** (*pernice bianca*) or snow grouse lives year-round on rocky ground at altitudes of 2000m to 2800m. It adapts superbly to its environment by changing colours at least three times during the year, from spotted grey in summer to pure white in winter. Its legs are protected by a special layer of insulating feathers. During winter it digs a hole in the snow for shelter and during the day potters about the slopes searching for food. As the spring thaw progresses it moves to snow-free ground in search of insects and new shoots on emerging plants.

The small **snowfinch** (*fringuello alpino*) adapts to its changing surroundings in the mountains; its brown back and black throat become paler during colder months. It's strictly an alpine species, never venturing below the limit of tree growth. It lives in large flocks on stony ground and in summer may be seen around the higher summits. The snowfinch will nest in sheltered crannies in buildings and in tiny crevices on rock faces. It lives on insects and seeds, but will scavenge around sites frequented by humans.

FLORA
Broad-leaved Trees
The **beech** (*faggio*) is one of the most plentiful broad-leaved trees in Italy. Almost pure forests of beech are found throughout the mountains, particularly on limestone. It's easily identified by the smooth, silver-grey bark and oval leaves, light green in spring, dark green and shiny in summer, then golden-brown to russet in autumn. The tree often reaches a height of 45m and can live for more than 300 years. Oil-rich beech nuts are an important food for many birds, squirrels and wild boar.

Beautiful **silver birch** (*betulla*) woods occur widely in mountain areas up to about 1800m. The tree, which grows to about 30m high, is white with large black, diamond-shaped markings in mature trees. The small roughly triangular leaves are shiny green with rough edges.

The **sweet chestnut** (*castagno*) grows throughout Italy between 300m and 1000m. It is a vigorous grower, making it suitable for coppicing (regular harvesting) to provide timber for various agricultural uses. A fairly tall tree, up to 30m, it has smooth, silvery-grey bark and longish, glossy, dark green leaves with toothed edges. The nuts (or seeds) are enclosed within a small rounded husk covered in spines. For centuries the nuts were a staple food for people in remote areas, and are still valued as the basis of luxurious desserts.

The **mountain maple** (*acero oppio*) can attain an age of 500 years and a height of 40m. Typically it has a broad crown above a thick, gnarled trunk. It prefers damp sites between about 1500m and 2200m, where it often colonises scree slopes. Being a particularly hardy tree, it is often planted along roadsides. In autumn its large leaves turn a striking golden yellow.

Not surprisingly in a country where wine is so important, the **cork oak** (*sughera*) is widely grown, mainly in the Apennines. It reaches a height of 20m. Its spongy, fissured, light grey bark, about 5cm thick, can be stripped every six to 12 years. The exposed trunk is rich red in colour.

The **holm oak** (leccio), typical of the Mediterranean *macchia* (scrub) vegetation, grows along the coast and up to 600m. It is an evergreen with glossy black-green leaves, which contrast attractively with the new silver-white and pale yellow foliage during spring.

Conifers

Also known as the Swiss stone pine, the **arolla pine** (pino cembro) has slender blue-green or dark green leaves bunched in groups of five. The small, bulbous cones, dark blue during summer and red-brown later, contain resinous nuts highly prized by birds, foxes and squirrels. The dark grey or orange-brown bark has shallow grooves and the branches turn up at the ends. It prefers higher altitudes, being rarely found below 1300m, and can survive at 2800m.

The hardy **Austrian pine**, also known as black pine, is common in central Italy and grows to about 30m. Its bark varies in colour from blackish-brown to purple-grey and is deeply ridged. The brownish cones have a distinctive pointed tip. The leaves are stiff and very dark, almost black, growing in pairs.

The very elegant **Italian cypress**, common along Mediterranean coasts, has a slender tapered profile. The dense, dark green foliage is a mass of tiny shoots growing in all directions and the oval cone is shiny green when young then dark reddish-brown.

Common juniper (ginepro) grows on acid and alkaline (limestone) soils in many areas, most commonly as a contorted, spreading shrub up to 6m high. Its short, sharply pointed, needle-like leaves are light grey with a greenish tinge. The globular fruit (berry) is green at first, then slowly turns blue, then black.

Unique among Europe's conifers, the **European larch** (larice) is deciduous, turning rich gold in autumn. In the mountains the tree grows to 40m tall and can reach a great age. It has huge boles and enormous canopies of thick branches, the lower ones upturned at the end. The brown cones are smallish and egg-shaped. It occurs right up to the limit of tree growth, usually in beautiful open forests. Its timber is extremely hard and weather resistant and has been the main building timber in mountain communities for centuries.

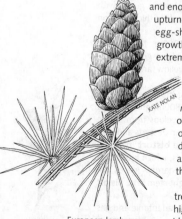

KATE NOLAN

The hardy **dwarf mountain pine** (pino mugo) generally grows at higher levels than most other trees, in broad dense thickets up to 2m high on stony ground and scree slopes. It has thick, deep green needles in tufts of two and the cones are egg-shaped. At lower altitudes, around 1500m, the dwarf pine can reach 20m in height.

The **European silver fir** (abete bianco) is a tall tree, up to 80m in height, which may be found as high as 2100m, often with the red spruce. It's easily

European larch cone

identified by its relatively large brown cones, which

have small, erect spines between the scales, and the whitish underside of its thick, dark green leaves, which are arranged along each side of the shoot. The dark grey bark develops ever more distinct small plates.

With its traditional Christmas tree shape, the **Norway spruce** (*abete rosso*) dominates commercial plantations up to about 1800m and also provides good shelter belts on open ground. It can reach a height of 40m and its stiff, pointed leaves hang downwards. The long cylindrical cone and the reddish or brown bark become cracked with age.

Shrubs & Flowers

Above the limit of tree growth and as high as 3000m, dense thickets of **alpenrose** (*rododendro ferrugineo*), up to 1.5m high, are scattered among rocky outcrops and clumps of grass. The small clusters of bell-shaped, deep pinkish-red flowers last through summer. An evergreen, it has deep green, shiny leaves with reddish undersides and curled edges.

The **Alpine aster** (*astro alpino*) has small, daisy-like, violet-blue or mauve flowers with a bright yellow centre. It is found only in limestone country, commonly on cliffs or well-drained mountain slopes, up to an altitude of 3000m. It blooms throughout summer.

Unlike many of its relatives, the **alpine buttercup** (*ranuncolo alpestre*) has a white flower, usually in small clusters. The shiny green leaves are generally round with small lobes. It has a liking for stony, damp ground, often along stream margins up to 300m. It flowers between June and October.

Alpenrose

The seemingly fragile **Alpine pansy** (*viola*) prefers meadows and stony sites no higher than 2200m. The long-stemmed, oval leaves are shiny green. The violet flowers have a short season – June and July.

With deep-green roundish leaves, and violet bell-shaped and fringed flowers, the **Alpine snowbell** (*soldanella alpine*) makes a seeming-ly miraculous appearance on the edge of melting snow. The delicate flowers on extremely slender stems (to 15cm long) move gently with the breeze. During succeeding weeks the plant develops thick mats on stony ground, at altitudes up to 3000m.

Usually found on wet stony ground up to 2200m, the **Alpine willow** has oval leaves, shiny green on top and bluish-green under-neath. Its short-stalked catkins (flowers) are pale yellow, and bloom in May and June.

With bright green leaves, slightly serrated along the edges, the **bil-berry** (*mirtillo*) is found on open ground up to 2800m, growing to a height of 60cm. The bluish-black berry, which develops from a pale pink flower during summer, is a popular ingredient in desserts and jam.

Prolific in damp, grassy mountain meadows, the **bistort** (*bistorta*) has dense, elongated clusters of bright pink flowers, which look like a single flower spike from a distance. The rather narrow leaves are darkish green on short stalks from the long, straight stem. The bistort blooms from June to October.

Broom (*ginestra comune*) occurs widely, is very adaptable and has masses of bright yellow, strongly scented flowers which bloom from

Bilberry

May to August. It is an evergreen shrub with long, thin branchlets. It is often used to consolidate areas that are subject to landslides.

The distinctive **bladder campion** (strigolo) is easily identified – the five white petals of its flower are deeply notched and spray out from a greenish, inflated, bladder-like tube. The roughly oval leaves are light green and set well down the stem. It stands to 60cm tall, blooms from May to September, and is found in mountain meadows and grasslands.

One of the higher growing plants, the **moss campion** (silene acaule) forms dense, bright green cushions of tiny leaves with clusters of equally small pink flowers dotted about the surface. It likes damp, rocky places and scree slopes up to 3700m, and flowers throughout summer. The moss campion is fully protected.

The **common columbine** (amor nascosto) is quite widespread in woods and meadows, especially in limestone areas. The violet-blue or purple flowers hang down; the outer petals, with long, backward-pointing and slightly hooked spurs, surround the inner bell-shaped cluster of petals. The small leaves are dull green. It blooms from May to July.

As early as March, at around 1000m, the hardy **white crocus** (croco albifloro) pushes its white, violet-tinged flowers straight through the thawing snow. The slender green leaves only begin to take shape once the flower is out. Until other species come into flower, carpets of crocuses dominate the scene, creeping up with the snow line as high as 2700m.

The much sought-after **edelweiss** (stella alpina) is a protected species. The small plant (to 20cm tall) prefers grassy or rocky slopes up to 3400m, and flowers between July and September. It's generally white or greyish-white in appearance with longish leaves. The small, yellowish-white flowers are surrounded by woolly bracts, resembling small leaves.

Meadows and marshy places up to 2700m are the preferred habitat of the **spring gentian** (genziana primaticcia). A very small plant, it has deep blue, five-petalled, star-shaped flowers, one to each slender stem, and is no more than 6cm high. The bright green leaves are arranged tightly around the base. It blooms from March to August.

The striking **trumpet gentian** (genzianella del Koch) has erect, deep blue or purplish blooms with tiny green dots inside; each measures up to 70mm long and seems to weigh down its short stem. It flowers from May to August and likes to keep its roots damp on rocky ground up to 3000m. It is fully protected.

With a striking, bright yellow, rounded flower, the tall **globeflower** (botton d'oro) grows in damp sites and along stream margins in upland meadows. It blooms during summer. The dark green, palm-shaped leaves cluster round the base of the 60cm-long stem.

The pretty **harebell** (campanula dello Scheuchzer) lasts right through summer and autumn in meadows and open woodlands up to 2200m. Single or small clusters of light blue, bell-shaped flowers wave about in the wind at the end of the slender, shortish stem. The rounded leaves form a mat at the base of the stem.

The fast-growing, prickly **common hawthorn** *(biancospino)* can grow up to 900m altitude and is often found in forests dominated by oaks. Elsewhere, on dry soils, this bush is rather stunted and is often found with broom and rockrose (cistus), forming the classic Mediterranean *macchia* type of vegetation. The spiny branches offer a safe haven for nesting birds; its white, perfumed flowers attract insects and its small, dark red fruit (rich in vitamin C), provide valuable winter food for birds.

The **spring heath** *(erica scopina)* grows to 40cm high and has urn-shaped, bright pink flowers and darkish green leaves. It's found in conifer woodlands and rocky places up to 2700m, and blooms from March to June.

Forming mats or tufts on rocky ground and scree, the succulent **mountain houseleek** *(semprevivo dei monti)* has thick oval leaves in tight, ground-hugging rosettes, and small, reddish-purple, star-shaped flowers on a longish stem. It blooms in July and August.

Lentisk *(lentisco)* is found throughout the Mediterranean basin, mainly in coastal areas as one of the species of the hardy *macchia* vegetation. An evergreen bush, it has dark green, leathery leaves and exudes a strong, resinous perfume. The yellow or reddish-brown flowers appear from March to June.

Between May and July, **St Bernard's lily** *(giglio di San Bernadino)* produces spikes of star-like, white flowers on a long, slender stem, around which cluster the thin grassy leaves. It's found in pastures and on dry rocky ground up to 1800m.

The **myrtle** *(mirto)* is an integral component of the Mediterranean *macchia*. It grows mainly on the coast in hot, dry areas. Both the leaves and flowers are intensely perfumed, and its essential oil is extracted for use in perfume-making. The aromatic fruit is a vital ingredient in grappa. The milky white flowers appear during July and August.

More than a dozen species of **orchid** *(orchide)* are found in mountainous areas and many more elsewhere. Many are threatened with extinction, being very vulnerable to disturbance of their habitats. Orchids are perennial herbs with simple stems and longish leaves. Typically they have dense flower spikes, in which the lowermost of three petals protrudes like a lip. A common species in the Alps is early purple orchid, which has purple, occasionally pink or white, flowers and narrow, black spotted leaves. The outer petals are spread out and the central petals form a hood. It is found in grassy meadows and woodlands up to 2600m.

Pasque flowers *(pulsatilla)* are members of the buttercup family are common in mountain areas from 1200m to 2700m. They generally flower throughout spring and summer. Pasque flowers are poisonous. The common pasque flower has large purple or mauve, bell-shaped flowers with bright yellow centres (anthers) and feathery leaves. It's found mainly in dry meadows up to 1500m. The low-growing spring pasque flower has white flowers with a pink or violet blush on the outside of the petals. The short stem is hairy and the

Endangered Species

Urbanisation, settlement in rural areas and especially along the coast, combined with the Italians' passion for *la caccia* (hunting) has rendered many species of native mammal and bird extinct, rare or endangered. Hunters are a powerful lobby group and continue to win the day in regular referenda on whether hunting should be banned.

During the 20th century at least 13 species became extinct, including the Alpine lynx, white-tailed eagle *(aquila di mare)* and the crane. According to a *Lista Rossa* (Red List) published by the WWF, 60% of vertebrates in Italy are at risk.

However, a raft of laws now protects many species and some are making a very slow comeback. These include the brown bear in the Brenta area of Trentino; the lynx in isolated areas in Friuli–Venezia Giulia and Abruzzo; and otters in Parco Nazionale del Cilento in Campania. Golden eagles and wolves are a little more widespread. The lammergeier or bearded vulture has been successfully reintroduced in Parco Nazionale del Gran Paradiso, thanks to an international cooperative programme.

KATE NOLAN

Lynx

---

small, pinnate (divided) leaves are evergreen. It's a common sight in meadows and on stony ground, often at the edge of snow banks in spring and as high as 3500m. The alpine pasque flower is a taller plant with large, white flowers, more spread out than its spring relative and with rather feathery, deeply divided slender leaves.

One of the most colourful plants on cultivated ground up to 1800m, the bright red **common poppy** *(rosolaccio)* brings huge splashes of colour to the fields between May and July. Each long, hairy stem has a single, four-petalled flower with a darkish centre.

The low, bushy **white rockrose** is abundant and colourful in Mediterranean areas, especially in exposed, dry sites on limestone. It's often found together with a close relative, pink rockrose.

The unusual-looking stemless **carline thistle** *(carlina segnatempo)* grows on rocky slopes and in open woodlands up to 2800m, prostrate in exposed places or up to 30cm high in sheltered positions. The conspicuous flower heads have a central, darkish brown disc fringed with small, white leaflets and surrounded by yellowish pointed outer ones. The spiny leaves lie flat beneath the flowers, which close up during bad weather. It blooms from July to September.

[Continued from page 22]

CLIMATE

Italy's diverse climate can be divided into three major zones, each with its own local variations.

Starting in the north, the alpine zone is warmer and drier at its western end than in the east. This is best summed up by the difference in the height of the snow lines: in Valle d'Aosta it's 3060m and to the east in the Julian Alps it's down at 2505m. A typical annual rainfall reading in the west is 660mm and in the east 1050mm. Rainfall is greatest in summer, and you can expect thunderstorms between May and October. Snow can fall at any time, but the heaviest falls are concentrated in the winter months (December to March). The foothills of the Alps, or the pre-Alps, including The Lakes, enjoy sunnier and warmer conditions during summer than the mountainous areas, and the winters are milder. In these foothills you may experience the föhn, (see the boxed text 'Windy Italy', p34).

Abutting the pre-Alps are the flat, low-lying Po valley and northern plains – all the way from Turin (Torino) to Venice and south to Ravenna, Bologna and Genoa. Summers are generally sunny and hot; the average summer temperature at Turin is 23°C. Winters are cold with plenty of frost, fog and snow; Turin's winter average is 0.3°C. Thunderstorms bring much of the summer and autumn rain, but the area is still fairly dry; Venice's average annual rainfall is 750mm.

Peninsular Italy can be subdivided into the mostly mountainous interior and the coast. In the Apennines temperatures are much lower (an annual average of around 13°C) and rainfall higher than along the coast, where hot, mainly dry summers are the rule. The highest temperatures are experienced in the south, where rainfall is minimal. The prevailing winds along the northwestern coast around Liguria are from the southwest; the area is protected from cold northerly winds by the Apennines. Sicily and Sardinia have mild winters and hot, dry summers; during July and August the maximum averages around 28° C but it can reach 40°C.

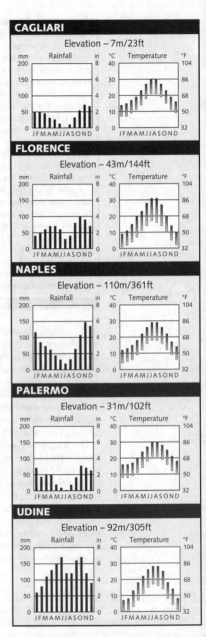

Signs of a Glacial Past

Many of the world's finest walks are through landscapes, which have been – or are being – substantially shaped by glaciers. As a glacier flows downhill its weight of ice and snow creates a distinctive collection of landforms, many of which are preserved once the ice has retreated (as it is doing in most of the world's ranges today) or vanished.

The most obvious is the *U-shaped valley* (1), gouged out by the glacier as it moves downhill, often with one or more bowl-shaped *cirques* (2) at its head. Cirques are found along high mountain ridges or at mountain passes or *cols* (3). Where an alpine glacier – which flows off the upper slopes and ridges of a mountain range – has joined a deeper, more substantial valley glacier, a dramatic *hanging valley* (4) is often the result. Hanging valleys and cirques commonly shelter hidden alpine lakes or *tarns* (5). The thin ridge, which separates adjacent glacial valleys, is known as an *arête* (6).

As a glacier grinds its way forward it usually leaves long, *lateral moraine* (7) ridges along its course – mounds of debris either deposited along the flanks of the glacier or left by sub-ice streams within its heart (the latter, strictly, an *esker*). At the end – or *snout* – of a glacier is the *terminal moraine* (8), the point where the giant conveyor belt of ice drops its load of rocks and grit. Both high up in the hanging valleys and in the surrounding valleys and plains, *moraine lakes* (9) may form behind a dam of glacial rubble.

The plains that surround a glaciated range may feature a confusing variety of moraine ridges, mounds and outwash fans – material left by rivers flowing from the glaciers. Perched here and there may be an *erratic* (10), a rock carried far from its origin by the moving ice and left stranded when it melted.

View of area before glacier's retreat

KATE NOLAN

Windy Italy

The fact that names are given to four winds which prevail over different parts of Italy at various times suggests that they're not just gentle breezes.

The **föhn** is a widespread phenomenon in mountain areas. Moist air rises across windward slopes, condenses as rain or snow and shrouds the ridges in cloud. The air then surges down the leeward slopes, becoming increasingly warm and dry. The föhn gives a great boost to windsurfers on the lakes, though walkers may be less impressed with the clouds.

The **mistral** is confined to the northwest and Sardinia; it's a cold, dry northwesterly, which rushes down between the Pyrenees (on the Franco-Spanish border) and the Alps.

At the opposite end of the scale, the **sirocco** is usually hot and humid, and makes life uncomfortable in the south during spring and autumn; it blows from the south and southeast, having developed as a dry wind over the Atlas mountains in north Africa. By the time it reaches Italy, it's laden with sand and with moisture from the Mediterranean.

The **bora** roars across the Adriatic coast from the Albanian mountains as a cold, dry easterly wind, gusting to 100km/h, usually during winter.

ECOLOGY & ENVIRONMENT

Since prehistoric times humans have left their imprints on Italy; in particular, forests have been felled and marshes drained to make way for grazing fields, crops and orchards. Throughout Italy, much of the landscape is a very pleasing blend of olive groves, vineyards, fields, and woodlands of conifers and deciduous trees. Truly wild country is mainly confined to the remote reaches of Sardinia and to the highest mountains, although even there you're likely to find *rifugi* or skiing developments. Nevertheless, The World Wide Fund for Nature (WWF) has classified 40% of Sardinia as wilderness, and identified substantial wilderness areas in Valle d'Aosta (Parco Nazionale del Gran Paradiso) and in Trentino-Alto Adige (Parco Nazionale dello Stelvio and adjacent protected areas).

Conservation

The Italian government's record on environmental issues is less than admirable. Although the Ministry for the Environment was established in 1986, environmental laws are not always stringently enforced. Environmental groups claim that one of the reasons why floods in northern Italy have been particularly devastating in recent years is that controls over building along river banks have been far too slack.

Environmental organisations have had some success in arousing awareness about a wide range of issues, although their membership remains small by comparison with similar organisations in some other European countries. Rubbish is a besetting problem almost wherever you go in Italy; in the late 1990s Naples and its hinterland in particular endured a crisis brought on by local authorities' dismal failure to provide adequate sites and resources for refuse disposal. Recycling is starting to be taken seriously, partly due to a campaign led by the organisation Legambiente.

Atmospheric pollution can make life very unpleasant in many cities, as Italians persist in using their cars, despite good public transport services. Car-free days in city centres have gained widespread support; one of Legambiente's major campaign issues is promoting sustainable means of public transport.

Over the years referenda to impose stricter controls on the hunting of wild animals (especially birds) have failed, thanks to the strength and determination of the hunting lobby. However, in Valle d'Aosta, an initiative launched in 2001 promises a more enlightened approach. A licensing scheme was introduced to stem the mass invasion of hunters during the first week of the hunting season (mid-September), which, in many places, literally terrified the residents of quiet villages. In addition, a quota scheme was launched to control the number of birds and mammals taken, coupled with a drive to reduce the number of wild boar, which wreak havoc in woodlands as they forage for food.

During 2001 the World Wide Fund for Nature drew attention to the attrition of protected areas where land was excised for developments, dubious or otherwise. Proposals to excise a substantial chunk of the Parco Regionale di Portofino in Liguria outraged environmental groups but went ahead anyway. Parco del Sasso Simone e Simoncello in Marche was trimmed when a *comune* (town council) caved in to pressure by hunting groups. On the other hand, 10 *comuni* sought to have Parco Nazionale dell'Aspromonte in Calabria enlarged from 785 sq km to 1020 sq km.

The year 2002 was declared the International Year of Mountains by the United Nations. Mountain peoples from many countries shared their common problems and drove home the message that every choice made about the future of the mountains had to involve the participation of the people who lived there. The Italian National Committee organised High Summit 2002, the first transcontinental multimedia conference dedicated to all the world's mountain regions; topics included water, cultural issues, economics and risks in mountain areas. A parliamentary group 'Friends of the Mountains', founded in the early 1990s, pushed these issues forward, despite the government of the day's apparent disdain for environmental issues. For more information, two interesting websites are w www.mountains2002.org or w www.montagna.org.

In addition to the CAI (see the boxed text 'Club Alpino Italiano', p36), Italy's leading environmental organisations include:

Amici della Terra Italia (☎ 06 686 82 89, fax 06 68 30 86 10; w www.amiciterra.it; Via di Torre Argentina 18, 00186 Rome) This is the Italian wing of Friends of the Earth. Its main concerns, at home and abroad, are nuclear power, climate change, environmental education, and disposal of waste and refuse.

Greenpeace Italia (☎ 06 572 99 91, fax 06 578 35 31; e info@greenpeace.it; Viale Manlio Gelsomini 28, 00153 Rome) This group directs its main activities against issues that are of national and international concern: genetically modified foods, pollution, loss of native forests and climate change.

Legambiente (☎ 06 86 26 81, fax 06 86 21 84 74; e legambiente@legambiente.com; Via Salaria 403, 00199 Rome) This is Italy's largest and most dynamic environmental organisation. It manages (jointly and independently) around 40 nature conservation areas throughout the country, and leads campaigns on a wide range of issues including sustainable transport, waste recycling and biodiversity in Italy's parks and reserves.

LIPU (☎ 0521 27 30 43, fax 0521 27 34 19; w www.lipu.it; Via Trento 49, 43100 Parma) The Lega Italiana Protezione Uccelli (Italian League for the Protection of Birds) was founded in 1965 and now has more than 40,000 members. It manages small natural areas to protect bird habitats and to enable people to see wildlife in natural settings, runs 'hospitals' where wounded wild birds are rehabilitated and conducts a wide-ranging environmental education campaign. Its website gives a comprehensive rundown on its activities.

World Wide Fund for Nature Italia (☎ 06 84 49 71, fax 06 855 44 10; w www.wwf.it; Via Po 25/C, 00198 Rome) This group has among its most pressing issues climate change, protection of native forests, safe transport and a ban on new *autostrade* (motorways). It also alerts members to, and organises petitions against, proposals for inappropriate developments in parks and reserves.

NATIONAL PARKS & RESERVES

Italy has slowly developed an extensive system of protected areas since the first national park was set aside in 1922 (see the boxed text 'Italy's First National Park', p114). A concerted drive to expand the number of parks, to provide secure habitats for endangered species and, ultimately, a system of linked or contiguous conservation areas, resulted in a very substantial increase in the area protected. Together the national parks now cover somewhere in the vicinity of 20,000 sq km or a little more than 6% of the country. The government is committed to eventually increasing the area of protected reserves to 10% of the country's landed area. The three principal categories of protected areas are *parchi nazionali* (national parks), *parchi naturali regionali e interregionali* (regional and interregional nature parks), and *riserve naturali statali e regionali* (state and regional nature reserves).

There are also wetland zones of international importance, special protection zones, special conservation zones and a range of smaller reserves, such as suburban parks, of which there are more than 230.

Within the Ministry of the Environment, the Nature Conservation Service is responsible, among other things, for preparing programmes for the protection and sustainable development of protected natural areas, investigating proposals for new national parks and state natural reserves, and paving the way for the inauguration of new protected areas. You can find out more about its activities (in Italian) at **w** www.scn.minambiente.it.

Each park is established by a separate enactment; administration and policy-making for a national park are usually the responsibility of a specially appointed council comprising representatives of a variety of interests. Management is handled by local park staff and/or forestry officers.

Club Alpino Italiano

Walkers visiting Italy can't help but be aware of the presence of the Club Alpino Italiano (*CAI;* ☎ *02 205 72 31, fax 02 205 72 32 01;* **w** *www.cai.it; Via E Petrella 19, 20124 Milan*), as owner and manager of mountain *rifugi*, and as the energetic waymarker of paths. The CAI is also the major player in the world of Italian walking, mountaineering, trekking and kindred winter activities.

The club was founded in October 1863 in Turin, following the example set a few years earlier by the establishment of The Alpine Club in London. However, from the outset there was a basic difference between the two organisations: would-be members of The Alpine Club had to demonstrate their competence in alpinism, whereas no such requirement applies in Italy – the club is open to all. On the eve of WWI, when the club celebrated its 50th anniversary with an ascent of Gran Paradiso, Italy's highest mountain, it had 7500 members. At the same time there were only 730 people in The Alpine Club. During the interwar years, the CAI continued to grow and by 1939 had 75,000 members. Numbers were halved during WWII but the club quickly recovered and in its centenary year had reached 89,000. Growth after 1970 was phenomenal; the 300,000 mark was passed in 1993. The total was 316,877 in 1997. Only the German Alpine Club is larger; the French equivalent has about 100,000.

The average age of CAI members is in the late 30s with the largest geographical concentration in Lombardy (Lombardia). The greatest strength is among younger people who make up nearly half the total membership. The club is decentralised from its head office in Turin, with more than 460 area groups, which are further organised into six regions. This arrangement has enabled closer cooperation with local government authorities. Volunteers are the foundation and strength of the CAI, and enable it to run many different activities.

It has more than 1000 national instructors in mountaineering, ski mountaineering and touring, climbing, trekking and activities specifically for young people. The club's success in sustaining the commitment of its volunteer members is the object of some admiration.

Local groups also undertake publication projects, such as the Amalfi Coast's Monti Lattari map.

The club is firmly apolitical – its members' allegiances embrace the diversity of Italy's colourful political spectrum. Even the appointment of high-profile politicians to senior positions has not compromised this stance; the club participates in ongoing debates about competitive mountain sports and environmental issues affecting the mountains.

Nowadays it seems the CAI is slightly embarrassed by the potential for conflict between its ownership of *rifugi* and its strong environmental protection policy. The commitment to maintaining the inheritance of the *rifugi* is strong, not least because they are generally regarded as the best in the world. The debate about extensions and new constructions continues. From the outside, it's easy to appreciate the dilemma. The *rifugi* are magnets for thousands of people, including young children, but eroded paths and problems of waste disposal loom large.

A website maintained by the **Federazione Italiana Parchi e Riserve Naturali** *(Italian Federation of Nature Parks and Reserves;* w *www.parks.it)* has, among other things, links to a database on all Italy's protected areas, in which many entries have a thumbnail sketch of the area's features.

National Parks

There are 20 *parchi nazionali* (with four more on the way), a number which increased significantly during the 1990s from the five which had been set aside between 1922 and 1992. National parks are terrestrial or marine areas containing at least one ecosystem that is intact or only partly modified by human intervention, and at least one geological, geomorphological or biological feature of international or national importance for scientific, aesthetic, cultural, educational or recreational purposes; the expectation is that such areas will benefit from state conservation-oriented management.

The parks are fairly widely distributed, although there are none on Sicily. The relatively few in the south include the country's largest, the 1926-sq-km Pollino, as well as Cilento e Vallo di Diano, Calabria and Vesuvio. More than half of the parks protect mountainous areas, in the Alps and Apennines, including two of the oldest and largest parks – Gran Paradiso (700 sq km) and Stelvio (1346 sq km).

In addition to Gran Paradiso, Stelvio and Vesuvio, this guide features Cinque Terre, Abruzzo, Gran Sasso e Monti della Laga, Majella and Monti Sibillini.

Natural Parks

These are areas of land, rivers or wetlands (and eventually coastal areas) of natural or environmental importance, which constitute a homogenous system with natural assets such as lakes, and/or are of value for peaceful recreation and artistic purposes, and contain traditional cultural settlements; they may extend across more than one region. There are 122 of these reserves, more than two-thirds in northern regions, notably Piedmont (Piemonte) and Lombardy.

Some of the walks in this book pass through important natural parks, including Sciliar, Dolomiti Ampezzane, Puez-Odle and Dolomiti di Sesto (Dolomites), Alpi Apuane (Tuscany), Portofino (Liguria), Etna, Nebrodi (Sicily), and Alpi Marittime.

Natural Reserves

There are more than 400 national and regional natural reserves. These are more evenly spread across the country, with several in Calabria, Basilicata, and on Sardinia and Sicily, as well as in the north. They are areas of land, rivers, wetlands or marine areas that contain at least one important species of each plant and animal, or at least one ecosystem of importance for biological diversity or conservation of genetic resources. Whether they are designated national or regional reserves depends on the significance of their individual features.

World Heritage Sites

Italy has 33 World Heritage sites of cultural or natural scenic importance, designated by Unesco as places of world significance that would be an irreplaceable loss to the planet if they were altered. This prestigious designation places an obligation on the government to ensure that nothing is done to compromise the qualities of the sites. A sizeable proportion of them are the great historic city and town centres (Florence, Naples), others include buildings and archaeological sites (notably Pompeii). The Cinque Terre on the Ligurian coast and the Amalfi Coast in Campania are featured in this book.

POPULATION & PEOPLE

Italy's population stood at an estimated 57,679,825 in 2001. The country's growth rate (0.09%) is one of the lowest in Europe, and is largely dependent on immigration, with the majority of new arrivals coming from Africa and Eastern Europe.

The most densely populated urban areas are around Rome, Milan and Naples, and the most populous regions are Piedmont, parts of Lombardy, Liguria, Veneto and Friuli-Venezia Giulia.

RELIGION

Around 85% of Italians profess to be Catholic. There are also large groups of Muslims, evangelical Protestants and Jehovah's Witnesses, and other smaller groups including a Jewish community in Rome and the Waldenses (Valdesi; Swiss-Protestant Baptists) living in small communities in Piedmont.

Although the fabric of Italian life is profoundly influenced by the presence of the Catholic church, surprisingly few Italian Catholics practise their religion. Church attendance is low – an average of barely 25% attend Mass regularly.

SOCIETY & CONDUCT

Most Italians identify with their region or town, rather than their nation, except, perhaps, at international sporting events. An Italian is always first and foremost a Sicilian or Milanese before being Italian. However, when meeting foreigners, Italians will energetically reveal a national pride not obvious in their relationships with each other. At the same time, they are particularly welcoming to people from the countries to which Italians have migrated en masse.

Particularly in the south, the family is still of central importance in Italian society. On weekends, in particular, you're almost certain to share a trattoria or pizzeria with large extended family groups, in which the oldest and youngest are easily the most important people.

Traditional Culture

Genuine, everyday instances of traditional cultural practices are largely confined to more remote valleys and uplands in the Alps and pre-Alps. In Valle di Gressoney, Val d'Ayas and Val Sesia you'll pass through many villages and tiny settlements comprised entirely of timber and stone houses, built in traditional Walser style (see the boxed text 'Walser Heritage', p131). You'll come across many *alpe*, upland farms where

cows are milked daily, and cheese is made and sold on site. The cattle and sheep are taken up to the high summer pastures as soon as the grass is long enough – a major community event when everyone turns out to watch the noisy parade of beasts, each one wearing a bell, barking dogs and shouting, laughing shepherds marching beside the herd.

In places machinery has still not completely taken over in the harvesting of grass for winter fodder; early in the morning people (most but not all older rather than younger) head off to the fields armed with scythes and long rakes. At least some of the cut grass is carried to the village in tall wicker baskets, shaped like the top half of an hour glass, with two narrow shoulder straps.

LANGUAGE

Although many younger Italians speak some English because they study it at school, English is more widely understood in the north than in the south. Some hotel, restaurant and bar staff speak a little English, but you'll get on much better if you at least initiate a conversation or transaction in Italian. You'll usually find someone who speaks English at tourist offices.

While Italian is the country's primary language, there are some areas where Italian is not necessarily used or even understood. German and the ancient Ladin language (see the boxed text 'The Ladin Tradition', p188) are spoken in the South Tyrol area, Slovene around Trieste, French in Valle d'Aosta and the old Walser language is being kept alive by small groups in Valle di Gressoney (see the boxed text 'Walser Heritage', p131). Most minority languages are protected by law and are used in all official communications.

The Language chapter (p355) offers a brief introduction to Italian, including basic phrases for everyday situations and common words you're likely to encounter. There is also a small section on (Austrian) German with common greetings and useful words.

Facts for the Walker

SUGGESTED ITINERARIES

With an excellent public transport system in Italy (see Getting Around, p351), getting from one walk to another is fairly easy. Allow at least one day for travelling between reasonably proximate areas but more for widely separated areas (eg, two to three days from Sicily to the Western Alps). You should also bear in mind seasonality (see When to Walk, p43) when working out an itinerary. Following are a few recommendations based on the amount of time you have to explore Italy's wonderful walking opportunities.

One Week

With a week to spare you could start by soaking up the sun along the Amalfi coast's spectacular Sentiero degli Dei and Capo Muro, then wander out to Punta Campanella on the Sorrento Peninsula and finish with Vesuvius, hoping the volcano is having a quiet day.

Alternatively you could immerse yourself in the mountains of Valle d'Aosta's Parco Nazionale del Gran Paradiso, starting with the scenic Alpe Money walk in Valnontey, then following the Alta Via 2 from Cogne to Rhêmes-Notre-Dame where ibex, chamois and marmots are part of each day's walk.

Two Weeks

With a bit more time you could spend a couple of days exploring Liguria's famous Cinque Terre, then escape from the crowds to the Apennines' highest peak Corno Grande. This is a good warm-up for the remote Maritime Alps where you can explore the magnificent limestone Marguareis massif or make the adventurous high-level crossing from Terme di Valdieri to Entracque.

Otherwise, discover Lago di Garda's wildflower-rich Monte Baldo then cross the lake to Limone and explore the awesomely rugged and historic Valle del Singol. For a complete contrast, head into the little-known Julian and Carnic Alps and try the Slovenian Two-Step on limestone and challenging Monte Carnizza on the Austrian border.

Long-Distance Walks

With extensive mountainous areas, countless existing paths, a strong tradition of walking and mountaineering, and excellent public transport, Italy has the ideal setting for long-distance walks.

This is exploited in numerous *alte vie* (high-level routes) in the Dolomites, Valle d'Aosta and Lago di Como, for example, and cultural or historical theme walks such as the Sentiero Walser in Valle d'Aosta. These routes can be followed from end to end in as few as four days or up to two weeks; highlights of some are featured in this book (in the Campania, Western Alps and Lake District chapters).

Yet there is much more to long-distance walking in Italy than this. The **Grande Traversata delle Alpi** wanders through the outliers of the Western Alps. The **Grande Escursione Appenninica** is a high-level route along the Tuscany-Emilia-Romagna border. The **E/1** (part of the European system of long-distance walks) goes from the Swiss border at Lake Lugano south to Genoa, east via the Apennines and down into Umbria. The **Sentiero Italia** is in a class all of its own, from Trieste towards Reggio Calabria, with planned extensions in Sicily and Sardinia.

It's rare to find dedicated waymarking for these long-distance routes, apart from the occasional signpost, so you need to be confident with your map reading.

However, these seriously long walks wouldn't fit into a conventional holiday and many walkers spend years doing manageable sections at a time, progressing towards the full distance.

Grande Traversata delle Alpi (GTA)

The GTA is a network of paths rather than a single continuous path through the Alps from Viozene, in the Maritime Alps, in the south to Valle Anzasca, east of Monte Rosa, in the north. About 1000km long, it involves the equivalent of several ascents of Mt Everest – 67,000m of climbing. Variants of many sections of the route considerably increase the potential distance.

More than 120 *posti tappa* (staging posts) are equipped with bunk beds, kitchens, water and power. Most are in villages or small towns where supplies and/or meals are available. Club Alpino Italiano (CAI) and private *rifugi* serve 16 of the 27 stages; elsewhere there may be hotels and pensiones. The best season for the route is mid-June to late September.

Nine sheets in the IGC 1:50,000 series (Nos 1, 2, 3, 6, 7, 8, 9, 10 and 17) cover the full length of the GTA with the route specially marked, including the alternatives. Experience indicates they aren't 100% reliable.

The **Associazione Grande Traversata delle Alpi** (☎ *011 562 44 77; Via Barbaroux 1, 10122 Torino*) issues two useful brochures: *Grande Traversata delle Alpi* (in English) and *Percorsi e Posti Tappa*, with maps and basic details of accommodation, public transport and facilities for each stage.

Grande Escursione Appenninica (GEA)

The GEA follows an undulating route along the spine of the Apennines for more than 400km, through small towns, villages, forests and across alpine areas, from Passo dei due Santi, north of La Spezia (on the Ligurian coast), to Bocca Trabaria, just south of the Tuscany-Umbria border.

The GEA is covered by more than 15 topographical maps from several publishers, ranging in scale from 1:15,000 to 1:70,000 – too many to list here. *GEA. Grande Escursione Appenninica*, by Alfonso Bietolini & Gianfranco Bracci, is a comprehensive guide to the walk with useful 1:30,000 maps. Up-to-date accommodation lists from tourist information offices are indispensable for planning a walk.

Contact the tourist offices in the towns nearest to the section of the GEA you are planning to explore for accommodation and transport information (eg, Pistoia, Lucca, Prato or Castelnuovo di Garfagnana). Spring and autumn are the best times for the GEA. Most, if not all, the route is accessible throughout the year, although snow and ice could be hazards during winter in the highest areas.

Continued on page 42

Long-Distance Walks

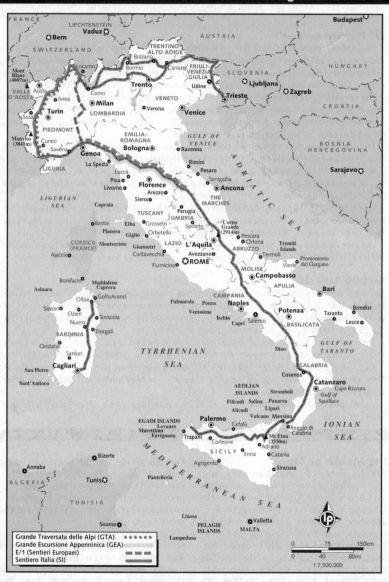

Grande Traversata delle Alpi (GTA) • • • • •
Grande Escursione Appenninica (GEA)
E/1 (Sentieri Europaei)
Sentiero Italia (SI)

0   75   150km
0   40   80mi
1:7,500,000

Long-Distance Walks

Continued from page 40

E/1 (Sentieri Europaei)

Through the Federazione Europea Turismo Pedestre more than 30 walking and mountaineering associations from 20 European countries cooperate in developing and promoting a network of 10 long-distance paths, totalling around 20,000km across the length and breadth of Europe. These link existing paths within the various countries to make continuous routes, most more than 2000km long.

The E/5 extends for 600km from Lake Constance on the Swiss-German border to the outskirts of Verona. The E/1 is in a different league, linking northern Europe to the Mediterranean, currently from central western Sweden, through Germany and the Swiss Alps, crossing into Italy at Porto Ceresio and extending to Scapoli on the Lazio-Molise border.

The E/1, between Lake Lugano and Genoa, is a walk of great variety – the lakes and the high plateau of Campo dei Fiori in the north, then the flat Ticino and Po valleys, back into the mountains with the Ligurian Alps, the full length of the Grande Escursione Appenninica and on to Parco Nazionale dei Monti Sibillini, ending, for the time being, at Scapoli. Beyond there the route is still just an idea, apart from about 100km in the Monti Picentini range north of Salerno.

Four 1:50,000 Studio Cartografico Italiano maps, Nos F13, F14, F15 and F16, cover the E/1 from Porto Ceresio to the Po; they should be available at good local bookshops. Further south, in the same series, Nos F1, F4, F6 and F11, plus the maps for the GEA, are useful.

The best source of information (especially the website) is the **Federazione Italiana Escursionismo** (☎/fax 010 46 32 61; **w** *www.fienazit.freeweb.supereva.it; Via La Spezia 58r, 16149 Genova*).

Sentiero Italia (SI)

The SI will eventually be a 5000km chain of paths from Trieste to Calabria, with extensions to Sardinia and Sicily. It will unite the Alps and the Apennines, and create an unbroken route of 350 stages – a year's continuous walking. The GTA and the GEA are important components, together with many other shorter routes. All the paths are accessible during most of the year.

The route is designed so there is somewhere to stay at the end of each stage – a CAI or private *rifugio*, or a purpose-built shelter with basic but adequate facilities in the Apennines and on the GTA.

Two special Kompass 1:50,000 maps, Nos 676 and 677, cover the Lombardy section of the SI. They come with a booklet outlining the route. Elsewhere you need the relevant maps in whichever series best covers the area.

The **Associazione Sentiero Italia** (☎ *011 33 12 00; Corso Rosselli 132, 10129 Torino*) is the best source of advice.

One Month or More

With the luxury of a month or more, you could concentrate on the warm and sunny south first with the Amalfi coast's historic paths and villages on the Valle delle Ferriere walk, then move west to the Sorrento Peninsula and wander out to beautiful Punta Penna. Cross to Sicily to experience the excitement of walking on rumbling Mt Etna and relax in the Sicilian countryside on the Nebrodi Lake circuit. Follow this with a week on Sardinia in the magnificent Gorropu Gorge and the beautiful coast of Golfo di Orosei. Tuscany, never short of sun, would be a fitting finale – enjoy the best of Italian food, wine and history-filled landscapes on the Medieval Hills and Chianti Classico walks.

For an adventurous mountain tour, start with the Northern Dolomites high-level walk, enjoying *rifugio* (mountain hut) hospitality and the natural wonders of the Dolomites' Parco Naturale di Sesto, then move west to Parco Nazionale dello Stelvio and the superbly scenic traverse over high passes from Val di Rabbi to Martelltal. You can't be in this part of Italy without trying one of the Brenta Dolomites' *vie ferrate*. Then make for Valle d'Aosta to finish with the exceptionally scenic Matterhorn and Monte Rosa walk, crossing passes between valleys in the shadows of these famous Alpine peaks.

WHEN TO WALK

From the range of walks presented in this book it's possible to find something for any time of the year.

Summer is the time to visit the Alps, Apennines, Apuan Alps, Julian and Carnic Alps, and the Lake District. The best months for the mountainous areas are late June, July and September; the season is a little longer around Lago di Garda, Lago di Como and Lago Maggiore. These months usually have the best weather and the hours of daylight are long – it's still light around 9pm. Light snow can fall over the highest ground at any time but rarely lies for very long in summer. *Rifugi* are usually open from mid-June to late September.

The cooler months of spring and autumn (April, May, September and October) are the best times to visit the coastal and lowland areas of Liguria, Tuscany, Campania, Sicily and Sardinia. Winter could also be worth considering if you don't mind the occasional very cold day but be prepared to adapt to short hours of daylight – darkness can fall as early as 5pm.

Remember that during August just about everyone in Italy is on holidays at the beach or in the mountains, along with huge crowds of other holidaymakers.

WHAT KIND OF WALK?

Walking in Italy is generally fairly organised. Italians prefer marked paths which are well served by *rifugi* or hotels, rather than treks in wilderness areas where it's necessary to carry a tent, sleeping bag, cooking equipment and food.

In popular walking areas, such as the Alps, Apennines, Apuan Alps, Lake District, Abruzzo and Chianti (in Tuscany), facilities are usually pretty good. It's possible to plan walks from a comfortable base in a town or village, or through walks with transport at each end and accommodation along the way.

In the south there are fewer *rifugi* and paths aren't always well marked. If you venture up Stromboli or into the interior of Sardinia without a guide, you might get lost and would have to extricate yourself unaided.

ORGANISED WALKS
Walk Operators in Italy

Guided walks, usually with cultural, historical or natural history themes, are organised in many national parks and by some local experts. You can obtain details of these from park and tourist information offices, details of which are given in the walk chapters.

There are also many walking clubs in towns and cities throughout Italy but, unless you can make contact through your own walking organisation, it's unlikely you'll get much help from them.

Mountain Guides You won't need a professional, qualified mountain guide to do any of the walks described in this book. However, if you want to have a go at one of the major peaks, such as Monte Rosa, Matterhorn, Monviso, Gran Paradiso or Mont Blanc (Monte Bianco), or tackle a high-level trek that includes glacier crossings, then a qualified guide is absolutely essential (unless, of course, you've done that sort of thing before).

The Unione Internazionale Associazione Guide Montagna (UIAGM), which is an international organisation for mountain guides, operates a qualification system and you should check that the guides you're contacting are entitled to wear the UIAGM's badge.

For contacts in the respective regions, see Guided Walks in the walk chapters or contact **Guide Alpine Italiane (W** *www.guidealpine .it; Via Petrella 19/a, 10124 Milan).*

Walk Operators Abroad

Many operators offer guided walking holidays in Italy; check outdoor magazines and websites such as **w** www.gorp.com for more information. Trips range from around five to eight days. Prices depend on the standard of accommodation and transport costs, but expect to pay from £500/US$750 to £750/US$1124 for eight days. Luxury operators such as Backroads charge up to US$3600 for six days.

The UK

ATG (☎ 01865 31 56 78, fax 01865 31 56 97; **w** www.atg-oxford.co.uk; 69–71 Banbury Rd, Oxford OX2 6PJ) This company offers several continuous walking trips (luggage transported) such as eight-day Unknown Umbria and Spoleto; and eight-day Montefeltro and Urbino; plus the popular destinations of Cinque Terre, Amalfi Coast and Tuscany.

Marmot Trails (☎/fax 020-8461 5516; 1 Farley Rd, London SE6 2AA) A small company, Marmot Trails has a string of eight-day walks visiting Stelvio National Park; Dolomites, with a wide range of walks from Val Pusteria; *vie ferrate* in the Dolomites; and Nebrodi National Park, Sicily.

Waymark Holidays (☎ 01753-516 477, fax 517 016; **w** www.waymarkholidays.com; 44 Windsor Rd, Slough SL1 2EJ) This is an experienced company offering holidays to popular areas, including Tuscany, Amalfi and the Dolomites; there is a seven- or 10-night Lago di Garda trip; and 10 days in Val d'Ayas on the north side of Valle d'Aosta, including non-technical ascents of high peaks.

Continental Europe

Active Tours (☎ 8374-5899 525, fax 5899 530; **w** www.activetours.de; Alpenrosenweg 20, 87463 Dietmannsried, Germany) Tours include the eight-day Dolomites hut to hut, from Rosengarten, and seven days of walking in Cinque Terre.

Terres d'Aventure (☎ 01 53 73 77 73, fax 01 43 25 69 37; **w** www.terdav.com; 6 rue Saint Victor, 75005 Paris, France) The company offers 13 trips to Italy, including Les Sentiers du Chianti de Florence à Sienne (seven days); Sardinia–Supramonte, including forests and gorges (seven days); and Lac du Come, focussing on Bellagio (six days). Other areas on the programme are the Adamello Dolomites (including *vie ferrate*), the Gran Paradis Haute Route and active volcanoes.

Trekking in the Alps (☎ 04 50 54 62 09, fax 04 50 54 63 29; **w** www.trekkinginthealps.com; Chemin des Biolles, 74660 Vallorcine, France). Run by an experienced Englishwoman, this company has six-day trips including Gran Paradiso High Route and Dolomites High Route.

The USA

Backroads (☎ 800-GO-ACTIVE, or 510-527 1555, fax 510-527 1444; **w** www.backroads.com; 801 Cedar St, Berkeley, CA 94710-1800) This company offers walking in style, staying at luxury accommodation – with prices to match. Walks head around Lago di Como (Cernobbio, Lenno, Bellagio); Cinque Terre (Sestri Levante and Portofino); and the Dolomites for eight days between Bolzano and Cortina d'Ampezzo.

Cross Country International (☎ 800-828 8768, fax 845-677 6077; **w** www.walkingvacations .com; PO Box 1170, Millbrook, NY 12545) This company offers an eight-day Amalfi Coast trip, based at Ravello and including a trip to Pompeii; and seven nights in Tuscany, southeast of Siena.

Wilderness Travel (☎ 1-800-368 2794, fax 510-558 2489; **w** www.wildernesstravel.com; 1102 Ninth St, Berkeley, CA 94710-1211) This company has an 11-day Sicily trip, including Madoine Mountains, Mt Etna and Zingaro Nature Reserve; an eight-day Lake Country trip visiting Lago di Orta and Lago di Como; and nine days along the Amalfi Coast based at Ravello and Amalfi; as well as visits to Tuscany, the Dolomites and Umbria.

Australia

interNATIONAL PARKtours (☎ 061-755 333 583, fax 061-755 333 683; **w** www.parktours.com.au; Binna Burra Rd, Beechmont, Qld 4211) This tour group offers a 22-day South Italian Sojourn visiting the Amalfi Coast, Sicily and Vesuvius, and staying in hotels.

RESPONSIBLE WALKING

Italy's countryside has been altered by the impact of many different human activities for thousands of years. However, the invasion by walkers (and other outdoors enthusiasts) during the past 30 years is probably unprecedented in scale.

Italy's rules for national and other parks serve to protect the environment and wildlife, while allowing low-impact recreational use, and have been summarised in the boxed text 'Country Code' (p45). Rubbish and human waste disposal are two unsightly problems in Italy and there's little evidence of any concerted attack. By following these guidelines for minimal impact walking and camping, we can all help to fulfil the responsibilities that go with the rights and privileges of walking in the Italian countryside.

Access

- Although it may not be obvious at the time, many of the walks in this book pass through private property, along recognised routes where access is freely permitted. If there seems to be some doubt about this, ask someone nearby if it's OK to walk through – you'll rarely have any problems.

Camping

- If camping near a farm or house, seek permission first.
- In remote areas, use a recognised site rather than create a new one. Keep at least 30m from watercourses and paths. Move on after a night or two.
- If your tent is sited away from hollows where water is likely to accumulate, it won't be necessary to dig damaging trenches if it rains heavily.
- Leave your site as you found it – with minimal or no trace of your use.

Washing

- Don't use detergents or toothpaste in or near streams or lakes; even if they are biodegradable they can harm fish and wildlife.
- To wash yourself, use biodegradable soap and a water container at least 50m from the watercourse. Disperse the waste water widely so it filters through the soil before returning to the stream.
- Wash cooking utensils 50m from streams, using a scourer instead of detergent.

Human Waste Disposal

- Bury your waste. Dig a small hole 15cm deep and at least 30m from any watercourse, 50m from paths and 200m from any buildings. Take a lightweight trowel or large tent peg for the purpose. Cover the waste with a good layer of soil and leaf mould.
- Do not contaminate water sources – contamination of water by human faeces can lead to the transmission of Giardia, a human bacterial parasite; gastroenteritis is probably caused by exposed human faecal waste.
- Toilet paper should be carried out. It can be burned, but this is not recommended in a forest, above the tree line or in dry grassland. Burying is a last resort – ideally use biodegradable paper.
- Sanitary napkins, tampons and condoms don't burn or decompose readily, so carry them out, whatever the inconvenience.

Rubbish

- If you've carried it in, carry it out – everything, including wrappers, citrus peel, cigarette butts and empty packaging, stowed in a dedicated rubbish bag. Make an effort to pick up rubbish left by others.

Country Code

- Respect those who live and work in the countryside
- Light fires only in fireplaces provided at picnic and camping areas
- Leave gates as you find them – open or closed
- Keep to defined paths and resist the temptation to take short cuts
- Use gates and stiles to cross fences and walls; if necessary, climb a gate at the hinged end
- Steer clear of livestock and machinery
- Take your rubbish home or to the nearest disposal point
- Avoid polluting water sources
- Leave all wild creatures and plants as your find them
- Drive and park considerately on country roads

- Don't bury rubbish – this disturbs soil and ground cover, and encourages erosion and weed growth. Buried rubbish takes years to decompose and will probably be dug up by wild animals who may be injured or poisoned by it.
- If you're camping, remove all surplus food packaging and put small-portion packages in a single container before leaving.

Other Walkers

- It's the custom and polite practice to greet other walkers on mountain paths. A simple *buongiorno*, *giorno* or *salve* (among aficionados) is fine. Germans you meet will usually greet you with a brisk *Grüss Gott* and most others settle for hello. This can become a little tiring when you meet a group of 30 walkers!
- It's usually a toss-up about who should give way on a narrow, steep path – walkers ascending or descending. It all comes down to common sense and courtesy.

ACCOMMODATION

Throughout this book, places to stay (and eat) at the end of each stage of a walk, or which could serve as a base for day walks, are specifically noted. Wherever possible at least two places are covered, although on extended walks there may be only one option, such as on a *rifugio* to *rifugio* walk in the mountains.

Many places offer half pension (dinner, bed and breakfast) and full pension (bed and all meals).

Local tourist offices can provide detailed lists of camping grounds, serviced accommodation and self-catering establishments in their area.

If you arrive at a large town with no bookings and after the tourist office has closed, you may find an after-hours accommodation service nearby – a video screen with a map and details of establishments, and a telephone which you can use to make free calls to the place of your choice.

Reservations

Many Italians holiday on the coast or in the mountains in August, so book early for those regions, especially if you're planning to stay in *rifugi*. In popular tourist areas such as Chianti and the Cinque Terre, accommodation is in strong demand year-round, so it's strongly recommended that you book well ahead. Hostels are nearly always busy, so bookings are advisable.

Camping

Many *campeggi* (camping grounds) in Italy are large, landscaped complexes with a swimming pool, restaurant and bar, shop, laundry – and places to park campervans, cars and caravans, and even pitch tents. Most also have a collection of small bungalows (cabins, chalets) and some static (on-site, fixed) caravans. Like hotels, they are graded according to a star system to indicate the facilities available.

At most places the tariff comprises a fee for each person (€6.20 to €9.30) plus a fee for the pitch/tent (€7.75 and beyond); you may have to pay extra if you have a car. It's not unknown to have to pay a small fee for a hot shower. This could end up costing more than a night in a hostel but less than a room in a one-star hotel.

Locations are usually attractive – with sea views on the coast or of mountains in the Alps. They're very sociable places and great for meeting people from all over the world, especially Europe. At busy times though, *campeggi* can become almost oppressively crowded.

The website **w** www.camping.it gives detailed information on camping grounds throughout the country. An English version is available.

Wild camping is generally not permitted in Italy and you might be disturbed during the night by the police. Out of the main tourist season, if you choose a spot out of sight of the nearest road, don't light a fire and generally keep a low profile, you shouldn't have any trouble. Always seek permission from the landowner if you want to camp on private property close to a house.

Camping is prohibited in national parks and nature reserves, except in recognised camping areas – of which there are very few.

Hostels

These are called *ostelli per la gioventù* and most are run by the Associazione Italiana Alberghi per la Gioventù (AIG), which is affiliated to Hostelling International (HI). You don't have to have an HI card to stay at a hostel but it does simplify things. Membership cards can be purchased at major hostels, AIG offices and from HI offices in your home country (see Hostel Card, p343).

Nightly tariffs range from €11 to €16.50, which may include breakfast; if not, it's an extra €1.55. Some hostels levy a fee for use of hot water and for heating in the cooler months, usually around €1. Evening meals are often provided, from €8.

Accommodation is in segregated dormitories; some hostels have family rooms, at a higher rate per person. Many hostels are in interesting and historic buildings (villas and small castles) and in scenic locations (overlooking lakes or the sea).

Some hostels close from 9am to 3.30pm, others at different times or not at all; check-in and curfew times vary from place to place.

Accommodation at the country's 85 hostels can be booked via the head office of the **AIG** (☎ *06 487 11 52, fax 06 488 04 92;* **w** *www.ostellionline.org; Via Cavour 44, 00184 Rome*), which also has an informative booklet about Italian hostels. Some can be booked via the London office of the **International Youth Hostels Federation** (**w** *www.iyhf.org*).

Independent hostels are virtually unknown in Italy outside Rome.

Rifugi

There's an excellent network of *rifugi* in the Alps, pre-Alps (hinterland of the Lake District), northern Apennines and Apuan Alps. There are fewer in the Maritime Alps and almost none in the south of the country, Sicily or Sardinia. *Rifugi* are marked on the topographical maps covering walking areas.

If you are counting on staying overnight at a *rifugio*, always phone ahead to make sure the place is open and has room, and to let the staff know approximately when you expect to arrive. *Rifugi* fill up quickly in midsummer, and occasionally one closes for repairs or burns down. *Rifugi* are also the first point of inquiry if someone goes missing in the mountains and staff are genuinely concerned for walkers' safety. Technically, *rifugi* may not refuse to provide shelter but they are also obliged to heed regulations, which state they cannot accommodate more people than there are beds. If full and there is enough time for you to reach the next *rifugio* before dark you will be sent on. If it's too late, you'll be allocated a space on the floor.

Some *rifugi* are privately run, many others are owned and run by the CAI (see the boxed text, p36). The CAI *rifugi* are usually cheaper and more likely to have mixed dormitory accommodation, either in largish rooms with long platforms on which a dozen or more bodies lie tightly packed, or in smaller rooms with individual bunks. Blankets are provided; you'll need a sleeping sheet and pillow case, although some *rifugi* have them for hire. A torch (flashlight) will probably come in handy – night-time lighting is minimal. Don't expect a hot shower at the end of the day – some *rifugi* provide only basins with cold water in the communal washrooms. Private *rifugi* may have smaller rooms with conventional beds. The average tariff per person (non-CAI member) for bed and breakfast ranges from €15.50 to €23.25.

Meals are always served – expect to pay €13 to €18. The meal usually consists of pasta or soup, a *secondo* (second or main course), which is almost always a meat dish with vegetables, and then dessert or cheese. Vegetarians should let the *gestore* (manager) know their requirements on arrival –

Do the Right Thing at *Rifugi*

It might seem old-fashioned but there are a few rules that CAI *rifugio* residents are expected to adhere to – not because the CAI is necessarily authoritarian but in the interests of a comfortable stay for everyone.

- Reservations must be taken up by 6pm, unless you've advised a later arrival time; after that the place will be allocated on a first-come, first-served basis
- You'll most likely be sent to bed at 10pm (at the manager's discretion); you can rise as early as 6am (or earlier by arrangement)
- Leave your boots in the entrance vestibule and change into your own sandals or runners, or use the slippers supplied
- Smoking is prohibited in dormitories and in the dining room
- Everyone is strongly urged to fill in the guest book with details of where they've come from and their destination next day – essential in the event of a search and rescue operation

you'll most likely be given an omelette instead of the meat dish. Drinks cost extra and are relatively expensive because of the cost of getting them there (helicopters, and sometimes mules, horses and people). Breakfast is simple: bread, butter, jam and coffee. You can usually obtain hot water if you want to fill a flask for hot drinks during the day; packed lunches may be available if ordered the night before.

Most *rifugi* are open full-time only from mid-June to late September. Those at lower altitudes or close to roads may also open on weekends from Easter until mid-October. Additional information, including contact details, can be obtained from local tourist offices and the CAI's website ( www.cai.it).

You could consider taking advantage of the reciprocal rights scheme (or Reciprocity Fund) that operates at CAI *rifugi*. By joining your national alpine or mountaineering club or association and obtaining a reciprocal rights card, you are entitled to pay CAI members' rates. The overnight tariff is just half that for nonmembers, and food and drink prices are between 60% and 75% of the full rate. In Britain, contact the **British**

Mountaineering Council (☎ 0161 445 47 47, fax 0161 445 45 00; e office@thebmc.co.uk; 177-179 Burton Rd, Manchester M20 2BB).

As well as the *rifugi*, there are *bivacchi* in more remote and often higher locations. A *bivacco* is a more basic shelter and not staffed by a *gestore*. Some are always open; for others it's necessary to arrange by telephone to collect a key before you head into the wilderness. Contact the nearest tourist office for details.

Hotels

Usually there isn't any obvious difference between a *pensione* and an *albergo* (hotel); in fact, some hotels use both titles. They are graded according to a system of one to five stars, indicating the range of facilities – from basic rooms with shared facilities to luxury establishments with everything that opens and shuts.

Meublé alberghi (furnished hotels) either have rooms with self-catering facilities or simply provide B&B; most hotels have their own dining room. *Locande* (inns) and *alloggi* or *affittacamere* (flats/apartments)

may be cheaper, but are not always given star gradings.

A *camera singola* (single room) or single occupancy of a double/twin room is relatively expensive – expect to pay from €15.50 in a one-star place to at least €30 in a three-star hotel. Some hoteliers will charge you the full room rate. A *camera doppia* (double room with twin beds) and a *camera matrimoniale* (double room with double bed) range from €20 to €42. Half pension is usually a good bargain – from €42 to €58 for dinner, bed and breakfast at a three-star hotel.

FOOD
Regional Food

What the world regards as Italian cooking is really a collection of regional cuisines; cooking styles vary markedly from region to region and significantly between the north and south.

Among the country's best known dishes are lasagne and tagliatelle *al ragù* (also known as spaghetti bolognese), both from Emilia-Romagna. In Trentino-Alto Adige the Austrian influence is strong and you'll

---

Pasta *al Dente*

Cooking pasta the Italian way is an art. The pasta must be top quality, salt is added to the boiling water before the pasta is thrown in and it must be cooked for precisely the correct length of time so that it is *al dente* (firm, almost crunchy). In a trattoria expect to wait the 10 to 12 minutes it takes to cook your order.

Pasta comes in hundreds of shapes and sizes, from spaghetti and linguine to tubes such as penne and rigatoni, as well as *conchiglie* (shells), *farfalle* (butterflies), *fusili* (corkscrew) and *orecchiette* (little ears). An important reason for this vast variety is that each shape absorbs or blends with sauces differently. Dried pasta is made with durum wheat and water. *Pasta fresca* or *pasta all'uovo* (fresh pasta) is made with eggs and flour and is used in stuffed pasta such as tortellini, fettuccine, cannelloni and ravioli, or cut into strips called tagliatelle, *taglionini* or *taglianini*. Egg pasta is usually served with slow-braised meats or sauces which are richer and creamier than those with dried pasta – usually tomato-based.

Sauce ingredients vary markedly between north and south. In the north they are richer, often creamy and often use red meat; the further south you go, the more you'll find vegetable-based sauces and, on the coast, seafood. In Sicily, eggplant is a popular addition to tomato sauces.

Freshly grated cheese is the magic addition for most pasta. *Parmigiano* (parmesan) is the most widely used, particularly in the north. Look for the name *Parmigiano Reggiano* on the rind to ensure you're buying the genuine article, rather than the similar but slightly inferior *Grana Padano*. In Sardinia the sharp *pecorino*, an aged sheep's cheese, is often used; *ricotta salata* (salted ricotta) is common in the south and in Sicily.

find *canederli* (dumplings) made with stale bread, cheese and, perhaps, liver. Polenta (corn meal) with all kinds of sauces, and/or with Fontina cheese is very popular in Valle d'Aosta. Two Ligurian specialties are pesto (sauce or paste of fresh basic, garlic, oil, pine nuts and sharp cheese) and focaccia (flat bread). In Tuscany the locals use plenty of olive oil and herbs, and regional dishes are noted for their simplicity, fine flavour and use of fresh produce. Among the staples of Tuscan cuisine are small white *cannellini* (beans).

As you go further south the food becomes spicier, and the cakes and pastries sweeter and richer. A pizza in or near Naples (where it was created), and local fish around Amalfi and Sorrento shouldn't be missed.

In Sicily try the *pesce spada* (swordfish); *melanzane* (eggplant) is popular here, in pasta sauces or filled with olives, anchovies, capers and tomatoes. Sardinia's treats include *carte musica* (thin crisp bread), eaten warm with oil and salt, and *pecorino* (aged sheep's cheese) sprinkled on pasta.

Where to Eat In towns and villages there's usually a choice of places to eat. A *tavola calda* is a self-service, offering inexpensive instant meat, pasta and vegetable dishes, and doesn't charge extra for you to sit down. A *rosticceria* usually offers cooked meats and other takeaway food. A pizzeria will, of course, serve pizza and usually has a full menu of pasta, fish and meat dishes; the best pizzas are *al forno* – cooked in a wood-fired oven. An *osteria* is the classic place to eat in Italy, usually a bar offering a choice from a small simple menu emphasising local food. A trattoria is essentially a more homely, less expensive version of a *ristorante* (restaurant) which, in turn, has more professional service and a greater range of dishes, although not necessarily of a higher standard than you'll find at a trattoria.

Menus are usually posted outside so you can check prices, as well as the *pane e coperta* (cover charge), which is usually around €1.50, and perhaps a service charge (around 15%). For opening hours see Business Hours (p347).

Vegetarians will have no problems eating in Italy. Specialist vegetarian restaurants are fairly rare, but vegetables, pasta, rice and pulses are staples of the Italian diet. Most eating places have a good selection of *contorni* (vegetable dishes) and *insalate* (salads), as well as meat-free *antipasti* (appetisers), soup, rice and pasta dishes and pizzas.

Unfortunately smoking is not banned in eating places in Italy, and you can expect other patrons to light up before, during and after a meal.

You can buy sandwiches at bars or have them made in *alimentari* (delicatessen/grocery shops) or a *panificio/panetteria* (bakery). A *pasticceria* (pastry shop) is the place to go for the accompanying cake or pastry. *Pizza a taglio* (pizza by the slice or massive slab) is sold in takeaway places. *Gelateria* (gelati shops) are plentiful everywhere; look out for those displaying a sign with the word *artigianale* (homemade), which should mean it is made on the premises and contains fresh ingredients.

On the Walk

For economy and safety it's a good idea to carry some of your own food on walks. Always carry emergency supplies: light, high energy items include nuts, dried fruits and chocolate. On many – but not all – walks you'll pass through a town or village during the day where you can stock up or have a light meal. In the mountains, *rifugi* are open during the day for snacks and drinks and a hearty lunch (see *Rifugi*, p 47).

Buying Food Snack foods, cheese, sliced meat, pate, bread, vegetables and fruit can be purchased at supermarkets, *alimentari*, and speciality fruit and vegetable shops and, if you're in the right place at the right time, open-air fresh produce markets. For fresh bread look for *panetteria/panificio* or *pasticceria.*

Cooking You can, of course, bring your own stove and cook meals at camping grounds and, perhaps, at *rifugi*, although this isn't a common practice and probably not very popular with the warden or other

Chianti, Lambrusco, Soave & Much More

The wine and food of each region tend to complement each other superbly, so always look for the local labels on a trattoria's wine list. It's surprisingly inexpensive – up to €7.75 for a commendable wine and €15.50 or more for a well-aged, limited production vintage. The best selections of wines are to be found in *enoteche* (wine stores), where tasting before buying is part of the ritual.

There are four main classifications to help ensure the standard of traditional Italian wines; these are prominently displayed on the bottle. *Denominazione di origine controllata* (DOC) means the wine has been subjected to regional controls over characteristics related to climate, soils and local tradition, and quality. *Denominazione d'origine controllata e garantita* (DOCG) is a guarantee of outstanding quality as these wines have been checked by government inspectors; very few wines earn this designation. *Indicazione Geografica Tipica* (IGT) certifies that the wine has the characteristics of its location. *Vino di tavola* (table wine) is the name given to all other wines, although such wines aren't necessarily inferior.

About 400 of the 1000 or more recognised grape varieties in Italy are in wine production. Each region's grapes are very much its own, so even if the same variety is used in two areas not far apart, their wines will be different. Following is an introduction to some of the best wines in the major wine producing areas.

Valle d'Aostawine

This is the smallest producer and also the claimed location of the highest classified vineyard in Europe, at Morgex. The Valle doesn't even meet the demands of local drinkers so it's unlikely you'll find any outside the region. Chambave Moscato is a dry white, best drunk young; look out for the *passito* version, a perfumed dessert wine. Among the reds, Donnaz (from the Nebbiolo grape) is light but ages well. See the boxed text 'Valdostane Gastronomy' (p111).

Piedmont

Wines from this region are widely regarded as being the equal best in Italy, along with Tuscany, and they come from local rather than well-known varieties. It has more than 40 DOC and DOCG wines, more than any other region.

Gavi is a flinty white with strong hints of citrus that goes well with *primi piatti* (entrées or first courses) and fish.

Barbera is a widely planted red, which produces anything from light *frizzante* (fizzy) to full-bodied wines. Barolo (from Nebbiolo grapes) produces outstanding reds, best drunk when well aged. If this is too expensive, try Nebbiolo d'Alba. Both go superbly with red meat and game. There's also Barbaresco, another Nebbiolo-based wine, softer than Barolo and more aromatic.

Asti is made from white Moscato grapes and dominates the export market. Moscato d'Asti for local consumption is completely different – fragrant and not too *frizzante*.

Lombardy

The main producing area is Valtellina (north of Lago di Como) where every possible square metre seems to be under vines, often on amazingly steep hillsides.

Methode Champenoise di Franciacorta is a sparkling white made from Chardonnay and Pinot Nero.

Valtelline Sfursat is a local specialty made from Nebbiolo, very spicy and best after a few years, with red meat and ripe cheese, as is Franciacorta Rosso, a blend of Cabernet Franc, Barbera, Nebbiolo and Merlot.

Trentino-Alto Adige

Here, too, the landscape, in many areas, is dominated by vineyards. The region produces a lot of DOC wine, and French varieties, including Merlot and Chardonnay, are widely used.

Chianti, Lambrusco, Soave & Much More

The region claims to be the original source of the grape that produces Traminer Aromatico (Gewürztraminer), the classic aromatic white. Try the Moscato with a slice of strudel.

Alto Adige Cabernet is intensely fragrant; while Terelego Rotaliano needs to age for a while to be at its best.

Veneto

The region produces 20% (by volume) of Italy's DOC wines and has two of the foremost wine regions in the country – Valpolicella and Soave, around Verona.

Soave is fresh and lively with a distinctive taste of the soil in which it was grown. Colli Euganei Moscato is very fragrant and good with desserts.

The famed Valpolicella is very easy to drink, while Amarone della Valpolicella is quite different, with a slightly bitter almond taste. Fragrant Bardolino is best drunk young with light *primi piatti*.

Emilia-Romagna

Although wine snobs look down their noses at Lambrusco Reggiano, the lightly *frizzante* red, it does go well with the region's rich food. Try Sangiovese di Romagna, fragrant and ruby red, with red meats.

The dry version of Albana di Romagna, a straw-coloured white, goes well with soups.

Tuscany

This region is most famously known for Chianti and the reds dominate the scene. Chianti Classico is the one to aim for, produced in the zone between Siena and Florence, with a DOCG rating to guarantee quality. From the hill town of Montepulciano there are the Rosso and Vino Nobile, predominantly from Sangiovese grapes. If you can afford it, Brunello di Montalcino is a rich and complex wine that must be aged for at least three years before accompanying red meats.

Vin Santo is one of Italy's best dessert wines, made from three varieties of grape, semi-dried and aged for three years.

Umbria

The region's best wine, Orvieto Classico, is a blend of five varieties of white to produce a dry or a semi-sweet wine. Sagrantino di Montefalco, as a dry red, mixes strength with velvety texture.

Abruzzo/Molise

Trebbiano d'Abruzzo, a fresh white, is best drunk cool rather than cold. The local Montepulciano d'Abruzzo grapes are used in a wine of the same name and in Biferno Rosso, both good with red meats, the former being the more robust and more in need of ageing.

Campania

Two ancient grape varieties, Greco and Aglianico, dominate the scene here; most of the wine isn't under any classification system.

Vesuvio Lacryma Christi is regarded as being more famous for its name than its taste; Greco di Tufo, a crisp white, is probably better. Taurasi, from the red Aglianico grape, has been called the south's Barolo and deserves long ageing.

Sicily & Sardinia

Marsala is Sicily's most famous wine. The dry style, with a woody aroma, is a superb *aperitivo* (aperitif) or with desserts. Among its table wines, Corvo is worth trying, as a white or red.

Sardinia's Vermentino di Gallure, from the Vermentino grape, is a strong-flavoured white; the dry version of Cannonau di Alghero, from Grenache grapes, is an excellent table wine.

guests. Inexpensive places to eat and superb fresh produce make the weight of a stove superfluous and the bother of buying fuel an unnecessary complication.

DRINKS
Alcoholic Drinks

Wine & Spirits For the great majority of Italians wine is an integral part of a meal, be it at lunch or in the evening, scarcely surprising since the country produces countless thousands of wines from every district. The boxed text 'Chianti, Lambrusco, Soave & Much More' (pp50–1) provides a short introduction to the wonderful world of Italian vino.

After dinner try a shot of grappa, a potent clear brew made from crushed grape skins and stalks, or an *amaretto*, an almond liqueur. Around Amalfi and in the Lake District, *limoncello*, made from fresh lemons, pure alcohol, sugar and water, is popular; it's sweet, powerful and all too easy to drink. In the Alps *genepy*, a very distinctive infusion of special herbs in alcohol, slides down beautifully after a rich meal.

Beer Italians don't drink a lot of *birra* (beer), although it is becoming popular with younger people. The most common Italian beers are crisp, light lagers, ideal for quenching your thirst on a hot day after a good walk. The major breweries are Dreher, Moretti and Peroni; bottled beer is probably more common than canned, and served in *birrerie* (bars) where you'll find beers *alla spina* (on tap), occasionally Italian but most likely German or British.

Moretti's Baffo d'Oro has a good malt flavour, although lacking in depth; Sans Souci is a superior lager in which the hops come through strongly. From Peroni the popular Nastro Azzurro is rather insipid, so if you like something more full-bodied, look out for the Gran Riserva Doppio Malto, quite a powerful drop at 6.6%. From Sicily, Messina is a refreshing brew, light and tangy with a sharp, hop-filled flavour.

Nonalcoholic Drinks

Drinking coffee is an essential ritual in Italian life. The boxed text 'Espresso, Cappuccino & *Macchiato*' (below) demystifies most

---

Espresso, Cappuccino & *Macchiato*

Along with pasta and vino, coffee is one of Italy's driving forces. But there's more to it than just a mug of black liquid made by pouring hot water on darkish brown granules or powder.

An espresso (made expressly for one person and nothing to do with speed) is a small, strong black coffee topped with a dense, light brown *crema* (foam); a *doppio* espresso is double the amount. If you want a bigger, weaker, watered-down black coffee, ask for a *caffè Americano, caffè grand* or *caffè lungo* or espresso *con molta acqua calda* (espresso with a lot of hot water). A *corretto* is an espresso with a dash of grappa or some other spirit, and a *macchiato* is an espresso with a small amount of milk. On the other hand, *caffè latte* or *latte macchiato* is milk with a spot of coffee (popular in *rifugi* and served in bowls). *Caffè freddo* is a long glass of cold black coffee, or a shot of coffee in cold milk.

Then there's cappuccino, coffee topped with hot, frothy milk; if you don't want the froth, ask for a *caffè latte* or cappuccino *senza schiuma*. Italians drink cappuccino only with breakfast and during the day, and never after meals or in the evening. Cappuccinos don't come piping hot, so if this is important, ask for it *molto caldo* and wait for the same frown that you attracted when you ordered an after-dinner cappuccino – the flavour comes through most strongly when coffee is *tiepido* (tepid).

of the different types of coffee, although there are variations from north to south.

Tè (tea) isn't widely drunk in Italy, and generally only in the late afternoon to accompany a few *pasticcini* (small cakes). You can order tea in bars and in restaurants; it usually arrives in the form of a cup or pot of hot water with one or a selection of tea bags; *tè con limone* (tea with lemon) is probably more common than *tè con latte* (tea with milk).

Tap water in hotels and houses is reliable throughout the country, but most Italians prefer to drink bottled *acqua minerale* (mineral water). It can be either *frizzante* or *con gas* (sparkling), or *naturale* or *senza gas* (still), and you will be asked in restaurants and bars which you would prefer. If you want a glass of tap water, simply ask for *acqua naturale* (water natural).

Supermarket shelves are loaded with soft drinks, many internationally known, but there is one Italian specialty worth looking for. Elisir di Rocchetta is a special mineral water flavoured with *pompelmino rose e fragoli* (pink grapefruit and strawberries), *tè verde* (green tea) or *mirtillo* (blueberries) with wild flower extracts, and several other thirst-quenching blends.

On the Walk

Water from *sorgenti* (fountains) in towns and villages, and from taps over troughs in the countryside is safe to drink, unless a sign stating '*acqua non potabile*' tells you that it isn't. There are mineral springs all over the place, usually easily identified by people filling bottles and containers.

Water from streams and rivers will almost certainly be polluted. In the mountains it's a temptation to drink from streams, but you can't be certain that there aren't animals – dead or alive – upstream. See Water Purification (p64) for advice on water purification methods.

WOMEN WALKERS

Experience suggests that it's safe for women to walk alone (and certainly in pairs or small groups) in Italy's most popular walking regions – the Alps, Dolomites, Tuscany and the Lake District. However, this practice isn't necessarily recommended in parts of Sicily and Sardinia, where the paths traverse remote country.

Solo women walkers may find themselves the object of unwanted attention by eager men, but are just as likely to be asked why they want to walk *da sola* (alone) without someone (male or female) to talk with during the day.

As for clothing, keep it simple. If you turn out in stretch top and shorts you'll attract a lot of attention – unwanted or otherwise. If you stick to simple, comfortable shorts and a T-shirt, you'll blend in with everyone else, although don't be surprised if you attract censorious glances from older women in rural areas. Always carry a pair of long pants on your walk, in case you want to visit a church; dress rules usually forbid bare legs and sometimes bare arms.

WALKING WITH CHILDREN

Many Italian families obviously enjoy walking together. Some carry babies in specially designed backpacks and it's not unusual to see children as young as six walking happily at high levels.

However, it you have never taken your child walking before, don't expect the introduction to be trouble-free. It may take some time and demand lots of patience to 'train' a child to go on walks of any duration. If you're bringing along inexperienced youngsters, choose areas where it's easy to find short walks, such as Tuscany, Liguria, the Amalfi-Sorrento area and parts of the Lake District.

Cable cars and chair lifts provide easy access to higher altitudes and, if you plan carefully, you could cover sections of some walks in the Dolomites (for example) without stretching your children unduly. In the mountains a 5m to 6m length of light rope with a minimum diameter of 8mm could come in handy on narrow ledges or when a short climb is necessary (although you may find they're more confident and sure-footed than you are). Lonely Planet's *Travel with Children* includes a comprehensive section on walking with children.

MAPS
Small-Scale Maps
Michelin publishes two good series of folded maps; No 988 covers the whole country at a scale of 1:1,000,000 (€6.20) and the 1:300,000 series (Nos 4280–433) comprises six maps giving country-wide coverage (€6.20 each). The Touring Club Italiano (TCI) has an excellent 1:200,000 regional series (13 maps), each with an index inside the cover (€6.20 each).

Large-Scale Maps
Several series of commercially-published maps of varying reliability cover Italy's recognised walking areas. Use 1:25,000 maps wherever available; they contain an enormous amount of detailed information, including waymarked paths, although the numbering may not be entirely accurate or up to date. Different publishers specialise in different parts of the country.

Kompass publishes both 1:25,000 and 1:50,000 series for most areas, many with a separate booklet of background information (usually in Italian and German, or Italian and French). However, Kompass' depiction of walking routes is often fanciful and needs to be treated with caution, and supplemented by other sources.

Tabacco produces a superb 1:25,000 series covering the Dolomites, Parco Nazionale dello Stelvio and the Julian and Carnic Alps. Edizioni Multigraphic produces a series of maps concentrating on Tuscany and the Apennines. Istituto Geografico Centrale publishes two series – 1:25,000 and 1:50,000 – for the Western Alps, Maritime Alps and Liguria. CAI maps are also quite common, particularly in the central Apennines and the Amalfi-Sorrento area.

In Sardinia it may be necessary to use the 1:25,000 Istituto Geografico Militare (IGM) maps, in the absence of any commercial publications. Contact the **IGM** (☎ 055 48 06 72, fax 055 48 97 43; w www.nettuno .it/fiera/igmi/igmit.htm; Viale Filippo Strozzi 10, 50122 Florence).

Taking Photos Outdoors

For walkers, photography can be a vexed issue – all that magnificent scenery but such weight and space restrictions on what photographic equipment you can carry. With a little care and planning it is possible to maximise your chance of taking great photos on the trail.

Light & Filters In fine weather, the best light is early and late in the day. In strong sunlight and in mountain and coastal areas where the light is intense, a polarising filter will improve colour saturation and reduce haze. On overcast days the soft light can be great for shooting wildflowers and running water, and an 81A warming filter can be useful. If you use slide film, a graduated filter will help balance unevenly lit landscapes.

Equipment If you need to travel light carry a zoom in the 28–70mm range, and if your sole purpose is landscapes consider carrying just a single wide-angle lens (24mm). A tripod is essential for really good images and there are some excellent lightweight models available. Otherwise a trekking pole, pack or even a pile of rocks can be used to improvise.

Camera Care Keep your gear dry – a few zip-lock bags can be used to double wrap camera gear and silica-gel sachets (a drying agent) can be used to suck moisture out of equipment. Sturdy cameras will normally work fine in freezing conditions. Take care when bringing a camera from one temperature extreme to another; if moisture condenses on the camera make sure it dries thoroughly before going back into the cold, or mechanisms can freeze up. Standard camera batteries fail very quickly in the cold. Remove them from the camera when not in use and keep them under your clothing.

For a thorough grounding in photography on the road, read Lonely Planet's *Travel Photography*, by Richard I'Anson, a full-colour guide for happy-snappers and professional photographers alike.

Gareth McCormack

Buying Maps

The best places to buy maps in Italy are newsagents, bookshops and *tabaccherie* (tobacconists; all-purpose shops where bus tickets and, often, phone cards are sold) in the towns and villages in walking areas. Major city bookshops (such as Feltrinelli) have map sections but the range is usually limited. Map prices range between €5.20 and €7.20.

PLACE NAMES

This book uses the common English (or other) name where it exists, and Italian place names and geographical terms otherwise. In some areas names in local dialect have also been used, particularly when a feature or place is known widely by that name. Things can get a bit confusing in the Dolomites, where three languages are spoken in some areas: Italian, German and Ladin. In South Tyrol – Parco Nazionale dello Stelvio for example – places must be referred to in Italian and German by law. Both French and Italian versions of place names are used in Valle d'Aosta.

PHOTOGRAPHY
Film

Numerous outlets sell and process film, but beware of poor-quality processing. Despite claims to the contrary, you'll rarely get your film processed in one hour. There's much to be said for hanging on to your film until you return home to trusted processors. Approximate costs are:

film	exp	cost (€)	processing (€)
print	24	4	9.55
print	36	4.65	15.50
slide	36	5.20	4.15

DIGITAL RESOURCES

Most local and regional tourist office websites, and those maintained by the national parks, have some information specifically about walking in their areas. The Lonely Planet website (w www.lonelyplanet.com.au) has information on Italy and a speedy link to many Italian websites; the Activities branch of Lonely Planet's Thorn Tree discussion board may contain other useful tips. Other sites to try include:

Adagio Gives walks descriptions from *Trekking* magazine, details map coverage of walking areas, lists tourist office contacts, has weather reports, and much more.
w www.adagio.it

Appunti di Viaggio Has hosts of useful links to organisations, tourist offices and sites with detailed walks information.
w www.escursionismo.org

Club Alpino Italiano Follow the *rifugi* link for an amazing number of links to regional, local, business and activity sites.
w www.cai.it

BOOKS
Lonely Planet

For comprehensive information about the country, use the *Italy* guide. For a sharper focus on a particular region, look out for *Florence*, *Milan*, *Turin & Genoa*, *Rome*, *Sicily*, *Sardinia*, *Tuscany* and *Venice*. *World Food – Italy* is a full-colour book with heaps of information on Italian food and drink, a useful language section and quick-reference glossary. The *Italian phrasebook* contains all the words and phrases you're likely to need in almost any conceivable situation in Italy. *Cycling Italy* gives a different perspective on Italy's byways, from Sicily to the Alps.

Historic Travel & Exploration

Three 'Grand Tour' classics are Johann Wolfgang von Goethe's *Italian Journey*, Charles Dickens' *Pictures from Italy* and Henry James' *Italian Hours*. DH Lawrence wrote three short travel books while living in Italy, combined in one volume, *DH Lawrence & Italy*.

For one facet of the early history of mountaineering in the Alps, hunt for a copy of *Scrambles Among the Alps*, by Edward Whymper, first to reach the summit of the Matterhorn (from the Swiss side).

Natural History

Mediterranean Wild Flowers and *Alpine Flowers of Britain & Europe*, by Christopher Grey-Wilson & Marjorie Blamey, are both beautifully illustrated flora guides; in the paperback editions they aren't too heavy to carry on day walks. The first has more than 2000 colour illustrations and useful information about habitats. The second also covers the Dolomites and includes the more common trees.

Also available in paperback: *Birds of Britain & Europe*, by John Gooders, has several illustrations for each species; *Birds of Europe*, by Lars Jonsson, is beautifully illustrated; and Keith Rushforth's *Trees of Britain & Europe* covers all the species native to Europe and imports. *Mammals of Britain & Europe*, by David MacDonald & Priscilla Barrett, is only available in hardback.

The pocket-sized Kompass guides *Fiori Alpini*, *Fiori di Prato*, *Animali delle Alpi* (which includes a few birds, reptiles and butterflies) and *Uccelli Canori*, with Italian text and full-colour photos, are good value and portable.

Buying Books

Most towns have a bookshop; in mountain areas they're likely to have a substantial section covering the mountains and related outdoor topics.

A few bookshops have small English-language sections (notably branches of the nationwide chain Feltrinelli). Rome's **Anglo-American Bookshop** (*Via della Vite 27*), off Piazza di Spagna, has a huge range of titles, especially travel literature.

Each of the walks chapters in this book includes details of where to buy relevant books (and maps) locally; see also Buying Maps (p55).

MAGAZINES

Three excellent, monthly Italian-language magazines focus on slightly different parts of the outdoors scene:

Trekking (€4) Has the highest proportion of articles related specifically to walking; articles can include walks descriptions and information about local history, culture, food and wine.

Montagna (€5.20) Has lots of news from the mountain world, articles discussing topical and environmental issues and natural history; the emphasis is more on climbing and mountaineering than walking.

Alp (€6.20) Is principally for climbers and mountaineers and is worth buying just for the photos in articles about areas and exploits, usually with some coverage of conservation issues and history.

WEATHER INFORMATION

Forecasts in the press and on TV are fairly generalised, but do give a basic idea of overall trends. Contacts for some local telephone forecast services are given in walks chapters. Some tourist offices and national park visitor centres display forecasts, which may not always be up to date. Useful Italian-language websites are:

Meteo Has a Europe-wide isobar chart, but only generalised forecasts.
w www.meteo.it

Meteo Italia The regional forecasts might be useful in lowland areas such as Tuscany and Campania, or in Sicily and Sardinia.
w www.meteoitalia.it

Nimbus Good forecasts for all the mountain regions, plus Tuscany, and reasonably detailed information for southern areas. For the mountains you get a detailed forecast including wind, rain and phenomena such as fog.
w www.nimbus.it

Clothing & Equipment

You don't need to spend a fortune on gear to enjoy walking, but you do need to think carefully about what you pack to make sure you're comfortable and prepared for an emergency. Taking the right clothing and equipment on a walk can make the difference between an enjoyable day out or a cold and miserable one; in extreme situations, it can even mean the difference between life and death.

The gear you need will depend on the type of walking you plan to do. For day walks, clothing, footwear and a backpack are the major items; you might get away with runners, a hat, shorts, shirt and a warm pullover. For longer walks or those in alpine regions, especially if you're camping, the list becomes longer.

We recommend spending as much as you can afford on good walking boots, a waterproof jacket and a sweater or fleece jacket. These are likely to be your most expensive items but are a sound investment, as they should last for years.

The following section is not exhaustive; for more advice visit outdoor stores, talk to fellow walkers and read product reviews in outdoor magazines.

CLOTHING

It's better to wear several thin layers rather than one or two thicker items. Layering allows you to add or remove layers as you get colder or hotter, depending on your exertion and the weather. Except in hot weather, begin with lightweight thermal underwear (made of wool or a wicking fabric such as Capilene or polypropylene, that moves the sweat away from your body). Your lightweight shorts/trousers and shirt make up the middle layer. Outer layers can consist of sweaters (jumpers), fleece jackets or down-filled jackets. Finally, there is the 'shell' layer, comprising waterproof jacket and overtrousers.

Look for clothes that offer warmth, but still breathe and wick moisture away from your skin. Avoid wearing heavy cotton or denim, as these fabrics dry slowly and are very cold when wet. When you are choosing clothes, prepare for the worst weather that a particular region might throw at you. The body loses most of its heat through its extremities, particularly the head; wearing a wool or fleece hat and gloves can prevent this warmth being lost.

When deciding between long or short sleeves and trouser legs, weigh up the advantages of sun and insect protection against discomfort in the heat.

Waterproof Jacket

The ideal specifications are a breathable, waterproof fabric, a hood which is roomy enough to cover headwear but still allows peripheral vision, capacious map pocket and a good-quality, heavy-gauge zip protected by a storm flap. Make sure the sleeves are large enough to cover warm clothes underneath and that the overall length of the garment allows you to sit down on it.

Overtrousers

Although restrictive, these are essential if you're walking in wet and cold conditions. As the name suggests, they are worn over your trousers. Choose a model with slits for pocket access and long ankle zips so that you can pull them on and off over your boots.

Footwear

Your footwear will be your friend or your enemy, so choose carefully. The first decision you will make is between boots and shoes. Runners or walking shoes are fine over easy terrain but, for more difficult trails and across rocks and scree, most walkers agree that the ankle support offered by boots is invaluable. If you'll be using crampons or walking in snow you need a rigid-soled walking boot.

Buy boots in warm conditions or go for a walk before trying them on, so your feet can expand slightly, as they would on a walk.

Most walkers carry a pair of thongs or sandals. These will relieve your feet from the heavy boots at night or during rest stops, and sandals are useful when you get your feet wet fording waterways.

Gaiters If you will be walking through snow, deep mud or scratchy vegetation, consider using gaiters to protect your legs and keep your socks dry. The best are made of strong fabric with a robust zip protected by a flap and an easy-to-undo method of securing around the foot.

Socks The best walkers' socks are made of a hard-wearing mix of wool (70–80%) and synthetic (30–20%), free of ridged seams in the wrong places (toes and heels). Socks with a high proportion of wool are more comfortable when worn for several successive days without washing. Spare socks are equally valuable, especially in wet conditions.

Check List

This list is a general guide to the things you might take on a walk. Your list will vary depending on the kind of walking you plan to do, whether you're camping or planning on staying in *rifugi* (mountain huts) or pensiones, and on the terrain, weather and time of year.

Clothing
- ☐ boots and spare laces
- ☐ gaiters
- ☐ hat (warm), scarf and gloves
- ☐ jacket (waterproof)
- ☐ overtrousers (waterproof)
- ☐ runners (training shoes), sandals or thongs (flip flops)
- ☐ shorts and trousers or skirt
- ☐ socks and underwear
- ☐ sunhat
- ☐ sweater or fleece jacket
- ☐ thermal underwear
- ☐ T-shirt and shirt (long-sleeved with collar)

Equipment
- ☐ backpack with liner (waterproof)
- ☐ first-aid kit*
- ☐ food and snacks (high-energy), and one day's emergency supplies
- ☐ insect repellent
- ☐ map, compass and guidebook
- ☐ map case or clip-seal plastic bags
- ☐ pocket knife
- ☐ sunglasses
- ☐ sunscreen and lip balm
- ☐ survival bag or blanket
- ☐ toilet paper and trowel

- ☐ torch (flashlight) or headlamp, spare batteries and globe
- ☐ water container
- ☐ whistle (for emergencies)

Overnight Walks
- ☐ cooking, eating and drinking utensils
- ☐ dishwashing items
- ☐ insulating mat
- ☐ matches, lighter and candle
- ☐ portable stove and fuel
- ☐ sewing/repair kit
- ☐ sleeping bag and bag liner/inner sheet
- ☐ spare cord
- ☐ tent, pegs, poles and guy ropes
- ☐ toiletries
- ☐ towel (small)
- ☐ water purification tablets, iodine or filter

Optional Items
- ☐ altimeter
- ☐ backpack cover (waterproof, slip-on)
- ☐ binoculars
- ☐ camera, film and batteries
- ☐ emergency distress beacon
- ☐ GPS receiver
- ☐ groundsheet (lightweight)
- ☐ mobile phone**
- ☐ mosquito net
- ☐ notebook and pen/pencil
- ☐ swimming costume
- ☐ walking poles
- ☐ watch

*see the First-Aid Check List (p64)
**see Mobile Phones (p346)

EQUIPMENT

You should always carry emergency food, a torch and a whistle on walks of more than a few hours.

Many Italian walkers also carry an umbrella, which may not be as silly as it seems, provided it isn't windy. You can see where you're going much more easily than if you're imprisoned inside a jacket hood and won't run the risk of overheating on a long ascent.

Backpack

For day walks a day-pack will usually suffice, but for multi-day walks you will need a backpack between 45L and 90L in capacity. Deciding whether to go for a smaller or a bigger pack can depend on where you will be walking, and whether you plan to camp or stay in *rifugi* etc. Your pack should be large enough that you don't need to strap bits and pieces to the outside, where they can become damaged or lost or, like foam mats, leave unsightly souvenirs in trackside bushes. However, if you buy a bigger pack than you really need there's the temptation to fill it simply because the space is there; its weight will increase and your enjoyment decrease.

A good backpack should:

- be made of strong fabric such as canvas, Cordura or similar heavy-duty woven synthetic, with high-quality stitching, straps and buckles, a lightweight internal or external frame, and resilient and smoothly working zips
- have an adjustable, well-padded harness that evenly distributes weight
- be equipped with a small number of internal and external pockets to provide easy access to frequently used items such as snacks and maps

Even if the manufacturer claims your pack is waterproof, use heavy-duty liners (garden refuse bags are ideal; custom-made sacks are available).

Tent

A three-season tent will fulfil the requirements of most walkers. The floor and the outer shell, or fly, should have taped or sealed seams and covered zips to stop water leaking inside. Weight will be a major issue if you're carrying your own gear so a roomy tent may not be an option; most walkers find tents of around 2kg to 3kg (that will sleep two or three people) a comfortable carrying weight. Popular shapes include dome and tunnel, which are better able to handle windy conditions than flat-sided tents.

Check you know how to pitch your tent before taking it away, and always check your poles and pegs are packed.

Sleeping Bag & Mat

You'll need a sleeping bag or an inner sheet for overnight stops in *rifugi*, which only supply blankets (see also *Rifugi*, p47). Inner sheets are compulsory in some youth hostels.

When buying a sleeping bag, choose between down and synthetic fillings, and mummy and rectangular shapes. Down is warmer than synthetic for the same weight and bulk but, unlike synthetic fillings, does not retain warmth when wet. Mummy bags are best for weight and warmth, but can be claustrophobic. Sleeping bags are rated by temperature; the given figure (-5°C, for instance) is the coldest temperature at which a person should feel comfortable in the bag. However, the ratings are notoriously unreliable. Work out the coldest temperature at which you anticipate sleeping, assess whether you're a warm or a cold sleeper, then choose a bag accordingly.

An inner sheet will help to keep your sleeping bag clean, as well as adding an insulating layer. Silk 'inners' are the lightest, but they also come in both cotton and polypropylene.

Self-inflating sleeping mats are popular and work like a thin air cushion between you and the ground; they also insulate from the cold and are essential if sleeping on snow. Foam mats are a low-cost but less comfortable alternative.

Stove

As a general guideline the stove you choose needs to be stable when sitting on the ground and to have a good wind shield. Fuel stoves fall roughly into three categories: multifuel, methylated spirits (ethyl alcohol) and butane gas.

[Continued on page 62]

NAVIGATION EQUIPMENT
Maps & Compass

You should always carry a good map of the area you are walking in (see Maps, p54), and know how to read it. Before setting off on your walk, ensure that you understand the contours and the map symbols, plus the main ridge and river systems in the area. Also familiarise yourself with the true north-south directions and the general direction in which you are heading. On the trail, try to identify major landforms such as mountain ranges and gorges, and locate them on your map. This will give you a better understanding of the region's geography.

Buy a compass and learn how to use it. The attraction of magnetic north varies in different parts of the world, so compasses need to be balanced accordingly. Compass manufacturers have divided the world into five zones. Make sure your compass is balanced for your destination. There are also 'universal' compasses that can be used anywhere in the world.

How to Use a Compass

This is a very basic introduction to using a compass and will only be of assistance if you are proficient in map reading. For simplicity, it doesn't take magnetic variation into account. Before using a compass we recommend you obtain further instruction.

1. Reading a Compass

Hold the compass flat in the palm of your hand. Rotate the **bezel** so the **red end** of the needle points to the **N** on the bezel. The bearing is read from the **dash** under the bezel.

2. Orientating the Map

To orientate the map so that it aligns with the ground, place the compass flat on the map. Rotate the map until the **needle** is parallel with the map's north/south grid lines and the **red end** is pointing to north on the map. You can now identify features around you by aligning them with labelled features on the map.

3. Taking a Bearing from the Map

Draw a line on the map between your starting point and your destination. Place the edge of the compass on this line with the **direction of travel arrow** pointing towards your destination. Rotate the **bezel** until the **meridian lines** are parallel with the north/south grid lines on the map and the **N** points to north on the map. Read the bearing from the **dash**.

4. Following a Bearing

Rotate the **bezel** so that the intended bearing is in line with the **dash**. Place the compass flat in the palm of your hand and rotate the **base plate** until the **red end** points to **N** on the **bezel**. The **direction of travel arrow** will now point in the direction you need to walk.

5. Determining Your Bearing

Rotate the **bezel** so the **red end** points to the **N**. Place the compass flat in the palm of your hand and rotate the **base plate** until the **direction of travel arrow** points in the direction in which you have been tramping. Read your bearing from the **dash**.

1	Base plate
2	Direction of travel arrow
3	Dash
4	Bezel
5	Meridian lines
6	Needle
7	Red end
8	N (north point)

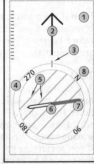

GPS

Originally developed by the US Department of Defence, the Global Positioning System (GPS) is a network of more than 20 earth-orbiting satellites that continually beam encoded signals back to earth. Small computer driven devices (GPS receivers) can decode these signals to give users an extremely accurate reading of their location – to within 30m anywhere on the planet, at any time of day, in almost any weather. The theoretical accuracy of the system increased at least tenfold in 2000, when a deliberate in-built error, intended to fudge the reading for all but US military users, was removed. The cheapest hand-held GPS receivers now cost less than US$100 (although they may have an in-built averaging system that minimises signal errors). Other important factors to consider are weight and battery life.

It should be understood that a GPS receiver is of little use to hikers unless used with an accurate topographical map – the GPS receiver simply gives your position, which you must locate on the local map. GPS receivers only work properly in the open. Directly below high cliffs, near large bodies of water or in dense tree-cover, for example, the signals from a crucial satellite may be blocked (or bounce off the rock or water) and give inaccurate readings. GPS receivers are more vulnerable to breakdowns (including dead batteries) than the humble magnetic compass – a low-tech device that has served navigators faithfully for centuries – so don't rely on them entirely.

Altimeter

Altimeters determine altitude by measuring air pressure. Because pressure is affected by temperature, altimeters are calibrated to take lower temperatures at higher altitudes into account. However, discrepancies can still occur, especially in unsettled weather, so it's wise to take a few precautions when using your altimeter.

1. Reset your altimeter regularly at known elevations such as spot heights and passes. Do not take spot heights from villages where there may be a large difference in elevation from one end of the settlement to another.

2. Use your altimeter in conjunction with other navigation techniques to fix your position. For instance, taking a back bearing to a known peak or river confluence, determining the general direction of the track and obtaining your elevation will usually give you a pretty good fix on your position.

Altimeters are also barometers and are useful for indicating changing weather conditions. If the altimeter shows increasing elevation while you are not climbing, it means the air pressure is dropping and a low-pressure weather system may be approaching.

[Continued from page 59]

Multifuel stoves are small, efficient and ideal for places where a reliable fuel supply is hard to find. However, they tend to be noisy and sooty, and require frequent maintenance.

Stoves running on methylated spirits are slower and less efficient, but are safe, clean and easy to use.

Butane gas stoves, although clean and reliable, can be slow, and the gas canisters can be awkward to carry and a potential litter problem. They are also more wasteful of resources than liquid fuel.

Fuel Super-refined petrol for stoves, known as Coleman fuel (Shellite in some countries; in Italy it's known as Coleman fuel or, less frequently, *benzina Coleman*) is available from outdoor shops; Coleman fuel costs from €6.20 for 500ml. Alternatively, *senza piombo* (unleaded petrol or gasoline) can be bought from any filling station.

Alcool denaturato (methylated spirits) is pink-coloured and widely available in supermarkets, hardware and outdoor shops, and costs around €1 for a 750ml bottle.

Gas or *cherosene* (kerosene) might be obtainable from shops that sell gear for Italy's abundant hunters and anglers. They usually have signs outside, which include the words *caccia* (hunting) and *pesca* (fishing). As a guide, a 250ml canister costs €4.90 and a 500ml one €7.50.

Carry your fuel in a clearly labelled, and sturdy plastic or aluminium bottle. Note that fuel cannot be carried on aeroplanes.

Walking Poles

Think about packing a pair of lightweight telescopic poles. They help you to balance and ease the jarring on your knees during steep descents.

Technical Equipment

The specialist equipment you will need for tackling the *vie ferrate* (iron ways) is discussed in the Via Ferrata special section (p203).

An ice axe, and possibly crampons, may be essential for crossing high mountain passes in late spring. It's essential to have had some experience in using them *before* you embark on high-altitude walks in Italy.

BUYING & HIRING LOCALLY

Some brands of Italian walking boots enjoy an excellent international reputation and it may be worth considering a purchase once you're in Italy. Prices are competitive, no matter where you come from.

Addresses of gear shops in towns near the walks described are given in the walk chapters. A useful source of addresses of outdoors shops is **w** www.outdooritalia.it, although few are readily accessible from areas covered in this book.

Apart from crampons, ice axes and *via ferrata* gear, hiring is virtually unknown.

Health & Safety

Keeping healthy on your walks and travels depends on your predeparture preparations, your daily health care while travelling and how you handle any medical problems that develop. While the potential problems can seem quite frightening, few travellers actually experience anything more than an upset stomach. The following sections aren't meant to alarm but are recommended reading before you go.

PREDEPARTURE PLANNING
Medical Cover
Citizens of European Union (EU) countries are covered for emergency medical care upon presentation of an E111 form, which you need to get before you travel. In Britain, it's available free at any post office. In other EU countries, obtain information from your doctor or local health service. Although the form entitles you to free treatment in government clinics and hospitals, you will have to pay for dental treatment, any medicines bought from pharmacies (even if a doctor has prescribed them) and possibly for tests. At home, you may be able to recover some or all of these costs from your national health service.

Australia (Medicare) has a reciprocal arrangement with Italy; you are entitled to subsidised health care for up to six months from the date of arrival. However, treatment in private hospitals is not covered, and charges are also likely for medication, nonurgent dental work and secondary examinations, including x-rays and laboratory tests. Medicare publishes a brochure with the details and it is advisable to carry your Medicare card.

Health Insurance
Make sure that you have adequate health insurance; Italy's private hospitals and clinics are good but expensive without insurance, and some treatments in public hospitals have to be paid for and can be expensive. See Travel Insurance (p342).

Physical Preparation
Some of the walks in this book are physically demanding and most require a reasonable level of fitness. Even if you're tackling the easy or easy–moderate walks, it pays to be relatively fit rather than launch into them after months of fairly sedentary living. Fitness is essential for the demanding walks (see Level of Difficulty, p13).

Unless you're a regular walker, start your get-fit campaign at least a month before your visit. Take a vigorous walk of about an hour, two or three times per week, and gradually extend the duration of your outings as the departure date nears. If you plan to carry a full backpack on any walk, carry a loaded pack on some of your training jaunts. Walkers with little previous experience should have a medical checkup beforehand.

Immunisations
No immunisations are required for Italy, but before leaving home it's worth ensuring that you're up to date with routine vaccinations such as diphtheria, polio and tetanus. It's particularly important that tetanus is up to date – the initial course of three injections, usually given in childhood, is followed by boosters every 10 years.

First Aid
It's a good idea to know the appropriate responses for a major accident or illness, especially if you are intending to walk for some time in a remote area. Consider learning basic first aid on a recognised course before you go, or taking a first-aid manual in your first-aid kit. Although detailed first-aid instruction is outside the scope of this book, some basic points are listed under Traumatic Injuries (p68). Preventing accidents and illness is vitally important – read Safety on the Walk (p70) for more advice. You should also know how to summon help should a major accident or illness befall you or someone with you – see Rescue & Evacuation (p71).

Other Preparations

If you have any known medical problems or are concerned about your health in any way, it's a good idea to have a full checkup before you go. It's far better to have any problems recognised and treated at home than to find out about them halfway up a

First-Aid Check List

This is a list of items you should consider including in your medical kit – consult a pharmacist for brands available in your country.

Essentials

- ☐ adhesive tape
- ☐ bandages and safety pins
- ☐ elasticised support bandage – for knees, ankles etc
- ☐ gauze swabs
- ☐ nonadhesive dressings
- ☐ paper stitches
- ☐ scissors (small)
- ☐ sterile alcohol wipes
- ☐ sticking plasters (Band-Aids, blister plasters)
- ☐ sutures
- ☐ thermometer (note that mercury thermometers are prohibited by airlines)
- ☐ tweezers

Medications

- ☐ antidiarrhoea and antinausea drugs
- ☐ antifungal cream or powder – for fungal infections and thrush
- ☐ antihistamines – for allergies, eg, hay fever; to ease the itch from insect bites or stings; and to prevent motion sickness
- ☐ antiseptic (such as povidone-iodine) – for cuts and grazes
- ☐ cold and flu tablets, throat lozenges and nasal decongestant
- ☐ painkillers – eg, aspirin or paracetamol (acetaminophen in the USA) – for pain and fever

Miscellaneous

- ☐ calamine lotion, sting relief spray or aloe vera – to ease irritation from sunburn, and insect bites or stings
- ☐ eye drops
- ☐ rehydration mixture – to prevent dehydration, eg, due to severe diarrhoea; particularly important when travelling with children

mountain. It's also sensible to have had a recent dental checkup since toothache on the *sentiero* (path) with solace a couple of days or more away can be a miserable experience. If you wear glasses, take a spare pair and your prescription.

If you need a particular medicine, take enough with you to last the trip. In case you do need more, take part of the packaging showing the generic name, rather than the brand, as this will make getting replacements easier. It's also a good idea to have a legible prescription or letter from your doctor to prove that you legally use the medication to avoid any problems at customs.

STAYING HEALTHY
Hygiene

To reduce the chances of contracting an illness you should wash your hands frequently, especially before preparing or eating food.

Take particular care to thoroughly dispose of all toilet waste when you are on a walk (see Human Waste Disposal, p45).

Food

The stringent food hygiene regulations imposed by the EU are in force in Italy, so you should feel confident the food you eat in restaurants is safe.

Water

In Italy, tap water is generally safe to drink. Water from *sorgenti* (fountains) in towns and villages, and from taps over troughs in the countryside is safe to drink, unless a sign stating '*acqua non potabile*' tells you that it isn't. There are mineral springs all over the place, usually easily identified by people filling bottles and containers. Water from streams and rivers will almost certainly be polluted. In the mountains it's a temptation to drink from streams, but you can't be certain that there aren't animals – dead or alive – upstream.

Water Purification If you have any doubts about the water, the simplest way to purify it is to boil it thoroughly. Vigorous boiling should be satisfactory, otherwise you can use a chemical agent. Chlorine and iodine are usually used, in powder, tablet or liquid form, available from outdoor equipment suppliers and pharmacies. Follow the recommended dosages and allow the water to stand for the correct length of time. Chlorine tablets will kill many pathogens, but not some parasites like Giardia and amoebic cysts. Iodine is more effective in purifying water. Follow the directions carefully and remember that too much iodine can be harmful.

Common Ailments

Blisters This problem can be avoided. Make sure your walking boots or shoes are well worn in before your visit. At the very least, wear them on a few short walks before tackling longer outings. Your boots should fit comfortably with enough room to move your toes; boots that are too big or too small will cause blisters.

Similarly for socks – be sure they fit properly, are specifically made for walkers and there are no seams across the widest part of your foot. Wet and muddy socks can also cause blisters, so, even on a day walk, pack a spare pair of socks. Keep your toenails clipped but not too short.

If you do feel a blister coming on, stop and apply a simple sticking plaster or, preferably, one of the special blister plasters, which act as a second skin; follow the maker's instructions for replacement.

Fatigue A simple statistic: more injuries of whatever nature happen towards the end of the day than earlier, when you're fresher. Although tiredness can simply be a nuisance on an easy walk, it can be life-threatening on narrow, exposed ridges or in bad weather. You should never set out on a walk beyond your capabilities on the day. If you feel below par, have a day off. To reduce the risk, don't push yourself too hard – take rests every hour or two, and have a half hour's lunch break. Towards the end of the day, slacken the pace and try to increase your concentration. You should also eat sensibly throughout the day; nuts, dried fruit and chocolate are good energy-giving snack foods.

Knee Strain Many walkers feel the strain on long, steep descents. It can be reduced but never eliminated by taking shorter steps with your legs slightly bent, ensuring that your heel hits the ground before the rest of your foot. Some walkers find tubular bandages help (although these could be uncomfortable in hot weather), while others use hi-tech, strap-on supports. Walking poles are very effective in taking some of the weight off the knees.

MEDICAL PROBLEMS & TREATMENT
Environmental Hazards

Walkers are at more risk than most groups from environmental hazards. The risk, however, can be significantly reduced by applying common sense – and reading the following section.

Altitude Lack of oxygen at high altitudes (over 2500m) affects most people to some extent. The effect may be mild or severe, and occurs because the air pressure is reduced, and the heart and lungs must work harder to oxygenate the body. In addition, fluid can build up in the lungs and brain causing extreme breathlessness – the person ultimately drowns in this fluid if he or she doesn't descend. Although the highest altitude reached on walks described in this book is 3292m (Col Lauson on the Valnontey to

Warning

Self-diagnosis and treatment can be risky, so you should always seek medical help. For emergency treatment, go straight to the *pronto soccorso* (casualty) section of a public hospital, where you can also get emergency dental treatment. Sometimes hospitals are listed in the phone book under Aziende Ospedaliere. The local tourist office or your accommodation host can usually recommend a local doctor or clinic.

We have used generic rather than brand names for drugs throughout this section – check with a pharmacist for locally available brands.

Rhêmes Notre Dame walk, p118) and the likelihood of suffering any significant effects is slight, it is still important to take precautions. Take a couple of days to acclimatise yourself to altitudes above 2500m if you're planning to cross the higher passes in the Western and Maritime Alps or Parco Nazionale dello Stelvio; do not ascend until your body has adjusted to the higher altitude. If symptoms, including breathlessness, headaches, nausea, dizziness, difficulty sleeping and loss of appetite, persist or are severe, it is essential to descend immediately.

Sun Protection against the sun should always be taken seriously; in the rarefied air and deceptive coolness of the mountains, sunburn develops rapidly. Slap on the sunscreen and a barrier cream for your nose and lips, wear a broad-brimmed hat, even on partly sunny days, and protect your eyes with good quality sunglasses with UV lenses, particularly when walking near water, sand or snow. If, despite these precautions, you get burnt, calamine lotion, aloe vera or other commercial sunburn relief preparations will soothe.

Snow Blindness This is a temporary, painful condition resulting from sunburn of the surface of the eye (cornea). It usually occurs when someone walks on snow or ice without sunglasses. Treatment is to relieve the pain – cold cloths on closed eyelids may help. Antibiotic and anaesthetic eye drops are not necessary. The condition usually resolves itself within a few days and there are no long-term consequences.

Heat Treat heat with respect! Take time to acclimatise to high temperatures, drink sufficient liquids and don't do anything physically demanding until you are acclimatised.

Prickly Heat This is an itchy rash caused by excessive perspiration trapped under the skin. It usually strikes people who have just arrived in a hot climate. Keeping cool, bathing often, drying the skin and using a mild talcum or prickly heat powder may help. Fungal infections of the skin also occur more commonly in hot, humid conditions – for more details, see Fungal Infections (p68).

Dehydration & Heat Exhaustion Dehydration is a potentially dangerous and generally preventable condition caused by excessive fluid loss. Sweating combined with inadequate fluid intake is a common cause among walkers, but other important causes are diarrhoea, vomiting and high fever – see Diarrhoea (p67) for appropriate treatment.

The first symptoms are weakness, thirst and passing small amounts of very concentrated urine. This may progress to drowsiness, dizziness or fainting on standing up and, finally, coma.

It's easy to forget how much fluid you are losing via perspiration while you're walking, particularly if a strong breeze is drying your skin quickly. Always maintain a steady fluid intake – the minimum recommended is 3L per day.

Dehydration and salt deficiency can cause heat exhaustion. Salt deficiency is characterised by fatigue, lethargy, headaches, giddiness and muscle cramps. Salt tablets are unnecessary; it's probably sufficient to add extra salt to your food.

Everyday Health

Normal body temperature is up to 37°C (98.6°F); more than 2°C (4°F) higher indicates a high fever. The normal adult pulse rate is 60 to 100 per minute (children 80 to 100, babies 100 to 140). As a general rule the pulse increases about 20 beats per minute for each 1°C (2°F) rise in fever.

Respiration (breathing) rate is also an indicator of illness. Count the number of breaths per minute: between 12 and 20 is normal for adults and older children (up to 30 for younger children, 40 for babies). People with a high fever or serious respiratory illness breathe more quickly than normal. More than 40 shallow breaths per minute may indicate pneumonia.

Heatstroke This is a serious, occasionally fatal, condition that occurs if the body's heat-regulating mechanism breaks down and the body temperature rises to a dangerous level. Long, continuous periods of exposure to high temperatures and insufficient fluids can make you vulnerable to heatstroke.

The symptoms are feeling unwell, sweating little or not at all, and a high body temperature (39°C to 41°C). When sweating has ceased, the skin becomes flushed and red. Severe, throbbing headaches and lack of coordination will also occur, and the sufferer may be confused or aggressive. Eventually the victim will become delirious or convulse. Hospitalisation is essential; meantime get the victim out of the sun, remove clothing, cover with a wet sheet or towel, and fan continually. Give fluids if the person is conscious.

Cold To much cold can be just as dangerous as too much heat!

Hypothermia This occurs when the body loses heat faster than it can produce it and the core temperature of the body falls.

It is frighteningly easy to deteriorate from very cold to dangerously cold due to a combination of wind, wet clothing, fatigue and hunger, even if the air temperature is above freezing. If the weather deteriorates, put on extra layers of warm clothing: a wind- and/or waterproof jacket, plus wool or fleece hat and gloves are all essential. Have something energy-giving to eat and ensure that everyone in your group is fit, feeling well and alert.

Symptoms of hypothermia are exhaustion, numb skin (particularly toes and fingers), shivering, slurred speech, irrational or violent behaviour, lethargy, stumbling, dizzy spells, muscle cramps and violent bursts of energy. Irrationality may take the form of sufferers claiming they are warm and trying to take off their clothes.

To treat mild hypothermia, first get the person out of the wind and/or rain, remove any wet clothing and replace it with dry, warm clothing. Give hot liquids – *not* alcohol – and some high-kilojoule, easily digestible food. Do not rub victims; instead, allow them to slowly warm themselves – it helps to put them between companions. This should be enough to treat the early stages of hypothermia. The early recognition and treatment of mild hypothermia is the only way to prevent severe hypothermia, a critical condition.

Infectious Diseases

Diarrhoea Simple things like a change of water, food or climate can all cause a mild bout of diarrhoea, but a few rushed toilet trips with no other symptoms are not indicative of a major problem. More serious diarrhoea is caused by infectious agents transmitted by faecal contamination of food or water, by using contaminated utensils or directly from one person's hand to another. Paying particular attention to personal hygiene, drinking clean water and taking care with what you eat are important in avoiding getting diarrhoea.

Dehydration is the main danger with any diarrhoea, particularly in children or the elderly as dehydration can occur quite quickly. *Fluid replacement* (at least equal to the volume being lost) is the most important thing to remember. Weak black tea with a little sugar, soda water, or soft drinks allowed to go flat and diluted 50% with water are all good. With severe diarrhoea a rehydrating solution is preferable to replace minerals and salts lost. Commercially available oral rehydration salts (ORS) are very useful; add them to water. In an emergency you can make up a solution of six teaspoons of sugar and a half teaspoon of salt to a litre of water. You need to drink at least the same volume of fluid that you are losing in bowel movements and vomiting. Urine is the best guide to the adequacy of replacement – if you pass small amounts of concentrated urine, you need to drink more. Keep drinking small amounts often. Stick to a bland diet as you recover.

Gut-paralysing drugs such as diphenoxylate or loperamide can be used to bring relief from the symptoms, although they don't cure the problem. Only use these drugs if you do not have access to toilets, eg, if you *must* travel. These drugs are not recommended for children under 12 years, or if you have a high fever or are severely dehydrated.

Seek medical advice if you pass blood or mucus, are feverish, or suffer persistent or severe diarrhoea.

Fungal Infections Sweating liberally, probably washing less than usual and going longer without a change of clothes mean that long-distance walkers risk picking up a fungal infection, which, while an unpleasant irritant, presents no danger.

Fungal infections are encouraged by moisture, so wear loose, comfortable clothes, wash when you can and dry yourself thoroughly. Try to expose the infected area to air or sunlight as much as possible, and apply an antifungal cream or powder like tolnaftate.

Tetanus This disease is caused by a germ, which lives in soil and in the faeces of horses and other animals. It enters the body via breaks in the skin. The first symptom may be discomfort in swallowing, or stiffening of the jaw and neck; this is followed by painful convulsions of the jaw and whole body. The disease can be fatal. It can be prevented by vaccination, so make sure your shots are up to date before you leave.

Insect-Borne Diseases

Lyme Disease This is a tick-transmitted infection. The illness usually begins with a spreading rash at the site of the tick bite and is accompanied by fever, headache, extreme fatigue, aching joints and muscles, and mild neck stiffness. If untreated these symptoms usually resolve over several weeks, but over subsequent weeks or months disorders of the nervous system, heart and joints may develop. Treatment works best early in the illness. Medical help should be sought.

Traumatic Injuries

Sprains Ankle and knee sprains are common injuries among walkers, particularly when walking over rugged terrain. To help prevent ankle sprains in these circumstances, you should wear an all-leather boot that has adequate ankle support. If you do suffer a sprain, immobilise the joint with a firm bandage, and, if feasible, immerse the foot in cold water. Distribute the contents of your pack among your companions. Once you reach shelter, relieve pain and swelling by keeping the joint elevated for the first 24 hours and, where possible, by putting ice on the swollen joint. Take simple painkillers to ease the discomfort. If the sprain is mild, you may be able to continue your walk after a couple of days. For more severe sprains, seek medical attention as an x-ray may be needed to find out whether a bone has been broken.

Major Accidents Falling or having something fall on you, resulting in head injuries or fractures, is always possible when walking, especially if you are crossing steep slopes or unstable terrain. Following is some basic advice on what to do if a major accident does occur; detailed first-aid instruction is outside the scope of this book. If a person suffers a major fall:

1. make sure you and other people with you are not in danger
2. assess the injured person's condition
3. stabilise any injuries, such as bleeding wounds or broken bones
4. seek medical attention – see Rescue & Evacuation (p71)

If the person is unconscious, immediately check for breathing – clear the airway if it is blocked and check for a pulse – feel the side of the neck rather than the wrist. If the person is not breathing but has a pulse, you should start mouth-to-mouth resuscitation immediately. It is best to move the victim as little as possible in case the neck or back is broken. Keep the person warm by covering them with a sleeping bag or dry clothing; insulate them from the ground if possible.

Check for wounds and broken bones; if the victim is conscious, ask where pain is felt. Otherwise gently inspect all over (including the back and back of the head), moving the body as little as possible. Control any bleeding by applying firm pressure to the wound. Bleeding from the nose or ear may indicate a fractured skull. Don't give the person anything by mouth, especially if unconscious.

Most cases of brief unconsciousness are not associated with serious brain damage. Nevertheless, anyone who has been knocked unconscious should be watched closely. Carefully note any signs of deterioration (eg, change in breathing patterns) to report to the rescuers/doctor.

Fractures Indications of a fracture (broken bone) are pain, swelling and discoloration, loss of function or deformity of a limb. Unless you know what you are doing, you shouldn't try to straighten an obviously displaced broken bone. To protect from further injury, immobilise a nondisplaced fracture by splinting it; for fractures of the thigh bone, strap it to the good leg to hold it in place. Check the splinted limb frequently to ensure the splint hasn't cut off circulation.

Fractures associated with open wounds (compound fractures) require urgent treatment as there is a risk of infection. Dislocations, where the bone has come out of the joint, are very painful, and should be set as soon as possible by a doctor.

Broken ribs are painful but usually heal by themselves and do not need splinting. If breathing difficulties occur or the person coughs up blood, medical attention should be sought urgently, as it may indicate a punctured lung.

Internal Injuries More difficult to detect, these cannot usually be treated outdoors. Watch for shock, which is a specific medical condition associated with a failure to maintain circulating blood volume. Signs include a rapid pulse and cold, clammy extremities. To manage shock raise the person's legs above heart level (unless their legs are fractured), loosen tight clothing and keep them warm. A person in shock requires urgent medical attention.

Cuts & Scratches

Even small cuts and grazes should be washed well and treated with an antiseptic such as povidone-iodine. Dry wounds heal more quickly, so where possible avoid bandages and dressing strips, which can keep wounds wet. Infection in a wound is indicated by red, painful and swollen skin margins. Serious infection can cause swelling of the whole limb and of the lymph glands, and a fever may develop; seek medical attention immediately.

Burns

Immerse the burnt area in cold water as soon as possible, then cover it with a clean, dry, sterile dressing. Keep this in place with plasters for a day or so in the case of a small, mild burn, longer for more extensive injuries. Seek medical help for severe and extensive burns.

Bites & Stings

Bees & Wasps These are usually painful rather than dangerous. However, people who are allergic to them may experience severe breathing difficulties and urgent medical care is required. Calamine lotion or a commercial sting relief spray will ease discomfort, and ice packs will reduce the pain and swelling.

Snakes To minimise your chances of being bitten always wear boots, socks and long trousers when walking through undergrowth where snakes may be present. Don't put your hands into holes and crevices.

A bite by any of the adders or vipers found in Italy is unlikely to be fatal. Even so, immediately wrap the bitten limb tightly, as you would for a sprained ankle, then attach a splint to immobilise it. Keep the victim still and seek medical assistance; it will help if you can describe the offending reptile. Tourniquets and sucking out the poison are now totally discredited treatments.

Ticks Always check all over your body if you have been walking through a potentially tick-infested area as ticks can cause skin infections and other more serious diseases. Ticks are most active from spring to autumn, especially where there are plenty of sheep. They usually lurk in overhanging vegetation, so avoid pushing through tall bushes if possible.

If a tick is found attached to the skin, press down around the head with tweezers, grab the head and gently pull upwards. Avoid pulling the rear of the body as this may squeeze the tick's gut contents through its mouth into your skin, increasing the risk of infection and disease. Smearing chemicals on the tick will not make it let go and is not recommended.

Hay Fever

If you suffer from hay fever, bring your usual treatment, as the pollen count in most areas covered by this book (except high in the mountains) is very high from May to July.

Women's Health

Walking is not particularly hazardous to your health; however, women's health issues can be a bit trickier to cope with when you are on a long walk.

Menstruation A change in diet, routine and environment, as well as intensive exercise can all lead to irregularities in the menstrual cycle. This, in itself, is not a huge issue and your cycle should return to normal when you return to your normal routine. It is particularly important during the menstrual cycle to maintain good personal hygiene, and regularly change sanitary napkins or tampons (for disposal options see Human Waste Disposal, p45). Antibacterial hand gel or pre-moistened wipes can be useful if you don't have access to soap and water. You can also use applicator tampons to minimise the risk of contamination, although these are quite bulky. Because of hygiene concerns and for ease while on an extended trip, some women prefer to temporarily stop menstruation. You should discuss your options with a doctor before you go. It is also important to note that failure to menstruate could indicate pregnancy! If concerned about irregularities seek medical advice.

Pregnancy If you are pregnant, see your doctor before you travel. Even normal pregnancies can make a woman feel nauseated and tired. In the third trimester, the size of the baby can make walking difficult or uncomfortable.

Thrush (Vaginal Candidiasis) Antibiotic use, synthetic underwear, tight trousers, sweating, contraceptive pills and unprotected sex can each lead to fungal vaginal infections, especially when travelling in hot, humid climates. The most common is thrush (vaginal candidiasis). Symptoms include itching and discomfort in the genital area, often in association with a thick white discharge. The best prevention is to keep the vaginal area cool and dry, and to wear cotton rather than synthetic underwear and loose clothes. Thrush can be treated by clotrimazole pessaries or vaginal cream.

Urinary Tract Infection Dehydration and 'hanging on' can result in urinary tract infection and the symptoms of cystitis, which can be particularly distressing and an inconvenient problem when out walking. Symptoms include burning when urinating, and having to urinate frequently and urgently. Blood can sometimes be passed in the urine. Drink plenty of fluids and empty your bladder regularly. If symptoms persist, seek medical attention because a simple infection can spread to the kidneys, causing a more severe illness.

SAFETY ON THE WALK

You can significantly reduce the chance of getting into difficulties by taking a few simple precautions. These are listed in the boxed text 'Walk Safety – Basic Rules'. A list of the clothes and equipment you should take appears in the Clothing & Equipment chapter (p58).

Crossing Rivers

Sudden downpours are common in the mountains and can speedily turn a gentle stream into a raging torrent. If you're in any doubt about the safety of a crossing, look for a safer passage upstream or wait. If the rain is short-lived, it should subside quickly.

If you decide it's essential to cross (late in the day, for example), look for a wide, relatively shallow stretch of the stream rather than a bend. Take off your trousers and socks, but keep your boots on to prevent injury. Put dry, warm clothes and a

Walk Safety – Basic Rules

- Allow plenty of time to accomplish a walk before dark, particularly when daylight hours are shorter.
- Don't overestimate your capabilities. Study the route carefully before setting out, noting the possible escape routes and the point of no return (where it's quicker to continue than to turn back). Monitor your progress during the day against the time estimated for the walk, and keep an eye on the weather.
- It's wise not to walk alone. Always leave details of your intended route, number of people in your group, and expected return time with someone responsible before you set off; let that person know when you return.
- Before setting off, make sure you have the relevant map and a compass – a GPS receiver should *not* be relied upon in remote areas. You should also make sure you know the weather forecast for the area for the next 24 hours.

towel in a plastic bag near the top of your pack. Before stepping out from the bank, unclip your chest strap and belt buckle; this makes it easier to slip out of your backpack and swim to safety if you lose your balance and are swept downstream. Use a walking pole, grasped in both hands, on the upstream side as a third leg, or go arm in arm with a companion, clasping at the wrist, and cross side-on to the flow, taking short steps.

Crossing Snow

High in the mountains, even in midsummer, you may find a stretch of late-lying snow. If it's soft and not too steeply angled, you should be able to march across, still taking care to ensure your feet are firmly placed with each step and using poles to keep your balance. However, if the snow is hard and icy, even if thinly decorated with a fresh fall, and the slope is steep, you need two or more of an ice axe, a rope, crampons, companions, a clear head and good balance. Walking poles are *no* substitute for an ice axe on hard snow. Remember that, once you start the crossing, it's awkward to reverse if the going gets too difficult. It may be possible to descend the slope to a narrower, gentler crossing – provided you can safely regain the path on the far side.

Dogs

During walks in settled and farming areas of Italy, you're likely to encounter barking dogs – tethered or running free. Regard any dog as a potential attacker and be prepared to take evasive action: even just crossing the road can take you out of its territory and into safety. A walking pole may be useful, though use it as a last resort, especially if the owner is in sight. Knowing your tetanus immunisation is up to date is reassuring.

Lightning

If a storm brews, avoid exposed areas. Lightning has a penchant for crests, lone trees, small depressions, gullies, caves and cabin entrances, as well as wet ground. If you are caught out in the open, try to curl up as tightly as possible with your feet together and keep a layer of insulation between you and the ground. Place metal objects such as metal-frame backpacks and walking poles away from you.

Rockfall

Even a small falling rock could shatter your hand or crack your skull, so always be alert to the danger of rockfall. Trail sections most obviously exposed to rockfall lead below cliffs fringed by large fields of raw talus – don't hang around in such areas. If you accidentally let loose a rock, loudly warn other walkers below.

Rescue & Evacuation

If someone in your group is injured or falls ill and can't move, leave somebody with them while another one or more goes for help. They should take clear written details of the location and condition of the victim, and of helicopter landing conditions. If there are only two of you, leave the injured person with as much warm clothing, food and water as it's sensible to spare, plus the whistle and torch. Mark the position with something conspicuous – an orange bivvy bag, or perhaps a large stone cross on the ground. Remember, the rescue effort may be slow, perhaps taking more than a day to remove the injured person.

Emergency Communications There are different emergency telephone numbers for different emergency services, all available nationally (see the boxed text 'Emergency Numbers', below). There are also regional search and rescue numbers for mountainous areas (see Search & Rescue Organisations, this page). In the mountains, telephones are available at most *rifugi*. For details on payphones and mobile phone coverage, see Telephone (p346). Only call out a rescue team in a genuine emergency – not for a relatively minor discomfort such as a lightly sprained ankle.

If no other emergency communications are available, use the international distress signal. Give six short signals, such as a whistle, a shout or the flash of a light, at 10-second intervals, followed by a minute's rest. Repeat the sequence until you get a response. If the responder knows the signals, this will be three signals at 20-second intervals, followed by a minute's pause and a repetition of the sequence.

Be ready to give information on where an accident occurred, how many people are injured and the injuries sustained, and, if a helicopter needs to come in, what the terrain and weather conditions are like at the place of the accident.

Search & Rescue Organisations The Corpo Nazionale Soccorso Alpino e Speleologico (CNSAS) is, by law, entrusted with the responsibility of search, rescue and saving of lives in the mountains. It is organised regionally with specific telephone numbers for several regions. For all other regions you should ring the national emergency number (☎ 118). The regional numbers may change, so you should check with **CNSAS** *(☎ 02 295 30 433, fax 02 295 30 364; w www.cnsas.it; Via E Petrella 19, 20124 Milan)* or local tourist offices for up-to-date numbers.

region	emergency number
Abruzzo	☎ 167 258 239
Alto Adige	☎ 0471 797 171
Campania	☎ 081 551 5950
Emilia Romagna	☎ 800 848 088
Friuli–Venezia Giulia	☎ 118
Liguria	☎ 0336 689 316
Lombardy	☎ 118
The Marches	☎ 118
Piedmont	☎ 118
Sardinia	☎ 070 286 200
Sicily	☎ 095 914 141
Trentino	☎ 118
Tuscany	☎ 0348 352 0408
Umbria	☎ 075 584 7070
Valle d'Aosta	☎ 0165 230 253
Veneto	☎ 118

Helicopter Rescue & Evacuation If a helicopter arrives on the scene, there are a couple of conventions you should be familiar with. Standing face on to the chopper

- Arms up in the shape of a letter 'V' means 'I/We need help'
- Arms in a straight diagonal line (like one line of a letter X) means 'All OK'

In order for the helicopter to land, there must be a cleared space of 25m x 25m, with a flat landing pad area of 6m x 6m. The helicopter will fly into the wind when landing. In cases of extreme emergency, where no landing area is available, a person or harness might be lowered. Take extreme care to avoid the rotors when approaching a landed helicopter.

Emergency Numbers

Wherever you are in Italy, these are the numbers to ring in an emergency:

Ambulance *(Ambulanza)*	☎ 118
Fire Brigade *(Vigili del Fuoco)*	☎ 115
Highway Rescue *(Soccorso Stradale)*	☎ 116
Police *(Carabinieri)*	☎ 112
Police *(Polizia)*	☎ 113

Liguria

The Ligurian coast was inhabited by Neanderthals about one million years ago and many remains have been unearthed in the area. Locals say the early inhabitants were lured by the beaches, which still exert a magnetic hold over the hundreds of thousands of tourists who flock to this narrow coastal region each year. There is more to Liguria (Ligure), however, than luxury resorts and beach umbrellas. With the majority of the population gathered along the coastline, a surprising amount of Liguria's mountainous hinterland, protected in several natural parks, remains rural and unspoilt. Woodlands cover more than half of Liguria, making it the most heavily forested region in Italy, and the coast still harbours precious pockets of undisturbed coastal vegetation. The walks in this chapter, all accessible from a base in the World Heritage listed Cinque Terre, combine some of the most popular and picturesque parts of the coastal fringe with wilder, less often visited stretches of the coast and immediate hinterland. However, Liguria also offers many other destinations to tempt the adventurous.

HISTORY

During a turbulent history marked by successive conquests and sea raids, the province of Liguria has been ruled by Greeks, Saracens, Romans, Venetians, Lombards and French, with strong early trade influences from as far afield as Sicily (Sicilia), North Africa and Spain. The many fortified buildings that dot the coast are a reminder that trade and prosperity came at a cost.

Liguria's fortunes have been closely tied to those of Genoa (Genova) since the town gained independence in 1162 and began to extend its influence along the coast. Successful expansion by the mercantile power between the 13th and 18th centuries transformed Liguria into a prosperous region of considerable maritime importance. Genoa reached its peak in the 16th century under the rule of imperial admiral Andrea Dora, and managed to benefit from Spain's American

Highlights

NICK TAPP

The Sentiero Azzuro, passing Vernazza and Monterosso, hugs the Cinque Terre coast

- Explore the five villages of the Cinque Terre on the fantastically scenic Sentiero Azzurro (p77)
- Wander off-the-beaten-track and enjoy coastal highlights on the Portovenere to Levanto Combination (p82)
- Discover the coastal plant communities, isolated farmlets, small villages and relatively undeveloped promontory of Parco Regionale di Portofino (p84)

fortunes by financing Spanish exploration. However, as the Mediterranean's importance declined, so too did the region's influence.

In 1796 Napoleon Bonaparte captured Genoa and in 1805 the Republic of Liguria became part of the French Empire. After 1814, with Napoleon's defeat at Waterloo, Liguria was absorbed into the kingdom of Sardinia-Piedmont (Sardegna-Piemonte). In 1861 Vittorio Emanuele II, king of Sardinia, became the first king of a still fragmented Italy. Genoa played a leading role in Italian unification during the remaining decades of the 19th century, and was the first northern city to rise against the German and Italian fascists towards the close of WWII.

In more recent times Genoa has become Italy's most important port, attracting a massive influx of workers from outlying regional areas and further abroad. Liguria itself has prospered from the post-war industrial expansion of the north and currently enjoys a good standard of living.

CLIMATE

Protected by both the Alps and the Apennines (Apennini) from cold northerly weather patterns, Liguria enjoys a mild, Mediterranean climate, with average daily maximum temperatures ranging between 10°C in winter and 28°C in summer. The annual rainfall is between 1000mm and 1250mm.

INFORMATION
When to Walk

With a pleasant climate year-round, walking in Liguria is recommended at any time. However, the most pleasant walking seasons are spring and autumn, when the summer heat and crowds abate.

Maps

The Touring Club Italiano's 1:200,000 map *Liguria* is helpful for planning your visit to the region.

Emergency

In the event of an accident while walking in Liguria, contact the *carabinieri* (police) on the national emergency number (☎ 112) or medical assistance on the national ambulance emergency number (☎ 118).

Cinque Terre

Recognised as a Unesco World Heritage site since 1998, the remarkable region of the Cinque Terre (Five Lands) owes its name to five villages – Monterosso al Mare, Vernazza, Corniglia, Manarola and Riomaggiore. The villages are perched along a precipitous stretch of the Riviera di Levante, the picturesque coast east of Genoa. While the steep hillsides are crowded with terraced vineyards and olive groves, and the

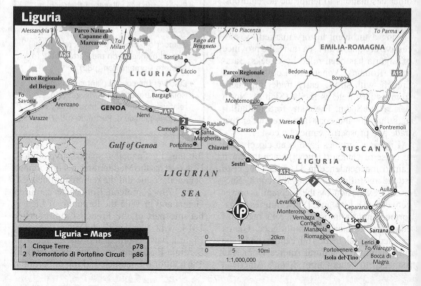

Liguria

Liguria – Maps

1:1,000,000

tiny, protected harbours are filled with fishing boats, it is tourism that now fuels the local economy. The Cinque Terre is fast becoming one of the most popular watering holes on the European circuit. Conversations in the villages' narrow, cobbled *carruggi* (alleyways) are as likely to be in German or English as they are in Italian.

While some Cinque Terre visitors come to eat, drink and loll beside the sea, many tackle at least a part of the Sentiero Azzurro (Blue Track), an often spectacular coastal walking route that connects the five villages. Fewer tackle the more challenging Sentiero Rosso (Red Track), a ridge-top route that climbs to 800m from the coast at Portovenere and returns to sea level at Levanto, looking down on the Cinque Terre from much of its length. Another option is to spread the walk over two days on the Portovenere to Levanto Combination, spending a night in one of the five villages and combining the best of the Sentiero Rosso with the whole of the Sentiero Azzurro.

NATURAL HISTORY

The Cinque Terre is part of the northwestern extremity of the Apennines. The hillsides of the Cinque Terre have been terraced and intensively cultivated for centuries, and little remains of the original coastal vegetation except at the southeastern extreme, towards Portovenere, and on Punta Mesco, between Monterosso al Mare and Levanto. Here there are extensive stands of Aleppo pine and patches of coastal *macchia* (scrub) – a well-established mixture of species such as myrtle, broom, arboreal heather and juniper. A little further inland, higher up on the ridge traversed by the Sentiero Rosso, cluster pines and broad-leaved trees, such as chestnuts, form almost pure forests, although walkers will also see the occasional cork oak.

There's not much large terrestrial fauna about – occasional signs that warn of hunting activities may explain the lack of mammals. However, a little birdlife survives and there's quite a variety of marine species along some stretches of the coast, in particular Punta Mesco and surrounds.

PLANNING
When to Walk

The crowd-shy would be wise to avoid the Cinque Terre during the peak summer months of July and August, when the area becomes inundated with tourists keen to experience its much-famed beauty first hand.

Maps

The Cinque Terre is well covered by maps, widely available in bookshops throughout the Cinque Terre and in surrounding towns. The Club Alpino Italiano (CAI) produces a good 1:40,000 *Cinque Terre e Parco di Montemarcello* map, with track notes (in Italian and German), and profiles on the back for the Sentiero Azzurro and Sentiero Rosso. There is also a 1:25,000 version of the same map, *Riviera Ligure: Le Cinque Terre da La Spezia a Lèvanto*. It is worth noting that not all the paths on the Sentiero Rosso are marked on these maps and a few that have been marked are not visible on the ground.

Occasionally more accurate, but more difficult to read, is the Kompass 1:50,000 map No 644 *Cinque Terre*, which has inset street maps of all five villages, plus Levanto and Portovenere, and comes with a slender, illustrated guide (in Italian and German) to the region. The Edizioni Multigraphic 1:25,000 *Cinque Terre, Golfo della Spezia, Montemarcello* has a guide in Italian printed on the reverse side.

Books

Cinque Terre shops sell a range of publications in different languages. Recommended is the *Guide to the Cinque Terre*, by Alberto Grani, with an accompanying 1:30,000 map. Designed for the less committed rambler, *Walking Through the Cinque Terre...*, by Antonio Cella, provides a short background description of each of the five villages and includes a number of easy walk itineraries.

Information Sources

The private Cinque Terre website (**w** home .sunrise.ch/avong/cinque_terre/index.htm), with up-to-date practical advice and recommendations from fellow travellers, is definitely worth a browse. The more official

Consorzio Turistico Cinque Terre website (W www.cinqueterre.it) is another good first port of call.

Leaving Luggage

You can leave excess gear at any train station while you do an overnight walk, but at €2.60 for every 12 hours or part thereof, this is an expensive business. Your hotel in town may store a spare bag for a day or two.

GETTING THERE & AWAY

All five Cinque Terre villages, plus Levanto, are served at less than hourly intervals between 6am and 11pm by La Spezia–Genoa trains. A trip anywhere within the Cinque Terre costs €1, from Levanto to La Spezia costs €1.35, and a special day pass allowing unlimited travel between La Spezia and Monterosso costs €2.85.

By car, the Cinque Terre is accessible from the A12 and the S1, which passes through La Spezia. While all the villages are accessible by car, some Cinque Terre roads are rough. You cannot drive right into the five villages but must park at the perimeter.

For a more romantic entry to the region, **Golfo Paradiso** (☎ 0185 77 20 91; W www .golfoparadiso.it) runs a ferry service (June to September) from a quay in the Mandraccio quarter of Genoa's Porto Antico to towns along the Riviera di Levante, including Monterosso and Vernazza in the Cinque Terre (€15.50) and Portovenere (€19).

There is also a **Golfo dei Poeti** (☎ 0187 77 77 27; W www.navigazionegolfodeipoeti.it) ferry service operating between the villages (not Corniglia), Portovenere and La Spezia (€11.50, four a day). Passengers have the option of paying for only a section of the trip on the legs between Monterosso and Vernazza, and Manarola and Riomaggiore.

ACCESS TOWNS

With the start and finish of the walks in this section easily accessed by train or boat from all Cinque Terre villages, you can base yourself in any of the five. For hostel accommodation in Manarola see under The Walk (p78), and for details on possibly the most fetching of the villages, see Vernazza (p83).

There are many more options than have been listed here, and plenty of locals rent out rooms on a more or less official basis – if you miss the telltale signs advertising *camere* (rooms) and *affittacamere* (rooms for rent), ask around in the bars. One word of warning, however: between April and October accommodation, even midweek, can be very hard to find, so you must book well in advance.

Riomaggiore

This classic Cinque Terre village comprises a mess of houses that slither down a ravine, which forms the main street. Tiny fishing boats line the shore and are stacked in the small square. The older part of town is a short walk south of the train station, through a long tunnel. For information contact the **Riomaggiore IAT** (☎ 0187 92 06 33; Piazza Unità). For transport options to/from Riomaggiore, see Getting There & Away (this page).

Places to Stay & Eat In front of the train station is the not-so-salubrious **Ostello Mamma Rosa** (☎ 0187 92 01 73; Piazza Unità; dorm beds €12.90), touted as a good meeting place for travellers and one of the few budget options in the Cinque Terre. At the beginning of the Sentiero Azzurro, **Edi** (☎ 0187 92 03 25, fax 0187 92 04 90; e edi-vesigna@iol.it; Via Cristoforo Colombo 111; doubles from €46.50, two-person apartments without/with balcony per week €310/362) has some sea views. The family-run **Ca' dei Duxi** (☎ 0187 92 00 36; Via Cristoforo Colombo 36; singles/doubles €82.65/103.30) is somewhat more expensive but has clean, quiet rooms.

For self-caterers, try **Coop 5 Terre** (Via Cristoforo Colombo), a community-run cooperative grocery store. Among restaurants in the main street, Via Cristoforo Colombo, are **La Grotta** (☎ 0187 92 01 87) and the budget **Veciu Muin**, serving very edible eat-in or takeaway pizzas from €3.60. The traditional Ligurian food of **Trattoria La Lanterna** (☎ 0187 92 05 89; Via San Giacomo 10) more than rewards the effort of booking a table. House specialities include octopus on a spring salad (€7.25) and crumbed scampi in a tomato sauce (€13.45).

Monterosso al Mare

An unusual feature of this village is the huge statues embedded into the rocks overlooking one of the few Cinque Terre beaches, a grey, pebbly affair. Information is available from the local **IAT office** (☎ *0187 81 75 06; Via Fegina 38*), below the train station. For transport options to/from Monterosso, see Getting There & Away (p76).

Places to Stay & Eat Close to the beach and train station, **Hotel Punta Mesca** (☎ *0187 81 74 95; Via Molinelli; doubles €67.15*) is clean and quiet. Breakfast is included in the rates. **Hotel La Colonnina** (☎ *0187 81 74 39; Via Zuecca 6; doubles €82.65*) is friendly and quiet, and has rooms with ocean views.

In historic Monterosso's centre, **Enoteca Internazionale** (☎ *0187 81 72 87; Via Roma 62*) is one of the best places in the Cinque Terre to munch on anchovy-topped bruschetta and sip sweet Sciacchetrà (a desert wine) or *limoncino* (a lemon liqueur made from Monterosso lemons).

Levanto

Situated on the western fringe of the Cinque Terre, Levanto can become predictably crowded in summer. Information is available from **Levanto IAT** (☎ *0187 80 81 25; Piazza Cavour*). For transport options to/from Levanto, see Getting There & Away (p76).

Places to Stay The Cinque Terre's closest camping option is **Acqua Dolce** (☎ *0187 80 84 65;* e *acquadolce@tin.it; Via Semenza 5; adult/tent/car €6.70/5.15/4.15*), conveniently located in the town centre. A new hostel in a restored historic building, **Ospitalia Del Mare** (☎ *0187 92 02 15; Via Riccobaldi 21; beds from €12.90*), 100m from the beach, has four-, six- and eight-bed rooms with bathrooms. **Hotel Garden** (☎ *0187 80 81 73; Corso Italia 6; doubles €41.35*) is right next to the beach.

La Spezia

Sitting at the head of the gulf of the same name, La Spezia is 100km southeast of Genoa. The construction from 1860 to 1865 of Italy's largest naval base propelled La Spezia from minor port to provincial capital, the ubiquitous blue sailor's uniform a constant reminder of its naval links.

The most useful information source (if an inconvenient distance from the train station) is **La Spezia APT** (☎ *0187 77 09 00;* w *www .aptcinqueterre.sp.it; Viale Mazzini 47*), which faces the waterfront. The helpful staff speak English, and there are plenty of brochures and maps. There is also an **information kiosk** (☎ *0187 71 89 97*) at the train station. There is a range of accommodation in La Spezia, but with the Cinque Terre so close, it is unlikely you'll want to stay here – ask at the APT for accommodation options.

Getting There & Away La Spezia is on the Genoa–Rome railway line, which follows the coast, and is also connected to Milan, Turin and Pisa. The A12 runs past La Spezia to Genoa and Livorno, and the A15 to Parma also connects with the main north-south route, the A1. The S1 passes through the city and connects with the S62 for Parma and the north. Ferries depart from La Spezia for Genoa and other coastal towns throughout the summer and occasionally on pleasant weekends during the rest of the year (see Getting There & Away, p76, for details of services).

Sentiero Azzurro

Duration	2½–5 hours
Distance	12km
Difficulty	easy–moderate
Start	Riomaggiore (p76)
Finish	Monterosso al Mare (p77)
Transport	train, boat, car

Summary The classic way to explore the extraordinary villages and cultivated hillsides of the Cinque Terre, while enjoying delightful coastal scenery.

Many people experience this fantastically scenic walk during the region's year-round tourist season. The Sentiero Azzurro (Blue Track) is named for its proximity to the blue Mediterranean or, strictly, the Ligurian Sea.

In October 2000, fierce storms, torrential rain and high seas caused some sections of the cliff-edge trail to collapse, including part of the lovely Via dell'Amore (Lovers' Lane) between Riomaggiore and Manarola. Closed for several months for repairs, the route is again open to the public.

Marked in part by blue-paint markers, the four stages of the track link the five villages of the Cinque Terre by the easiest route. Owing to the precipitous nature of the terrain, however, even this route is airy and somewhat strenuous in parts, with a total of 440m of ascent. Many of the holiday-makers who tackle the Sentiero Azzurro complete only the easiest section between Riomaggiore and Corniglia. To a seasoned walker, however, the Sentiero Azzurro is a delightful, undemanding day's outing along, arguably, some of the finest coastline in Italy.

The route is described from southeast to northwest because, with a reasonably early start, you'll have the sun behind you. Be aware the walking becomes progressively more difficult as you proceed in this direction, so if you are finding the going tough, it might be a good idea to finish the day early. You can, however, start at either end.

From Riomaggiore to Monterosso, as the seagull flies, is little more than 8km. The route winds and twists, but it's not a long walk. Signposts and maps give an 'official' walking time of five hours and 10 minutes, but many reasonably fit, experienced walkers will cover the distance in half that. However, with an almost continuous supply of photogenic vantage points, captivating medieval villages and restaurants to sample along the way, be prepared to make slow progress.

THE WALK

Although it's possible to walk out of the train station at **Riomaggiore** and head immediately up the coast towards Manarola, it's worth first exploring the most interesting part of this, the easternmost of the five

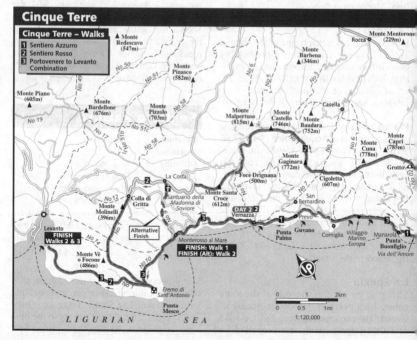

villages of the Cinque Terre. To do so, turn right outside the station entrance and follow the footpath beside the railway line through a tunnel for 150m. Once you emerge into daylight, passages lead down to the right to the waterfront, where small fishing boats are stacked in a tiny piazza, while the pedestrian main street leads left up the steep-sided Valle di Riomaggiore.

The Sentiero Azzurro proper, also known as No 2, begins back at the piazza outside the train station, where a staircase (left) leads over the railway line to the beginning of the excessively famous **Via dell'Amore**. This cliffside path between Riomaggiore and Manarola passes through a roofed gallery, something of a shrine on the theme of *l'amore* (love), which also serves the more practical purpose of protecting walkers from falling rocks. At the end of Via dell'Amore a 150m tunnel leads from the **Manarola** train station into the village, about 30 minutes from Riomaggiore.

If you plan to stay in the village, **Ostello Cinque Terre** (☎ *0187 92 02 15, fax 92 02 18; *w* www.cinqueterre.net/ostello; Via Riccobaldi 21; dorm beds/family rooms from €16/64*), roughly 300m north of the train station, is a well-run, popular choice, so you'll need to book ahead. The charge for an organic breakfast is €3.5.

From the end of the tunnel, head left, down towards the picturesque waterfront with its rocky boat landing and tiny harbour protected by a breakwater. From here follow the marked and rerouted footpath round the small headland (maps still show the old and now fenced-off route that climbed up past the Manarola cemetery). The way ahead, carved into the steep hillside, is clear. The path soon gains the route once followed by the old railway line, now colonised along some of its length by the low-key holiday resort Villaggio Marino Europa, then passes under the present-day line and alongside the platforms of the Corniglia train station. A

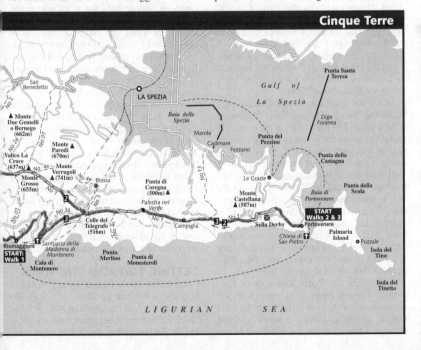

Cinque Terre

365-step brick staircase zigzags up to the ridge top where the village of **Corniglia** is perched above the sea, roughly 3km and one hour from Manarola. The Sentiero Azzurro keeps the centre of Corniglia on its seaward side, passing the 14th-century **Chiesa di San Pietro** with its grey Gothic facade and marble rose window, and crossing the sealed road to San Bernardino.

Two small bridges mark the beginning of the climb to Prevo. The hillside above the tiny grey-sand beach of Guvano is steep and somewhat unstable. Even so, the buildings of Prevo soon come and go, and the track proceeds more gently again through olive groves. As Vernazza nears, the views across the village and along the coast to Monterosso are truly grand.

The buildings of **Vernazza** (p83), about 1½ hours from Corniglia, cluster improbably on a headland, dominated by the tower of the Castello Belforte, and a breakwater extends across the entrance of a small harbour where colourful boats are moored in rows. The Sentiero Azzurro winds down through narrow laneways and crosses the main pedestrian street, which runs from east to west, between the waterfront piazza – well worth a detour – and the train station. By now it's likely to be lunch time, and there's a variety of fairly pricey cafés to choose from.

Leave the village on a well-formed track beside the church, Chiesa di Santa Margherita d'Antiochia. The track climbs away steeply and gives excellent views far back, eventually, as Corniglia and Riomaggiore. It levels out and becomes narrower and not as well maintained, but remains generally well marked and is not difficult to follow all the way to **Monterosso al Mare**, about 1½ hours from Vernazza. Once in Monterosso, after skirting the seaward side of an upmarket hotel, you come to a sheltered beach separated by the railway line from Piazza Garibaldi in the old village, where the Sentiero Azzurro officially ends.

The Golfo dei Poeti boat service (see Getting There & Away, p76) leaves from the western end of the beach. To reach the train station, continue round the waterfront and through a tunnel under the headland to an-

other, longer beach. The train station is upstairs in buildings that face the sea, approximately halfway along.

Sentiero Rosso

Duration	9–12 hours
Distance	38km
Difficulty	moderate
Start	Portovenere
Finish	Levanto
Nearest Towns	La Spezia (p77), Riomaggiore (p76), Levanto (p77)
Transport	bus, train, ferry

Summary An end-to-end, ridge-top traverse of the Cinque Terre along shady woodland paths with sweeping coastal views.

Few of the holiday-makers who invade the Cinque Terre venture along the Sentiero Rosso, making this walk a delightful opportunity to retreat from the madding crowd. Although its highest point is barely 800m above sea level, this ridge-top route is as close as the Cinque Terre gets to a true *alta via* (high-level walking route), and it is sufficiently long and has enough ascent/descent (1150m) to deter casual strollers. As a challenging day walk it offers the satisfaction of a complete traverse of the highest part of the Cinque Terre. Navigational difficulties are minimal, and experienced walkers, especially those fresh from more demanding alpine terrain, will find the 'official' walking times posted along the route generous.

For those interested in completing only a section of the Sentiero Rosso (and it should be stressed that the entire route is an ambitious day's outing), there are several options for leaving the trail early, finishing the day in the pleasant surrounds of Riomaggiore, Vernazza or Monterosso al Mare.

GETTING TO/FROM THE WALK

From La Spezia's Piazza Giuseppi Verdi, near the waterfront (a 2km walk from the train station), you can catch an **ATC** (☎ 0187 52 25 22) bus to the beginning of the walk at Piazza Bastreri (where the bus turns around) in Portovenere (€0.80, 30 minutes, every half hour); the daily service starts at 4.45am (5.45am Sunday).

THE WALK (see map p78–9)

From Piazza Bastreri, the Sentiero Rosso or No 1 begins with a brisk climb up the staircase beside the town's 16th-century castle. On days when the air above the Gulf of La Spezia sheds its characteristic brown haze, there is a magnificent view across the water to the Alpi Apuane in northern Tuscany (Toscana). The 13th-century Chiesa di San Pietro, perched dramatically at the seaward end of the promontory in Portovenere, also appears to good advantage as the track climbs past the castle. Ignore track 1a off to the left, which returns 600m later at a hairpin bend on a sealed road. Continue on the lower arm of the hairpin, past an abandoned marble quarry, and take a marked foot track on the right, which cuts off one of the road's numerous switchbacks. The road leads around to the left into Sella Derby, where signposts near a building at the extreme left of another big bend point left into the coastal vegetation and up a small spur with fine coastal views.

The Sentiero Rosso, now a foot track, touches a further hairpin bend, where the Alta Via del Golfo (p88) heads off to the right along the road, then continues up the crest of the ridge. Yet another loop of road appears out of the pine forest and vanishes again before the track joins the road into Campiglia. At a small soccer pitch on the left on the outskirts of the village, the track detours left through pines and climbs gently into the little piazza beside the Chiesa di Santa Caterina in Campiglia.

Follow signs through the village (there's a good **shop** on the right for coffee, focaccia, cheese, fruit etc), then left up stairs at a junction. Track 1 climbs quite steeply up a ridge, then levels out and proceeds along the crest, passing an array of curious-looking sculptures: the exercise stations of Palestra nel Verde (Gymnasium in the Forest). From the **La Pineta** bar, the track joins, then leaves, a made road on the way to **Colle del Telegrafo** (516m), where several roads and tracks meet, two to three hours from Portovenere. From

here, track 3 descends left to Riomaggiore (see Day 1, p83, of the Portovenere to Levanto Combination for a description of this trail). **Bar Trattoria Da Natale** offers a last opportunity to replenish supplies before the Santuario della Madonna di Soviore, another four to six hours away.

From Colle del Telegrafo, cross the road and head back into the trees up the foot track labelled '1'. This soon gives characteristic Cinque Terre views all the way along the coast to Monterosso al Mare. After 10 minutes a telegraph tower appears ahead atop Monte Verrugoli, while down to the left Riomaggiore clings impressively to the sides of a canyon. The route follows a pleasantly shady vehicular track through chestnut forest, past track 4e on the right, and into the small saddle of Valico La Croce, where track 01 (not to be confused with track 1) crosses the ridge.

Heading to the left here, away from the vehicular track, continue along the crest of the main ridge, passing a grotto, then the junction with track 02 and, a few minutes later, a sign that points to the Menhir di Monte Capri. This standing stone lies, rather than stands, 50m off to the right. Some 15 minutes later the track switches back to the west side of the ridge and the first significant descent of the day begins. The track drops steadily into a saddle where it meets track 6, then continues more levelly into a grassy clearing that makes a pleasant spot for lunch. A few minutes further on, signposts announce the saddle known as **Cigoletta** (607m), where track 7 comes in from the right. You are roughly halfway to Levanto.

Tracks 1 and 7 merge for a short distance, then No 1 doubles back to the right and heads uphill, with brief glimpses of the coast below. The trail swings north for a way, then west again, in a wide arc round the head of the drainage basin that feeds Rio Vernazzola. Chestnut forests give welcome shade and the Sentiero Rosso reaches its highest point on the ridge of **Monte Malpertuso** (815m). Descend, on and off a vehicular track, to a three-way intersection of sealed roads. Follow the markers along the road that leads west to a larger road at

Foce Drignana and a sign on the left for track 8. This track leads down to Vernazza, for an early end to the day.

If continuing on, cross the road and head up a spur. The foot track rounds Monte Santa Croce on its north side, continues through a saddle and along the ridge, then descends to meet a major sealed road. A sign points left down the road towards Genoa, Levanto and Monterosso. This road is the route for the next 3.5km with the exception of a brief detour, after 1.5km, through the grounds of the **Santuario della Madonna di Soviore**, the oldest sanctuary in Liguria. The **bar** on the terrace (with views as far as Corsica on the right day) serves drinks, snacks and meals until 10.45pm. For the weary traveller, the bar is a good point at which to leave the Sentiero Rosso (see Alternative Finish: Monterosso al Mare, this page).

Another 2km down the road at Colla di Gritta, Levanto comes into view. Cross the road ahead, enter the car park beside **Ristorante Albergo Il Bivio** and go left to find track 1 as it leaves the car park by a set of stairs. The track climbs a pine-clad ridge with occasional views back to the southeast along the coast. It rises and falls over some minor peaks, including Monte Molinelli, then descends into a saddle, 2.8km from Colla di Gritta, where track 14 heads right. Straight ahead is Monte Vè o Focone, but the track swings left (south) round it towards Punta Mesco. Just short of the point, track 1 doubles back to the right towards Levanto. It's worth continuing for five minutes (100m) along track 10 to the ruins of an old hermitage, **Eremo di Sant'Antonio** (dating from the 11th century), and an old *semaforo* (beacon), with an uninterrupted view back along the Cinque Terre coast.

Back at the sharp bend in track 1, go left and make the gradual 5km descent, through pine forest and then cultivated land, briefly joining a sealed road along the way, to Levanto. A final staircase below the 13th-century walls of a Malaspina family castle leads down to the grey-sand beach. To reach the train station, head north along the waterfront for 500m, then follow the main street, Corso Roma, away from the beach for 1km.

Alternative Finish: Monterosso al Mare
45 minutes–1 hour, 7km

For the weary walker this is a welcome early finish to the day – an easy, shady descent down a paved mule track (No 9), still used by pilgrims to the Santuario della Madonna di Soviore. Leaving from the edge of the terrace outside the sanctuary bar, follow the track as it descends steeply through forest, past the ruins of a hexagonal chapel, and continues across the main access road to Monterosso. A little further on the trail joins a small sealed road for a short distance. The road peters out but the trail continues its descent to Monterosso. It finally emerges at Via Roma (the exit point is marked by an iron cross). Follow the Via Roma down to Monterosso's eastern beach. The Golfo dei Poeti boat service (see Getting There & Away, p76) leaves from the western end of the beach. To reach the train station, continue round the waterfront and through a tunnel under the headland to another, longer beach. The train station is upstairs in buildings that face the sea, approximately halfway along.

Portovenere to Levanto Combination

Duration	2 days
Distance	30km
Difficulty	easy
Start	Portovenere
Finish	Levanto
Nearest Towns	La Spezia (p77), Riomaggiore (p76), Levanto (p77)
Transport	bus, train, ferry

Summary Walk the Cinque Terre from end to end, with time to explore the villages, and remarkable natural and cultivated scenery for which the region is justly famous.

This two-day walk combines the off-the-beaten-track scenic highlights of the Sentiero Rosso – its beginning and end – with the entire Sentiero Azzurro. It gives you time to explore the full length of the Cinque

Terre with an overnight stop in Vernazza, perhaps the most fetching of the villages.

GETTING TO/FROM THE WALK

See Getting to/from the Walk (p80) for Sentiero Rosso.

THE WALK (see map p78–9)
Day 1: Portovenere to Vernazza
4–6 hours, 20km, 900m ascent

Follow the Sentiero Rosso from Portovenere to Colle del Telegrafo, as described under The Walk (p81) for Sentiero Rosso.

From the Colle del Telegrafo, the Sentiero Rosso proceeds along the main ridge and track 3a follows a minor road to the left towards Riomaggiore. Find No 3, a foot track that heads to the left of No 3a from just in front of **Bar Trattoria Da Natale**. Heading down the hill, this track is well marked, and there's a good chance you'll meet walkers coming from the opposite direction, from Riomaggiore to Portovenere. At intervals, as it winds about, the track overlooks the main La Spezia–Riomaggiore road, but the views also include coastal cliffs, blue water and built-up, terraced vineyards. You will also see the ingenious monorails that carry the locals to and from the *vendemmia* (grape harvest), and transport the picked grapes down to the villages on the coast.

Continue down the hill to emerge through a gap in a wall at a very rustic, but adequately marked, T-junction. Track 3a heads up to the east here to meet the minor road that descends from Colle del Telegrafo. A further 500m downhill to the west, with fine views, is the **Santuario della Madonna di Montenero**, a fine former church that now houses an elegant restaurant. From here the roughly paved track swings back towards the east then northeast, into a gully which eventually feeds down into the canyon that becomes the main street of Riomaggiore. Head back to the west again, down the gully, and cross the La Spezia road. Continue down the left (south) side of the gully, following red-and-white markers and descending a long flight of stairs to meet the made road on the outskirts of **Riomaggiore**. Cross here and

follow the Valle di Riomaggiore, which now becomes the main thoroughfare through the village, down to the entrance to the railway tunnel, just above the water.

Head through the tunnel on the footpath beside the train line to the piazza outside the train station, where the Sentiero Azzurro begins. Follow the route described under The Walk (p78) to **Vernazza**.

Vernazza

Possibly the most fetching of the villages, Vernazza makes the most of the sea, with a promenade and piazza on the water. The village's main cobbled lane, Via Roma, links the piazza with the train station. For transport options to/from Vernazza, see Getting There & Away (p76).

Places to Stay & Eat If you want sea views try **Albergo Barbara** (☎ 0187 81 23 98; *Piazza Marconi 30; doubles from €41.30).* Alternatively there is **Franca Maria** (☎ 0187 81 20 02; *doubles from €33.60),* in the same building, or **Da Martina** (☎ 0187 81 23 65; *Piazza Marconi 36; doubles from €36.15).*

Trattoria Gianni Franzi (☎ 0187 82 10 03; *Piazza Marconi 5; doubles from €41.35)* also has rooms to rent and serves up plates of steaming, home-made ravioli, among other tasty delicacies, in the atmospheric surrounds of Piazza Marconi. Another meal option is **Trattoria Bar il Baretto** (*Via Roma 31),* which has *primi* (first courses) from €6.20 and *secondi* (second courses) from €7.75. There are several *gelaterie* (ice-cream parlours) in Via Roma.

Day 2: Vernazza to Levanto
2½–3½ hours, 10km, 485m ascent

Continue along the Sentiero Azzurro (see The Walk, p78) to the train station in **Monterosso al Mare**. From here track 10 heads west along the waterfront to a huge sculpture known as *Il Gigante*, a rather tortured-looking Neptune. The track begins to climb, keeping the sculpture between it and the water, following signs towards a little tower. It passes some impressive buildings, then emerges beside a road. Walk beside the road, then on it for a couple of minutes, before heading up a set of stairs at a bend in the road. There are lovely views back along the Cinque Terre as the track continues to climb and, less than an hour from Monterosso, comes to a junction where signs point left to Punta Mesco. The 100m detour left, to the abandoned **Eremo di Sant'Antonio** and old *semaforo*, is worthwhile on a good day. From here, follow the last stage of the Sentiero Rosso (see The Walk, p81) into Levanto.

Parco Regionale di Portofino

Portofino is an unlikely place to find relatively undisturbed coastal terrain. Portofino, the town, is one of the most fashionable seaside hang-outs in Italy, where the country's rich and famous come to get away from it all – or, at least, do it in a different setting. Portofino, the natural park, is small (11.5 sq km) but set on a beautiful and relatively undeveloped promontory ringed by dramatic cliffs and small coves.

The promontory rises to a high point of 610m at Monte di Portofino, and its limestone and conglomerate soils support a wide variety of plant species. The southern slopes of the promontory experience a predominantly Mediterranean climate, and the vegetation is dominated by pine, oak and other species of the coastal *macchia*. North of the ridge of hills that cross from west to east, however, the hours of sunlight are reduced, the prevailing winds are continental ones, and the plant species that thrive are those usually associated with cooler climates further north. The two air currents, one warm and humid and the other cool, collide above the ridge and frequently give rise to cloud or fog about the tops.

Many bird species are found here, including a number of migratory ones that call in twice a year on their way back and forth between continental Europe and Africa. The waters off the promontory are one of the richest marine habitats in the Mediterranean and are protected in a marine reserve.

Promontorio di Portofino Circuit

Duration	5–6½ hours
Distance	18km
Difficulty	moderate
Start	Camogli
Finish	Santa Margherita Ligure
Nearest Town	Rapallo (p85)
Transport	train, bus, ferry
Summary	Explore a picturesque, unspoiled coastal park and the tiny, remote settlement of San Fruttuoso with its historic abbey, finishing on a trail through luxury resorts.

The Parco Regionale di Portofino is laced with well-established, marked walking tracks. This very panoramic walk around the coastline combines a series of those tracks. While by no means an Alpine challenge, it is a reasonably long walk, and negotiates several short but steep ascents (900m total ascent). Fixed wire cables have been placed in a couple of places where the trail crosses exposed terrain.

For walkers seeking a more relaxed experience, the route can be shortened by taking a boat from San Fruttuoso back to Camogli or on to Portofino, which is connected to Santa Margherita by bus.

PLANNING
Maps
The Sagep 1:10,000 *Guida al Parco di Portofino* map is sold with a detailed guidebook to all the marked tracks in the park. If you can't find it, the Euro Cart 1:25,000 *Tigullio Carte dei Sentieri* map also covers the walk.

Books
Sagep's guide to the promontory, *Guida al Parco di Portofino*, by Alberto Girani, now translated into English, provides a good introduction to the park and a number of walk itineraries. Alternatively, Sagep also publishes a cheaper booklet on the park, *The Park of Portofino Quick Guide*, by Fabrizio Calzia & Alberto Girani, with maps and descriptions for several day walks.

What to Bring

The walk crosses terrain with little shade, so bring plenty of water, sunscreen and a hat with a brim. Weather permitting, don't forget to pack a swimming costume.

NEAREST TOWN
Rapallo

The smart, seaside town of Rapallo is one of the less exorbitantly expensive options on the exclusive Portofino strip, dubbed by the Italian press as 'the richest promontory in Italy'. With its Roman origins, Rapallo boasts a bridge supposedly used by Hannibal during the Carthaginian invasion of Italy in 218 BC.

Information For accommodation information and walking maps, try the **IAT tourist office** (☎ 0185 23 03 46, fax 0185 6 30 51; Lungomare Vittorio Veneto 7), 50m west of Piazza Pastene. **Libreria Agorà** (Via Milite Ignoto 22) has a good selection of Liguria guides and maps.

Places to Stay & Eat For the camping grounds in the hills near Rapallo, take the Savagna bus from the train station. Two options are **Miraflores** (☎ 0185 26 30 00; Via Savagna 12; two people with tent €17; open Apr-Oct) and **Rapallo** (☎ 0185 26 20 18; Via San Lazzaro 4; two people with tent €16.55; open June-Sept).

The cheap-end pick of the many hotels in Rapallo is the popular **Bandoni** (☎ 0185 5 04 23, fax 0185 5 72 06; Via Marsala 24; singles/doubles without bath from €28.40/ 46.50), right on the waterfront. In Santurario di Montallegro, a short trip from Rapallo by cable car, **Albergo Ristorante il Pellegrino** (☎ 0185 23 90 03; singles €31; open May-Aug, Easter & Christmas) offers B&B with stunning views in highly atmospheric surroundings. At the deluxe end of the market, sample the plush comforts of the **Astoria** (☎ 0185 27 35 33, fax 0185 6 27 93; ₩ www.Eurose.it/astoria; Via Gramsci 4; singles/doubles €105/155).

Ristorante da Monique (☎ 0185 5 05 41; Lungomare Vittorio Veneto 5), on the harbour, has a very respectable seafood menu. More upmarket and touted as one of the best seafood restaurants in Rapallo is **La Goletta** (☎ 0185 66 92 81; Via Magenta 28; a la carte €31). There are numerous small alimentari (grocery shops) in the streets back from the waterfront.

Getting There & Away Rapallo is served daily at regular intervals by trains from Genoa (€1.90), La Spezia (€3.55) and Rome (€30.75). By car, Rapallo is accessible from both the A12 (take the Rapallo exit) and the S1, which passes through La Spezia.

GETTING TO/FROM THE WALK

Camogli can be accessed by road from the A12 (take the exit at Recca). Not all La Spezia–Genoa trains stop in Camogli but if you get off in Santa Margherita Ligure, where most do stop, it's possible to swap to a local train for the short hop across the promontory to Camogli. Trains of both varieties run frequently.

Tigullio Trasporti (☎ 0185 23 11 08) operates buses at frequent intervals between Rapallo, Santa Margherita and Camogli, leaving from the bus terminal next to the train station in Rapallo, and from Piazza Vittorio Veneto in Santa Margherita.

From the walk's finish at Santa Margherita, there are frequent trains to Rapallo (€0.90). Alternatively, you can catch a Tigullio Trasporti bus (€0.70). The same company also runs a service from Portofino to Rapallo (€1.05), for an earlier end to the walk. Portofino, Santa Margherita and Rapallo are all on the S227, which services the eastern coast of the promontory.

Between April and October, **Servizio Marittimo del Tigullio** (☎ 0185 28 46 70) ferries stop at San Fruttuoso on the hour between 11.30am and 5.30pm, en route from Camogli to Santa Margherita and Portofino. Tickets from San Fruttuoso to Portofino and Santa Margherita cost €5.15 and €6.70 respectively.

THE WALK

From the station in Camogli, cross the road and turn left (south) down Via Nicolò Cuneo. At the first hairpin bend take the left turn into a lane, Via San Bartolomeo, between two buildings. Within 200m the lane comes to the Torrente Gentile and crosses to its west bank. A gentle, sometimes winding ascent of a little more than 1km, between old houses and stone walls following trail markers (two red-painted dots), leads to **San Rocco di Camogli**, 30 minutes from the start of the walk. Around to the right of the parish church, which is decorated in the trompe l'oeil style seen in many Ligurian towns, is a *bivio* (fork) in the track. Take the right branch and then, after another 200m, the left branch, signed Via Mortola, and proceed along a reasonably level track (No 5), marked periodically with the two red

dots. Ignore track 3, marked with two red triangles, which goes off to the left towards Semaforo Nuovo after 1km. After another 1km track 5 comes to a grotto on a headland with good views of rocky Punta Chiappa below and, on a clear day, back up the coast to Camogli and beyond. Just round the bend, the remains of a WWII German anti-aircraft gun emplacement sit beside the track in an area known, simply, as **Batterie**.

Conglomerate cliffs now rise above the track, and from time to time a wire cable fixed to the rock offers protection and reassurance over an exposed section. Passo del

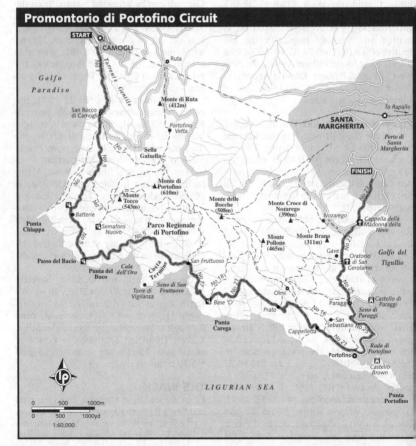

Promontorio di Portofino Circuit

START — CAMOGLI

Golfo Paradiso

Torrente Gentile

San Rocco di Camogli

Ruta

Monte di Ruta (412m)

Portofino Vetta

To Rapallo

SANTA MARGHERITA

Porto di Santa Margherita

Sella Gaixella

FINISH

Monte di Portofino (610m)

Monte Tocco (543m)

Monte delle Bocche (508m)

Monte Croce di Nozarego (390m)

Nozarego

Cappella della Madonna della Neve

Batterie

Punta Chiappa

Semaforo Nuovo

Parco Regionale di Portofino

Monte Pollone (465m)

Monte Brano (311m)

Gave

Oratorio di San Gerolamo

Golfo del Tigullio

Passo del Bacio

Punta del Buco

Cala dell'Oro

Costa Termine

San Fruttuoso

Seno di San Fruttuoso

Torre di Vigilanza

Base 'O'

Prato

Olmi

Cappelletta

San Sebastiano

Paraggi

Castello di Paraggi

Seno di Paraggi

Punta Carega

Portofino

Rada di Portofino

Castello Brown

LIGURIAN SEA

0   500   1000m
0   500   1000yd
1:60,000

Punta Portofino

Bacio gives more fine views. Across the steep-sided Cala dell'Oro to the southeast is a rocky headland topped by a 16th-century *torre di vigilanza* (watchtower), built for defence against raiders from North Africa. The track follows the contours into and out of several gullies, and into the valley at the head of the Cala dell'Oro, then climbs steeply to the crest of the Costa Termine ridge.

It's a straightforward descent from here, with occasional glimpses of the Seno di San Fruttuoso and the *torre di vigilanza*, to the tiny and very picturesque settlement of **San Fruttuoso**, nestled among olive trees and some magnificent pines. Two to 2½ hours from Camogli, this is roughly the halfway point of the walk. The grey beach is lined with foldout chairs, and ferries from Portofino and Camogli dock one after another at the tiny quay, bringing visitors to the **Abbazia di San Fruttuoso di Capodimonte** *(admission €5.15; open 10am-6pm June-Aug, shorter hours other times)*, a Benedictine abbey that houses the Doria family crypt and a small museum. A selection of **eateries** is clustered around the beach.

Continue over a small promontory and through another small group of waterfront buildings, up a gully, past a helipad and around the coast, climbing to a track junction shown on the Sagep map as Base 'O'. From here go east, still on the track marked by two red dots. Pines and Mediterranean *macchia* dominate the headlands, and broadleaved vegetation abounds in the gullies. The coastal scenery is impressive. From Prato to the Olmi turn-off the trail is lined with street lamps. Continue to a four-way junction and turn right on a signed path to Cappelletta. Follow the path to a T-junction, where a left turn leads to Cappelletta. At the small hamlet, go left rather than down towards the sea. A couple of minutes later the trail reaches another T-junction, where you go right (southeast) down a series of stone stairs (a less distinct track goes straight ahead towards San Sebastiano). The stairs lead, steeply at times, down a gully to the main road through **Portofino**.

From here it's a pleasant walk to Santa Margherita. The official time of one hour

and 50 minutes is generous, but if you're tired of walking, there's a bus stop beside the parish church on the south side of the main road. Directly over the road from here, steps lead up to the beginning of the path to Paraggi and Santa Margherita. The path almost immediately forks. Ignore the left fork to San Sebastiano and keep following the trail signed with three red dots as it heads roughly east at first, among elegant residences just above the road. A short distance further on the path meets a sealed road. Turn right down the road then almost immediately veer left, up beside an imposing gateway. From here the track proceeds without fuss, staying above the road but within sight of it, until it descends to meet the road at the attractive harbour at **Paraggi**.

When you reach the road go left (north) for just one short block to Hotel Argentina. Turn left here, then right behind the hotel and up narrow stairs between stone walls, sometimes roofed by greenery. The going is again straightforward and there is only the odd track junction to watch out for. Track marking is adequate. Follow the three dots arranged in a triangle to the hillside hamlet of Gave and its restored chapel, the Oratorio di San Gerolamo. As you continue north down the hill, on a track marked with '+' signs, Santa Margherita is visible ahead. After going right at a fork, the track comes to a road, goes right and descends a ramp to the road, then follows it to the tiny chapel of the Madonna della Neve below the settlement of Nozarego. The track passes to the left of the chapel and continues down a spur through increasingly suburban surroundings to its signposted end at the southern corner of the boat harbour in Santa Margherita. The bus to Rapallo stops on the far side of the waterfront road. The train station is on the north side of the port, just a few blocks uphill from the water.

Other Walks

LIGURIAN ALPS & APENNINES
The mountains of the Ligurian hinterland – Colle di Cadibona, behind Savona, marking the division between the Alps to the west and the Apennines

to the east – reach no great heights, but contain several natural and regional parks. These are crisscrossed by walking tracks and dotted with *rifugi* (mountain huts). Both the tracks and *rifugi* are maintained, for the most part, by branches of the Club Alpino Italiano (CAI). Those branches are the best sources of information on the considerable possibilities for walks in the local hills. Even so, such information is not easy to come by. Visitors are generally welcomed to CAI clubrooms and libraries, but finding the rooms and then finding the information you seek, can be quite difficult – ask at visitor centres for local CAI contact details.

Alta Via dei Monti Liguri

This 44-day, 440km walk is the result of an ambitious project to connect the entire length of the province from Ventimiglia, in the west, to Ceparana, near La Spezia, in the east. Following in part the routes of the Grande Traversate delle Alpi (GTA) and the Grande Escursione Alpino (GEA), the *alta via* (high-level walking route) passes through Nervia, Argentina and Arroscea valleys, rising to a high point of 2200m at Monte Saccarello. Details of the trail have been published in the *Guide Alta Via dei Monti Liguri*, which includes a detailed walk description, and plenty of colour photos and maps at 1:50,000. An English-language version has been promised in the future. If you cannot find a copy of the guide in Ligurian bookshops, contact **Unioncamere Liguri** (☎ *010 2 47 18 76; Via San Lorenzo 15/1, Genoa*). For more information on the Ligurian long-distance walk, the **Associazione Alta Via dei Monti Liguri** can be contacted on the same telephone number.

GULF OF LA SPEZIA
Alta Via del Golfo

Beginning at Bocca di Magra, southeast of La Spezia, the Alta Via del Golfo (AVG) follows ridge tops around the Gulf of La Spezia only a kilometre or two from the coast, avoiding La Spezia and finally meeting the Sentiero Rosso at Campiglia and descending to Portovenere. The route is shown on the CAI 1:40,000 *Cinque Terre e Parco di Montemarcello* map but not on the Kompass 1:50,000 *Cinque Terre* map. The 'official' walking time of just over 15 hours, while likely to be well on the conservative side, suggests that the AVG might best be done over two days. Finding somewhere to stay in Buonviaggio or Sarbia might not be easy; check with the APT or CAI in La Spezia before you set off.

PORTOFINO PROMONTORY
Portofino Hinterland

This is a challenging, nine-hour walk through the heart of the Portofino hinterland, beginning in Ruta and finishing in Chiavari, on the coast to the east of the promontory. En route it takes in several hill sanctuaries, some magnificent coastal panoramas and pockets of coastal *macchia*. The walk climbs to a high point of 801m at the summit of Monte Manico del Lume; landmarks along the way include Passo dei Quattro Pini, Passo del Gallo, Passo della Serra, the small village of Chignero, Monte Lasagna and Monte Pegge. A detailed route description is in *The Park of Portofino Quick Guide*, by Fabrizio Calzia & Alberto Girani, available from bookshops in the area. The Euro Cart 1:25,000 *Tigullio* map shows the route, but as it combines several different tracks, you will need the Sagep guide to follow the walk accurately.

Maritime Alps

The Maritime Alps (Alpi Marittime), the southernmost wag in the tail of the mighty Alps, are a range full of surprises. Accessible yet wild in character, they shelter high meadows, streams and tarns in glacial valleys separated by rugged ridges and numerous peaks of more than 3000m.

The northern limit of the Maritime Alps is Colle della Maddalena, at the head of Valle Stura, 55km west of the provincial capital of Cuneo in southern Piedmont (Piemonte). From here they extend southeast in a meandering arc to Colle di Cadibone, behind the Ligurian coastal city of Savona, where they give way to the Apennines. The Maritime Alps east of Colle di Tenda are also known as the Ligurian Alps (Alpi Liguri). For much of their length the Maritime Alps straddle the border between Italy and France.

On the Italian side of the mountains are a number of nature reserves. The two largest are the 280-sq-km Parco Naturale delle Alpi Marittime, home of the highest peaks in the range, and the 66-sq-km Parco Naturale dell'Alta Valle Pesio e Tanaro, which protects an area of rugged cliffs and limestone formations above ground and extensive karst cave systems below. This chapter describes four walks in these two parks. All four follow the Grande Traversata delle Alpi (GTA; see the boxed text 'Long-Distance Walks', pp40–2) for at least part of their length. In summer it's possible to link the two parks on a three-day walk along the GTA.

The walker from afar is likely to receive a warm if somewhat incredulous reception in the Maritime Alps, especially outside the peak holiday season. Visitors are increasingly common, but locals still seem accustomed to the relative obscurity of their corner of the Alps. The area's relative isolation is a major ingredient of its charm. While not wishing to spoil the appeal, the Maritime area is recommended as both a fine introduction to the Alps and a worthy destination in its own right.

Highlights

NICK TAPP

Piano del Valasco with the Testa del Claus (2889m) behind

- Enjoying Maritime Alps *rifugio* (mountain hut) culture: conversation, good food, wine, coffee and grappa

- Exploring the magnificent Alpine valley, waterfalls and glacial lakes on the Lago di Valscura Circuit (p94)

- Crossing three substantial passes (and making side trips to two more) on the four-day Terme di Valdieri to Entracque walk (p96)

- Admiring the awesome views of the Marguareis massif from Rifugio Garelli (p108)

HISTORY

Archaeological discoveries point to the occupation of the Vei del Bouc Valley, southeast of San Giacomo, by shepherds during the Bronze Age. A better known site from the same period is Vallée des Merveilles (Valley of the Marvels), south of the border in France's Parc National du Mercantour, where there is an extensive collection of rock engravings that date from about 1800 BC to 1500 BC. Grazing livestock in the valleys and meadows of the Maritime Alps continues, although many of the *gias* (herders camps) walkers visit are now abandoned.

The profusion of walking routes across the Maritime Alps from north to south testifies to the centuries-old commerce between southern Piedmont and France. People, ideas and goods have crossed the Alps freely here since before the days of the Roman Empire. Even the dominant language on both sides of the Alps was for a long time the same – *l'occitano* or *langue d'oc*. Track M11 over Colle di Finestra is sometimes referred to as the Sentiero del Sale or 'Salt Route' due to its former status as the main thoroughfare between Cuneo and the coast.

Colle di Finestra has more recent, tragic historical resonances. In September 1943 several hundred Jews fleeing the Nazi occupation of southern France crossed the Alps here on foot in search of a safe haven in Italy. Most were captured and first interned in a concentration camp at Borgo San Dalmazzo, then transported to camps in Germany and never seen again.

All the walks in this chapter have stages in common with the GTA. Some of these date from the mid-19th century, when the Argentera was a huge royal hunting reserve, and follow hunting trails built for Vittorio Emanuele II, king of Sardinia-Piedmont and the first king of a united Italy. Lodges occupied by the king's hunting parties can be seen at Terme di Valdieri (p94), on Piano del Valasco (p95) and near San Giacomo (p101). Other sections of the GTA follow roads built, or enlarged, for military purposes between the world wars – the wide, stone-paved track between Lago Inferiore di Valscura and Lago delle Portette on the Lago di Valscura Circuit (p94) is a good example. For details on the GTA, see the boxed text 'Long-Distance Walks' (pp40–2).

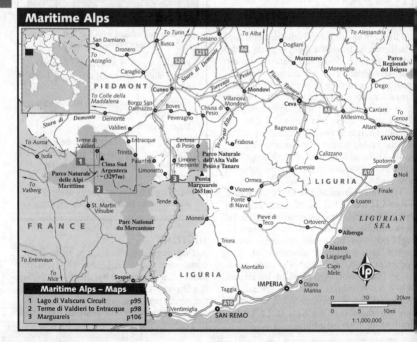

Maritime Alps – Maps

CLIMATE

The position of the Maritime Alps exposes them to Mediterranean as well as continental weather patterns. This, combined with their somewhat lower altitude, means that the weather here is generally milder than in the mountains further north. They become free of snow somewhat earlier than more northerly parts of the Alps, but snow-covered in winter they certainly are.

INFORMATION
Maps

Although the Maritime Alps are in southern Piedmont, the Touring Club Italiano (TCI) 1:200,000 map *Liguria*, which is widely sold in bookshops, is good for planning and access information. See the Planning sections of individual walks for specific map requirements.

Books

Wild Italy, by Tim Jepson, has a good section on Maritime Alps flora and fauna. Two attractive new park guides in Italian are widely sold in the region – see the individual park sections later in this chapter for details. The Club Alpino Italiano (CAI) guide to the area is called *Valli Cuneesi: Pesio, Gesso e Stura*. Larger bookshops in the region should carry these titles.

Place Names

Place names in Italian, French and local dialects are at times used interchangeably. The local word *gias*, found on signposts and maps throughout the region, refers to a summer pasture where a herder brings livestock to graze. A *gias* will usually consist of a stone building or two in better or worse repair, and perhaps a pen or corral, in a relatively flat, grassy area. There's generally water nearby, but don't rely on a *gias* for shelter as some of the buildings are roofless, and those that keep the weather out may be occupied.

The Parco Naturale delle Alpi Marittime used to be known as the Parco Naturale dell'Argentera. Both names may appear on maps of the region, in books and, rarely now, on signposts.

Emergency

For medical assistance the **national emergency number** (☎ *118*) can be contacted 24 hours a day.

Weather Information

A regional weather report in Italian is available on ☎ 011 318 55 55.

GATEWAYS
Cuneo

The provincial capital, Cuneo, makes a good base for all the walks described.

Information Visit the **IAT tourist office** (☎ *0171 69 32 58; Via Roma 28;* **w** *www .cuneotourism.com)* for local bus timetables (recommended reading) and a somewhat out-of-date brochure about the Maritime Alps in English, but little else of particular value to walkers.

Reliable sources for local walking maps and guidebooks are **ICAP** (☎ *0171 69 89 89; Piazza Galimberti 10)* and **Antica Libreria Salomone** (☎ *0171 69 25 62; Via Roma 64D).* Park visitor centres and *rifugi* (mountain huts) also sell them, but you are likely to want at least a map before you get that far.

Supplies & Equipment A range of books and outdoor gear, including everything needed for *vie ferrate* (iron ways) is available at **Ravaschietto Sport** (☎ *0171 69 20 81; Via Roma 32).*

The walks described stop overnight at *rifugi*, which can supply dinner, breakfast, packed lunch and snacks. Consequently there's no need to carry a fuel stove or much food. To stock up on lunch and snacks at town prices, Cuneo has supermarkets, including **GS** *(Corso IV Novembre)*, two blocks northeast of the train station, and **Maxisconto** *(Via Ponza di San Martino)*, just off Piazza Galimberti, as well as numerous bakeries.

Places to Stay & Eat At the southern edge of town, with mountain views and a pool is **Campeggio Bisalta** (☎ *0171 49 13 34; Via San Maurizio 33; camping per person/ tent €3.85/3.85).* Local bus 4D goes there from the train station – get off and walk to

MARITIME ALPS

the right where the bus goes left onto Via San Maurizio, a couple of stops after the Ipercoop shopping centre.

Albergo Cavallo Nero (☎ *0171 69 20 17; Piazza Seminario 8; singles/doubles with private bathroom €41.30/51.65)* includes breakfast. Slightly smarter **Albergo Ligure** (☎ *0171 68 19 42; Via Savigliano 11; singles/ doubles €43.90/62)* is in a quiet part of the old town. **Hotel Royal Superga** (☎ *0171 69 32 23; Via Pascal 3; singles/doubles with bath from €51.65/67.15),* at the other end of Piazza Seminario from the Cavallo Nero, is one star more comfortable and will store a bag while you're away walking.

Albergo Cavallo Nero and Albergo Ligure both have good **restaurants**, and **Trattoria Zuavo** *(Via Roma 23)*, also merits a visit. **Pizzeria Il Veliero** *(Via Savigliano 18)*, just north of Piazza Galimberti, is quiet, good value for lunch or dinner and popular with locals. There are many **cafés** on Piazza Galimberti, Via Roma and Corso Nizza.

Getting There & Away Cuneo is readily accessible by train, bus or car. There are regular trains to and from Saluzzo, Turin, San Remo, Ventimiglia and Nice (France). Various bus companies run services from Saluzzo, Turin, Imperia, Savona and towns in Valle Stura. If travelling by car from Turin, take either the SS20 direct or the A6 as far as Fossano, then the SS231 to Cuneo.

Parco Naturale delle Alpi Marittime

This park was established in 1995, combining Parco Naturale dell'Argentera and Riserva del Bosco e dei Laghi del Palanfrè. For 35km, along the French border, it abuts Parc National du Mercantour (see the boxed text 'Parks Without Borders', p93). Both parks have their origin in a huge hunting reserve created in 1857 for Vittorio Emanuele II.

Two walks are described, one of a day's duration and the other of four days. Both visit lakes and waterfalls and give superb views of the highest peaks in the Maritime Alps.

NATURAL HISTORY

The park is dominated by a number of granite massifs with peaks over 3000m, in particular the Argentera group, which gave the park its previous name and whose highest point is Argentera Cima Sud (3297m). To the northwest, separated from the Argentera group by Vallone del Valasco and Valle Gesso della Valetta, is the massif topped by Monte Matto (3097m). To the southeast, on the French border and accessible from both countries, is the Gelas group, which includes Monte Gelas (3143m), Cima della Maledia (3061m) and the southernmost 3000m mountain in the Alps, Monte Clapier (3045m).

The park also harbours the most southerly glaciers in the Alps. These persist high on the north-facing slopes of the peaks along the French border. They are much reduced in extent, and consist of little more than a névé, where the falling snow collects and lies permanently. Heavy snowfalls in the winter of 2000–01 gave these glaciers a reprieve, but their continued existence is tenuous.

The dominant vegetation types above the tree line are peat bogs, grasses, abundant wildflowers and low, wiry Alpine heathland plants including the dwarf pine and bilberry. Most of the forests on the lower slopes of the park are almost pure stands of *faggio* (beech). Many of the rest consist of conifers such as the silver fir, red spruce, arolla pine and European larch.

There are a number of smaller plants endemic, or nearly so, to the park, including a species of gentian, a violet found only here and on Corsica, and the so-called ancient king, a rare plant that grows slowly in cracks in the rock high in the mountains, takes decades to reach maturity, flowers once and then dies.

More than 400 of the park's plant species, and their habitats, are represented in the Giardino Botanico Valderia in Terme di Valdieri (p94).

The open higher slopes and ridges of the Maritime Alps are home to the *stambecco* (ibex) – reintroduced earlier this century – and the more numerous *camoscio* (chamois). Walkers can sometimes approach both species quite closely as they graze, although they'll often keep their distance. The rarer *mouflon* (mountain sheep) crosses into the area from Parc National du Mercantour in France but is seldom seen.

Alpine *marmotte* (marmots) are both seen and heard here. Fox, badgers, martens, squirrels, ermine and snow hares are also found, and wolves have recently returned after an absence of several decades.

Flocks of *gracchi* (choughs) wheel and whistle overhead in the higher parts of the park, and you may spot an *aquila reale* (golden eagle). Reintroduction of the *gipeto barbuto* (lammergeier or bearded vulture), once hunted to extinction in the Alps, is still in progress. At lower altitudes, forest birds include the black woodpecker and eagle owl.

Animal life on a smaller scale is abundant, and includes butterflies of all shades, from drab through to conspicuous blue, that flit about the grassy valley floors and slopes.

PLANNING
Maps & Books

The best map for both walks is the Blu Edizioni 1:25,000 *Parco Naturale delle Alpi Marittime*, available in bigger bookshops in the region. On the back are extensive park notes in Italian and useful information such as telephone numbers of *rifugi*.

There are also the older Istituto Geografico Centrale (IGC) maps – the 1:25,000 No 113 *Parco Naturale Alpi Marittime* and the 1:50,000 No 8 *Alpi Marittime e Liguri*, which covers a larger area, including the Marguareis group.

Blu Edizioni and the park authorities publish an attractive guidebook in Italian, *La guida del Parco Alpi Marittime*, with information on flora, fauna and human history, and track notes to 20 short walks. It's available from the bookshops in Cuneo (p91).

Information Sources

There's no single outstandingly useful place to go for information on the park. Administrative and technical functions are spread between the towns of Valdieri and Entracque at the **park headquarters** (☎ 0171 973 97, fax 0171 975 42; Corso Dante Livio Bianco 5, Valdieri • ☎ 0171 97 88 09, fax 0171 97 89 21; Via Provinciale 1, Entracque). The park also has a website (Ⓦ www.parks.it/parco.alpi.marittime). More useful and more

---

Parks Without Borders

In practical recognition of the fact that wildlife does not respect national frontiers, the Parco Naturale dell'Argentera, as it was then, and France's Parc National du Mercantour joined forces in 1987 to co-operate in their natural and cultural conservation work. The link was formalised in 1998 when a three-fold charter was signed to improve the understanding and preservation of the area's heritage, and to bring people together. The ultimate aim is to create a single large European park under European law.

Back in 1993 the parks' efforts had been rewarded with the Council of Europe's coveted Diploma Europeo, given to internationally important reserves for their nature conservation achievements. The Diploma was renewed in 1998, testimony to the parks' successes in involving the forestry and pastoral sectors and in preparing management plans.

Among the most notable successes has been the reintroduction of species long absent from the Maritime Alps. The handsome *stambecco* (ibex) was hunted virtually to extinction in Italy in the 19th century, and fared little better in France. It was first reintroduced to the Valle Gesso between 1920 and 1932. From the descendants of that group a number were released, between 1987 and 1995, at several other sites in the Alpi Marittime and Mercantour parks. Breeding has been successful and numbers are steadily increasing. Since 1986, 80 *gipeti* (bearded vultures) have also been released. Some have formed breeding pairs, and in the last few years a small number of young have hatched.

For walkers, the Italian-French guide *Montagne Senza Frontiere* comprises a guidebook and four 1:50,000 maps. A great deal of background information sets the scene for descriptions of a variety of walks, the routes of which ignore the dotted Italy-France border line on maps.

conveniently placed for walkers using public transport are **visitor centres** *(opposite Albergo Turismo, Terme di Valdieri •* ☎ *0171 97 86 16; Piazza Giustizia e Libertà 2, Entracque).*

ACCESS TOWN
Terme di Valdieri

Both walks in the park begin in the tiny spa town of Terme di Valdieri. During July and August it's not only possible, but quite convenient, to do both walks from a base in Cuneo using regular local buses to Terme. If you feel like spending a night in Terme before or after a walk, the more affordable accommodation option is **Albergo Turismo** *(*☎ *0171 973 34; singles/doubles €20.65/ 41.30; open mid–May–late Oct)*, at the southwestern end of town. It offers half board and is the best place for an evening meal or lunch. For a sneak preview of the diverse plant species awaiting you in the park, the **Giardino Botanico Valderia** *(admission €2.60; open mid-June–mid-Sept)* is worth a visit.

Terme is served by **Nuova Benese buses** *(*☎ *0171 69 29 29)* from Cuneo (€2.58, two per day Monday to Saturday, July to August). Outside July and August, from early June to early September, a reduced service (one per day) operates. Buses leave the west side of Cuneo's Piazza Galimberti and also call at the train station. In Terme they return from an area between the Grande Albergo Royal and the upper village. By car, take Corso Francia to Borgo San Dalmazzo, then follow the signs to Terme.

Popular Geothermics

No doubt there's a scientific explanation for the origin of the healing waters of Terme di Valdieri. According to one local walker, the popular version goes like this. A long, long time ago, the devil used to live in this valley. Then one day a good angel came down from above and ordered the devil to get back where he belonged. The earth split open, the devil disappeared, and up through the hole in the earth bubbled the hot waters that gave Terme di Valdieri both its name and its enduring popularity.

GETTING TO/FROM THE WALKS

In addition to the Nuova Benese bus services between Cuneo, Terme di Valdieri and Entracque described elsewhere in this chapter, **Alpibus minibuses** *(*☎ *0171 973 97)* take chartered groups to other destinations in the area from June to August. This service might widen your options if you want to vary the walks described.

Lago di Valscura Circuit

Duration	5–6 hours
Distance	21km
Difficulty	moderate
Start/Finish	Terme di Valdieri (p94)
Transport	bus
Summary A superb day walk, with mountain views and a historic track, to glacial lakes at the head of a picturesque Alpine valley.	

A fine introduction to the Argentera area, and hard to beat for those with limited time in the Maritime Alps, this walk begins and ends near the park visitor centre in Terme di Valdieri. It follows the GTA along a former hunting road of Vittorio Emanuele II to Piano del Valasco, an Alpine meadow in a magnificent glacial valley, and then climbs almost to the French border. It visits three scenic lakes and offers excellent views of the Argentera massif before returning to the valley. It is described here as a day walk but could be extended over two days, with an overnight stay at Rifugio Questa, to allow more time to explore. It's an ascent of 1020m from Terme to Rifugio Questa, the highest point of the walk.

PLANNING
When to Walk

During July and August a second daily bus to Cuneo leaves Terme at 6pm, giving you plenty of time to do the walk in a day from Cuneo, if you catch the early bus (8.10am) to Terme. Outside these months you may have a better chance of getting a bed at the Albergo Turismo in Terme (this page) – take your pick. Outside mid-June to early September, Terme is accessible only by private transport.

THE WALK

From the southwestern end of Terme di Valdieri, just uphill from the park visitor centre, follow the rocky road southwest, then west. After a few bends up and away from the river, the remains of a substantial mule track offer a shorter and steeper route than the road. Both reach the same destination, the lower end of the beautiful **Piano del Valasco**, an hour or so from Terme.

The fire-damaged **Reale Casa di Caccia** (Royal Hunting Lodge) is visible further up the plain, a short detour from the main track. Restoration works were in progress at the time of writing.

From a signpost on the upper end of Piano del Valasco (1814m), where a handsome waterfall has carved a small gorge, a bridge crosses the stream and another track goes southeast towards Colletto del Valasco. Stay beside the stream on its west side, following signs towards Rifugio Questa, and rejoin the old road after a few hundred metres. About 30 minutes from the lower end of the plain, the way divides and a signpost indicates two routes to the *rifugio*. Take the right fork, which leads north past some small waterfalls, doubles back and through a tunnel in the rock, and then winds generally northwest up a glacial valley, past rocks scored by an ancient glacier and ruined military buildings, to **Lago Inferiore di Valscura** (2274m), in a pretty cirque, after another 50 minutes or so. Just north of the waterfalls a clearly marked alternative route on the left zigzags up a restored mule track. This avoids a long traverse, and the tunnel, and is perhaps less exposed to rockfall.

From the lake, ignore a signposted track which leads around its north side towards Bassa del Druos (2628m). Follow the GTA to the left as it climbs out of the valley and heads roughly south towards Lago del Claus. The partly paved track – a military road built between the world wars – is wide and level as it crosses a large jumble of

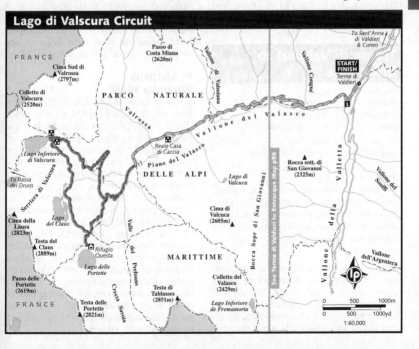

Lago di Valscura Circuit

FRANCE

Cima Sud di Valrossa (2797m)

Colletto di Valscura (2520m)

Passo di Costa Miana (2620m)

Vallone di Valmiana

To Sant'Anna di Valdieri & Cuneo

Vallone Congné

START/FINISH
Terme di Valdieri

PARCO   NATURALE

Valrossa

Vallone del Valasco

Reale Casa di Caccia

Lago Inferiore di Valscura

Piano del Valasco

DELLE   ALPI

Serriera di Valscura

To Bassa del Druos

Cima della Làusa (2823m)

Lago del Claus

Testa del Claus (2889m)

Rifugio Questa

Lago delle Portette

Passo delle Portette (2619m)

FRANCE

Testa delle Portette (2821m)

Cresta Savoia

Valle del Prefouns

MARITIME

Lago di Valcuca

Cima di Valcuca (2605m)

Rocca Sopr di San Giovanni

Rocca sott. di San Giovanni (2325m)

Valletta

Vallone del South

Vallone della Argentera

Testa di Tablasses (2851m)

Colletto del Valasco (2429m)

Lago Inferiore de Fremamorta

See Terme di Valdieri to Entracque Map p98

Vallone   della

0   500   1000m
0   500   1000yd
1:60,000

scree. There are fine views of the Argentera massif away to the east and, closer at hand, back down Vallone del Valasco.

Around 40 minutes from Lago Inferiore di Valscura, the track passes by some lakelets and into a glacial basin where cliffs surround the deep, clear waters of **Lago del Claus** (2344m). After another 20 minutes south, a zigzagging descent leads to a track junction where a signpost points up the hill to **Rifugio Questa** (☎ *0171 973 38; half board around €38; open mid-June–mid-Sept*), perched above the steep-sided Lago delle Portette. The *rifugio* sleeps 45 people and serves drinks and food, including hot lunches.

Back at the signpost below Rifugio Questa, head down to the north on the GTA, leaving the more substantial track which heads east. The GTA is always adequately marked with red-and-white squares as it descends in 45 minutes back to the three-way junction you passed through earlier on the route. Go right, and in less than two hours, returning by the way you came, you will be back in Terme di Valdieri.

Terme di Valdieri to Entracque

Duration	4 days
Distance	45km
Difficulty	demanding
Start	Terme di Valdieri
Finish	Entracque
Nearest Towns	Terme di Valdieri (p94), Cuneo (p91)
Transport	bus

Summary Pass crossings and an easy summit on the French border among 3000m-plus peaks and retreating glaciers. The challenging Passo dei Ghiacciai requires experience and caution, but can be avoided.

Because of the rugged nature of the ridges in the Argentera region, most walking routes follow valleys, or link valleys by means of pass crossings. This walk could be dubbed 'the five passes route'. It crosses three significant passes and makes side trips to another

Warning

Consult *rifugio* staff about current conditions before attempting to cross Passo dei Ghiacciai (see Day 3, p100). Snow slopes may make it hazardous unless you're equipped with crampons and an ice axe and are familiar with their use. The crossing should not be attempted in poor visibility. If in doubt, take the longer but more straightforward Alternative Route: via San Giacomo (p101), or complete the walk in three days by descending from Rifugio Soria-Ellena through San Giacomo to Entracque.

two, and an easy peak of nearly 3000m, on the border with France. Of the five passes, only one is technically challenging, and we describe an alternative route that avoids it should weather or snow conditions dictate.

The walk begins in the tiny spa village of Terme di Valdieri and ends in the larger centre of Entracque. There is no wild camping in the park, and overnight accommodation is in *rifugi*. Additional stops, at Rifugio Morelli-Buzzi and the Foresteria in San Giacomo, could extend the walk by a day each and shorten the first and last days respectively.

PLANNING
When to Walk

The best period in which to do this walk is from mid-June until mid-September, when all *rifugi* are open, and especially July and August, when regular public transport reaches Terme di Valdieri. At the risk of stating the obvious, these months also tend to have the best weather. Buses operate to a restricted timetable at other times, and much accommodation closes down.

It's impossible to predict when conditions will be best for the Passo dei Ghiacciai crossing (see 'Warning', this page). Late in the summer, the snow slopes that make it, as they say, *una cosa alpinistica* (one for the alpinists) may be dangerously firm but relatively narrow. Earlier in the season, while there's likely to be more snow, the crossing may be easier because the snow slopes receive more sun and are therefore softer. Always approach the crossing with respect.

What to Bring

Provided you phone ahead and reserve a place at each night's *rifugio*, there's no need to carry camping equipment, or food other than snacks and perhaps some lunches. CAI regulations require that you use a sleeping sheet and pillowcase at *rifugi*. Light footwear to put on at the day's end is optional as most *rifugi* have a supply of 'hut slippers'.

Rifugio staff will usually ask to see your passport (or CAI membership card) when you arrive, and may keep it overnight.

See the boxed text 'Warning' (p96) regarding Passo dei Ghiacciai. Bring crampons and an ice axe – and make sure you know how to use them – if you intend to cross the pass.

GETTING TO/FROM THE WALK

See Terme di Valdieri (p94) for information on getting to the start of the walk from Cuneo. At the other end, Nuova Benese buses (€2.05, up to five per day mid-June–early Sept) return to Cuneo from Entracque.

THE WALK
Day 1: Terme di Valdieri to Rifugio Genova-Figari

5½–6½ hours, 11.5km, 1160m ascent, 510m descent

The start of the track is well signposted where it leaves the main road on the south-east (true right) bank of the Torrente Gesso della Valletta, about 50m downhill from the Grande Albergo Royal in Terme di Valdieri. Within a few minutes the track crosses on a footbridge the stream that enters from the southeast, turns up the northeast (true right) bank of the stream and begins to climb on switchbacks. Deciduous forest, with occasional clearings that offer views back to Terme, gives way to pines. After about an hour, there are views across the valley to Monte Stella (3262m) and to the dramatic couloir of **Canalone di Lourousa**.

Another 25 minutes of straightforward walking leads to Gias Lagarot, a stone-walled, tin-roofed hut and a stockyard. After a further 10 minutes, near a memorial cross beside a beautiful stream, a track branches off to the right, across the valley

and up to Bivacco Varrone, now visible near the foot of the couloir. Ignore this and continue up the valley to surmount a big moraine wall which brings first Colle del Chiapous, then at 2351m, **Rifugio Morelli-Buzzi** (☎ *0171 973 94; half board around €40; open mid-June–late-Sept*) into view. The *rifugio* serves hot meals and drinks – including coffee, of course – and makes a good spot for lunch or to stay overnight. A set of switchbacks up a moraine wall comes into view 20 minutes further on. The ascent is less strenuous than it looks, and from the top it's only a short distance to the signpost that marks the top of the grassy **Colle del Chiapous** (2526m). From the pass the track crosses a mass of moraine, then zigzags

After-Dinner Drinks

An evening at table in an Alpine *rifugio* can be a gastronomic and cultural adventure. Food tends to be simple, but none the worse for that, and the society can be a highlight of a walk. After dinner, two important ingredients often fuel the conversation.

Grappa, a strong, clear grape spirit, is a perennial favourite. Often it's flavoured with mountain herbs, flowers, berries or pine cones, which you may see steeping in bottles of sugar and water in sunny spots around the *rifugio*. *Genepy*, flavoured with artemisia leaves, is towards the sweeter end of the spectrum, while *genziana* or *genzianella*, made with gentian root, is often decidedly bitter.

The other standard is coffee, sometimes taken *corretto* – with a shot of grappa. A variation on this theme is *grolla valdostana*, the name of which betrays its origins in the villages of Valle d'Aosta. *Grolla* is a dark concoction of black coffee, grappa and sugar, sometimes with lemon zest or cloves added, which is served in a carved wooden vessel with a number of spouts – one for each person partaking – and traditionally comes to the table flaming. You won't find *grolla* on the drinks board everywhere – it's a job to prepare, and probably wouldn't help enforce a 10pm curfew either – but it may be available on request.

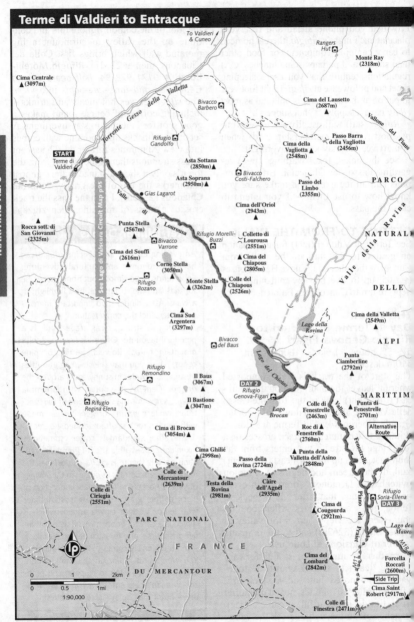

Terme di Valdieri to Entracque

To Valdieri & Cuneo

Rangers Hut

Monte Ray (2318m)

Cima Centrale (3097m)

Torrente Gesso della Valletta

Bivacco Barbero

Cima del Lausetto (2687m)

Rifugio Gandolfo

Passo Barra della Vagliotta (2456m)

Vallone del Fiuss

START
Terme di Valdieri

Asta Sottana (2850m)

Asta Soprana (2950m)

Bivacco Costi-Falchero

Cima della Vagliotta (2548m)

PARCO

Gias Lagarot

Valle di Lourousa

Passo del Limbo (2355m)

Rocca sott. di San Giovanni (2325m)

Punta Stella (2567m)

Cima dell'Oriol (2943m)

NATURAL

Bivacco Varrone

Rifugio Morelli-Buzzi

Colletto di Lourousa (2551m)

della Rovina

Cima del Souffi (2616m)

Corno Stella (3050m)

Cima del Chiapous (2805m)

Valle

DELLE

Rifugio Bozano

Monte Stella (3262m)

Colle del Chiapous (2526m)

Cima della Valletta (2549m)

See Lago di Valscura Circuit Map p95

Cima Sud Argentera (3297m)

Lago della Rovina

ALPI

Bivacco del Baus

Punta Ciamberline (2792m)

Rifugio Remondino

Il Baus (3067m)

Lago del Chiotas

MARITTIM

Rifugio Regina Elena

Il Bastione (3047m)

DAY 2
Rifugio Genova-Figari

Lago Brocan

Colle di Fenestrelle (2463m)

Punta di Fenestrelle (2701m)

Alternative Route

Cima di Brocan (3054m)

Roc di Fenestrelle (2760m)

Vallone di Fenestrelle

Cima Ghilié (2998m)

Passo della Rovina (2724m)

Punta della Valletta dell'Asino (2848m)

Rifugio Soria-Ellena
DAY 3

Colle di Mercantour (2639m)

Testa della Rovina (2981m)

Càire dell'Agnèl (2935m)

Cima di Cougourda (2921m)

Piano del Praièt

Lago dei Mauri

Colle di Ciriegia (2551m)

PARC NATIONAL

M18

FRANCE

Cima del Lombard (2842m)

Forcella Roccati (2600m)

Side Trip

DU MERCANTOUR

Cima Saint Robert (2917m)

Colle di Finestra (2471m)

0   1   2km
0   0.5   1mi
1:90,000

MARITIME ALPS

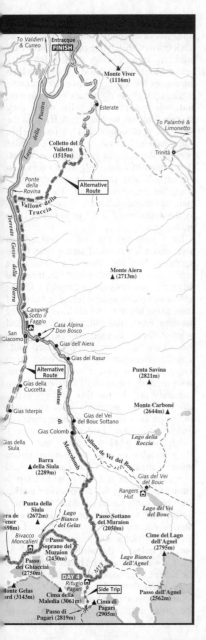

down below cliffs, first on the west side of the valley, then on the east. **Lago del Chiotas**, nearly 550m below the pass, is artificial but still spectacular. The track drops down the valley until almost level with the top of the dam wall, makes its way southeastwards around to the wall and crosses it.

Once across, follow the occasional red-and-white GTA markers down a short stretch of road, through a tunnel, then up and around the southeastern end of Lago del Chiotas on a rough road, to **Rifugio Genova-Figari** (☎ *0171 97 81 38; half board around €37.50; open mid-June–mid-Sept*), at 2015m, between Lago del Chiotas and the naturally occurring Lago Brocan. Phone ahead to be sure of a bed and a place at the table. (Note the signpost, halfway round the lake, indicating the start of the following day's route over Colle di Fenestrelle.)

Day 2: Rifugio Genova-Figari to Rifugio Soria-Ellena
3–3½ hours, 7km, 490m ascent, 660m descent

From the *rifugio* return to the signpost that points towards Colle di Fenestrelle, and follow that track as it climbs gently, then somewhat more steeply, to the east. After about 90 minutes of zigzagging ascent around the north and east sides of the Vallone di Fenestrelle, the track crosses a false pass over a spur, descends to cross a gully where there may be some snow, then climbs for another 20 minutes to the signposted **Colle di Fenestrelle** (2463m).

The descent from the pass is well defined and adequately marked. Ibex and chamois often graze in this open, grassy valley. Lower down towards Piano del Praiet you may hear the piercing alarm cries of marmots and spot them scampering for cover. Cowbells are another common sound here. On the valley floor a signpost points the way to **Rifugio Soria-Ellena** (☎ *0171 97 83 82; half board €40; open mid-June–mid-Sept*), which looms atop a knoll at 1840m, on the east side of the stream. Phone ahead to reserve a spot. The 40m climb from the river bank to the *rifugio* is the steepest ascent of the day.

MARITIME ALPS

Side Trip: Colle di Finestra
2½–3 hours, 6km, 690m ascent

On a clear day it's well worth following the track that leads south, up the valley beyond Rifugio Soria-Ellena, to Colle di Finestra (2471m) on the French border. From the *rifugio*, return to the valley floor and follow the well-defined track south, which soon begins to climb and, after a couple of switchbacks, reaches a signposted junction where track M18 goes left towards Pera de Fener. This is the Day 3 route to Passo dei Ghiacciai and Rifugio Pagarì (this page). Take the right fork (M11) and ascend gradually south for 20 minutes to the remains of a building (2090m) on the east side of the track, then for perhaps another hour to **Colle di Finestra**. Beyond lies France. The track continues south through Parc National du Mercantour past Lac de Fenestre, visible less than 1km away, to the GR52 long-distance track and Refuge Madone de Fenestre.

Retrace your steps from the Colle di Finestra to Rifugio Soria-Ellena.

Day 3: Rifugio Soria-Ellena to Rifugio Pagarì
4½–6 hours, 7.5km, 1160m ascent, 350m descent

From the *rifugio* drop to the valley floor and follow the track south towards Colle di Finestra for 20 minutes, as far as the signpost to Pera de Fener. Go left here, and follow the well-defined track M18, marked with occasional cairns, red paint stripes and arrows, as it zigzags up a spur, keeping a

series of rocky cascades on its left (north) side. About an hour from the *rifugio* the track crosses, then twice recrosses, a stream tumbling from a wide, scree-filled gully below Monte Gelas Nord (3143m), which dominates the skyline above. Continue to zigzag up the true right bank of the stream, and sidle into the wide gully, which may contain some snow. Pass a faint track on the right (at spot height 2441m on the Blu map), which climbs towards the spectacular Forcella Roccati. As you climb eastwards, views open of Lago della Maura down on the left side and, further back to the northwest, the Argentera massif. The track remains clear and well marked, and continues to the remains of a stone building on a grassy area.

On a good day the pass is visible from here, only a few hundred metres away to the northeast. Note that there is a lower, more precipitous notch further north on the same ridge; the route does not go through it. Cairns now lead up and around unstable slopes of scree to the top of the knoll above the ruined building. From this knoll, rocky terraces lead below cliffs towards the pass. Depending on the season, the cairned and marked route may be interrupted by several quite steep tongues of snow. Late in summer, these remain in shade for much of the day and consequently may be too firm to cross safely unless you are equipped with crampons and/or an ice axe. An alternative route can sometimes be found by descending on rocky ground, skirting below the snow and scrambling up below the pass to rejoin the marked route. Cairns and red paint markers lead around to the left and finally up to a dip in the narrow, rocky ridge top where marker flags on a cable have been fixed to the rock. Below and to the left (north) is Bivacco Moncalieri, and below it are two lakes, Lago Bianco del Gelas and a smaller, unnamed one. Far below to the northeast, beyond the lakes, a walking track can be seen snaking up the side of Vallone del Vei del Bouc.

To cross **Passo dei Ghiacciai** (2750m), follow cairns and red markers north along the crest until a straightforward, well-marked descent leads directly to **Bivacco**

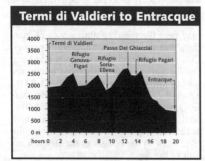

Termi di Valdieri to Entracque

[Elevation profile chart showing the route from Termi di Valdieri to Entracque, with marked points: Termi di Valdieri, Rifugio Genova-Figari, Rifugio Soria-Ellena, Passo Dei Ghiacciai, Rifugio Pagarì, and Entracque. Vertical axis in metres (0 m to 4000), horizontal axis in hours (0 to 20).]

Moncalieri (2710m) in a splendid setting. This basic 11-bed hut remains open during summer. Ibex often graze nearby.

From here the track is indistinct at times, though marked with cairns and splashes of red paint, as it leads down from the uphill side of the *bivacco* across the loose moraine below Ghiacciaio Nord-Est del Gelas, then down to cross the outlet from Lago Bianco del Gelas. The remains of Rifugio Moncalieri, destroyed by avalanche in 1975, are visible on the north side of the lake. The route towards Rifugio Pagarì leads to the right, between the two lakes, on the downhill side of the smaller, unnamed one and along the moraine wall which dams it. Follow cairns and paint markers left (north), over the lip of the moraine and across the outlet stream from the unnamed lake, which vanishes under rocks here for a short distance. Alternating patches of grass and rocky ground lead generally east across a couple of stream gullies and around the base of a big bluff. At a prominent red paint marker, the track veers northwest for a short way, down the toe of a spur through scrubby alpine vegetation. It then doubles back to the east at more markers and traverses into a big, scree-filled basin, where it stays high below cliffs, avoiding the worst of the scree. A climb of 15 to 20 minutes leads to a ridge top and **Passo Soprano del Muraion** (2430m). The Vallone del Muraion and the track from Rifugio Pagarì down the valley to San Giacomo now appear below, and across to the east is Lago Bianco dell'Agnel.

A winding, ascending traverse leads across a broad gully to another ridge, where the *rifugio* comes into view. Ten minutes later the main track down the valley goes off to the left. Go right, and just over the brow of the hill, with the impressive north-east face of Cima della Maledia (3061m) behind it, is **Rifugio Pagarì** (☎ 0171 97 83 98; *half board around €40; open mid-June–mid-Sept*). Also known as Rifugio Federici-Marchesini, this *rifugio* is the highest in the Maritime Alps at 2650m. Outside the normal opening period, contact ☎ 0171 94 49 43 or e maayaa@libero.it.

Alternative Route: via San Giacomo
6½–7½ hours, 15km, 1435m ascent, 625m descent

To avoid Passo dei Ghiacciai take this route. From the *rifugio*, retrace your steps back to the Piano del Praiet signpost. From here head northeast on a wide, rocky track above the true left side of the river. Punta della Siula (2672m) comes into view above a wide valley on the right, and after 30 minutes a signpost indicates that you are passing Gias della Siula (1480m). A further 15 minutes down the valley is Gias Isterpis, recently rebuilt, where you can sometimes buy cheese. The deep Vallone di Moncolomb soon appears on the right, coming in from the east. The track, which is now an unsealed road, zigzags down through lovely beech forest, past a waterfall on the Torrente Gesso della Barra and into **San Giacomo** (1213m).

The **park information centre** (☎ 0171 97 84 44; *open daily June–early Sept*) is on the left as you enter the village. In the same building (the Foresteria) and on the same telephone number is a comfortable **posto tappa** (*staging post; half board around €25*) run by the park. **Baita Monte Gelas**, on the right, serves meals, snacks and drinks. **Camping Sotto il Faggio** (☎ 0171 97 87 04; *camping per person/tent €2.60/3.60*) is across the bridge just below the village.

At the bridge in San Giacomo turn east across the river, past the camping ground, and reverse the route description given for the start of Day 4 (p102) to reach Rifugio Pagarì in 4½ to 5½ hours. From the *rifugio* you can tackle Cima di Pagarì.

Side Trip: Cima di Pagarì
2–3 hours, 2.5km, 255m ascent

On a good day, this makes a fine farewell to the high Maritime Alps. For the best chance of clear views, do it first thing in the morning before descending to Entracque – and go during autumn. From the flagpole in front of the *rifugio*, follow red markers and cairns south to **Passo di Pagarì** (2819m) and the international border. There may be some low-angled snow to cross. A path of military origin leads towards the top from the north side of the pass, but it's not essential you find it. Just head up to the northeast over rocky but easy terrain, and the summit (2905m) with its many cairns will appear before long. Just above the col, a dry-stone battlement in excellent condition overlooks the valley on the French side. During WWII this position was held first by German troops, then Italian Fascists, and finally partisans, all of whom sheltered in the rifugio. The **summit** offers views in all directions – north over the *rifugio*, northwest to the Argentera massif, southeast to Monte Clapier and south over France's Parc National du Mercantour. On a really clear day, look for the coast and Corsica.

To return, retrace your steps to the *rifugio*.

Day 4: Rifugio Pagarì to Entracque
5–6 hours, 19km, 1750m descent

From the *rifugio* the well-marked track M13 zigzags in a northeasterly direction at first, down a rocky spur with good views towards Passo dell'Agnel and the peaks that surround it, away to the east. The track then swings a little west of north and follows the

side of Valle Muraion for a couple of kilometres, winding without difficulty through Passo Sottano del Muraion and finally dropping to the valley floor, and a signpost, about 1½ hours walk from the *rifugio*. A couple of minutes on from the signpost is a lovely pool where a stream cascades across the track from the southwest.

Proceed roughly north down the valley, here referred to as Vallone di Moncolomb, and cross to the east side and Gias del Vei del Bouc Sottano. Here a signpost indicates the start of the track up Valle del Vei del Bouc that is visible from Passo dei Ghiacciai. Continue north along a grassy plain, Prà del Rasur, which extends for 1km or more, to the *gias* at its northern end. The track then enters the first patches of beech forest and soon passes Gias dell'Aiera.

The main track, now a little-used road, winds along the north bank of the river, which twists and cascades below. Several pedestrian short cuts avoid bends, though the distance saved is not great. The road passes through a former royal hunting lodge, now the **Casa Alpina Don Bosco**, among tall

---

All the Way with the GTA?

The 1st edition of *Walking in Italy* contained a boxed text entitled 'Track Rage'. This described a failed attempt, in 1997, to follow the GTA from San Giacomo to Entracque, and raged against 'tracks' that existed in theory but were a nightmare to walk in practice.

In researching this edition we went back there, and found the GTA north of San Giacomo in better shape than it had been in 1997 – but not by much. It was often indirect, overgrown or uneven, and still needed work, and much more traffic, to bring it up to the standard of other sections of the GTA. Further north, however, closer to Vallone della Truccia, it joins an old trout fishing track and becomes truly pleasant.

Then it swings east, up the valley, and becomes very steep. Very steep indeed. Laughably steep, in fact, if you were fit, confident and in a laughing mood, but steep enough to be demoralising, or worse, if you were not. And it remains steep for quite a distance.

For the purpose of this book, it came down to this: Is this track suitable to recommend to a visitor from halfway round the world? The straight answer is no. There's a perfectly good, level road on the other side of the Torrente Gesso della Barra. There seemed no valid reason to take such an arduous, contrived alternative.

Yet, for this walker at least, there was a sneaking pleasure in the climb, and the situation once near the top of the ridge, overlooking Lago della Piastra more than half a kilometre below, was exhilarating. We can't recommend you go there. But if you do, and you too find it perversely fun, even exhilarating – well, remember who warned you.

Nick Tapp

pines and beeches, and five minutes later crosses a bridge over the Torrente Gesso della Barra just below **San Giacomo** (see Alternative Route: via San Giacomo, p101).

From here you can follow the GTA to Entracque (see Alternative Route: via the GTA, below) or continue along the road down the west side of the river, the best onward route. It's 4km from San Giacomo to Ponte della Rovina, where there's a trough and running water. A further 3km takes you the length of Lago della Piastra and brings you to a signposted turn-off down to the right towards Entracque. Follow this road back towards the base of the dam that holds back the lake, then north through a peaceful rural setting to **Entracque**, which should take another 30 minutes or so.

Alternative Route: via the GTA
4–5½ hours, 14km
For something a little different (see the boxed text 'All the Way with the GTA?', p102) walk the GTA to Entracque. The usual red-and-white GTA markers lead into the woods beside the office of Camping Sotto il Faggio on the east bank of the Torrente Gesso della Barra in San Giacomo. The track downstream of this point is sometimes indistinct and overgrown, and evidently receives little traffic. After following the river to Vallone della Truccia almost opposite Ponte della Rovina, the path climbs (extremely steeply) up the valley side, then sidles more gently to Colletto del Vailetto (1515m) and descends to Esterate. From Esterate it's just 2km by back roads to Entracque.

Parco Naturale Alta Valle Pesio e Tanaro

This park, only 10km east of Parco Naturale Alpi Marittime, might almost be in another mountain range, so different is the landscape – thanks mainly to its distinct underlying geology. The peaks of the Argentera and Gelas massifs are clearly visible from the summit of Punta Marguareis (2651m), the highest point in the park and the highlight of

the Marguareis Circuit (p104), which begins and ends in Limone Piemonte.

The 66-sq-km park was founded in 1978, but the valley's environment has been carefully managed since the 12th century, when Carthusian monks founded the Certosa di Santa Maria (Certosa di Pesio) charterhouse, now near the northern edge of the park, where the Rifugio Garelli walk (p108) begins and ends.

NATURAL HISTORY
Whereas the Argentera and Gelas mountain groups are granite formations, the Pesio Valley is limestone country. The north-facing ramparts of Punta Marguareis and its satellite peaks are the most impressive of many cliffs in the area, and the surrounding valleys and plateaus are riddled with caves. Some of these, below the Conca delle Carsene karstic basin to the west of Punta Marguareis, have been plumbed to depths in excess of 600m. In all, more than 150km of caves have been explored in the region. Rainfall is abundant but, instead of forming streams and clear, deep lakes, surface water here tends to disappear underground. Sometimes it reappears later in spectacular fashion, as in the Piscio del Pesio waterfall, where an underground river gushes from a cliff.

Though robbed by the porous terrain of much of the rain, the upper slopes of the park harbour a wide variety of plant species, including lilies, gentians and alpine pasqueflowers. By contrast, the deep valleys are well watered and densely wooded. There are extensive pure stands of silver fir, sweet chestnut, beech and European larch as well as mixed broad-leaved forests.

Some Alpine animals are found here too, in particular the Alpine marmot, the chamois and, at lower altitudes, wild boar, roe deer and red deer. You may spot a golden eagle riding the thermals from Rifugio Garelli.

PLANNING
Maps & Books
The best map for all walks in the park is the Blu Edizioni 1:25,000 *Alpi Liguri – Parco Naturale Alta Valle Pesio e Tanaro*, available in bigger bookshops in the region.

Also useful is the older IGC 1:25,000 map No 114 *Limone Piemonte – Valle delle Meraviglie – St Dalmas de Tende*. The IGC 1:50,000 map No 8 *Alpi Marittime e Liguri* covers a larger area, including the Argentera group. Neither of these shows the route from Porta Sestrera to Lago Rataira or the track through Colle Palù to Punta Marguareis.

Blu Edizioni and the park authorities also publish a guidebook in Italian, *La Guida del Parco Alta Valle Pesio e Tanaro*, with information on natural and human history, and track notes to 16 short walks. You'll find it at bookshops.

Information Sources

You'll find bits of information here and there if you search, but little or nothing that's crucial to the success of a visit. The **park headquarters** (*Ente di Gestione dei Parchi e delle Riserve Cuneesi;* ☎ *0171 73 40 21;* ⓦ *www .parks.it/parchi.cuneesi; Via Sant'Anna 34, Chiusa di Pesio*) has little information of general interest. The APT office in Limone Piemonte (this page) has more information of use to walkers.

Marguareis Circuit

Duration	2 days
Distance	35km
Difficulty	moderate–demanding
Start/Finish	Limone Piemonte (p104)
Transport	train

Summary Climb above ski slopes to the karst country of the Alta Valle Pesio and a fascinating mountain *rifugio* with grandstand views of the limestone cliffs of Punta Marguareis, and enjoy further sweeping views from the top.

This two-day walk – two *big* days – begins and ends just outside the park, among the groomed slopes and condominiums of Limone Piemonte. It soon climbs above the lifts onto the dramatic ridge that overlooks Limone, then heads east across karstic plains and drops into Vallone del Marguareis at the foot of the Marguareis massif. Rifugio Garelli offers outstanding views

of these cliffs. On the second day, the walk climbs to the summit of Punta Marguareis, then returns to Limone after making a minor incursion into French territory.

PLANNING
When to Walk

In conjunction with the weather, the factor that determines the best time for this walk is the availability of accommodation at **Rifugio Garelli** (☎ *0171 73 80 78; half board €36; open 15 June-15 Sept; open weekends only mid-May–mid June & mid-Sept–mid-Oct with accommodation Sat night only*). While you can obtain a key and let yourself in at other times (call ☎ *0174 447 30*) the opening periods give a fair indication of when the weather is likely to be good.

What to Bring

Camping gear is not required provided you reserve a place at Rifugio Garelli, but a sleeping sheet and pillowcase are. You'll also need your passport or other identity document.

French Visa If you want to cover every contingency, and are a citizen of a country whose nationals require a visa to enter France, you might obtain one for this walk. In practice, the walk traverses 4km of a remote corner of France, crossing the border from Italy and back again within a couple of hours, at two windswept cols far from human habitation.

Place Names

Those used here are generally in line with the Blu Edizioni map and guide. Local names do vary: Lago Rataira, for instance, may be referred to by any of three different names according to whether the speaker is from the Pesio, the Tanaro or the Ellero Valley.

NEAREST TOWN
Limone Piemonte

Both days of the Marguareis Circuit are long, and you may be glad of the little extra time gained by staying in Limone Piemonte before or after the walk. Limone is one of the most popular downhill ski resorts in the southern Alps. The **APT office** (☎ *0171 921 01; Via Roma 30*) in Limone Piemonte has transport and accommodation options as well as some information on the park and the GTA.

Places to Stay & Eat A 900m walk uphill from the train station, opposite the bottom of the Sole ski lift is **Hotel Petit Meublé** (☎ 0171 92 61 32; Via Genova 59; rooms per person from €20.65); the rate includes breakfast. More central is the three-star **Hotel Marguareis** (☎ 0171 92 75 67; Via Genova 30; singles/doubles €41.30/62).

There are many places to eat in the centre of Limone. Good choices include **Ristorante La Diligenza** (Via Cuneo 3), just off the main street, and **Pizzeria La Giara**, on a piazzetta by the river, down a set of steps from the main piazza.

Getting There & Away Limone lies on the train line from Cuneo to Ventimiglia and Nice (France). Numerous trains make the journey from Cuneo every day (€1.85, 29km).

THE WALK (see map p106)
Day 1: Limone Piemonte to Rifugio Garelli
5–6 hours, 14km, 1560m ascent, 595m descent

From Piazza Risorgimento, in front of the train station in Limone, head under the railway bridge and quite steeply uphill to the east along Via Almellina. This dwindles to an unsealed road as it climbs up the Valle Almellina for 2km or so to a cluster of buildings, **Casali Braia**.

Follow the road as it bends back to the south and, within a few minutes, passes under a ski lift, next to its bottom station. After a few switchbacks up the line of the lift, the track heads south around a spur through a patch of beech forest to emerge onto open slopes near a lodge, Capanna Chiara, at the bottom of another two lifts. Take a faint track that leads up a small spur, roughly parallel with the more northerly of the two lifts, passing Gias Gorgia, to the lift's top station, after about an hour's walking.

Continue climbing, under the top of the lift you first encountered down near Casali Braia and away from the resort infrastructure, on a track that snakes up grassy slopes

with ever-expanding views. The track rounds a spur and becomes more easterly, passing through a lush, damp hollow, then winds its way into an eroded gully system, where the trickle emitted by Fonte di Carlaccio may be the only water. Continue to the northeast up this gully system on very faint tracks, then up grassy slopes to meet a prominent track on the ridge top just south of Punta Melasso (2079m), an hour from the top of the lifts.

Turn south on this track. Despite the presence of Limone in the valley to the west, the walk now takes on an increasingly wild feel, thanks to the imposing formations of Rocce del Cros straight ahead and Roccia il Pulpito across Valle Pesio to the northeast. The track passes the sheep-trodden Fonte Paciot, then skirts below the cliffs of Cima Baban (2102m) and heads for Monte Iurin (2192m) before sidling around its eastern slopes. To the southeast, through a low saddle and across the limestone plain of Conca delle Carsene, Punta Marguareis looms. The track winds easily down to the valley floor, then climbs again for a short distance beside a last, low set of cliffs to the saddle, **Colle del Carbone** (2019m).

A faint route now continues down through the col, in a direction slightly north of southeast, to meet the GTA with its reassuring red-and-white markers. Go left on the GTA (to the right, uphill, is the way to Capanna Morgantini) and follow it east, passing the new Gias dell'Ortica, and the remains of the old one, just south of the track, and then a signpost where track F11 heads north. The GTA swings down to the valley floor, then climbs to a small pass south of Testa di Murtel. It follows a scenic, pine-clad ridge top and passes a scantily fenced-off sinkhole before a final switchback leads to **Passo del Duca** (1989m) after another 50 minutes from Colle del Carbone.

The track drops into a small saddle, Colle del Prel (1925m), where track H10 heads north. Stick to the GTA as it swings spectacularly around to the south below Testa del Duca, then tends gradually east and descends for half an hour to the bottom of Vallone del Marguareis. Head southeast up the valley for 40 minutes to the pretty **Laghetto** di **Marguareis**. This lakelet was becoming shallower each year as the flow of water from melting snow scoured the bed of its outlet stream deeper, but some discreet engineering works now maintain the level. Here the track nearly doubles back on itself and sidles to the northwest across the north side of the valley. Just around a ridge, at 1965m, sits the palatial **Rifugio Garelli** (see When to Walk, p104) its steeply pitched roofs mirroring (in more ways than one) the shape of the limestone cliffs opposite. This modern structure sleeps up to 94 people and has excellent facilities, including hot showers.

Day 2: Rifugio Garelli to Limone Piemonte
6–7½ hours, 21km, 1145m ascent, 2110m descent

From a signpost on the edge of Pian del Lupo, the tiny plain behind the *rifugio*, follow red-and-white GTA markers uphill to the east. They lead up the left (north) side of a valley to **Porta Sestrera** (2225m) after 30 minutes. Proceed for a few minutes down the broad, grassy valley ahead, until a well-defined but less clearly marked track diverges to the right towards a cairn in a saddle. From here the very broad Colle del

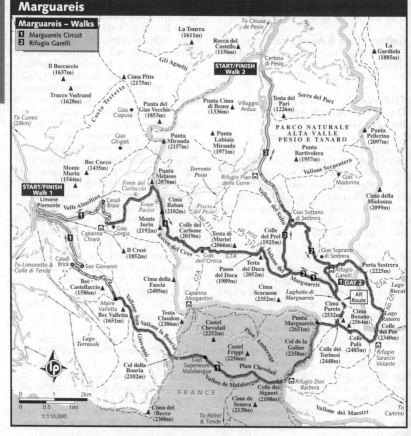

Pas is visible to the south. Cairns and occasional red paint markers persist as the track contours a little east of south. If you get off route, continue south and don't lose too much height. Head for a standing stone on the lip of the depression which hides Lago Rataira (Lago Ratauoloira on the Blu map). In poor visibility it would be not too inconvenient a detour to follow the GTA as far as Lago Biecai and then head back to Lago Rataira along track G5. At Lago Rataira you join track G5, and paint markers lead south over a little spur and up to **Colle del Pas** (2340m), 45 minutes from Porta Sestrera.

Head through the pass and down towards a grassy plain, just west of Rifugio Saracco Volante, and the dark entrance to one of this region's many deep caves. Descend from the pass for 10 minutes, passing an indistinct fork on the left which leads to the *rifugio*, until signs prominently painted on two large rocks point the way to 'Marguareis'. Follow a minor track west, in the direction indicated by the signs, up grassy slopes, then cunningly through some bands of rock to **Colle Palù** (2485m) after 30 minutes.

The mighty whaleback of Punta Marguareis, with its prominent summit cross, is 1km to the west. After negotiating a short section of steeper, rocky ground to the right (north) of the pass, a well-defined track leads across rounded, grassy slopes, up and across a broad rocky spur, across a gully and up to the summit of **Punta Marguareis** (2651m). From here on a clear day you'll see the Argentera group to the west and solitary Monviso (3841m), source of the river Po, further away to the northwest.

From the summit, follow the open crest south until it drops steeply into Col de la Galine (2358m). Here a well-defined, marked track crosses the ridge. Follow it to the right (southwest), around a knoll and down into a gully, then through a maze of limestone formations, to reach **Colle dei Signori** (2108m) about an hour from the summit. Rifugio Don Barbera is tucked away to the northeast, below the col, and has water – but may be closed.

The route now ducks across French territory for a few kilometres. A road leads

through Colle dei Signori and circuitously towards Col della Boaria. Leave this road a few metres north of Colle dei Signori, and drop to the west on a rough track onto the grassy Plan Chevolail. The walking is easy but yellow paint markers are few until the track passes through a narrowing at the western end of the plain, then up through a gap to the right of a plug of rock. Continue west above bluffs and around the head of a succession of gullies which drain to the south – look for markers, and don't lose height too soon. About 40 minutes after leaving the col, the track finally descends to the floor of Vallon de Malabergue to meet a track that comes up the valley from Rèfrei and Tende. Follow this, still on the north side of the stream bed, until a tributary gully enters from the north. Cross here to the south side of the main gully and continue slightly to the north of west, past a *gias* on the opposite bank, until a signpost points back down the valley to Rèfrei and Tende.

Head west from the signpost for 50m, along a tributary gully that leads towards Col della Boaria, then follow yellow markers up

Rifugio Phoenix

The original Rifugio Piero Garelli, perched above Vallone del Marguareis on Pian del Lupo (Plain of the Wolf), was totally destroyed by fire in 1987. Over the next two summers, volunteers from the Mondovì section of CAI, and others, built the present *rifugio* in its place.

During the 1988 season they constructed the outer shell – walls, roof and shutters – so that it would be able to weather the winter. The following year they completed and fitted out the interior of the building. In all, helicopters made about 1000 trips to transport materials from the nearest roadhead to Pian del Lupo at an altitude of nearly 2000m.

At the opening ceremony, the symphony orchestra of Cuneo played from the forecourt of the *rifugio* to a crowd of thousands, who sat in the sun on the natural amphitheatre of the ridge to the south. The albums of photos that document the process are proudly displayed inside.

onto a small rocky spur on the south side of the gully. The track leads deviously up and emerges on grassy slopes within sight of the road from Colle dei Signori. Ten minutes further west, the track rejoins the road, and some ruined buildings and a signpost indicate that you've reached **Col della Boaria** (2102m).

In Italy once more, leave the road again and follow a marked track northwest from the col, down Vallone la Boaria. The track drops quite steeply at times and eventually swings west into the broader Valle San Giovanni about 30 minutes from the col. The track swings north again and remains above the river as it tumbles through a short gorge, then 100m further downstream winds down to the river and crosses to the true left (west) bank. Signs of civilisation become more frequent as the track leaves the river and winds through pastures on the north side of the craggy Bec Valletta to a T-junction above a cluster of buildings at Maire Valletta.

Go left for 50m, then right at another junction, following yellow markers down the hill to the northwest on a very rustic track. This soon joins a dirt road, which continues down Valle San Giovanni. It's a pleasant walk down the road, which is sealed below Casali Brick, to a tiny church in the tumbledown village of San Giovanni. From here it's a further couple of kilometres back to the bright lights of Limone.

Alternative Route: Punta Marguareis via Canalone dei Torinesi

1½–3 hours, 3km

There's a more challenging and direct route up Punta Marguareis from Rifugio Garelli than the one described via Porta Sestrera and Colle Palù. The Canalone dei Torinesi, a deep gully to the west of Marguareis' subsidiary summit Cima Pareto, is the *via normale* (normal route) to the top from the north side. In good conditions, this option might save you an hour or more on Day 2 of the Marguareis Circuit; if snow-filled, however, it can be all but impassable without crampons and an ice axe. Check with *rifugio* staff what condition the route is in before you attempt it.

It's 50 minutes to an hour's walk from the *rifugio*, via Laghetto di Marguareis and then a faint track up the valley to the southeast, to the scree fan at the foot of the Canalone. Here paint markers on a big boulder indicate the way, unmistakably, up. The route steepens from this point, the ground underfoot is loose, and the narrow confines of the upper part quite often hold snow until at least early summer. Rockfall is another potential hazard.

In short, don't underestimate the seriousness of the *via normale*. If you're ready for it, though, another 50 minutes should bring you to Colle dei Torinesi (2448m) at the top of the gully. From here, a faint, cairned track leads south and skirts around the west side of some depressions to meet the track from Colle Palù. From Colle dei Torinesi to the summit of Punta Marguareis is less than 1km and takes 30 minutes or so.

Rifugio Garelli

Duration	4–5 hours
Distance	18km
Difficulty	easy–moderate
Start/Finish	Certosa di Pesio
Nearest Town	Cuneo (p91)
Transport	bus

Summary A return trip from an ancient but still functioning charterhouse, to a fascinating *rifugio* with great mountain views.

A fine way to sample this lovely park with less expenditure of effort than the Marguareis Circuit is to visit Rifugio Garelli from Certosa di Pesio. The walk to and from the *rifugio* alone is worthwhile, for the grandeur of Marguareis' cliffs and perhaps especially for the return journey down the Marguareis Valley. However, the walk could be extended to an easy two days with an overnight stay at the *rifugio*, or to a moderate three days, with a day trip to the summit of Punta Marguareis by either of two routes (see Day 2 of the Marguareis Circuit, p106), and a second night's stay at the *rifugio*.

It's a climb of just over 1100m from Certosa di Pesio to the *rifugio* at 1965m.

PLANNING
When to Walk

As for the Marguareis Circuit, a major factor in planning an overnight, or longer, trip is the opening period of Rifugio Garelli (see When to Walk, p104) The day walk can, however, be done earlier or later provided you can reach Certosa di Pesio.

What to Bring

If staying at the *rifugio*, you won't need a tent or sleeping bag, but you will need a sleeping sheet and pillowcase, your passport or other identity document. Outside Rifugio Garelli's opening season you'll need to carry all food for the walk.

GETTING TO/FROM THE WALK

Certosa di Pesio, where the walk starts and finishes, is accessible via the buses of **Autolinee Valle Pesio** (☎ 0171 73 44 96) from Cuneo (two per day mid-June–mid-Sept). Buses leave the west side of Cuneo's Piazza Galimberti at 8.25am and 2.45pm (though several more daily go as far as Chiusa di Pesio). The last bus out of Certosa on the return trip leaves at 5.30pm.

THE WALK (see map p106)

Two roads, one on each side of the Pesio, lead south up the valley from the car park where the bus from Cuneo turns around, just across a bridge from Certosa itself. It's possible to follow either as far as Rifugio Pian delle Gorre, or to cross above Villaggio Ardua, about halfway there. The roads on the west side are quieter. Either way, it's a straightforward walk, a shade over 3km, to Pian delle Gorre, and takes about 45 minutes.

From Pian delle Gorre, at a barrier and information board, a substantial, drivable track (the left fork if you've followed the east bank of the Pesio) leads roughly southeast for a kilometre or so, and ends at a small turning area labelled 'Il Salto'. Here take the left fork again. This time it's a foot track, which soon gives the first views of the Marguareis massif ahead, and climbs rather more steeply through fine mixed forest before it emerges at Gias Sottano di Sestrera, where there's a water trough and another parting of ways.

Yet another left fork now leads up Vallone di Sestrera, and climbs steadily, with views of the *gias* across the valley to the east, then of the cliffs and gullies of the Marguareis group. The next major landmark is Gias Soprano di Sestrera. Once you're here, after about two hours of climbing from Pian delle Gorre, **Rifugio Garelli** (see When to Walk, p104) is within view, only a few hundred metres further on. You can make the *rifugio* your lunch stop, or make it your base for a night or more.

The return journey begins by reversing part of the Marguareis Circuit (see Day 1, p105) – following the GTA, first to Laghetto di Marguareis, then down the valley to the foot of the descent from Passo del Duca. From here, continue down the true left bank of the Marguareis (although the Blu map shows the track on the true right bank for a short distance). Eventually the track enters beech forest, then crosses the pretty stream on a bridge shortly before returning you to Gias Sottano di Sestrera. From here, retrace your steps past Rifugio Pian delle Gorre to Certosa.

Other Walks

Other walk options, both long and short, abound in the Maritime Alps, especially from mid-July to mid-September. As long as transport services run and accommodation remains open, the GTA and its network of *rifugi* and other places to stay, known as *posti tappa* (staging posts), are an excellent basis for walks of almost any length. For example, three stages of the GTA connect Trinità, near Entracque at the end of the Terme di Valdieri to Entracque walk, via the villages of Palanfrè and Limonetto, to Rifugio Garelli. Further east beyond Rifugio Garelli, two more stages reach the end of the GTA at Viozene. It would thus be possible, just for example, to follow the GTA for eight days, from Viozene to Terme di Valdieri or vice versa, linking much of the territory covered by the walks in this chapter. Minor tracks make many variations possible. And just over the border on the French side of the range, linked via a number of passes to the Italian system, is a comparable network of French tracks and huts. Some walks here, in the Parc National du Mercantour, are described in Lonely Planet's *Walking in France*.

Western Alps

Italy's oldest national park and highest mountain, two of the best-known mountains in Europe, footpaths to high passes, lakes and alpine meadows, welcoming *rifugi* (mountain huts), an immensely rich variety and quantity of flora, and some tame wildlife – all these are found in Parco Nazionale del Gran Paradiso (PNGP) and the valleys north and south of Valle d'Aosta in the heart of the Western Alps. This generous portfolio of assets also includes the rare combination of accessible but remote areas, only lightly touched by modern developments.

From a huge range of possible walks, a small selection of the finest is described here. There are walks of varying length, exploring the national park and following parts of two long distance routes – the Alta Via 2 (AV2) and Alta Via 4 (AV4). An adaptable excursion of up to six days links the valleys on the northern side of Valle d'Aosta and extends into Valsesia in Piedmont (Piemonte). See Valle d'Aosta to Valsesia (p141) for both these areas.

NATURAL HISTORY

Within the vast chain of the Western Alps, stretching from the far southwest corner of mountainous northern Italy to Lago Maggiore, Valle d'Aosta separates the Graian Alps to the south from the Pennine Alps to the north. The Gran Paradiso massif (the heart of PNGP) is the most significant range in the Graian Alps, with 15 glaciers and 10 major summits, topped by Gran Paradiso (4061m). The park consists essentially of deep lateral valleys and separating ridges extending south from Valle d'Aosta. These valleys were cut by glaciers pushing north towards Valle d'Aosta where they dumped huge masses of moraine. The Pennine Alps are dominated by the chain of peaks between the Matterhorn (Il Cervino; 4478m) and Monte Rosa (4637m). Long, deep, glaciated valleys extend generally southwards from the range to Valle d'Aosta; Valsesia to the east is oriented southeast in its upper reaches.

Highlights

SANDRA BARDWELL

Majestic Gran Paradiso (4061m), Italy's highest mountain, above Valsavarenche

- Close encounters with tame ibex and friendly marmots in Parco Nazionale del Gran Paradiso (p115)

- Enjoying breathtaking views of the awesome Gran Paradiso massif and its glaciers in Valsavarenche between Valnontey and Rhêmes Notre Dame (p118)

- Walking amidst colourful carpets of wildflowers in alpine meadows on the Lakes & Wildlife walk (p123)

- Feeling the dominating presence of the mighty mountain massifs of the Matterhorn and Monte Rosa (p132)

The Dora Baltea, Valle d'Aosta's river, and Fiume Sesia are both tributaries of the Po, Italy's longest river. Granitic gneiss is the most common rock type throughout; there are relatively small outcrops of other rocks, notably the distinctive greenstone, and compass-distorting magnetite near Cogne.

The patterns of trees and flowering plants change with altitude. In the valleys are fields, some still used for crops, and mixed woodlands. The lower reaches of the mountainsides' meadows, rich in wildflowers, may be grazed by cattle and sheep, and are separated by woodlands of oak and chestnut. Further up, between 800m and 1000m, woodlands of beech, larch and spruce are widespread. In the subalpine zone – between 1600m and 2000m – spruce, larch, Arolla pine and mountain pine mark the tree line.

Above the tree line, alpenrose, dwarf juniper and bilberry are the easiest to identify. In the grasslands up to 2400m you'll find gentians, arnica, primulas, pasque flowers and tormentil. On the cliffs and screes in marginal growing conditions, many of the species are dwarf, cushion-forming perennials. In the high alpine zones, yellow genipi, saxifrages and moss campion survive; algae and mosses occur on the snow line.

Its fauna population is what makes PNGP special among Italy's national parks. There are about 3700 ibex and 8400 chamois, greater numbers of marmots, and small populations of ermine, weasels, badgers, voles and white hares. However, in the valleys of the Pennine Alps it's unusual to see anything more than marmots. Among the 100

Valdostane Gastronomy

Valdostane (peculiar to the Valle d'Aosta) wine, spirits, cheese, game, fruit and honey are excellent reasons for an extended visit to Valle d'Aosta; these delights are best appreciated – or justified – after the energy-burning walks in the Parco Nazionale del Gran Paradiso and its surrounds.

Valdostane wines enjoy Italy's first *denominazione di origine controllata* authentication system; labels bear the letters DOC, which can be used for at least 20 wines produced in the region. Most of the vineyards are in the main valley; the principal varieties of white grapes are Chardonnay and Müller-Thurgau and the reds include Pinot Noir, Torrette, Chambave Muscat and Pinot Gris. Enfer d'Arvier is a particularly fine wine, which should appeal to anyone keen on robust, full-flavoured Australian reds. A very drinkable bottle costs up to €5 and you can pay up to €26 for a well-aged wine.

Genepy (or *genepi*) is a Valdostane specialty and once tasted, becomes an indispensable conclusion (with a good espresso) to a day in the mountains. This herb-rich nectar is an infusion of an alpine plant *Artemesia glacialis* which grows on moraine edges. For around €3 you can savour a generous nip in the bar; a bottle of the delectable Herbetet brand costs around €16.

Fontina cheese is also protected against imitations by the *denominazione* system, using the distinctive motif of the silhouette of the Matterhorn and the words *Consorzioni Produttori Fontina*. It's made by traditional methods, with unpasteurised milk and no colouring agents. After a long maturation process this full-fat cheese has a unique flavour, which must owe a lot to the diet of the local cows that graze the flower-rich meadows where artificial fertilisers seem to be unknown. Fontina pops up all over the place on restaurant menus. It's basic to *zuppa* Valdostane (slices of dark bread soaked in stock and thick Fontina sauce) and polenta Valdostane.

For carnivores, two common items on restaurant menus are *camoscio* (chamois) and *cervo* (venison).

Apples and pears are grown locally; look out for bottles of Puro succo di mele Renetta e Golden, a delicious fruit juice. Each 1L bottle (€2.20) is made from 2kg of apples and is additive-free.

Local honey is derived from various flowers, including rhododendron (recommended), clover, acacia, thyme, eucalyptus and mixtures of whatever the bees found, called *millefiori*, *bosco* and *montagna*.

Caffe alla Valdostane is a trap for the unwary. It's a heady concoction of strong, sweet black coffee, orange curacao and local grappa, which can give you a flying start after lunch or put all thought of further activity beyond comprehension.

For further gastronomic exploration look for a copy of *Valle d'Aosta Gastronomica*, by Bovo, Sanguinetti and Vola. It is an excellent guide (in Italian) to the history and traditions of local wines and other delights, with about 100 recipes.

WESTERN ALPS

species of nesting birds recorded, you're most likely to see royal eagles, ptarmigan, alpine choughs and alpine accentors.

CLIMATE

Conditions in the valleys to the north and south of Valle d'Aosta and in upper Valsesia are markedly cooler than at lower altitudes, although in summer temperatures well into the 20°Cs are common. Even so, the mean annual temperature at Aosta is just 10°C. Frost is likely above 1800m at any time. Rainfall is concentrated in summer; May and September are usually comparatively

dry. Each valley experiences its own pattern of prevailing winds, and the Gran Paradiso and Monte Rosa massifs create their own climates. Snow can fall at any time, although it is uncommon during July and August.

INFORMATION
When to Walk

Conditions vary widely from year to year, but walks reaching 2500m should be accessible, without the use of ice axe or crampons, from late May to late September. Snow usually lies above 2500m until mid-June, or even later (see the boxed text 'Warning', this

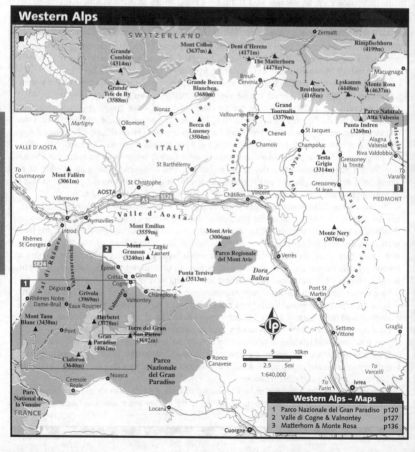

page). From about mid-July until late August the area is very busy and accommodation is at a premium. Public transport services are more frequent during summer; camping areas are generally open from late May to mid-September. A few *rifugi* are open in April; most are open during May (at least at weekends), and all should be open from early June until mid-September.

Maps
For access to and within the area, Touring Club Italiano's 1:200,000 map *Piemonte e Valle d'Aosta* is very good. Studio FMB's 1:100,000 map *Valle d'Aoste*, in the Euro-cart series, is also adequate. Both are available at newsagents and bookshops.

Books
Numerous Italian-language guides to walks and climbs throughout the area are available. *A Piedi in Valle d'Aosta,* by Stefano Ardito, comes in two volumes, each describing more than 90 walks. German publisher Rother has a *Guide Escursionistica* to Valle d'Aosta, and the map publisher Istituto Geografico Centrale (IGC) offers a two-volume set of guides, *Il Parco Nazionale del Gran Paradiso,* to accompany its maps of the area. *I Laghi della Valle d'Aosta,* by Sergio Piotti, includes descriptions of 185 walks.

The Kompass series of *Guide Naturalistiche* includes *Animali delle Alpi, Fiori Alpini* and *Fiori di Prato*. These economical guides contain 70 colour photos with brief descriptions of the most common species.

Many newsagents and bookshops in Aosta stock maps.

Information Sources
It's worth calling at the **PNGP park office** (☎ *0165 950 55, fax 0165 959 75;* **w** *www.parks.it/parco.nazionale.gran.paradiso/; Loc Champagne 18; open Mon-Fri),* a few kilometres west of Aosta. It's easily accessible by car, on the S26, not the autostrada, about 300m west of the village of Villeneuve. Or catch the Courmayeur bus from Aosta to Villeneuve (€2.20 return). The office provides general information as well as detailing accommodation throughout the park.

Warning

The winter of 2000–01 hit the valleys particularly hard, after the disastrous October floods (see the boxed text '15 October 2000', p117).

Snow piled up to record depths – so much so that paths, passes, *rifugi* and even roads that would normally be open by mid-June (2001) were still closed, making it impossible (unless in the company of a local mountain guide) to follow any higher-level routes. Amazingly, Rifugio Savoia near Col del Nivolet (above Valsavarenche), usually thronged with car-borne visitors by then, was still surrounded by 0.5m of slowly thawing snow.

The thaw created more hazards: swollen, fast-flowing streams and tumbling stones.

In mid-September another 20cm of snow fell at 2500m, making pass crossings hazardous.

Whether the big freeze and the unusual autumn snows were isolated, freak events or whether they signal a change of the local – or wider – climate, only time will tell. Contact the local tourist information or national park office for advice.

Place Names
French and Italian versions of place names are used throughout the area, with a tendency for French to be favoured the further west you travel, eg, Colle della Finestra and Col Fenêtre between Val di Rhêmes and Valgrisenche are one and the same place.

Emergency
In Valle d'Aosta call the **mountain rescue service** (☎ *0165 23 02 53).* For medical assistance call the **national number** (☎ *118).*

GATEWAY
Aosta
The busy, sprawling town of Aosta is the capital of the autonomous region of Valle d'Aosta. It's the hub of the excellent bus services and the train terminus.

Information Useful for accommodation lists, free road and town maps, and weather forecasts is the **UIT** (☎ *0165 23 66 27, fax 0165 346 57;* **e** *uit-aosta@regione.vda.it;*

Piazza Chanoux 8; open Mon-Sat & Sun morning). Some of the staff speak English. The region's website, w www.regione.vda .it/turismo, is in Italian only, and has loads of similar information.

Local weather forecasts (☎ 0165 441 13, fax 0165 402 56) are available, in Italian only, from Aosta airport.

Brave the smoky atmosphere of the **Bar Snooker** (☎ 0165 23 63 68; e media@evo.it; *Via San Lucat 3; open Thur-Tues)* to check email (€5 per hour).

Libreria Aubert *(Via E Aubert 46)* and **Minerva** *(Rue de Tillier 24)* have plenty of Italian-language books about walks, and natural and cultural history.

Supplies & Equipment You can stock up on stove fuel, buy maps and replace worn-out socks at **Meinardi Sport** *(Via Edouard Albert 23; open daily; closed Mon morning)*, five minutes' walk west from Piazza Chanoux.

Hire an ice axe and crampons (early or late in the season) from **Calzature Baroli** *(☎/fax 0165 950 20; Via A Cerlogne 15, Villeneuve).* Each item costs around €10.35 to hire for two days or €18.10 for seven days.

For supplies there are two **Standa supermarkets** *(Piazza Plouves • Via Chambery; both open daily; closed Sun siesta).* There are many smaller *alimentari* (grocery shops) in Via San Anselmo east of Piazza Chanoux.

Places to Stay & Eat For good grassy pitches with valley views campers should head to **Ville d'Aoste** *(☎ 0165 36 13 60; Viale Gran San Bernardo 76; camping per person/site €4.15/8.25; open June-Sept),*

Italy's First National Park

The ibex, Europe's largest alpine wild animal, is at the heart of the history of PNGP. Desire for its preservation motivated the park's creation and it has been the focus of a long-term conservation project there.

Climate change and hunting drove ibex into the mountainous areas in prehistoric times. The first attempt to protect it was a hunting ban in the early 19th century but the ruling House of Savoy was exempt. King Vittorio Emanuele II of Piedmont (Piemonte) – later the first king of Italy – regularly visited the Gran Paradiso area. A royal hunting reserve of 22 sq km was created in 1856 for his exclusive use. Some say his motive was to protect the ibex, others that it was pure selfishness. However, local people benefited. To create the reserve, locals had forfeited their hunting rights to the king, and in return could join special new corps of wardens whose job it was to curtail poaching, or become porters or gamekeepers who were paid to get rid of the lynx and bearded vulture, regarded as predators.

Paths (or *mulattiere*) were built to hunting lodges and across mountain passes. Of the former hunting lodges, Lauson is now Rifugio Sella (above Valnontey) and Nivolet is Rifugio Savoia (near Col del Nivolet, above Valsavarenche).

In 1919, faced with rising maintenance costs, the revival of poaching during WWI and the consequent decline of the ibex population, King Vittorio Emanuele III surrendered his hunting rights and gave the property to the state so that a national park could be established. This eventually happened on 3 December 1922. The park's purpose was to preserve flora, fauna and natural beauty.

The PNGP's area is around 700 sq km, of which about 90% belongs to small land owners and *comunes* (town councils). The park's administrative council must approve all building work and land-use changes within the park, so new developments generally harmonise with traditional architectural styles. Park staff aim to instil an understanding of how people, wildlife and the landscape are interrelated, through guided walks within the park.

In 1972, PNGP was twinned with neighbouring Parc Nationale de la Vanoise in France, making a truly European park of 1230 sq km. As far as possible, the two parks are managed as one – as *uno parco senza frontiere* (one park without borders).

conveniently located on the SVAP bus route No 4 (Variney–Charvensod), close to the GS Bernardo ang Betulle stop (€0.80). At the train station buy tickets at the bar or newsagent, and catch the orange bus opposite. Otherwise it's a 30-minute walk.

Of Aosta's numerous and varied hotels **La Belle Époque** (*π/fax 0165 26 22 76; Via d'Avise 18; singles/doubles €31/57*) is in the heart of the old town. It's an older-style place with decor reflecting its name.

Gelato (ice cream) addicts should take in the *gelateria* (ice-cream parlour) in Via Trottechien (west of Piazza Chanoux).

La Cave de Tillier (*π 0165 23 01 33; Via De Tillier 40*), in a lane off Via E Aubert, is highly recommended for a break from pizza and spaghetti. It offers set menus (such as three fish courses for around €18) and a wide choice from the superb *zuppa della casa* (soup of the day) to polenta and gnocchi.

Crowded with locals, the excellent **Pizzeria Moderna** (*π 0165 356 69; Via E Aubert 21*) has numerous pizzas including regional specialties such as Tirolese, Valdostana and Siciliana. The menu also offers a range of salads and the usual pasta and gnocchi dishes; servings are generous.

Family run since 1957, **Ristorante da Nando** (*π 0165 444 55; Via di Tillier 41*), in old vaulted cellars, offers traditional Valdostane cuisine plus pasta, pizzas and polenta; you'll eat well for around €18.

Getting There & Away Aosta's bus station (*π 0165 26 20 27; Via Giorgio Carrel*) is diagonally opposite the train station. **SADEM** (*π 011 300 06 06; W www.sadem.it*) operates buses from Milan's Piazza Castello (€11.60, 2½ hours, once a day) and from Corso Castel Fidardo in Turin (Torino; €6.45, two hours, three a day). Both travel to Courmayeur via Aosta.

Normally, approaching Aosta by train the service from Turin is direct (€5.70, two to 2½ hours, more than 10 per day), while coming from Milan (Milano) you change at Chivasso (€10.10, three hours, several a day). However, the floods of 2000 (see the boxed text '15 October 2000', p117) swept away sections of the line. At the time of writing restoration was not complete. In the meantime, trains from Chivasso terminate at Borgofranco where connecting buses take you to Aosta at no extra charge. Contact **Aosta station** (*π 0165 26 20 57*).

By car, the A5 through Valle d'Aosta bypasses Aosta; access roads link it with the town just to the north.

The A5 and the S26 connect Aosta with Chamonix in France via the Mont Blanc tunnel. From the north, the S27 links Switzerland with Valle d'Aosta via the Gran San Bernardo tunnel.

The most spectacular way to reach Aosta is to fly with **Air Vallée** (*π 0165 23 69 66, W www.airvallee.com*). Operating from Aosta's small airport at Sant'Christophe, 4km east of the town centre, it flies from/to Roma Fiumicino (standard return/APEX €242/151, twice a day except Saturday). Catch the local VAT bus No 8a from the airport to the town centre (€0.80).

Parco Nazionale del Gran Paradiso & Nearby

Gran Paradiso must surely rank among Italy's top three national parks. Lying south of the town of Aosta, with Valle di Cogne and Vallone di Urtier forming its northern boundary; it extends south to Valle dell'Orco and the French border, has the town of Ronco Canavese midway along its eastern border and in the west is bounded by Valle di Rhêmes. Scenically it's stunning and marvellously varied, with dozens of peaks exceeding 3500m, including Gran Paradiso (4061m) the highest mountain entirely within Italy, numerous glaciers, scores of lakes, and long, deep, glaciated valleys sheltering small villages. You can count on seeing ibex, chamois and marmots every day. From the limits of plant growth to the beautiful larch and pine woodlands and the grassy meadows, the displays of wildflowers are truly superb. PNGP is Italy's oldest national park (see the boxed text 'Italy's

WESTERN ALPS

First National Park', p114) and protects many historic features, most importantly for walkers, an extensive network of paths linking the valleys via high passes.

This section describes two flexible, linked two- to three-day walks within the park, and three-day walks from Cogne (on the edge of the park) and the nearby village of Valnontey. The Vallone di Grauson walk is just outside the park but is no less scenic and offers superb views of the central Gran Paradiso massif. Suggestions for other walks in and near the park are also provided (see Parco Nazionale del Gran Paradiso & Nearby, p140).

PLANNING
Maps
Kompass' 1:50,000 No 86 *Gran Paradiso, Valle d'Aosta* is useful for general orientation, but the depiction of paths is not always accurate; the accompanying booklet (in Italian and German) is very informative.

Studio FMB's 1:50,000 *Gran Paradiso* is clear but also contains errors in the location of features and paths. The information on the reverse side, in Italian, about natural and mountaineering history, makes it worthwhile.

IGC's 1:50,000 No 3 *Il Parco Nazionale del Gran Paradiso* map is easy to read and reliable enough. It has a companion two-volume guide with the same title.

In Cogne, several shops along Via Bourgeois sell maps. Two good bookshops (which also sell maps) are **Montagne di Carta** *(Via Dr Grappein 56)* and **Cavallo** *(Viale Cavagnet 51)*, with shelves of Italian titles about walks, and natural and cultural history.

Guided Walks
There are some good options for guided walks in PNGP. As an indication of costs, guides based at Cogne lead groups of five people to the summit of Gran Paradiso for €98 per person per day, which includes half board at a *rifugio*. Mont Blanc (Monte Bianco) is more expensive – €264 per person covering half board and the guide's services for just two people. Trekking trips in the Gran Paradiso area are also provided, including a five-day circuit from Cogne around Gran

Paradiso, with the summit as an optional extra, for €340 per person in a group of five. Contact the **Società Guide Scuola di Alpinismo** (☎ 0328 137 37 28) for details.

ACCESS TOWNS
Cogne
This very small town is strongly oriented to tourism year-round, without really spoiling its character as a long-established mountain centre.

Information The AIAT office (☎ 0165 740 40, fax 0165 74 91 25; Piazza Chanoux 36; open daily; closed Sun afternoon) offers an accommodation list, a map and a multilingual brochure *Try the Trails* outlining 47 local walks. Beware – the walks are numbered differently in the brochure than on the ground. Another multilingual brochure is *Discovering Colonna's Mines* (see Colonna, p140). Limited information can be gleaned about the condition of local paths (a little English is spoken) but it's far better to ask either at Ezio Sport, a *rifugio*, or your hosts. The daily weather forecast, in Italian, is displayed in the office. Outside office hours, you can check accommodation availability and telephone your choice (free) from a video information point around the corner from the office. The local website **w** www.cogne.org includes a comprehensive list of accommodation for Cogne and Valnontey.

A programme of half-day and day-long guided walks (in Italian) runs from early July to early September, visiting such places as the Colonna mine and Rifugio Sella. Details are available from the AIAT office.

Tracce (☎ 0165 74 96 16; Via Dr Grappein 61; open daily) is an interesting 'nature' shop where you can also check email (30 minutes costs around €3).

Supplies & Equipment The place to go for stove fuel, outdoor equipment and clothing is **Ezio Sport** *(Via Mines de Cogne 66)*.

Pick up supplies at the smallish **Despar supermarket** *(Via Bourgeois)* and, 250m east from there, two *alimentari* and a fruit and vegetable **shop**.

Places to Stay & Eat Cogne has plenty of hotels to choose from, though few at the lower end of the price scale. **Hotel Bouton d'Or** (☎ 0165 742 68; fax 0165 74 91 98; Viale Cavagnet 15; B&B from €50) has an uninterrupted view across the meadows towards the mountains; all rooms are en suite.

Hotel Sant'Orso (☎ 0165 748 21, fax 0165 74 95 00; w www.cognevacanze.com; Via Bourgeois 2; B&B doubles from €31, with half board from €56.80) has superbly fitted out, spacious rooms, many with a balcony. Half board is excellent value. The four-course evening meal, always includes Valdostane specialties.

Several restaurants in the town enthusiastically uphold Valdostane traditions. **Hostellerie de l'Atelier** (☎ 0165 743 27; Via Dr Grappein 102; open Fri-Wed) is a busy, informal place where the briskly efficient staff will explain the mysteries of favé (a superb pasta dish), crespelle alla Valdostana (crepes), and recommend from the exclusively Valle d'Aosta wine list. Expect to pay up to €18.60 for two courses plus drinks.

Getting There & Away Buses run by **SAVDA** (☎ 0165 26 20 27, fax 0165 36 12 46) travel between Aosta and Cogne (€2.10, 50 minutes, six a day). Tickets can be purchased at the Aosta bus station or on board.

By car, take the Aymavilles exit from the S26, 6km southwest of Aosta; continue on SR47 from Aymavilles village to Cogne, 20km further on.

Valnontey

This compact historic village is 3km south of Cogne, deep in its valley. During summer the number of visitors each day vastly outnumbers the residents. Valnontey (val-non-**tay**) doesn't have its own tourist office – the AIAT in Cogne (see Information, p116) looks after its interests.

Places to Stay & Eat With a homely feel **Camping Gran Paradiso** (☎ 0165 74 92 04; camping per person/tent €3.90/5) is just beyond the southern end of the village. You can pitch a tent on the grassed terraces. There's a bar for drinks and snacks, and a

shop – don't forget a bag of tegole (the local biscuit treat) – it's much cheaper than in Cogne. Within the national park, camping is permitted only in formal sites such as this.

Bar La Clicca (☎ 0165 741 57; Fraz Valnontey 31; dorm beds €25.80) has small bright bunkrooms, each with balcony and private facilities; rates include breakfast. The bar offers a vast range of drinks and serves snacks.

Albergo Paradisia (☎/fax 0165 741 58; Valnontey 36; half board €63) overlooks the oldest part of the village and is delightfully informal and idiosyncratic. Most rooms have private facilities and a good view. The

---

15 October 2000

The people of Valle d'Aosta, including the Cogne area, will probably never forget October 2000. It rained continuously with tropical intensity for four days, dumping 12 months worth of rain. These monsoonal rains were the product of an inrush of warm African air, evaporation on a grand scale over the Mediterranean and a strong blocking anti-cyclone over the Balkans.

The Cogne comune received warning of hugely devastating floods (named Alluvione Josefine) and called all citizens from Lillaz, Cogne, Gimillan, Cretaz and Epinel to gather at the village centre.

On 15 October terrifying avalanches of water, rock, fallen trees and debris swept down the mountainsides and through the valley, ripping out sections of road and dumping masses of rock and silt along the widened course of the river. Miraculously, no lives were lost in Cogne, but homes were flooded and the road to Aosta was cut for six weeks. Supplies were brought in by helicopter.

Even by midsummer 2001, one section of the road was still causing some concern, despite heroic efforts to rebuild it. A massive amount of work has been put into repairing roads and bridges and many of the paths, but the awesome scars of the many landslides will take decades to heal and stabilise as trees and plants slowly colonise their bare faces.

excellent three-course evening meal is especially good for soups and vegetable dishes.

For self caterers there is a small *alimentari*.

Petit Dahu (☎/fax 0165 741 46; set menu around €18), almost next door to Albergo Paradisia, excels in Valdostane specialties – try the set menu; reservations are essential.

Getting There & Away A bus service travels between Cogne (from near the Aosta bus stop in Via Bourgeois) and Valnontey (€0.80, 10 minutes, frequent daily service from late June to mid-September). A timetable is available from the AIAT office in Cogne. When the bus service isn't operating it is possible to walk from Cogne, see the Cogne to Valnontey Alternative Start (p121). The road to Valnontey (3km) branches from Via Bourgeois in the centre of Cogne.

Valnontey to Rhêmes Notre Dame

Duration	2 days
Distance	30.5km
Difficulty	moderate–demanding
Start	Valnontey (p117)
Finish	Rhêmes Notre Dame-Bruil (p118)
Transport	bus

Summary The two most dramatic and spectacular days of the Alta Via 2, over the highest and most challenging pass, with scores of ibex, chamois and marmots for company, in the heart of the national park.

This is an outstandingly varied and challenging walk, with 3030m of ascent. From Valnontey, the route crosses Col Lauson (3296m) on the Grivola–Gran Paradiso Range, the highest pass in the park accessible to walkers (see the boxed text 'Col Lauson – Warning', p119), then descends into isolated Valsavarenche at Eaux Rousses. From there it's over the easier (less demanding) Col di Entrelor and down into Val di Rhêmes and the village of Rhêmes Notre Dame-Bruil. Each of the days can be self contained; with public transport available.

The route is described from east to west, because it's potentially less unnerving to climb to Col Lauson from the east than to descend that way.

When the seasonal bus service from Cogne to Valnontey isn't operating, it is possible to start the walk in Cogne (see Alternative Start: Cogne to Valnontey, p121).

The walk follows part of the Alta Via 2 (AV2; see the boxed text 'Mountain Odysseys – Long Distance Routes', p130) and there's a good case for claiming they are the best two days for scenery, wildlife and ease of access. Much of it follows paths built in the 1860s to make ibex hunting easier for royal parties (see the boxed text 'Italy's First National Park', p114). Waymarking and signposting of the paths is generally reliable. Ibex are now back in force and you can expect to see them in many places, together with chamois and marmots.

It's possible to vary the route of this walk, and spread the long ascent to Col di Entrelor over a couple of days, see the Alternative Route: Pont to Laghi Djouan (p122).

PLANNING
Maps

Two IGC 1:25,000 maps, Nos 101 *Gran Paradiso, La Grivola, Cogne* and 102 *Valsavarenche, Val di Rhêmes, Valgrisenche*, are at the ideal scale although path information is not universally accurate. See also Maps (p116).

NEAREST TOWNS

See Valnontey (p117).

Rhêmes Notre Dame

This locality is actually a collection of very small villages deep in the upper reaches of Val di Rhêmes. In Rhêmes Notre Dame-Chanavey you will find a **PNGP Visitor Centre** (☎ 0165 93 61 93; admission €1.55; open daily June-Sept), which is open less frequently at other times and has excellent displays, particularly featuring 'Gipeto' (the bearded vulture). Free Internet access is available here, but you'll probably have to queue.

Places to Stay & Eat The first village you'll reach at the end of the walk is Rhêmes Notre Dame-Bruil where the **Hotel Galisia** (☎/fax 0165 93 61 00, half board to €38.75) is popular with Italian families and has plain but decent-sized rooms. Half board includes a generous three-course evening meal.

Hotel Chez Lidia (☎ 0165 93 61 03; half board €46.50), opposite Hotel Galisia and not immediately obvious, is usually more peaceful.

There's a wider choice between more expensive hotels, in Rhêmes Notre Dame-Chanavey, 1km north of Rhêmes Notre Dame-Bruil. Full details are provided in the Valle d'Aosta accommodation list available from the UIT in Aosta (p113).

There's a small **shop** selling food, maps and souvenirs beside Hotel Chez Lidia in Rhêmes Notre Dame-Bruil, and another down in Chanavey.

Getting There & Away A bus service is operated by **SAVDA** (☎ 0165 26 20 27) between Aosta and Rhêmes Notre Dame-Bruil (€2.30, one hour, three a day from July to mid-September, three a day on Monday to Saturday at other times).

By road from Valle d'Aosta, turn off S26 to Villeneuve, 11km southwest of Aosta and follow SR23 west then south through Introd; a couple of kilometres further on, turn off along SR24 to Rhêmes Notre Dame-Bruil (19km from Villeneuve).

THE WALK (see map p120)
Day 1: Valnontey to Eaux Rousses
7½–8 hours, 17km, 1630m ascent

From the far side of the bridge over Torrente Valnontey in Valnontey village, follow the broad path waymarked 2 for the AV2. The path winds up through forests and its comfortably graded zigzags take you deeper into Vallone del Lauson and past numerous waterfalls on Torrente Lauson. It gradually leaves the trees behind and leads into open ground, bare except for innumerable wildflowers. When **Alpe Gran Lauson**, across the *torrente*, is occupied and the cows are busily grazing, it's possible to buy milk, cream, butter and cheese there. The ascent to **Rifugio Sella** (☎ 0165 743 10; ᴡ www .rifugiosella.com; nonmembers €33; open early April-late Sept) takes two to 2½ hours; drinks and snacks are served either in the smallest building or the main one. The *rifugio* is an extremely popular day's outing from Valnontey. Snacks and drinks are available all day and a substantial lunch is served. To spend a night in this magnificent location it's essential to book well ahead. The website has an on-line booking service.

From the signposted path junction close to the PNGP's Casotto del Lauson, continue in the direction of Col Lauson and shortly bear right with a 2 waymarker, which may seem like the wrong direction, but the old path soon swings round to make a fine traverse of the mountainside above the *rifugio*. The path then leads into an impressively huge amphitheatre walled with rugged colourful peaks and glaciers to the south. Next you cross a classic hidden valley, gaining height comfortably towards the seemingly impregnable cliffs. A bridge crosses the *torrente*; the path then bears leftish (west), up and across the steep slope. Continue past the turnoff (right) for route 26b (to Col de la Rousse and Col de la Noire) and into a silent world of scree, rock and sparse vegetation. The route leads on through a long, narrow

Col Lauson – Warning

Parts of the upper reaches of the path from Rifugio Sella to Col Lauson cross erosion-prone, loose and friable rock and fine scree and are very narrow and slightly exposed. There are at least four artificial sections, where small landslips have been filled in; there are no fixed chains or ropes.

You need to be sure-footed and calm – after all, hundreds of walkers make this exhilarating crossing.

It does become a more serious proposition if the ground freezes (which it can do on cold nights) and/or if there's more than a few centimetres of snow.

The initial descent from Col Lauson towards Eaux Rousses is less precipitous and the scree relatively stable, but considerable care is still required.

valley then zigzags up the ever-steepening boulder-scree slope at the valley head.

Having exhausted the scope for zigzags, the path narrows and rises steeply to a false col, and the exciting part of the ascent comes into view. There's a series of built-up lengths of path, between small bluffs, around which the exceedingly narrow path creeps; then a steep section over fine scree and you can collapse with relief at small Col Lauson (3296m; two hours from Rifugio Sella). The magnificent prospect westwards is filled with peaks and glaciers in layers separating the depths of Valsavarenche and Val di Rhêmes. The most striking peak to the southeast is Torre del Gran San Pietro (3692m), crowning the ridge along Valnontey's eastern side.

The descent starts steeply – follow the yellow (and occasionally red) waymarkers for the safest route, though small landslips can occasionally blur its line. The route heads down towards the towering cliffs of Grivola

(3969m), crosses reddish boulders and scree and soon starts a series of zigzags. Then comes a steep bit and another section through boulders; from the first patch of grass the old path, with its comfortable gradient, becomes consistently easy to follow. Around here, to the left (south) are good views of Gran Paradiso's glaciers and snowfields and the spiky peaks of Becca di Montandayne (3838m) and Herbetet (3778m). The path soon starts to work its way towards Torrente Levionaz.

The path winds down in long zigzags across broad spurs, then steepens, winds in and out of a rock-filled gully, and into the main valley, passing the signposted turn-off for a route to Rifugio Chabod on the left. A bit further on, you may find the ground around the path unusually bare of vegetation and the path itself more eroded – this is a favourite grazing area for ibex. Continue down and cross the bridge over Torrente Levionaz (1¼ to 1½ hours from Col Lauson) and go on down to riverbank level.

About 1.5km further on there's a short climb to the PNGP base at Levionaz (30 minutes from the bridge). Skirt the buildings and shortly pass a tiny *oratorio* (oratory) on the right.

Then come a few hundred eroded metres of path. Beyond the turnoff for route 10 (to the right) the path contours a boulder field then leads into woodland. Further down, the path has been carefully rebuilt where it crosses a very long landslip several times. About an hour from Levionaz you cross a massively gouged-out stream, then stay in the open for the last 30 minutes of descent, latterly on a walled path between fields to the main road through the valley. The bus stop is 50m to the right, at the junction of the road leading to the hotel at Eaux Rousses.

Eaux Rousses & Around

This handful of buildings is right on the normal route of the AV2, just above the main valley road. Its name comes from the iron deposit in the cliffs, down which the local waterfall cascades.

A curious place, **A L'Hostellerie du Paradis** (☎ 0165 90 59 72, fax 0165 90 59 71; **w** www.hostellerieduparadis.it; annexe dorm beds with half board €36.15, hotel rooms with half board €77.50) has split-level floors and rooms covered in paintings and photos. The evening meal is excellent.

There is also accommodation at Pont (p123) about 5km up the road; at Bien, about 1km down the road; and at Dégioz (**day**-gosh) a couple more kilometres down the valley. Details are available on **w** www.valsavarenche.org or in the Valle d'Aosta accommodation list available from the UIT in Aosta (p113).

At Dégioz there is also a small **shop**, a *tabaccheria* (tobacconist and all-purpose shop) and a **PNGP visitor centre** (☎ 0165 90 58 08; admission €1.55; open daily July-Aug, Sun only June & Sept); the display features predators.

There's a **SAVDA** (☎ 0165 26 20 27) bus service between Aosta and Eaux Rousses (€2.50, one hour, three a day mid-June to mid-September, and Monday to Saturday at other times). By road from Valle d'Aosta,

turn off S26 to Villeneuve, 11km southwest of Aosta and follow SR23, west then south, through Introd. A couple of kilometres further, at a junction, continue along SR23 to Eaux Rousses, 20km from Villeneuve.

Alternative Start: Cogne to Valnontey

40 minutes, 3km, 130m ascent

Walk across Piazza Chanoux (with the AIAT office on your left) and follow a well-used path across the spacious meadows between the town and Torrente Valnontey to a bridge over the river, and turn left. Follow the wide vehicle track upstream to the bridge over the stream on the western edge of Valnontey. The path to Rifugio Sella leads off to the right.

Day 2: Eaux Rousses to Rhêmes Notre Dame-Bruil

6½–7 hours, 13.5km, 1400m ascent

Normally you'd start this day by following the AV2 from the hotel, but at the time of writing the path was closed on account of forestry work. Thus our main route, which is clearly signposted, is via the hamlet of Créton 2km down the valley.

When things return to normal the mapped alternative route will be the one to take. The AV2 is also a *sentiero natura* (nature path/ walk) from Eaux Rousses to Champlanaz (above Montagna Djouan). The features of this walk include the iron-rich mineral spring, forest trees, glacial features and alpine grazing settlements. A descriptive leaflet is available locally – try **A L'Hostellerie du Paradis** or the **PNGP visitor centre** at Dégioz.

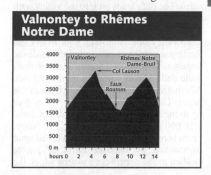

Valnontey to Rhêmes Notre Dame

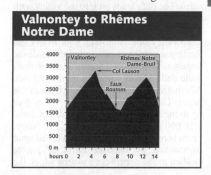

WESTERN ALPS

To reach Créton, walk north down the main road from Eaux Rousses for about 1km to a point opposite the more northerly side road to the hamlet of Bien (where there is a bus stop) and turn left towards Créton; cross the bridge and turn right, passing **Camping Grivola** (☎/fax 0165 90 57 43; camping per person/site €5/10; open mid-June–mid-Sept), on the left, and **Hotel Grivola** (☎/fax 0165 90 57 43), on the right. Follow the minor road up through the old village of Créton and about 30m past a car park on the right, turn left along a signposted path in the direction of Col di Entrelor and AV2. Soon the path ascends fairly steeply through forest to the meadows of ruinous Alpe Ruja; go to the left of it and up, past a tiny *oratorio*. The path gains height sharply past a single derelict building on the right then, approaching the next one, bends to the right to pass in front of a stone building, then rises into woodland. The path zigzags up and soon you come to a junction with the official AV2 route (1¼ to 1½ hours from Eaux Rousses). Then a steep section takes you to PNGP's **Casa Reale** at Orveille (see the boxed text 'Italy's First National Park', p114), which was a favourite royal hunting lodge in the late 19th century. Skirt this and continue gaining height. The views from here are spectacular in all directions, but particularly of the soaring spires of Grand Nomenon (3488m) and Grivola (3969m), above the opposite side of Valsavarenche. Continue up to **Montagna Djouan**, occupied in summer.

Go on to a deserted stone building at Champlanaz (Alp Tsoplanaz on the 1:25,000 map). The path leads on into the valley with Col di Entrelor at its head. Continue steadily upwards on the narrow path traversing the steep valley side. Almost an hour from Casa Reale you come to a path junction beside the largest of the Laghi Djouan, route 9 from Valle delle Meyes comes in on the left (see Alternative Route: Pont to Laghi Djouan this page). The path leads on up the valley (not up to the stone building as the 1:25,000 and 1:50,000 maps show) to sombre Lac Noire. From here it rises in zigzags up a broad spur, overlooked by massive cliffs of Pointe Gollien to the northwest, towards which the path narrows determinedly. It keeps close to the cliffs to the final steep ascent through a boulder field to **Col di Entrelor** (3007m; 1¼ to 1½ hours from Laghi Djouan). The inspiring view includes the great peaks on the opposite side of Val di Rhêmes, topped by Grande Rousse (3607m).

To start the descent, bear right through boulders, carefully following the yellow waymarkers; soon there's a short, slightly exposed bit to negotiate, then it's down again through boulders, towards the cliffs on the northern side of Vallone di Entrelor. A longish stretch down over scree brings you to the start of the clearly defined path. It keeps as close as possible to the cliffs until the valley starts to widen, then heads more towards the middle of the valley. At a path junction by the ruinous Alpe Plan des Feyes (Alp Plan de la Feya), bear left with the AV2 and route 10 (route 7 goes to the right). Further down, keep to the path on the northeast side of the valley, descending past the neat, extensive fields of Alpages d'Entrelor on the left. At the bottom of these fields, where there's a large timber crucifix, the wide path swings to the right (north) to descend through larch woodland. After about 1km bear right along a narrower waymarked path, which continues to lose height steadily. It reaches a vehicle track (not on the 1:25,000 map) – follow this for just 10m then drop down to the right along a path. Cross the bridge almost opposite the end of the path and you've reached Rhêmes Notre Dame-Bruil (2¾ to three hours from Col di Entrelor).

Alternative Route: Pont to Laghi Djouan
7½–8 hours, 18km, 810m ascent, 1290m descent

To tackle the ascent to Col di Entrelor in a more moderate two days, staying overnight at Rifugio Savoia, start at Pont and follow the Lakes & Wildlife walk (p123). Instead of bearing right at path 9a towards Meyes d'en Haut on Day 2, continue to Laghi Djouan via Valle delle Meyes. At the lakes you join the main route. The bus to Eaux Rousses (p121) continues to Pont (three a day in summer).

Lakes & Wildlife

Duration	2 days
Distance	22km
Difficulty	moderate
Start/Finish	Pont (p123)
Transport	bus

Summary Lakes, wildflowers and wildlife are the highlights of this magnificently scenic walk, with the chance to stay at a historic *rifugio* and a choice of routes to minimise the amount of ascent.

There's much more to walking in PNGP than crossing high passes with long ascents and descents. Numerous tarns and high valleys, amazingly rich in wildflowers can be linked by good paths, and the views of the highest peaks are unfailingly spectacular.

This walk starts and finishes in upper Valsavarenche and offers a choice of routes from Pont up to the beautiful alpine meadows of Piano del Nivolet. The main route does involve 1785m of ascent and a fairly high pass – Grand Collet (2832m) – but the amount of ascent is less than the daily stages on the Valnontey to Rhêmes Notre Dame walk (p118), and most importantly for your knees, involves a great deal less descent. The vistas of the Gran Paradiso Range from this ascent are truly magnificent.

A side trip to most of the lakes sitting in a hanging valley above Rifugio Savoia and Laghi del Nivolet, is described. This is just one of several possible routes around this fascinating area, where you can follow paths or find a way across country. The return is via the beautiful, wild Valle delle Meyes where you're almost certain to see herds of ibex and chamois.

If time is very short, it's possible to go direct to Rifugio Savoia from Pont, do the side trip and return to Pont in one day. The walk also offers an alternative approach to Laghi Djouan on the Day 2 route of the Valnontey to Rhêmes Notre Dame walk, see Alternative Route (p122).

Paths are generally good, apart from the odd rockfall; signposts are extremely minimal, though waymarking is adequate.

PLANNING
What to Bring
You'll need to carry food and drink for both days – there are no settlements between Pont and Rifugio Savoia.

Maps
The IGC 1:25,000 No 102 *Valsavarenche, Val di Rhêmes, Valgrisenche* is best, though its depiction of paths and other features isn't entirely accurate. For orientation and identification of features outside the scope of the 1:25,000, choose between the FMB 1:50,000 *Gran Paradiso* or the Kompass 1:50,000 No 86 *Gran Paradiso, Valle d'Aosta*.

NEAREST TOWN
Pont
At the end of the road through Valsavarenche and close to the head of the valley, Pont is tiny – just two hotels, a camping ground and a few old buildings, some seemingly used as holiday homes. A small **information office** (☎ 0165 953 04; open daily July-Aug) is most useful for advice on local weather and the condition of paths. Valsavarenche's website (ｗ www.valsavarenche.org) has details on accommodation in the valley.

Places to Stay & Eat The spacious **Camping Pont Breuil** (☎ 0165 954 58, fax 0165 950 74; Fraz Pont 23; camping per person/site €4.15/9.30; open June-Sept) has stunning views. The facilities are better than average.

Friendly **Hotel Genzianella** (☎ 0165 953 93, fax 0165 953 97; ｗ www.genzianella .aosta.it; Fraz Pont 1; half board €58), is about 500m short of the end of the road. It has great character and there are artefacts and fascinating photos to peruse. The rooms are spacious and the three-course supper generous.

Next to the camping area is a small *alimentari* (open June-Sept), with a modest range of supplies.

Hotel Gran Paradiso (☎ 0165 954 54), near Camping Pont Breuil, offers reasonably priced meals either in the bar or the informal restaurant.

Getting There & Away A bus service operated by **SAVDA** (☎ 0165 26 20 27) runs between Aosta and Pont (€2.70, 1¼ hours, daily mid-June to mid-September). From late September to early June, the bus terminates at Eaux Rousses, 5km down the road.

By road from Valle d'Aosta, turn off S26 to Villeneuve, 11km southwest of Aosta and follow SR23, west then south, through Introd. A couple of kilometres further on at a junction, continue along SR23 to Pont, 25km from Villeneuve.

GETTING TO/FROM THE WALK

See Getting There & Away (p123) for Pont. If you want to leave or join this walk midway a very limited bus service is operated by **SATTI** (☎ 800 21 72 16; **w** www.satti.it; Corso Turati 19/6) from Turin bus station to Col del Nivolet, near Rifugio Città di Chavasso (one on Sunday during school holidays).

THE WALK (see map p120)
Day 1: Pont to Rifugio Savoia via Grand Collet

3½–3¾ hours, 9km, 1015m ascent

From the large car park at Pont, skirt the camping ground and follow the riverbank path upstream for about 15 minutes to a signpost pointing to Grand Collet along route 2a. The narrow, rocky path rises steeply and directly for a few hundred metres then starts to traverse the precipitous slope through scattered boulders, thickets of alpenrose and across grass. At length, an easy stretch along a grassed slope brings you to the deserted **Alpe de Seyvaz** (an hour from the riverbank path). This spectacular viewpoint affords perhaps the most impressive views of all of the Gran Paradiso Range, seemingly at arm's length across the valley.

From the wooden crucifix just north of the Alp, bear slightly right along a faintish path which soon becomes clearer and ascends straight up the steep mountainside, through a few shallow valleys; waymarkers are sparse so follow cairns, more or less in line of sight, for the best way up. If in doubt, remember that the route tends to the right (north). Cross a shallow valley with a large scree slope sprawled across its northern side; bear up to the right to another partly

grassed area and then edge right across it. From here, either continue up a grassy ramp and bend to the right at the top of the crag to rejoin the cairns, or climb through a small cliff to a bare, flat area at the foot of the final ascent. This is a zigzag path up the steep, gravel slope to the relatively wide **Grand Collet** (an hour from Alpe de Seyvaz).

From the northern end of the col descend along the edge of a gravel slope then follow a clear, cairned path through scree and boulders down to the valley floor. Keep to its right (northern) side for about 200m then bear left, following cairns. The views of the massive peaks, along the Italian-French border west of Col del Nivolet, are superb. The main part of the descent then falls into two sections: initially across grassy slopes, then much more steeply via a rocky path down to Alpe du Grand Collet (45 minutes from the col).

Follow the well-used path leading southwest across Piano del Nivolet, where most of the stream crossings are bridged. The path draws you towards the road on the right, passing beneath power lines and along the shore of the larger of the Laghi Nivolet, to reach the road close to the *rifugio* (about an hour from Alpe du Grand Collet).

The main building of **Rifugio Savoia** (☎ 0165 941 41; per Arturo Dayné, Via Chanoux 12; half board €36.15; open mid June-late Sept) is an original 19th-century hunting lodge. More luxurious accommodation in a modern annexe is available in midsummer only. Be prepared for enormous servings at the three-course evening meal.

Rifugio Città di Chivasso (☎ 0124 95 31 50; per Via S Maurizio 9, Gassino Torinese; rooms €16.55; open Apr-May & June-Sept), a CAI establishment near Rifugio Savoia, is an alternative.

Alternative Route:
Via La Croix d'Arolley

2¾–3 hours, 8km, 580m ascent

Follow the signposted path starting behind Hotel Gran Paradiso at Pont, up to La Croix d'Arolley (Cross of Arolley; 55 minutes). Continue along the well-used path into a broad valley, across a sheltered basin then up through a series of rock slabs and meadows, and eventually into the broad expanses of Piano del Nivolet. The path can be boggy in places until you reach ruinous Alpe du Grand Collet (45 minutes from the cross). From here follow the main route to Rifugio Savoia.

Side Trip: Laghi Rosset, Chanavey and Tre Becchi
3–3½ hours, 8km, 470m ascent

The dissected plateau sitting high above Rifugio Savoia and the Laghi Nivolet cradles several lakes, ranging from the relatively large Lago Rosset to Lacs Chanavey, a chain of ponds overlooked by a rugged array of peaks and a glacier or two. Several paths crossing the plateau en route to two difficult cols (Rosset and Leynir) can be linked by lesser paths and some cross-country walking to make a scenic tour. The IGC 1:25,000 map isn't much help with the location of the paths.

On the northern side of Rifugio Savoia a battered sign points along a well-used path which angles generally north up the slope above the *rifugio*. Then follow a cattle-trampled path up to Alpe Riva. Bear left here, contour the slope on the right and cross a stream (with difficulty after heavy rain) and gain some height. The path then bends to the right and crosses a stream. Follow the path marked with yellow arrows, recross the stream and ascend to the shore of **Lago Rosset**. Continue along the shore but bear left shortly to pass above Lago Leità (an hour from the *rifugio*). Cross the slope above its feeder stream, ascend for a few minutes then turn sharp right across the slope. The clear path zigzags up, with a small lake below on the left, then crosses a flat, broad spur to the foot of the final steep climb to Col Rosset (a route into upper Val di Rhêmes) – a strange, barren and quiet place (45 minutes from Lago Leità).

Then head eastwards cross-country, above **Lacs Chanavey** in a rather deep basin on the right, and along the crest above its eastern side. Descend this spur, with excellent views of Lago Rosset, and rejoin the path followed a while ago. On the next steep descent you can see a narrow path leading east; follow it until it fades, then descend and cross a shallow valley. Continue along the base of the slope on the right and the path reappears on the left; follow it up to a shallow gap. Cross the gap and follow the path, now above Lago Rosset, to meet a well-defined path. For a good view of **Laghi Tre Becchi**, just continue east for about 100m (about an hour from below Col Rosset). Return to the clear path and follow it above Lago Rosset. After a while it bends to the right; a path joins it from the left, then almost immediately, a lesser path diverges to the right; ignore it and follow the main path to Alpe Riva and on down to Rifugio Savoia (about 30 minutes from the point above Laghi Tre Becchi).

Day 2: Rifugio Savoia to Pont
4¾–5 hours, 13km, 100m ascent, 670m descent

Walk northeast from the *rifugio* along the scenic, almost-level road to a signpost on the right with faint lettering 'Pont'. Turn left here following a 3a waymarker and yellow arrows (an hour from the *rifugio*). Ascend to a junction marked by large cairns and bear right (another 20 minutes). Fairly soon the path forks; normally you'd go right to cross a nearby stream; if the water is high, bear left for an easier crossing. Then comes a vague stretch across a potentially boggy area, beyond which the path is clear. After about 30 minutes, Valle delle Meyes comes into view. Descend to a path junction beside a huge boulder encrusted with red-orange lichen (55 minutes from the junction marked by large cairns).

Bear right here (path 9a), soon passing beside a tarn. As the path starts to drop sharply watch for a waymarked path on the right and follow it; about 10 minutes further, on a bend, follow a path to the left to reach the stone buildings of **Meyes d'en Haut**, a favourite ibex haunt. The path then drops steeply past a lone stone building to another cluster of stone buildings, **Meyes d'en Bas**, complete with a tiny chapel. Follow triangular waymarkers for route 4 down to the end of a gravel road, which makes easy walking, through a 400m long-tunnel (you can see each end in the middle), and down to the main road beside Hotel Genzianella (2½ hours from Valle delle Meyes).

Alpe Money

Duration	5¾–6¼ hours
Distance	15km
Difficulty	moderate–demanding
Start/Finish	Valnontey (p117)
Transport	bus

Summary An outstandingly scenic walk to traditional alpine grazing huts below the edge of a glacier, and around the glacier-ringed head of Valnontey; ibex encounters almost guaranteed.

On good paths almost all the way, this walk is a dramatic introduction to Valnontey and the magnificent Gran Paradiso Range. It is best walked in the direction described so that you're heading towards the best views. The ascent from Valnontey is steep (750m for the day) but the path, narrow in places, is well graded, adequately signposted and waymarked.

It is quite common for places to be named 'Money' around Valle d'Aosta; this is of ancient origin and believed to mean shared, or perhaps common, pasture.

PLANNING
See Maps (p116).

When to Walk
Several stream crossings would make the walk extremely hazardous, if not impossible, during the spring thaw and after heavy rain. The simple bridge over the youthful Torrente Valnontey regularly falls victim to its turbulent waters – check locally that it exists before setting out. If there's any doubt, the walk to Alpe Money and back is well worthwhile; allow about six hours. Until about late June, snow drifts may linger on the route from Alpe Money to the head of the valley.

THE WALK (see map p127)
From the cluster of signposts by the Valnontey village bridge, set out along the broad vehicle track (following route 23). On the eastern side of the river pass Camping Gran Paradiso, then head through conifer woodland. Soon you pass the miniscule settlement of **Valmianaz** where a restored house on the right displays some fine timberwork.

About 45 minutes from Valnontey the track narrows to path width, and 10 minutes further on you reach a junction. Turn left up the path marked 20. It rises steeply to a line of cliffs, with magnificent views of the valley and enclosing peaks, then finds an ingenious route up through the cliffs, across open ground, above another cliff line and into a wide valley with the leading edge of Ghiacciaio di Patri looming almost overhead. On a broad platform breaking the steepness of the mountainside, the path then crosses huge rock slabs to **Alpe Money** (about one hour from the path junction). At an altitude of 2325m, there are at least five recognisable structures, one roofed and seemingly liveable. The magnificent view across the valley to Gran Paradiso and its spectacular satellites and glaciers dictates a lunch stop here.

The path onwards (route 21) is easy to follow, with cairns and yellow waymarkers, southwards over narrow spurs and across the intervening streams. One of these streams may be bridged – logs were waiting to be installed when the walk was surveyed. Patches of crimson-flowering alpenrose and dwarf willow bring colour to a landscape of greys and whites. About an hour from Alpe Money, descend the narrow crest of a long spur northwestwards, cross two streams and more moraine to the bridge over Torrente Valnontey (approximately two hours from Alpe Money).

Head downstream close to the river for about 50m then go through a patch of larches and continue boulder-hopping downstream for about 100m. The route then gradually swings away from the river; about 25 minutes from the bridge, at a prominent path junction, keep to the right along path 23. It makes for relatively easy walking down the valley, with mighty cliffs soaring above. About 30 minutes from the path junction, cross substantial Ponte dell'Erfaulet over Torrente Valnontey; it's then just on an hour to Valnontey village.

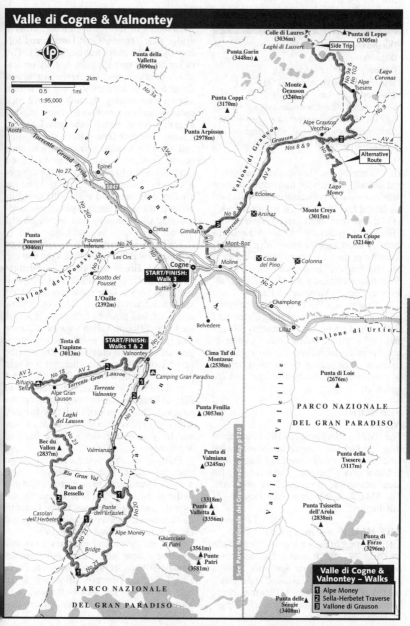

Valle di Cogne & Valnontey

0   0.5   1   2km
0   0.5   1mi

1:95,000

Valle di Cogne & Valnontey – Walks

1. Alpe Money
2. Sella-Herbetet Traverse
3. Vallone di Grauson

WESTERN ALPS

Sella-Herbetet Traverse

Duration	6¾–7¼ hours
Distance	15km
Difficulty	demanding
Start/Finish	Valnontey (p117)
Transport	bus

Summary An incredibly exhilarating and scenic traverse high on the precipitous western side of Valnontey, along a narrow path, exposed in places, with plenty of wildlife for company.

This is one of *the* classic walks in PNGP, and all Valle d'Aosta for that matter. It starts with an ascent to popular Rifugio Sella (see the boxed text 'Italy's First National Park', p114); between there and Casolari dell'Herbetet (a park rangers base to the south) there's a short, airy traverse with a length of chain for protection, where you need a good head for heights. The day's ascent is 1180m. From the casolari, it's downhill virtually all the way back to Valnontey village.

The views across the valley to the spiky peaks and small glaciers lining the eastern skyline and around to the mighty Ghiacciaio Tribolazione below Gran Paradiso itself, are awesome indeed. Herds of ibex and chamois graze peacefully on steep patches of grass and you should also hear and see marmots.

PLANNING
Maps
The IGC 1:25,000 map No 101 *Gran Paradiso, La Grivola, Cogne* has a somewhat fanciful depiction of route 23 (Rifugio Sella to Casolari dell'Herbetet) but it is useful for identification of features along the route. The FMB 1:50,000 map *Gran Paradiso* is satisfactory.

THE WALK (see map p127)
The first stage of the walk up to **Rifugio Sella** (☎ 0165 743 10; ⓦ www.rifugiosella.com; nonmembers €33; open April–late Sept) is straightforward and is described under Day 1 (p119) of the Valnontey to Rhêmes Notre Dame walk, where full details of Rifugio Sella are also given.

To continue from Rifugio Sella, go to the left (south) of the main building, cross a bridge over Torrente Gran Lauson and follow the wide path (waymarked 23). The rather broken-up path goes directly up and across the slope, over the crest of a spur and down a bit as Valnontey opens up ahead. Then it's up steadily, through massive rock outcrops and on into a wide valley, passing a small pond on the left – the main Lago del Lauson. The path then skirts a small valley and rises to a large cairn where it ends on the crest of a spur of Bec du Vallon (2837m), 35 to 40 minutes from the *rifugio*. It's worth pausing here, before tackling the serious stuff ahead, to absorb the magnificence of the view: the peaks lining the eastern side of Valnontey and the depths of Vallone di Grauson beyond Cogne.

The traverse starts with several metres across awkwardly angled rock, then you can cling to a firmly anchored, head-height chain, where handholds are scarce and footholds only a little more plentiful, until you reach a wooden ramp. Then the narrow and much less exposed path zigzags across the folds of Bec du Vallon's southern slopes. The path contours easily across steep grassed slopes and crosses two streams (the second of which could present a slight problem after heavy rain). Then it's across a boulder field to the welcome flatness of **Pian di Ressello** (about two hours from the *rifugio*). This is an extraordinary balcony with cliffs above, precipitous slopes below and truly awesome views to the head of Valnontey.

Follow the path southwest and down from the edge of Pian di Ressello. Beyond a small stream, the path narrows and the nothingness to the left is momentarily apparent. Soon enough you reach **Casolari dell'Herbetet,** another magnificent lookout (30 minutes from Pian di Ressello).

The path then twists and turns down to a junction – bear left; it eventually reaches Ponte dell'Erfaulet (locally known as Ponte Erfollet) over Torrente Valnontey. From here it's easy going back to the village of Valnontey (2¼ hours from Casolari dell'Herbetet).

Terraced vineyards and famous villages – the Cinque Terre's Vernazza spills into the Ligurian Sea

Colourful Portofino, where Italy's rich get away from it all

Sentiero Azzuro in Manarola

Peaceful Torrente Valnontey

The Marguareis massif, Parco Naturale dell'Alta Valle Pesio e Tanaro

Picking *lamponi* (raspberries) on the descent from Rifugio Pagarì to San Giacomo

Cloud fills Vallone del Muraion, Parco Naturale delle Alpi Marittime

Spectacular Valle d'Aosta

Vallone di Grauson

Duration	7¾–8¼ hours
Distance	20km
Difficulty	demanding
Start/Finish	Cogne (p116)
Transport	bus

Summary A choice of beautiful alpine lakes, high above meadows carpeted with colourful wildflowers, and with awesome views of peaks above Valnontey and Valle di Cogne.

Vallone di Grauson reaches deep into the range of peaks northeast of Cogne and is just outside PNGP. Its lower reaches are rugged and precipitous, with small meadows and patches of larch woodland between the cliffs; Torrente Grauson thunders down in waterfalls and cascades. Higher up, the valley widens and looks relatively benign with its grassy expanses divided by low moraine ridges and streams, and dotted with stone huts, some still used by herdsmen during midsummer cattle grazing.

Laghi di Lussert, a chain of three tarns, the highest at 2907m, lies below the colourful cliffs of Punta di Laures (3367m) and Punta di Leppe (3305m) and is the objective for this longish, exceptionally scenic day. The daunting amount of ascent (1400m) comes in stages and is generally on good paths. The route is waymarked and signposted, though you need to be aware of the local geography to interpret some of the signs. Route 4 (in a triangle) is the long distance route AV4 (see the boxed text 'Mountain Odysseys – Long Distance Routes', p130).

The walk can start in either Cogne or the village of Gimillan, about 2km to the north.

PLANNING
What to Bring
Carry some water; there's a *sorgente* (spring) at Alpe Grauson Vecchio (1¼ hours from Cogne), which produces delicious water almost too cold to drink.

Maps
There's no 1:25,000 coverage of this walk so you have to use either the Kompass or FMB 1:50,000 maps (see Maps, p116). The *Try the Trails* leaflet from the AIAT at Cogne (p116) lists this walk as No 32.

GETTING TO/FROM THE WALK
See Getting There & Away (p117) under Cogne. You can save at least 45 minutes and 250m of ascent by catching the bus to Gimillan (€0.80, 12 minutes, frequent daily service late June to mid-September, once a day Tuesday and Friday mornings at other times). By car, the Gimillan road winds up from a crossroads immediately over the bridge at the eastern end of Cogne. There is a large car park on the left of the road at the edge of the village, about 2.5km from Cogne.

THE WALK (see map p127)
To reach Gimillan on foot, head east along the road through Cogne and follow it across the bridge over Torrente Grand Eyvia. Cross the main Cogne–Lillaz road to the corner of the Gimillan road and walk up a path signposted to Gimillan. Turn left at a road by an old hospital and follow it for about 250m to a path on the left way-marked 8. Go up beside some conifers on the right and on to the road. Turn left for about 20m, cross the road and ascend a path with a field on the left, to the road again. Then it's left for just 20m; cross and continue up a path ahead to the road; cross it once more and go straight up to meet the road close to a large car park on the left at the edge of Gimillan. Walk past the car park and bus stop and on up the road to a clutch of footpath signs on the right. Bear right between houses, pass a small car park, cross the road and follow the signposted path (routes No 8 and 9) up through fields. At a T-junction, it's right, the path quickly taking you into the embrace of Vallone di Grauson. Keep right at a fork then descend to a bridge over Torrente Grauson (1¼ hours from Cogne).

Cross the bridge and turn left along a path, bypassing the old buildings of **Ecloseur**, up the valley. A line of cliffs ahead across the valley is easily surmounted. Then you cross a small meadow, skirt the southeast

WESTERN ALPS

end of low cliffs, traverse another meadow and continue along the steep mountainside. Just over an hour from the Torrente Grauson bridge, you reach a large crucifix and then a path junction. This is the parting of the ways if you're heading for Lago Money (see Alternative Route: Lago Money, p131).

For Laghi di Lussert, head down into the spacious valley towards the neat group of stone buildings that is **Alpe Grauson Vecchio**. Shortly before a bridge, a small sign points to the *sorgente* on the right. Head upstream beside Torrente Grauson (on your left) to another bridge; cross it to a sheltered meadow then ascend beside a stream to a

Mountain Odysseys – Long Distance Routes

To really get to know the Alps you need to spend a week or more walking over the passes and through the valleys, free from the confines of a busy itinerary.

Four high-level waymarked routes in the area covered by this chapter offer opportunities to do just this. You could spend up to four weeks following at least two of these, with side trips to summits and other features thrown in. The routes are: Valle d'Aosta's Alta Via 1 (AV1), Alta Via 2 (AV2) and Alta Via 4 (AV4), and the Tour of Monte Rosa (TMR). All are essentially walking routes; the few sections (such as glacier crossings) requiring special equipment and skills can be avoided. They're all strenuous – in the space of a week you could easily climb a couple of Everests. The high passes (some above 3000m) usually hold snow until mid-June, so the ideal time to walk is from late June to mid-September.

An immense variety of superb scenery is guaranteed all the way and wildlife encounters (with ibex, marmots and chamois) are certain in PNGP. Although the routes mainly follow paths, all involve some road walking on gravel or bitumen; if this is anathema it's possible to devise a route that almost completely avoids roads. Accommodation is in *rifugi* with the chance to stay in hotels in villages along the way. Public transport access points are plentiful.

The routes are marked on the 1:25,000 and 1:50,000 topographic maps (see under Maps for individual walks), although you'll almost certainly find some diversions, necessitated by landslides and floods. Good maps are essential – waymarking varies from good to nonexistent, though it is better for the AV1 and AV2 than the other two routes. Two Cicerone guides are useful, if a bit dated: *Long Distance Walks in the Gran Paradiso & Southern Valdotain* by JW Akitt and *The Grand Tour of Monte Rosa* (Vols 1 & 2) by CJ Wright. Gillian Price's *Walking in Italy's Gran Paradiso* covers the AV1 in outline and in many separate walks. *Valle d'Aosta Alta Vie 1, 2*, a booklet available free from Aosta AIAT and PNGP offices, contains 1:50,000 topographic maps plus handy tables showing times between major staging points and facilities available. You'd also need the accommodation guides issued by the UIT in Aosta (p113). The routes are:

AV1 goes from Gressoney St Jean to Courmayeur via St Jacques, Valtournenche, uppermost reach of Val Sant' Barthélemy, Valpelline, Val del Gran San Bernardo and Val Ferret. Allow seven to nine days; no pass is over 2800m.

AV2 goes from Courmayeur to Château Champorcher via Val Veny, Col des Chavannes, La Thuile, Rifugio Deffeyes, Passo Alto, Col de la Crosatie, Planaval, Valgrisenche, Col di Finestra, Rhêmes Notre Dame, Col di Entrelor, Eaux Rousses, Col Lauson, Valnontey, Cogne, Lillaz, Finestra di Champorcher and Dondena. Allow nine to 10 days; the highest pass is Col Lauson (3296m).

AV4 comprises several diversions from AV2: from above Val Veni; between La Thuile, Valgrisenche and Val di Rhêmes; an alternative route to Valsavarenche; from Valnontey to Gimillan and on to Dondena. Four passes lie above 3000m; allow at least six days.

TMR is a Swiss-Italian route; the Italian section links Valpelline and Valsesia. It partly follows the AV1 and elsewhere goes higher up the valleys; many variations are possible. Two passes higher than 3000m are optional; allow at least seven days.

signposted path junction. Following paths 9 and 9a go up (generally north), over flowery meadows. Where the path divides go left, soon passing a lone stone building, and up to another junction on the edge of a basin. Here, bear left towards Colle di Laures along the route numbered both 9 and 102. The path takes you up to the row of well-maintained stone buildings that is **Alpe Tsesere** (an hour from Alpe Grauson Vecchio).

Continue on path 9a/102; having crossed two small streams, go right at a path junction with a 9a waymarker. This takes you up into a spacious valley; cross its wide expanses, passing the rather amorphous low-ermost Lago Lussert. The middle lake is about 300m further west; go up the left hand (southern) slope, then head northwest to reach the upper lake (an hour from Alpe Tsesere), from where Colle di Laures is easy to pick on the skyline to the northeast (see the Side Trip, p132).

Retracing your steps to return; it takes about 3½ hours to reach Cogne. Views of the Gran Paradiso Range spread across the skyline constantly seize your attention.

Alternative Route: Lago Money
5½–6 hours, 16km, 1000m ascent

On the southern side of Vallone di Grauson, Lago Money, cradled below an arc of peaks (topped by Penne Blanche, 3254m), is a less taxing objective than Laghi di Lussert. Follow the main route to the path junction near the crucifix above Alpe Grauson Vec-chio, then take path 8a, gaining height quickly to a wide valley. Just around a bend leave the wide path and go right, up a spur, and follow yellow arrows along a narrower path. This leads up to a split level basin,

Walser Heritage

Between the 12th and 15th centuries Walser people migrated south from Switzerland and settled the more intractable and remote reaches of Val d'Ayas, Valle di Gressoney and Valsesia. At that time the climate was mild enough to make high-level settlement possible. Until the climate cooled in the 18th century, a settlement in Val d'Ayas was among the highest in Europe, at 2072m.

Many Walser villages survive and the landscape still bears the mark of their activities. Walser ham-lets were clusters of two-storey timber-and-stone houses, each with the dwelling, storage and ani-mal shelter under one roof and with ingenious design features allowing ventilation and heat conservation. Most hamlets had a communal oven and forge, and a chapel. Forests were cleared to provide timber for building and space for grazing and cultivation on terraces. Canals were labori-ously dug; some are still used.

Colle di Valdobbia and Colle Pinter were on frequently used routes between the valleys; sections of the paths were lined with upended stones or timber fences – some are still intact.

As the Industrial Revolution progressed during the 19th century, the people left the valleys and agriculture began a long decline, only halted recently. Tourism began to bring back some prosper-ity to the valleys from the 1950s, but at the price of attrition of Walser traditions. Now in Valle d'Aosta the traditions live on in Valle di Gressoney, while Alagna Valsesia is the stronghold in Valsesia. Houses are being restored, relatively remote villages remain inhabited and the Walser heritage has become a tourist attraction.

The Sentiero Walser (SW) draws much of this together. It's a long-distance route from Colle di San Teodulo, northeast of Valtournenche, to St Jacques, over Colle Pinter to Gressoney La Trinité and Gressoney St Jean and up to Colle di Valdobbia. The route, signposted at crucial junctions, is easy enough to follow and there are elaborate information boards at many interesting features along the way. A booklet, *Il Grande Sentiero Walser*, is available from local tourist offices. The excellent **Museo Walser** (☎ 0163 92 29 35; admission €2.10; open afternoons daily in midsummer; Sat, Sun & holiday afternoons at other times) in the village of Pedemonte, close to Alagna, houses a vast number of artefacts in a typical Walser building and is worth a visit.

WESTERN ALPS

divided by a massive moraine bank. Continue across the basin, and go up the bank to the shore of the tarn. Retrace your steps back to Gimillan and Cogne.

Side Trip: Colle di Laures
1 hour, 2km, 130m ascent
In midsummer very fit walkers should be able to climb from the topmost lake of Laghi di Lussert, over snow-free but rather steep and rocky ground to Colle di Laures (3036m), for great views into Valle d'Aosta.

Valle d'Aosta to Valsesia

This section takes in three valleys – Valtournenche, Val d'Ayas, Valle di Gressoney – on the northern side of Valle d'Aosta, and upper Valsesia in Piedmont, all reaching down from the long mountainous chain forming the border with Switzerland and dominated by the Matterhorn and Monte Rosa. This area is not in a national park – as is obvious from the multifarious and incongruous developments for skiing, epitomised in the artificial town of Breuil-Cervinia at the head of Valtournenche. Yet the scenery is truly magnificent in scale, diversity and extent: *pics*, *puntas* and *testas* (all mountain peaks of subtly differing shapes), dominated by the Matterhorn and Monte Rosa. Wildlife is scarce, apart from ubiquitous marmots, but the countless meadows are exceptionally rich in wildflowers.

In three of the four valleys – Ayas, Gressoney and Sesia – the history and traditions of the Walser people are an integral part of the landscape and proudly upheld. They offer many fascinating insights into a tough, enduring way of life now rare in Western Europe (see the boxed text 'Walser Heritage', p131).

This section is devoted to a flexible three-day walk from Valtournenche to Riva Valdobbia or Alagna Valsesia; for suggestions for further walking in Valtournenche and from Alagna Valsesia see Valle d'Aosta to Valsesia (p141).

Matterhorn & Monte Rosa

Duration	3 days
Distance	50km
Difficulty	demanding
Start	Valtournenche (p133)
Finish	Alagna Valsesia (p134)
Transport	bus

Summary An exceptionally scenic walk linking four contrasting valleys, in the presence of two Alpine giants: the Matterhorn and Monte Rosa; the Walser people's history and culture provide a unifying theme.

This is essentially a valley-to-valley walk, crossing passes, none of which is above 3000m, between each of the valleys. It is *not* an ascent of the two Alpine giants!

The walk starts in the town of Valtournenche, in the valley of the same name (with the Matterhorn at its head) and finishes in either Riva Valdobbia or Alagna Valsesia, in upper Valsesia, below Monte Rosa's southeast faces. Total ascent is 3725m. The route follows part of the AV1 (see the boxed text 'Mountain Odysseys – Long Distance Routes', p130), from Valtournenche to Gressoney St Jean, then the Sentiero Walser (SW; see the boxed text 'Walser Heritage', p131) from St Jacques to Colle di Valdobbia. The walk then follows a waymarked route to Riva Valdobbia and up to Alagna Valsesia.

Waymarking and signposting of the routes varies from excessive to rare, along paths, tracks and short stretches of quiet road. Point to point times given on signposts seem to match those taken by fit walkers. In several places, small landslides had ripped out sizeable chunks of path when the walk was surveyed (July 2001) but it was still possible to pass. Some sections of path are more like scree slopes than paths.

If you're interested in adapting the route, each of the three days of walking is self-contained, with public transport available. A more leisurely itinerary could be spread over as many as six days.

In each of the valleys, there's a choice of accommodation, in either *rifugi* or hotels.

Camping would be a heroic option, considering the amount of ascent.

PLANNING
When to Walk
The passes on the route of this walk should be clear of snow from mid-June until late September. The *rifugi* are open for approximately the same period.

What to Bring
Before mid-June an ice axe may be necessary and gaiters are recommended. During summer, it can be unbelievably hot, so a hat, sunglasses and sunscreen are essential.

Maps
On all but the local maps, path numbers may differ from those on the ground. You'll be able to find at least some of the following maps in the villages and towns en route.

For positive identification of features, the IGC 1:25,000 series is superior: maps Nos 108 *Cervino-Breuil Cervinia-Champoluc* and 109 *Monte Rosa-Alagna V-Macugnaga-Gressoney*.

In the Kompass 1:50,000 series, the maps are Nos 87 *Breuil-Cervinia-Zermatt* and 88 *Monte Rosa*. These include detailed notes in German and Italian.

In IGC's 1:50,000 series, easier to read than Kompass, the maps are No 5 *Cervino-Matterhorn e Monte Rosa* and No 10 *Monte Rosa, Alagna e Macugnaga*.

Two local maps are also valuable. The Comune di Valtournenche's 1:25,000 *Alta Valle* comes in several languages and shows all the waymarked paths in the valley. It's available free from the tourist office in Valtournenche (this page). *Gressoney Monte Rosa* is a 1:35,000 map covering the area from Monte Rosa to the town of Gaby and showing all the waymarked paths and many others. It is available from the *tabaccheria* in Gressoney St Jean (p138). Check with the tourist office about damaged paths which were officially closed after the October 2000 floods.

Information Sources
Each valley has a tourist office, and most are useful for accommodation information; contact details are listed with town information. Alternatively, the accommodation guides available from the UIT at Aosta (p113) cover all but Valsesia.

Place Names
Many places have dual Italian-French or Italian-German identities. The Italian names are used here, except where another name is better known to English-language speakers, ie, the Matterhorn rather than Il Cervino. Some variations exist between the spelling of names in the maps quoted and local signposts; the local spelling is given here as far as possible.

Guided Walks
The **Corpo Guide Alagna** (*☎/fax 0163 913 10; *ⓦ www.guidealagna.com; Piazza Grober*) in Alagna Valsesia has a long and honourable history of guiding on Monte Rosa. You can join a group of four to climb to Capanna Margherita (4559m and the highest *rifugio* in the Alps); it will cost around €180 for the guide and equipment, plus the night at the *rifugio* and use of the Monrosa *funivia* (cable car) and chair lift.

NEAREST TOWNS
Valtournenche
This is the name of both the long valley extending to the foot of the Matterhorn and this attractive small town, which is still a traditional mountain village at heart. The surrounding housing developments, mainly to lure winter skiers, aren't too incongruous, although some ski lifts and facilities wouldn't win architecture prizes.

In Piazza della Chiesa, alpine history enthusiasts will be interested in the walls that are covered with memorial plaques to early mountain guides and alpinists.

For tourist information try **UIAT** (*☎ 0166 920 29, fax 0166 924 30; *ⓔ valtournenche@ netvallee.it; Via Roma 45; open daily*).

Places to Stay & Eat Many of the hotels have their own restaurants and offer half board, which is good value since eating is otherwise largely confined to pizzerias in the main street.

WESTERN ALPS

Camping Glair (☎ *0166 920 77, fax 0166 920 80;* e *campingglair@netvallee.it; Loc Glair; camping per person/site €4.65/4.75),* 3km south of the town, has a bar, restaurant and laundry.

Hotel Montana (☎ *0166 920 23, fax 0166 931 31; Via Roma 37; half board €41)* is a welcoming establishment, with slightly old-fashioned, but clean and spacious rooms. Some of the rooms have a balcony and valley views. The hotel's substantial three-course evening meal usually includes local specialties.

For self-caterers there is a **CRAI super-market** *(open Tues-Sun),* two *alimentari (open daily)* and two **greengrocers**, all in the main street.

Getting There & Away First you have to reach Chatillon in Valle d'Aosta. Trains on the Chivasso–Aosta line stop here (several daily). **SADEM** (☎ *011 300 06 06)* buses from Milan and Turin to Courmayeur (see Getting There & Away, p115) stop here. The SADEM Aosta–Ivrea bus also goes to Chatillon (€1.80). Make sure you alight at the bus station, which is some distance from the train station.

From the Chatillon bus station, **SAVDA** (☎ *0165 26 20 27)* buses go to Valtournenche (€1.80, one hour, seven a day).

By car, Chatillon is 24km east of Aosta via S26 or the A5; from there SR406 takes you the 19km to Valtournenche.

Alagna Valsesia

A convenient base for local walks, Alagna Valsesia is a small town with its mind very firmly oriented towards Monte Rosa. At Alagna's **Pro Loco Tourist Office** (☎ *0163 92 29 88, fax 0163 912 02; Piazza Grober; open daily)* you can pick up a guide to local services, a brochure about Walser villages, a basic map of local paths, and transport information. The office is also the point of contact for the Corpo Guide Alagna (see Guided Walks, p133) if you fancy tackling Monte Rosa. Maps and books are sold at **Bazar-Souvenir** *(Via Centra).* Stove fuel is available from **Articoli Sportivi** opposite Ristorante Stolemberg.

Places to Stay & Eat At the southern end of the town, near the junction of the bypass and town centre roads, is **Campeggio Alagna** (☎*/fax 0163 92 29 47;* w *www.campeggio alagna.com; camping per person/site €3.90/ 3.60).* It has limited space for tents, close to the river. **Residence Mirella** (☎*/fax 0163 92 29 65; rooms €38.80),* a lively and friendly place, is close to the Monrosa *funivia.* Each room has a compact kitchen. The rooms are above a busy *pasticceria* (cake shop), thronged with climbers and walkers; the coffee, snacks and cakes are superb.

There are two *alimentari (Via Centro).* One of Alagna's several restaurants, **Ristorante Stolemberg** (☎ *0163 92 32 01; Via Centro 40),* confronts you with an enormous pizza, excellent ravioli and a good espresso.

Getting There & Away The bus service operated by **ATAP** (☎ *015 848 84 11, fax 015 40 13 98)* between Alagna Valsesia and Vercelli stops at Varallo (€2.50, one hour, five a day); buy tickets at the *tabaccheria* next to Hotel Cristallo. The bus stops at Riva Valdobbia, but on the main road not in the village. At Varallo you can connect with trains to Novara (€8.25, 1¼ hours, four a day) from where there are good connections to Milan and Turin. At Varallo buy train and bus tickets from the bar on the station.

Baranzelli (☎ *0163 83 41 25)* buses travel between Alagna and Milan (Piazza Castello) via Varallo and Novara (three a day). Buy a ticket on board.

STN (☎ *0321 47 26 47)* buses link Novara train station and Milan Malapensa airport (€6.70, six a day).

By road, Alagna is at the end of the S299, which branches from S142 at Romagnano (between Biella and Arona); alternatively leave the A26 at the Romagnano exit; Alagna is 23km further.

THE WALK
Day 1: Valtournenche to St Jacques
5¾–6¼ hours, 15km, 1275m ascent
Towards the southern end of Valtournenche village, join the AV1 at a junction of the main road with a road signposted to Cretaz. A few

metres along this road take the first right, signposted to Cheneil. Follow this minor road for about 250m, then go left up steps between houses in Cretaz and shortly turn right along a narrow lane; 150m along continue ahead at a junction. The path crosses Torrente Cheneil and soon leads into forest; bear left at a Y-junction. It's a steep climb; follow waymarkers at the next two junctions. About 45 minutes from Valtournenche, cross a gravel road and go up to the gently sloping meadows and scattered houses of Promindoz. Cross the gravel road diagonally left and go up a wide path signposted to Cheneil. About 50m further on, the path swings right across a field; then on the edge of a forest ascend steeply left beside a stream. Shortly, ignore a path left and continue up to the edge of spacious meadows and on to the signposted path junction at **Cheneil** (40 minutes from Promindoz). Have a drink on the terrace at **Hotel Panorama Bich** (☎/fax 0166 920 19; e cheneil@libero.it; half board €41.30) and contemplate the Matterhorn in all its glory. In this tall, traditional stone building some rooms have Cervino-gazing balconies; facilities are shared. The evening meal is first-rate, and may include genuine minestrone. Advance booking is recommended. Cheneil comprises a few chalets, the hotel and a small chapel.

Continue straight (southeast) on a wide path that soon leads into the beautiful upper reaches of the valley, dotted with larches and alpenrose. At Champsec, a long, low deserted building set into the slope, go up to the left; the path continues to gain height, skirting a small basin – good marmot country – and on to **Col des Fontaines** (2700m, one to 1½ hours from Cheneil). On a good day, the magnificent view takes in the multitudinous peaks of PNGP to the southwest.

Then it's east down the path towards the head of the valley below. The path soon starts to regain height and reaches **Colle di Nana** (2775m), 40 minutes from Col des Fontaines. The outlook is eternally memorable – the sprawling glaciers, snowfields and cliffs of the Monte Rosa massif, nearby to the northeast, and the mountains south of Valle d'Aosta's depths in the opposite direction.

The descent starts with the path worming through boulders and down a narrow cleft. It's then slightly exposed for about 100m across a precipitous slope; the rest of the descent to a gravel road is straightforward (40 minutes from Colle di Nana).

Rifugio Grand Tournalin (☎ 0125 30 70 03; beds €25.80, half board €36.15), built in the late 1990s, is a few minutes up to the left. At lunchtime, it offers pasta, minestrone, torte and drinks.

Continue down the gravel road; from the second derelict stone building on the right, follow a waymarked diversion. Further down, cross the road and go down through fields. When you reach the road again, go right for a few metres and take another waymarked shortcut, then another down towards an *alpe* (mountain pasture) to a grassed vehicle track. Turn left and after 20m, bear right down a path which descends through conifers to a road. Then it's left for about 25m and down to the right to another house. Descend past a tiny shrine on the left, on a clear path across fields, past a wooden crucifix and back into forest briefly. Then, via more fields, you reach some houses; go between two on the left and one on the right and follow the path down to a bitumen road. Cross the bridge here and you've reached St Jacques (1½ hours from Rifugio Tournalin).

St Jacques

This tiny village, where time seems to have stood still, has many fascinating buildings – well worth a wander. The nearest camping ground, **Sole e Neve** (☎/fax 0125 30 66 10; camping per person/site €5/8), is at Morenex (Ayas), about 10km southwest of the village. In St Jacques, **Hotel Genzianella** (☎ 0125 30 71 56, fax 0125 30 81 47; w www.hotelgenzianella.it; Place de la Grotte 5; half board €75) offers good rooms, most with private bathroom.

Bar Fior Roccia offers snacks and light meals. **Bar Lago Blu** is near Place de la Grotte. There's a small *alimentari* and **La Cretza**, which sells phone cards and maps.

Information for Valle d'Ayas is available at Champoluc **AIAT** (☎ 0125 30 71 13, fax 0125

30 77 85; e info@libero.it; Via Varasc 16; open daily), a five-minute bus ride down the valley. Champoluc is a sizeable town with a far greater choice of accommodation and you can join the route for Day 2 there – the price of Champoluc's comforts is 120m extra ascent.

Valdostana Impresa Trasporti Automobilistici (VITA; ☎ 0125 96 65 46) operates services between St Jacques and Verrès in Valle d'Aosta (one hour, seven a day), from where there are connections within the valley and to Milan and Turin. See Getting There & Away (p134) for Valtourneche.

Day 2: St Jacques to Gressoney St Jean
7½–8 hours, 17km, 1350m ascent

If you're starting from Champoluc, it's best to locate waymarked route 13 to Crest in the town centre.

In St Jacques, a few steps downhill from the bridge, turn left along Chemin de Resy (with a waymarker for route 9 and sign for Rifugio Frachey). Beyond the small cluster of traditional houses, follow route 9 up towards Resy (as signposted). The wide path gains height in conifer forest, crosses a meadow below a lone house, then goes

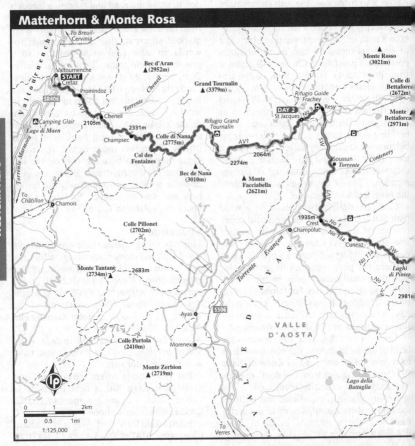

Matterhorn & Monte Rosa

To Breuil-Cervinia

Valtourneche

Valtournenche
START
Cretaz
Promindoz

Camping Glair
Lago di Maen
Torrente Marmora

2105m
Cheneil

Bec d'Aran
(2952m)

Cheneil

2331m
Champsec

Colle di Nana
(2775m)

Col des Fontaines

To Châtillon
Chamois

Colle Pillonet
(2702m)

Monte Tantanè
(2734m) 2683m

Grand Tournalin
(3379m)

Rifugio Grand Tournalin

Bec de Nana
(3010m)

2274m

2064m

Monte Facciabella
(2621m)

Rifugio Guide Frachey

DAY 2 No 9 Resy
St Jacques

Monte Rosso
(3021m)

Colle di Bettaforca
(2672m)

Monte Bettaforca
(2971m)

Soussun
Torrente

AV1

SW

Contenery

1935m
Crest
Champoluc

No 1
No 13a

Cuneaz

No 11a
No 1

SW

Laghi di Pinter

2981

Ayas

Colle Portola
(2410m)

Monte Zerbion
(2719m)

Morenex

Torrente Evançon

VALLE D'AOSTA

Lago della Battaglia

To Verres

0   1   2km
0 0.5 1mi
1:125,000

WESTERN ALPS

above it and past two older buildings. The steep ascent persists to the settlement of **Resy** from where there are excellent views down Val d'Ayas (50 minutes from St Jacques).

At Resy, the **Rifugio Guide Frachey** (☎ *0125 30 71 89, fax 0125 30 71 65;* **e** *kauft@libero.it; B&B around €40)* offers a possible alternative to staying in St Jacques. There's also **Rifugio Ferraro** here, but at the time of writing it was closed for repairs.

To continue, head south and about 50m beyond Rifugio Ferraro, follow the signposted Sentiero Walser (SW; destination Crest), down fields to a narrow path which

contours a small valley, then leads to a very shaky bridge. Cross it and continue along a vehicle track. About 15 minutes from Resy, turn right and go down a wide track; about 150m beyond the end of a ski lift, turn right at a junction and descend to a gravel road. Here a SW signpost points you ahead towards Crest. Beyond various skiing installations, the road ascends to a junction; bear right here with the SW. A few minutes further on, stay above the traditional buildings of the hamlet of Soussun and contour to a gravel road. Shortly you pass the remains of a water mill where you can make out the

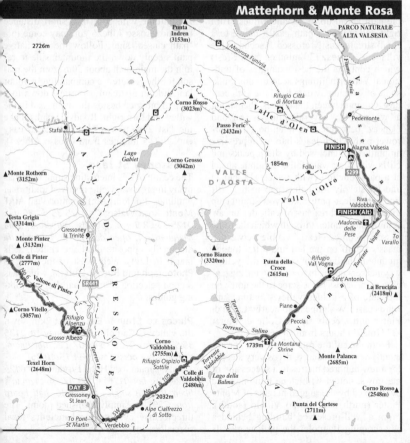

Matterhorn & Monte Rosa

date 1601 on a timber beam. The vehicle track descends to cross Torrente Contenery, then regains the height fitfully. Around a bend, you come to a SW sign directing you down to the right towards Crest; the path may be overgrown but can be bypassed in the adjacent field. Turn right at a gravel road for 60m then go left, indicated by a signpost to Colle Pinter, and you will soon reach a chapel. From here go down through the old village of **Crest** to a water trough liberally decorated with waymarkers (1½ hours from Resy).

Continue on the path up Valle di Cuneaz (waymarked 13a and 1); cross a gravel road a few hundred metres further on and stay on the path ahead up to a vehicle track. Turn right and follow a path past a house to a small stream, easily crossed. Ascend to the village of **Cuneaz** (30 minutes from Crest) which contains the best examples of traditional Walser buildings seen on this walk, some of which may date from the 15th century. Go up between the houses, then along a wide path; several minutes beyond Cuneaz, bear left at a junction on a narrower path which leads into an impressive amphitheatre, enclosed by sharp peaks and cliffs with long waterfalls. Continue ahead at a path junction (with routes 11a and 1) and up steeply through a gap in the cliff line. The clear path takes you straight up these uppermost reaches of Valle di Cuneaz. A miraculous notch through which the route passes becomes clearly visible between a massive bluff on the left and a flat-topped mountain on the right. Follow the yellow waymarkers up the extremely steep, zigzagging path, across loose scree to the notch on the edge of a hidden valley. Continue upwards past SW signposts to nearby Laghi di Pinter and steeply up to Colle di Pinter (2777m, 2¼ hours from Cuneaz).

From the col the rocky path, most prominently waymarked as 6, drops very steeply for a few hundred metres to a succession of meadows, dotted with stone buildings and overlooked by the rugged heights of Monte Pinter (north) and Corno Vitello (south). From a well-preserved building behind a sky-scraping flagpole, the path works its way down the centre of steep-sided Vallone di Pinter. About an hour from Colle di Pinter, the floor of Valle di Gressoney comes into view as the path drops across a small stream and down the southern side of the valley to an *alpe*. Head straight down the slope (east-southeast) and make for a rectangular stone ruin, from where the way onwards along path 6 becomes clear. Descend across flowery meadows to stone and timber buildings and continue to the right with a SW signpost to **Grosso Albezo** – the Walser name for the next hamlet. Here you can find Rifugio Alpenzu, an attractive but, at the time of passing, lifeless timber building (1¾ hours from Colle di Pinter).

Continue with path 6; a short distance beyond Grosso Albezo you may come to a 'path closed' sign. Follow the alternative path steeply down the mountainside to rejoin the main path about 50m from the reason for the closure – a comparatively minor landslide in a stream. Continue down to a strip of bitumen beside the main road in the valley and turn right. Roadside paths make the last 2km to Gressoney St Jean easy enough (45 minutes from Grosso Albezo).

Gressoney St Jean

The centre of this interesting small town has many impressive, well-preserved traditional buildings. For tourist information visit **AIAT Monte Rosa Walser** (☎ 0125 35 51 85, fax 0125 35 58 95; e aptwalser@libero.it; Villa Margherita 1; open daily). The *tabaccheria* diagonally opposite the large church, sells maps. In Linty Weg, west of the *platz* is **Photograph und Bücher-Libreria**, which has a good selection of maps and Italian walking guides.

Places to Stay & Eat About 2km down the valley is **Camping Gressoney** (☎ 0125 35 52 64, fax 0125 35 64 07; Loc Bielciuken; camping per person/site €4.15/10.35).

On the main road **Hotel Lyskamm** (☎ 0125 35 54 36, fax 0125 35 59 17; e thyman@libero.it; B&B singles from €36, half board from €39) has simply furnished rooms. The three-course evening meal includes local specialties and is good value.

Hotel Grünes Wasser (☎/fax 0125 35 54 03; e camisasca@gressoney.it; B&B with shared facilities from €38.80), also on the main road, is a tall old building on the northern edge of the town.

There are two well-stocked **alimentari** on and near the central Obre Platz.

There are several not exactly inexpensive restaurants from which to choose, all focussing on local dishes. If you're suffering from pizza deprivation **Pizzeria Ristorante Principe** (☎ 0125 35 51 17), a popular spot on the eastern side of the main road, offers more than 25 varieties, including Gressonara, a formidable presentation with lots of local Fontina cheese.

Getting There & Away There are **VITA** (☎ 0125 96 65 46) buses from Pont St Martin in Valle d'Aosta to Gressoney (55 minutes, seven a day). Pont St Martin is on SADEM's Aosta–Ivrea and Milan/Turin–Aosta bus routes. Chivasso–Aosta trains stop here.

Day 3: Gressoney St Jean to Alagna Valsesia

6½–6¾ hours, 18km, 1100m ascent

Cross the bridge over Torrente Lys in Gressoney St Jean and walk south down the main road; on the far side of ornate **Villa Margherita** turn left along a path with a SW sign. It leads across a stone bridge and through the hamlet of Verdebbio. About 800m from the Villa, at Ondro Verdebbio, turn left up a path with a SW signpost to Colle di Valdobbia (for centuries an important trade and smuggling route), with waymarkers for routes 11 and 105. The path winds up the steep, wooded mountainside with good views down the valley. About 1¼ hours from Gressoney St Jean, the path swings to the east and into a deep valley. Within 10 minutes you should catch sight of the Colle – the pronounced dip between the skyline peaks, with a large building (Rifugio Ospizio Sottile) squatting in the middle.

Soon the route passes below **Alpe Cialfrezzo di Sotto** (where you could buy fresh butter and cheese) and then a simple footbridge takes you over the east branch of the torrente (river). Turn sharp right on the far side. The path zigzags up meadows and passes above Alpe Cialfrezzo di Sopra, then goes up the middle of the valley. In the upper reaches of the stream, where the path has been swallowed by a small landslip, it may be safer to cross downstream. Then it's straightforward although steep up to **Colle Valdobbia** (1½ hours from Alpe Cialfrezzo di Sotto). **Rifugio Ospizio Sottile** (☎ 0163 919 65) was closed at the time of writing. It'd be a great place to stay, with superb mountain-filled views east and west. A signpost here suggests it takes 2¾ hours to Riva Valdobbia, but this would necessitate seriously fast walking.

The path dives down from the edge of the col into the hanging valley below, then leads above Torrente Valdobbia thundering through a gorge. Beyond a boulder slope it winds down, and about 45 minutes from the col, comes to a junction. Ignore the narrow path ahead across a grassy spur and bear left – there are faint red and yellow waymarkers – soon alongside a stream, then down through cliffs and trees and on to a meadow with stone buildings. Go straight down to the right of the original line of the path, overgrown but marked by two rows of boulders. Here you can pause to take in the spectacular setting – long waterfalls on Torrente Rissuolo to the north and other streams framed by spiky peaks.

Continue a short distance and cross a bridge. Pass a small shrine; the path soon crosses a meadow between lines of boulders. Watch out for overgrowing nettles on the next stretch through woodland. Pass **La Montana shrine** (dated 1678) and go down to the dramatic merging of Torrente Sulino on the left and Torrente Vogna in the deep main valley (about two hours from the col). The wide path soon passes a chapel, then the village of **Peccia** with many fine Walserstyle buildings. About 15 minutes from the confluence, the path becomes a vehicle track and another 30 minutes brings you to the start of a bitumen road at the village of **Sant'Antonio**. Here you'll find **Rifugio-Bar-Trattoria Val Vogna** (☎ 0163 919 18; dorm beds around €9.80); booking is essential during July and August.

The quiet road steadily descends Val Vogna, past a couple more hamlets. About 2.2km from Sant'Antonio, just past the **church** of Madonna delle Pese, take the path to the right signposted 'Via delle Capelle', to cut off a wide bend. Back on the road, go downhill for 50m and diverge again for another short cut, and continue down to a road junction at the northwest end of **Riva Valdobbia** (45 minutes from Sant'Antonio), an alternative finish for the walk. With luck you'll be greeted by an awesome view of Monte Rosa presiding over upper Valsesia. This largish but compact village of mainly traditional-style buildings at the meeting of Val Vogna and Valsesia has a **bar**, *tabaccheria* and two small *alimentari*. **La Locanda della Ribebba** *(☎ 0163 910 31, fax 0161 27 14 66; e gigi.alessio@libero.it; half board €38.80)* has only six rooms; ring ahead to secure one. To find it, follow signs from the large church in the centre of Riva. The friendly owner speaks English. The bus serving Alagna Valsesia (see Getting There & Away, p134) stops here, but on the main road, not in the town.

To reach **Alagna Valsesia**, 2km further on, cross the road and go down to the main road (S299). Cross a footbridge over Fiume Sesia then turn left with a sign 'Sentiero per Alagna'. This road soon becomes a vehicle track and leads to the river bank. Follow this up to a footbridge; on the far side, turn right along the main road for about 250m to a side road next to the *municipio* building. This minor road leads to Via Centro (30 minutes from Riva); turn right to find the Pro Loco office and accommodation, or left to reach the *campeggio*.

Other Walks

PARCO NAZIONALE DEL GRAN PARADISO & NEARBY
Colonna
The earliest recorded mine was operating in Val di Cogne in 1679, but full-scale exploitation lasted for barely a century until 1979. The Colonna mine (at 2400m) was the centre of underground operations and the main output was magnetite, a source of iron ore. Innovations in transport, especially a *funivia*, overcame most of the problems of high-level operations, but the mine finally closed in 1979.

An informative brochure *Discovering Colonna's Mines* from the AIAT at Cogne describes the history of the mine at Colonna and outlines a circular walk from the **museum** *(☎ 0165 74 92 64)*, set to reopen along with restored mine buildings in 2003, to the mine site and back to Moline, near Cogne. However, this walk contains an extremely hazardous section across a precipitous rocky gully near the mine buildings and is not recommended.

Fortunately you should be able to reach Colonna from Moline, just across the bridge beyond the eastern end of Cogne. The path has yellow waymarkers – ignore occasional outbreaks of red-and-white stripes. Allow about four hours for the 8km return walk, which involves 860m ascent; it's well worth the effort for the superb views of Cogne and Valnontey. Use the IGC 1:25,000 map No 101 *Gran Paradiso, La Grivola, Cogne* map. The mine buildings are an anticlimax – they're too fragile for safe access. But the views and the experience of visiting a place that must have demanded nothing short of heroism to develop and maintain are good reasons for doing the walk.

Pousset
Punta Pousset's extraordinary tower of rock (3046m) is an attention-riveting feature of the view westwards from Cogne. Below its formidable slopes is a network of paths, along which a medium day walk from Cogne (or the downstream villages of Cretaz and Epinel) can take you through the woodlands on the southwest side of Val di Cogne up to the beautiful Vallone del Pousset, right below the Punta. The route is shown on the *Try the Trails* leaflet, available from the AIAT office in Cogne (p116).

The best map to use is the FMB 1:50,000 *Parco Nazionale Gran Paradiso*, though it doesn't show all the paths. It's worth noting that route 26b from Buttier (immediately across Torrente Valnontey from Cogne) to Les Ors was washed away in October 2000.

Allow about 5¾ hours from Cogne for the 13km walk; 850m of ascent is involved. Between the end of July and mid-August, the walk can be shortened by about 1½ hours by catching the bus from Cogne to Cretaz at the start, and from Epinel to Cogne at the finish.

Rifugio Walk
Rifugio Frederico Chabod and Rifugio Vittorio Emanuele II (a former royal hunting lodge) are perched high above Valsavarenche in the shadow

of Gran Paradiso and are popular bases for summit ascents. It is possible to visit them without any aspirations for the big climb, on a fine 14km high-level walk with 1250m of ascent; allow 6½ to seven hours. The walk also offers spectacular views of the glaciers of Gran Paradiso and crosses moraine ridges and boulder fields. It can fit into a fairly strenuous day, or be spread over two days by staying at one of the *rifugi*. Booking is essential during July and August, and highly advisable at other times at both **Rifugio Chabod** (☎ *0165 955 74;* **w** *www.rifugiochabod.com; beds €15.50, half board €31; open late Mar-early May & late June–mid-Sept)* and **Rifugio Vittorio Emanuele** (☎ *0165 959 20; beds €15.50, half board €31; open late Mar-late Sept).* The morning bus from Aosta to Pont drops you at the start of the path to Rifugio Chabod; a bus leaves Pont early in the evening. The IGC 1:25,000 map No 102 *Valsavarenche, Val di Rhêmes, Valgrisenche* is the one to take.

VALLE D'AOSTA TO VALSESIA
Valtournenche's Gran Balconata
The Gran Balconata is a circular waymarked route with Breuil-Cervinia and Torgnon as its northernmost and southernmost points respectively. It keeps well above the floor of the valley, passes through a few villages and hamlets, and is extremely scenic with the Matterhorn as a constant presence. There are also views of Monte Rosa, and a variety of terrain from steep mountainsides to meadows and grassland. It takes at least three days to go the full 40km distance; alternatively, it's easy to join and leave the route at several places and to return to your base by bus. There isn't much to choose between a clockwise direction or the reverse – the views are great either way.

The Kompass 1:50,000 map No 87 covers the whole route. The locally produced Comune di Valtournenche 1:25,000 map *Alta Valle* (available from the tourist office in Valtournenche) gives more detail, but cuts off a few kilometres north of Torgnon.

Valle di Otro & Valle d'Olen
Extending west from Alagna Valsesia, these two magnificently scenic valleys provide striking contrasts between Valsesia's past and present. In Valle di Otro are reputedly the finest Walser villages in the Alps, including Follu with its beautifully decorated church; Valle d'Olen shelters the Monrosa *funivia* and chairlifts, kept busy carrying skiers and climbers to Punta Indren (3260m) on Monte Rosa. The two valleys can be linked by crossing Passo Foric (2432m) from where, on a fine day, the heights of Monte Rosa and the arc of peaks, passes and snowfields above upper Valsesia are in full view. This 13km circular walk from Alagna takes about seven hours and involves 1290m of ascent. You could take two hours off this by returning on the *funivia* from Alpe Pianalunga in Valle d'Olen.

For refreshments (and accommodation), there are **Ristoro Alpino zar Senni** (☎ *0163 92 29 52)* in Valle di Otro, a traditional Walser house; **Rifugio Città di Mortara** (☎ *0163 92 29 96)* and **La Baita** (☎ *0163 92 29 91),* not far below the *funivia* station.

The map of local walks from the Pro Loco office at Alagna is more up-to-date than the IGC 1:25,000 map No 109 *Monte Rosa-Alagna V-Macugnaga-Gressoney,* although the latter is far better for identifying landmarks. Waymarking (red and yellow plus a number) is erratic; there are also a few signposts. The paths and tracks are not unduly rough, although they may be overgrown in places; the route includes about 1km of road walking.

Lake District

It is all too easy to dismiss Italy's Lake District as an area with many fine natural assets that has sacrificed its soul on the altar of mass tourism and become an exotic outpost of England, Germany or the Netherlands. Yet it's not difficult to find small, unspoiled towns and timeless villages in the remote valleys. For walkers, there's enough scope around Lago di Garda, Lago di Como and Lago Maggiore to occupy half a lifetime. The variety of locales for walks of all standards takes in mountain summits both benign and rugged, ridges and valleys, forests, meadows, alpine uplands, cultivated terraces and farmland. Almost everywhere there are reminders of a long history and of the importance of religious belief in people's lives.

CLIMATE
The lakes generally enjoy warm, sunny summers (up to nine hours of sunshine daily) and cold winters. Summer is the wettest season, with frequent thunderstorms. July is usually the warmest month, with an average maximum temperature of 20°C, and daily maxima in the low 30s being quite common.

Föhn winds (see the boxed text 'Windy Italy', p34), blowing from the north, usually during the morning, are common, attracting hordes of windsurfers, but often shrouding the mountains in fog.

Snow can lie on sheltered slopes of Monte Baldo (above Lago di Garda) and on the mountains northwest of Lago di Como until early June. However, it is rarely very deep.

INFORMATION
Maps
Touring Club Italiano's 1:200,000 *Lombardia* map covers the entire Lake District and is ideal for finding your way round.

Emergency
For urgent medical assistance in the Lake District, call the **national emergency number** (☎ 118).

Highlights

DENNIS JONES

While walkers explore the paths around Lago di Como, others explore its depths

- Rambling through olive groves, tall forests and alpine pastures beneath towering peaks around Monte Baldo (p143)

- Enjoying exceptionally rich displays of wildflowers during spring and early summer on Monte Baldo (p143)

- Taking in magnificent panoramic views while exploring old paths high above Lago di Como (p152)

- Walking among traditional stone buildings in the valley villages above beautiful Lago Maggiore (p159)

Lago di Garda

Lago di Garda lies apart from Lago di Como and Lago Maggiore to the west, and its cultural, geological and geographical affinities are closer to the Dolomites and southern Austria than the Alps. The walks described in this section are in two areas: around the Monte Baldo Range, rising to 2000m above the eastern shore of the lake, and at Limone sul Garda close to rugged Valle del Singol and surrounding peaks on the western side.

NATURAL HISTORY

With an area of 370 sq km, Lago di Garda is the largest of the three lakes. About 40% of its depth (346m at its deepest) is made up of moraine deposits, the legacy of its glacial origins. This massive deposit pushed the lake south beyond its confining valley, out into the Po Valley. The surrounding peaks may be lower than those around Lago di Como and Lago Maggiore, but they lack little in grandeur. Monte Carone (1621m) above Valle del Singol dominates the complex topography of ridges, spurs and valleys in the northwestern corner. Monte Baldo's elegantly

The Partisan Movement

During the later stages of WWII, the Lake District was the theatre for many of the Partisan movement's activities. Beginning in Piedmont (Piemonte) soon after Mussolini was ejected in September 1943, troops from disbanded regiments joined groups of civilians to fight for the overthrow of the German army and of Fascism. Political allegiances were less important than the common aim; partisans might otherwise have been communists, socialists, Christian democrats or members of the Party of Action (nonsocialist and republican).

Despite the daunting odds against taking on the professional army of a ruthless state, the partisans were very successful in guerrilla operations and supplied the allies with much strategic information. They clashed with Fascist forces around Lago di Como near the Swiss border, and memorials at Le Biuse above Valle Cannobina point to similar action there. The short-lived Free Republic of Domodossola, set up by partisans during 1944, extended east to Valle Cannobina.

It was fitting, given the area's partisan links, that Mussolini was finally captured and summarily shot by partisans at Dongo beside Lago di Como in April 1945.

simple long sweep, with steep western slopes and more gentle gradients in the east, stands in striking contrast. Geologically, Garda is dominated by limestone formations.

PLANNING
When to Walk

May and September are the best times, when the weather is mild to warm and most likely to be settled. July and August are usually hot, and the area is very crowded with tourists.

Monte Baldo

Duration	6½–7 hours
Distance	13km
Difficulty	moderate
Start/Finish	Monte Baldo cable car station
Nearest Towns	Malcesine (p146), Navene (p147)
Transport	cable car

Summary An outstanding mountain ridge walk with far-ranging lake and alpine views, and abundant wildflowers.

Monte Baldo is a long, rugged ridge paralleling the middle part of Lago di Garda's eastern shore. From its broad extremities, the ridge narrows dramatically to a knife-edge crest, punctuated by several precipitous peaks, the highest being Cima Valdritta (2218m). Popular with skiers in winter and mountain bike riders in summer, Monte Baldo is also a magnet for walkers, and a well-used path traverses the ridge. The extensive network of waymarked paths, in conjunction with the *funivia* (cable car) and local buses, provide many opportunities to explore the mountain. Signposts at path junctions give times to destinations; fit, younger walkers should find it easy to better them. Waymarking, with CAI (Club Alpino Italiano) red and white stripes, is reasonably reliable. The main path followed in the walk described here is No 651.

The route described is an out-and back walk, with a total ascent of 750m, but variations are possible. The approach from lake level at Navene (see Alternative Start, p148)

LAKE DISTRICT

gives a much better sense of actually arriving on the mountain than you feel by taking the *funivia* up to the main ridge – but it's a long climb. If you take the *funivia*, you could return to the lake on foot, via either Col di Piombi (Co di Piombi; see Navene to Malcesine, p165) or Val Dritta (p165).

NATURAL HISTORY

The range is composed of a layer of limestone laid down between 135 and 220 million years ago and later folded by upheavals in the earth's crust. Although Lago di Garda was formed by glacial action, the Monte Baldo range escaped direct impact of the Ice Age, adding to its ecological importance.

Up to 350m olive and citrus groves and oak woodlands are widespread. Sweet chestnuts take over between 350m and 900m; next come beech and conifers in more open woodland. These give way above 1400m to grassy alpine meadows, thickets of mountain pine (spreading as wide as they are high) and alpenrose with small, deep pink bell-shaped clusters of flowers.

Monte Baldo is popularly known as Italy's botanic garden. Three of the most striking species you're likely to see are the deep blue

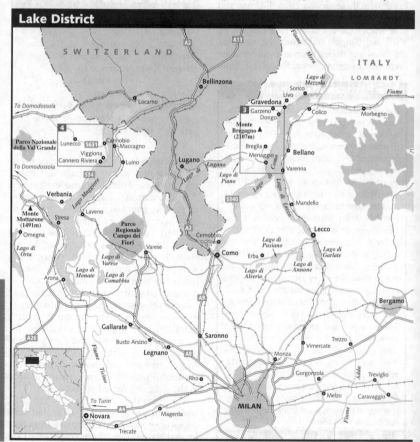

Lake District

rumpet gentian; its more delicate relative, pring gentian; and the bright yellow globe-lower. Two small *riserve statali* (state reerves) – Gardesana Orientale on the lower lopes above Navene, and Lastoni Selva 'ezzi extending right along the ridge crest – re intended to protect fauna and flora.

PLANNING
What to Bring

Valking poles, or even an ice axe, are essential in May as sections of the paths may e under snow. Large snow drifts can lie on Monte Baldo until early June.

German is widely spoken around the lake, and you're quite likely to have prices in shops quoted in German, even if you've used Italian to start the transaction, so Lonely Planet's *German phrasebook* will be as useful as the *Italian phrasebook*.

Maps

The Kompass 1:25,000 map No 690 *Alto Garda e Ledro* is the best of the bunch, although it contains some errors in the location of paths and junctions. The Gruppi Alpinistici's 1:25,000 *Carta dei Sentieri Monte Baldo* comprises two maps and a

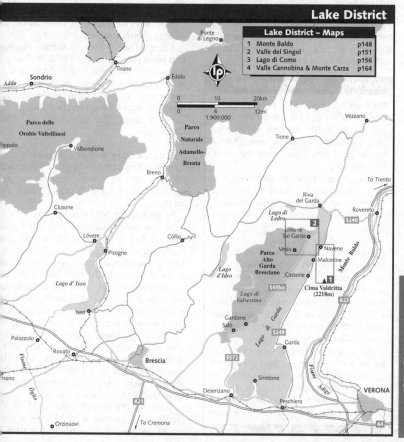

Lake District

0   10   20km
0   6   12mi
1:900,000

LAKE DISTRICT

booklet in Italian with notes about more than 50 walks; it's rich in accurate detail, although awkward to use. The locally produced 1:20,000 *Walks Map, Monte Baldo, Malcesine* has notes in English, German and Italian on about seven walks in the area and is OK.

Various shops in Malcesine (this page) sell maps but the best source is **Klaus Giornali e Libri** (*Via Statuto 19, Malcesine*); which also stocks local history and natural history guides and foreign-language newspapers.

Place Names

There are some differences between names signposted along the paths and those on the maps listed; the maps also differ in some spellings. The signposted names are given here, with the more common map name in brackets at the first mention.

Warning – Mountain Bikes

The tracks crisscrossing the slopes of Monte Baldo, from the main ridge to the lake shore, and the old tracks (and even some paths) around Valle del Singol on the western side of the lake are extremely popular with mountain-bike riders.

Many of these tracks are wide enough to allow riders to pass walkers safely, but many are not. Some riders even take to paths barely wide enough for one person on foot, let alone a bike.

Many riders religiously stick to a 'good riding code' – on catching sight of walkers ahead the leader calls out to following riders to either move to one side to continue, or to stop and wait until the approaching walkers have passed. Other cyclists are not so inclined and clearly believe that their speed and weight justify their headlong descent, regardless of walkers on the path.

This warning is offered with bicycles in mind, but the author also encountered a motorbike on one of the narrower, steeper paths on the southern slopes of Valle del Singol, as the rider manoeuvred down the fragile slopes oblivious to the destruction of large chunks of the path.

Weather Information

You can phone for **local weather forecast** (☎ 1678 603 45).

NEAREST TOWNS
Malcesine

This busy lakeside town on the lower mountain slopes has an old centre and modern, though not ugly, periphery. It may have sold its soul to pizza producers and *gelato* (ice cream) manufacturers, but it's a convenient base for the area.

The **IAT office** (☎ 0457 40 00 44, fax 0457 40 16 33; ⓦ www.aptgardaveneto.com; Via Capitanato 6-8; open Mon-Sat) issues a town map and accommodation guide. The website also has plenty of information, including transport timetables.

There's a handy **accommodation reservation office** (*Via Gardesana*) beside the bus station on the main road. Outside there's an automated, after-hours service showing availability and location of numerous local establishments with a free phone to call them.

Pesca Sport (*Via Gardesana 56*) sell Campingaz.

Places to Stay & Eat Centrally located **Camping Priori** (☎ 0457 40 05 03, fax 0457 58 30 98; Via Navene 31; camping per person/site €5.15/5.15) is rather small and cramped.

Hotel Pelèr (☎ 0457 40 02 03, fax 0456 50 02 30; ⓔ peler@malcesine.com; Via Gardesana 84; doubles up to €56.80), has immaculately clean, pleasantly furnished rooms facing the lake, or the heights of Monte Baldo. An ample buffet breakfast is included.

Malcesine has numerous rather un-Italian pizza and pasta restaurants catering to the numerous German visitors. The choice comes down to outlook as much as anything else.

There's a large **supermarket** (*Piazza Statuto; open Mon-Sat*) and a **Despar supermarket** (*Via Navene; open Mon-Sat*). Opposite the latter is a **fruit and vegetable shop**. A good bakery is **Il Fornaio** (*Via Antonio Bottura*), off Piazza Statuto.

Garden Ristorante (☎ 0457 40 04 40; Via Garibaldi; 2 courses €15-23) has a view across the lake that's sufficient reason to at here, even if it's not a scintillating gourmet experience. The extensive menu, in which fish is prominent, doesn't neglect vegetarians.

Getting There & Away Malcesine is a very accessible place, by land and water.

Bus Departing from the bus station opposite Verona train station, APT (☎ 045 800 41 29; w www.apt.vr.it) operates a Verona–Riva del Garda (route 62–64) service via Malcesine (€4.55, 1¼ hours, at least 10 per day). In Verona, buy tickets or grab a timetable from the APT office at the bus station. At Malcesine, buy tickets at the bus station or from the machine outside. **Atesina** (☎ 0461 82 79 2; w www.atesina.it) operates a bus service from Trento to Riva del Garda (€3.80, one hour and 37 minutes, at least three per day).

Train On the Milan–Venice line, you can catch a train to Desenzano and then a ferry connection, or to Peschiera where you can connect with the APT bus (Verona–Riva del Garda) or the ferry to Malcesine. From the Rome–Bologna–Verona–Trento (and beyond) train line, buses depart from near Verona station. Coming from the north, you could alight at Trento to connect with buses to Riva del Garda.

Ferry Operating services to many lakeside towns is **Navigazione Lago di Garda** (☎ 800 5 18 01). You can reach Malcesine from Desenzano (ferry/hydrofoil €7.30/10.30, even per day) or Peschiera (ferry/hydrofoil 7.30/10.30, two per day). You can also reach Malcesine from Riva del Garda at the northern end of the lake (ferry/hydrofoil 5.15/7.40, one hour and five minutes by hydrofoil, 21 per day).

Car From the A4 (Milan–Venice) along the southern shore of Lago di Garda, take the Peschiera exit to the S249, which hugs the eastern shore of the lake, to Malcesine (5km). The A22 (Modena–Brennero) parallels the eastern shore, at a distance; take the Lago di Garda Sud exit a few kilometres northwest of Verona, or the Lago di Garda

Nord exit near Rovereto, then follow signs to Malcesine (48km/23km). As a guide to tolls, you'll pay €5.95 for the Milan–Peschiera stretch on the A4.

Navene

This lakeside village is 5km north of Malcesine and (apart from the traffic) much quieter, though with minimal facilities.

Places to Stay & Eat With ample space for tents on tiers of terraces with superlative views, **Camping Navene** (☎/fax 0456 57 00 09; Via Gardesana Nord 62; sites €10.35 plus per person €5.15, bungalows from €25.80) also offers fresh bread daily; order from the office.

The nearest *alimentari* is in the village of Campagnola, about 2km towards Malcesine. At Navene, the kiosk next to the lakeside bus stop sells wine and beer.

Pensione & Bar Navene (☎ 0457 40 0797; B&B doubles €41.30) is the place to which outdoors folk gravitate. Most of the simple rooms in the pensione have a good view. The bar serves generous meals of excellent quality for around €7, including crisp pizzas, spaghetti and salads.

Getting There & Away Navene is on APT's Verona–Riva del Garda bus route (see Bus, this page, for Malcesine). You can buy tickets locally at Bar Paola, almost opposite the bus stop.

GETTING TO/FROM THE WALK

Several APT buses on the Verona–Riva route link Navene and Malcesine (€0.85). The **Monte Baldo Funivia** (☎ 0457 40 02 06), which has been extensively upgraded and has a much greater capacity than the old cable car, does not run strictly to the timetable but responds to demand, although the times of the first and last departures from the three stations are fixed. The first departure from Malcesine is at 8am and the last from Monte Baldo at 6.45pm (earlier before mid-April and after mid-September). The single/return fares between Malcesine and Monte Baldo are €8.50/13, and between Malcesine and San Michele are €3.50/6.

THE WALK

From the *funivia* station head down a wide track, following the red and white signs (including route 651), past **Baita dei Forti restaurant** to Bocca Tratto Spino (Bocca Tredespin). Keep going up, still following route 651, generally along a rocky ridge to the tops of two ski tows, where you keep to the right of a large building. About 100m further on you enter the Riserva Statale Lastoni Selva Pezzi. Gently rising alpine meadows soon give way to low mountain pine and heather. The ridge narrows and the ascent steepens. About 1¼ hours from the

Monte Baldo

start, pass a sign 'Cima Pozzetta' pointing up to Cima Pozzette (2132m), not a particularly prominent feature. The path then narrows and steepens and is slightly exposed in places. Another steep climb takes you past a sign to Cima Longina (Cima del Longino). The summit of **Cima Longina** (2179m) is a bit further up, topped by a crucifix (about 30 minutes from the Pozzetta sign). It's a stupendous view – mountains near and far with Malcesine directly below.

Continue down to a gap then regain most of this lost elevation through pines. Follow along to the start of the traverse of the extremely steep, eastern flank, below Cima Val Finestra. The narrow, mildly exposed path is even more fun with a covering of snow. It then continues to contour the precipitous craggy slopes, clad with clumps of low mountain pine, crosses a gully and a spur, then a mighty view of huge rock walls rising from Val Dritta opens up ahead. Descend slightly to the unmarked junction of the path to the summit; it's easy enough along a narrow spur to reach crucifix-topped Cima Valdritta (2218m; 1½ to two hours from Cima Longina). With luck you can enjoy the magnificently dramatic views of deep valleys and towering cliffs nearby and the great expanses of the lake framed by ranges of alpine peaks to the north and northwest.

Retrace your steps to return to the *funivia* (2½ to three hours)

Alternative Start: Navene to Funivia Station

4¼–5 hours, 7km, 1690m ascent

From **Bar Navene** follow waymarked path 634 (which shares the road then well-used vehicle track with routes 4 and 6). Once you pass the turn-offs from paths 4 and 6, route 634 is bike free, as it climbs through forest to Bocca di Navene (1517m; three to 3½ hours). Here you'll find **Rifugio Bocca di Navene** (☎ 0457 40 17 94) and can sample their excellent *torta* (cake) or something more filling, with hot or cold drinks.

Walk up the road for a short distance to an unmarked path on the right (not shown on the Kompass 1:25,000 map), which leads up to a wide gravel road. Follow this to a point about 40m beyond a large information board welcoming you to Monte Baldo. Take signposted route 3, (which is also route 651); ignore a path to the right where route 3 leads to Cima di Ventrar and ascend the steep slope to an unnamed point (1751m). Continue south on a broad path across open Colma di Malcesine, where wildflowers are very plentiful, to **La Capannina** where you can have drinks and sandwiches, or more substantial polenta and pasta. Descend slightly, past ski lifts and buildings, to the *funivia* station (1¼ to 1½ hours from Bocca di Navene).

Valle del Singol

Duration	6¼–6½ hours
Distance	21km
Difficulty	moderate–demanding
Start	Vesio
Finish	Limone sul Garda
Nearest Town	Limone sul Garda (p149)
Transport	bus

Summary A superbly scenic walk around the rim of spectacular Valle del Singol, following old tracks and paths past many WWI historic sites.

On the northwestern shore of Lago di Garda, Limone sul Garda (Limone) is an ideal base for exploring an extensive network of paths and roads built during WWI. You can feel deep in the mountains, even though the vast expanses of Lago di Garda aren't far away. Valle del Singol provides the ideal mountain walk – following the rim of a valley right around its watershed. This particular valley reaches deeply into the mountains, a vast amphitheatre of limestone crags and towers, and narrow ledges with precariously perched trees.

Both Limone and Valle del Singol are in the northeast corner of Parco Alto Garda Bresciano, a large reserve (383 sq km) extending for around 40km along the western shore of Lago di Garda and west into the mountains. It protects a wide variety of ecosystems from lakeside to alpine, extensive woodlands, traditional mountain settlements and 18th-century villas.

This walk, with 900m of ascent, could be spread over two days by staying overnight in Baita Bonaventura Segala. The recommended ascent of Monte Carone (p166), an alternative rim-hugging route around Valle del Singol (see Valle del Singol Alternative, p165) and an exhilarating excursion through Val Pura (see Valle del Singol & Val Pura, p165) offer further options.

PLANNING
What to Bring

If staying at Baita Bonaventura Segala bring a sleeping bag and food. Carry plenty of water as there are no natural sources; you may find bottled drinks at Baita Segala.

Maps

The Kompass 1:25,000 map No 690 *Alto Garda e Ledro* has some useful notes on the reverse side and is better than the same publisher's 1:50,000 map No 102 *Lago di Garda/Monte Baldo*.

The 1:12,500 *Carta Turistica*, published by the local Mountain Troops Veterans Association (ANA), has multilingual notes outlining walks along numerous waymarked paths in the area. It is a useful supplement to any of the other maps listed here.

The best place to look for maps is the **tabaccheria** *(Piazza Garibaldi)* near the Limone ferry port.

NEAREST TOWN
Limone sul Garda

Popular with package-tour operators and tourists generally, especially from Germany and Britain, many overpriced 'baits', such as souvenir shops and boat trips, are set by Limone's entrepreneurs to trap the unwary.

The *comune* (town council) **information office** *(☎ 0365 91 89 87, fax 0365 95 47 20; Via IV Novembre 2/c; open daily)* issues an accommodation guide, booklet with handy town map, bus timetables and tickets, and information about guided walks. Almost adjacent to the office is a limited after-hours hotel booking service.

Places to Stay & Eat There are a shop and restaurant on site at **Campeggio Garda**

(☎ 0365 95 45 50, fax 0365 95 43 57; Via 14 Novembre 10; camping per person/site €6.20/11.90, chalets from €67.15). The camping ground is about 15 minutes walk south from the town centre. Some of the pitches on shady, grassed terraces have lake views.

Hotel Sole (☎ 0365 95 40 55, fax 0365 95 47 03; Via Lungolago Marconi 36; rooms to €41.30) charges very reasonable rates for tastefully decorated, spacious rooms, many with a lake view. A plentiful buffet breakfast is included.

War in the Mountains

Italy entered WWI in 1915 on the Allied side, hoping to extend its northern borders by liberating the Alto Adige and Trentino regions, not far north of Lago di Garda. Limone was evacuated for the duration since the border with the Austro-Hungarian empire generally followed the rim of Valle del Singol. Many battles were fought in the area; remains of the *fortini* (barracks, gun emplacements and other wartime paraphernalia) can still be seen beside the road between Passo Nota and Baita Segala and near the track up to Monte Carone.

Baita Segala and the nearby chapel were built by members and friends of the local Associazione Nazionale Alpini (ANA; Mountain Troops Veterans Association) on the ruins of wartime buildings. Mass is held in the tiny chapel from time to time.

The ANA also built paths to Monte Carone and rebuilt the large crucifix on the summit. This is made of long metal spikes and barbed wire with a soldier's helmet resting on each end of the horizontal arm. The wording of the plaque at the base of the cross is simple: it was erected in the name of peace and fraternity. The summit is surrounded by stark white stones; the remains of a fortified village.

The cemetery near Passo Nota, even more poignant, was also restored by a local ANA group. Within a low stone wall, surmounted by a striking, harsh fence of barbed wire and metal spikes, are several anonymous headstones and three large memorials to soldiers who died during the war.

For supplies there are the excellent **Alimentari Martinelli** (Piazza Garibaldi) and a **Despar supermarket** (Via IV Novembre). The **Coop Agricola Possidenti Oliveti**, near Despar, is the place to go for local olive oil, wines, cheese and bread (and who needs more?). The various **fruit and vegetable stalls** (Lungolago Marconi) are probably cheaper than the **greengrocer** in Via Comboni. The best place for the daily *gelati* (ice cream) is **Pink Panther** (Via Comboni).

Al Pirata (☎ 0365 95 43 85; Via Comboni 38) is a justifiably popular pizzeria in a semi-garden setting from where you can just see the slopes of Monte Baldo. Crisp, well-filled *al forno* (cooked in a wood-fired oven) pizzas and pasta (both to €6.70) make an excellent meal; only German beer is served.

Al Torcol (☎ 0365 95 41 69; cnr S45 & Lungolago Marconi) has better views than Al Pirata, and more pizzas on its menu, but is rather more expensive – you'd eat well here for €20.

Getting There & Away Limone is easy to reach whether you're coming from the north or south.

Bus A service is operated by **SIA** (☎ 030 22 37 61) between Brescia and Limone (€4.90, two hours, one per day Monday to Saturday). Brescia bus station is near the train station. From the north, **Atesina** (☎ 0461 82 79 22) operates between Trento and Riva (€3.80, at least three per day). From Riva an **APT** (☎ 045 800 41 29) service to Desenzano passes through Limone (18 minutes, six daily).

Train Approaching from the south, Brescia (for bus connections) is on the busy Milan–Verona–Venice line. From the north, at Trento on the Brennero–Verona line you can connect with a bus to Riva and on to Limone.

Ferry Operating services to many lakeside towns is **Navigazione Lago di Garda** (☎ 800 55 18 01). You can reach Limone from Desenzano (ferry/hydrofoil €7.30/10.30, seven per day) or from Peschiera (ferry/hydrofoil

€7.30/10.30, two per day). You can also sail from Riva at the northern end of the lake (ferry/hydrofoil €5.15/7.40, 35/21 minutes, 21 per day) and between Malcesine and Limone (ferry/hydrofoil €3.50/5.60, 13/10 minutes, 21 per day).

Car From the south, leave the A4 Milan–Venice by the Brescia East exit and follow signs to Salo and Limone along S45bis. From the north, leave the A22 Modena–Brennero at Rovereto Sud/Lago di Garda Nord exit and continue to Riva del Garda on S240 then S45bis to Limone.

GETTING TO/FROM THE WALK

The walk starts near Vesio, a village 9km southwest of Limone. There is one morning SIA bus from Limone to Vesio at 9am (€1.45, 25 minutes). Alight at the stop on the southeastern edge of the village or in the village itself.

THE WALK

From the southeastern (lower) edge of Vesio, walk northwest for about 600m until a T-junction, then right along Via Orsino to a major junction where a road leads north (to Passo Nota) and where there is a car park

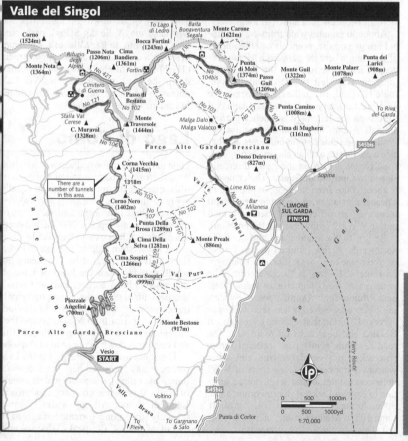

and picnic area. Follow Via Dalvra northeast for 100m to a bend and continue on a gravel road signposted Sentiero Angelini. About 50m further along, turn left between stables and fields, a red and white sign reassuringly indicating that you are on route 106 to Passo Nota, now a wide gravel road through forest. The road gains height in a stack of tight bends; once it levels out (below Bocca Sospiri) you can begin to appreciate the dramatic views of rugged mountains surrounding Valle di Bondo to the west. After about two hours of generally very scenic walking, with some fine views of Valle di Bondo and the surrounding rugged peaks, the road burrows through six tunnels in quick succession, all between 20m and 30m long.

About 30 minutes walk from the last tunnel brings you to a point about 800m north of the point where the path from Monte Traversole meets the track on the right, and a junction. Bear left (west) downhill along route 121 (path 102 to the right bypasses the wartime cemetery ahead). Pass Stalla Val Cerese on the left, used to shelter grazing animals. About 700m from the junction, opposite some ruined stone buildings and beside a picnic site with an enormous barbecue fireplace, is a path on the right, discreetly signed to **Cimitero di Guerra**. The cemetery is about 200m from the road, at one side of a peaceful meadow, and contains graves and memorials to officers and men who died during WWI (25 minutes from the junction).

Return to the main track and continue northwards. A few hundred metres further on you come to a major junction; bear right on route 421 towards Bocca Fortini. The wide gravel road soon crosses Passo Nota; here **Rifugio degli Alpini**, a possible watering hole, was closed when this walk was surveyed. Continue steeply up over Passo di Bestana and bear right on route 421. The road descends gently past scattered *fortini* (barracks, gun emplacements and other wartime paraphernalia), remnants of WWI defences. Continue past a signposted junction to Lago di Ledro at Bocca Fortini; about 300m further on, Sentiero Tosi Agostino, route 105 to Monte Carone, takes off to the left. This is a *via ferrata* (iron way).

After another 250m you reach **Baita Bonaventura Segala** (an hour from the *cimitero*). Built by the local ANA in the shadow of Monte Carone, this is a smallish place in the style of a *rifugio* (mountain hut), open to walkers on a first-come, first-served basis. Visitors are asked to stay for one night only and to leave a donation in an honesty box. It has a gas cooker and lighting; bottled water, beer and wine are provided (payment goes into the honesty box). Contact the tourist office in Limone for up-to-date information about the water supply.

Continue along the road generally southeast, beneath the towering cliffs of Punta di Mois, across Passo Guil and on to route 101. This path winds down through cliffs and woodland into Valle del Singol, past some **lime kilns** ruins, to **Bar Milanesa**, a pleasant place for a drink and excellent apple strudel (1¾ hours from Baita Segala). Continue down the road, which becomes Via Caldogno, to the main road (Via IV Novembre) in Limone (about 30 minutes).

Lago di Como

Lago di Como's renowned scenic beauty and crystal-clear air have inspired volumes of often extravagant praise, which can equally apply to the area's attractions for walkers. From the shore rise an extraordinary array of mountains, many topping 2000m, and deep, steep-sided valleys extend far inland.

On the western side of the lake two distinct areas are separated by Val Menaggio, which extends from the head of Lago di Lugano (partly in Switzerland) to Como's shore. South of this valley the topography is quite complex; to the north a horseshoe-shaped ridge rises from Menaggio and then sweeps north, via Monte Cardinello (2521m) and eastwards down to the head of the lake.

The small town of Menaggio is the base for the walks described here. Its accessible hinterland offers perhaps the widest variety of walks in any one compact area around Lago di Como. All the walks, from a leisurely stroll along Torrente Sanagra to an ascent of one of the peaks, share scenic landscapes replete with evidence of a long history of settlement, with striking, mostly harmonious contrasts between old and new. The paths and mule tracks surviving from centuries of high-level summer grazing, and still used for this purpose, are ideal for walking – for pleasure rather than necessity.

NATURAL HISTORY

Lago di Como's origins are glacial; a few million years ago, the Adda glacier carved out the upper lake basin, then split on either side of a promontory to cut the two arms that give the lake its inverted Y-shape. Two rivers flow into the lake in the north – the Mera and the Adda. The latter is the sole outlet from Lago di Lecco, the eastern arm. The stem of the Y is sometimes called Lago di Colico; the name Como commonly applies to the western arm, and to the lake as a whole, through Lario (the older name, from the Roman Lacus Larionus) is also used. Como has the longest shoreline of the three lakes – more than 270km – and enters the record book as Italy's deepest lake with a depth of 410m near Argegno on the western arm.

Geologically, the Como basin is an area of both limestone and crystalline (gneiss) rocks. Monte Grona, above Menaggio, is the northernmost of the dolomitic (limestone) peaks in the southern pre-Alps.

The Como basin's mild climate is ideal for the cultivation of olives and vines and of colourful flowering shrubs in many towns around the shores. In the extensive deciduous woodlands on the steep mountainsides, sweet chestnut and oaks are prominent, many of massive proportions; there are also hazel, silver birch and beech.

The limestone country supports a colourful variety of flora. During early spring, trumpet gentians, spring heath and rock mezereon brighten the rocky ground. In summer, clusters of the well-named yellow globeflower, the orange lily and columbine stand out among dozens of species readily seen.

PLANNING

Spring and autumn are the best times to visit the area; snow lingers on the highest peaks until early June. Thunderstorms and heavy rain are likely from June until September. During July and August, the warmest months, the lakeside towns are very crowded.

If camping bring plenty of fuel for your stove as it can be difficult to source locally.

The marking of paths can be infuriatingly inconsistent. You can find markers lavishly and unnecessarily painted on trees, rocks and walls, but entirely lacking, obscurely placed or overgrown at crucial junctions, in village alleys or around featureless meadows. Even so, it's better to stick to the marked paths, rather than hope that a beguiling line on a map will lead to where you want to go – without suddenly being confronted by an irate landowner with barking dogs.

Maps

The best available map is the Kompass 1:50,000 No 91 *Lago di Como, Lago di Lugano*, which comes with a booklet in Italian and German. It's useful for general orientation but unreliable for the location of paths, showing many which do not exist.

The useful *Via dei Monti Lariani* booklet contains basic planimetric maps of this long-distance walk (see the boxed text 'Is the Via Viable?', p157) and a generalised description of the route between villages, settlements and distinctive features, and is available from the IAT in Menaggio (this page).

Il Ritrovo (*Via Calvi 10*), a bookshop in Menaggio, is a good source of maps and Italian- and German-language guidebooks.

Weather Information

The **Swiss Meteorological Service** (☎ 0041 91 162) provides local weather forecasts in Italian and German.

ACCESS TOWN
Menaggio

This beautiful lakeside town is in a superb location, overlooked by towering peaks, and boasts fine views of the rugged mountains across the water. Its many handsome old buildings are well preserved and the concessions to modern tourism that rob many other towns of their Italian character are absent.

You can obtain information about local walks at the **IAT office** (☎/fax 0344 329 24;

LAKE DISTRICT

e *menaggioinfo@tiscalinet.it; Piazza Garbaldi 8; open Mon-Sat)*, as well as a list of local accommodation (posted outside after office hours).

Places to Stay & Eat North of town, **Camping Lido** (☎ *0344 311 50; Via Roma 4; camping per person/tent €4.65/7.75)* occupies a one-time soccer pitch. An on-site bar serves snacks. Be warned – the bus depot is next door and buses are on the go from 6am.

La Primula (☎ *0344 323 56, fax 0344 316 77;* e *menaggiohostel@mclink.it; Via IV Novembre 86; B&B €10.85)* is a youth hostel at the southern end of town with a lovely view of the lake. An excellent three-course evening meal costs around €7.75.

Of the several hotels, some of which are on the serious side of expensive, **Hotel Garni Corona** (☎ *0344 320 06, fax 0344 305 64;* e *manueladi@interfree.it; Largo Cavour 3; doubles to €56.80)* is conveniently located next to Piazza Garibaldi. Many of the simply furnished rooms have lake views.

For food shopping, there are two supermarkets: **CompraBene** off Via Roma at the northern end of town and **Consorso Agrario** *(Via Lusardi)* near the ferry port. **Clerici** *(Via Loveno)* is an excellent fruit and vegetable shop and almost opposite is **Il Fornaio**, a first-class bakery. Possibly the best *gelato* in Italy comes from **Panne e Cioccolato** *(Via Calvi)*. Only fresh ingredients and fruit in season are used; the *limoncello* is delicious.

La Giara Pizzeria Ristorante (☎/fax *0344 322 59; Via Roma 22)*, next to Camping Lido, is a shrine at which all pizza connoisseurs should worship. An imaginative range of *al forno* pizzas (to €7.75) includes several with fresh local produce (such as *boletus* mushrooms); antipastos (to €7.25) include earthy *mozzarella di bufala* (buffalo cheese).

Trattoria Le Sorelle (☎ *0344 323 90; Via Camozzi 16)*, in a narrow lane off Piazza Garibaldi, is an informal, family-run place. It specialises in pasta (to €6.20); fish dishes (to €8.80) include tasty trout.

Getting There & Away Reaching Menaggio by public transport takes time linking connections; a ferry trip is recommended.

Bus An **SPT** (☎ *031 24 71 11)* bus service links Milan's Malpensa airport and Menaggio (€12.90, one hour and 55 minutes, one per day).

From Como train station, SPT's C10 bus to Colico stops at Menaggio (€2.45, one hour and 10 minutes, 13 per day). Buy tickets at the *tabaccheria* on the station. At Colico, purchase tickets from the newsagent on the train station; the bus stop is nearby.

Train Como is on the Milan–Chiasso line (€7.75, 43 minutes). The Milan–Sondrio/Tirano train service goes through Varenna (€5.95, one hour) and Colico, ports on the lake's ferry network. There are plenty of trains daily on both lines. At Colico you can connect with the bus to Menaggio.

Ferry By water, **Navigazione Lago di Como** (☎ *800 55 18 01)* offers services from Varenna (ferry/hydrofoil €2.50/3.80, 10/five minutes, at least six per day) or Colico (ferry/hydrofoil €4.70/6.80, one hour and 32 minutes/40 minutes, at least three per day).

Car Leave the A9 Milan–Passo Sant'Gottardo at the Como Nord exit to join the S340 along the western shore of the lake. Menaggio is 34km from Como.

Monte Grona

Duration	4½–5 hours
Distance	9km
Difficulty	moderate
Start/Finish	Breglia
Nearest Town	Menaggio (p153)
Transport	bus
Summary	A steep climb to a rocky summit is rewarded by magnificent panoramic views of Lago di Como and the surrounding mountains.

The dramatic cluster of dolomite crags towering above Menaggio to the west is surprisingly easy to reach on this walk, which includes a total ascent of 990m. The well-trodden route from Breglia, high above Menaggio, follows clearly waymarked paths and relatively short sections of vehicle track. Rifugio Menaggio, at the foot of Monte Grona's rocky southern face, is at the halfway mark and a pleasant staging point. It could also serve as a base for a leisurely exploration of the ridge to Monte Bregagno (2107m) and even beyond, following part of the Alta Via dei Monti Lariani (see Side Trip: Monte Bregagno, this page, and the boxed text 'Is the Via Viable?', p157).

There are two routes to the *rifugio* from Breglia: the Sentiero Basso (the longer route, partly through woodland) and the shorter, steeper, more scenic Sentiero Alto Panoramico described here. The return section of the walk is via the chapel of Sant'Amate on the Monte Bregagno ridge. The Alternative Finish to Menaggio (this page) is a pleasantly varied alternative to catching the bus and is not unduly strenuous.

PLANNING

Water is available at *sorgenti* (drinking fountains) between Breglia and the *rifugio*, and at the *rifugio* itself.

GETTING TO/FROM THE WALK

The SPT bus route C13 links Menaggio (Piazza Garibaldi) and Breglia (€1.20). Buy tickets in Menaggio at the **newsagent** *(Piazza Garibaldi)*.

THE WALK (see map p156)

From the bus stop in Breglia, walk up the road signposted to Rifugio Menaggio. After a couple of bends, turn right up a path signposted to the *rifugio*. Here, and at several successive junctions, follow the eye-catching red-and-yellow waymarkers and/or signs to the *rifugio*. Above a *sorgente* and some picnic tables (on the right), a sign directs you up to the right along Sentiero Alto Panoramico. Around here the path crosses the contact zone between greyish crystalline rocks and smooth, grey-white limestone (dolomite). The path then leaves the spur and makes a fine rising contour around a valley, up to the *rifugio* (1¼ to 1½ hours from Breglia).

Rifugio Menaggio *(☎ 0344 372 82, 0161 21 37 51; beds for non-CAI members €15.50; open mid-June–mid-Sept plus weekends &* *holidays year-round)* offers lunch, snacks and drinks during the day; expect to pay around €12.90 for the evening meal.

Directly above the *rifugio*, prominent red-and-yellow signs indicate the way to the Forcoletto and Monte Grona, and then Via Direttissima (which ascends very steeply) and Via Normale. Follow Via Normale up to Forcoletto – the saddle on the ridge linking Monte Grona and Monte Bregagno. Continue gaining height, now over small crags; after several minutes the path divides to cross Monte Grona's northern face. The upper and lower paths are about equally narrow and very mildly exposed, and reunite at a small gap just short of the summit's rock tower. A firmly anchored wire cable provides some assistance for the final climb to the top (an hour from the *rifugio*). With luck you won't have to share the summit with the local wild goats and can identify the peaks marked on the topographic plate in odourless peace.

Return to Forcoletto and head northeast and north towards Sant'Amate, along a clear path on or just below the ridge crest. From the old **chapel**, take on the Side Trip to Monte Bregagno (below) or take the descent path, signposted to Breglia. It crosses the steep grassy eastern flank of the ridge. About 30 minutes' walk brings you back to the path you took up to the *rifugio*. Breglia is about an hour further on. If you're walking all the way to Menaggio (see Alternative Finish, below) you need to turn off southwest just before you reach the main road in Breglia.

Side Trip: Monte Bregagno
1½ hours, 6km, 600m ascent
From Sant'Amate chapel, follow the waymarked path up the grassy ridge north to the crucifix-topped summit. The highlights of the view are Lago di Como, almost at your feet, and Monte Rosa on the western skyline.

Alternative Finish: Menaggio
2 hours, 7.5km, 100m ascent, 650m descent
This alternative to catching a bus back to Menaggio starts at a path junction on the road from Rifugio Menaggio. Just above the main road in Breglia, beside a large tree, turn southwest down a lane with a route 3

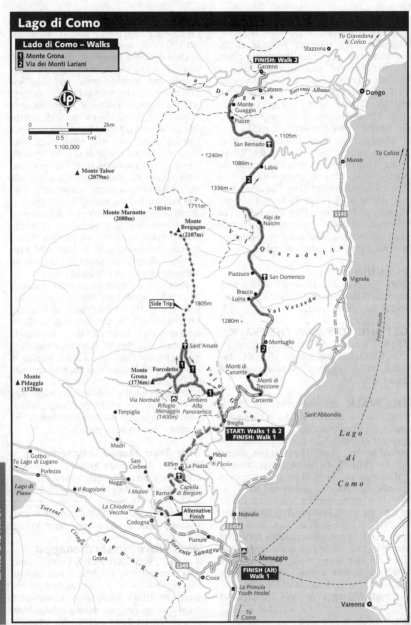

Lago di Como

Lado di Como – Walks
1. Monte Grona
2. Via dei Monti Lariani

0 1 2km
0 0.5 1mi
1:100,000

To Gravedona & Colico

Stazzona

FINISH: Walk 2
Garzeno

Catasco

Torrente Albano

Dongo

Monte Guaggio

Piazze

+ 1105m

San Bernado

Musso

To Colico

+ 1240m 1086m + Labiu

2

1336m +

▲ Monte Tabor (2079m)

Alpi de Nalcim

S340

1711m + 1804m

▲ Monte Marnotto (2088m)

Monte Bregagno (2107m)

Val

Quaradella

Piazzuco San Domenico

Vignola

Side Trip

1805m

Bracco Luina

Val Vezzedo

1280m +

Sant'Amate

2

Montuglio

Monte Grona (1736m) Forcoletto

1

1

Monti di Carcente

▲ Monte Pidaggia (1528m)

Via Normale

1

Rifugio Menaggio (1400m)

Sentiero Alto Panoramico

Monti di Treccione

Carcente

Sant'Abbondio

Timpiglia

No 3

Breglia

START: Walks 1 & 2
FINISH: Walk 1

Madri

Plesio
Plesio

Lago

Gottro
To Lago di Lugano Porlezza

Sass Corbee

835m + La Piazza

Naggio

di

Il Rogolone I Molini

Barna

Capella di Bergum

Como

Lago di Piano

La Chioderia Vecchia

Alternative Finish

Torrente Menaggio

Codogna

Nobialio

S340d

Val

Torrente Sanagra

Pianure

▲ Grona

Croce

S340

Menaggio

FINISH (Alt) Walk 1

La Primula Youth Hostel

To Como

Varenna

ed-and-white waymarker (Via dei Monti Lariani). After a few minutes, bear left where here's a sign to Sorgente Chiarella; the path oon leads into woodland. Cross a stream, hen don't be tempted to go down to the left at a junction but ascend on the main path. About 150m past a *sorgente* bear left to pass below a white, two-storey stone house. A wide track then leads into woodland and descends to a road. Turn left and go down to La Piazza, a scattering of mostly old stone houses fringing some meadows.

Next, pass roadside **Capella di Bergum**. About eight minutes further on, go left around a bend (not straight ahead) and up. Only 12m further on, drop down to the right, with a house on the left, on a narrow path that drops to the edge of the village of Barna. At a T-junction turn right and descend. Below a gushing fountain, turn left to reach the church piazza. Cross this, passing a war memorial, and go right along a path (with Casa del Padre Mio on the left), down between houses

then diagonally right across a small piazza and along a cobbled lane for about 30m. Take the second turn left, down to a stream, but don't cross it. Instead, turn left and continue down to a wide track, which drops to a road at **La Chioderia Vecchia** where you can stop for a beer inside the well-preserved old building (once a nail factory) or outside under trees. Then follow the path beside Torrente Sanagra to a bridge and go up to the left along a vehicle track which eventually takes you to the open expanses of Pianure. Continue down the road from here. Beyond the sports centre, turn right down Piazza Wacks Mylius, past a large church and on to a junction with an *alimentari* on the left. Walk down Via N Sauro for about 30m then go right, down a steep path. At the bottom turn right along the road and take the first left beyond the bridge over Torrente Sanagra, walking up a path (Via Castellino), now in Menaggio, which takes you down to Via Calvi – at the far end of which is Piazza Garibaldi.

Is the Via Viable?

The Via dei Monti Lariani is a 125km-long waymarked route along the western side of Lago di Como between the towns of Cernobbio (6km north of Como) and Sorico, close to the head of the lake. It passes through several villages, including San Fedele, Croce, Breglia, Garzeno, Peglio and Livo, from some of which there are bus services to lakeside towns. The Via was developed several years ago and is maintained principally by the Comunità Montana Alto Lario Occidentale and the CAI (Club Alpino Italiano) Dongo branch. It follows age-old paths linking mountain settlements, vehicle tracks and, occasionally, minor roads. It's a middle-level rather than high-level route, only occasionally rising above 1000m.

Villages (rather than towns) where walkers can find refreshments and accommodation are quite widely spaced and some have only one hotel or bar. It's possible to complete the full distance in six fairly strenuous days, with a minimum of around 800m ascent per day.

A brochure *Hiking on the Via Dei Monti Lariani* and an annually updated accommodation list, available from the IAT office at Menaggio (p153) are invaluable for planning. Two Kompass 1:50,000 maps cover almost all the route: No 91 *Lago di Como* and No 92 *Chiavenna. Val Bregaglia*.

It's an extremely scenic, varied and interesting route. However, at the time of writing natural events, including landslides in the valley of the Rio Bares, Val Inferno and at Tabbidello, as well as the washing away of the bridge over Torrente Vincino in the Liro Valley, had temporarily made it impossible to complete the full distance. Furthermore dozens of unbridged stream crossings become difficult after only 24 hours of heavy rain – from ankle to knee deep and fast-flowing. Another difficulty is waymarking, with red-white-red bands and the section number (1-4) of the Via. Markers are often not well placed and it's easy to miss a crucial change of direction.

However – it's far from being all bad news – the section described here is a truly outstanding walk, as is that between Garzeno and Peglio, once the Torrente Vincino bridge is restored. In other words – don't miss it! Always inquire about current conditions at the IAT office at Menaggio.

Via dei Monti Lariani

Duration	8–8½ hours
Distance	22.5km
Difficulty	moderate–demanding
Start	Breglia
Finish	Garzeno (p159)
Nearest Town	Menaggio (p153)
Transport	bus

Summary A magnificently scenic route above Lago di Como, following paths through several old settlements and beautiful woodlands.

The section of the Via dei Monti Lariani (see the boxed text 'Is the Via Viable?', p157) between Breglia and Garzeno on the northern side of Val Dongana offers an outstanding day's walk, with 950m of ascent. The route traverses the mighty eastern and northeastern flanks of Monte Bregagno then descends into Val Dongana. Streams in Val Quaradella and those draining Bregagno's north slopes could be difficult to cross after heavy rain and the area is prone to minor landslides.

With an early start it might be possible to reach Garzeno in time to catch the last bus down to Dongo (see Getting To/From the Walk, this page) on the shore of Lago di Como. Otherwise there's just one *albergo* (hotel) in Garzeno (p159) a large village full of fascinating old buildings.

The route is, with a few exceptions, adequately waymarked with rectangular red-white-red markers (most marked '3' to indicate the third section of the Via). Here and there you will need to check that you are still on the route by looking back to see signs placed for people following the path in the opposite direction.

PLANNING

There's nowhere to enjoy a refreshment stop, other than several *sorgenti*, so you need to be self sufficient.

The Kompass 1:50,000 map No 91 *Lago di Como* shows the route in very generalised fashion. The booklet about the Via, available from the IAT in Menaggio (p153), is useful though it does not provide a detailed route description.

GETTING TO/FROM THE WALK

An **SPT** (☎ 031 24 72 47) bus service (C13) links Menaggio and Breglia (€1.20, 25 minutes, at least eight a day Monday to Saturday). Early departures (5.50am and 8.30am) are from the bus depot at Piazza Roma (at the northern end of town), thereafter from the central Piazza Garibaldi.

From Garzeno, SPT service C17 operates to Dongo (€1.20, Monday to Saturday). The last departure is at 6.27pm. At Dongo you connect with the SPT C10 Colico–Como service to Menaggio (23 minutes, 13 per day).

THE WALK (see map p156)

From the bus stop in Breglia, walk up the road signposted to Rifugio Menaggio for about 30m then turn right along a lane. This soon descends into Val di Greno, crossing a bridge over the main stream. About 40 minutes from Breglia you come to Carcente, a hamlet where most of the buildings seem to be part-time residences. The Via follows a lane, up left then bending left and into woodland. A well-graded path takes you up to Monti di Carcente (40 minutes from Carcente) where you'll find a *sorgente* and many restored buildings. Then follow a nearly level path to Monti di Treccione. The next turn – left and downhill – is indistinct; 50m further on take a right turn uphill. From this point and for the next hour or so, constant care is necessary to follow the waymarkers. Continue past a *sorgente* and 25m further on go left up to a vehicle track and turn right. After barely 10 minutes, pass the houses of Montuglio and continue along the vehicle track. Immediately past a red fire hydrant on the left, bear left up the grassy slope, across some open ground. Continue ahead, keeping more or less level and without markedly changing direction, through birches, to a scattering of substantial, restored stone buildings. Cross meadows to a car park, walk up a bitumen road to the left for a short distance and continue on a gravel road to a T-junction and turn right. This path makes its way up and into Val Vezzedo, and soon narrows. Then come three stream crossings, which might be difficult after heavy rain, then it's on to the settlement of Luina (an hour from Montuglio).

Now the Via takes you across the lower reaches of some meadows, with houses above and magnificent views below. Soon you reach Bracco where there's a left turn by a house named 'Carolina'. Ascend steeply to the small **church** of San Domenico, with more awesome views, and continue uphill. About 250m above the church, you reach the settlement of Piazzuco (about 30 minutes from Luina). The narrow path then dives into wild Val Quaradella. Here two stream crossings are potentially hazardous; about 100m beyond the second, go steeply up to the left to more open ground. Pass below a stone wall, go up to a fountain then up a steep, grassy slope. The path then contours to Alpi di Nalcim (about an hour from Piazzuco).

The path continues contouring, passes through trees and crosses a stream. About 750m further on, turn right downhill; cross two streams and descend right beside the second. You soon pass a couple of houses then reach a larger settlement. Near a large two-storey house with a fenced enclosure, go down right for 30m then left across the slope, keeping right at a vague junction. Go on to a pair of stone buildings with two large trees; bear right to contour downhill and reach a larger settlement – Labiu (Labbio; about 1¼ hours from Alpi di Nalcim). Here you have to be on the lookout for a turn up to a two-storey house with solar heating panels. Keep ascending to a path on the right, which, 700m further on, merges with a wider path and takes you up to the large grey **church** of San Bernardo (30 minutes from Labiu).

Drop down to a saddle below the church and descend generally westwards into Val Dongana, across grassy spurs and small streams. At the first encounter with the buildings of Piazze, turn right and descend to an unmarked junction; waymarking is poor around here. Go down to the right towards a stream but don't cross it; bear slightly left. The frequency of signs then improves as you lose height through trees to the next settlement. Make a right turn, passing in front of Ritrovo Alpino Monte Guaggio. The Via takes you between houses, around to the left and down to a road, concreted for part of the way to a bridge across Torrente Albano. A

wide path then leads on and up steeply to a road at the village of Catasco. Keep ascending to the left along a narrow road and you eventually reach Garzeno (about 1¾ hours from San Bernardo church).

Garzeno

A prominent three-storey building, **Albergo de Jean** (*☎ 0344 880 22; Via Roma 54; doubles €23.25*) is on a sharp bend in the main road at the eastern end of the village. It has basic rooms, some with mountain views. In the large dining room next to the bar, you can feast (for around €5.15) on generous serves of pasta and an excellent *al forno* pizza.

Lago Maggiore

Lago Maggiore may not be dominated by dramatic peaks as is Lago di Como, but at its northern end, close to the Swiss border, are fine peaks offering superb wide views. There are also secluded valleys where tightly clustered villages preserve a wealth of traditional stone buildings and wayside shrines. Tourism is much less pervasive here than around Lago di Garda – you see people going about their everyday lives, growing vegetables, cutting grass, coppicing chestnut trees. The walks in this section centre on the old town of Cannobio, at the entrance to Valle Cannobina where a network of age-old paths offers many opportunities for both easy and strenuous walks. Make sure you take a ferry ride on the lake, to fully appreciate the town's superb setting at the end of its long wooded valley.

NATURAL HISTORY

At 65km, Lago Maggiore is the longest of the three lakes, though generally on the slender side – no more than 4km at its widest point.

Glacial in origin, its main feeders are Fiume Ticino, coming in from the north and carrying through to become the only outflow at Sesto Calende; Fiume Toce, flowing from the west to a bay between Verbania and Stresa; and Fiume Tresa to the east, which arrives at Luino via Lago di Lugano. The highest and most rugged peaks are in the north and northwest, set well back from the lake: Limidario (2187m) on the Swiss border, flanked by the towering rock walls of the Gridone, and Monte Zeda (2156m) in Parco Nazionale della Val Grande, well west of the small town of Cannero Riviera. Elsewhere, the ranges around the lake are much lower and make for less dramatic, though still very attractive landscape.

Chestnuts dominate the extensive woodlands on the mountainsides, accompanied by oaks, beech, European larch and rhododendrons. For centuries chestnuts were a valuable resource in the valleys although an immense amount of effort was involved in harvesting them, removing the husks, drying them in special buildings, then removing an outer skin and finally an inner skin

Wayside Shrines

Throughout the mountains around Lago Maggiore (and in many other parts of the country), in villages and at roadsides, wayside shrines testify to the importance of religious belief in people's lives. Some are simple – just a crucifix on a stone base. Others are elaborate structures the size of a small room, with altar and cloth, frescoes, statues, flowers and candles.

In Valle Cannobina, numerous shrines were built on the orders of San Carlo, Archbishop of Milan (1564–84). A great reformer, he devised a hierarchy of shrines (or sanctuaries), churches, chapels and crosses to bear witness to the divine presence in people's lives.

Near the old settlement of Bronte, high above the valley, is a particularly interesting shrine, visited on the Valle Cannobina walk (p161). Timber-roofed, it spans the path and protects a weather-beaten wooden crucifix. A sign explains that this was once carried in processions between the Monday and Wednesday before Pentecost (a Christian festival 50 days after Easter). On the Tuesday, the route followed was from a church high in the valley of Rio di Orasso, a tributary of Torrente Cannobina, a few kilometres northwest of the shrine. The procession then moved towards La Piazza (east of Olzeno above Rio Cavaglio), then to two other localities and back to the shrine, whereupon celebrations began.

protecting the precious kernel. This wa then pounded into a fine flour.

Around the lake shores, the mild climate fosters the cultivation of citrus groves and the widespread growth of palms and olean ders in public gardens and along promenades

PLANNING
None of the walks described here goe above 1800m, so the best times to visit ar May to early July, and September to earl October; July and August are the busies and warmest months.

Many of the signposts at junctions and other crucial places along the paths in the area show the average time to the named destination. The pace seems inconsistent - it's easy to match or better some and diffi cult to match others.

Maps
The locally published 1:25,000 map Valle Cannobina, Itinerari Escursionistici show the routes of numerous waymarked path and is the best one for this area.

The IGC 1:25,000 map No 12 Laghi Maggiore d'Orta e di Varese shows most of the paths, but lacks the path numbering scheme as does the Kompass 1:50,000 map No 90 Lago Maggiore, Lago di Varese, which i otherwise useful for general orientation.

If you're a cartophile, it's worth huntin for the Carta Nazionale della Svizzera 1:25,000 No 1332 Brissago – a beautifu map with all the paths but no path numbers

Maps can be purchased at the IAT office in Cannobio (this page) and at various shop in the town, notably the Libreria at the south ern end of Piazza Indipendenza.

Place Names
There are differences between the spelling of many names on the various maps and signposts. Here the signpost version is given first, followed by the Valle Cannobina, Itin erari Escursionistici map version.

ACCESS TOWN
Cannobio
This largish town, filling the lowermos reaches of Valle Cannobina, is the base fo

relaxing near Rifugio Menaggio above Lago di Como

Lake District delicacies

al dei Forni's vast glacier, the largest in the Central Alps, is part of Parco Nazionale dello Stelvio

raditional polentina cake

Lakeside living at Cannero Riviera on Lago Maggiore

Ruins of a WWI fort (left) guard the Dolomites' Cristallo group

Sunset on Tre Cime di Lavaredo

Mountain mirror – the Dolomites reflected on a *rifugio* (mountain hut) window in the Croda del Lago

Sunset lights up the rocks around Forcella Denti di Terrarossa

Mystical Tre Cime de Lavaredo

the walks. Accommodation is limited else-where in the valley and Cannobio has vir-tually all the facilities you're likely to need.

The **IAT office** (*☎/fax 0323 712 12; Viale Vittorio Veneto 4; open Mon-Sat plus Sun afternoon*) is where you can buy maps and bus tickets, and obtain an accommodation brochure and bus timetable.

You can buy Campingaz from **Al Bute-gun del Burg** (*Via Antonio Giovanola 23*) or the nearby, similar 'we-have-everything' shop (*Via Antonio Giovanola 39*).

Places to Stay & Eat On the peninsula be-tween Torrente Cannobino and the lake shore, **Camping Riviera** (*☎/fax 0323 713 60; Via Casali Darbedo; sites €10.35 plus per person €5.95, caravans €51.65, bungalows from €82.65*) has grassed, shady pitches and excellent facilities. There's an on-site **shop** (*open daily*), useful for drinks and bread which can be ordered). Also on site is **Ris-torante Riviera**, which is very informal and good value; pasta and gnocchi are average, but the pizzas have a good crust (to €6.20). A substantial breakfast is also served.

Surrounded by a camping ground, **Albergo del Fiume** (*☎ 0323 73 91 21, fax 0323 701 92; e delfiume@libero.it; Via Darbedo 26; doubles €82.65*) has comfortable, reason-ably priced (by local standards) double rooms with terraces giving good views.

For self catering there are two, centrally lo-cated **supermarkets** (*Viale Vittorio Veneto*) and a larger **Conad supermarket** (*Via Al ago*). There are also several specialty *ali-mentari* (*Via Antonio Giovanola*), a good **fruit and vegetable shop** (*Via Umberto I*) and a de-servedly popular **bakery** (*Piazza San Vittore*).

Ristorante da Nuccia (*☎ 0323 722 93; Via Magistris 43*) enjoys perhaps the best views of the several lakeside restaurants. The chef clearly understands that garlic needs to be tasted if it's listed as an ingredient in a pizza (to €7.25); top up with a generous serve of pasta and finish with an excellent espresso.

Getting There & Away There is no dir-ect, simple way to reach Cannobio by pub-lic transport. The most easily negotiated connections involve catching a train from

Milan Piazza Garibaldi to Gallarate (fre-quent) then changing for Luino (€7, one hour and 35 minutes, frequent). From there **Navigazione Lago Maggiore** (*☎ 800 55 18 01*) operates a ferry service to Cannobio (€2.30, 17 minutes, roughly hourly).

Alternatively, use the Milan Central to Domodossola train service to Stresa (€9.30, one hour and 11 minutes, frequent). Catch a bus to Verbania Intra (roughly hourly) from outside the train station, or walk to the ferry at the lakeside and enjoy a voyage to Ver-bania Intra (€3.90, one hour, every hour). There are also ferries all the way to Canno-bio (€6.45, one hour and 10 minutes, two per day).

The **ASPAN** (*☎ 0323 51 87 11*) Verbania Intra–Brissago bus service, which stops at Cannobio, and a service to Cannobio only (€1.45, 30 minutes, at least six daily), de-part from a stop close to the Intra ferry wharf. Buy tickets from the nearby bar.

By car, follow the A8/26, which skirts the southern end of Lago Maggiore, and the A8 towards Domodossola. Take the Arona exit to the S34; continue for 27km to Cannobio.

Valle Cannobina

Duration	8–9 hours
Distance	24km
Difficulty	demanding
Start/Finish	Cannobio (p160)
Transport	bus, ferry

Summary An ancient network of superbly built paths winding up the valley, past timeless villages, delicate shrines and remains of old settlements in extensive woodlands.

This walk makes for a full day but is rich in interesting features and fine views. It fol-lows old paths and some vehicle tracks, tra-versing the lower northern slopes of Valle Cannobina and returning via a higher level route down the valley of Rio Cavaglio. It has a total ascent of 1340m.

It's possible to do the walk in two stages, breaking at Spoccia, which isn't too far from a bus route to/from Cannobio. The bus stops at Ponte Spoccia, which is reached by a path (800m in distance and 200m in descent) that starts just west of the village. There is an early afternoon bus to Cannobio (Monday to Friday) and from Cannobio to Ponte Spoccia (Thursday mornings).

For refreshments, there's an *alimentari* in Traffiume and in Cavaglio's Piazza San Donnino. You'll pass signs pointing to **Bar Circolo Agli** as you go through Cavaglio; a similarly signposted **bar** in Spoccia was closed at the time of writing.

GETTING TO/FROM THE WALK
To reach an alternative starting point at Traffiume, catch the **ASPAN** (☎ 0323 51 87 11) bus from Cannobio (€0.85). There's a convenient 8.20am departure on Monday, Wednesday, Thursday and Saturday. Back from Traffiume, the bus departs at 4.58pm Saturday and 5.33pm Monday to Friday.

THE WALK (see map p164)
Set out from the southern end of the bridge on the main road over Torrente Cannobino and follow a riverside path to a footbridge; cross it and bear right, then follow Via Curioni to the Traffiume road, which leads to a piazza by a large church. Continue along Via alla Parrocchia, then turn right at a junction to Piazza Municipale, from where you continue along Via Sant'Anna to a car park and the start of a signposted footpath by a large shrine (about 30 minutes from Cannobio).

The path leads up into woodland and soon settles down to contour above the gorge of Torrente Cannobino. Eventually it descends to cross Rio Cavaglio then zigzags up to a road; turn right to reach Cavaglio (an hour to 1½ hours from Traffiume). Signposts opposite a small war memorial indicate the direction to **Gurrone**, initially along a lane then up a very quiet road. This compact village of traditional stone and timber houses is 30 minutes from Cavaglio.

Follow a sign to Spoccia, then bear left along a path where the road bends to the right. A few hundred metres further on keep left at a junction, then, after 30m, go right towards Spoccia. The path wanders up and down and contours past scattered stone

buildings. Nearly an hour from Gurrone you come to a **topographic plate** naming the prominent features in the view, including Monte Zeda to the southwest and the village of Orasso to the northwest. Further on, beyond a few stream crossings, go up to a road; cross diagonally and ascend a bit more to emerge by Spoccia's war memorial (nearly two hours from Gurrone). To reach Ponte Spoccia, turn left when you reach the road (instead of crossing it diagonally) and head west to find the path directly down to Ponte Spoccia. If this fails, then just follow the road all the way to Ponte Gurro, also a bus stop.

Nearby signs point the way onwards – head for Bronte, and again at the next junction, and soon you're above the village car park. Continue up steps and along the path above the car park. The broad path leads on across a stream and up, soon past a beautifully kept **shrine** associated with a traditional Pentecost procession (see the boxed text 'Wayside Shrines', p160). At the next junction continue towards Bronte. Further on, skirt a meadow and continue to gain height to the hamlet of Bronte (an hour from Spoccia).

Follow a narrow path up, behind a building housing an aerial cableway (used to transport everything from shovels to sheep), then pass below some stone ruins. Contour the slope just above some trees; cross a stream and continue briefly through trees, then go up to a path junction. Continue more or less ahead towards Tre Confini. It's up most of the way to this saddle on a long timbered spur (about 45 minutes from Bronte). Follow the path to the right towards Le Biuse. The path becomes a vehicle track at this scattered settlement, where most of the houses have been restored – complete with solar heating panels! About 1km further on, marked paths cut off two bends in the road. Then you need to take a path to the left, through a thicket of yellow-flowering broom, down towards another restored village, Olzeno (40 minutes from Tre Confini). Follow waymarkers between houses and at a small building with a sloping roof (the one-time washing place) turn right and continue past vegetable gardens to a cableway building, from where a clear path descends to a road. Cross the road and set out on a long descent, via stone steps, to Cavaglio (an hour from Olzeno). Here, cross Piazza San Donnino and turn left for the path to Traffiume (1¼ hours from Cavaglio). Retrace your steps to Cannobio (30 minutes) or catch the bus.

Monte Carza

Duration	5½–5¾ hours
Distance	11km
Difficulty	moderate–demanding
Start/Finish	Cannobio (p160)
Transport	bus, ferry

Summary An age-old church and somnolent village, long lake views from a mountain summit, meadows and magnificent chestnut woodlands.

This walk explores the southwestern corner of Valle Cannobina, passing through timeless villages, notably Carmine Superiore with its ancient church, and reaches its highest point at Monte Carza (1116m). Paths and waymarking are generally good throughout. There's an ascent of 1050m.

For refreshments, you'll find an *alimentari* and the small bar-trattoria **Circolo Martiri Viggionese** in Viggiona, for drinks, snacks and more substantial local dishes including polenta.

An Alternative Route (p165) and an Alternative Finish (p165), offering shorter versions of the walk, are outlined. One bypasses Carmine Superiore, the other descends to Cannero Riviera from Carmine Superiore.

THE WALK (see map p164)

From the southern end of the centre of Cannobio set out along the main Valle Cannobina road (S631); about 200m along, turn left along signposted Via Cuserina then shortly left up Casali Bagnara to a sharp bend, where it's left again towards Viggiona. The path ascends into chestnut woodland. About 25 minutes from Cannobio, bear right along a wider track and go up to a road. Walk up past a house surrounded by a high fence and turn left along a lane signposted to Trarego-Viggiona. The ascent continues, past restored farmhouses, to the hamlet of Mulinesc (Molineggi). A fine path then takes you up to a junction – continue straight on towards Carmine Superiore (or turn right here for the Alternative Route, p165). Then it's mostly down until you reach **Carmine Superiore** (see the boxed text, below). Cross a small stream to a path junction. To visit the church go left here, up steps to the piazza in front of the 14th-century building (about one to 1½ hours from Cannobio).

From the junction, walk up a cobbled alley, then turn right at the next two junctions. (At the second junction continue straight if you're descending to Cannero Riviera on the Alternative Finish, p165.)

Carmine Superiore – Pilgrims' Village

Overlooking Lago Maggiore from an unrivalled perch between Cannobio and Cannero Riviera, Carmine is typical of the old villages around the lake. Solidly built houses, separated by tight passageways, cluster intimately around a large church. Some of the houses are empty and decaying; many more have been faithfully restored. This renaissance has helped to reverse the seemingly terminal decline of the village after many residents left during the interwar years. Superiore refers to the village's location above Carmine Inferiore, not to its alleged status.

Carmine and its church of San Gottardo stand on a site first occupied more than 1000 years ago. Construction of the church began in 1300 and was completed a century or more later. The church was the heart of the village and a safe haven for the inhabitants in times of strife. Frescoes by Lombard artisans and dating from the late 14th century still adorn the outside and interior of the church. Those outside are now very faded but the faint colours of the images on the cream walls still convey much of their beauty. At the time of writing a project was underway to restore the interior frescoes. The forecourt – the best place for views of the lake – was the village cemetery until 1875.

About 50 minutes steady ascent brings you to a cobbled lane; continue to Piazza Pasque in **Viggiona**. To reach the **shop** and **bar** in Piazza Vittorio Veneto, walk up Via Tarchetti and take the first left (Via Luigi Canones), which leads to the piazza.

Return to Via Tarchetti and follow it for about 200m then bear right in front of a three-storey house. Go up a few steps then left along a narrow path for about 25m, and left again between farm buildings; continue up past a house with a mural to a road – turn right. Go up past a house on the left then around to the left; a broad path soon materialises. At a junction where a small sign points right to Madonnina, turn left. A narrow path gains height through trees, crosses a small meadow and brings you to a junction where you bear right towards Pro Redond (about 45 minutes from Viggiona). A superb path leads on across a deep gorge to Pro Redond's open spaces and a large farmhouse. Follow a prominently waymarked

path steeply up to the left (generally south) to a vehicle track. The grassy summit of **Monte Carza** isn't much further on, to the left (45 minutes from Pro Redond). It's a magnificent view – the vastness of Lago Maggiore, mountains in most directions, and high-level villages punctuating the deep green woodlands clothing the slopes.

Return to Pro Redond then head down the path signposted to Cannobio. Turn right below the lone house on a wide path, descending through open woodland. About 30 minutes from Pro Redond, turn left at a not particularly prominent junction, and soon turn right in the direction 'Sorgente' and continue down. (The *sorgente* is very sulphurous and really only for mineral water addicts.) Descend to a vehicle track and turn right for 40m, then left down a path. Cross a vehicle track and keep to the path down to the vehicle track again; this time turn right along it. Follow the track around a few bends and bear left down a path which soon

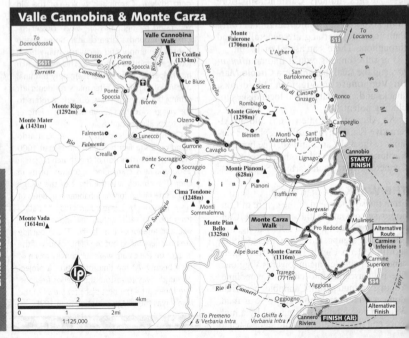

lands you back at a junction just above the Valle Cannobina road, on the edge of Cannobio, nearly 1½ hours from Pro Redond.

Alternative Route: Mulinesc to Viggiona
45 minutes–1 hour, 2km, 240m ascent
If time is short or you would prefer a less strenuous route, you can bypass Carmine Superiore and go direct from Mulinesc to Viggiona. At the junction above Mulinesc turn right. Follow the path up through woodland and eventually past Viggiona's 13th-century church and the adjacent cemetery, and along a lane lined with small shrines to Piazza Pasque in Viggiona, where you can rejoin the main walk.

Alternative Finish: Cannero Riviera
1 hour, 3.75km
For an easier day out and to reach Cannero Riviera, worth a look in its own right, head generally south from Carmine Superiore. Follow the waymarked path from the northern edge of the hamlet, down through trees to the main lakeside road, just east of Cannero Riviera. Cross diagonally, descend steps to a lane and go on to the lakeside. The **ASPAN** (☎ 0323 51 87 11) bus service from Verbania Intra to Brissago passes through Cannero Riviera and will take you back to Cannobio (€0.85, 12 minutes, about hourly). Alternatively, catch the ferry (€2.65, 28 minutes).

Other Walks

LAGO DI GARDA
Navene to Malcesine
Lookouts giving excellent views over Lago di Garda and the mountains to the west are scattered through the tall forest reaching high up the slopes of the Monte Baldo Range. Many different routes can be devised along the network of paths through the forests, such as the 14km one between Navene and Malcesine, via Col di Piombi (Co di Piombi) and Malga Fiabio, involving 1100m of ascent (allow 5½ to six hours) Any of the recommended maps will do (see Maps, p145). Paths are waymarked but you'll need to be sharp-eyed in places. You can expect to meet mountain-bike riders along some of the paths.

Malcesine and Navene, on the main lakeside road, are well served by the APT Verona–Riva del Garda bus (see Getting There & Away, p147, for Malcesine).

Val Dritta
From above Lago di Garda, the connoisseur's approach to Cima Valdritta on the Monte Baldo Range must surely be via the awesome Val Dritta immediately to the west of the peak. The valley could also provide the descent route from the peak, having climbed it via the ridge route from the Monte Baldo *funivia*, as described in the Monte Baldo walk (p143). The 16km (six to 6½ hour) walk offers beautiful beech woods and stupendous views across Lago di Garda. The amount of ascent involved, even by starting from the San Michele *funivia* station, is formidable: 1270m to La Guardiola overlooking Val Dritta and another 270m to the main ridge. The Kompass 1:25,000 No 690 *Alto Garda e Ledro* covers this walk.

This is definitely a route for experienced and confident walkers; the valley holds snow late, so walking poles or an ice axe are essential. If you don't have the experience or the equipment, it would be a beautiful walk just up to the valley and back – a real sense of wildness and unspoiled beauty, no power lines, roads or ski tows.

Valle del Singol & Val Pura
Though it doesn't reach any high points, this is a magnificently scenic loop from Limone, into an awesome valley with the most amazing and improbable path in the area. It involves a couple of minor scrambles, one of which bypasses the crossing of a cliff face where a cable is insecurely fixed to the rock, and a steep descent on a scree-covered path into Val Pura. Allow about four hours for the 8.5km walk; the ascent totals 950m. Carry either the Kompass 1:25,000 No 690 *Alto Garda e Ledro* or the local 1:12,500 *Limone sul Garda* map; neither shows the junction of paths 110 and 109 correctly.

Valle del Singol Alternative
Another highly scenic route around the rim of Valle del Singol is possible. It is more strenuous, but takes less time, than the Valle del Singol walk (p149). Starting and finishing at Limone, it covers 16km and involves about 1500m ascent; allow at least 6½ hours. The paths are well waymarked; carry either the local 1:12,500 *Limone sul Garda* map or the Kompass 1:25,000 No 690 *Alto Garda e Ledro*, though the latter's path numbers and junctions are inaccurate. The route takes you to the foot of Mt Traversole (worth climbing for the magnificent view), to the saddle between Corna Vecchia and Corno Nero, to Baita Segala

and back to Limone via the meadows of Malga Dalo and Malgo Valacco.

Monte Carone

The highest peak overlooking Valle Singol, Monte Carone (1621m), can be reached on a 13km day walk from Limone. Allow about seven hours return; it involves about 1600m ascent. From the summit, with its crucifix (see the boxed text 'War in the Mountains', p150) and flag pole, the views of the Monte Baldo Range are superb. The Kompass 1:25,000 No 690 *Alto Garda e Ledro* map gives an idea of what's involved but the locally produced 1:12,500 *Limone sul Garda* map is more useful.

LAGO DI COMO
Sass Corbee & Il Rogolone

Sass Corbee is a huge boulder sitting in an impressive canyon on Torrente Sanagra, several kilometres upstream from Menaggio. It's the objective of a comparatively easy half-day walk from the town (around three hours, 10km, with 300m ascent). The route follows quiet roads and paths.

Sass Corbee can be combined with a 10km walk to Il Rogolone, an ancient oak tree in a clearing about 2km northwest of Codogna. The tree is traditionally associated with local law-making as far back as the 16th century. Allow about 1½ hours return from La Chioderia Vecchia, a bar-trattoria and trout farm on the Sass Corbee route.

Both routes are described in a leaflet *Hiking in the Areas around Menaggio* available from the IAT in Menaggio (p153).

Val di Darengo

This spectacularly rugged and wild valley, cradling Torrente Livo, reaches deep into the mountains north from the village of Livo (on the Via dei Monti Lariani) and high above the lakeside towns of Gravedona and Domaso. From Livo the CAI has waymarked a route through the valley, with signposts and red dots, as far as Rifugio Como on the edge of Lago di Darengo (1790m).

When an attempt was made to survey this walk in 2001, the path immediately above the next bridge upstream from Ponte di Borgo was blocked by a landslide and flooding. Nevertheless, the walk to this point is highly recommended. Allow five hours return from Livo; about 14km and 500m ascent is involved. It's described in a leaflet *Lago di Darengo* available from the IAT in Menaggio (p153), where you should be able to obtain advice about the condition of the route through to Rifugio Como.

For access, you can catch an SPT bus (route C18) from Dongo or Gravedona to Livo (€1.20).

LAGO MAGGIORE
Monte Faierone & Monte Giove

Towering over the lower reaches of Valle Cannobina, Monte Faierone (1706m) affords excellent views of Lago Maggiore and the surrounding mountains, and a rare opportunity in the area to enjoy walking through open grassland. Starting from Lignago and finishing in Cannobio, the 14km walk involves 1500m ascent and should take 7½ to eight hours. Take the local 1:25,000 *Valle Cannobina, Itinerari Escursionistici* map, available from the IAT office in Cannobio (p160). The route follows waymarked and signposted paths. The bus from Cannobio to Sant'Agata (€0.85, Tuesdays and Fridays only) saves you 270m ascent and about 45 minutes.

Monte Giove (1298m) is an outlier of Monte Faierone to the southeast and rising directly from lowermost Valle Cannobina. It also provides excellent panoramic views and a shorter, less strenuous walk than that to Monte Faierone. Allow about six hours; 1100m ascent is involved. It is reached by starting out on the Monte Faierone route, and turning off near Rombiago. Return via Biessen, Sant'Agata and Traffiume.

Crealla & Monti Sommalemna

There are many very well-preserved stone buildings among the chestnut woodlands between Gurrone and Lunecco on the northern side of Valle Cannobina. On the opposite side of the valley, from Crealla to Socraggio, there are also many beautiful shrines, plus superb views of the upper valley. East from Socraggio, paths link several high meadows – reminders of another aspect of the valley's history – affording magnificent views. All this can be linked in a long, 20km day's walk starting and finishing at Traffiume; allow 7¾ to 8¼ hours; 1410m ascent is involved.

The paths are well signposted and waymarked. Though not entirely accurate, the 1:25,000 *Valle Cannobina, Itinerari Escursionistici* map is the one to carry. The walk could also be divided into stages by using the infrequent bus services in Valle Cannobina. Visit the IAT office in Cannobio (p160) to buy the map or inquire about bus services to/from Traffiume, Lunecco and Socraggio.

Walk from Cannobio to Cavaglio and Gurrone as per the Valle Cannobina walk (p161). Continue through Lunecco, Crealla (with its beautifully preserved church and shrines), Luena (a deserted hamlet with superb views, Corte and on to peaceful Socraggio. The route then takes in Voias (Aurasco), Voia (Monti Voja), the spacious meadows of Monti Sommalemna, and Pianon before returning to Traffiume.

Stelvio

Parco Nazionale dello Stelvio is Italy's third-largest national park, protecting 1346 sq km of mountainous country in the regions of Trentino-Alto Adige or South Tyrol (Südtirol) and Lombardy (Lombardia). Bordering the Swiss National Park in the northwest, and the contiguous Parco Naturale Adamello-Brenta and Parco Regionale dell'Adamello in the south, it forms the larger part of a vast, protected area of around 2634 sq km. The core of the national park is the Ortles-Cevedale mountain massif, essentially an array of huge ridges arranged roughly east to west and culminating in the park's highest peaks, Monte Cevedale (Zufallspitze, 3769m), Gran Zebrù (Königspitze, 3851m) and Orles (Ortler, 3905m), towering over sprawling glaciers and snowfields. Reaching into the heart of the massif are deep valleys, forested and settled on the lower slopes, and meadows, boulder fields, vast moraine deposits and rock above.

Diverse cultural traditions are exceptionally important in the park – one of its purposes is to protect and uphold them. South Tyrol, once part of the Austro-Hungarian empire, was shifted into Italy at the end of WWI, but differences in language and culture endure (see the boxed text 'An Alpine Battlefield', p170). German is generally the preferred language in South Tyrol, while Italian comes first in Lombardy and Trentino to the south.

The park was established in 1935 and extended to its present area in 1977. A national park council decides on management policies and rules. These are carried out by three regional or provincial directive committees, which delegate the day-to-day running of the park to forestry officers.

Stelvio is extremely well organised for walkers with hundreds of kilometres of well-marked and generally well-maintained paths. There is also an extensive network of *rifugi* (mountain huts) and plenty of accommodation in villages.

Highlights

Gran Zebrù (3851m) towers above Val di Cedec in the heart of Stelvio National Park

- Witness social and cultural contrasts between German-speaking South Tyrol and Italian Lombardy
- Explore fine paths over high passes and through deep valleys on the Val di Rabbi to Martelltal walk (p170)
- Wander through beautiful cool pine and larch woodlands, not so dense as to hide the spectacular views
- Climb commanding mountain peaks overlooking a spectacular glacier in Val dei Forni (p178)

This chapter introduces the huge range of walks available with a three- or four-day tour from Val di Rabbi in the southeast to Martelltal (Val Martello) in the central north. Other Walks (p178) outlines a flexible 1½- or two-day walk around Val dei Forni and Val di Cedec in the west, near the town of Bormio.

CLIMATE

Stelvio's climate is predominantly alpine in character. July and August are the wettest months (around 100mm each month), the rain borne mainly on southerly or easterly winds. Afternoon thunderstorms are common, presaged by towering cumulus then lower, flatter nimbus clouds. The rainfall for May and September is considerably lower, as little as half that of the summer months. Heavy snowfalls typify winter, although snow can fall at any time of the year.

In summer the average temperature is well into the 20s in the valleys but decreases markedly with altitude. It's not uncommon for summer days to dawn fine and clear, but become cloudy over the mountains during the warmest part of the day.

During April and May, in particular, the föhn, a warm, dry wind, can affect the area. The temperature rises rapidly, possibly triggering avalanches and accelerating the thaw of winter snow.

INFORMATION
When to Walk

In most years snow should have retreated from all but the highest ground by mid-June, and heavy and persistent snow should not return until early October. Lower-level walks in the valleys should be accessible from May to October.

Maps & Books

The Touring Club Italiano's 1:200,000 map *Trentino-Alto Adige* is ideal for general planning and access information in the wider Stelvio region.

Among the Italian-language titles, *Escursioni Parco dello Stelvio Trentino e Alto Adige*, by Paolo Turetti & Tiziano Mochan, and *Escursioni Parco dello Stelvio Alta Valcamonica e Alta Valtellina*, by Paolo Turetti, have planimetric maps and lots of background information, plus walk descriptions. They're available at national park visitor centres.

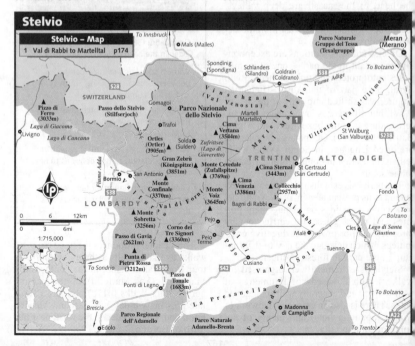

Place Names

Italian names are either used exclusively or given precedence over German names in Trentino and Lombardy, but German is preferred over Italian names in South Tyrol (eg, Martelltal/Val Martello). However, in Stelvio you'll find some path signposts with both or only one (commonly German) version, and even with different spellings in the one language of the same place (eg, Passo Soy and Forcella di Soi). The locally preferred version is given precedence in this chapter.

Emergency

If you need emergency assistance in the Malè area, you can contact the local **mountain rescue** (☎ 0339 630 51 33). If on the west side of the park, you can contact the Bormio based **mountain rescue** (☎ 0342 90 46 86). In South Tyrol you can also contact the regional search and rescue branch of the **Corpo Nazionale Soccorso Alpino e Speleologico** (☎ 0471 79 71 71). Otherwise, for medical assistance contact the **national emergency number** (☎ 118).

GATEWAYS
Bormio

The nearest sizeable town on the western side of the park is Bormio (just beyond the boundary), with a wide choice of accommodation.

Information The **APT office** (☎ 0342 90 33 00; e aptbormio@provincia.so.it; Via Roma 131B) issues an accommodation guide and plenty of other useful information. The **park headquarters** (☎ 0342 91 01 00, fax 0342 91 90 63; w www.stelviopark.it; Via Roma 26) has leaflets about the park and topo maps, and can give fairly reliable information about local conditions. The website offers an informative introduction to the park's natural and cultural history.

Places to Stay & Eat Among the numerous hotels, **Hotel Stella Alpina** (☎ 0342 91 03 97, fax 0342 90 47 41; e hotelstella@ tiscalinet.it; Via Roma 101; B&B around €38.75) is a typical midrange establishment offering unpretentious, comfortable rooms.

Ristorante-Pizzeria Contado (☎ 0342 90 34 34; Via della Vittoria 6) is the place to go for an *al forno* (cooked in a wood-fired oven) pizza (to €7.75) and local specialities. **Trattoria Notte e Di** (☎ 0342 90 33 39; Piazza Cavour 15) is quite different. Local dishes are prominent on the menu; you'll pay around €15.50 for two substantial courses.

There are an *alimentari* (grocery shop) and a *macelleria* (butcher) on Piazza Cavour, and two **supermarkets** in Via Nesini and Via Fiera.

Getting There & Away To reach Bormio from the south, a regular train service runs from Milan Central to Tirano (€11.90, 2½ hours). This connects with a **Perego** (☎ 0342 70 12 00, 0342 90 50 90) bus service to Bormio (€2.60). Buy tickets at the bus station or on board.

From the north, **SAD** (☎ 800 84 60 47) operates one of the most exciting bus rides in Italy. From July to mid-September at least three buses daily go from Schlanders (Silandro) in Vinschgau (Val Venosta) to Stilfserjoch (Passo dello Stelvio), via Spondinig (Spondigna). The fare is about €4.40. This should connect at the pass with the equally enthralling Perego service down to Bormio (€1.70).

By road, Bormio is on the S38, which links Bolzano with the northern end of Lago di Como, via Passo dello Stelvio, Bormio, Tirano and Sondrio.

Malè

A smallish old town in Val di Sole, Malè is close to the threshold of Val di Rabbi and outside the park.

The well-organised **APT office** (☎ 0463 90 12 80, fax 0463 90 29 11; w www.valdisole .net; Piazza Regina Elena; open daily) issues a comprehensive *Useful Information* booklet in several languages, as well as a trekking booklet for Stelvio and nearby Parco Naturale Adamello-Brenta, outlining walks between *rifugi*. Accommodation information is also available.

Maps can be purchased from the *tabaccheria* (Via E Bezzi) near the large church.

Places to Stay & Eat Conveniently close to the train and bus station, the **Hotel Alle Alpi** (☎ *0463 90 11 45, fax 0463 90 19 41;* W *www.hotelallealpi.com; Via Garibaldi 12; doubles with half board €43.90)* has simply furnished rooms. The rate represents good value and includes a substantial three-course evening meal of simple, unpretentious fare. An altogether different place is **La Segosta** (☎ *0463 90 13 90, fax 0463 90 06 75;* e *segosta@tin.it; Via Trento 59; B&B doubles €41.30),* with modern, tastefully decorated rooms. Local specialities are prominent on La Segosta's menu. The barley soup is almost a meal by itself and the

An Alpine Battlefield

At the outbreak of WWI, Italy looked north from Lombardy into Südtirol, in the Austro-Hungarian empire, and saw water resources, industrial development opportunities and a conduit into central Europe. What's more, it was believed that since Südtirol was on the Italian side of the Alps, the area belonged in Italy.

The Ortles-Cevedale range (now within Stelvio) became the highest battleground of the war, known as the Cevedale front. Both sides dug in, overcoming the rugged terrain and severe winter weather.

Remnants of the defences can still be seen in several places in the park: at Rifugio Corsi high up in Martelltal, above Val di Cedec and especially around Passo dello Stelvio. There's a small and fascinating museum at the pass, in the bank's premises.

At the end of the war, national boundaries were abolished and a new, coldly logical line drawn between Italy and Austria, along the watershed north of Vinschgau (Val Venosta), ignoring the language and culture of the people affected. Part of the Austrian province of Tirolo became Südtirol (later Alto Adige) in Italy. Further south, Trentino was returned to Italy, where it felt much more at home.

Trentino-Alto Adige is now an autonomous Alpine region, the union of two quite different provinces in a lucrative arrangement to protect their identities and to appease nationalists on both 'sides'.

gnocchi are feather-light. Expect to pay around €18.10 for two courses.

For supplies, there's a **supermarket** *(closed Sunday afternoon)* at the western end of town.

Getting There & Away A private company, **Ferrovia Trento-Malè** (☎ *0463 90 11 50),* operates a train service between Trento (on the FS Verona–Bolzano–Brennero line) and Malè (€3.70, one hour and 35 minutes, several trains daily); Trento station is about 250m from the FS platforms. The train also connects with the FS line at Mezzocorno, between Trento and Bolzano. The Verona to Trento fare is €7.25.

SAB (☎ *035 28 90 11)* bus group operates a service from Milan (Piazza Castello) to Malè (5½ hours, once a day Monday to Saturday), arriving midevening.

By road from the east, turn west off the A22 at the San Michele junction (between Trento and Bolzano) and follow S43 and then S42 north and west respectively to Malè, a distance of 41km.

Val di Rabbi to Martelltal

Duration	4 days
Distance	55km
Difficulty	moderate–demanding
Start	Bagni di Rabbi
Finish	Martell
Nearest Towns	San Bernardo & Bagni di Rabbi (p171), Martell (p172)
Transport	bus

Summary An exceptionally scenic and varied tour on excellent paths and tracks, through valleys and over high mountain passes with several possible variations.

This walk traverses valleys and intervening ridges in the east part of the park, within the Trentino and South Tyrol sections. It's a wonderfully varied excursion; cultivated valleys dotted with well-tended farms and Tyrolean-style villages, pine woodlands, open mountainsides and ridges with fantastic views of peaks and glaciers, and mountain tarns.

The reservoirs in Ultental (Grünsee and Weissbrunnsee) and Martelltal (Zufrittsee) may seem out of place in a national park, but the abundant waters from the glaciers and streams are an invaluable resource for the low-lying, intensively cultivated Vinschgau (Val Venosta) to the north. Geologically, metamorphic rocks are the most widespread type – mica schists to the west of Val di Rabbi, quartz-phyllite extending from Monte Cevedale along the Ultental-Martelltal ridge, with limestone and dolomite further west. Apart from marmots, wildlife is elusive; domestic grazing animals are far more common up to high levels in the valleys.

The valleys are deep and the linking passes high, so this is an energetic walk, with a total of 3640m ascent. The paths and minor vehicle tracks followed are almost all well maintained, so the walking is never difficult; waymarking, using a numbering system, and signposting are excellent throughout.

Day 4, not essential to completing the overall tour, is a highly recommended, comparatively easy walk from Enzianhütte, high up in Martelltal, down the valley to Martell; a fascinating bus journey links the end of Day 3 and Day 4.

You can vary the described route to make easier days. From Bagni di Rabbi you can:

1) go direct to Rifugio Stella Alpina, a half-day walk, allowing for a late start;
2) ascend to Rifugio Stella Alpina then go down to St Gertraud for the first night; or
3) stay at Rifugio Dorigoni on the first night, then follow route 107 to Rifugio Canziani, bypassing Rifugio Stella Alpina and St Gertraud. From Rifugio Canziani, go straight to Soyscharte and down to Martelltal.

Some alternatives are included in the route description, and you can enter or exit the walk from San Gertraud at the end of Day 2.

PLANNING
When to Walk
Those parts of the route above 2600m should normally be free of snow between June and late September, although an unseasonable fall of snow at the beginning of September when the walk was surveyed

made it difficult to follow the waymarkers on the descent from Soyscharte (Day 3).

What to Bring
No special equipment is required during the recommended season but gaiters and an ice axe would probably be welcome, if not necessary, at other times. You'll find refreshment places during the course of each day's walk, but it would still be wise to carry some food and drink to tide you over.

Maps & Books
Unfortunately, complete coverage of the walk at the ideal scale of 1:25,000 isn't available. The best map is the Tabacco 1:25,000 No 08 *Ortles-Cevedale/Ortlergebiet*, which covers the earlier and middle parts of Day 1, the end of Day 3 and Day 4; some path junctions are incorrect.

The Kompass 1:50,000 map No 072 *Parco Nazionale dello Stelvio* covers the entire area but isn't always accurate. Some of its place names are, well, unique; with a 1:500,000 map and notes in Italian and German on the reverse, it's good for planning.

The Kompass 1:25,000 map No 637 *Cevedale-Valle di Pejo-Alta Valfurva* covers Day 1 as far as the peak Gleck (Collècchio).

Guida Escursionistica Val di Sole, published by Kompass, is an Italian-language guide describing 49 outings, of which 10 are in Val di Rabbi. It has reduced 1:50,000 maps on which the route is superimposed.

NEAREST TOWNS
San Bernardo & Bagni di Rabbi
Several small villages and hamlets are spread out along Val di Rabbi, the largest of which is San Bernardo, 3km from the start of the walk at Bagni di Rabbi.

Information The San Bernardo **Ufficio Turistico** (☎/fax 0463 98 50 48; ⊞ www .valdirabbi.com; open Mon-Sat June-Sept) is useful for accommodation information. In Bagni di Rabbi, the **Stelvio visitor centre** (☎ 0463 98 51 90; ⊞ www.stelviopark.it; open daily) sells maps, reference books and walking guides; a detailed weather forecast is posted outside.

Places to Stay & Eat Beside the road, about 250m downhill from the bus stop at Bagni di Rabbi, is **Hotel-Garni Alpenrose** (☎/fax 0463 98 50 98; e hotelalpenrose@ tin.it; B&B/half board €30.50/40.30). Also in the village is **Bar Rosa delle Alpi** and a **supermarket** (open daily). In San Bernardo there are several **bars** and **cafés**.

Getting There & Away Private company **Ferrovia Trento-Malè** (☎ 0463 90 11 50) operates a daily bus service from Malè to Bagni di Rabbi (€1.55), via San Bernardo, with at least five buses each way. Buy tickets at the Malè bus station or on board. By road, SP86 branches off S42 about 2km northeast of Malè; Bagni di Rabbi is 11km up the valley.

Martell (Martello)

In the Martelltal, the area of greatest interest to walkers is around the village of Martell (also known as Dorf), above the main road through the valley. The small **Pro Loco** office (☎ 0473 74 45 98, fax 0473 74 46 98; w www .martell.suedtirol.com; Dorf 96; open mornings only Mon-Fri) can help with accommodation information, local guidebooks (in Italian and German) and maps.

Places to Stay & Eat The most convenient, although far from the most scenically located, of several hotels is **Gasthof Waldheim** (☎ 0473 74 45 45, fax 0473 74 45 46; e waldheim@rolmail.net; St Maria in der Schmelz 16; B&B/half board €28.40/38.75). It's a modern, typically Tyrolean establishment beside the main road.

Scenically located is the **Gasthof Premstl** (☎ 0473 74 47 66; Ennetal 228; B&B/half board €22.20/33.60) at Premstlhof. If you reach Martell by bus, it's not impossibly far to walk up to this friendly place. It offers smallish, simply furnished rooms with great valley views. The substantial evening meals have a distinctly Tyrolean bias. The host is a qualified Alpine guide of some renown.

There are several other well-located and welcoming establishments on the valley slopes, notably the **Niederhof Agriturismo** (☎ 0473 74 45 34), which charges similar rates to Gasthof Premstl. It can be reach from the valley road via signposted paths and tracks from a bridge about 250m down (northeast) the main road from the **Hölderle Café**, where meals are available.

For supplies, there's a small **shop** in Martell.

Getting There & Away From Schlanders, SAD (☎ 800 84 60 47) operates buses to Martell (€1.80) at least four times daily; buy tickets on board. This service connects with the frequent SAD service through Vinschgau (Val Venosta) between Meran (Merano) and Mals (Malles). Meran is at the end of the train line from Bolzano, which is on the Verona–Brennero line.

By road, turn off the busy S38 at Goldrain (Coldrano; 24km west of Meran, 28km southeast of Mals); it's 12km to Martell. To reach Premstlhof from Martell, follow roads to Ennetal (Valdene) and Walderg (Selva).

GETTING TO/FROM THE WALK

To get to the start of the walk, see Getting There and Away (this page) for San Bernado & Bagni di Rabbi. If you're walking straight up to Rifugio Stella Alpina (see Alternative Route: via Malga Palude Bassa, p175), catch a bus to Piazzola (only some of the Bagni di Rabbi services go there). If driving, there is a large car park at Somrabbi, a short distance up the road from Bagni di Rabbi, and others further up the valley along a gravel road. If you're going to Rifugio Stella Alpina and back, the dedicated car park is reached by turning off SP86 for Piazzola about 1km north-west of San Bernardo and continuing via Piazze, following signs to the car park.

For transport options from the finish of the walk, see Getting There & Away (this page) for Martell.

THE WALK
Day 1: Bagni di Rabbi to Rifugio Stella Alpina

7–7¼ hours, 16km, 1600m ascent

From the bus stop at Bagni di Rabbi, set off along the bitumen road up the valley. After about 25 minutes you come to a signposted junction on the left for a *percorso alternativo* (alternative route) to 'Coler', 'Stablasolo' (Malga Stablasol) and 'Saent' (Cascate di Saènt). Cross Torrente Rabbiès on a footbridge and follow this path for about 1km, then as it peters out, bear right to the valley road. Go to the right of the road, cross the bridge over the stream and take a path to the left, signposted to 'Malga Stablasolo' and 'Cascate di Saent'; there's a large car park nearby. Continue up the road, past **Albergo Fontanin** (☎ 0463 90 20 80), then follow a riverbank path for 20 minutes to a signposted junction; cross a bridge and head towards 'Malga Stablasolo', via slabs through a boulder field and a track up to the *malga* (herders' summer hut), where you can enjoy a drink overlooking the depths of the narrow valley.

Press on, up the vehicle track signposted to Rifugio Dorigoni; the valley is wider now and unrelentingly rugged with extremely steep cliffs separated by precipitous grassy slopes on which are glued clumps of pines. A short distance along the track, follow a path signposted 106 and you soon come to a small **national park visitor centre**. This houses a wonderful (free) display starring marmots, the most numerous wildlife in this part of the park – 7000 of them at last count. Rejoin the path behind the visitor centre; it climbs steeply to 'Dosso dell'Cros' (Dosso del Cros), 30 minutes from Malga Stablasol. Dosso del Cros is a national park outstation where there's a spring and a superb view of Cascate di Saènt.

Go through a gate above Dosso del Cros and bear left at a path junction, towards Rifugio Campisol. (The path to the right, route 106, descends to Val Saènt, then continues up to Rifugio Dorigoni.) The narrow path rises steeply though open larch forest with occasional views of the cascade and the peaks above. About 45 minutes from Dosso del Cros, you reach Rifugio Campisol, locked but with picnic tables outside. The path to Rifugio Dorigoni (now 128), leads on across boulders, through a narrow gap and across a steam. It then sets out on a superb, undulating traverse across scree, boulders and grass. Beyond a small stream with stepping stones, the path rises steeply through crags to a grassy basin. Cross it, then go up the slope on

the right, across a broad spur, and down into the main valley. Continue to a signposted junction; the path on the right is 106, the alternative route from near Dosso del Cros. Turn left, soon cross a stream then climb to **Rifugio Saènt Silvio Dorigoni** (☎ 0463 98 51 07; **e** info@rifugiodorigoni.it; beds €16.55), which charges an extra €3.60 for a shower. A filling three-course dinner adds up to another €15.50 or so. The *rifugio* is perched on a shelf below a massive crag-covered hill (1½ hours from Rifugio Campisol).

Follow a waymarked path from the valley side of the *rifugio*, across the slope (eastwards), past a pond, across a stream and then a grassy, flat area. You soon come to a junction; signposts point right for route 130 (Malga Artise) and left for 107. There's a separate sign nearby for route 145 to Rifugio Lago Corvo [*sic*]; this is now your number. The clear path leads towards dark cliffs, then over scree and up across a very steep, boulder-strewn slope. Nearly two hours from the *rifugio*, you reach the crest of the ridge (at 2833m) enclosing Val di Rabbi to the northeast and east; signposts indicate the way onwards, following route 145 along the ridge. For a direct route to Rifugio Canziani from here, drop down to the east with route 107. This descends steeply past Lago Nero in the valley of Valschauser Bach (Rio Valsura) and meets the route of Day 2 of this walk near Langsee (Lago Lungo).

To continue to Rifugio Stella Alpina, head along the ridge, gaining some height. If the weather is fine, diverge to **Gleck** (Collècchio; 2957m), signed as 'Cima Collècchio', for even wider views; the way up is marked by large cairns and the destination painted on a boulder. The main path continues along the ridge for a shortish distance, then bears down left, below a minor summit on the right; the steep descent now starts in earnest. Eventually, once on relatively level ground, you pass one of the larger of the Laghi Corvo near its outlet; continue down past a path junction, across a stream, to the *rifugio* (1½ to 1¾ hours from the ridge).

The **Rifugio Stella Alpina al Lago Corvo** (☎ 0463 98 51 75; B&B/half board €19.65/ 35.10) is a friendly, homely place; bedrooms

STELVIO

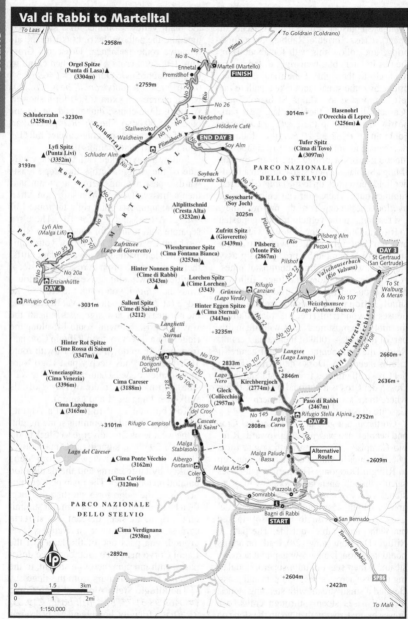

Val di Rabbi to Martelltal

To Laas

To Goldrain (Coldrano)

+2958m

No 11

No 8

Martell (Martello)
FINISH

Orgel Spitze
(Punta di Lasa) ▲
(3304m)

Ennetal

Premstlhof

+2759m

No 244

Rio

Schluderzahn
(3258m) ▲

+3230m

No 26

3014m +

Hasenohrl
(l'Orecchia di Lepre) ▲
(3256m)

No 15

No 32

Niederhof

Schludertal

Stallweishof

Hölderle Café

END DAY 3

Lyfi Spitz
(Punta Livi)
(3352m)

Waldheim

Plimabach

Soy Alm

Tufer Spitz
(Cima di Tovo)
▲ (3097m)

Schluder Alm

No 34

Soybach
(Torrente Soi)

PARCO NAZIONALE
DELLO STELVIO

3193m +

R o s i m t a l

No 0

Soyscharte
(Soy Joch)
3025m

No 142

Altplittschnid
(Cresta Alta)
(3232m) ▲

Pilsberg Alm

Pilsberg
(Monte Pils)
(2867m) ▲

(Rio

Pozza)

DAY 3
St Gertraud
(San Gertrude)

Lyfi Alm
(Malga Lifi)

No 8

Zufrittsee
(Lago di Gioveretto)

Zufritt Spitz
▲ (Gioveretto)
(3439m)

Pilbach

Pilshof

No 12

Valschauserbach
(Rio Valsura)

P e d e r t a l

No 35

No 20

Wiessbrunner Spitz
(Cima Fontana Bianca)
(3253m) ▲

To St
Walburg
& Meran

No 70

M A R T E L L T A L

No 20a

Enzianhütte
DAY 4

Hinter Nonnen Spitz
(Cime di Rabbi)
(3343m) ▲

Lorchen Spitz
(Cime Lorchen)
(3343)

Grünsee
(Lago Verde)

Rifugio
Canziani

No 107

Weissbrunnsee
(Lago Fontana Bianca)

Rifugio Corsi

+3031m

Hinter Eggen Spitze
▲ (Cima Sternai)
(3443m)

No 12

Kirchbergtal

(Valle di Montechiesa)

2660m +

Sallent Spitz
(Cime di Saènt)
(3212)

Langhetti
di
Sternai

+3235m

No 107

Langsee
(Lago Lungo)

2636m +

Hinter Rot Spitze
(Cime Rossa di Saèmt)
(3347m) ▲

Rifugio
Dorigoni
(Saènt)

No 107

2833m

No 107

No 130

No 12

2846m

Veneziaspitze
(Cima Venezia)
(3396m) ▲

Cima Careser
(3188m) ▲

No 106

No 128

Lago
Nero

Kirchbergjoch
(2774m)

Paso di Rabbi
(2467m)

No 108

Cima Lagolungo
(3165m) ▲

Dosso
del Cros

Gleck
(Collècchio)
(2957m)

Rifugio Stella Alpina
+2752m
DAY 2

+3101m

Rifugio Campisol

Cascate
di Saènt

No 145

2808m

Laghi
Corvo

No 108

Lago del Càreser

Cima Ponte Vécchio
(3162m) ▲

Malga
Stablasolo

Malga Palude
Bassa

**Alternative
Route**

+2609m

Cima Cavión
(3120m) ▲

Albergo
Fontanín

Coler

Malga Artise

Piazzola

Somrrabbi

PARCO NAZIONALE
DELLO STELVIO

Bagni di Rabbi
START

San Bernado

Cima Verdignana
(2938m) ▲

+2892m

Torrente Rabbies

+2604m

+2423m

SP86

0   1.5   3km
0   1   2mi

1:150,000

To Malè

have two, four or five beds; facilities, including a hot shower (€2.60), are shared. The three-course evening meal is substantial and filling.

Alternative Route: via Malga Palude Bassa

2¾–3 hours, 5km, 1230m ascent

From the upstream side of the national park visitor centre, follow a path signposted 'Piazzola' up to a road; turn right and walk along the road, through a small piazza (where there's a bus stop for the Malè service) and **Bar Rosa delle Alpi**; 50m further on there's a **supermarket**. Continue to a road junction where there are signs to various places, including 'Laghi Corvo' via route 108. Walk left along this road for a few hundred metres to a junction and go left again with route 108. The road gains height between meadows; continue along a vehicle track from the end of the bitumen and, further up, pass the car park for the *rifugio* on the right. A few minutes further on, diverge left up a waymarked path, which ascends steeply through two crossroads to a gravel road; keep following the red and white waymarkers.

About 1½ hours from the start, you come to a gravel road more or less in the open; turn right and you soon reach the ruinous buildings of **Malga Palude Bassa**. A couple of minutes further on, turn up to the left, as waymarked, through trees; at the next gravel road, go right for a short distance then bear left again up a path. About 25 minutes from the *malga* cross a stream to a path junction where 108 goes both ways. The route to the right is longer, slightly less steep, and, in its upper reaches, eroded and bare. The path to the left goes straight up the valley to the *rifugio*, another 45 minutes.

Day 2: Rifugio Stella Alpina to St Gertraud

5¼–5¾ hours, 12km, 1540m descent, 640m ascent

There are two routes to St Gertraud (San Gertrude) from the *rifugio*. Described here is the longer, more scenic route. The direct approach follows route 108 down Kirchbergtal (Valle di Montechiesa) on a vehicle track most of the way. This leads you to a road near the centre of the village; the bus stop is down to the right. To reach the accommodation listed, follow small signs marked 'Kirche' (church) up to the left.

It is now necessary to go all the way down to St Gertraud because the very conveniently located hotel beside Weissbrunnsee was closed when this walk was surveyed in September 2001. The alternative would be to stay at Rifugio Canziani.

From Rifugio Stella Alpina, retrace the previous day's steps for about 250m to a path junction by a stream crossing and follow path 12 to the right (north). This route now follows a different line from that shown on the Kompass 1:50,000 map. The faintish path crosses a sheep-cropped meadow towards the cliffs of the Kirchbergjoch ridge, then makes a rising traverse through crags and across grass, below the cliffs. About 45 minutes from the *rifugio*, on a rocky spur, the path turns sharply left (don't be seduced by the clear onward path) and ascends to a **pass** at 2846m (one to 1¼ hours from the *rifugio*). The fine view northwards is painted in greens, dull red and greenish grey: the lakes in the valley below, artificial Grünsee (Lago Verde) beyond, overlooked by the soaring heights of Hinter Eggen Spitze (Cima Sternai; 3443m) to the west and Pilsberg (Monte Pils; 2867m) to the east, with Rifugio Canziani sitting quietly on the shore of Grünsee.

The well-made path makes relatively easy work of the descent through scree, then it's across rocky meadows to a succession of easy stream crossings. The fourth, however, may

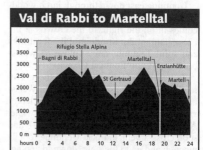

Val di Rabbi to Martelltal

dictate a minor diversion of about 30m downstream to keep your boots dry. About 45 minutes from the pass, you meet route 107 at a path junction. A few metres further on, the path divides; bear left (route 12). The path to the right is 107, which can be followed down to the valley of Valschauserbach (Rio Valsura), bypassing Rifugio Canziani and joining the main route above Weissbrunnsee; not as the Kompass 1:50,000 maps shows it, with route 107 skirting the lake.

Continuing towards Rifugio Canziani, ascend to overlook Grünsee and a substantial slice of Ultental (Val d'Ultimo) stretching away northeastwards. Then descend slightly and continue on an extraordinary path of huge flat slabs up to the reservoir wall. Cross the wall and go up to a path junction; the *rifugio* is nearby to the left (1¾ to two hours from the pass).

Considered elegant by *rifugio* standards, **Rifugio Canziani** *(Höchsterhütte; ☎/fax 0473 79 81 20; e info@rifugiocanziani.it; 39010 St Gertraud, Ultental; beds €15.50)* is a CAI establishment. The bright dining room is very tempting; the modern bedrooms have from three to 10 beds.

To continue, pass the electricity authority installations and descend a wide track, which soon becomes a well-used path (route 140), zigzagging down the steep slope. About 45 minutes from the *rifugio*, pass the turn-off to the left for route 12 to Pilsberg Alm. If you're following this route to Soyscharte (Soy Joch), pick up the main route in the description of Day 3 at a junction above Weissbrunnsee; allow 1¼ to 1½ hours to reach this junction.

Continue east down through larch woodland, passing a junction where route 107 comes in on the right, to the crowds at the bar-restaurant **Zur Knödelmoidl** – for drinks and solid Teutonic fare – close to Weissbrunnsee (Lago Fontana Bianca).

To reach St Gertraud, follow the gravel road just above the southern shore of Weissbrunnsee, signposted as route 107, which provides the novelty of level walking for a while. After 10 minutes bear right with 107 and soon cross a vehicle track. Continue to a T-junction and go to the right, down to another

T-junction and again bear right along a forest road for about 250m. Then it's left down a path (still route 107) and the real descent starts, through pine forest, eventually to a T-junction on the edge of fields. Turn right along the vehicle track and follow it to a bitumen road with beautiful white, red-spired **St Gertraud church** above. Accommodation is about 200m up and slightly to the right (1¼ to 1½ hours from Weissbrunnsee). To reach the centre of the village, shop and bus stop, follow the path below Pension Ulternhof down, past stations of the cross, to a minor road then descend steeply between houses to the main Ultental road.

St Gertraud (San Gertrude)

A typical Tyrolean village, St Gertraud is picturesquely scattered around the head of the Ulten valley. Here German is the language of first choice – Italian is either unknown or not readily used.

With valley or mountain views, **Pension Ulternhof** *(☎ 0473 79 81 17, fax 0473 79 80 00; 114 Ulten; B&B/half board €31/43.90)* offers spacious, fairly plain rooms. Breakfast is a substantial affair and the evening meal likewise. The village **shop** has a good range of supplies. The **SAD** *(☎ 800 84 60 47)* bus service from Meran in Vinschgau provides at least four buses daily, more on workdays.

The **tourist office** *(☎ 0473 79 53 87)* for Ultental is at St Walburg, 13km down the valley from St Gertraud.

Day 3: St Gertraud to Martelltal

7–7½ hours, 15km, 1400m ascent

Follow route 108 and signs to 'Kirche' up to Pension Ulternhof, then go down the bitumen road below the church. On a sharp bend continue down a vehicle track for about 200m to a signposted turn-off to the left into pine forest. The well-graded path ascends to a vehicle track; turn right for about 250m then left with a sign for route 107. At the next junction turn right along a level track. Continue straight on at the next intersection and follow the level track around the shores of Weissbrunnsee to the road near the former Berggasthaus Enzian (1¼ to 1½ hours from St Gertraud).

Continue up the vehicle track on the uphill side of the hotel, signposted as route 12. About 40m along, bear left up steps with route 12 waymarkers. The narrow, rocky path gains height. After about 20 minutes a path (from the direction of Rifugio Canziani) merges from the left. Nearly an hour from Weissbrunnsee you emerge into the open meadows at Pilshof and come to a timber cabin with a picnic table inside. The path leads on, back into forest; two stream crossings on stepping stones could be slightly difficult after heavy rain. The next stream, Pilsbach (Rio Pozza), is bridged. Soon the path traverses a rugged, forested slope to Pilsberg Alm (30 minutes from Pilshof). Fresh water is available here; the isolated, superbly sited place is usually occupied. A sign points the way to Passo Soy/Soy Joch [sic] and to San Gertraud [sic] down to the right, via an extremely steep route.

Head north up to a prominent signpost on a spur and turn left towards the pass following route 142. The path, faint in places, leads up over a stony meadow and keeps to the left (south) of a huge hill of scree and boulders, ascending to a grassy shoulder. This marks a dramatic transition from open meadows to a wild, cliff-enclosed valley. The path goes up the right side, and ascends scree and boulders in a series of longish zigzags, to the flat pass, mapped as Soyscharte (two hours from Pilsberg Alm).

The route descends steeply through boulders; watch the waymarkers (142) carefully as they're not always in line of sight. Then drop down a steep, gravel slope to the slightly easier ground of a long moraine spur. Descend the spur and, after a while, cut across to the left to another spur, following it down on a now clear, waymarked path. Reach a small stream on the right and cross it, then another and follow a spur down, past a path junction on the right, to another junction. Bear right here and follow clear paths on to Soy Alm, usually open for refreshments (two hours from Soyscharte).

From here the path (now route 4) drops into forest, crosses a bridge over Soybach and descends steeply. Well down, just past a stream crossing, bear right and descend a path to the main road through Martelltal (Val Martello), next to Hölderle Café (45 minutes from Soy Alm). The bus stop is about 200m to the left; there is a bus at about 5pm to Martell (p172) but the last one going up passes here in the early afternoon.

Day 4: Martelltal – Enzianhütte to Martell

4¾–5¼ hours, 12km, 300m ascent, 750m descent

It's worth noting that none of the available maps show all the paths and junctions on this section accurately.

First of all, you need to reach Enzianhütte (Hotel Enzian); there's a bus from Martell (€1.80) at around 9.30am that takes you to the hotel on an amazing journey up a series of very tight hairpin bends.

From the hotel, walk down the road for about 100m to a signposted vehicle track on the left. Go up past deserted buildings and on the far side of the last one on the left, turn left up a path (route 20, Pedertal). The path gains height quickly through open pine woodland. About 25 minutes from the start, cross a bridge over the main stream in Pedertal, then a few minutes further on, at a junction, bear right (20a) towards 'Malga Lifi' (the same place as Lyfi Alm and Malga Livi on other signposts). Then it's only a short distance to the open spaces of Pederalm and another junction; continue ahead on a path marked 20a and 35. A small hut here is locked but there are seats under the wide eaves. The route then descends to another junction; stay with 35, crossing a meadow then generally descending to scenically located Rifugio-Bar-Ristorante Lyfi Alm (☎ 0473 74 47 08), about an hour from the start. The extensive menu includes sustaining barley soup (€4.65), local cheese (€8.25) and excellent strudel (€2.85).

Continue along route 8 across a stream, past the turn-off for route 10 (to the road by Zufrittsee) then through meadows. The path soon descends in pine forest, negotiating a small cliff via timber steps, across a stream and down past a junction (where route 0 would take you down to the valley road). Cross an open stretch of path preceded by a sign warning you to hurry across here if it's raining, as rockfalls are likely. From a junction further on (about an hour from Lyfi Alm) the path climbs to a bridge over the main stream in Rosimtal. Continue up, past a small hut; a larger hut nearby is firmly locked. Ascend steeply to a path junction with fine views up Rosimtal. The path (route 8) rises steeply from here for several hundred metres, then descends via steps and timber ramps into Schludertal and across the stream. A little further on, at Schluder Alm, route 34 (right) leads down to Waldheim. Continue with route 8, generally losing height across slopes where signs warn of falling stones, to **Stallwieshof** (about 1¼ hours from Rosimtal) – a possible refreshment stop.

Walk along the road for about 100m, cross a stream with an old **water mill** nearby, and turn left along a vehicle track with routes 15 and 32. The track, evidently extended since the maps were published, has annihilated chunks of the waymarked path. Just past the turn-off to the right for route 32 (to Niederhof), bear right along a path (15), which generally descends in pine forest. Forty minutes from Stallwieshof you reach a path junction, the configuration of which is quite different from that on the maps. Turn right to follow 24 (to Plattmahd) and 26; a short distance along, turn sharp left downhill with route 24 (don't be tempted by the clearer path ahead to Suchbuhl) and drop steeply to a junction where you could go right to Niederhof and Hölderle Café or left for Premstlhof. In the latter case, follow a well-graded path down to a junction just above a road. A short path on the right towards Premstlhof avoids a bit of road walking, then continue down it. Just before a gate, take a short cut on the left down to Premstlhof (1¼ hours from Stallwieshof).

To reach Martell, walk down the road; take a couple of steep short cuts signposted as routes 8 and 11. The last one lands you in the courtyard of the Gasthof Edelweiss; the bus stop is about 150m up the road to the right (30 to 35 minutes from Premstlhof).

Other Walks

Val dei Forni

The vast Forni glacier, in the heart of the Lombardy section of the park, is the largest glacier in the entire Central Alps. This awesome mass of ice, plus two of the park's three highest peaks (Monte Cevedale and Gran Zebrù) are the stunning highlights of walks in Val dei Forni and its upper reaches, Val di Cedec. A good network of well-waymarked paths and tracks provides opportunities for not too strenuous excursions through the valleys with the glacier and the peaks and their impressive satellites almost constantly in view. The best map to use is the Tabacco 1:25,000 sheet No 08 *Ortles Cevedale*.

From the bus stop in Santa Caterina, the direct route to **Albergo Ghiacciaio dei Forni** (☎/fax 0342 93 53 65; 23030 Santa Caterina, half board €43.90), high up Valle dei Forni, is 4.5km along a bitumen road all the way. This involves 450m ascent and takes 1¼ to 1½ hours.

A moderate 11km circuit from Albergo Forni takes in **Rifugio Branca** (☎ 0342 93 55 01; beds €15.50), which has un unrivalled view of Forni glacier, following path 28a, then 28c most of the way up Val di Cedec to **Rifugio Pizzini Frattola** (☎ 0342 93 55 13; beds €15.50), which crouches at the foot of Gran Zebrù. The return is along an unnumbered but signposted path along the western side of Val di Cedec, past Rovine Caserma (ruins of WWI barracks) and down to Albergo Forni. This takes 3¾ to 4¼ hours with 620m ascent. A 3.5km return side trip (400m ascent) from Rifugio Pizzini Frattola up to Passo Zebrù following path 30, to overlook spectacular Val Zebrù, is highly recommended; allow about 1¼ to 1½ hours.

To vary the return to Santa Caterina, you could choose the relatively straightforward route on the northern side of Val dei Forni, along path 27a from above Albergo Forni to Ables, then down route 34 to Santa Caterina. This 7.5km route takes 2¼ to 2½ hours and involves 350m ascent. Alternatively, on the opposite side of the valley, an unnumbered and at times elusive route descends from below Albergo Forni to a point opposite **Rifugio Stella Alpina** (☎ 0342 93 5 88; 23030 Valfurva; beds with half board €33.60); from here follow 24b to Losseda and then route 35 to Santa Caterina. This 6km route takes 2½ to 2¾ hours with around 450m descent.

Dolomites

Rich in ancient culture and tradition, offering some of Italy's most spectacular peaks and largely protected as regional parks, the mountains and valleys of the Dolomites (Dolomiti) are crisscrossed by a vast network of well-marked trails. Not surprisingly, tourism is one of the principal resources of the region, and there are excellent accommodation, restaurant and public transport facilities. There is also an excellent network of *rifugi* (mountain huts) for high-altitude walkers.

While the walks in this chapter are in the northern section of the Dolomites, largely part of Alto Adige or South Tyrol (Südtirol), the entire Dolomites range extends well into Trentino to the south and Veneto to the east. Trentino–Alto Adige forms an autonomous Alpine region, but the two provinces are best thought of as two distinct areas – culturally, linguistically and historically separate.

South Tyrol was part of Austria until ceded to Italy in 1919. The people, mostly of Germanic descent, predictably favour the German language (68%) over Italian (28%), although Ladin, an ancient Latin-based language, is also spoken in some areas (see the boxed text 'The Ladin Tradition', p188). Trentino, however, was a reluctant part of the Austrian and Austro-Hungarian empires for about a century until it was returned to Italy after WWI. The people have a strong Italian identity, although German is also spoken.

HISTORY
That the Alpine valleys were frequented by humans in prehistoric times, even at high altitudes, has been well-documented by archaeological finds dating back to the 8th millennium BC (the Mesolithic period). In September 1991, the body of Otzi, the nickname given to him at the Bolzano (Bozen) museum, was discovered in Val Senales, northeast of Merano (Meran). Yielded up by the Similaun glacier, the body was perfectly preserved along with clothes and tools. Otzi was probably a hunter or merchant who lived around 5300 BC (the Neolithic period).

Highlights

JEFF CANTARUTTI

Tre Cime di Lavaredo, one of the most beautiful places in the Dolomites

- Walking in the undulating pastures of the Alpe di Siusi high plain, overshadowed by the spectacular Sciliar (p183)

- Descending into the magical atmosphere of the karst amphitheatre known as the Alpe di Fanes on the Northern Dolomites walk (p187)

- Sunset illuminating the peaks of the Tre Cime di Lavaredo on the Crode Fiscaline Loop (p198)

- A cup of delicious hot chocolate served with fresh cream at the rustic Malga Ra Stua in Parco Naturale delle Dolomiti d'Ampezzo (p201)

By the time the region was absorbed into the ancient Roman Empire, it had already developed a long history of intense intercultural and commercial exchange. Then, as today, this area was a slice of Italy where the cultural diversity of the different minorities that inhabited it created an unusual backdrop. The Ladin ethnic group, which developed over the centuries in the Badia (Gadertal), Gardena (Grödnertal) and Fassa valleys, and in the Ampezzo basin, are descendants of the Celts. Romanised under the Emperors Augustus and Claudius in the first decades after Christ, they still maintain their own Romance language, as well as a social system founded on the model of the *viles* – clusters of family houses where several agricultural activities were carried out in common.

In the northernmost valleys, the original South Tyrol populations, Germanic in language and culture, preserve to this day the system of *maso chiuso* – single-family farms and land that, each generation, are passed down to the first-born son. The South Tyrol territories were administered in the Middle Ages by Germanic bishops or feudal lords. They were subsequently made part of the Kingdom of Bavaria and finally of the Austro-Hungarian Empire of the Hapsburgs. In 1919, with the defeat of the Hapsburgs at the end of WWI, South Tyrol was annexed by Italy. The population, after suffering a forced attempt at integration under Mussolini, today enjoys an autonomous government status along with Trentino.

At the beginning of the 19th century, the Dolomites figured prominently in the first explorations and early triumphs in Alpine mountaineering, which laid the foundations of the region's current tourism.

NATURAL HISTORY

Geographically the area of the Dolomites, within the borders of South Tyrol, forms an 80km-long rocky strip that extends east-west between Val d'Isarco (Eisacktal), northeast of Bolzano, and Val di Sesto (Sextental), southeast of San Candido, and is defined to the north by Val Pusteria (Pustertal).

To the explorers of the 19th century, influenced by a romantic and heroic vision, these mountains were especially atmospheric. The bizarre, vertical shapes – steeples, pinnacles and towers of white rock – standing out among brilliant green forests and grassy slopes, dotted here and there with tidy farms, captured their imaginations.

The Dolomites owe their name to the French geologist Deodat de Dolomieu, who first described their composition in 1788. De Dolomieu found that the Dolomites were largely made up of extensive stratification of calcium and magnesium rock – all that remained of trillions of sponges and coral of an ancient tropical sea (see the boxed text 'Coral Reefs at 3000m', p182).

One of the most obvious qualities of the Dolomites is their colour; the great vertical peaks are softened by the pale shades of the minerals of which they are composed. In the sunlight they go from whitish to blue-grey,

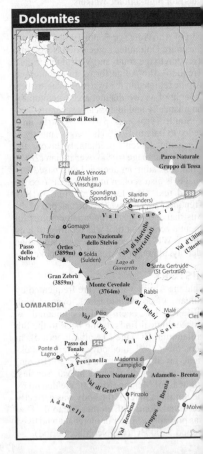

and then turn rose and purple as the sun sets. A series of natural habitats, determined principally by altitude, can be distinguished in horizontal strips on the slopes.

Typical Alpine carnivores like the bear, lynx, wolf and lammergeier (bearded vulture) have been extinct in the area since the beginning of this century. Projects are now underway to reintroduce these animals to their natural habitats, although you are unlikely to see any. Minor carnivores, hoofed herbivores (some of which have been reintroduced) rodents, mustelids, reptiles and many bird species inhabit the high-altitude woods and prairies. You are most likely to encounter them in the early morning or at sunset. See Watching Wildlife (p23) for detailed information on these animals.

CLIMATE

The dominant climate is typically continental Alpine, with long, harsh winters and short, temperate summers. As a general rule, precipitation levels increase with altitude. Snow falls between October and December and begins to melt between March and April; depending on the exposure of the slope it can last until July or August. January is the

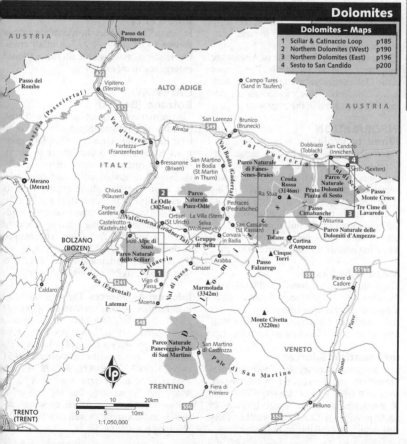

Dolomites

Dolomites – Maps	
1 Sciliar & Catinaccio Loop	p185
2 Northern Dolomites (West)	p190
3 Northern Dolomites (East)	p196
4 Sesto to San Candido	p200

DOLOMITES

Coral Reefs at 3000m

The Dolomites are incredibly rich in marine fossils from an ancient tropical sea, known as the Tethys, that existed some 250 million years ago. The bed of this sea consisted of layers of organic sediments, in some areas 1km thick, which accumulated over a period of 120 million years. At the start of the Tertiary period (70 million years ago), the pressure of the African plate on the European plate compressed and pushed up what remained of the coral reefs and sediment to form a magnificent mountain range.

coldest month, with an average temperature of below 0°C; the warmest period is usually July to August, which has an average temperature around 20°C.

Be aware, after the middle of August the temperature can drop suddenly. The climate in the Dolomites can be unpredictable, with sunny mornings giving way to sudden, violent thunderstorms in the afternoon.

INFORMATION
When to Walk
The walking season is June to September/October. *Rifugi* provide food, lodging and assistance to walkers from mid-June to mid-September (depending on the weather). This is the best time for low-risk walking. August is more stable than June weather-wise, but the *rifugi* are usually full and the area can get crowded. September is more tranquil, while in October the days begin to shorten.

Maps & Books
The Touring Club Italiano's 1:200,000 map *Trentino-Alto Adige* is ideal for route planning and general orientation.

Gillian Price's *Walking in the Dolomites* is a useful reference for other walks in the area.

Information Sources
The **Regional Agency for Environmental Protection and Prevention in the Veneto** (Arpav; ☎ 0436 792 21, fax 0436 78 00 08; w www.arpa.veneto.it; open 15 June-15 Sept) provides a Dolomites weather forecast, which is available in English.

Regulations
Within the protected park territory it is prohibited to remove certain plant and animal species (included seeds, insects, butterflies, larvae, chrysalises, nests and eggs of any species), as well as fossils and minerals.

Place Names
Many places in the Dolomites are referred to in German and Ladin (see the boxed text 'The Ladin Tradition', p188), as well as Italian. Some maps use all three, some use two, others only use one. In this chapter, where appropriate, we have included the German or Ladin spelling for place names.

Emergency
In South Tyrol contact the **mountain rescue service** (☎ 0471 79 71 71) or, in all areas, for medical assistance call the **national emergency number** (☎ 118).

GATEWAY
Bolzano (Bozen)
The provincial capital of South Tyrol, Bolzano is unmistakably Austrian. You'll hear Italian and German spoken but, aside from concessions to the former in street, hotel and restaurant signs, there are precious few reminders of Italian rule here. The town's small historic centre, with its engaging Tyrolean architecture and arcaded streets, harbours numerous outdoor cafés and restaurants, making it a very pleasant place to spend a few days. The **Museo Archeologico** (☎ 0471 98 20 98; via Museo 43) is worth a visit, in particular to see Otzi (see History, p179) and his equipment.

Information Sources The regional information office, **Alto Adige Marketing** (☎ 0471 99 99 99, fax 0471 99 99 00; w www.hallo .com; Piazza Parrocchia 11; open 9am-6pm Mon-Fri), provides a regional online accommodation booking service. **Bolzano AAST** (☎ 0471 30 70 00, fax 0471 98 01 28; w www .bolzano-bozen.it; Piazza Walther 8; open Mon-Fri & Sat morning) has regional information about accommodation, museums, activities and transport, as well as walking and climbing possibilities.

Supplies & Equipment The best equipped of Bolzano's outdoor shops, **Sportler** (☎ 0471 97 40 33; w www.sportler.it; Via Portici 37) specialises in mountain technical gear, including clothing and maps.

The bookshop **Athesia** (☎ 0471 92 71 11; w www.athesialibri.it; Via Portici 41) offers a good selection of mountain books and maps.

Places to Stay & Eat Towards Merano (Meran), the **Moosbauer camping ground** (☎ 0471 91 84 92; e info@moosbauer.com; Via San Maurizio 83; camping per person/tent/car €5.75/4.90/4.90) is 5km northwest of Bolzano.

Hotel Feichter (☎ 0471 97 87 68; e hotel.feichter@dnet.it; Via Grappoli 15; singles/doubles €51.65/77.45) is good value for money, with breakfast included. **Hotel Figl** (☎/fax 0471 97 84 12; e info@figl.net; Piazza del Grano 9; singles/doubles €72.30/92.95) has good rooms.

You can pick fresh fruit, vegetables, bread and cheese from the open **market** (Piazza delle Erbe; open Mon-Sat). In the same area, there are numerous **bakeries**, **pastry shops** and **cafés**, as well as a small **supermarket**.

While you can eat pizza and pasta if you wish, Bolzano's best restaurants specialise in Tyrolean food. **Cavallino Bianco/Weisses Rosslwirt** (☎ 0471 97 32 67; Via Bottai/Bindergasse 6; full meals €15.50) is extremely popular and reasonably priced.

Getting There & Away Flying out of **Bolzano airport** (☎ 0471 25 52 55; w www.abd-airport.it), **Air Alps** (☎ 0512 29 27 29; w www.airalps.at) has services to Rome (daily) and the Austrian town of Innsbruck (Friday and Sunday).

SAD buses leave from the bus terminal in Via Perathoner, near Piazza Walther, for destinations throughout the province. For South Tyrol transport details, including timetables and fares, contact **SIT** (☎ 800 84 60 47; w www.sii.bz.it; Mon-Fri 8am-7pm, Sat 8am-1pm); information is available in Italian, German and English.

Regular trains connect Bolzano with Merano, Trento (Trent), Verona (1½ hours), Milan, Rome, Innsbruck (two hours) and Munich (Germany). You can also catch a train from Bolzano to Brunico (Bruneck) and San Candido (Innichen) in Val Pusteria.

Bolzano is well served by the A22 (the Brennero *autostrada*), which leads to the Brennero Pass and northern Europe.

Sciliar & Catinaccio Loop

Duration	4 days
Difficulty	moderate–demanding
Start/Finish	Compaccio
Nearest Towns	Castelrotto (p183), Compaccio (p184)
Transport	bus
Summary	A scenic walk, from the undulating pastures of the Alpe di Siusi to the jagged peaks of Torri del Vajolet and Catinaccio.

The Alpe di Siusi (Seiser Alm), part of the Altipiano dello Sciliar, rise high above the villages of Castelrotto (Kastelruth) and Siusi (Seis). There's something magical about the view across the Alpe di Siusi to Monte Sciliar (Schlern), with undulating green pastures ending dramatically at the foot of towering peaks. The area offers something for walkers of all ages and expertise. As a bonus, you can plan walks to ensure that you reach a *malga*, an alpine hut where graziers make butter and cheese in summer, for a lunch break.

The jagged peaks of the Catinaccio group provide many challenging walks, including the popular *via ferrata* (iron way) Santner.

PLANNING
Maps
The excellent Kompass 1:25,000 map No 629 *Rosengarten-Catinaccio-Latemar* covers the walk, except the start from Compaccio to the Hotel Panorama, which is usually covered by chairlift. The Tabacco 1:25,000 map No 5 *Val Gardena-Alpe di Siusi* covers only the northern section.

NEAREST TOWNS
Castelrotto (Kastelruth)
A picturesque town, Castelrotto is a popular tourist centre. The **Associazione Turistica**

DOLOMITES

Sciliar Castelrotto (☎ 0471 70 63 33; W www .castelrotto.com; Piazza Kraus 1) has regional and local information, as well as hotel lists and prices. The ski and climbing school **Dolomiten** (☎ 0471 70 53 43, fax 0471 71 14 80; W www.dolomiten-alpin.com; Via Vogelweidergasse) offers guided, seven-day treks and via ferrata excursions.

Places to Stay & Eat There are plenty of hotels and pensiones in all the local towns. In Castelrotto, **Albergo Torre** (☎ 0471 70 63 49; W www.zumturm.com; singles €36.15-56.80) has a restaurant offering typical meals for around €18.10. Breakfast is included in the room rates. **Silbernagl** (☎ 0471 70 62 22; Via

Legend of the Roses

The Legend of the Roses explains why the Catinaccio (Rosengarten) mountains turn red at dusk, a common phenomenon in the Dolomites. It tells the story of the dwarf king Laurens, whose kingdom is a virtual garden of red roses, the *rosengarten* (rose garden). Peace-loving and wealthy, Laurens wants for nothing but the hand in marriage of Similda, a beautiful princess from a neighbouring kingdom. His request refused, Laurens uses magic to kidnap the princess and holds her prisoner for seven years – until her brother discovers her whereabouts and sets off with his men to rescue her. In the ensuing battles, Laurens is eventually defeated and taken prisoner. Only after many years does he manage to escape and return to his kingdom in the mountains where, on his arrival, he sees the beautiful rose garden. Realising that the roses had led his enemies into his kingdom, Laurens casts a spell to turn the rose garden into stone, saying that the roses must not show themselves day or night. But Laurens forgot to include dusk in his spell, so every evening at sunset the enchanted garden becomes visible, casting a beautiful red glow over the Dolomites. If you're lucky, perhaps you will meet some elves, fairies or witches during the walk – at the very least you will have no trouble imagining them!

Stefano Cavedoni & Helen Gillman

Oswald Von Wolkenstein 10) is a well-stocked supermarket. For a quiet restaurant with open-air tables, try **Liftstuberl** (☎ 0471 70 68 04; Via Marinzen 35).

Getting There & Away Castelrotto is accessible by SAD bus from Bolzano (€2.60, 50 minutes, Monday to Friday half-hourly, Saturday hourly and Sunday every two hours), Ortisei (St Ulrich; €2.60, 30 minutes, five a day) and Bressanone (€2.60, 50 minutes, four a day). By car, exit the A22 at Bolzano Nord and head north on the panoramic road to Fiè (Völs), Siusi and Castelrotto. From the north, exit the A22 at Chiusa and head south on the S12 to Ponte Gardena, then turn left for Castelrotto.

Compaccio (Compatsch)

A popular winter and summer resort, there are plenty of accommodation options in Compaccio. For information contact **Associazione Turistica Alpe di Siusi** (☎ 0471 72 79 04; W www.seiseralm.net). Convenient to the start of the walk, the **Hotel Panorama** (☎ 0471 72 79 68, fax 0471 72 79 45; W www .alpenhotelpanorama.it; half board €59.40) is serviced by the Panorama chairlift (see Day 1, this page).

Getting There & Away A regular bus (every 20 minutes from 8am to 7pm) operates from Castelrotto and Siusi to Compaccio. Some of Castelrotto's hotels provide guests with a special Buxi card, which entitles them to free bus travel.

From May to October the roads to Alpe di Siusi are closed to normal traffic, but customers of the area's hotels can obtain a permit. Ask the hotel owner for assistance.

THE WALK
Day 1: Compaccio to Rifugio Alpe di Tires
5–7 hours, 957m ascent, 378m descent

You can walk from Compaccio, heading southeast along No S-10 and then turn right (southwest) onto trail 10. Continue until it intersects with a dirt road (No 5) on the left (southeast), which you follow to Malga Saltner. However, the best option is to use the **Panorama chairlift** (€3.10; open 8.30am-5.30pm). From the upper station near the Hotel Panorama, walk right (southwest) on the dirt road, marked as trail S, reaching Malga Laurinhütte, where the proper trail S starts on your left (south). Follow it downhill to reach the dirt road (No 5) where you turn left (south), cross a bridge and continue to the evocative **Malga Saltner** (one hour from the top station of the chairlift). Enjoy an apple strudel with whipped cream before continuing.

From Malga Saltner continue along trail 5, known as Sentiero dei Turisti, which joins

No 1. Follow this trail west as it snakes its way up to the Monte Sciliar (Schlern) high plain. Once you arrive at the plateau (two hours), you'll find trail 3-4 on your left. To continue to Rifugio Alpe di Tires, turn left (southeast) on trail 3-4, which crosses the Monte Sciliar high plain. Walk across the south face of Cima di Terrarossa, descending into a deep valley. At a junction make sure you stick to trail 4 on your left (don't take No 3, which goes down to Val Ciamin) until you reach **Rifugio Alpe di Tires** (☎/fax 0471 72 79 58, 0471 70 74 60); two hours from the junction of trails 1 and 3-4.

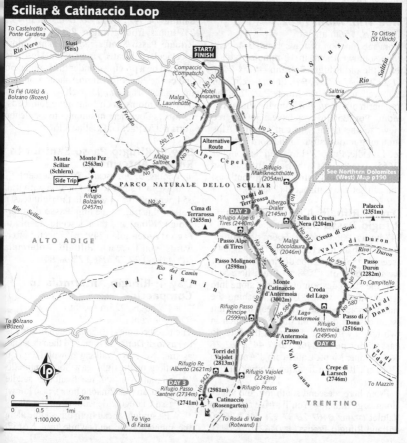

Sciliar & Catinaccio Loop

Alternative Day 1: via Forcella Denti Di Terrarossa

1–2½ hours, 669m ascent, 59m descent
If time is limited, you can take this shorter route. From Hotel Panorama head west on the dirt road and after a few metres you'll find trail 2 on your left (south). Follow it down and up, crossing a peculiar peat-meadow, until you reach a trail junction (just before a dirt road, about 10 minutes) where you'll turn right (south) on No 2. Following this trail you'll ascend to **Forcella Denti di Terrarossa** (an excellent sunset lookout) and, in 15 minutes, you'll descend to the Rifugio Alpe di Tires.

Side Trip: Monte Pez

1¼ hours, 156m ascent
From the junction of trails 1 and 3-4, continue southwest and, in 10 minutes, you'll reach the old **Rifugio Bolzano** *(☎/fax 0471 61 20 24; 0471 72 40 94)*. From here it's an easy walk up to nearby Monte Pez. Take the trail north of the *rifugio*. From the summit of **Monte Pez** (2563m) you have a 360-degree view: to the north you can see the Alps stretching into Austria; to the northeast you see Le Odle, Puez (2913m) and Sassongher (2665m); to the east is the Sella group, Sasso Lungo and Sasso Piatto (2964m); southeast you can see the Catinaccio (2981m).

Day 2: Rifugio Alpe di Tires to Rifugio Passo Santner

5–7 hours, 905m ascent, 606m descent
Head south along a rocky trail (No 3a-554), ascending to Passo Alpe di Tires and nearby **Passo Molignon** (2598m). From here you start the steep descent on a scree slope into a rocky alpine valley. Before reaching the valley floor, the trail forks. Keep to the left (southeast) and stay on trail 554, which in two hours will take you up to the **Rifugio Passo Principe** *(☎ 0462 76 42 44, 0462 76 46 31)* under Monte Catinaccio d'Antermoia (3002m). It is worth taking a break at this tiny *rifugio*.

From here, descend south into the valley along large trail 584. You'll arrive at **Rifugio Vajolet** *(☎/fax 0462 76 32 92, 0462 76 90 45)* and **Rifugio Preuss** *(☎ 0462 76 48 47)*,

the latter being a bar-restaurant open during the day only. From here you go right (west), up the steep and rocky trail 542s to the Catinaccio hidden valley. Those without mountaineering experience will find this part of the walk challenging, but it is equipped with an iron cord for security. You will arrive in an evocative rocky world with a tiny lake and **Rifugio Re Alberto** *(☎ 0462 763 428, 0462 76 35 48;* e *b.deluca@rolmail.net)*, just in front of three sharp pinnacles called **Torri del Vajolet**, famous among climbers. Walkers who have booked for the night can call Rifugio Re Alberto from the Rifugio Vajolet and send their backpack up on the cableway.

Follow trail No 542s up to **Rifugio Passo Santner** *(☎ 0471 64 22 30, 0462 57 35 13)*, 2¾ hours from Rifugio Passo Principe. Rifugio Passo Santner is one of the most spectacularly located *rifugi* in the Alps. It is perched on a precipice under the Catinaccio and on the edge of an almost sheer drop into the valley. The *rifugio* itself is tiny, with only two rooms, each containing four beds. Climbers flock here in summer to tackle the Torri del Vajolet and Catinaccio.

Day 3: Rifugio Passo Santner to Rifugio Antermoia

4–5 hours, 529m ascent, 766m descent
Retrace your steps to the junction with trail 554, where No 584 veers to the right (east). Follow this trail to the high **Passo d'Antermoia** (2770m) and then descend steeply to **Lago d'Antermoia** (2495m). Shortly afterwards you'll reach **Rifugio Antermoia** *(☎ 0462 60 22 72, 0462 75 04 80)*.

Day 4: Rifugio Antermoia to Compaccio

3½–4½ hours, 225m ascent, 890m descent
The trail becomes No 580, which heads east to **Passo di Dona** (2516m) and then descends as trail No 578. Walking downhill, ignore deviations on the right (east) for Campitello-Mazzin, and you will reach another saddle, **Passo Duron** (2282m, one hour), also known as Passo Ciarégole depending on the map.

Walk straight ahead from this saddle along the mountainside and, while trail No 578 veers down to the right (east) for Valle di Duron-Campitello, continue left on the narrow and wild No 555. This trail will take you in a northwesterly, slippery descent along the northern slopes of the Croda del Lago group. Before the trail joins a dirt road (No 532), near the group of herders' shelters known as Malga Dòcoldaura (2046m), you have to ford the (usually easy) Rivo Duron. Follow No 532 north to Sella di Cresta Nera (2204m) and descend to **Albergo Dialer** (formerly Casa del TCI; ☎ 0471 72 79 22, fax 0471 72 78 62) at 2145m, about two hours from Passo Duron. Walk north along the dirt road for 10 minutes and turn left (west) on trail No 7, veering north after a small creek. This trail will take you down and then up to the **Rifugio Mahlknechthütte** (formerly Rifugio Molignon; ☎ 0471 72 79 12, fax 0471 72 78 63; e mahlknechthuette@cenida.it), about 30 minutes from Albergo Dialer. The rifugio and the hotel are good alternatives for an overnight stop.

From Rifugio Mahlknechthütte the trail becomes dirt road No 7 (in some sections corresponding to No 12). It will take you to the Hotel Panorama and chairlift, about an hour from the rifugio, and then to Compaccio, another 40 minutes' walk.

Northern Dolomites

Duration	7 days
Distance	70km
Difficulty	easy–moderate
Start	Ortisei
Finish	Hotel Dolomitenhof
Nearest Towns	Ortisei (p187), San Candido (p188)
Transport	bus

Summary This beautiful, high-level route follows well-marked, mostly easy trails, although some exposed passages make the adventure more exciting.

From the beautiful Ladin areas of Val Gardena and Val Badia, rich in ancient traditions and colourful legends (see the boxed text 'The Ladin Tradition', p188), this walk takes

you to the wide meadows of Prato Piazza and the great views of Tre Cime di Lavaredo, one of the most beautiful places in the Dolomites.

The walk has been described as a seven-day trip, with a maximum of six hours' walking per day. For strong walkers happy to spend up to eight hours on the trail, the walk can be done in six days, but this leaves little or no time for side trips. While none of the sections require real technical skills, some have exposed passages.

PLANNING
Maps
Make sure you carry good maps – the Tabacco 1:25,000 Nos 05 *Val Gardena*, 07 *Alta Badia*, 03 *Cortina D'Ampezzo* and 010 *Dolomiti di Sesto* are recommended.

NEAREST TOWNS
Ortisei (St Ulrich)
Culturally rich Ortisei is a picturesque, Alpine town, which boasts a pedestrian only central area with an extensive system of escalators and moving walkways. It is in the heart of Val Gardena, an enclave that has managed to preserve the ancient Ladin traditions. The valley's other claim to fame is its woodcarving artisans, known for their statues, figurines and toys. The **tourist office** (☎ 0471 79 63 28; w www.valgardena.it; Str Rezia 1) has information about accommodation, guided walks and rock-climbing schools.

Places to Stay & Eat Located close to Seceda cable car, **Garni Irma** (☎/fax 0471 79 60 34; e irma@val-gardena.com; Via Resciesa 19; singles €31) is a convenient accommodation option. Breakfast is included.

Warning

Sections of the following walk are equipped with steel cables or chains to assist walkers with little experience in Alpine mountaineering, especially those who have trouble crossing exposed passages. While none of these sections require real technical skills, you might feel more confident carrying proper *via ferrata* equipment (see Equipment, p204).

DOLOMITES

There is a supermarket, **Despar** *(Via Rezia 230)*, which is centrally located. For a simple meal try **Terrazza** *(☎ 0471 79 63 66; Str Sneton 9)*.

Getting There & Away Daily SAD buses arrive from Bolzano, some of them via Siusi and Castelrotto, and connect all the villages of Val Gardena (€4.15, 1½ to two hours, high/low season 14/10 runs Monday to Saturday from 7.40am to 7.15pm, fewer on Sunday). If you're driving, take the A22 north from Bolzano, turning right into Val Gardena after 30km. Continue east along this road to Ortisei.

San Candido (Innichen)

The Alta Pusteria valley takes in Dolomiti di Sesto, Tre Cime di Lavaredo and the resort towns of San Candido and nearby Sesto. In San Candido don't miss the Romanesque **Collegiata**, a church built in AD 769. The **tourist office** *(☎ 0474 91 31 49, 0474 91 31 56; w www.altapusteria.net; Piazza Magistrato 1)* can help with information on the valley.

Places to Stay & Eat The nearest camping ground is **Caravan Park Sexten** *(☎ 0474 71 04 44; w www.caravanparksexten.it; Via San Giuseppe 54, Sesto; person/tent plus car €9.50/5)*, southeast of Sesto on the road to Passo Monte Croce. The relaxing **Hotel Passo Monte Croce** *(☎ 0474 71 03 28, w www.passomontecroce.com; half board with bath from €56)*, 7km southeast of Sesto at Passo Monte Croce, is at the top of the quality scale.

In San Candido itself, try **Villa Waldheim** *(☎ 0474 91 31 87, fax 0474 91 44 02; Via Pascolo 1; half board €62)*. A supermarket, **Despar Schafer** *(Piazza San Michele 8)*, is centrally located.

Getting There & Away You can take the train from Bolzano to San Candido (€7.75, two hours, 10 a day), changing at Fortezza. There are SAD bus services between Bolzano and San Candido, with a change in Brunico or Bressanone. To get to Rifugio Auronzo at the Tre Cime di Lavaredo, catch the bus from San Candido (departures 8, 8.30 and 10.30am). By car, San Candido is

---

The Ladin Tradition

The Ladin language and culture can be traced to around 15 BC, when the people of the Central Alps were forcibly united into the Roman province of Rhaetia. The Romans, of course, introduced Latin to the province, but the original inhabitants of the area, with their diverse linguistic and cultural backgrounds, modified the language to such an extent that, by around AD 450, it had evolved into an independent Romance language, known as Raeto-Romanic. Today the language and culture are confined mainly to the Val Gardena and Val Badia areas, where about 90% of the locals declared in the 1981 census that they belonged to the Ladin language group. Along with German and Italian, Ladin is taught in schools, and the survival of Ladin cultural and linguistic identity is protected by law.

The Ladin culture is rich in vibrant poetry and legends, set amid the jagged peaks of the Dolomites, and peopled by fairies, gnomes, elves, giants, princesses and heroes. Passed on by word of mouth for centuries and often heavily influenced by Germanic myths, many of these legends were in danger of being lost. In the first decade of this century, journalist Carlo Felice Wolff spent 10 years gathering and researching the local legends, listening as the old folk, farmers and shepherds recounted the legends and fairytales. Instead of simply writing down what he was told, Wolff reconstructed the tales from the many different versions and recollections he gathered. Wolff's book *Legends of the Dolomites* is available in English at the **Delago bookshop** *(Piazza S Antone 82, Ortisei)*.

The medieval tor (gate) castle at San Martino in Badia houses the **Museum Ladin** *(☎ 0474 52 40 20; w www.museumladin.it; Via Tor 72)* and is definitely worth a visit if you are interested in Ladin culture.

easily accessible from the A22 via Bressanone and from Cortina on the S51.

GETTING TO/FROM THE WALK

The walk starts at the base of the cable car at Via Roma in north Ortisei. From the end of the walk at Hotel Dolomitenhof, you can walk the 5km to Sesto, or buses run to Sesto and San Candido (hourly in high season, from 8.30am to 6pm).

THE WALK
Day 1: Ortisei to Rifugio Puez

4–6 hours, 10km, 450m ascent,
431m descent

The initial climb from Ortisei is easy and spectacular, thanks to the two-section **Seceda cable car** (☎ 0471 79 65 31; €11; open 8.30am-12.15pm & 1.45pm-5.30pm daily; 8.30am-5.30pm 22 July-2 Sept). The view from the gondola is memorable, taking in the spiky pinnacles of the Odle group and Sass Rigais (3025m) to the northeast; the massive Sella group and Sasso Lungo (3181m) to the southeast; and the green, high plain of the Alpe di Siusi at the foot of Monte Sciliar (2563m) to the southwest.

From **Ristorante Seceda** at the top station of the cable car, take trail 2b, which heads east at mid-slope through lush green, sloping pastures dotted with wooden *malghe*. Keep to the descending trail 2b, recently renamed from 2a and brick paved in some slippery sections. It takes you, avoiding numerous deviations, to a lovely area known as **Prera Longia**, where you'll find a romantic *malga* selling milk in a surreal landscape dotted with huge boulders. In the early morning it is likely that you'll see marmots, roe deer and lots of small birds, such as the alpine finch. Stay on trail 2b until you arrive at **Plan Ciautier**, where a number of trails ascend north towards canyons where there are several *vie ferrate*. From here No 2b descends to cross a small river bed and then to the convergence of Val Mont da l'Ega and Val Forces de Sielles, 1½ hours from Seceda. The convergence forms the beginning of the large riverbed of the Ruf de Cisles, where water flows only when it rains. Cross the riverbed and climb up Val

Forces de Sielles. On the way up to the Forcella Forces de Sielles, the trail changes from No 2b to No 2-3 and then No 2; it is a tough, semi-vertical walk. Don't take the trail that descends southwest (the western branch of No 2-3) for Rifugio Firenze (20 minutes). At **Forcella Forces de Sielles** (one hour from the convergence of the valleys) you will see a section of picturesque Vallunga to the southeast and there is a spectacular view over the Odle group to the northwest. By this time you will probably be ready for a rest, so save your snacks and drinks for this scenic spot!

Return to trail 2 and follow it to the left (north). You will come to several short sections of exposed trail, equipped with iron cords, but don't panic – you don't need any equipment. Just hold on to the cord if you need help crossing any of these sections. Turning east with the trail, you'll pass a crest (2600m), the highest point of the day, and then descend to a rocky green balcony above the U-shaped glacial valley of Vallunga. Descending again, trail 2c, from Forcella Nivea, comes in from the left. The trails merge in a wide flat grassy area, inhabited by sheep and horses. Continue east along the trail. If you plan to make this walk a one-day loop, you can take trail 16, which descends on the right (southwest) to the Vallunga (see Alternative Finish: Selva p190). Otherwise, remaining on No 2, you'll soon reach **Rifugio Puez** (☎ 0471 79 53 65, 0471 84 70 59; open 15 June-1 Oct), 2¾ hours from Forcella Forces de Sielles. At the *rifugio* you can take a well-earned hot shower (coin operated) and rest.

If you are feeling energetic and daylight is on your side, you can finish the day with the Side Trip to Piz de Puez (below).

Side Trip: Piz de Puez

2–2½ hours, 438m ascent/descent

From Rifugio Puez take the unnumbered steep trail that heads northwest, passing to the left of Col de Puez. Climb uphill to the small saddle below the Puez peak. In a few minutes you'll reach the summit (2913m), from where you can enjoy the wonderful panoramic views.

DOLOMITES

Alternative Finish: Selva

2–2½ hours, 886m descent

If you plan to complete this walk as a one-day loop, follow No 16, which descends steeply (southwest), eventually reaching the bottom of the Vallunga, where it joins a small dirt road marked as No 14. Turn right (southwest) and meander down the pretty Vallunga with its alpine vegetation. If you walk quietly you should come across small animals such as fawns, squirrels, roe deer and many birds. The contrast between the majesty of the high mountains and the gentle environment of the valley creates a memorable effect and provides a fitting end to the walk. Once at the St Sylvester chapel, it takes about 15 minutes to reach the town of Selva, from where you can catch a bus back to Ortisei.

Day 2: Rifugio Puez to La Villa

4–5 hours, 73m ascent, 1116m descent

Follow No 2-5-15 southeast, crossing an arid high plain inhabited by white partridges to Passo Gardenaccia (2548m). The trail then merges with No 11 and descends east to old style **Rifugio Gardenaccia** (☎ 0471 84 92 82, 0471 83 96 61; e info@miramontihotel.it) two hours from Rifugio Puez.

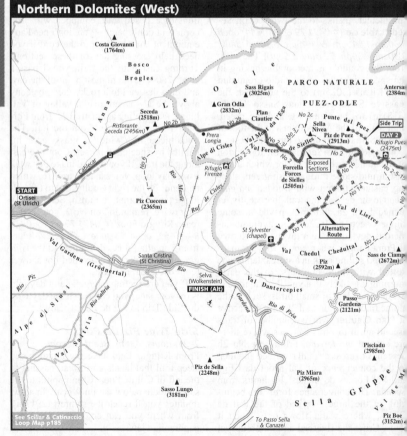

Northern Dolomites (West)

From Rifugio Gardenaccia descend south-east along trail 11 into the Gardenaccia valley. Walk through a forest, coming out near Maso Ploten, from where you descend to a church on the outskirts of La Villa (1433m), 1½ to two hours). From the church take the paved road, curving downhill to reach SP244 and the helpful tourist information office.

La Villa (Stern)

Situated at the southern end of Val Badia, the most authentic stronghold of the ancient Ladin culture, La Villa is one of the most fascinating and efficient tourist resorts in the Dolomites. Some of northern Italy's most renowned restaurants and hotels can be found in the area. For more information, ask at the helpful **tourist office** (*☎ 0471 84 70 37; *w** www.altabadia.org; Via Picenin 10).

Places to Stay & Eat The nearest camping ground is **Sass Dlacia** (*☎ 0471 84 95 27; *e** sassdlacia@altabadia.it; Via Sciarè 11; camping per person/tent with car €5/6.50), 4km from San Cassiano on the southeast road to Passo Falzarego. In La Villa try **La Villa** (*☎ 0471 84 70 35; *e** lavilla@altabadia.it; Boscdaplan 176; singles €31-61.95), rates

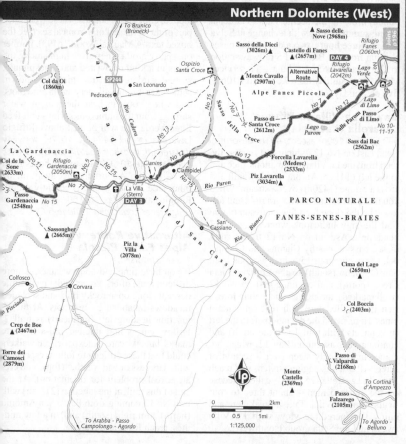

Northern Dolomites (West)

To Brunico (Bruneck)

Col da Oi (1860m)
San Leonardo
SP244
Pedraces
Rio Cadera
Val Badia
La Gardenaccia
Col de la Sone (2633m)
Rifugio Gardenaccia (2050m)
Passo Gardenaccia (2548m)
No 15
No 71
No 5
No 11
Cianins
La Villa (Stern)
DAY 3
Ciampidel
No 12
No 13
No 15
Sassongher (2665m)
Piz la Villa (2078m)
Colfosco
Corvara
Crep de Boe (2467m)
Torre dei Camosci (2879m)

Ospizio Santa Croce
Sasso della Dieci (3026m)
Castello di Fanes (2657m)
Sasso delle Nove (2968m)
Rifugio Fanes (2060m)
Monte Cavallo (2907m)
Alpe Fanes Piccola
DAY 4
Rifugio Lavarella (2042m)
Lago Verde
Lago di Limo
No 7
No 7
No 12
Passo di Santa Croce (2612m)
Lago Parom
Valle Parom
Passo di Limo
No 10-11-17
Sasso della Croce
Forcella Lavarella (Medesc) (2533m)
Piz Lavarella (3034m)
Sass dai Bac (2562m)
Rio Paron
Valle di San Cassiano
San Cassiano
Rio Bianco
PARCO NATURALE
FANES-SENES-BRAIES
Cima del Lago (2650m)
Col Boccia (2403m)
Passo di Valpardia (2168m)
Monte Castello (2369m)
Passo Falzarego (2105m)
To Cortina d'Ampezzo
To Agordo - Belluno
To Arabba - Passo Campolongo - Agordo

0   1   2km
0   0.5   1mi
1:125,000

include breakfast. The hotel also has a good restaurant. A more expensive option if you are planning to splurge a little is **Relais & Chateaux Rosa Alpina** (☎ 0471 84 95 00; ⓦ www.rosalpina.it; Via Micurà de Ru 20, San Cassiano; singles €113.60-263.40). The rates include breakfast. The restaurant is considered one of the best in Italy. For self caterers there is a central supermarket, **Sport Tony** (Strada Colz 56).

Getting There & Away Daily SAD buses reach all the valley villages from Bolzano, with a change at Bressanone or San Lorenzo (€8.80, three hours, eight a day Monday to Saturday from 7.45am to 5.15pm, two a day Sunday), or via the scenic Passo Gardena, during summer only, with a change at Selva (€6.20, three hours, two a day). SAD buses also run from the Brunico FS railway station to Corvara (€4.65, 1½ hours, 11 services Monday to Saturday from 7.55am to 7.10pm, five on Sunday).

Day 3: La Villa to Rifugio Lavarella (Lavarela)

5–7 hours, 1100m ascent, 491m descent
Head east on No 12, which starts across the road from the La Villa information office and to the left of Hotel Aurora. Go downhill and cross a bridge (1420m) over a stream. When you reach the asphalt road, turn right and follow it up the slope for a few metres until you find the sign indicating where trail 12-13 heads left. Ascend on No 12 to the right (east), passing nearby Cianins and Ciampidel. Cross over trail 15, which ascends from San Cassiano (south) to the Ospizio Santa Croce (north), and continue east on No 12 (well marked), through an enchanting forest, rich in birdlife, until you reach mountain pines. Here, avoid the deviation off to the left (it connects with trail 15 to the north) and continue your ascent on trail 12, which becomes increasingly steep over a section of scree. After a zigzagging stretch, you reach **Forcella Lavarella** (2533m) – called Medesc on the Tabacco map – about three to four hours from La Villa. Take a break here and enjoy the incredible view with La Villa (west) and the Sella group (southwest).

Continue descending northeast on No 12, avoiding deviations, until this trail merges in a flat meadow with No 7, which comes from Passo di Santa Croce. Turn right (east) and follow No 7-12 for about 100m to another Y-junction (30 minutes from Forcella Lavarella). Here you have a choice: the more difficult option is No 7 on the left (see Alternative Route, this page). Otherwise, on the right (southeast) is No 12, which is the main, well-marked route. Follow this trail past **Lago Parom** (which is sometimes there and sometimes not). You are likely to see carpets of edelweiss here. The trail descends along a strange, silent river bed through a landscape of plume-shaped rocks that, when tapped, emit glassy sounds. These were once part of the coral reef of a tropical sea (see the boxed text 'A Magical World', p193). Further on, sparse arolla pines grow high among the rocks in a kind of twisted and inhospitable, surreal garden. The trail meanders down, sometimes through slippery arolla pine roots, and when you can hear the roar of water surging from the numerous springs that feed Lago Verde you will be just above **Rifugio Lavarella** (☎/fax 0474 50 10 79; ⓦ www .lavarella.it; bed/half board from €15/34.60; open 15 June-10 Oct), 1½ to two hours from the Y-junction. A short distance away, on the other side of the stream, is recently rebuilt **Rifugio Fanes** (☎/fax 0474 50 10 97; ⓔ info@ rifugiofanes.com; open 15 June-5 Oct).

Alternative Route: via Alpes Fanes Piccola

1½–2½ hours
If you have time and good weather, a more difficult route offers a spectacular panoramic descent along open rocky hills and secluded meadows inhabited by marmots. At the Y-junction heading left (northeast) is trail 7. Follow cairns and unclear red-and-white marks, but take care – inexperienced walkers could find these difficult to follow, especially with darkness or bad weather (fog could create a real problem for orientation). At the end of this trail, at the junction (2150m) with trail No 13 coming from Passo San Antonio (north), turn right (south) and, in a few minutes, reach Rifugio Lavarella.

Alternative Finish: Podestagno

3–3½ hours, 132m ascent, 760m descent

If you wish to finish your walk at this point, it is possible to head to Cortina d'Ampezzo or Dobbiaco. From Rifugio Fanes take the dirt road No 10 up to Passo di Limo and then down into the gorgeous **Valle di Fanes**, taking a shortcut to avoid the hairpin bends of the road. Continue along the road and pass a deep gorge at **Ponte Alto**. A brief detour for a visit to the impressive **Fanes Falls** is recommended. Follow the road to the S51 road at Podestagno, where you can catch a bus south to Cortina (9km) or north to Dobbiaco (23km). Turning right (south) on the S51, in 20 minutes you reach **Hotel Fiames** (☎ 0436 23 66; e fiames@tiscali.it; Fiames 13; half board €51.65), 150m north of the shuttle bus stop. A further 1km south is **Camping Olympia** (☎ 0436 50 57).

Day 4: Rifugio Lavarella to Rifugio Biella

5–7 hours, 809m ascent, 534m descent

Follow the dirt road (northeast), which corresponds with trail 7 (also marked with the blue, triangular Alta Via No 1 signs). These roads are occasionally used by 4WD vehicles ferrying customers between the *rifugi* Lavarella–Pederù €7.75, Lavarella–Pederù–Sennes €12.90). The road descends steeply into the small valley of Rio San Vigilio and, after a wide curve on the right (east), you come across the first of three shortcuts on the left, which cut across hairpin bends. However, it is just as easy to stick to the road, especially if it is raining, all the way to **Rifugio Pederù** (☎/fax 0474 50 10 86; open 15 June-10 Oct), about 1½ to two hours. Following this route you also pass the start of the Alternative Route via Banc dal Sè (p194). It is possible to exit from the walk at Rifugio Pederù. A road descends into the beautiful Valle di Rudo, reaching San Viglio di Marebbe in two to three hours. Alternatively, take a shuttle bus from the *rifugio*. In San Viglio you can connect with a bus to Alta Badia or Brunico.

From Rifugio Pederù, take the road (east) that climbs in a series of sharp hairpin bends to a plateau. Once at the top you'll

find a shortcut (left), indicated by signs. From here you can also continue along No 9 (right fork) to reach Rifugio Fodara Vedla, which is a great place to spend an extra night and do the Side Trip to Malga Ra Stua (p194). Otherwise, follow the shortcut to **Rifugio Sennes** (☎/fax 0474 50 10 92; e sennes@rolmail.net; open 9 June-20 Oct), about two to 2½ hours away. The *rifugio* is beside Lago di Sennes and surrounded by *malghe*. There is a 4WD for customers only from Pederù (€7.75).

From Rifugio Sennes you can either head east following the dirt road Alta Via No 1 (this is the longer route but affords great views) or cut northeast on trail 6, to rejoin the Alta Via in sight of the old **Rifugio Biella** (☎ 0436 86 69 91, fax 0436 87 87 83; open 20 June-30 Sept), set in an unforgettable lunar landscape. If you take trail 6, Rifugio Biella is about an hour from Rifugio Sennes.

Side Trip: Croda del Becco peak

2–3 hours, 483m ascent

From Rifugio Biella head north up the technically easy, steep trail to Croda del Becco (2810m). Sections of the trail are equipped with iron cord.

A Magical World

You are now in the magical world of the Fanes, an imaginary people of ancient folk legend. Hidden among these dry, windswept rocks, the Fanes people are waiting to rebuild their kingdom.

Ecologically speaking this area is very special indeed – it is a great karst amphitheatre where *anidride carbonica* (carbon dioxide) dissolved in rainwater has split the limestone rock to form fissures, wells, depressions that periodically become ponds, and curious formations of flat rock plains on almost level ground furrowed by numerous channels.

While walking through the Alpe di Fanes, you will be struck not only by the unique beauty of the place, but also by the silence. It is as though this great, high plain absorbs not only water but sound.

Warning

The Banc dal Sè route is definitely not recommended in darkness or during bad weather conditions. It is a narrow and slippery mountain route that requires a safe step. The route is at the base of a vertical mountain face and is crossed by several water courses. When it rains, there can be rockfalls and landslides.

Alternative Route: via Banc dal Sè

4–5 hours, 751m ascent, 491m descent

This alternative trail ascends northeast into the heart of the semi-wilderness of the Bancdalsè group. It's an atmospheric route that saves as least an hour of walking, but sections of the trail are a bit exposed and should not be attempted in poor weather or fading light (see 'Warning', above).

Following the dirt road from Rifugio Lavarella, about 10 minutes past **Lago Piciodèl** (right) you will see a huge boulder (1814m). Shortly after the road begins to descend, look to your right (northeast) for a cairn. This marks the turn-off for the unmarked trail called **Banc dal Sè**, which ascends steeply northeast through the scree. It's marked on some maps with black dots and dashes. Do not attempt this trail in poor weather or fading light. There are several steep ascents and descents before arriving at the very picturesque **Rifugio Fodara Vedla** (☎/fax 0474 50 15 38; ⓦ www.fodara.it; open 15 June-5 Oct), two to 2½ hours from the turn-off. The *rifugio* is surrounded by a village of traditional *malghe* with a tiny wooden chapel. It offers comfortable rooms and a great terrace where you can relax and enjoy the magnificent scenery. If you have time you can spend an extra day here and visit Rifugio Malga Ra Stua (see Side Trip: Rifugio Malga Ra Stua, this page).

To continue on to Rifugio Sennes, from Rifugio Fodara Vedla head north on the dirt road (No 7-1). After a few hundred metres it comes to a fork, where you head right. This way you avoid the busy road and cross a high plain where it is not uncommon to encounter chamois. Eventually you rejoin the dirt road No 7-1 and the main route to Rifugio Sennes (approimately one hour from Rifugio Fodara Vedla).

Side Trip: Rifugio Malga Ra Stua

3½–4 hours, 448m ascent

Take trail 9 (east), which follows an old WWI military road down into the Val Salata. When you reach an intersection, turn right (southeast) along a dirt road to reach **Rifugio Malga Ra Stua** (☎ 0436 57 53, ⓦ www.malgarastua.it; open 10 June-20 Oct), about one to 1½ hours from Rifugio Fodara Vedla. It is possible to sleep here or just enjoy a pleasant lunch on the deck before heading back to Rifugio Fodara Vedla At the least, try a marvellous hot chocolate topped with fresh whipped cream.

From the *rifugio* walk back (northwest) along the dirt road No 6 through the beautiful Val Salata. Continue to just before Rifugio Sennes (1½ to two hours), cut across (southwest) on trail 7 and then head south to reach Rifugio Fodara Vedla (one hour from Rifugio Sennes).

You can link this loop (from Rifugio Malga Ra Stua) with the Parco Naturale delle Dolomiti d'Ampezzo route (p201).

Day 5: Rifugio Biella to Rifugio Vallandro

5½–6½ hours, 323m ascent, 600m descent

Head southeast up No 28, with great views of Lago Grande di Fosses. The trail follows the mountain crest towards the Croda Rossa a majestic mountain inhabited by golden eagles and ibex. Once you reach Forcella Cocodain (one hour), descend left (north) on No 28, a difficult, slippery and rocky route to a junction (2195m, one hour) where you pick up No 3. The area offers an amazing landscape. From the junction ascend north along combined trail 3-28 until you reach another junction with No 4, coming from the northwest. Ascend to the right on trail 3-4 28 and then turn right (east) again on trail 3 4. Walking through pastures, you will reach a junction (2260m). From here descend southeast to **Malga Cavalli di Sopra** (also called Casera Cavallo di Sopra), about an hour from Forcella Cocodain, where you can enjoy refreshments from the rustic café while enjoying a fabulous view of the imposing Croda Rossa.

Continue along No 3, ascending southeast along the north face of the Croda Rossa. The trail narrows and there is a sheer drop, but there are fixed iron cords to hold onto for safety. This section is quite exposed and might pose some difficulty for inexperienced walkers. It requires a careful step and, during storms, is not advisable (see Alternative Route: via Hotel Ponticello, this page). Trail 3 continues to its highest point (2300m), about an hour from the *malga*, and then descends towards the valley.

When you reach a junction (1965m), where trail 18 descends to the left (northwest) towards Ponticello, continue ascending northeast along No 3. You will pass nearby **Malga Stolla**, a rustic wayside café offering a delicious yoghurt and myrtle berry drink, and trail 18 heading right (southeast) to Passo Cimabanche on the S51, where there is a bar and bus stops for Cortina (15km) and Dobbiaco.

Taking trail No 3a, you will soon reach the wide meadows of Prato Piazza in front of the **Hotel Hohe Gaisl** (☎ 0474 74 86 06; ⓦ www.hohegaisl.com), one hour from the high point, and the nearby **Rifugio Pratopiazza** (☎/fax 0474 74 86 50). Turn right and take the road up to **Rifugio Vallandro** (☎ 0474 97 25 05; open 1 June-1 Oct), about 40 minutes. The small, old-style *rifugio* has great views of the Croda Rossa (west) and Cristallo (south), and is still 'guarded' by the ruins of a WWI Austrian fort. Try to get up before dawn so you can see how the Croda Rossa earned its name.

Side Trip: Picco di Vallandro
4 hours, 848m ascent/descent
It is worth making the ascent to the summit (2839m) on trail No 40, which starts from the chapel next to Rifugio Pratopiazza.

Alternative Route: via Hotel Ponticello
2½–3 hours, 500m ascent, 700m descent
From Malga Cavalli di Sopra, descend in a northeastly direction along the steep dirt road to **Hotel Ponticello** (☎ 0474 74 86 13, fax 0474 74 87 57; ⓦ www.hotel-brueckele .it), 1½ hours. To exit from the walk at this point, take the bus from Ponticello to Lago di Braies or Villabassa–Monguelfo–Brunico (seven a day from 10.40am to 5.30pm).

To continue, from Hotel Ponticello walk south up the road and take trail 18 (right) to a junction (1965m) with trail 3. Heading left (northeast) you rejoin the main route across Prato Piazza to Rifugio Vallandro.

To avoid the steep ascent from Hotel Ponticello, the shuttle bus up to Prato Piazza (€1.05, seven a day from 10am to 4.25pm) might be a better bet.

Day 6: Rifugio Vallandro to Hotel Tre Cime
2–2½ hours, 172m ascent, 794m descent
There are some very exposed sections, which are equipped with iron cords, along this route. If this worries you try the Alternative Route via Carbonin (p197).

Northern Dolomites

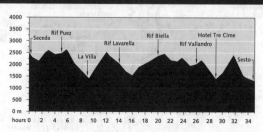

From Rifugio Vallandro take the dirt road No 34, which ascends north, or the trail, also numbered 34, that heads uphill (east) from just behind the *rifugio*, cutting up to a ruined fort and Sella di Monte Specie (2200m, 40 minutes). Avoid the trail on the right, which heads up to the summit of Monte Specie (2307m, 30 minutes); this trail is signed 'Heimkehrer Kreuz' after the war memorial *kreuz* (cross) at the summit. Make the steep descent on No 34, dug into rocks by Austrian soldiers as a strategic military road during WWI and offering breathtaking views. Along the trail there is a very

exposed section, with a narrow ledge with a sheer drop to one side. These sections are equipped with iron cord for security. Interesting features along the trail include the ruins of a military cableway station, a roughhewn short tunnel, fortifications in the rock face and caves.

At the S51 cross the stream and turn left (north) to **Hotel Tre Cime** (☎ 0474 97 26 33, fax 0474 97 23 30; W www.trecime.net), two hours from Sella di Monte Specie. From the car park there are good views of the summits of the Tre Cime di Lavaredo to the east. Here you can have a pleasant walk

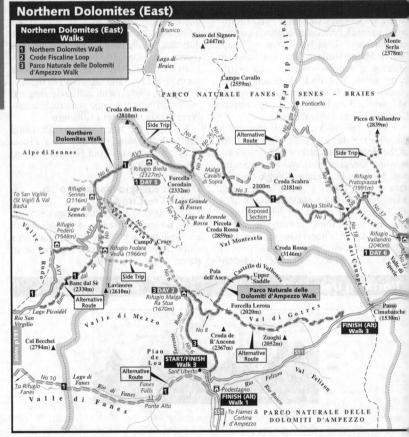

Northern Dolomites (East)

Northern Dolomites (East) Walks
1 Northern Dolomites Walk
2 Crode Fiscaline Loop
3 Parco Naturale delle Dolomiti d'Ampezzo Walk

round nearby Lago di Landro. From Hotel [T]re Cime buses connect with Dobbiaco [(1]0km) or with Cortina (24km).

Alternative Route: via Carbonin
[3]–4 hours, 622m descent
[F]rom Rifugio Vallandro, descend southeast [o]n the dirt road, shortened by trail 37. [Y]ou'll reach Carbonin (one hour) on the [S]51, and the bus stops for Cortina and Dob[b]iaco. To rejoin the main trail, turn left on [th]e road and walk 3km north to Hotel Tre [C]ime. There is a parallel trail following the [e]ast side of Lago di Landro.

Day 7: Hotel Tre Cime to Hotel Dolomitenhof
5–7 hours, 999m ascent, 1105m descent
Cross the road and from the car park take the dirt road No 10-102 east for a long pleasant walk along Fiume Rienza Nera. The trail climbs steeply along the Valle di Rinbon, up to the high plain with great views of the northern faces of Tre Cime di Lavaredo (Cima Grande, 2999m) to the south. A number of trails depart along here; continue to follow No 102 northeast to **Rifugio Locatelli** (☎ 0474 97 20 02, low season ☎/fax 0474 71 03 47; open 1 July-30 Sept), three to five

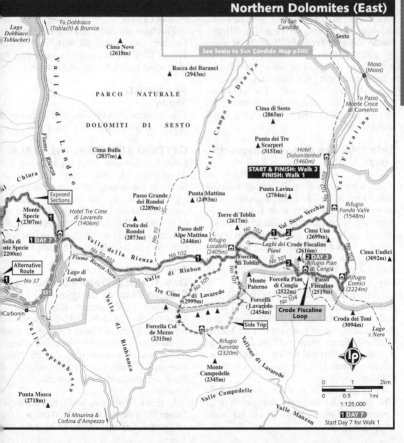

Northern Dolomites (East)

DOLOMITES

hours. This is one of the most beautiful and most visited places in the Dolomites. Even though the *rifugio* has 60 beds and 100 bunks, it is popular with large groups and you should book in advance.

If you decide to stop at Rifugio Locatelli, use your extra day to explore the Tre Cime di Lavaredo area (see Side Trip: Tre Cime di Lavaredo Loop, this page) or link with the Crode Fiscaline Loop (this page).

From Rifugio Locatelli continue northeast along No 102, which descends into the steep Val Sasso Vecchio. On the way down you'll pass the picturesque **Laghi dei Piani**. Note the pinnacles of Monte Paterno to the south, particularly the profile of the Frankfurter Würstel, a rocky spur shaped like a sausage! Once you arrive at the **Rifugio Fondo Valle** (☎/fax 0474 71 06 06; **w** www .rifugiofondovalle.com), about 1½ to two hours from Rifugio Locatelli, you can take a break and enjoy the wonderful views of Croda dei Toni to the south. From the *rifugio* follow the forest road north and, after about 30 minutes, you will reach the Hotel Dolomitenhof.

Side Trip: Tre Cime di Lavaredo Loop
2–3 hours, 271m ascent, 271m descent
If you want to finish up the day by taking a closer look at the Tre Cime, remember that crowds of people arrive daily from Rifugio Auronzo, on the southern side of the peaks, ferried up by buses on the controversial, paved toll road from Misurina. Early in the morning this loop is definitely more enjoyable and could be perfect as an addition to Day 7.

From Rifugio Locatelli take trail 105 southwest, passing some lovely small lakes under the north face of the Tre Cime and then heading up to Forcella Col de Mezzo (2315m). From here you can descend to Rifugio Auronzo and return to Rifugio Locatelli on trail 101, via Forcella Lavaredo (2454m).

From this saddle you can also take trail 104 east to the romantic Rifugio Pian di Cengia and link with the Crode Fiscaline Loop (this page).

Crode Fiscaline Loop

Duration	2 days
Difficulty	easy
Start/Finish	Hotel Dolomithof
Nearest Town	San Candido (p188)
Transport	bus

Summary A high-altitude loop to the amazing pinnacles of Crode Fiscaline.

This walk starts in Val Fiscalina, one of th most impressive approaches to Tre Cime c Lavaredo. It takes in some amazing roc formations, passes some WWI trenches an includes a night in the lovely, tiny Rifugi Pian di Cengia.

This look can easily be combined with th Northern Dolomites walk (p187) or the Sid Trip to Tre Cime di Lavaredo (this page) fc truly spectacular, longer alternatives.

PLANNING
Maps
The Tabacco 1:25,000 No 010 *Dolomiti a Sesto* is recommended for this walk.

GETTING TO/FROM THE WALK
From San Candido head southeast on S5 passing through Sesto (7km). Just after th Sesto, in the village of Moso (Moos), tur right onto the Val Fiscalina road headin southwest. Hotel Dolomitenhof is at the en of this road, 5km from Sesto. Regular buse run between San Candido, Sesto and the hote (hourly in high season from 8.30am to 6pm

THE WALK (see map p197)
Day 1: Hotel Dolomitenhof to Rifugio Pian di Cengia
4–5 hours, 1124m ascent, 47m descent
Take the dirt road No 102-103 south to wards the spires of Croda dei Toni. As yo set out near the hotel, note the unusual fresc on the wall of a house depicting the giant Huno and Hauno, who figure in several an cient legends about the founding of Sa Candido.

In about 30 minutes you'll reach **Rifugi Fondo Valle** (☎/fax 0474 71 06 06; **w** ww .rifugiofondovalle.com). From here the trai scends to a fork; head right on trail No 102 scending 850m over the rocky ledges of Val asso Vecchio before reaching the Forcella i Toblin and **Rifugio Locatelli** (☎ 0474 97 '0 02, 0474 71 03 47; open 1 July-30 Sept), bout two hours from Rifugio Fondo Valle. Rifugio Locatelli is in a large, 1950s-style building with the disconcerting look of an rmy barracks, but a marvellous terrace view. To the south are the Tre Cime di Lavaredo which, on closer inspection, prove to be our peaks, not three), dominating a vast, neavily furrowed limestone high plain. The place is very special and everyone knows his. If you're not fortunate enough to arrive n a moment of calm, the chaos is worth enduring for the sake of the view, and the afternoon light all but guarantees outstanding photos.

From the *rifugio* descend southeast on rail No 101, passing above Laghi dei Piani, hen ascend among loose rock to Forcella Pian di Cengia (2522m). From the saddle continue left (east) along trail No 101, passing old military trenches, to reach **Rifugio Pian di Cengia** (☎ 337 45 15 17), 1½ hours rom Rifugio Locatelli. The lovely, tiny Rifugio Pian di Cengia has a 15-bunk dormitory on the upper floor, accessible through a trap door at the top of a ladder.

Day 2: Rifugio Pian di Cengia to Hotel Dolomitenhof
4-5 hours, 1218m descent

Follow trail 101 east among more WWI trenches to **Passo Fiscalino** (2519m), where you find great views. From here it is a short walk left (north, blind alley) to the amazing pinnacles of **Crode Fiscaline**, about 1½ hours return. To continue, from Passo Fiscalino descend east to a fork where you go eft (northeast) to **Rifugio Comici** (☎ 0474 '1 03 58, 0474 71 04 13; open 20 June-15 Sept), one hour from the saddle and set at he gravelly base of the crag. From here go north, descending the steep trail 103 to Rifugio Fondo Valle, 1½ hours, with the Cima Undici on your right and the wonderful Croda dei Toni behind you. On the dirt road again, return to Hotel Dolomitenhof 30 minutes).

Sesto to San Candido

Duration	2½-3 hours
Difficulty	easy
Start	Sesto
Finish	San Candido
Nearest Town	San Candido (p188)
Transport	bus, train

Summary A low-altitude, pleasant forest stroll with spectacular Dolomites views.

This delightful walk starts in Sesto in Val di Sesto, in the heart of Parco Naturale Dolomiti di Sesto, and ends in San Candido in Val Pusteria, on the northern edge of the Dolomites. The present-day Austrian border is only 8km east of San Candido, which developed at the meeting point of Val di Sesto and the Fiume Drava.

PLANNING
Maps
The Tabacco 1:25,000 No 010 *Dolomiti di Sesto* is recommended for this walk.

GETTING TO/FROM THE WALK
From San Candido head southeast on S52 to reach Sesto (7km). Regular SAD buses run between San Candido and Sesto (hourly in high season, from 8.30am to 6pm).

THE WALK
From Sesto's *municipio* (town hall), take Via San Vito uphill. At the church entrance turn right (east). After about 30m you come to a wide intersection where there is a sign indicating numerous different trails. Take No 4d, also known as the Sentiero di Meditazione (Meditation Path), for Cappella del Bosco (Waldkapelle). Follow the sign on the paved road that, after a house, becomes a grassy trail heading to a wooden bridge. Before the bridge turn left (north) ascending alongside a stream. When you reach the asphalt, cross the road and take northwest Via Hosler. It ascends gently, affording magnificent views over gentle pastures dotted with wooden *fienili* (haysheds).

In a few minutes you come to a farm where Via Hosler ends. Following the 4d trail signs,

DOLOMITES

you'll pass under the ramp of a hayshed and find yourself facing the frescoed facade of a house. Pass along the right side of the house and pick up the path that heads into the woods. Climbing a steep incline among fir trees and moss-covered boulders, you'll pass two of the numerous **wooden sculptures** that mark the meditation stops along the way. When you reach a hayshed, ascend right, take a break at the little wooden table (1470m, 50 minutes) and enjoy the spectacular east to west panorama of Croda Rossa di Sesto, Croda dei Toni, Tre Scarperi and Rocca dei Baranci in the background.

Take up the trail that heads northwest through the wood. After about 20m you'll find a path on the right marked 'Pietre Preistoriche'. It's a 30-minute return deviation to visit the site of a prehistoric place of worship – two **stone slabs** with strange incisions typical of Neolithic rock carving in the Alps.

Continuing northwest, the main trail climbs a small, rocky valley, until it reaches

the **Cappella del Bosco** (10 minutes), a lo[...] chapel built in 1917, after locals had to b[...] evacuated from the valley due to the Italia[...] bombing of what was then Austria. From th[...] chapel continue up the path until you com[...] to a fork where you descend to the left ont[...] a dirt road, following the sign for trail 4 t[...] San Candido. It's a pleasant descent throug[...] the lush woods of the crest all the way to Sa[...] Candido. Avoiding any deviations, descen[...] first through the firs and then, after a shar[...] curve to the right, some Scots pines. If yo[...] proceed quietly, you might even surprise [...] fawn or a squirrel or two skipping amon[...] the branches. Still walking along trail 4, ig[...] nore the fork to the left for No 5 to Sest[...] You'll come to another little table (1400m[...] with a fantastic view over Val Campo d[...] Dentro, with the Torre dei Scarperi to th[...] left (south) and the Croda dei Rondoi to th[...] right. Continuing on you will come to a for[...] without signs – go straight ahead downhil[...] avoiding the dirt road that ascends to th[...]

Sesto to San Candido

ight. After 30 minutes you'll come to another fork where the road ascends to the right. At this point head downhill on a shortcut, which will bring you to a playground, from where a short zigzagging ramp on the left (west) leads down to the northern side of San Candido.

Parco Naturale delle Dolomiti d'Ampezzo

Duration	2 days
Difficulty	easy
Start/Finish	Sant'Uberto
Nearest Town	Cortina d'Ampezzo (p201)
Transport	bus
Summary	A return walk taking in Rifugio Malga Ra Stua, Forcella Lerosa and an upper outlook at Pala dell'Asco.

This walk, through the Parco Naturale delle Dolomiti d'Ampezzo is suitable for all walkers and ideal for families. It provides a good introduction to some of the Dolomites' more scenic peaks, notably Croda Rossa.

PLANNING
Maps
For this walk the Tabacco 1:25,000 map No 03 *Cortina d'Ampezzo e Dolomiti Ampezzane* is recommended.

NEAREST TOWN
Cortina d'Ampezzo
The **Cortina APT** (☎ 0436 32 31; W www .apt-dolomiti-cortina.it; *Piazzetta San Francesco 8*) provides information. Parco Naturale delle Dolomiti d'Ampezzo is operated by the **Comunanza delle Regole d'Ampezzo** (☎ 0436 22 06; W www.regole.it; *Via del Parco 1*), an ancient consortium of families dating back to the first Celtic/Roman settlements in the valley. The group manages the collective use of the pastures and forests according to tradition, and provides information about the park. The consortium's **summer information office** (*open June-Sept*) is at the Fiames entrance to the park.

Supplies & Equipment A central shopping centre, **La Cooperativa** (*Corso Italia 40*), includes a grocery shop. For quality equipment try **K2 Sport** (☎ 0436 86 37 06; W www .k2sport.com; *Via Cesare Battisti 2*).

Places to Stay & Eat About 3.5km north of Cortina at Fiames, **International Camping Olympia** (☎ 0436 50 57; *camping per person/tent from €4.50/7*) is served by the No 1 local bus (see Getting to/from the Walk, below). Bungalows are also available. **Hotel Fiames** (☎ 0436 23 66; e fiames@tiscali.it; *Fiames 13; half board €51.65*), 150m north of the shuttle bus stop, is as cheap and basic as it gets.

In Cortina you'll struggle to find reasonably priced accommodation. The best deal is **Casa Tua** (☎ 0436 22 78, 335 656 75 57; W www.casatuacortina.com; *Zuel 100; beds €31-51.65*), about 2.5km south of Cortina in a quiet area with gardens. Rates include breakfast. To get there take bus No 2 from Piazzale Roma, departing every 30 minutes in the high season and hourly during the rest of the year.

For a good meal or a pizza, try **Ariston** (☎ 0436 86 67 05; *via Marconi 10; full meal €15.50*), in front of the bus station.

Getting There & Away Cortina's bus station is in Via Marconi. **SAD** (☎ 800 84 60 47) buses leave Cortina at 8.45 and 10am, and 12.40, 4 and 6.50pm for Hotel Fiames, Passo Cimabanche, Carbonin, Dobbiaco (change for Brunico and Bolzano), Braies or San Candido. **Dolomitibus** (☎ 0435 321 55) travels west to Passo Falzarego or southeast to Calalzo, where you can catch a FS train for Belluno-Venezia.

GETTING TO/FROM THE WALK
From the Cortina bus station, local bus No 1 (*€0.80*) reaches the Fiames car park (a former airstrip), on the S51, about 4km north of Cortina and 150m before the Hotel Fiames. From 9 July to 9 September the road up to Rifugio Malga Ra Stua is closed to normal traffic and a shuttle service (*€3.65, 8am to 7pm*) runs from the Fiames car park (former airstrip).

DOLOMITES

THE WALK (see map p196)
Day 1: Sant'Uberto to Malga Ra Stua

1 hour, 4km, 247m ascent

If you decide to walk up to Rifugio Malga Ra Stua and prefer to avoid the small busy road, from the eastern side of the S51 switchback, in an area known as Sant'Uberto, take the unnumbered trail that heads uphill and follow the southern slope of Croda de R'Ancona. In one hour you'll arrive at **Rifugio Malga Ra Stua** (☎ 0436 57 53; w www.malgarastua.it; open 10 June-20 Oct), at the beginning of Val Salata, where it's worth staying overnight. This lovely alpine valley is perfect for spending the rest of the day in with a relaxing walk northwest to the nearby Campo Croce. More serious walkers can continue to the end of Val Salata, ascend to Rifugio Sennes and pick up sections of the Northern Dolomites walk (p187), notably the Rifugio Malga Ra Stua Side Trip on p194.

Day 2: Malga Ra Stua to Sant'Uberto via Pala dell'Asco

4–5 hours, 606m ascent/descent

From Rifugio Malga Ra Stua continue ascending along Val Salata for about 150m and take the dirt road to your right (east), which ascends for about 250m. At the fork take the branch of trail 8 that heads to the right (southeast) – it's longer but easier and far more scenic. Pass a wooden bridge with a gate and follow the series of switchbacks winding uphill past ancient fir trees – at certain points there are panoramic views across the Fanes high plain. You will reach a small, flat valley where, if you approach quietly, you might see the resident chamois and squirrels. Follow the trail around the valley, avoiding the deviations, which head off to the right. In front of you now is the majestic Croda Rossa, one of the most beautiful peaks in the Dolomites. The trail will bring you to a little wooden house with a water fountain at the edge of a dirt road in a wide valley called Valbones, west of Forcella Lerosa (one hour).

If you want more adventure head north across the pastures, rich in marmot dens, to reach another small wooden house (2039m). From here ascend north, progressively turning east, with an easy climb on the fascinating slope of **Pala dell'Asco**, made up by rocky stripes dotted by Arolla pines. You soon reach the upper saddle (2274m, 40 minutes) above an inner rocky basin called Castello di Valbones, at the foot of the imposing reddish peak of Croda Rossa (3146m), usually inhabited by a herd of chamois. Enjoy the astonishing view southwest and descend the slippery grassy slopes in a southwesterly direction in order to return to the Forcella Lerosa dirt road.

At this point you have three options. The first is to turn right (northwest) and follow the dirt road No 8 back down to Rifugio Malga Ra Stua (one hour). This route is a slippery shortcut and less attractive than the ascent so, if you're in no hurry, you can return the way you came. Otherwise see the Alternative Finish below.

Alternative Finish: via Val di Gotres

1 hour, 5km

A third option is to turn left (southeast), still following No 8, to Forcella Lerosa and descend the picturesque walk along the Val di Gotres. After about 5km you will reach the S51, just 1km southwest of Passo Cimabanche, 14km from Cortina.

At the time of writing, buses passed Passo Cimabanche for Cortina at 8.15 and 10.35am and 4.05 and 6.25pm. Buy tickets on the bus. Check with the **bus information office** (☎ 0436 86 79 21).

VIA FERRATA

A *via ferrata* (iron way; plural *vie ferrate*) uses intriguing and often ingenious combinations of ladders, metal brackets, chiselled footholds and even bridges to allow progress on steep or vertical cliffs. Steel cable is bolted to the rock at waist level. The cable acts as both a handhold and security, with walkers clipping onto it with a lanyard and karabiner system.

HISTORY

The protection of climbing routes in the European Alps, and in particular the Dolomites, began as long ago as the 1860s, but it was not until WWI that a large number of *vie ferrate* was constructed. They proved to be an excellent means of moving troops and military equipment quickly and safely over difficult terrain. After WWI some routes were left to rust away, but many were adopted by climbers to speed access to more difficult free climbs.

The Brenta Dolomites never had *vie ferrate* constructed for military purposes. However, their great beauty and dramatic rock faces attracted the attention of local and foreign climbers, and during the 1930s the construction of a *via ferrata* to the base of difficult climbs began. Work on what was to become the Bocchette continued after WWII, and this eventually developed into one of Italy's classic *vie ferrate*. Multiple sections of ladders and narrow ledges now wind along the base of some of the most impressive rock peaks in Europe.

Elsewhere in the Dolomites, CAI (Club Alpino Italiano) directives to use *vie ferrate* only as a means of access were at times ignored, and several famous routes were constructed all the way to the summits of previously difficult peaks. While maintenance of *vie ferrate* continues, the CAI has placed a ban on construction of new routes.

GARETH McCORMACK

Right: Climbing in the breathtaking Brenta Dolomites on one of the many *vie ferrate*.

203

EQUIPMENT

The core of the *via ferrata* system is a climbing harness and a *via ferrata* kit. The kit has two specially designed karabiners tied on either end of a length of dynamic (shock absorbing) rope, commonly referred to as a lanyard. This rope passes through a simple, but extremely important, energy-absorbing device, which in turn is attached to the harness with a locking karabiner. See the boxed text 'Technique & Safety' (below) for more on the energy absorber.

You can use a straightforward 'sit' harness for a *via ferrata*, but many people use a waist and chest harness combination. This is especially recommended for children and for climbers with heavy packs, so that in the event of a fall they are prevented from flipping upside down (with the associated risk of head injuries). Although not essential, a helmet is strongly recommended. *Via ferrata* kits can generally be rented from most equipment shops in the Dolomites for around €2.60 per day.

If you want to buy your own gear, it's best to do so in Italy; expect to pay up to €50 for the full kit. Alternatively, it should be possible for

Essential *via ferrata* ge
– helmet, harness,
karabiners, dynamic ro
and energy absorber

Technique & Safety

You don't need mountaineering experience to use *via ferrata* equipment, though proper attention to safety and technique is essential. Before even setting out you should familiarise yourself with your harness and equipment. Always check to make sure that your harness waist strap is doubled back through the buckle. Use a specifically designed energy-absorbing device – most belaying devices or figure-of-eight abseil devices are not sufficient. In the event of a fall this device will hugely reduce the impact on your equipment and body.

Once on the route you must ensure that you are clipped into the wire cables with one of your two karabiners at all times. When you come to a bracket, use your free karabiner to clip into the cable on the other side of the bracket before unclipping the first karabiner and continuing. On ladders it makes life easier to loop your lanyard over your forearm whilst climbing. On vertical sections of cable and on ladders, always unclip one of the karabiners after you have 'leapfrogged' a bracket. Falling with both karabiners attached will prevent your energy absorber from working.

More experienced and confident walkers only clip into the cable on the most difficult sections and can therefore move extremely quickly. The decision whether to clip in or not on any given section is ultimately your own.

GARETH McCORMACK

Keep one 'clipped' at all times

Warning

Vie ferrate can never be guaranteed to be safe. Rock fall, lightning, avalanche, sudden weather changes, icing on the rock and cables and inattention whilst clipping the cable, are all factors which can lead to serious accidents. While the equipment on popular *vie ferrate* is generally sound, it is not fail-safe. Above all you need to remain alert and use your judgment.

gear shops in other countries to order kits from the manufacturers; **Petzl** (w *www.petzl.com*) and **Camp** (w *www.camp.it*) are two of the biggest.

INFORMATION
Maps & Books
Höfler and Werner's *Via Ferrata: Scrambles in the Dolomites* is one of the best English-language guides, detailing 89 routes.

Walking maps (normally 1:25,000) of areas where *vie ferrate* are common usually have the routes marked, and it is advisable to carry a map with you just as you would on a normal walk.

THE BRENTA DOLOMITES
The spectacular Brenta group, just north of Lake Garda and to the west of the main Dolomite range, offers classic *vie ferrate*. The group is part of the Parco Naturale Adamello Brenta, which is Trentino's largest protected area, covering 618 sq km and incorporating 50 lakes. Here we detail two easier sections of the Bocchette *via ferrata* – one of the most famous routes ever constructed.

PLANNING
When to Walk
The routes described here should be snow-free snow by early June. Late September sees the *rifugi* (mountain huts) shut and the first snows of winter are normally not far behind.

Maps
Use the Kompass 1:25,000 map No 688 *Gruppo di Brenta*.

Information Sources
Weather forecasts for the Brenta are posted daily at many camping grounds, *rifugi* and walking equipment stores.

Contact **Parco Naturale Adamello Brenta** (☎ *0465 67 49 89;* w *www.parcoadamellobrenta.tn.it*) for park information.

ACCESS TOWN & FACILITIES
Madonna di Campiglio
An attractive and popular ski resort, Madonna di Campiglio retains its liveliness during summer with plenty of visiting walkers and climbers. The **APT office** (☎ *0465 44 20 00,* w *www.campiglio.net; Via Pradalago 4; open 9am-noon & 3pm-6.30pm Mon-Sat, 9am-noon Sun*)

is off Piazza Brenta Alte, in the village centre. Staff at the **Casa delle Guide Alpine** (*☎ 0465 44 26 34; Via Cima 3*) can provide up-to-date condition reports on popular *via ferrata* routes. There are numerous gear shops in the centre, and **Olimpionico Sport** (*☎ 0465 44 12 59; Piazza Righi 15*) hires *via ferrata* equipment.

Accommodation in Madonna is not cheap; near the centre of town the quite adequate **Hotel Palù** (*☎ 0465 44 16 95; w www.hotelpalu .com; Via Vallesinella 4; half board low season/high season €28.50/ 59.50*) is one of the cheaper options.

There are plenty of good places to eat; try **Ristorante/Pizzeria Le Roi** (*☎ 0465 44 30 75*). For *panini* (bread roll with filling) and other snacks the **L'Azzurro** bar is excellent. There are several well-stocked **supermarkets** in the centre of town.

Atesina (*☎ 0461 98 36 27*) operates a bus service between Madonna di Campiglio and Trento (two hours, six times a day). Trento is on the busy Verona–Bolzano–Brennero train line.

Camping Faé

The closest camping ground to the *vie ferrate*, 5km down the valley towards Trento, is Camping Faé (*☎ 0465 50 71 78; 2 people €22.70*).

Rifugio Tuckett

At the start of both routes, Rifugio Tuckett (*☎ 0465 44 12 26; half board €31; open June-Sept*) is open for lunch, snacks and drinks.

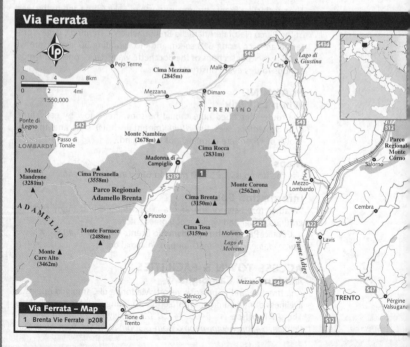

Via Ferrata

Via Ferrata – Map
1 Brenta Vie Ferrate p208

Via Ferrata SOSAT

Duration	2½–3 hours
Distance	4.5km
Difficulty	beginner
Start	Rifugio Tuckett
Finish	Rifugio Alimonta or Rifugio Brentei
Nearest Town	Madonna di Campiglio (p205)
Transport	cable car

Summary A good first-timer's route, offering a taste of most *via ferrata* techniques and including an exciting crux section.

Built in 1961, the SOSAT is mainly a high-level walking path, with just one concentrated and relatively short section of *via ferrata*. It offers a well-protected and relatively easy introduction for confident first timers. The protected section is interesting and varied, involving gullies, ladders and ledges, and the crux (most difficult part of a climb) is an exposed vertical ladder that is enough to set most people's blood coursing. The route is well marked throughout.

GETTING TO/FROM THE ROUTE

To reach the start of the walk at Rifugio Tuckett, take the **Grostè cable car** (☎ 0465 44 77 44), 1km northwest of Madonna di Campiglio on the main road to Dimaro, to the top station. The first car leaves at 8.30am and the last one leaves the top station at 5pm (return €7.50). From the top station head southwest along path 316, which is signed to the Rifugio Tuckett. The hut is reached after 1½ hours of walking.

THE ROUTE

Follow the well-marked path 303 east from **Rifugio Tuckett** and keep right at two junctions. About 700m from the *rifugio* a third junction is reached, and a sign indicates the SOSAT to the right. Descend south and cross the moraine beneath the Vendretta di Tuckett to reach a plaque marking the official start of the Via Ferrata SOSAT. A series of low rock ledges lead around the northwest side of the Punta di Campiglio; wire cables are in place to protect several steps and ledges early on, though many people don't clip on here. The route is then essentially a rough walking path for 1.5km, with paint splashes marking the way through the jumble of boulders.

The descent of an easy, unprotected gully is an indication of the onset of a difficult section. After another 200m you round a corner and the route disappears into a second gully, this time protected. Metal staples provide footholds. The cable then leads along the steep western face of the Punte di Campiglio, descending several ladders and crossing short ledges as it makes its way towards a corner where two cliff faces meet. A large boulder lies wedged in the gully between these cliffs, providing a natural bridge from one to the other. One ladder descends to the boulder, then another, longer ladder (with 51 rungs!) climbs vertically up to a **narrow ledge** on the opposite cliff wall. This is the crux of the route. The cable continues to protect the ledge for a

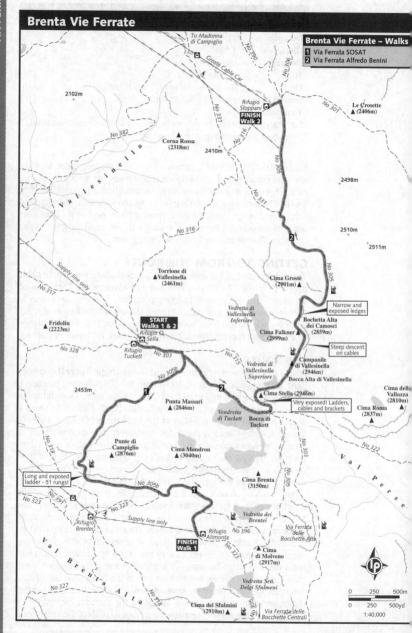

Brenta Vie Ferrate

Brenta Vie Ferrate – Walks
1. Via Ferrata SOSAT
2. Via Ferrata Alfredo Benini

To Madonna di Campiglio

Groste Cable Car

No 390

No 306

Rifugio Stoppani
FINISH Walk 2

No 301

Le Crosette
▲ (2406m)

2102m

No 382

No 331

Corna Rossa
(2318m)

2410m

No 316

2498m

No 331

2510m

2511m

Torrione di
▲ Vallesinella
(2461m)

Cima Grostè
(2901m) ▲

Vedretta di
Vallesinella
Inferiore

Bochetta Alta
dei Camosci
(2859m)

Narrow and
exposed ledges

No 317

Supply line only

Fridolin
(2223m)

START Walks 1 & 2
Rifugio Sella

Rifugio Tuckett

No 328

No 303

No 305b

Cima Falkner
(2999m)

Campanile
di Vallesinella
(2946m)

Bocca Alta di Vallesinella

Steep descent
on cables

No 375

Vedretta di
Vallesinella
Superiore

Cima della
Vallazza
(2810m)

2453m

Punta Massari
▲ (2846m)

Vendretta
di Tuckett

Cima Stella (2946m)

Bocca di
Tuckett

Very exposed! Ladders,
cables and brackets

Cima Roma
(2837m) ▲

Punte di
Campiglio
▲ (2876m)

Cima Mondron
▲ (3040m)

No 303

V a l   P e r s e

No 322

Long and exposed
ladder - 51 rungs!

No 318

No 391

No 323

Rifugio
Brentei

No 305b

No 323

Supply line only

Cima Brenta
(3150m)

Vedretta dei
Brentei

No 396

Rifugio
Alimonta

FINISH Walk 1

No 323

Cima
di Molveno
(2917m)

Via Ferrata
delle
Bocchette Alte

V a l   B r e n t a   A l t a

No 327

Cima del Sfulmini
(2910m) ▲

No 378

Vedretta Sett.
Delgi Sfulmeni

Via Ferrata delle
Bocchette Centrali

0   250   500m
0   250   500yd

1:40,000

short distance until the cliff gives way to easier ground, and a path leads around and into the Val Brenta Alta, with wonderful views of the Brenta ridge opening up at the head of the valley.

The worst of the difficult sections are now over. Pass a low overhang and then descend two short ladders through a gully, after which a short walk brings you to a trail junction. The orange-roofed **Rifugio Brentei** (☎ 0465 44 12 44; half board €34; open June-Sept) is about 15 minutes down the valley to the southwest, while the **Rifugio Alimonta** (☎ 0465 44 03 66; half board €34; open June-Sept) lies a 30-minute climb away to the east. Both *rifugi* are well signed.

Via Ferrata Alfredo Benini

Duration	3½–4½ hours
Distance	7km
Difficulty	beginner–intermediate
Start	Rifugio Tuckett
Finish	Grostè cable car
Nearest Town	Madonna di Campiglio (p205)
Transport	cable car

Summary A sustained initial section leads through a wide variety of terrain before reaching easier ground in a wonderful high-level situation.

The Benini forms the northern section of the Via ferrata delle Bocchette and provides more challenging and exposed *via ferrata* sections than the SOSAT. However, it is well within the capabilities of most confident *via ferrata* first-timers given good weather, plenty of time and the prerequisite of freedom from vertigo. It is also an excellent route to try after the SOSAT. It is possible to follow straight onto the Benini from the SOSAT if you start from the Rifugio Alimonta or Rifugio Brentei (see above).

The Benini is described travelling south to north, because this is arguably the easiest direction for a beginner. From the southern end of the Benini at the Bocca del Tuckett you can see the most difficult section of the route climbing diagonally above the Vendretta di Tuckett on a series of ladders, brackets and airy ledges. If this all proves too much it is easy to turn back, and if you get through you can continue in the knowledge that the other sections will be no more difficult. The majority of traffic comes north to south, with the Rifugio Tuckett often the intended destination.

PLANNING
What to Bring
It is possible, though unlikely, that an ice axe and crampons may be necessary to climb the Vendretta di Tuckett to the Bocca di Tuckett; check at **Rifugio Tuckett** (☎ 0465 44 12 26).

GETTING TO/FROM THE ROUTE
See Getting to/from the Route (p207) for Via Ferrata SOSAT.

THE ROUTE

Follow path 303 (well marked) east from the Rifugio Tuckett towards the Vendretta di Tuckett. Ignore an unmarked path running off to the right and then pass another path heading left towards a prominent gully. This second path (the Sentiero Attrezzato Dallagiacoma, 315) provides rather tortuous walking access onto the Benini just west of Cima Sella, cutting out the initial section of *via ferrata* from the Bocca di Tuckett. However, this path is normally only used when the Vendretta di Tuckett is icy. Continue on path 303 past a signposted turnoff for the SOSAT, and climb steadily across rock shelves to reach the foot of the glacier (30 minutes from the Rifugio Tuckett). The glacier is not crevassed and is gently angled, providing a 20-minute climb to the **Bocca di Tuckett** (ice axe and/or crampons are not usually needed).

The Benini sets off up the imposing cliffs to the north, immediately using ladders to connect narrow and exposed ledges. You're soon above the glacier and after climbing a high, vertical ladder you drop down onto several brackets leading to a short traverse along a tiny foot ledge. This section is tremendously exposed, but well protected, with each search for a new foothold also forcing you to contemplate the vertical space beneath. Climb a short ladder and onto another exposed ledge before reaching less exposed ground in a wide gully. Scramble up to the base of some easy ladders and climb these to reach the end of this section on the west shoulder of **Cima Sella** (2946m). There is a marked junction here with trail 315.

Degrees of Difficulty

Whether or not you'll enjoy a *via ferrata* is likely to be determined by your reaction to 'exposure' (proximity to a large vertical drop). A well-maintained *via ferrata* is normally a thrilling but safe outing for a properly equipped and suitably experienced walker. However, many routes feature vertical ladders and sections along narrow ledges with several hundred metres of vertical drop beneath. The psychological demands are significant, and walkers prone to even mild vertigo will find an average *via ferrata* terrifying. Most people do find this uncomfortable to begin with, but it is possible to develop your comfort levels by starting on easier routes and progressing onto more challenging and exposed routes. There is no recognised grading standard for *vie ferrate* but the following is a general guide applied to the *via ferrata* descriptions in this book:

Beginner – Suitable for confident walkers with a sound general awareness of mountain conditions and safety. The route will feature exposed sections and perhaps some ladders, but difficult sections will be short. Much of the route may simply be a rugged walk.

Intermediate – May feature several sustained sections on ladders, cables and artificial footholds. Narrow ledges and significant exposure are common. Will only suit those who are confident.

Advanced – These routes may be complicated by snow gullies, glaciers and tremendous exposure. Generally mountaineering experience is required.

Walk up to the Bocca Alta di Vallesinella and cross over to the east side of **Campanile di Vallesinella** (2946m), where a stunning view opens up encompassing from right to left: the summit of Cima Brenta (3150m), the dark depths of the Val Perse, the castellation of Cima Roma and, in the distance on a clear day, the rest of the Dolomites. Easy ledges lead down into a gully from where another well-protected scrambling section leads up a **rocky nose** in a tremendously exposed situation (two hours from the Rifugio Tuckett). The ledge at the top of this marks the high point of the route (2900m) and the end of the difficult section. Descend steeply using cables and narrow ledges to reach a long traverse on ledges round the east face of Cima Falkner (2999m) to the Bochetta Alta dei Camosci, and then a similar section around Cima Grostè to the end of the Benini. The Grostè cable car is then within sight, 45 minutes easy walking away. The ledge sections (around Cima Falkner and Cima Grostè) are only protected where they are particularly narrow, so stay alert on the wider ledges, which are still very exposed.

the jagged peaks of the ruppi di Brenta (Brenta Group), from the Via ferrata delle Bocchette

OTHER ROUTES

There are literally hundreds of *via ferrata* routes in Italy, most of which are concentrated in the Dolomites. The following is a very small selection.

BRENTA DOLOMITES
Via ferrata delle Bocchette Alte
An advanced *via ferrata*, the Bocchette Alte is probably the hardest route in the Brenta and requires basic alpine skills to cope with crossing steep snow gullies. It begins at the Bocca di Tuckett (continuing south from the Benini) and is sustained and exposed for most of the way to the Rifugio Alimonta. Its height means that ice is a common problem towards the end of the season.

Via ferrata delle Bocchette Centrali
An excellent intermediate route, the Centrali links the Rifugio Alimonta (and the Bocchette Alte) with the Rifugio Pedrotti. It is well protected and very popular, featuring spectacularly exposed ledges and ladders.

NORTHERN DOLOMITES
Sass Rigais
This 3025m peak can be climbed using a well-maintained *via ferrata* on the south face. Rated beginner to intermediate, this route can be accessed from Ortisei (p187) or Santa Cristina. An exposed ridge leads to the summit, where views extend right across the Dolomites.

Via ferrata Ivano Dibona
Approached from Cortina, this spectacular but technically straightforward route takes you to the summit of Monte Cristallo. This mountain saw extended and fierce fighting between Italian and Austrian troops during WWI and *vie ferrate* were constructed to move troops and equipment. The Ivano Dibona, however, is a relatively new construction featuring cables, ladders and bridges. The route should suit those at beginner to intermediate levels, but becomes very crowded on summer weekends.

Julian & Carnic Alps

'Austria 7, Slovenia 11' – it's not the score-line from an action-packed football international but the wording on a road sign in Tarvisio. This is the main town in the valley between the rugged Julian Alps (Alpi Giulie), a range Italy shares with Slovenia, and the eastern end of the more gentle Carnic Alps (Alpi Carniche), which straddle the border with Austria, east of the Dolomites.

This far northeastern corner of Italy – wedged between borders, a meeting place of territories and cultures, and for centuries a natural route for human traffic – has a turbulent history. Long fought over, it's now at the cutting edge of the trend towards integration within Europe. You can order your lunch in a variety of languages and, before the introduction of the euro, could pay the bill in any of several currencies.

To the walker, this background lends an intriguing, if sometimes sobering, air to a visit here. You're bound to notice traces of two world wars, even in improbably high, remote corners, and it's hard to be unmoved by the thought of men living and fighting in such an environment – especially in winter. These days, though, the mood in the mountains is friendly, and walkers come and go across borders at will. On trails in the Carnic Alps it's as common to be greeted with the German 'Grüss Gott' as the Italian 'Salve', and in parts of the Julian Alps you'll hear the occasional Slovene 'Dober dan', as well as the Italian 'Buondì'.

Greetings in any language, though, are far from frequent. Once away from places where walkers' paths converge – trailheads, passes and some of the more popular *rifugi* (mountain huts) – you're likely to have even the most spectacular terrain pretty much to yourself.

A major attraction of walks in the Julian Alps is the beauty and relative integrity of the natural environment. It's a heavily forested area, mostly free of large-scale development (there are ski resorts but quite small ones) and just over the border in Slovenia is Triglavski

NICK TAPP

Looking northwest from below Sella Robon to the plains of Altipiano del Montasio

- Winding forest paths, picturesque lakes and soaring Alpine rock walls on the Fusine-Mangart Loop (p217)

- Exploring the rich flora and stark, stony landscape of high limestone plateaus on the Slovenian Two-Step (p218)

- Rifugio Corsi, in a spectacular natural amphitheatre at the foot of mighty Jôf Fuart (p221)

- Wide, open spaces and airy ridge-tops around Monte Carnizza (p223)

Narodni Park. This huge national park is credited with harbouring much of the wildlife that crosses the border into the Italian Julian Alps. No less appealing or important are the lush uplands of the Carnic Alps, along the Austrian border, which host a great variety of wildflowers and offer walking in a rounded, rolling landscape reminiscent of other, less vertical parts of the world.

This chapter covers the western Julian Alps and the eastern Carnic Alps – a compact area reasonably accessible from Tarvisio. Both ranges extend further – the Julian Alps to the south, as well as east into Slovenia; and the Carnic Alps west as far as the Dolomites. There's ample scope to explore much further than is covered here.

CLIMATE

An Alpine climate prevails across the region. Summers are cool and rainy, though fine spells are not uncommon. Winters can be bitterly cold – pre-Alps to the south block warmer air currents from the Mediterranean – and snowfall is abundant. Snow depths reach 2m in Tarvisio, at less than 800m altitude, and snow banks may lie across higher trails well into the summer. Avalanches are common in spring. Conditions vary markedly between the warmer, more sheltered valley floors and the exposed tops, and between sunnier slopes with a southerly aspect and colder, north-facing ones. A couple of glaciers cling to existence on the northern slopes of Monte Canìn and Jôf di Montasio in the Julian Alps.

INFORMATION
Maps

Any number of maps are good for planning and information about access, including the 1:250,000 map *Friuli-Venezia Giulia: carta turistico-stradale*, distributed free by tourist offices in Udine and elsewhere. The Tabacco 1:150,000 *Friuli-Venezia Giulia* map is more detailed and accurate.

Books

Wild Italy, by Tim Jepson, has an enticing couple of pages on the area's natural history. There are numerous publications in Italian, including a comprehensive CAI guide to the marked trails. Free from the APT in Tarvisio, and particularly strong on geology, are the 'Discover Nature' series of

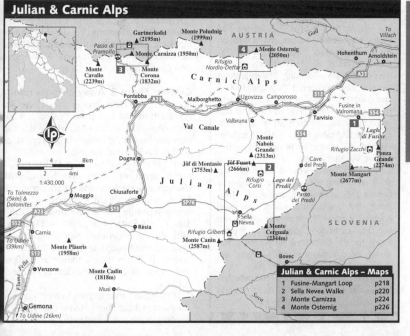

Julian & Carnic Alps

JULIAN & CARNIC ALPS

leaflets describing short walks in the Julian and Carnic Alps – including some of those described in this chapter.

Emergency

The **national emergency number** (☎ 118) can be contacted 24 hours a day. Outside populated areas, making a telephone call will generally mean using a mobile or reaching a *rifugio*.

Weather Information

There's a **telephone weather service** (☎ 800 86 03 77) for all of Friuli-Venezia Giulia. The tourist office in Tarvisio posts up-to-date local weather bulletins – most days.

GATEWAYS
Udine

Udine has a very attractive old centre and makes an interesting destination in its own right, but is an optional stopover for walkers. A couple of **bookshops** in the old centre

sell Tabacco maps and have a better range of Italian-language guidebooks than you may find in Tarvisio. It's worth arranging any onward or return bus/train tickets from Tarvisio here, if you haven't already, since the train station at Tarvisio Boscoverde is a few kilometres out of town and inconvenient to get to without a car.

Information Sources The **ARPT office** (☎ 0432 29 59 72, fax 0432 50 47 43; *Piazza Primo Maggio 7*) has detailed information on accommodation in Tarvisio, and some general information on walks in the Julian and Carnic Alps.

Places to Stay & Eat Comfortable **Hotel Principe** (☎ 0432 50 60 00, fax 0432 50 22 21; *Viale Europa Unita 51; singles/doubles with bath & air-con from €43.90/72.30*) is very convenient to the train and bus stations. A bit further away and cheaper, **Albergo Al Vecchio Tram** (☎ 0432 50 25 16; *Via Brenari 32; singles/doubles without bath €18.10/28.40*) is near Piazza Garibaldi.

There are ample options for eating out, including **Odeon Pizzeria** (*Via Gorghi 1*), a few blocks north of the station, and **Spaghetteria da Ciccio** (*Via Grazzano*) and **All'Allegria** (*Via Grazzano*).

Getting There & Away Udine is readily accessible by train, bus or car. There are regular trains to and from Venice and Vienna (Austria). Various bus companies run services from most centres in the region, as well as Padova and Taranto.

If travelling to/from the Dolomites, a combination of trains and buses, with changes at Conegliano and Calalzo, connects Udine with Cortina d'Ampezzo (€9.45, 4 hours depending on connections). There's also a daily **Saita** (☎ 0432 60 14 31) bus in each direction between San Candido and Trieste, which stops at Udine (€7.75, 4½ hours). It leaves San Candido at 3.30pm and, in the other direction, leaves Udine at 8.15am.

If travelling by car from Venice, take the A4 northeast for about 90km, then the A23 heading north towards Austria.

Via Alpina

The Via Alpina is a new long-distance trail linking Trieste on the Adriatic and Monaco on the Mediterranean. There are five routes passing through eight countries with 344 days or 5000km of walking. The majority of the trail stays between 1000m and 3000m, and doesn't involve glacier crossings or technical climbing. It has been organised so that accommodation and food a day's walk apart. Existing paths form a continuous chain; established signposts are being given the distinctive Via Alpina logo.

The direct Trieste–Monaco route (the Red Trail), comprising 161 daily stages, will greatly benefit the Julian and Carnic Alps, where recognised long-distance routes have been scarce. The trail will visit remote villages and spectacular limestone scenery. From there it heads for the Dolomites; further on it traverses Val d'Aosta, then the Maritime and Ligurian Alps (all covered in this book).

For more information, contact **Grande Traversée des Alpes** (☎ 04 76 42 08 31; **w** www .via-alpina.com; Grenoble, France).

Tarvisio

Picturesquely positioned in Val Canale between the eastern Carnic Alps and the western Julian Alps, Tarvisio is fairly well provided with accommodation and transport options. It makes a logical base for walks in both ranges. Through traffic (to/from Austria and Slovenia) can jam the narrow roads leading east out of town.

Information The **APT office** (☎ 0428 21 35; w www.tarvisiano.org; Via Roma 10), over the road and just west of the bus stop in the middle of town, has plenty of useful information, including SAF bus timetables and a simple town map, and posts local meteorological bulletins on a board outside – most days. The bookshop opposite sells Tabacco and other maps, as well as some guidebooks.

Supplies & Equipment If you've forgotten, lost or run out of anything vital, **Lussari Sport** (☎ 0428 404 74; Via Alpi Giulie 44), on the right on the way into Tarvisio from Udine, stocks gear and clothing for skiing and cycling, and would be worth a visit.

For general needs, there's a **Supercoop** supermarket (Via Vittorio Veneto 184) and numerous general stores, often labelled 'Alimentari/Lebensmittel'.

Places to Stay & Eat The nearest camping facilities are about 70km away at **Camping Ai Pioppi** (☎ 0432 98 03 58; w www.camping.it/english/friuli/aipioppi), in Ospedaletto, on the northern outskirts of Gemona.

Within walking distance from Tarvisio's main bus stop, at the less congested, western end of town, are several perfectly adequate places to stay, such as **Albergo Regina** (☎ 0428 20 15; Via Diaz 2; singles/doubles without private bath €19.10/35.65). Relatively new **Albergo 2000/Duemila** (☎ 0428 64 42 23; Via Parini 4; singles/doubles with bath from €36.15/56.80) is the next place after Albergo Regina. Further up the hill is **Hotel International** (☎ 0428 64 41 90, fax 0428 64 46 45; Via Diaz 74; singles/doubles with bath €49.10/67.15). There are other options in and around the heart of town – the APT office has details.

All three hotels have **restaurants**, as do most of their competitors. The one at **Albergo Haberl** (Via Roma 16) is central and good, as are **Bar Caffè Tschurwald** (Via Roma 8) and **Pizzeria Trattoria Raibl** (Via 4 Novembre 12).

Getting There & Away Tarvisio Boscoverde station, 2km east of town, is on the train line from Udine to Vienna (Austria), but only infrequent Eurostar services stop there Monday to Saturday (more frequent services Sunday). More useful is a combination of train (from/to Udine) and **SAF** (☎ 0428 21 34) bus (to/from Tarvisio), with a change at Carnia or Gemona. Some SAF buses also make the complete journey. Buses come and go from Tarvisio Città, the bus stop on Piazza Unità in the middle of town. Train stations at both ends sell combined tickets for €7.90, and Bar Commercio, opposite the bus stop in Tarvisio, sells bus tickets. The trip takes about 1¾ hours.

Tarvisio is just off the A23 to Villach (Austria), which connects south of Udine with the A4 between Venice and Trieste.

Julian Alps

The Julian Alps *seem* like the real thing. The forests are dense and ancient, the lakes deep and scenic, the rivers clear and the limestone mountains steep, rugged and impressively big. Picturesque towns and villages nestle in valleys, their belltowers visible above the trees before anything else comes into view. So where are all the people?

To be sure, the A23 tollway carries a steady stream of through traffic up and down Val Canale. Tarvisio gets busy, especially at its eastern end, where a market attracts bargain-hunters from far afield. Out of town, one or two easily accessible, scenic spots, such as the immediate surrounds of the Laghi di Fusine, also draw crowds on a fine day. And certain *rifugi* are well visited by the *via ferrata* (iron way) set. Elsewhere, trails are quiet and the walking is a joy amid marvellous, wild scenery. That's what a slightly out-of-the-way location, and the greater drawing power of more famous neighbours – in this case, the Dolomites – can do.

Even the road approaches to some of the walks, through the renowned forests of Tarvisio, are delightful. Before you leave, if you have your own transport and a spare hour on a fine day – preferably late in the afternoon – head just a few kilometres west from Tarvisio and turn south through Valbruna. Continue along the sealed road up Val Saisera, and soak up the views of Monte Nabois Grande and Jôf Fuart, on the left, and then Jôf di Montasio, at the head of the valley.

Local Hero

Spend time in the Julian Alps, and you're bound to come across the name, the likeness and the words of Julius Kugy. There's a street named after him in Tarvisio, while in Valbruna his sayings are recorded on stone plaques and the main piazza bears his name – you can even drop in for an espresso at Bar Julius Kugy.

Born in Gorizia in 1858, Kugy is said to have been captivated by mountains from childhood, and during his years as a law student devoted much time and energy to climbing in the Julian Alps with a couple of close friends – a fine tradition still upheld in universities everywhere. It's not clear what became of his legal career but his course through life as a mountaineer was now set.

In the decades before WWI, Kugy explored the Julian Alps in the company of local herdsmen and hunters. These men of the mountains were his guides and, when war came, some of them were recruited to serve beside him as Alpine guides to the Austrian army. Kugy honoured their exploits, as well as the beauty of the mountains, in books such as *Anton Oitzinger, vita di una Guida Alpina*. At least one title has been translated into English, but they're hard to track down. It's easier if you read Italian – bookshops in the region carry recent re-editions of some of his works.

A humble museum, just off Piazza Julius Kugy in Valbruna, houses exhibits from Kugy's life, mostly from the time of the war.

PLANNING
When to Walk

This region becomes a skiing destination in winter. The summer walking season extends, roughly, from early June to the end of September. That's when *rifugi* are open and SAF buses run to a summer schedule.

Maps & Books

The Tabacco 1:25,000 No 19 *Alpi Giulie Occidentali Tarvisiano* is the map of choice for all the Julian Alps walks. It's available in bookshops in Udine and Tarvisio.

Alpi Giulie: Quaranta panoramiche da portare nello zaino, by Furio Scrimali, is a neat idea and attractively produced. As the title suggests, it is a portable photo-guide of 40 panoramas, extracted from a pictorial book by the same author-photographer, to help you identify features you'll see while walking in the mountains.

Those interested in *vie ferrate* and high Alpine routes in general should look up a mini-guide (in Italian) titled *Sulle orme di Julius Kugy* (In the Footsteps of Julius Kugy), produced by local mountain guides and tourism authorities. It is available online (w www.tarvisiano.org/pdf/Kugy.pdf) or as a free booklet from tourist offices in Udine, Tarvisio and elsewhere. The mini-guide describes and illustrates seven classic, equipped routes established in the high Julian Alps around the turn of the 20th century by Kugy and his band of mountain guides (see the boxed text 'Local Hero', this page), as well as an ambitious six-day ring around the Montasio, Fuart and Nabois massifs. The mini-guide promotes guided trips, but also contains interesting background and practical information for independent types as well.

Place Names

The Julian Alps extend well into Slovenia as the Julijske Alpe, and dual naming in Italian and Slovene is widespread along the international border. In this section preference has been given to the Italian names.

The highest peak in the Italian part of the range, Jôf di Montasio, is one of just a handful labelled with the term 'Jôf' (meaning 'peak' or 'mountain'). Some people say it's a Friulian word; others, that it came south from German-speaking lands.

Emergency
The **national emergency number** (☎ 118) operates in the Julian Alps but you can also contact **local emergency services** (Cave del Predil ☎ 0335 741 36 21 • Sella Nevea ☎ 0443 540 25) directly.

Fusine-Mangart Loop

Duration	3–4 hours
Distance	11km
Difficulty	moderate
Start/Finish	Lago Superiore di Fusine
Nearest Town	Tarvisio (p215)
Transport	bus

Summary Fine tracks wind through delightful forests and natural rock gardens, from a pair of picturesque lakes to the foot of an imposing Alpine wall.

Picture yourself in the pages of a favourite bedtime story of a certain genre – enchanted forest, winding path – and you're ready for the climb from Lago Superiore di Fusine to Rifugio Zacchi. As CAI track 512 winds up through the forest, it would come as no surprise to meet Snow White and co marching the other way. Beyond the *rifugio* the going is more rugged, crossing the base of huge scree slopes below the towering north face of Monte Mangart, before a serpentine descent through more forest leads back to the valley floor. The walk begins and ends at a height of 930m, and reaches 1475m before descending.

The lakes themselves are very picturesque and are protected by the tiny Parco Naturale di Fusine. They are also very popular with day trippers. Pleasant, easy trails (not described here) lead around both lakes – the northern shore of Lago Inferiore, in particular, gives pretty views of the Mangart group.

Monte Mangart and the crest west of Rifugio Zacchi are surmounted by several *vie ferrate*. The *rifugio* makes a suitable base for anyone with the inclination, experience and equipment to attempt them.

GETTING TO/FROM THE WALK
From June to late September, **SAF** (☎ 0428 21 34) buses go from Tarvisio Città to the Laghi di Fusine (€1.35, 25 minutes, three a day). The first leaves Tarvisio at 8.50am, and the last returns from the Lago Superiore car park at 6pm. By car, take the S54 east towards Slovenia for just over 6km, through Fusine in Valromana, then turn right and follow the sealed road for 3.4km to park beside Lago Superiore.

THE WALK
Track 512 leaves the Lago Superiore car park heading southwest, past **Bar Ai Sette Nani**, where drinks and snacks are sold. At this stage it's a comfortable, gravelled road and already there are fine views of Monte Mangart to the south. Once you're past a boom gate and heading south, red-and-white CAI track markers appear. Within 10 minutes a signpost indicates track 517a (initially track 513) to the right, which you'll descend later in the day. Continue along track 512, which soon narrows and begins a sometimes steep ascent. After a couple of minor, signposted junctions, it settles down to climb steadily through beautiful forest, and within about an hour gains a road. Beside this, at a height of 1380m and with great views of the cliffs, sits **Rifugio Zacchi** (☎ 0428 611 95; half board around €38).

Continue south along the road. Within 10 minutes, at a well signposted junction, track 513 leaves the road and goes left. Follow it, ignoring a climbers' route to the west towards Sella Strugova on the Slovenian border, through forest to the Alpe Vecchia, an area populated by dwarf vegetation at the foot of scree slopes. Another climbing route, the Via della Vita, soon goes left in the direction of a CAI *bivacco* (shelter) high on the ridge above, while track 513 swings west and remains reasonably level before a signposted junction with track 517 on the left, half an hour or so from the road. Track 513 continues easily back to the lake from here.

Faint at first, track 517 winds and climbs through forest and shortly emerges near the base of large cliffs. Cairns and red paint

JULIAN & CARNIC ALPS

markers now persist even when the track itself is hard to make out. It heads west and crosses patches of bare scree alternating with areas being reclaimed by pioneer vegetation. A final, short climb over a spur covered in dense, low plants leads to a big boulder where markers point back towards Rifugio Zacchi and up towards Bivacco Nogara. It's 40 minutes or so to here from the start of track 517.

The Laghi di Fusine nestle in the valley to the north and track 517a leads down the spur in the same direction. It enters forest, and winds improbably and steeply down to emerge into the open again, rejoining track 513, at Alpe Tamer, about half an hour from the boulder. Continue northward across the clearing and bear right at the first fork. This soon merges with a road on the right that descends from Capanna Ghezzi and Rifugio Zacchi. Within half an hour from Alpe Tamer you will arrive back at the car park by Lago Superiore.

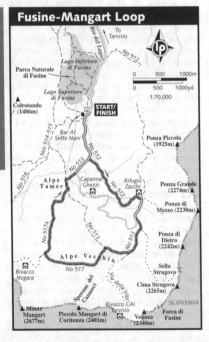

Fusine-Mangart Loop

Slovenian Two-Step

Duration	4–5½ hours
Distance	12km
Difficulty	moderate
Start/Finish	Funivia Canìn car park
Nearest Town	Tarvisio (p215)
Transport	bus

Summary A cable car gives easy access to a karst plateau rich in wildflowers, where scenic tracks lead to two passes on the Slovenian border, then back to the leafy valley floor.

Sella Nevea is a popular but compact winter resort. Lift lines rise on both the north and south sides of the valley, running west from the geographical *sella* (saddle). The Funivia Canìn cable car takes the sting out of the start of this walk, from Sella Nevea to the base of Piano del Prevala, which is in a spectacular setting below the imposing cliffs of Bila Pec (meaning 'White Rock' in Slovene).

You then continue climbing on foot to Sella Prevala, along what was once the most convenient route from Sella Nevea to Bovec (Slovenia). From Sella Prevala the trail crosses a broad plateau devoid of surface water but rich in low Alpine flora thanks to plentiful precipitation. Taller growth is limited by the quantity of snow and the frequency of spring avalanches. The plateau and the mountains above are composed of whitish-grey limestone, much shaped by glaciation and erosion. Caves in the area have been surveyed to depths of 560m. A second pass into Slovenia, Sella Robon, marks the start of a long descent back to the mixed coniferous and broadleaved forest of the lower valleys.

Thanks to the Funivia Canìn cable car, the day's walk involves only 489m of ascent and 1198m of descent. The 'Canìn' in the name of the cable car is from Monte Canìn (2587m), on the Slovenian border west of Sella Prevala. Its summit is accessible by a number of challenging routes – most directly, from Rifugio Gilberti along track 632 and the Ferrata Julia, established by Julius Kugy in 1903.

PLANNING
What to Bring

Carry plenty of water as you're unlikely to find any along the route.

GETTING TO/FROM THE WALK

It's up with the sparrows unless you have your own transport or are a *very* fast walker. There's an **SAF** (☎ *0428 21 34*) bus to Udine that leaves Tarvisio Città at 6.10am and reaches Chiusaforte at 6.53am (€2.48), then another service that leaves Chiusaforte at 7.15am and arrives in Sella Nevea around 8am (€1.70). For the fleet of foot, another combination leaves Tarvisio at noon and Chiusaforte at 1.20pm, reaching Sella Nevea at 2.05pm.

By car, take S54 south from Tarvisio for 11km through Cave del Predil, then turn right onto SP76 and continue another 11km to Sella Nevea. Park at the base of the Funivia Canìn cable car (signposted).

THE WALK (see map p220)

The **Funivia Canìn** (☎ *0433 540 26*) does most of the day's climbing – from Sella Nevea (1122m) to a height of 1831m, just below Rifugio Gilberti – in just a few minutes. In summer, cars go every 20 minutes from 9am to 12.30pm and 1.30pm to 4.45pm Monday to Saturday, and until 6pm Sunday. The one-way adult/concession fare is €6/5.

From the top station of the cable car it's only a short distance (signposted) to **Rifugio Gilberti** (☎ *0433 540 15; half board around €38*) at 1850m, past a small chapel in memory of members of the Italian Alpine regiments who fought here during WWI. Track 636 skirts behind and below the *rifugio*, and heads east, down into the wide, open Piano del Prevala. Until relatively recent times there was a glacier here, and there may be snow, even groomed ski trails, well into summer.

It's a straightforward but substantial climb, firstly on the north side of the valley and then the south, up bare slopes to **Sella Prevala** (2067m), about an hour from the top of the cable car and the first chance to step over into Slovenia.

Track 636 turns briefly northward and sidles below ruined barracks to a minor, higher col (2109m) with more fine views. It then cruises downhill to the northeast, through a harsh but lush landscape (if that's possible) of green growth and colourful flowers against a glaring, whitish-grey backdrop of weathered limestone. Deep holes and weird rock formations abound.

The steep south face of Monte Poviz looms ahead. At a three-way junction, half an hour from the minor col, track 636 descends northwest towards Sella Nevea. Continue on to Sella Robon, turning sharply back to the east onto track 637. This heads across an even lusher karst plateau with fine views north to the Montasio and Fuart mountain groups across the upper Val Rio del Lago.

About 45 minutes from the junction, after traversing extensive scree slopes below Monte Cergnala, the track drops into a gravelly bowl, where signs point left (northwest) towards Sella Nevea. Continue east, climbing briefly through a series of switchbacks to **Sella Robon** (1865m). To the east are the peaks of Slovenia's Triglavski Narodni Park. Having come this far, you might want to explore nearby Monte Robon (see Side Trip, p221).

To descend to Sella Nevea, retrace your steps and find track 637 as it heads northwest, through the gravelly bowl, past a prominent '637' on a boulder and down the rocky bed of Rio Robon for a short way. When the stream bed drops away steeply, the track swings to the true right side of the gully, below cliffs on the west face of Monte Robon, then back to the west to recross Rio Robon.

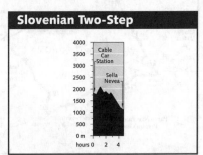

Slovenian Two-Step

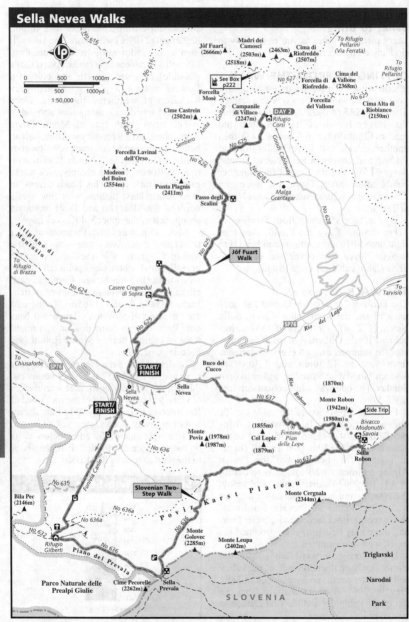

JULIAN & CARNIC ALPS

The track is easier to follow now, although sometimes slippery as the terrain becomes damper and more densely vegetated, especially in the soggy hollow of Fontana Pian delle Lope, where water seeps from rock walls. About 90 minutes from Sella Robon the steady descent becomes briefly steep and loose, as the track drops to an unsealed road, which leads west for 500m to join SP76.

Continue west along the road; it's 1.5km through Sella Nevea to the car park at the base of the Funivia Canìn.

Side Trip: Monte Robon Middle Peak
35 minutes, 1.5km, 77m ascent

From Sella Robon a track leads north along the west side of the ridge past the ruins of a tiny WWI outpost and a cavers' shelter, Bivacco Modonutti-Savoia, in a small saddle. It sticks to the vegetated west side of the ridge for a bit further, then climbs a staircase (literally!) through a cleft onto the rocky top. A devious route marked with cairns and red paint continues, more or less on the west side, until it swings east round a big chasm to reach Monte Robon's second-highest summit (1942m) and some spectacular views. The main summit (1980m) is visible from here, just to the west looking back the way you've come, but is guarded by steep ground. Retrace your steps carefully to Sella Robon.

Jôf Fuart

Duration	2 days
Distance	12km
Difficulty	moderate
Start/Finish	Sella Nevea
Nearest Town	Tarvisio (p215)
Transport	bus
Summary	A relaxed trip to a *rifugio* in the spectacular heart of the rugged Julian Alps.

Along with Montasio, Mangart and Canìn, Jôf Fuart is a peak emblematic of the Italian Julian Alps. The ascent of its northeast face,

from Rifugio Pellarini, is a 'real climb', and even the normal route to the summit, above Rifugio Corsi, holds difficulties that demand specialised *(via ferrata)* equipment and put it beyond reach for most walkers.

This walk offers a close-up look at Jôf Fuart without technical requirements, rounding a couple of ridges in unlikely fashion to enter the spectacular valley below the mountain's southeastern faces. Along the way, wartime fortifications, once impregnable but now decaying by natural causes, recall the area's not-so-distant past as fiercely contested ground.

It's possible to visit Rifugio Corsi, have a good look around and return to Sella Nevea in a day but, in a region rich with fine day walks and challenging routes, it is an excellent opportunity to stay a night in one of those grand locations that inspire people to build *rifugi*. The *gestore* (manager) and staff at Rifugio Corsi are a fount of knowledge regarding all the routes in the area – that is provided you can muster some Italian.

PLANNING
When to Walk
The ideal time to walk is when Rifugio Corsi is open, from the start of June until the end of September.

What to Bring
Provided you phone ahead and arrange to eat and sleep at Rifugio Corsi, all you need to bring is lunch and snacks. To include any *vie ferrate* in your itinerary, you'll need a helmet and the other equipment described in the Via Ferrata section (p203).

GETTING TO/FROM THE WALK
See Getting to/from the Walk (p219) for the Slovenian Two-Step. The later bus combination leaves ample time to reach the *rifugio* if staying overnight, but not much time to look around and return the same day. With your own car, park near the start of the walk, just behind the Guardia di Finanza building, on about the only minor road on the north side of SP76, or at the foot of the nearby ski lift.

THE WALK (see map p220)
Day 1: Sella Nevea to Rifugio Corsi
2½–3 hours, 6km, 795m ascent, 96m descent

Track 625 begins near the Guardia di Finanza building. Look for red track markers and the first of numerous signposts indicating 'Giro delle Malghe Cregnedul'. A ski lift starts up the hill, just to the east, and the track crosses the lift line after only 100m or so. The next section of the track was being transformed into something grander at the time of writing, with trees being cut down and tracks widened into roads. However, after 15 minutes or so, the red markers lead left, up the hill, leaving the roadworks behind.

The track markers and 'Giro delle Malghe' signs continue through forest, until the tree cover begins to thin allowing views of the cliffs above. The track then leads to **Casere Cregnedul di Sopra**, about 45 minutes from the start. These buildings were once summer quarters for shepherds. The uppermost one is open to walkers for use as a shelter; you are allowed to stay overnight but there is no telephone and no *gestore*. There's water inside.

Head roughly east, through a gate, and after 100m or so a sign at a three-way junction shows you've rejoined track 625. Continue north up the valley to some ruins, then follow the track as it swings east. After half an hour of sidling and a brief flurry of switchbacks, the track rounds a spur and emerges from the trees onto a wide, open slope that faces southeast. About 1km to the north is a rocky crest, which is crossed, after another burst of zigzags, at **Passo**

Ledge of the Gods

The Sentiero Anita Goitan is a favourite among the many *vie ferrate* that link passes, peaks and ledges in the mountains around Rifugio Corsi. It begins at Forcella Lavinal dell'Orso as a track ascending a grassy hillside, but it's a narrow track and a steep hillside, and you wouldn't want to tackle even this without sure feet and a steady head. Once it gains the crest of Cime Castrein, and especially once it approaches the precipitous Forcella Mosè, Sentiero Goitan is no longer a mere walk.

Nor, however, is it a technically demanding climb. The protected sections around Forcella Mosè aren't technically difficult or long, and they lead to a straightforward traverse of the southeastern slopes of Jôf Fuart. Once there, the side trip to the 2666m summit is almost irresistible – little more than a plod, but with terrific views and real mountain atmosphere.

Then comes the Cengia degli Dei (Ledge of the Gods). On this traverse around the towers known as the Madri dei Camosci, on a ledge of variable width (from 2m to practically nothing) and through precipitous clefts between the pinnacles, most people will think seriously about using the equipment nearly every *via ferrata* enthusiast carries.

Many will connect themselves to the extensive safety cables here; others won't feel the need, or will argue that the security the cables offer is illusory – a view supported by the occasional eye-bolt that dangles loose on the end of a cable, pulled free of the rock it had been fixed to.

Nearly all, though, will don a helmet, for protection from falling rocks or should they themselves fall. Rocks can be dislodged unwittingly by people above – including your own companions – or by ibex and chamois as they bound about without concern for your safety. And sometimes, of course, rocks simply fall.

Partway along this imposing ledge (once you're completely committed to it) a metal box houses a log book to record your passing. It's a nice touch, the equivalent of a summit log for a route with no summit.

On returning to Rifugio Corsi, it's fun to look up and try to trace where you've just been. Then look in a special Julian Alps issue of the Italian mountain magazine *Alp*, kept in the *rifugio*, for photographs from the first, and to date only, traverse of the Cengia degli Dei *in winter*.

legli Scalini (1970m). Jôf Fuart, Rifugio
Corsi and the unlikely-looking track to the
rifugio now come into view – a view that's
ven better from a short distance east along
he crest.

The track ahead is milder than it looks –
vith a little help from wartime engineering.
t passes turn-offs on the left (track 626 to
'orcella Lavinal dell'Orso) and right (track
528 to Malga Grantagar) before skirting
velow a rocky tower, Campanile di Villaco,
and dropping to **Rifugio Corsi** (☎ *0428 681
3; half board around €38*). The *rifugio*
1874m) is perched in a valley ringed by
ugged limestone peaks.

Day 2: Rifugio Corsi to Sella Nevea

½–2 hours, 6km, 96m ascent,
*95m descent

Retrace your steps via Passo degli Scalini to
Sella Nevea. The detour to Casere Creg-
edul di Sopra is optional.

Carnic Alps

The Carnic Alps form the watershed between
Austria's Black Sea catchment to the north
and that of the Adriatic, on Italian territory to
he south. The border between the two coun-
ries follows their crest – walking tracks and
he frontier sometimes share the same markers. Until WWI the border was further south,
out after 1919 much Austrian territory was
eded to Italy. On the two walks described
nere, there is a sense that you could be in
Austria even when you're not.

Greener, less jagged and rounder than
he Julian Alps, and at slightly lower alti-
udes in general, the Carnic Alps offer less
esistance to walkers and are popular with
ocals for just that reason. They do, however, reward the effort of climbing to their
ops with fine views and are rich in wild-
lowers. The Carnic's sedimentary rock
ields many fossils and has been exten-
ively shaped by glaciers.

The walks described here are quite short
out take in some of the most scenic country
asily accessible (by car, at any rate) from

Tarvisio. There's plenty more walking further west, beyond the scope of this book. If
you're looking for a longer alternative, the
walks described share ground with the
Traversata Carnica, a long-distance track
which takes about seven days to walk. It
begins in Sesto, strays onto both sides of the
international border, and has both an Italian
and an Austrian finish, in Tarvisio and just
over the border in Unterthörl, respectively.

PLANNING
When to Walk

The walking season extends, roughly, from
early June to the end of September. Outside
that time, bring your skis.

Place Names

Dual naming of geographical features, in
German and Italian, is widespread along
the border between Italy and Austria. We
have given preference to the Italian names
in this section.

Monte Carnizza

Duration	3–4 hours
Distance	9km
Difficulty	moderate
Start/Finish	Passo di Pramollo
Nearest Town	Tarvisio (p215)
Transport	private

Summary Warm up on rustic roads, then
climb above pastures to the Austrian border
and take an airy ridge-top route with a foot in
each country and views in all directions.

This pleasant ramble (and a bit of a scramble) on the Italy-Austria border takes advantage of the sealed road that connects Val
Canale with the Gail valley in Austria across
Passo di Pramollo (1530m) – or Nassfeld
Pass, to give it its Austrian name. In both
languages the name refers to the wet,
marshy environs of the pass. Stausee, the
small lake at the pass, has only been there
since 1962, when an earthen dam was built.

The walk sets out on an unsealed road –
part of the long-distance Traversata Carnica –

through pastures where cattle still graze in summer. Once it climbs to the border, ski lifts on the Austrian side are a constant presence. But the ridge-top traverse to Monte Carnizza is thoroughly enjoyable, and the views on a good day extend from the Dolomites to the Julian Alps.

The area around Passo di Pramollo, on both sides of the border, is renowned for its wildflowers, and especially for a rare figwort, *Wulfenia carinthiaca*, which grows only here and in the mountains between Albania and Yugoslavia. There is plenty of mixed coniferous forest around, but for much of its distance the walk passes through pastures or follows a ridge largely clear of trees.

Rocks in the area are rich with fossils that date from the range's origins, hundreds of millions of years ago, as a stretch of tropical coast. Along the narrow crest of Monte Carnizza, several different rock types, including limestone and quartz conglomerates, can be found in the space of a few hundred metres.

The route ascends and descends 720m, with the option of an additional 40m up and down Monte Auernig.

PLANNING

Maps

The recommended map is the Tabacco 1:25,000 No 18 *Alpi Carniche Orientali. Canal del Ferro*. It's sold in bookshops in Udine and Tarvisio.

NEAREST TOWN & FACILITIES

See Tarvisio (p215).

Passo di Pramollo

Right at the start of the walk, both **Albergo Ristorante Wulfenia** (☎ 0428 905 06) and **Ristorante Hotel Al Gallo Forcello** (☎ 0428 900 14; w www.galloforcello.com; half board in low/high season €35/45) serve meals all day from 11.30am. You'd also find a telephone here should you need one.

GETTING TO/FROM THE WALK

There's no bus to Passo di Pramollo from the Italian side. You could conceivably take a taxi from Tarvisio but a rental car is a more convenient option; to arrange either service call **Mauro Collini** (☎ 0347 260 26 36). From Tarvisio take the S13 west to Pontebba (21km), then follow signs north up the valley of the Rio Bombaso. Park beside the

road near the hotels, which are right by Stausee and just before the pass itself.

THE WALK

From the north side of Ristorante Hotel Gallo Forcello, take the road that leads east past a barrier. It climbs briefly, then levels out and soon comes to Casera Auernig and a junction on the north side with track 501. This is the way you'll descend later from Monte Auernig.

Continuing east it's a straightforward and pleasant walk along the road, losing some height, with views towards Monte Malvueric to the south. At a signposted junction about 3km from the pass, take the foot track that climbs away from the road on the north side. It contours to the east, then around towards the south, to join an unmade road that leads to a small group of *malghe* (herders' summer huts) at Casera For.

Beyond here the track wanders east, then swings north and climbs through low vegetation to a meadow just below the top of Monte Corona (1832m). Even Daisy the cow has conquered Monte Corona but its quaint, flat summit gives good views. Just below the summit, at a T-junction (marked with a painted 'T' on a rock), the ridge-top traverse west to Monte Carnizza begins.

First the track drops into grassy Sella Carnizza. From here a trail heads south to Casera For and another descends on the Austrian side to Garnitzenalm. Continuing west, narrow but distinct and well-marked track stays close to the crest (and the international boundary) as it climbs above the top station of an Austrian ski lift. By this point the crest is narrow, and it narrows and steepens further as it drops into a saddle (1836m) before the final scramble to the airy top of **Monte Carnizza** (1950m). If the weather is kind, you'll have great views in all directions – into Austria, with the ski lifts around Gartner Sattel (1863m) and Gartnerkofel (2195m) close at hand, west past Monte Cavallo (2239m) towards the Dolomites, and southeast to the peaks of the Julian Alps.

Heading west from Monte Carnizza, the ridge is less precipitous, and tracks lead off on the Austrian side. After 30 minutes, at a signpost in a second, broad saddle (1823m), track 501 heads down to the south towards 'Auernig Alm' (Casera Auernig). Monte Auernig is not far away (see Side Trip, below). From the saddle it's an easy enough 15-minute descent on track 501 to Casera Auernig and the road west back to Passo di Pramollo.

Side Trip: Monte Auernig

25 minutes, 600m, 40m ascent

After Monte Carnizza, Monte Auernig does not present much of a challenge – but, on a nice day, why not stay high a little longer? The summit gives a good view over Passo di Pramollo, which has remained hidden hitherto. There's also an interesting variation on the usual summit marker! From the second saddle west of Monte Carnizza, where track 501 begins its descent to Casera Auernig,

---

Humble Pie, Please

One look at the map on the wall in the *rifugio* would have done it. I'd have seen track 507a crossed out with a black felt pen and the words 'Non praticabile' written beside it. A simple 'Buongiorno' to someone behind the bar and they'd have given me the details.

But this particular *rifugio* didn't look all that inviting. There were walkers and horse riders milling about outside. Horse dung! Dust! It was already 10am, I had a map and I thought I knew what I was doing; so I walked past.

Later that day, after some unplanned map-and-compass navigation down a trackless, densely forested spur, I went into the *rifugio* for an espresso and a glass of water, and to ask about the track. There it was on the map: 'Non praticabile'. The *gestore* gave me the details.

At least I hadn't simply screwed up and got lost. But the moral of the story is that *rifugi* and the people in them are a storehouse of knowledge – up-to-date, local knowledge – and it's there for the asking. So go in and ask. I wish I had.

Mind you, if I hadn't been coming down the spur, I never would have seen that deer bound away through the forest...

Nick Tapp

Austrian track 411 leads along the broad, scrubby ridge to Auernig's summit (1863m) – and then, when you're done, back again.

Monte Osternig

Duration	3–3½ hours
Distance	11km
Difficulty	easy–moderate
Start/Finish	Rifugio Nordio-Deffar
Nearest Town	Tarvisio (p215)
Transport	private

Summary A steep climb leads to open pastures and a high point on the Austrian border.

Not unduly strenuous, this walk takes you to the wide, open spaces above the tree line and some fabulous views. Like some other summits in the Carnic Alps, Monte Osternig's rounded bulk brings to mind – of all places – the Australian Alps.

The Austrian influence is strong. Trail signs sponsored by competing breweries lure you towards *Gasthäuser* ('guesthouses' or 'inns' in German) just over the border in Austria. It wouldn't happen on the French border!

The route is easy to follow and not long. It might be graded 'easy' if it wasn't for the height gained and lost (872m) and the sometimes steep gradients. You could avoid more than a third of the climbing, although not the steepest sections (they're right at the start) by going no higher than Sella Bistrizza.

PLANNING
Maps
The Tabacco 1:25,000 map No 19 *Alpi Giulie Occidentali Tarvisiano* is recommended for this walk.

NEAREST TOWN & FACILITIES
See Tarvisio (p215).

Rifugio Nordio-Deffar
At the start/finish of the walk, this CAI *rifugio* (☎ *0428 600 45*) serves meals, snacks and drinks all day from 6am to 10pm. There's a telephone here too.

GETTING TO/FROM THE WALK
There are no buses to Rifugio Nordio-Deffar, where the walk begins. You could conceivably take a taxi from Tarvisio but a rental car is a more convenient option; to arrange either

Monte Osternig

service, call **Mauro Collini** (☎ *0347 260 26 36*). By car, take the S13 west from Tarvisio to Ugovizza (9km). At the sign to 'CAI Rifugio Fratelli Nordio', turn right onto Via Uqua, which leads through the village and up the valley of the Torrente Uqua. Follow the narrow, sealed road until the sealed surface ends at the *rifugio*.

THE WALK

From Rifugio Nordio-Deffar, the unsealed road continues steeply northwards up the valley until a fork, where one way continues north to Sella di Lom. Swing east towards Osternig Alm (Feistritzer Alm) and climb steadily, with many switchbacks, up the north side of a valley. Forty-five minutes or so from the *rifugio*, the track emerges from the trees and, in another 10 minutes, you arrive at bustling Sella Bistrizza, where the Gasthaus Oisternig does a roaring trade in meals and beer.

Track 481 (northwest) to the summit of Monte Osternig is unmistakeable. It leads steadily up, through a couple of major zigzags, until some ruined fortifications appear on the right (north) side of the track.

Head north here, following painted arrows, up the final slopes to the summit (2050m), about 40 minutes above Sella Bistrizza. The views include the Dolomites to the west beyond Monte Cavallo and Gartnerkofel, the Julian Alps to the south, and snowy Austrian peaks to the north. It's a pleasant wander east along the ridge to the lower summit (2035m), marked by a prominent cross, then down to the southwest to rejoin the main route near another wartime ruin.

Once back in Sella Bistrizza, a track leads south along the Austrian side of the ridge and, in just five to 10 minutes, reaches a saddle and the tiny chapel of **Madonna della Neve**, with poignant memorials inside to members of an ill-starred local family. Back on the Italian side, the route drops quite steeply but straightforwardly for another five to 10 minutes into Sella Pleccia.

From here follow track 507 west down the valley of Torrente Pleccia to Rifugio Nordio-Deffar. At the time of writing track 507a (south of Sella Pleccia) did not continue west of the 'Rotonda' to the valley floor, as shown on the Tabacco map (see the boxed text 'Humble Pie, Please', p225).

Tuscany

It can be rightly claimed that the province of Tuscany (Toscana) has the best of everything – art, architecture, some of Italy's finest fresh produce and best known wines, and beautiful countryside, which has captivated artists and tourists alike for centuries.

You can certainly programme a few wine-tastings while following the trails of the Chianti Classico walk. The region also has some of Italy's most impressive medieval towns, including Certaldo, San Gimignano and Volterra, which are featured in the Medieval Hills walk.

If you prefer more challenging mountain walks, you'll want to head for the Apuan Alps (Alpi Apuane), bordered on one side by the Tuscan coastline and on the other by the vast valley of the Garfagnana. The Apuan Alps have been mined for their precious marbles since Roman times and nearby is Carrara, where Michelangelo selected white marbles. A regional park regulates land use here to some extent, but the landscape in some parts of the mountains has been utterly destroyed by mining. The walks in this chapter go to both spoiled and unspoiled parts of the Apuan Alps – judge for yourself which you prefer.

Travelling in Toscana is easy and all the walks detailed in this chapter are easily accessible by public transport. However, the region's popularity with tourists can make accommodation hard to find in peak periods. It is best to book in advance, especially if you plan to tackle the Chianti Classico.

Chianti

Chianti is that bit of countryside between Florence and Siena, renowned the world over for its excellent wine and olive oil, where an ever increasing number of tourists come each year in search of a peaceful holiday in a villa, a quaint village or even a winery. Although prices tend to be high, the area does offer an unusually high concentration of art and history, as well as plenty of opportunities for romantic walks.

Two easy walks are described in this section. The charm of the landscape and the lodgings along the way, in hotels or *agriturismo* (farmstays), make them long, relaxing rambles, enriched by historical sites, delicious meals and celebrated wines. The walks are suitable for the whole family and could also be adapted for cyclists.

HISTORY

Etruscan civilisation blossomed in these valleys from the eighth century BC until it was absorbed by the expansion of Rome. In medieval times, the Chianti area was on the main route, called the Via Francigena, from northern Europe to Siena and Rome. Later, as Florence and Siena grew in size, the two cities faced off in Chianti, building castles on every hilltop they could find. In 1384, the Lega del Chianti (Chianti League) was formed for defence purposes by Radda, Castellina and Gaiole. Finally, in 1550, Florence defeated Siena and the great dukedom of Tuscany was established. The area then lost its strategic importance and the people were able to dedicate themselves entirely to agriculture. Chianti was already exporting wine to England in the 16th century. The aristocratic families, who owned entire districts, built countless luxurious country villas, many of which have now been reborn as wineries.

NATURAL HISTORY

The Chianti ridge is a system of harmonious wooded hills between Florence and Siena, bordered by Val d'Arno to the east and Val d'Elsa and Val di Pesa to the west. To the west of Certaldo and Val d'Elsa are San Gimignano and Volterra, situated in an area known as the Medieval Hills, and featuring extensive woods and fields of grain.

The Chianti and the Medieval Hills areas are composed predominantly of sandstone or clay-type sedimentary rock, and of layers of sand and gravel. In fact, 200 million years ago the area was covered by a sea. Starting in the Miocene epoch (20 million years ago), the pressure of the African plate on the Euroasiatic plate began to push up the land, forming hills where, in some areas, you can still find marine fossils. Where the sea was shallow, near present-day Volterra, the evaporating water left gypsum crystals, one variety of which is the alabaster now mined in the area.

The woods are dominated by four species of oak tree, including the holm oak. There are also maples, chestnuts, hazelnuts, alders, stone pines, cluster pines and black pines. In the areas of Mediterranean scrub,

there are the typical gum tree, strawberry tree and myrtle associated with the holm oak. Elegant rows of cypresses, noble grape vines and olive trees complete the picture.

The largest mammal in the forests of Chianti is the *cinghiale* (wild pig), stalked intensively by its only dangerous predator – people. The Tuscan hunter is also fond of the resident pheasant, hare, fox, badger, weasel, beech-marten, squirrel and the bizarre *istrice* (porcupine), which was imported from Africa by the ancient Romans. Among the birds there are woodpidgeons, jays, blackbirds, hoopoes, kestrels, buzzards, crows and tits. Among reptiles there is the lizard and the innocuous water snake. In rocky areas you can run into poisonous vipers.

CLIMATE

The climate of Chianti and of the Val d'Elsa is mild and temperate. The average annual temperature is around 15°C, with peaks of 35°C in summer and the rare sub-zero winter day. Snow and fog occur only in exceptional cases.

PLANNING
When to Walk

In spring (March to May) and autumn (September to November) the climate is sunny and mild, and the palettes of seasonal colours are wonderful. At the beginning of October there is the *vendemmia* (grape harvest). In January and February, Chianti virtually closes down; summer is the least suitable for walking due to the sultry heat.

TUSCANY

Emergency

For urgent medical assistance in the Chianti region, contact the **national emergency number** (☎ 118).

ACCESS TOWNS
Florence

Cradle of the Renaissance and home of Machiavelli, Michelangelo and the Medici, Florence seems unfairly burdened with art, culture and history. As such, the city attracts millions of tourists each year and accommodation can be quickly booked out in the peak season.

Information The **APT office** (☎ 055 29 08 32/3, fax 055 276 03 83; ⓦ www.firenze .turismo.toscana.it; Via Cavour 1r; open 8.15am-7.15pm Mon-Sat year round, 8.30am-1.30pm Sun Apr-Oct) is just north of the *duomo* (cathedral). There are other information offices in Florence, but this one should have everything you need.

Supplies & Equipment A well stocked outdoor shop is **Climb** (☎ 055 324 50 74 ⓦ www.climbfirenze.com; Via Marigliano 149/151). If you are looking for maps or books, **Libreria Stella Alpina** (☎ 055 41 16

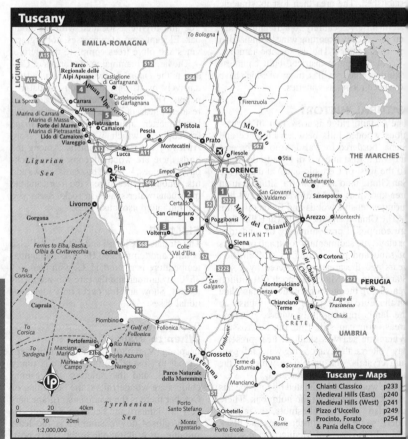

Tuscany – Maps	
1 Chianti Classico	p233
2 Medieval Hills (East)	p240
3 Medieval Hills (West)	p241
4 Pizzo d'Uccello	p249
5 Procinto, Forato & Pania della Croce	p254

88; W www.stella.alpina.com; Via Corridoni 14B/r) specialises in Italian-language maps, travel books and guides.

Places to Stay & Eat With an adjacent camping ground, **Ostello Villa Camerata** (☎ 055 60 14 51, fax 055 61 03 00; Viale Augusto Righi 2-4; B&B €14.45) is an HI hostel; a meal costs €7.75. In the town centre, **Locanda Starlight** (☎ 055 28 70 12; W www .locandastarlight.it; Via Guelfa 59; doubles €49.05) is a quiet place with five modern-style frescoed doubles and two external bathrooms. Rates are without breakfast.

Getting There & Away You can reach Florence by train from any major city in Italy.

The towns along the Chiantigiana (S222), which connects Florence and Siena, are accessible by **SITA** (☎ 800 37 37 60) buses from the terminal in Via Santa Caterina da Siena, near the main train station. From the same terminal, SITA also runs a direct bus to Siena, via Tozzi, almost every hour from 6.45am to 9.05pm.

Siena

An enchanting city, Siena's medieval centre is bristling with majestic Gothic buildings. It is also a popular tourist destination and accommodation can be difficult to find during the peak season around August. For information try the **APT office** (☎ 0577 28 05 51, fax 0577 27 06 76; W www.siena.turismo .toscana.it; Piazza del Campo 56; open 8.30am-7.30pm Mon-Sat, 9am-3pm Sun early Apr-end Oct; 8.30am-6pm Mon-Sat rest of year). At the **Sport Centre** (☎ 0577 461 23; Viale Sclavo 210), 500m from the train station, you'll find a limited range of outdoor equipment and clothing.

Places to Stay & Eat A non-HI hostel, **Guidoriccio** (☎ 0577 522 12; Via Fiorentina 89; B&B €12.90) offers meals for €8.80.

Getting There & Away Siena is not on a major train line. If you're coming from Rome, change at Chiusi, or from Florence change at Empoli.

There are direct bus services from Rome to Siena (€13.95, three hours, eight a day) run by **SENA** (☎ 800 93 09 60) departing from Piazzale Tiburtino in Rome, accessible from Termini, the main train station, on the Metro Linea B (get off at Stazione Tiburtina). **Tra-in** (☎ 0577 20 42 45) and **SITA** (☎ 800 37 37 60) run more than 10 direct buses daily between Florence and Siena's Piazza Gramsci, where Tra-in buses also depart for Castellina, Gaiole and Radda in Chianti.

Chianti Classico

Duration	3 days
Distance	48km
Difficulty	easy
Start	San Fabiano
Finish	Vagliagli
Nearest Towns	Florence (p230), Siena (p231), Vagliagli (p232)
Transport	bus

Summary A pleasant walk, mainly on country roads, past vineyards, olive groves, *borghi* (ancient villages) and evocative forests. Enchanting, panoramic views of Badia a Passignano and the Chianti hills.

This is a classic tour through the landscape, culture and tastes of the world famous Chianti region. Although long, it is a relatively easy walk, mostly along dirt roads, with minimal climbing. The Chianti area slopes down to the west in a sequence of valleys mostly oriented from northwest to southeast, where the crests maintain a height of between 300m and 500m. The highest point of Chianti is Monte San Michele at 892m, in the eastern crest known as Monti del Chianti.

The walk includes a bus link between Grieve in Chianti at the end of Day 1 and Pieve di Panzano at the start of Day 2. If you wanted to shorten the walk by starting at Pieve di Panzano, you could easily catch the linking bus from Florence, where it originates (see Getting to/from the Walk, p232, for details of the service).

TUSCANY

PLANNING
Maps
The SELCA 1:70,000 map *Il Chianti, terra del vino* is detailed enough for this walk. Multigraphic's 1:25,000 map No 512 *Chianti Classico, Val di Pesa, Val d'Elsa* does not, unfortunately, cover the very beginning of the walk.

NEAREST TOWNS
See Florence (p230) and Siena (p231).

Vagliagli
A small town 11km north of Siena, Vagliagli has a *tabaccheria* (tobacconist), a **bar** and a good restaurant, **La Taverna** *(☎ 0577 23 25 32; meals around €25.80)*. At the bus stop in Corsignano, 4km south of Vagliagli along the main road for Siena, is the hotel **Casa Lucia** *(☎ 0577 32 25 08, fax 0577 32 25 10; e info@casalucia.it; doubles €72.30-82.65)*. Nearby you'll find the restaurant **Nonna Luisa** *(☎ 0577 32 27 40; meals around €20.66)*.

Getting There & Away From the town piazza in Vagliagli, **Tra-in** *(☎ 0577 20 42 45)* bus No 34 goes to Piazza Gramsci in Siena (€1.25, 40 minutes, four a day at 1.50pm, 2.25pm, 4.10pm and 7.15pm Monday to Saturday). You can buy tickets at the bar in the piazza.

GETTING TO/FROM THE WALK
To get to the start of the walk at San Fabiano, take the **SITA** *(☎ 800 37 37 60)* bus from the terminal in Via Santa Caterina da Siena, near the main train station in Florence (€2.30, one hour, eight a day at 7.15am, 9.15am, 12.55pm, 1.50pm, 4.05pm, 5.50pm, 6.35pm and 7.35pm Monday to Saturday, three a day at 9.15am, 4.05pm and 7.35pm Sunday and public holidays).

From Greve (Piazza Trento) to Pieve di Panzano, the starting point of Day 2 of the walk, take the SITA bus for Lucarelli and get off 2km south of Panzano at Pieve di Panzano (San Leolino; 15 minutes, three a day at 7.55am, 12.50pm and 5.55pm Monday to Friday, two a day at 12.50pm and 2.30pm Saturday). Be sure to take the right bus because

most terminate at Panzano (17 buses a day) On Sunday, from Greve or Florence, it is possible to get only as far as Panzano (seven a day from 8.15am to 9.15pm).

THE WALK
Day 1: San Fabiano to Greve in Chianti
4–5 hours, 16km, 350m ascent
San Fabiano is a tiny *borgo* featuring a Romanesque façade, which is all that remains of the local church. From San Fabiano head back downhill towards Florence along the surfaced road. After about 250m, turn left into Via Fornace Casavecchia, a dirt road that passes through picturesque olive groves with a panoramic view to the hills across the Val di Pesa. Below, to the right, is the Palagio, a small, medieval castle, and further ahead you can see the bell tower of the Pieve di Santo Stefano a Campoli.

In 10 minutes you reach an ancient **kiln**. Follow the dirt road straight uphill (south) into the trees, and skirt a fine *casale* (farmhouse) and fountain. After another 10 minutes you reach a shrine at the corner of the buildings of La Cava. Here follow the road to the right through the yards of two *casali* and, in five minutes, you'll reach the Romanesque **Pieve di Santo Stefano a Campoli** (337m). The grassy churchyard, surrounded by cypresses, provides a pleasant setting for the contemplation of this ancient country church, built in the 10th century AD. Turn left (south) and follow the made road. Fortunately there is little traffic and in about 30 minutes you'll reach a large intersection, where you turn left. Passing between vineyards and *casali*, in another 15 minutes you'll reach Santa Maria Macerata (363m). Following the descending road you'll reach a triple junction with a cemetery and a shrine among the cypresses that marks the place where the asphalt turns into dirt road (350m).

Follow the dirt road down to the right and then make the steep ascent to the turn-off to the left for Valigondoli (443m) marked by an oak tree. Take the right fork; the road soon begins to descend, affording a view of the Badia a Passignano. The abbey is among the most beautiful in Tuscany, majestic and

Chianti Classico

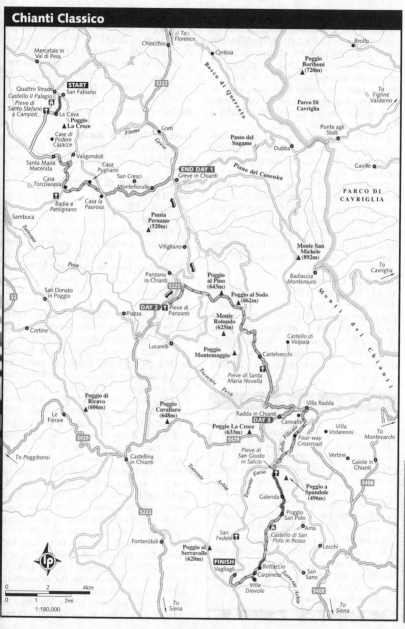

evocative with its two crenellated towers defended by a ring of lush cypresses. Continue past the tower-house called Tracolle and you'll reach the paved road near the abbey at Casa Torcilacqua (354m). At the time of writing the **abbey** (☎ 055 807 16 22) was being restored and visits were suspended indefinitely, but the village is still worth visiting (see the boxed text 'The Badia a Passignano', below).

From Casa Torcilacqua, take the ascending road to the left for Greve in Chianti, which offers further excellent views. After passing the Casa Pugliano you reach Casa la Paurosa (496m) and the paved road that links the town of Mercatale with Panzano; turn to the right and after 200m turn left and head downhill on the recently paved road towards Greve (5km). There are panoramic views of the Chianti hills. The ancient, small town below you is Montefioralle.

Greve in Chianti

About 20km south of Florence on the S222, Greve is in the heart of the Chianti hills. The **information office** (☎ 055 854 62 87, fax 055 854 42 40; e info@chiantie.chianti .it; Viale G da Verrazzano 59; open 10am-1.30pm & 5pm-8pm summer, 10am-1.30pm winter) can provide maps and information in English.

The Badia a Passignano

This imposing monastery was probably founded by the Lombard Kingdom. Here rests San Giovanni Gualberto, who started the monastic reform of Vallombrosa in the first half of the 11th century. In the dining hall is a precious fresco of the Last Supper painted by Ghirlandaio in 1476; the chapel of San Michele Archangelo in the church was painted in 1598 by Domenico Cresti, called 'il Passignano' for his having been born and raised in the nearby house of Pugliano. Notable also are the 1470 cloister and the imposing 14th-century fireplace in the monk's kitchen. There are some places to eat in the village, which surely merits a visit for its incomparable atmosphere.

Places to Stay & Eat The two hotels in town are on the main piazza. **Giovanni da Verrazzano** (☎ 055 85 31 89; e verrazzano@ ftbcc.it; Piazza Matteotti 28; singles/double in high season €72.30/82.63) has a restaurant with a beautiful terrace overlooking the piazza. **Del Chianti** (☎ 055 85 37 63; e info@ albergodelchianti.it; Piazza Matteotti 86; doubles €92.96) has a pool and a garden.

Getting There & Away Greve is served by frequent **SITA** (☎ 800 37 37 60) buses from Florence (€2.80, one hour, 23 a day).

Day 2: Pieve di Panzano to Radda in Chianti

4–5 hours, 16km, 344m ascent,
279m descent

On the opposite side of the road to the bus stop, there's a small paved street that leads up to the borgo, then continues up to the 10th-century **Pieve di Panzano** (457m) and 16th-century colonnade. Inside there is a 12th-century painting of the Madonna Enthroned and a 14th-century triptych by the Master of Panzano. Outside, enjoy the splendid panoramic view of the Val di Pesa, then visit the evocative 14th-century cloister.

Go back to the borgo and take the fork heading slightly uphill to the right; pass Hotel Villa Barone and continue on past a cemetery until you come to a stop sign (471m). Go right towards Montemaggio along a dirt road with a wide panorama looking south. After about 800m you pass a shrine on the right and, going down towards some cypresses, wonderful vistas open up to the north as well. Shortly afterwards is a triple fork where you take the central, uphill road towards Montemaggio-Castelvecchi. The road snakes off into the woods, passing the large iron gate of the Cennatoio farm on the right.

You soon reach a meadow and continue comfortably along level ground, with extensive views south, until you come to a fork among the fields and oak trees of Poggio a Sodo (662m), featuring a sign for Lamole. Turn to the right and begin the descent into the woods towards Montemaggio, following the dirt road marked 'SP114 Traversa de Chianti'. After 300m, at another fork (659m)

follow the signs to Radda in Chianti as you continue to descend, keeping to the right.

Here the road narrows and after about 800m you'll come to the Montemaggio turn-off (625m); continue descending to the left, keeping to the main road. After 2.4km the pine wood is interrupted by some cypresses and then thins out into some beautiful meadows and cultivated fields, arriving at the romantic *borgo* of **Castelvecchi**. You can see Castello di Volpaia off to the left, built into the slope at the edge of the wood. From here the road was recently paved, and twists down among olive groves and vineyards to the charming **Pieve di Santa Maria Novella** (478m), which retains its original Romanesque structure of three apses.

The descent gets steeper here and reaches a fork in the road. Go right towards Radda, cross the bridge (351m) over Torrente Pesa, and head uphill to the east for Lucarelli and Panzano, then go left towards Radda in Chianti. You'll need to walk 1.7km on this busy road until you come to an unusual red-brick bridge. Pass under it, then immediately turn off to the left and swing back over the bridge towards Radda, which is now 1km away. The village of Villa Radda lies straight ahead along the road.

Radda in Chianti

About 10km east of Castellina and 17km south of Panzano in Chianti, Radda is an old village and a good base from which to reach the best spots in Chianti. The **tourist office** (☎ 0577 73 84 94; ℮ proradda@chiantinet.it; *Piazza Ferrucci 1; open 10am-1pm & 3pm-7pm summer, 10am-1pm winter*) offers information about accommodation, cooking courses, independent walking tours and guided tours to wineries. For free advice, join the online Chianti Club (ⓦ www.chiantinet .it), recently established by Gioia Milani. Gioia works in tourism in Chianti, is very enthusiastic and well-informed, and will help travellers plan a tailor-made itinerary in the area.

Places to Stay & Eat One of the cheapest options is to rent a room in a family home in the centre of Radda. At **Da Giovannino**

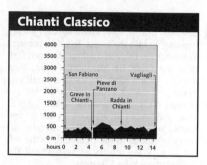

Chianti Classico

(☎/fax 0577 73 80 56; *Via Roma 6-8; singles/ doubles €49.06/67.14*) the rooms are clean and breakfast is included. Otherwise, a minimum two-night stay in one of the delightful old **farmhouses** in the Radda area costs from €51.65 per night for a small apartment. Check in advance with the Radda tourist office or contact Gioia Milani. You'll find Giovannino in his delicatessen **La Bottega** *(Via Roma 6)*, where you can pick up supplies.

Getting There & Away Bus services operated by **SITA** *(☎ 800 37 37 60)* run from Radda to Florence (twice a day at 7.15am and 8.50am) and from Florence to Radda (twice a day at 7am and 5pm). **Tra-in** *(☎ 0577 20 42 45)* buses travel from Radda to Florence (once a day at 6.10pm), with a change at Lucarelli, and from Radda to Siena (five a day at 6.55am, 8.50am, 1.50pm, 3.35pm and 6.40pm).

Day 3: Radda in Chianti to Vagliagli
5–6 hours, 20km, 500m ascent

Retrace your steps downhill and continue east on the busy paved road to Villa Radda, 1km east of Radda. Find the red-and-white sign painted on the left corner of the hotel Villa Miranda, marking trail 68 for San Giusto, and turn off here.

Trail 68 is actually a pleasant, little country road that heads south into a small, cultivated valley. Following the red-and-white signs, you'll pass the ancient tower of **Canvalle** on the right as you head up the other side of the valley. After a few metres, the main road descends to the right at a junction,

TUSCANY

marked by a cypress with a sign for an *agriturismo*; instead, you continue straight on, heading up into the forest. In a few minutes you reach the ridge and a three-pronged fork near the Casa Beretuzzo; go right, then straight on and more or less level, until you reach a wooden cross encircled by cypresses. Take care to stick to the marked trail and avoid deviations. After a few metres you can enjoy the view over the territory of Radda to the right and, to the left (southeast), the towers of Vertine and the 16th-century Villa Vistarenni.

Continue through a wide, grassy clearing with a four-way crossroads (530m). Go straight ahead here, following the main dirt road downhill (it curves slightly to the right) until you reach a T-junction (485m) where you'll turn right downhill in the direction of San Giusto in Salcio. Shortly afterwards, you'll see the elegant Romanesque bell tower of Pieve di San Giusto in Salcio peeping out of the trees on the other side of the valley. The road now descends in steep curves through fields and cypresses, continues to descend to the right at a Y-junction, crosses a little bridge over a stream and leads to the paved road at the valley bottom, where you will turn left (378m).

A Taste of Tuscany

The Fattoria Dievole (Dievole farm) is at the centre of extensive vineyards and produces an excellent Chianti DOCG. The panorama here is among the most beautiful in Tuscany.

Call ahead to organise a wine tasting. You'll be welcomed by Andrea Annichini, the courteous *sommelier* (wine host) of the farm. While recounting the history of Dievole and its wine, he will guide you through the cellars, sustaining you with sips of the various reds and whites, as well as some snacks.

Accommodation in **Villa Dievole** (☎ 0577 32 26 13, fax 0577 32 10 18; **e** villa.dievole@ dievole.it; doubles from €123.95) is an excellent way to spend some leisurely days in a real villa among the hills and vineyards of Chianti. It is a minimum two-day stay and there is also a swimming pool.

About 100m along the road there's a turnoff for Vagliagli-San Fedele on the right. Ignore it and continue on the paved road you'll cross a bridge over Torrente Fosse delle Filicaie and, after walking anothe 200m, turn right onto the cypress-lined dir road to reach **Pieve di San Giusto in Salci** (419m). This 11th-century, triple-apsec church is marvellously positioned among th ancient farmhouses, grassy courtyards anc centuries-old trees of a tiny *borgo*. Continue past the church and walk uphill until you meet up with a dirt road, marked by a red and-white sign on a tree, where you turn left

After 20m you'll reach a three-pronged fork with two parallel dirt roads in front of you (480m); follow the right one for Galenda-Ama. The path follows an ancient stone wall offering a lovely view and winds downhill into the forests. Avoid two diversions on your left before crossing the shallow stream (440m). Then follow the path uphill to reach **Galenda** (485m), a delightful rural *borgo* where you can make a pleasant rest stop among the cypresses.

Leave the *borgo* through the vaulted passageway between the houses and, heading south, follow the grassy path that traverses the side of the slope among the fields. Note the **small shrine** on your right. Walk downhill to the bottom of the small valley, cross the stream (450m) and continue to follow the path uphill (southeast) again into the bush. When you reach an iron gate go to the right and follow the fence as you descend. Then continue uphill along the grassy tractor trail until you reach a ghastly modern building. Here you will find a little road on the left, which takes you among the lovely houses of Poggio San Polo (527m). Of interest is the ancient *parata*, a kind of vaulted garage for housing farm equipment, which has been transformed into an elegant country home. There is a good restaurant here, I **Poggio** (☎ 0577 74 61 35, fax 0577 74 61 20; closed Monday Jan-Feb; meals without wine around €25.80).

Continue descending on the asphalt road towards Castello di San Polo in Rosso, now following CAI route 66 instead of No 68. The road becomes a pleasant cypress-lined dirt road, which passes through a forest and leads to a small cemetery. There is a splendid view of San Polo in Rosso and the Sienese Chianti.

Pass an elegant *casale* with a portico surmounted by a rustic, double-arched window. You then reach the ancient **Castello di San Polo in Rosso** (456m), founded in AD 1000 as a *pieve* (parish church), fortified in the 13th century and later embellished with a Renaissance loggia. Unfortunately, the castle is closed to visitors.

Take the dirt road that heads downhill beside the parking area, passing a house with a lovely staircase supported by a column. The dirt road veers to the left and then winds down into the forest, affording a view of the *pieve* from the south. The dirt road continues its long descent through the forest towards Torrente Arbia and you'll begin to notice the rich birdlife. As the road approaches the bottom of the valley, it crosses a grassy bridge spanning a secondary stream, and continues among the poplars maintaining a distance from the true left of the river. In a few minutes you'll come to a junction marked with a small shrine, where turning right you'll soon come to a field. Here the dirt road turns into a trail, which veers to the right and leads to an **abandoned bridge** (see 'Warning', above), overgrown and damaged by floods.

After crossing the bridge, go uphill to the left. The old road, used by vehicles until 30 years ago, is now a path consumed by rain water. The path ascends into the forest in steep, sharp curves. When you reach a great oak tree at a fork, veer left and continue uphill a few metres to a dirt road and the beautiful, restored *casale* of **Bottaccio** (392m) with a double *parata* next to the entrance. From here you can enjoy the panorama with San Sano nestled among the vineyards.

Continue ascending and at a fork in the path, marked by a tree, go right. After passing a wall take the steps to the left to reach the courtyard and Renaissance chapel of the tiny *borgo* of **Carpineto** (413m). As you continue uphill on the road you now have a view of the remarkably beautiful Crete Senese.

Follow the road on the ridge, ignoring the first deviation to the left, and after a few metres you'll reach a semicircle of cypresses. Here you can take the dirt road to the left, descending to the elegant manor house of **Villa Dievole** (420m; see the boxed text 'A Taste of Tuscany', p236), adorned with a little 17th-century chapel as elegant as it is tiny.

To continue to Vagliagli, follow the dirt road uphill to the asphalt road and turn right. Vagliagli is 1.8km from the semicircle of cypresses.

Medieval Hills

Duration	3 days
Distance	48km
Difficulty	easy
Start	Certaldo (p238)
Finish	Volterra (p238)
Transport	train, bus

Summary A peaceful and panoramic walk, taking in medieval villages, solitary country churches and the abandoned fortress of Castelvecchio.

As its name implies, this is an atmospheric ramble across typical Tuscan countryside and through historic towns and villages, including Europe's best-preserved medieval city, San Gimignano.

Described as a three-day walk, it can easily be extended by stopping at picturesque *borghi* along the way but be aware, not all *agriturismo* and hotels will take visitors for just one night, especially in high season and weekends, so you must plan well ahead if you plan to stay in these places. It is also well worth spending some time exploring the unique delights of the larger towns. In

TUSCANY

Certaldo, San Gimignano and Volterra, there are city and environmental guides; ask for information at the local tourist offices.

The walk can also be shortened by combining the first two days into a demanding, single stage.

PLANNING
Maps
The SELCA 1:50,000 *Dolce Campagna Antiche Mura* map is ideal for this walk. Multigraphic's 1:25,000 map No 513 *S. Gimignano, Volterra* does not, unfortunately, cover the start.

NEAREST TOWNS
Certaldo
About 40km from both Florence and Siena, this perfectly preserved, medieval town originated in the 12th century, when the counts of the Alberti family built the castle. Preserved in Certaldo are the reconstructed house (it was severely damaged during WWII) and tomb of Giovanni Boccaccio (1313–75), the celebrated author of the *Decameron*, one of the first poetic works in vernacular Italian. The walled, historic section of town sits high on a hill overlooking the Val d'Elsa and the Via Francigena.

Information Sources The information office (☎ 0571 66 49 35; e girasolecstac@tin.it; Via Cavour 32; open 9.30am-12.30pm & 3.30pm-6.30pm Apr-Oct; reduced hours Oct-Dec) is in the new town.

Places to Stay & Eat A couple of kilometres from the centre of Certaldo, **Fattoria Bassetto** (☎/fax 0571 66 83 42; e info@bassettobackpack.com; dorm beds/doubles €19.65/70), just off the main road to Poggibonsi, is a 14th-century Benedictine convent that has been transformed into a beautiful farm with a manor house and garden. A section of the convent has been converted into a hostel, with rooms that sleep three to six, an external bathroom and a communal kitchen. In the adjacent 19th-century manor house, once home of the Guicciardini duchess, there are six romantic rooms replete with antique furniture (shared bathrooms). Booking

is recommended. You can reach the Fattoria Bassetto on foot from the Certaldo train station, or contact the owners and arrange to be picked up.

The **Osteria del Vicario** (☎ 0571 66 82 28; e info@osteriadelvicario.it; Via Rivellino 3; singles/doubles with bath €56.80/82.65) next to the Palazzo Pretorio, is in Certaldo's historic centre. Breakfast is included. The hotel's excellent restaurant boasts a magnificent terrace on the bastions of the ancient walls and a meal costs from €41.30.

Il Delfino (☎ 0571 65 27 47; Via Roma 83; pizzas from €5.15) is in the new town.

Getting There & Away Certaldo is easily accessible by train from both Florence (€2.90, one hour, 20 a day Monday to Saturday, 12 a day Sunday) and Siena (€2.50, 42 minutes, 15 a day Monday to Saturday, 12 a day Sunday). The S429, which runs along the Val d'Elsa, connects Poggibonsi with Empoli, passing by Certaldo.

Volterra
The Etruscan settlement of Velathri was an important trading centre, a status that continued under the Romans. A long period of conflict with Florence, starting in the 12th century, ended when the Medici took possession of the city in the 15th century. Perched on top of a huge plateau, the city looks almost forbidding because of its well-preserved medieval ramparts.

Information Certaldo's information office (☎/fax 0588 872 57; w www.volterratur.it, Piazza dei Priori 20) is in the main square.

Places to Stay & Eat The best deal is at **Ostello della Gioventù** (☎/fax 0588 855 77, Via del Poggetto 3; dorm beds €10.35), near the Guarnacci Etruscan Museum. **Seminario Vescovile** (☎ 0588 860 28, fax 0588 907 91; Viale Vittorio Veneto 2; doubles with bath €35.10) is a religious institution, which offers large, clean rooms.

Near the town walls, **Ristorante La Pace** (☎ 0588 865 11; Via Don Minzoni 55; full meals €18.10) is a lovely restaurant with a friendly atmosphere.

Getting There & Away Buses operated by CPT (☎ *0588 861 86)* connect Volterra to San Gimignano, Florence and Siena, via Colle Val d'Elsa (€2.20, one hour, four a day Monday to Saturday), Pisa, via Pontedera (€4.91, two hours, nine a day Monday to Saturday) and Cecina, via Saline di Volterra (€3.50, one hour, at least three a day Monday to Saturday). FS trains or buses connect Saline di Volterra, a small town 9km southwest of Volterra, with Cecina on the Tyrrhenian coast, from where you can get a train to Pisa or Rome. **SITA** (☎ *800 37 37 60)* operates services from Volterra to Florence, via Castelfiorentino-Montespertoli, and **Tra-in** (☎ *0577 20 42 45)* runs from Colle Val d'Elsa to San Gimignano, Siena and Florence.

THE WALK
Day 1: Certaldo to San Gimignano
3–4 hours, 14km, 380m ascent, 130m descent

From the centre of Certaldo Nuovo (new Certaldo) follow the signs for San Gimignano. Cross a bridge and then immediately after a second bridge go left on the paved road for San Gimignano. After less than 1km you'll come to an ERG petrol distributor, the hotel/restaurant **Latini** and a paved road on the right, with a blue sign indicating Pancole and Fattoria del Monte (Villa del Monte). The walk follows this road, rising gently southeast among new houses, then vineyards and olive groves, and immediately affords a beautiful view of Certaldo to the northeast and San Gimignano to the south. After about 1km of climbing on the road, you reach the little church of **Canonica**, where a double row of cypress trees lines the road up to the majestic **Villa del Monte** (202m), from where you can enjoy a wide panorama east over Val d'Elsa and the hills of Chianti.

The undulating road continues for 2.5km to the quaint *borgo* of **La Piazzetta** (222m), and then reaches the church and *borgo* of **Pancole** (272m), a 17th-century sanctuary rebuilt after WWII. There are two accommodation options, **Fratelli Vagnoni** (☎ *0577 95 50 77, fax 0577 95 50 12; Pancole 82;*

doubles with bath €41.30) and **Hotel Le Renaie** (☎ *0577 95 50 44;* e *lerenaie@iol.it; Pancole 108; singles with half board €70.25, doubles with breakfast €98-118.80),* where you can also get a good meal in the restaurant from €20.65.

About 1km past Pancole, at a bus stop with a red-and-white trail marker, leave the road and turn right onto a dirt road for **Collemucioli** (350m). Take the next fork to the left, following the dirt road around the recently restored *borgo* with its lovely tower. Continue along this road, passing under an archway and heading uphill – at this point there is a beautiful view of San Gimignano. You then come to a wide clearing across from the splendid **Pieve di Cellole** (385m), about 45 minutes from Pancole. The little church, unfortunately open only on Sunday and holidays from 10am to noon, has rows of cypresses in front of its elegant 13th-century façade. Descend south on the little, now paved road that, after 300m meets up with provincial road 63, where you turn left. Being careful of the traffic, walk along the road the final 3.5km to San Gimignano.

San Gimignano
Originally an Etruscan village, San Gimignano became a *comune* (local government area) in 1199. Attesting to the wealth and power of the city's medieval families, some 72 towers were built, of which 14 remain. Ravaged by plague in 1348, the town's population was decimated and its infrastructure collapsed. This led to the town's submission to Florence in 1353. Today San Gimignano has the feel of a museum and is one of Europe's best-preserved medieval cities. In summer and at weekends year-round it is crowded with tourists.

Information In the main square, the **Associazione Pro Loco** (☎ *0577 94 00 08;* w *www .sangimignano.com; Piazza Duomo 1; open 9am-1pm & 3pm-7pm Mar-Oct, 9am-1pm & 2pm-6pm Nov-Feb)* offers extensive information on accommodation, public transport, car and bicycle rentals and many other services.

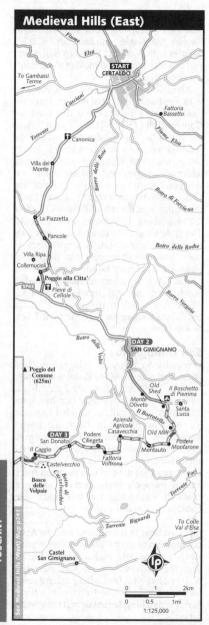

Medieval Hills (East)

Fiume
Elsa
START
CERTALDO
To Gambassi
Terme
Casciani
Fattoria
Bassetto
Canonica
Torrente
Fiume Elsa
Borro delle Roie
Villa del
Monte
Botro di Forciano
La Piazzetta
Pancole
Botro delle Roche
Villa Ripa
Collemucioli
Poggio alla Citta'
SP83
Pieve di
Cellole
Borro Vergaia
Botro delle Volle
DAY 2
SAN GIMIGNANO
Poggio del
Comune
(625m)
Old
Shed
Il Boschetto
di Piemma
Monte
Oliveto
Il Borratello
Santa
Lucia
Azienda
Agricola
Casavecchia
Old Mill
DAY 3
Podere
Podere
San Donato
Ciliegeta
Montauto
Montarone
Il Caggio
Castelvecchio
Fattoria
Voltrona
Bosco
delle
Volpaie
Botro di Castelvecchio
Torrente
Foci
Torrente Riguardi
To Colle
Val d'Elsa
Castel
San Gimignano
0   1   2km
0   0.5   1mi
1:125,000

See Medieval Hills (West) Map p241

Places to Stay & Eat There is a camping ground, **Il Boschetto di Piemma** (☎ 0577 9 03 52; e bpiemma@tiscalinet.it; campin per person/tent/car €4.70/5/2.10; open Apr-mid-Oct) 2km south of San Gimignano'southern gate, towards Santa Lucia, on th actual walk route. Inside the walls of Sai Gimignano, **Ostello della Gioventù** (☎ 057. 94 19 91; e franchostel@ftbcc.it; Via delle Fonti 1; dorm beds from €15.50) is at th northern edge of town. Breakfast is include in the rates. Lock-out is from 9am to 5pm and curfew is 11.30pm.

Getting There & Away In San Gimignanc buses depart from Piazzale Martiri di Mon temaggio, outside the city's southern wal gate, Porta San Giovanni.

SAP (☎ 0577 93 81 15) runs a service tc Certaldo (€1.35, 20 minutes, three a day Monday to Saturday) and **Tra-in** (☎ 0577 2C 42 45) operates to Poggibonsi (€1.35, 2C minutes, at least 10 a day). From both Certaldo and Poggibonsi you can catch a bus oi train for Florence, Siena, Colle Val d'Elsa and Volterra.

Between 6.30am and 7.30pm, a local bus runs to Santa Lucia (€0.85, seven minutes eight a day Monday to Saturday), where the second day of the Medieval Hills walk starts. The bus stops almost in front of the entrance to the Il Boschetto di Piemma camping ground.

Day 2: San Gimignano to San Donato

2½–3 hours, 8km, 174m ascent

Leave San Gimignano by **Porta San Giovanni** (324m), the city's main gate on the southern wall. Head south, descending to the right along a main road. At an intersection turn right onto the road for Volterra and then, almost immediately, turn left for the village of Santa Lucia. After less than 1km you'll pass the convent of **Monte Oliveto**, which is on the right, and soon after you'll see the entrance to the camping ground, Il **Boschetto di Piemma** (☎ 0577 94 03 52; e bpiemma@tiscalinet.it; open Apr–mid-Oct), to the left. Santa Lucia is another 500m further along the road.

TUSCANY

About 200m past the camping ground entrance there is dirt road on the right, marked with a red-and-white trail marker. Take this road and in 30m you reach an old shed. Do not follow the dirt road that turns right, but descend straight (south) into the woods between the shed and an iron gate on a steep, rambling trail with a red-and-white trail marker. After about 50m you come to a T-junction (with the dirt road you didn't follow before), where you go left (east). When you reach another dirt road turn right and make a wide, curving descent into the valley.

The road ends in the courtyard of an old mill, which has been restored as a holiday home. Descend to the left of the building and its lovely garden (there is a red-and-white trail marker) and, after a few metres, you reach the shady ford over Il Borratello (180m) – which you can jump over. On the other side (south) follow the marked trail, which ascends and soon exits the woods. You'll reach a dirt road at the *agriturismo* **Vallebuia di Montauto** (☎ *0577 94 12 39;* e *vallebuia@vallebuia.com; Vallebuia 13; camping per tent €25.80, doubles €90.40).* You can also rent a tent in the garden. Follow the cypress-lined road south, ascending

to **Podere Montarone** (229m), an abandoned farmhouse. Continue along the dirt road to the right (west), ascending among vineyards and olive trees to a little church in the tiny, peaceful *borgo* of Montauto. Here you can find accommodation in two farm holiday centres, **Borgo Montauto** (☎*/fax 0577 94 10 54; Montauto 9; doubles with breakfast €46.50)* or **Montauto Vacanze** (☎ *0577 94 08 38, fax 0577 93 82 14; Montauto 6A; doubles with bath €51.65, four-person apartments €67.15).*

From Montauto, take the road down to the left of the church and, after about 300m, leave the main road (which continues north to San Gimignano), turning left onto the dirt road marked with a trail map on a signpost. After 50m turn right and follow the dirt road for 1km to the Azienda Agricola Casavecchia (275m). After passing some houses the road becomes little more than a tractor trail. Continue along this marked trail for about 30m and then descend sharply to the left (south) into the valley, skirting a vineyard. After swinging left (south), at the bottom of the valley the trail finally veers right, enters the trees (marked with a trail marker) and crosses a sandy creek bed (225m), which is

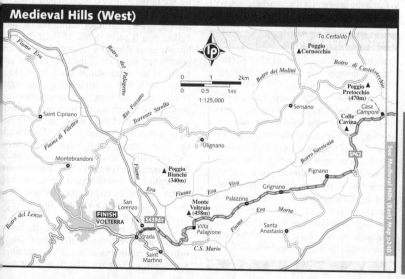

Medieval Hills (West)

usually dry. Climb the other side, continuing south along the tractor trail among the fields.

The tractor trail becomes a dirt road at the first of two houses you'll pass before reaching **Fattoria Voltrona** (☎ *0577 94 31 52;* e *info@voltrona.com; Montauto 50; doubles with breakfast €56.80*), near a small lake. As you continue along the dirt road, you can see the outline of Castel San Gimignano to the south. Pass **Podere Ciliegeta** (302m) and you will soon arrive at the delightful little *borgo* of San Donato. A section of this tiny village operates as **Fattoria San Donato** (*☎/fax 0577 94 16 16;* e *fattoriasandonato@iol.it; doubles €77.50*). Breakfast is included and a meal costs €20.65.

If you have the energy, you can follow the directions at the start of Day 3 to reach the ruins of Castelvecchio (see the boxed text, below) and then return to San Donato (three to four hours).

Day 3: San Donato to Volterra
6–7 hours, 22km, 670m ascent,
383m descent

From the elegant little Romanesque church of San Donato, head southwest along a paved road in the direction of Castel San Gimignano to reach the provincial road – where you will notice a lamppost marked with a trail marker.

Castelvecchio

Originally the Etruscan temple of an agricultural community, the cliff-side Castelvecchio was fortified after the Roman era. In the 13th century it was one of 20 castles that formed a defensive belt around San Gimignano. The only entrance, on the western side, was protected by a huge tower that still exists. The population of no greater than 100 people lived in the area between the tower and the church of San Frediano, the fascinating ruins of which are visible near the grain deposit. Farm animals and vegetable gardens were kept on the far eastern end of the cliff. Up to the 15th century the fortress was strategically important, but gradually fell into disuse and was ultimately abandoned after a plague epidemic.

Turn right onto the road and, after about 30m, turn left and ascend a steep dirt road, following the trail marker. When the dirt road emerges onto a rocky crest, you can see the ruins of Castelvecchio beyond the narrow, wooded valley. Shortly after, the dirt road descends steeply and then goes uphill to a clearing in the woods in front of the farm of Il Caggio (390m), about 30 minutes from San Donato. From here descend southeast on the steep, sharply curving trail (No 18) to reach a ford (285m) over Botro di Castelvecchio. On the other side continue west along the trail. After a brief but tiring climb, you come to a clearing where there is a dirt road closed with a chain. If you want to visit the interesting ruins of **Castelvecchio** (379m; see the boxed text, this page), turn left (east) and hop over the chain. The ruins are about 600m away and you'll need about 30 minutes for a decent exploration.

If you don't want to visit the ruins, turn right (west) at the clearing and ascend on the dirt road. Cross through woods, ignoring all turn-offs, until you reach a plain. The road then passes under some high tension wires, veers left and gradually descends until it reaches the intersection with the access road for the farmhouse of Casa Campore (440m) on your right. Follow the main dirt road to the left (west) and after a little more than 1.5km you'll reach SP62 (520m), locally known as di Poggio Cornocchio. Turn left (south) and walk along the road (watch out for cars) on a panoramic crest for 1.1km. Here you'll find a dirt road on the right (west), marked with two stone wayside posts. Descend among the trees and you will soon meet another dirt road, where you head right (west). Follow this cypress-lined walk up to the stupendous *borgo* of **Pignano** (502m), with its lovely, 12th-century church **Romanesque Pieve di San Bartolomeo Apostolo** and double access ramp, adorned with a palm and a cherry tree. If you want to stay here try **Pignano Vacanze** (*☎ 0588 350 32;* e *bcazac@tin.it*).

Follow the main dirt road, which descends sharply southwest, to a small bridge (370m) offering a panorama over the wooded territory south of Volterra. The route continues

ascending west and then descends slightly along the ridge to the buildings of Grignano. For overnight accommodation here try **Grignano** (☎/fax 0588 350 53; ℮ cherob68@ tin.it; doubles with bath from €41.30). Continuing southwest, in 1.3km you arrive at Palazzina with its abandoned 12th-century **San Lorenzo** chapel. A little more than 2km further on you reach the Medici-style villa of Villa Palagione (two hours from Pignano). Built in 1598 right under the rocky hump of Monte Voltraio, **Villa Palagione** (☎ 0588 390 14, fax 0588 391 29; ℮ info@villa-palagione .com; doubles with bath €41.30-72.30) is a cosy and well-organised holiday centre and an option for an overnight stay. It's 15km from San Donato and 7km from Volterra.

If you have the energy, you might like to climb **Monte Voltraio** (458m, see the boxed text, this page). There is a path just across the road from the entrance to Villa Palagione (50 minutes return).

From Villa Palagione continue on the dirt road, which descends in steep, sharp curves southward. Cross a bridge (205m) over the Fiume Era Morta, continuing northwest until you reach S439dir, with signs for Pontedera to the right and Saline di Volterra to the left. Turn left onto the winding state road and, after about 20m, you'll note trail markers on the guard rail and on a tree, indicating trail 21 to the right. The trail is actually a bit difficult to see because it is hidden by the undergrowth. Ascend through thick vegetation and annoying, prickly bushes for about 300m, until you reach a junction with a narrow, paved road. To the right is elegant **Agriturismo San Lorenzo** (☎ 0588 390 80; ℮ info@ agriturismosanlorenzo.it; doubles with bath €82.65), which offers meals for €20.65. There is also a little 13th-century church here.

To continue to Volterra, go straight on and ascend among the fields until you reach an intersection with another narrow, paved road. Turn left and, in a few metres, you'll be on the S68 at Strada. If you're tired, from Strada there is a **CPT** (☎ 0588 861 86) bus for Volterra (at 7.20am, 10.10am, 3.15pm and 6.50pm). Otherwise, turn right and continue along the road. In 2km you'll reach Volterra, passing under the Medici fortress.

> ### Monte Voltraio
>
> Upon this strange mountain, which is shaped like a truncated cone and rich in fossils, there once stood a fortress. Built late in the 1st century AD, it was where the bishops of Volterra hosted the powerful men of the time. Of the fortress there remains only a few evocative traces, but it is worth the climb to enjoy the view from the summit.

Apuan Alps

The sub-Apennine range known as the Apuan Alps (Alpi Apuane), in the far northwestern corner of Tuscany, has given the Western world the raw material for some of its grandest monuments and works of art. The pure white marble of Carrara and Massa, and the many other shades of marble extracted from different parts of the Apuan Alps, have been favoured for buildings and sculptures since the days of the Roman Empire. Most famously, Michelangelo travelled to the quarries behind Carrara to select the blocks of stone from which he carved many of his greatest works.

The Apuan is also a range of real natural beauty. It forms a continuous ridge approximately 30km in length, but a ridge that divides here and there and wanders from its main axis. It also includes almost disconnected peaks such as Monte Pisanino, the highest in the range at 1947m. The peaks are often described as 'dolomitic' in appearance and are separated in many cases by deep valleys.

One of the greatest challenges for the administration of the 543-sq-km Parco Regionale delle Alpi Apuane, established in 1985 in response to growing disquiet about the impact of human activity on the mountains, has been to try and balance environmental values with the ongoing economic health of the region. Around 22,000 people live within the borders of the park, many of them reliant to some degree on the marble industry. In an attempt to clarify the park's priorities, three levels of protection have been established, in which scenic, economic and

TUSCANY

natural values, respectively, take precedence. An area of 124 sq km has also been set aside for special protection in a series of *riserve naturali* (natural reserves). Walkers quickly become aware, however, that protection of the park's natural, and even scenic, resources is frustratingly difficult to ensure.

Two longish walks, known as Apuane Trekking and Garfagnana Trekking, cover much of the best of the Apuan Alps. The latter also explores the Garfagnana valley, east of the Apuan Alps, and the Orecchiella mountains further inland. Both trails link a series of *rifugi* (mountain huts) and other cheap places to stay. Two shorter walks, of two and three days respectively, are described in this section. They incorporate the precipitous Pizzo d'Uccello (1781m) in the north of the park, and the spectacular formations of Monte Procinto and Monte Forato with Pania della Croce (1858m) in the south.

NATURAL HISTORY
More than anything else, it is the geology of the Apuan Alps that has made them famous.

The Price of Glory

If the Apuan Alps have indirectly achieved fame and glory by serving for centuries as a source of fine marble, the cost to the natural environment has been high. Commentators wax lyrical about sunsets on the Apuan Alps, seen from the coast, when the warm rays are reflected off the marble scraps on the vast slopes, as though they were covered in snow. Nor is there any denying the beauty of a smooth, cool facet of marble, as can be seen in 300 or more quarries, large and small, throughout the range. But there's beauty, if you focus narrowly enough, in the rings of a sawn-off forest giant or the reflections on the surface of the reservoir that drives a hydroelectric power station. A marble quarry enhances the Apuan Alps the way a hillside of tree stumps enhances a forest or a concrete dam improves a river valley. Glowing sunsets and sculpted masterpieces have their price.

Nick Tapp

The raw materials of today's marble, limestone and sandstone were laid down on the sea bed over hundreds of millions of years, and underwent severe compression and folding during the Tertiary period (beginning about 60 million years ago). At one time covered by a layer of sedimentary rock known as the Falda Toscana (Tuscan Layer), the Apuan Alps, now metamorphosed, were pushed up and the Falda Toscana slid off and became the Appennino Tosco-Emiliano range. The elements, principally water in the form of rain and then ice (during the last glacial period, which ended about 10,000 years ago), carved the new range into something like its current shape.

This modelling went on, and still goes on, below ground as well as above. Under the Apuan Alps is the largest cave system in Italy, and one of the largest in the world. It contains a number of deep, predominantly vertical *abissi* (abysses) – one of these, Abisso Olivifer, is the deepest cave in the country at 1215m. There is also the extensive complex of Antro del Corchia (with more than 60km of tunnels) and many caverns rich in beautiful formations. Some of the finest examples are accessible to the general public in the Grotta del Vento, near Fornovalasco.

One peculiarity of the geology of the Apuan Alps is that the predominantly calcareous rock quickly absorbs most of the plentiful rain that falls, feeding it into underground watercourses. This leaves the surface comparatively arid and almost without permanent running water. This has practical implications for walkers, who must carry all the water needed for a day's walk

Because of the range's geological diversity and its dramatic rise from the Ligurian Sea to a height of nearly 2000m in less than 20km, there is a great variety of plant communities. Species of the Mediterranean *macchia* (scrub) give way over a relatively short distance to alpine varieties. Vegetation types can also change, quite discernibly to the experienced eye, at the boundaries between different geological zones. On top of all this human activities (aside from quarrying for marble) have over the centuries had a significant impact on the original vegetation.

In the lower valleys, up to an altitude of about 800m, the sweet *castagno* (chestnut) tends to dominate. While originally a naturally occurring species, the chestnut was spread during centuries of cultivation by local people, who depended on it for sustenance and income. Although cultivation has all but ceased since WWII and the number of trees has been reduced by disease, chestnut forests now cover something like 20% of the Apuan Alps. On seaward slopes at these altitudes, the *pino marittimo* (cluster pine) is more common.

The most common tree of the higher slopes, from 800m to 1700m or so, is the *faggio* (beech). This is despite the beech being exploited for firewood and now covering less of the Apuan Alps than it once did. Birch and oak are also found in this altitude band. Grasses and other low-growing species, a number of them endemic to the Apuan Alps, occupy the highest slopes and cling to cracks in the cliffs.

In spring and summer, the forest floors and upper slopes support magnificent displays of wildflowers, including jonquils, crocuses, anemones, gentians and a number of orchid species, and, late in summer, pink cyclamens.

Badgers, martens, fox and other small mammals live in the Apuan forests, but are seldom seen. A variety of small forest birds also live here, and above the tree line walkers may see choughs in large colonies, falcons and the occasional golden eagle.

CLIMATE

The Apuan Alps are among the wettest places in Italy, with an annual rainfall in some areas of more than 3000mm. The two sides of the range, however, receive very different weather. The southwestern slopes enjoy mild, humid Mediterranean conditions, with warm summers and mild winters, and an annual average temperature of roughly 15°C. On the northeastern side of the range, summers are hot and winters are cold, with significant snowfalls. On the highest peaks and internal ridges of the mountain range, winter can extend to more than four or five months of the year, with average temperatures falling below 7°C.

PLANNING
When to Walk

Rifugi and some other accommodation options remain open from mid-June until mid-September, and bus companies operate to an expanded summer timetable for roughly the same period, making this the most convenient period to walk. During winter, snow cover and prohibitive mountain weather make walking impractical.

What to Bring

Always pack wet- and warm-weather clothing, no matter how clear the forecast, as the weather in the Apuan Alps can change dramatically with little warning.

Maps

To help with planning and to give you a good overall picture of the layout of the Apuan Alps, pick up a copy of the Touring Club Italiano 1:200,000 map *Toscana*, widely available in Italian bookshops.

The most detailed map of walking tracks and *rifugi* is the Edizioni Multigraphic 1:25,000 map No 101/102 *Alpi Apuane* in the Carta dei Sentieri e Rifugi series. Edizioni Multigraphic's 1:50,000 Carta Turistica e dei Sentieri map *Parco delle Alpi Apuane* is less detailed, but the fact that the entire range is displayed on one sheet makes it easier to use. The maps have some discrepancies in mountain heights and some track inaccuracies, but nothing that should affect navigation. Both list *rifugi* details and are available from bookshops in the major towns in the area.

Books

There are few books published in English on the Apuan Alps but many in Italian. Accompanied by sketch maps of each route, *Le Alpi Apuane: Ambiente, Storia, Cultura*, by Mario Vianelli, details a four-day traverse of the Apuan and more than 40 different day walks in the region. Of special interest is the section on walks following the often spectacular but no longer used *vie di lizza* (marble transportation routes). Two other books that contain handy background information, if your Italian is up to it, are *Alpi Apuane: Guida al territorio del Parco*, by Frederick Bradley & Enrico Medda, and *Alpi Apuane*, by F Ravera.

Information Sources

The Parco Regionale delle Alpi Apuane has three main **visitor centres** (☎ 0585 31 53 00; Via Corrado del Greco 11, Forno • ☎ 0584 75 61 44; Piazza delle Erbe 1, Seravezza • ☎ 0583 64 42 42; Castelnuovo di Garfagnana). The official Parco delle Alpi Apuane website (**w** www.parks.it/parco.alpi.apuane/Eindex .html) provides a brief English-language introduction to the park, listing places to stay in the area along with publications available for purchase from the park's administration by mail order.

Emergency

If you strike trouble in the mountains (and can get to a telephone), contact the *carabinieri* (police) on the **national emergency number** (☎ 112) or for medical assistance call the **national ambulance number** (☎ 118).

ACCESS TOWNS
Massa

While fairly unremarkable in itself, the province's administrative capital, at the foot of the Apuan Alps, provides a comfortable base from which to explore the mountains. The **APT** (☎ 0585 24 00 63; Viale Amerigo Vespucci 24) is in an old seafront villa. There is also a **summer-only centre** (☎ 0585 63 31 15; Via delle Pinete 77). You can leave excess gear at the Massa train station while you walk, although, at €2.60 for each item per 12 hours or part thereof, this is an expensive business.

Places to Stay & Eat Most of Massa's accommodation is near the beachfront of Marina di Massa. There are dozens of camping grounds; book through the APT offices.

In shady grounds, **Ostello Internazionale Turimar** (☎ 0585 24 32 82; Via Bondano a Mare 64; dorm beds €18.10, with half/full board €25.80/31) is one of the newer hostels. **Hotel Frjsco** (☎/fax 0585 24 22 35; Viale Roma 410; singles/doubles €33.60/67.15, singles with half/full board €49.05/54.25) is a comfortable, family-friendly place on the

No 60 bus route. Closer to the centre of Marina di Massa is **Hotel Parma Mare** (☎ 0585 24 10 44, fax 0585 24 46 32; Via delle Pinete 102; singles/doubles €46.50/67.15, singles with half/full board €59.40/62). Right on the seafront in a converted villa, **Hotel Villa Carla** (☎ 0585 86 94 54, fax 0585 24 02 44; Via Mazini 18; singles/doubles €36.15/51.65, rooms with full board €51.65) has pleasant rooms with bathroom. It tends to be heavily booked in summer, so reservations should be made well in advance.

There are a large number of **bars** and **pizzerias** along the waterfront on Viale Amerigo Vespucci, and a **supermarket** (Via delle Pineta) and **alimentari** (grocery; Via delle Pineta). In the centre of Marina di Massa, **Il Farfarello** (Via Colombo 30) is cosy and serves some refreshing variations on a familiar seafood theme. **La Locanda del Sole** (☎ 0585 86 97 17; Via A Zini) is more traditional and upmarket.

Getting There & Away Massa is on the railway line between Pisa (€3) and La Spezia (€2.50), with trains continuing to Rome (€28.05) and Genova.

By car, Massa is accessible from the A12 which connects Genova and Rosignano (via La Spezia, Pisa and Livorno). Running parallel to the autostrada, the S1 (Via Aurelia) services towns along the coast from the Monaco border to Livorno.

Pietrasanta

With something of an international reputation as a marble centre, Pietrasanta has a steady stream of students visiting each year to attend master classes and workshops. The **visitor centre** (☎ 0584 79 55 60, fax 0584 79 55 60) is in the very pleasant Piazza del Duomo – the town's only real attraction. If you haven't already equipped yourself, **Libreria Santini** (Via Mazzini 79) sells a number of maps and books on the Apuan Alps.

Places to Stay & Eat On the coast at Marina di Pietrasanta is **Hotel La Pigna** (☎ 0584 74 58 88; Via Don Bosco 15; rooms with half/full board €62/67.15). In Pietrasanta proper there is **Da Piero** (☎ 0584 79 00 31;

TUSCANY

Via Traversagna 3/5; singles/doubles from €31/46.50), two blocks from the bus station. It offers simple but clean rooms, with a cafe-restaurant downstairs. **Agriturismo da Pio** (☎ 0584 79 02 66; Via Traversagna 54; camping per person €7.75, singles/doubles €56.80/72.30), 1km out of town, is a charming converted farmhouse. It offers home-cooked evening meals (€12.90). Camping is available next to the house.

Near the train station, **Dimeglio supermarket** (Piazza della Repubblica) is a convenient stop for food supplies. A popular meeting place, **Pizzeria Betty** (pizzas around €6.20) is in the picturesque setting of the Piazza del Duomo. For more expensive meals try **Il Vaticano** (Via Marzocco). There are many other places to eat in the streets around the piazza.

Getting There & Away Pietrasanta is 10 minutes from Massa by train on the Pisa–La Spezia line. **CLAP** (☎ 0584 701 36) buses also run at frequent intervals between the towns, leaving from the bus terminal near the train station. CLAP buses leave for Marina di Pietrasanta roughly every 30 minutes.

Pizzo d'Uccello

Duration	3 days
Distance	29.5km
Difficulty	moderate
Start	Resceto
Finish	Castelpoggio
Nearest Town	Massa (p246)
Transport	bus

Summary Traverse of the northern Apuan Alps, with the full gamut of park experiences from marble quarries to shady beech wood, and a breathtaking ridge walk past the spectacular, sheer face of Pizzo d'Uccello.

At just 1781m, Pizzo d'Uccello is not the highest peak in the Apuan Alps, but its isolated position at the northwestern end of the range and the steepness of its faces and ridges make it one of the most imposing. Pizzo d'Uccello's north face, which drops approximately 700m from the summit, appeared in the records of English mountaineer FF Tuckett in 1883. He considered it one of the most impressive rock walls in the Apuan Alps, but at least four decades were to pass before it was first climbed. Opinion differs on whether the honour went to two *Genovesi* (from Genoa) in 1927 or two *Milanesi* (from Milan) in 1940. Today the face sports many Alpine rock climbing routes. Among them are some of Italy's hardest and repeat ascents are few.

This walk views the north face of Pizzo d'Uccello from close range and includes the option of a side trip to its airy summit by the easiest route. This calls for a steady head but no special skills as a rock athlete. Val Serenaia, into which the walk descends on the first day, is one of the most extensive glacial valleys in the Apuan Alps and is enclosed by the major peaks of the northern Apuan: Pizzo d'Uccello, Monte Pisanino (1947m), Monte Cavallo (1888m), Monte Contrario (1790m) and Monte Grondilice (1805m). Its upper reaches, in particular the area covered in beech forest known as Orto di Donna (Lady's Garden), are rich in plant species. The trail also skirts areas devastated by the scourge of the Apuan Alps environment, the marble extraction industry, at Passo della Focolaccia, on the Cresta Garnerone and at Foce di Pianza. However, it also provides many of the glorious views, both mountainous and coastal, for which the Apuan Alps are, in their own small way, justly famous.

As described, the walk is in three stages, but Day 3 is short. The walk could be extended and made into a circumambulation of Pizzo d'Uccello with additional overnight stops in Ugliancaldo and Vinca. Alternatively, it could be extended south past Monte Tambura to link up with the southern part of the Apuane Trekking route and the Procinto, Forato & Pania della Croce walk (p252).

GETTING TO/FROM THE WALK

Resceto, at the start of the walk, is accessible by **CAT** (☎ 0585 85 21 24) bus from Massa (€1.50, 30 minutes). Unfortunately, the only bus convenient for an early start leaves Massa at the enthusiasm-dampening time of 6.30am, Monday to Saturday, from outside the ticket office on Largo Matteotti,

TUSCANY

just off Viale Chiesa. The first bus on Sunday and public holidays is not until 2pm.

By car, Resceto is only a short drive north (10km) of Massa up into the valley of the Torrente di Renana.

At the end of the walk, frequent CAT buses leave from opposite Bar Liviana on Castelpoggio's main street for Carrara (€1.05, 30 minutes); buy your ticket on the bus. The first bus departs at 7am (9.55am on Sunday and public holidays). Buses on Sunday and public holidays are less frequent.

Castelpoggio is roughly 5km north of Carrara along the S446d. Massa is another 5km southeast of Carrara along the S1 (Via Aurelia), with frequent CAT buses (leaving from the Piazza Allende bus terminal) connecting the two.

THE WALK
Day 1: Resceto to
Rifugio Val Serenaia

4–5 hours, 9.5km, 1185m ascent, 520m descent

From the car park just above Resceto, where the bus from Massa turns around, an unsealed road continues up the valley of Canale di Resceto. Red-and-white paint markers label it as track 35. Follow the road north, past a junction (left) where track 170 heads towards Foce Vettolina. After 10 minutes or so, at a small quarry, the road gives way to a narrower but still impressively steep track, once a *via di lizza* down which marble blocks were lowered from the quarry above (see the boxed text 'La Lizzatura', p250). A few hundred metres further on is another track junction, 1km from Resceto. Here track 35, the remarkable **Via Vandelli**, crosses Canale Pianone to the east and begins its tortuous zigzag ascent of nearly 1000m to Passo della Tambura.

Continue up the west side of the valley on track 166, past yet another impeccably signposted track junction, this time where track 166b departs on a higher route to Passo della Focolaccia. After another half-hour of slow climbing, track 163 heads off to the east at a clearly marked junction. Stay on track 166, which heads left here and up some grassy slopes, then begins to negotiate gullies full

of marble 'scree'. A short scramble past cairns and painted markers, and along the occasional stretch of well-engineered track, leads to the lower edge of Cave Magnani, a functioning marble quarry. The western slopes of Monte Tambura (1895m) loom across the valley to the east.

The final climb to the pass follows the zigzagging road through the quarry – interesting if unattractive – past some buildings on the right and then a junction where track 166b rejoins the route. **Bivacco Aronte**, the oldest walkers' shelter in the Apuan Alps, appears a short distance off to the left, just below the pass, and is equipped with a wood stove and sleeping platforms for emergencies. (Note that the location of this shelter is not marked accurately on the Carta dei Sentieri e Rifugi map). The rocky crest just west of Bivacco Aronte, including the elegant needle of Punta Carina, sports a number of classic rock climbs.

Although approaching it through a quarry is good mental preparation, **Passo della Focolaccia** (1642m) still comes as a shock. The original pass has disappeared, engulfed by a huge pit from which slabs of the precious white stone are probably being carved out and carried away before your eyes. At the time of writing, the walking trail descended to the right, smooth and white underfoot, along the road round the main pit (the red trail markers may be difficult to spot in overcast weather) and down to the bottom of the quarry. Above the quarry to the southeast, Monte Tambura wears a somewhat forlorn look.

Track 179 leaves the road only a short distance beyond Passo della Focolaccia and contours to the northwest, joining up with track 178 on its way to **Foce di Cardeto** (1670m). The start of the track (where it leaves the road) is not clearly marked, and if you suspect you've missed it – in particular, if you reach the point where the road switches back to the south, downhill – head uphill from the road to regain the track and follow it to the pass. The lush Val Serenaia now lies ahead to the northwest, and towering beyond the valley is Pizzo d'Uccello. All along the western side of the valley

Pizzo d'Uccello

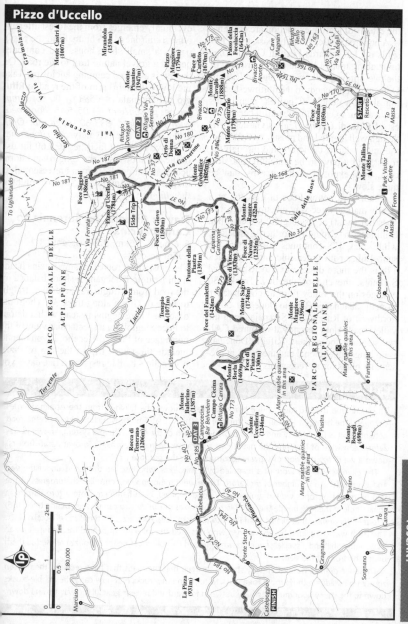

reaching up to rugged Cresta Garnerone, the effects of marble extraction are obvious.

A hundred metres from the pass, track 179 splits off left towards Foce di Giovo. Continue along track 180, the more northerly of the two options, following a sign to Rifugio Donegani. It descends to the northwest, staying above a couple of gullies, then heads down a spur to enter the beautiful beech forest of **Orto di Donna** (Lady's Garden). Although well marked and mostly well defined, the track takes a devious route through the forest, and it pays to be watchful. The descent, over exposed rock outcrops, can be quite slow.

About 1km below Foce di Cardeto, at a clearly marked three-way junction, track 180 goes left (west) across a gully system, then continues in a roughly northerly direction, while track 178 continues north down the spur. Either path is feasible, although track 178 is the more direct route to Rifugio Val Serenaia, the end of the day. Track 180 emerges on the valley floor a short distance from the abandoned Rifugio Donegani, 500m northwest of Rifugio Val Serenaia along the valley road. Until recently a favoured CAI-run stopover for walkers, Rifugio Donegani is no longer operational and there are, at present, no plans for its reopening.

Continuing its leafy descent, track 17? eventually emerges from the forest after another 1km (one to 1½ hours from the pass) passes a small stone house and continue next to a gravel nature trail to the road. O? the left is a fenced camping enclosure. Tak? the lower (eastern) arm of the road to **Rifugio Val Serenaia** (☎ 0583 61 00 85; *camping per person/tent €1.05/5.15, dorm bed with half board €33.60; open Apr-Oct)* 100m away. The privately run *rifugio* ha? primitive camping facilities (€2.60 for us? of the hot showers at the *rifugio*) and dorm accommodation. Bookings are essential a? the owners do not always stay overnight a? the *rifugio*.

Day 2: Rifugio Val Serenaia to Campocecina

5–6 hours, 15km, 825m ascent,
655m descent

The most direct route to Campocecina head? from Rifugio Donegani, a short distance u? the road from Rifugio Val Serenaia, straigh? to Foce di Giovo along track 37. The rout? described here begins instead with a detou? to Foce Siggioli for a spectacular view of th? north face of Pizzo d'Uccello. If you plan t? include the return trip to the top of Pizz? d'Uccello – hard to resist on a fine day – yo?

La Lizzatura

The technique used to lower huge blocks of marble down the hillsides from the Apuan quarries changed little between Roman times and the 1960s. At that time construction began on the road network that is used today and trucks took over much of the work. The old system, known as *lizzatura*, consisted of lowering the marble on a *lizza* (wooden sled), which slid over *parati* (rollers) down a *via di lizza*, a kind of slipway constructed for the purpose.

The exercise was the work of a team led by a *capolizza*, who inserted the rollers under the sled and gave orders to a number of *mollatori*. These were the men who controlled the progress of the sled by means of ropes wound around *piri* (wooden pegs), each hammered into a *foro da piro*, a square hole in the rock beside the *via di lizza*. Examples of *fori da piro* can be seen beside track 166, a former *via di lizza* that climbs from Resceto to Passo della Focolaccia on the Pizzo d'Uccello walk. The team was completed by several men who retrieved the rollers from behind the sled as it made its way downhill and a specialist *ungino*, who greased the rollers before the *capolizza* reinserted them under the front of the sled.

These *vie di lizza* were often very steep – so steep that the roads that have replaced them often zigzag up hillsides with no room for a truck to turn, and the trucks that now carry the marble blocks down to the valley floor must alternate between forward and reverse gear all the way up and down.

hould make a reasonably early start in order
o reach Campocecina in good time.

From Rifugio Val Serenaia follow the road
ack (southeast) to the hairpin bend and then
ound and upwards to Rifugio Donegani.
Continue north beyond the *rifugio* for 500m
o a second sharp bend in the road, past a
ign marking the boundary of the *cava di
marmo* (marble quarry). A short distance on,
markers on rocks indicate the start of track
87, which heads back towards the north-
est at an acute angle from the road. A sign,
'Pericoloso, Sentiero Altrezzato', warns of
he occasionally airy sections to come along
his trail. Passing first through lovely beech
orest, then angling up more open slopes
ith views to the right across the Alta
Garfagnana, the track comes to **Foce Siggi-
li** (1386m), 40 minutes and 300 vertical
netres from Rifugio Donegani. The uninter-
upted view of the sheer north face of Pizzo
'Uccello, just a stone's throw away, fully
arrants the detour. A few metres north
long the Cresta di Capradosso ridge is the
op of a *via ferrata* (iron way), which offers
nose with the necessary equipment and ex-
erience a strenuous but spectacular route up
rom the valley floor more than 500m below.

The well-marked track 181 leads south
long the picturesque ridge top for a two
ninutes, then leaves the crest and traverses
teep hillsides, where beech forest alternates
ith rocky, open spurs and gullies. A few
hort sections of the track are somewhat ex-
osed and are equipped with metal cables –
kind of miniature *via ferrata* – but in good
eather should not present problems to
noderately experienced walkers; no special
quipment or technical skill is required.
.fter 30 minutes from Foce Siggioli the
ack regains the ridge top at a small saddle
1497m), where track 191 heads down to
ie west and an unnumbered route leads
orth towards the summit of **Pizzo d'Uc-
ello**. If it's a fine day and you have a good
ead for heights, you'll probably be tempted
 climb to the top (see Side Trip, p252).

To continue towards Campocecina, head
outh for an easy 500m to **Foce di Giovo**
1500m), the main weakness in the Cresta
arnerone ridge connecting Pizzo d'Uccello

with Monte Grondilice. A descent of less than
10 minutes to the northwest brings you to a
track junction above a group of ruined buildings marked on some maps as 'Capanne del
Giovo'. Ignore track 175, which continues
towards Vinca. Instead take No 37 on a long,
descending traverse to the south. After nearly
2km in the open below the rocky Cresta Garnerone, the track enters mixed forest. Only a
few minutes into the forest is the locked metal
bulk of the Capanna Garnerone, 45 minutes
from the Foce di Giovo. Just below the hut is
a reliable source of piped water.

Track 37 is now joined by No 173 from
Vinca and continues through a forest now
dominated by introduced pines. After 15
minutes track 38 heads downhill on the
right. To enjoy the scenic crest that connects Monte Rasore and Monte Sagro, continue uphill for another five minutes to the
ridge top and a junction with tracks 168 and
186. Follow No 37/173 west along the north
side of the ridge, past a narrow gap where
No 37 peels away to the south, then touch-
ing the crest at another low point, before
reaching **Foce di Vinca** (1333m), roughly 30
minutes from Capanna Garnerone.

From here make your way attentively
down to the north, bearing left at every opportunity, still on track 173. This heads generally west, becoming more clearly marked
and with spectacular views of Pizzo d'Uccello, crossing scree slopes and encounter-
ing abandoned machinery in a gully. A
climb up this gully, steep and crisscrossed
with fixed cables towards the top, leads to
a ridge and a patch of eerie forest. The track
swings to the west below the cliffs of Monte
Sagro and 1km from the top of the gully,
after several sections equipped with fixed
cables, emerges at the **Foce del Fanaletto**
(1426m). The scene to the west is one of
monumental destruction – or of busy production, depending on your point of view.

It is now necessary to skirt the south side
of the quarry that fills the intervening valley. Markers lead south at first, round the
steep western slopes of Monte Sagro, then
across the head of the valley, up onto a spur
and along it to meet the road through Foce
di Pianza (1300m).

TUSCANY

The final 30 minutes from Foce di Pianza is a pleasant coda to the day's exertions as the trail leaves the rumble of heavy machinery behind. From the pass, cross the road and follow track 173, north at first, up and round the eastern flank of Monte Borla. Signs are faint to begin with but lead quickly into a beech wood and along a clearly marked path to the broad, open slopes of Campo Cècina. The track crosses the open pasture and descends to the scattered buildings of **Campocecina**. Just above the road is **Rifugio Carrara** (℡/fax 0585 84 19 72, 339 460 57 96; half board €34.60) with 18 beds.

Side Trip: Pizzo d'Uccello Summit
1¼–1¾ hours, 290m ascent, 290m descent
Painted markers on rocks lead all the way up the south ridge of Pizzo d'Uccello from the saddle at 1497m. The gradient is gentle at first. As it steepens, the route seeks out the line of least difficulty and becomes less direct. The ridge is increasingly airy, and it is necessary to use your hands on the steepest sections and look carefully where you place your feet, but there is no great climbing skill required. The markers continue, so if faced with an impossibly sheer-looking stretch of rock, look about you for a splash of red paint. After an unhurried 45 minutes from the saddle, the summit cross appears ahead on a knoll. After a final clamber down into a dip and up the other side, you are there.

On a clear day, the summit of **Pizzo d'Uccello** or 'Bird's Peak', is a spectacular eyrie, with views of the snow-capped Alps away to the north and northwest, the Gulf of La Spezia to the west and, closer at hand, the rest of the Apuan Alps, including the highest point, Monte Pisanino, just across the valley to the east. With the benefit of familiarity, the descent to the saddle takes little more than half the time it took to get up there – but take your time and take care.

Day 3: Campocecina to Castelpoggio
1½ hours, 5km, 770m descent
This short, straightforward, downhill amble is a pleasant way to finish the walk. Follow the track from the front of Rifugio Carrara down hill to the northwest to meet the road opposite a car park. Continue past **Bar Belveder** then, just before a little bridge, follow red and-white markers down the hill to the west. The track winds between fields, fences, caravans and buildings for a few minutes, the proceeds down the side of a ridge. Track 4 joins from the north, then a few minutes late departs to the south at a grotto. Follow trac 185, which swings north down a spur amon interesting rock formations, including a archway that may be partly natural, before meets a sealed road and the intersection several walking tracks at Gabellaccia.

Cross the road and continue downhill the west on track 185. Track 184 soc branches off south towards La Pianacc and Gragnana, followed by No 46 toward Ponte Storto. After a gently descending tra verse of 2km, No 185 rounds a spur an passes beneath power lines, then merge with an unsealed vehicle track and make its way into **Castelpoggio**, perched pic turesquely on a spur.

Procinto, Forato & Pania della Croce

Duration	2 days
Distance	26km
Difficulty	moderate
Start	Stazzema
Finish	Ponte Stazzemese
Nearest Town	Pietrasanta (p246)
Transport	bus
Summary	Glorious ridge-top walking past the spectacular formations of Monte Procinto and Monte Forato to the summit of the 'queen' of the Apuan Alps, with an overnight stop in a cosy *rifugio*.

Pania della Croce (1858m), together wi Pania Secca (1709m) and Pizzo delle Saet (1720m), forms the southernmost of the re ally big Apuan massifs. Its airy summ ridge is a magnificent place to be when th light slants across the Apuan Alps, eithe early or late in the day, and sets off th mountain peaks against the haze-filled valleys. The summit itself, topped by a massive iron cross, gives wonderful views up and down the crest of the range and across to the Ligurian Sea only 15km away.

This walk approaches Pania della Croce by way of two lower, but also noteworthy, mountains. Monte Procinto is a splendidly steep-sided, limestone pinnacle, which juts from a ridge a little to the west of the main Apuan crest. Much commented on by poets and artists over the centuries, it was first climbed in 1879. A *via ferrata* makes the summit accessible to those who are properly equipped and with sufficient experience. All the other routes to the top of the Procinto are the province of rock climbers. Monte Forato is one of the strangest and most visible examples of the natural forces at play in the Apuan Alps. Erosion by wind and water has worn a hole, 30m across, in the ridge and left a remarkable rock bridge between the two summits of the mountain.

The walk begins in the village of Stazzema – or, rather, just below it – 7km as the crow flies, but further by road, from Pietrasanta. It finishes at Ponte Stazzemese, beside the Fiume Vezza on the valley floor below Stazzema. Buses also pick up passengers from Pruno or Cardoso, further up the valley, if the prospect of a final leg along a sealed road does not appeal.

It is possible during summer to fill in the gaps between this walk and the Pizzo d'Uccello (p247), combining the two into a long traverse of the entire Apuan Alps closely following the marked Apuane Trekking route from Pietrasanta to Carrara.

GETTING TO/FROM THE WALK
On the way to Stazzema, Ponte Stazzemese is served by **CLAP** (☎ *0584 701 36*) buses from Pietrasanta (€1.80, 25 minutes), departing from the bus station on the other side of the railway line from the train station and accessible by a pedestrian underpass. The most convenient bus leaves at 7am (7.15am on Sunday and public holidays). The next bus is not until 10am. From Ponte Stazzemese, **Fratelli Verona Autolinee** (☎ *0584 74 57 37*) buses travel to

Stazzema (20 minutes, twice a day at 8am and 10.25am); the buses should connect. There are no buses for this leg on Sunday or public holidays, so be prepared to walk 3km to the start of the walk.

Ponte Stazzemese is a short, if circuitous, drive from Pietrasanta up into the foothills of the Apuan Alps via the town of Seravezza. Stazzema is another 3km uphill from Ponte Stazzemese along a sealed road.

Returning to Pietrasanta from the end of the walk, afternoon buses leave from the main piazza in Ponte Stazzemese (three a day at 3.50pm, 5.55pm and 8pm Monday to Saturday, twice a day at 1.55pm and 5.40pm Sunday and public holidays), near the turn-off up the hill to Stazzema. There are also several afternoon buses from Pruno (Monday to Saturday only) and Cardoso, 4km and 2km respectively along the walk trail from Ponte Stazzemese.

THE WALK
Day 1: Stazzema to Rifugio Enrico Rossi
4½–5½ hours, 13.5km, 1300m ascent, 90m descent

Tracks 5, 5b and 6 set off from the last sharp bend in the road from Pietrasanta, below the village of Stazzema. Monte Procinto (1147m) rises prominently above to the northeast. Markers lead up a made road towards Monte Procinto and Rifugio Forte dei Marmi. This climbs gradually round the hillside and switches back first to the west, then to the east again. In less than half an hour, at a signposted junction only a short

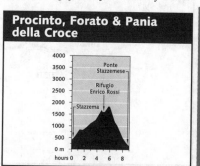

Procinto, Forato & Pania della Croce

Procinto, Forato & Pania della Croce

Pizzo delle Saette (1720m)

Pania Secca (1709m)

Rifugio Enrico Rossi

DAY 2

Vallone dell'Inferno

Uomo Morto

Monte Corchia (1676m)

Foce di Mosceta

Pania della Croce (1858m)

No 126

No 9

Canale delle Verghe

No 727

No 9

No 131

No 7

Rifugio del Freo

No 125

Costa Pulita

No 7

Antro del Corchia

No 124

Foci di Valli

To Levigliani

No 9

No 122

Valle

Canale

Deglio

Collemezzana

No 124

Canale delle

To Retignano

No 123

(1209m)

Natural Archway

No 12

Canale della Capriola

Monte Forato (1223m)

Via Ferrata

No 122

Canale

No 12

No 124

Foce di Petrosciana

Pruno

Cardoso

Monte Croce (1314m)

No 124b

No 109

Volegno

Canale dell'Oreto

Canale Versiglia

Fiume Vezza

No 8

No 8

Foce delle Porchette

To Pietrasanta

FINISH

Ponte Stazzemese

No 6

No 5b

I Bimbi del Procinto

Monte Procinto (1147m)

Via Ferrata

il Monte (591m)

No 5

Monte Nona (1279m)

Stazzema

START

Mulina

Rifugio Forte dei Marmi

Fosso

No 221

Pomezzana

Rifugio Albergo Alto Matanna

Monte Matanna (1317m)

0   500   1000m
0   500   1000yd
1:50,000

TUSCANY

distance after the second major bend, a marked walking track branches off on the south side of the road.

A few hundred metres after it leaves the road, the walking track divides. Track 6 goes left and is the more direct route to Monte Forato. However, it is worth going right to visit the picturesque Rifugio Forte dei Marmi. Follow No 5 for a further 45 minutes to meet track 121. At the track junction is a stone shelter and water fills a stone tank nearby. Two hundred metres to the right (southeast) from here, with a dramatic view of Monte Procinto, is the welcoming **Rifugio Forte dei Marmi** (☎ 0584 77 70 51; open 15 June-15 Sept daily, Sat-Sun only rest of year), with bar, restaurant and 52 beds.

From the track junction follow markers uphill on track 121 (not No 5b, which descends). This passes below the cliffs of **Monte Procinto** and round the western end of a group of smaller towers known as I Bimbi del Procinto. Monte Forato (1223m) and Pania della Croce (1858m) now dominate the view across the valley to the north. Track 6 comes in from below, followed by No 8 from Cardoso (at the opposite angle to that shown on Multigraphic maps of the area); the latter soon splits off and climbs to Foce delle Porchette. Continue along track 6, ignoring first No 124b on the left, then No 109 on the right and No 124 on the left, to Foce di Petrosciana (931m). Plans to build a road through this pass, connecting the Versilia region to the south with the Garfagnana to the north, have never been realised.

An unnumbered, and less obvious, track now leads northwest from the pass, straight up a spur. (This is not accurately depicted on the Carta dei Sentieri e Rifugi map, which shows the track leaving from below the pass). It passes the start of a *via ferrata*, then traverses round the eastern side of **Monte Forato** to the startling **natural archway**, approximately 30m across, which pierces the ridge between its two summits and gives the 'Mountain With a Hole' its name. The lower, more northerly peak (1209m) is easily accessible a few minutes above the intersection with track 12. Those with a head for heights who wish to take

their lives into their own hands should be particularly wary of loose rocks as they make the obvious, narrow 'skyline traverse' to the higher summit.

The saw-toothed ridge, approximately 1.5km long, that extends north from Monte Forato towards Pania della Croce is a gem. The still unnumbered track – so faint that you will have to rely on blue paint trail markers in places – stays close to the ridge top, which is by turns grassy, rocky and clad with patches of beech forest. There are lovely views back beyond Monte Forato's two summits to Monte Nona, and ahead to the huge, open southeastern slope of Pania della Croce, known as 'Costa Pulita'. The track leads down through Foci di Valli to the base of the Costa Pulita and a four-way track junction. Follow track 7 as it climbs steadily up and across the Costa Pulita to the eastern shoulder of Pania della Croce, an ascent of 400m.

From here the trail descends roughly north, past junctions with track 126 (tomorrow's route) and then No 139. After a further five minutes of relatively level walking some solar panels on the left announce the cosy **Rifugio Enrico Rossi** (☎ 0583 71 03 86; bunks nonmembers €28.40; open 16 June-10 Sept daily, Sat-Sun only rest of year) at 1609m. It has a bar, restaurant and 22 bunks; rates include dinner and breakfast. *Pannini* (bread rolls) and chocolate bars can be provided for lunch on the trail.

Day 2: Rifugio Enrico Rossi to Ponte Stazzemese

3½–4 hours, 12.5km, 250m ascent, 1700m descent

Retrace your steps southwest for 500m, past the signed start of track 139, to the point where track 126 goes west. Follow it steeply up through the tumbled rock landscape of the evocatively named Vallone dell'Inferno (Valley of Hell) to the ridge top. Except perhaps on the windiest of days, you should reward yourself with a straightforward detour to the summit of **Pania della Croce** (1858m) and its massive cross, just 200m south (actually, a few degrees east of south) along the crest of the ridge. On a good day, this is an exhilarating viewpoint with the sea just 15km away to the southwest and the Apuan Alps stretching in both directions parallel to the coast.

The track descends north along the ridge top towards Pizzo delle Saette (1720m) for about 200m, then drops off to the west and begins the long, gradual descent to **Foce di Mosceta**. At this saddle, track 125 comes in on the left from Foci di Valli, then, a few minutes on, where a stone shelter stands beside the track, No 127 goes right (north) and No 122 heads left (south). Straight ahead across a little gully is the large and comfortable **Rifugio del Freo** (☎ 0584 77 80 07; e mosceta@interfree.it; beds nonmembers €26.85; open 15 June-15 Sept daily, Sat-Sun only rest of year); rates include dinner and breakfast. Relatively accessible by road, the rifugio is a popular weekend getaway.

Turn south on the well-defined track 122. To the northeast is Monte Corchia (1676m), beneath which is the deepest and most extensive limestone cave system in Italy, known as Antro del Corchia. In a small saddle 1km from Foce di Mosceta, track 9 drops steeply off the ridge to the west, heading for the village of Levigliani, and after a

little over 500m, in another small saddle track 122 heads south towards Pruno while No 123, not as defined but more clearly marked than No 122, continues to the southwest towards Retignano.

Leave the ridge on track 122, dropping past some small clusters of decrepit buildings, and one or two well maintained ones. Track markers are infrequent but the walking is easy. Half an hour from the ridge top the track joins a steep, winding, sealed road but after only a couple of minutes leaves it again at a red-and-white marker painted on the corner of a building on the left. A further 15 minutes, mostly spent on a venerable stone-paved mule track, brings you to Pruno, where track 122 descends a flight of concrete steps to meet the asphalt at a car park and a park information board.

From Pruno it's sealed road all the way. In clear conditions Monte Forato is seen to good advantage above and to the east. Once on the valley bottom, which you reach at the lower end of Cardoso (30 minutes from Pruno), it's an unappealing trudge of 2km down the valley, past buildings still showing evidence of the extensive damage done by floods in 1996, to Ponte Stazzemese.

sea of pink in the Julian Alps

la Prevala's glaciated view

Range upon range – Monte Mangart in the Julian Alps

dge of the Gods – the Sentiero Anita Goitan *via ferrata* (iron way)

Essential *via ferrata* equipment

A classic Chianti hills scene – rustic buildings, vineyards and gentle, wooded slopes

Late afternoon in the Apuan Alps, looking north from the summit ridge of Pania della Croce

Dense beech forests cover the valleys and slopes of Tuscany's Apuan Alps

Central Apennines

The Apennines form the backbone of the Italian peninsula, extending for 1300km from the Ligurian Alps in the northwest of the country all the way to the Strait of Messina and into Sicily. This lengthy chain is grandest in a 200km section that straddles three regions: Abruzzo, the Marches (Le Marche) and Umbria. Within this area lie four national parks; including the second national park created in Italy (the Parco Nazionale d'Abruzzo), and three newer parks created in 1993 to expand protected habitat for endangered species and create a linked system of conservation zones. Together these parks and their associated nature reserves form an almost contiguous zone of protected land 6000 sq km in size.

The wild scenery begins in the southern area of the Marches with the bald summits and craggy ridges of the Parco Nazionale dei Monti Sibillini. High walks can be found on the area's long, narrow ridges, while thousands of feet below, the famous limestone gorge of L'Infernaccio offers shady pockets of cool air on hot summer days.

Slightly further south lies the Parco Nazionale del Gran Sasso e Monti della Laga also known as Gran Sasso-Laga), in northern Abruzzo. The Gran Sasso Range features impressive mountain scenery, with the undisputed centre point being the rock pyramid of Corno Grande (2912m), the highest summit in the Apennines. Often overshadowed by such superlatives, the adjoining Monti della Laga attracts walkers to the gentler pleasures of exploring waterfalls deep within forested valleys.

To the southeast of Gran Sasso, the remote Parco Nazionale della Majella is characterised by rounded, scree-covered summits and a long history of human habitation. To the southwest, the Central Apennines culminate in the woodland and ridges of the Parco Nazionale d'Abruzzo.

All these national parks are fringed by a network of valleys and scattered hill villages, and the whole region has the feel of

Highlights

GARETH McCORMACK

High on the western ridge of Corno Grande (2914m), the Apennines' highest summit

- Crossing a long, narrow and airy ridge, and several panoramic peaks on the Sibillini Traverse (p263)
- Scrambling to the summit of the highest mountain in the Apennines on the Corno Grande walk (p268)
- Keeping an eye out for bears in the forested valleys of the Parco Nazionale d'Abruzzo (p273)

a place passed over by the fast-moving commercialism of modern life. The downside of this is that visitor conveniences such as public transport, tourist centres and well-stocked equipment stores can be few and far between (make sure to bring all equipment for your trip). But if getting away from it all and seeking out little-visited mountain scenery and traditional ways of life seems attractive, then the Central Apennines are definitely for you.

Central Apennines

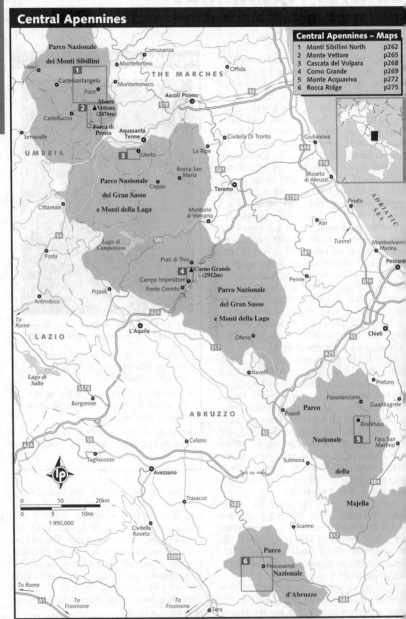

Central Apennines – Maps

1	Monti Sibillini North	p262
2	Monte Vettore	p265
3	Cascata del Volpara	p268
4	Corno Grande	p269
5	Monte Acquaviva	p272
6	Rocca Ridge	p275

CLIMATE

The Apennines offer an interesting mix of alpine and Mediterranean climate. Summers are warm and dry, with daytime temperatures in the valleys and slopes normally in the mid-20°Cs. Temperatures are lower on the summits but the strength of the sun may still make it feel hot, especially with so little shade available. Snow may fall on the higher ground from October to June, with the eastern side of the range receiving the lion's share. Maximum daytime temperatures during the winter can be as low as 3°C in the highest inhabited areas; such cold weather has enabled Europe's most southerly glacier to survive beneath the northeast face of Corno Grande.

INFORMATION
Maps & Books

Touring Club Italiano's 1:200,000 map *Umbria e Marche* and *Abruzzo e Molise* are ideal for general orientation. See the Planning section of individual walks for specific map requirements.

Stephen Fox's *Central Apennines of Italy: Walks, Scrambles & Climbs*, published in the UK by Cicerone, suggests a range of day walks within the Sibillini and Gran Sasso-Laga national parks.

Emergency

For medical assistance contact the **national emergency number** (☎ 118). In Abruzzo here is also the **mountain rescue service** (☎ 167 25 82 39).

GATEWAY
Pescara

A heavily developed beach resort and commercial centre, Pescara is the main eastern transport hub for the Marches and Abruzzo. The **IAT office** (☎ 085 42 90 02 12; Via Nicola Fabrizi 171) can provide full accommodation listings.

Places to Stay & Eat At the cheaper end of the scale are **Albergo Nuova Locanda** (☎ 085 69 37 47; Via Orazio 86; doubles €25.80) and **Albergo Aterno** (☎ 085 69 04 0; Via Bastioni 26; doubles €25.80).

Cross the River Pescara to find the reasonably priced restaurant/pizzeria **Pinguino** (☎ 085 628 69; Corso Manthonè 36). **Cantina di Jooz** (☎ 085 451 88 00; Via delle Caserme 61) is more expensive but offers more subtle cuisine.

Getting There & Away Pescara is on the main train line along the Adriatic coast, and is easily accessible from most other Italian cities, with direct services to centres such as Bologna, Ancona and Rome. **ARPA** (☎ 085 421 50 99) has bus services to destinations throughout Abruzzo, and several companies offer around five services daily to/from Rome (2½ hours). Buses leave from outside the train station on Piazzale della Repubblica.

Pescara is at a major road junction, with the A14 leading north and south along the Adriatic, and the A25 leading west to Rome.

Parco Nazionale dei Monti Sibillini

In the southwest corner of the Marches, the Parco Nazionale dei Monti Sibillini covers almost 710 sq km and encompasses more than 20 peaks over 2000m in height. The highest point of the Monti Sibillini range is the summit of Monte Vettore (King's Mountain; 2476m). The park was established in 1993, and over 16,000 people live in small, traditional communities within its boundaries.

NATURAL HISTORY

The park is home to 1800 species of plant, 50 species of mammal and 150 species of bird. Wolves, porcupines, wildcats and martens roam the area, while snow voles remain, a relic of the last ice age. The chamois (a cross between a goat and an antelope) is a recent reintroduction. Among the more charismatic bird species here are golden eagles (also successfully reintroduced), sparrowhawks and eagle owls. The park also marks the northernmost habitat in Italy of Orsini's viper. The lower slopes are characterised by forests of oak and beech, with the tree line generally around 1750m.

PLANNING
Maps & Books
The CAI (Club Alpino Italiano) map *Parco Nazionale dei Monti Sibillini* and Edizioni Multigraphic's map *Parco Nazionale dei Sibillini* both cover the park at 1:25,000, and are suitable for walking. There's also the Kompass 1:50,000 map No 666 *Monti Sibillini.*

Parco Nazionale dei Sibillini: Le Piú Belle Escursioni, by Alberico Alesi & Maurizio Calibani, details a variety of walks within the park, but is available in Italian only.

Information Sources
For further information on the area contact the **park headquarters** *(Ente Parco Nazionale dei Monti Sibillini; ☎ 0737 97 27 11; w www .sibillini.net; Largo GB Gaola Antinori, 1-62039 Visso).*

ACCESS TOWNS & FACILITIES
Montemonaco
On the eastern boundary of the park, Montemonaco (1080m) is a picturesque hilltop village that receives a surprising number of visitors during the summer.

The **park office** *(☎ 0736 85 64 62; Via Roma)* is in the centre of the village, while maps and guidebooks for the area are available from both the **general store** and the *alimentari* in the main square. The nearest **petrol station** is 8km to the north in Montefortino.

A Mythological History

Today's national park sits atop the mythical kingdom of Sibilla Cumana, infamous throughout Europe for its necromancers and devilish connections during the 15th and 16th centuries. Queen of horrors was Sibilla herself, a prophetess and communicator with the dead who lured brave knights to their deaths. Sibilla's lair was a cave on the slopes of Monte Sibilla. When the evil enchantress finally died legend has it her body was dragged into the waters of Lago di Pilato (beneath Monte Vettore) by a herd of buffalo, where it was consumed by red waves.

Places to Stay & Eat In the centre of the village is **Albergo Sibilla** *(☎ 0736 85 61 44 Via Roma 52; twins €38.75).* The **Albergo Carlini** *(☎ 0736 85 61 27; Via Roma 18; twin €43.90)* is nearby. Both include breakfast

Around 5km northwest of town, **Rifugio Sibilla** *(☎ 0736 85 64 22; dorm beds/half board €10.35/38.75)* is up a steep grave road, just off the road to Isola S Biagio. The location of the *rifugio* (mountain hut) at an altitude of 1540m and almost beneath the peak of Monti Sibilla, is impressive.

Almost all the hotels in Montemonaco have **restaurants** offering evening meals and **La Scampagnata** *(☎ 0736 85 63 92; Vi Don Settimio Vallorano)* has good pizza.

Getting There & Away Montemonaco i reasonably well served by buses. **Co Tra VA** *(☎ 0734 22 99 03)* runs from Rome to Aman dola via Montemonaco (four hours and 1 minutes, two a day). **Mazzuca** *(☎ 0736 40 2 67)* buses travel to Ascoli Piceno (three day), from where there are frequent connec tions east to Pescara.

Camping Montespino
About 4km north of Montemonaco toward Montefortino (along the road signed t Amandola) is Camping Montespino *(☎ 073 85 92 38; 2 people with tent/cabins €13.45 28.40).* The bus service from Rome to Aman dola (see Getting There & Away, above, fo Montemonaco) passes this camping ground

Castelsantangelo
This small village lies beneath the stee slopes of Monte Bove. There are limited fa cilities within the village, but it makes good base for walks in the area. The **par office** *(☎ 0737 97 00 89; Via Roma 19)* is o the main road at the north end of the village There are several small *alimentari,* bu maps, guidebooks and petrol should all b bought in Visso, 7km to the north.

Places to Stay & Eat The closest accom modation to Castelsantangelo is **Alberg dal Navigante** *(☎ 0737 98 10 60; double €46.50),* in Nocelleto, 2km south of the vil lage. Breakfast is included.

Otherwise **Hotel La Fiorita** (☎ 0737 983 ?1; half board €43.90) is about 7km south-ast towards Castelluccio, but is even closer o the mountains. The closest camping ;round, **Monti Prata** (☎ 0737 97 00 62; 2 *people with tent €15.80)*, is 5.5km south ilong the road to Castelluccio. All these ac-ommodation options have **restaurants** on ite, though **Il Bucaneve** (☎ 0737 981 12), in the main road at the south end of the vil-age, is a traditional-style alternative.

;etting There & Away Use **Contram SPA buses** (☎ 0737 63 24 02) to travel to and rom Visso (seven a day), where there are connections to Rome (three a day).

La Gola dell'Infernaccio

Duration	3 hours
Distance	8.5km
Difficulty	easy
Start/Finish	L'Infernaccio trailhead
Nearest Town	Montemonaco (p260)
Transport	private

Summary An easy and justifiably popular walk through a deep and twisted limestone gorge. Continuing to the head of the valley provides escape from the sightseers and offers good mountain views.

.a Gola dell'Infernaccio is probably the nost impressive gorge in the Apennine Range. The start of the walk is a short drive rom Montemonaco, and the most dramatic part of the gorge is only a few minutes' valk from the parking area. Such easy ac-ess attracts plenty of people and the early tages of the walk are marred by the poor oilet habits of some visitors! Overlooking his, the continuation of the path leads gen-ly up through pleasant beech forest, cross-ng the rushing stream several times to arrive at an open meadow at the head of the valley. For an easy half-day walk involving 350m of ascent, simply return along the ame route. If you prefer more of a chal-enge take up one of the options given for xtending this walk.

PLANNING
When to Walk
The walk will be at its most impressive dur-ing the thaw from May to late June, when the stream is full. To escape the worst crowds avoid weekends and walk early or late in the day.

What to Bring
Bring water as the stream should not be trusted without filtering.

Maps
Although it isn't strictly necessary to carry a map unless you plan to go beyond the head of the valley, the best map for the walk is the CAI 1:25,000 *Parco Nazionale dei Monti Sibillini*.

GETTING TO/FROM THE WALK
Public transport will take you only as far as Montemonaco, 6km from the start. From there follow signposts for the village of Isola S Biagio, and then for L'Infernaccio itself. The final 2km are along a gravel road, with plenty of room to park at the end.

THE WALK (see map p262)
Follow the wide track as it descends steeply beneath the limestone cliffs. After 10 or 15 minutes you reach a bridge crossing the Fosso Tenna at the mouth of the gorge. Drips from the overhanging limestone walls on the left provide a refreshing shower even in late summer. Cross the stream and climb steeply into the **gorge**, descending to a sec-ond bridge between rock walls only a few metres apart. The stream cuts a virtual tun-nel through the rock here, and the path de-tours around to the left to recross the stream via a third bridge (particularly impressive and noisy if there is a lot of water).

From this bridge the path is forced away from the stream and climbs around a house-size boulder, while the water passes through a narrow defile to its left. Climb past a fourth and fifth bridge to where the gorge widens out and shady beech forest takes hold. A side path climbs through the trees to the right, signposted for the natural springs at San Leonardo. This path also leads to the high-level route that traverses the slopes above the north walls of the gorge.

On the main trail, the gorge soon begins to close in once again. On the left, two tributaries flow down from spectacular gorges cut into the southern walls. Cross again to the right (north) side of the Fosso Tenna and climb more steeply through attractive woodland reaching the meadows at **Cerasa**, 1½ to two hours from the start. An obvious hill with a small ruin on the left gives splendid views back down L'Infernaccio and also across the slopes of the surrounding mountains.

Retrace your steps to the start, or more ambitious walkers can extend the route from the meadow along several different trails. One option is to return to the start by climbing up to either of the trails traversing the steep slopes on the north and south sides of the gorge (allow four to five hours). Alternatively, by climbing higher still on the south side, walkers can join up with the Sibillini Traverse (p263) and enjoy several kilometres of airy ridge walking, returning to either the start of La Gola dell'Infernaccio, or to Montemonaco (allow five to seven hours for each option).

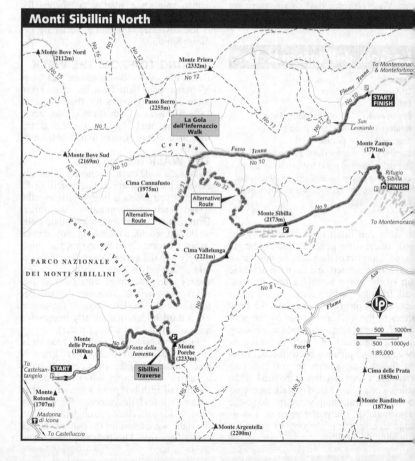

Sibillini Traverse

Duration	4½–6 hours
Distance	13km
Difficulty	moderate–demanding
Start	Monte delle Prata parking area
Finish	Rifugio Sibilla
Nearest Towns	Castelsantangelo (p260), Montemonaco (p260)
Transport	private

Summary A long, narrow ridge crosses the Sibillini Range, offering great views and very memorable walking.

This route traverses the heart of the Parco Nazionale dei Monti Sibillini, offering vistas across most of its peaks and giving a wonderful overview of the area. However, the views around you will often take second place to what is going on underfoot, because the terrain covered is impressive to say the least. The main ridge section of the route stretches for over 4km along a continuously narrow spine of rock. Almost entirely airy without being dangerously exposed, there are three short rock steps that demand the use of hands and perhaps deserve a 'hard' grading, around the peak of Monti Sibilla. The ridge crosses three major summits and nine intermediary peaks over 2000m in height, with the first peak, Monte Porche, providing the highest point at 2233m. The day's ascent is 975m.

Unless you have two cars, the A-to-B format of this walk can cause difficulties as no public transport connects the start and finish. Another option is to start from either end and go as far as you choose along the ridge before returning to your starting point. Or you could make two days of it, see the Alternative Route: via Valle Langa (p264).

PLANNING
When to Walk
The ridge is exposed to the elements and has few escape routes; avoid walking in high winds and if lightning is possible. Wet weather will also lessen the friction of the rock, making it slippery.

What to Bring
No water is available between the Fonte della Iumenta spring towards the beginning of the route and the Rifugio Sibilla at the end – be sure to carry plenty.

Maps
The best map for the walk is the CAI 1:25,000 *Parco Nazionale dei Monti Sibillini*.

GETTING TO/FROM THE WALK
From Castelsantangelo, take the road southeast towards Castelluccio. After around 10km of climbing the Forca di Gualdo and the little church of Madonna di Icona are reached. From here, take the paved road leading east, signed to Monte Prata, following it for 2.5km to the large gravel Monte Prata parking area.

From the Rifugio Sibilla it is 5km to Montemonaco. Follow the winding gravel access road down to a paved road and turn right. Follow signs to the left 1.5km later to reach the centre of the village.

THE WALK (see map p262)
Take the gravel track that leads east from the parking area, passing around a vehicle barrier soon after the start. Look out for trail 6 as the track contours around the southeastern slopes of Monte Prata. This path is not marked or obvious, and many people simply continue along the track to arrive at the Fonte della Iumenta, where they rejoin trail 6. A footpath – faint at first – leads off to the north of the spring. Red paint splashes and an increasingly worn trail soon reassure you that you are on trail 6.

Wide switchbacks lead up a hillside to a shoulder, where the path veers southeast to begin the climb of Monte Porche's west face. Join trail 1 at a cairn shortly before reaching the ridge between Monte Porche and Monte Argentella. From the ridge, turn sharp left and begin the steep climb north up open terrain (no path) to the summit of **Monte Porche**. Allow two to 2½ hours to reach this point. An incredible panorama of the Sibillini Range awaits at the summit cairn, including an impressive view of the ridge on which you are about to embark. Do not be put off – it is rarely the knife-edge that it might appear.

Cross a small rise to the northeast of the summit and pick up the path that descends onto the ridge itself. The terrain is generally rocky underfoot as the ridge undulates towards and past Cima Vallelunga (2198m). The path is obvious throughout, sometimes using the top of the ridge and sometimes dropping off to contour just below it on either side. Intermittent red paint splashes and old signposts mark the way, and views down into the valleys on either side are continually impressive. The only easy escape route is at a col beneath Monte Sibilla, 3km along the ridge from Monte Porche, where a gravel track leads down to the Rifugio Sibilla. Following this track will avoid the most difficult (but perhaps the most enjoyable) terrain around Monte Sibilla.

Monte Sibilla (2173m) is undoubtedly the most visually impressive summit on the ridge, and the narrow fin of pink rock can look intimidating on the approach. Again, it is easier than it looks, although hands will be called on for one or two short sections of easy scrambling on the final climb to the top. A black memorial cross marks the summit, reached around 3½ to 4½ hours from the start. From here the ridge is generally grassy, with the exception of a rock step just a few hundred metres below the summit. Hands will be called on again to negotiate this, and a short metal cable provides assistance.

The path is well worn, and marked by blue as well as red paint, as it descends gently over the grassy ridge. Around 1.5km from Monte Sibilla the path leaves the ridge and contours around the southern slopes of an unnamed peak, eventually returning to the ridge at a saddle. One more short rise is climbed before the path to the **Rifugio Sibilla** (see Montemonaco, p260) leads off the ridge to the east. Descend on this path as it zigzags down through a hollow, with the *rifugio* soon coming into sight below.

Alternative Route: via Valle Langa
3–5 hours, 8km

To overcome the lack of public transport connecting the start and finish points, you can overnight at Rifugio Sibilla, and return by trails 32 and 31 for a change of scenery.

Monte Vettore

Duration	4–4½ hours
Distance	10km
Difficulty	moderate–demanding
Start/Finish	Forca di Presta
Nearest Towns	Castelsantangelo (p260), Montemonaco (p260)
Transport	private

Summary The highest mountain in the Sibillini Range, Monte Vettore can be climbed in a few hours by a strenuous path rising from the Forca di Presta.

Local walkers would probably not consider the 10km (942m ascent) route from the Forca di Presta to be the connoisseur's approach to Monte Vettore, since the longer and harder route from the Valle Lago di Pilato is undoubtedly less crowded and more scenic. However, the Forca di Presta route has much to offer. The well-formed trail and relatively high starting point mean that it is the easiest and most straightforward option and it does give fantastic and almost immediate views south across the Monti della Laga. Once on the shoulder at the basic and unstaffed Rifugio T Zilioli there are also great views down the Valle Lago di Pilato. The ascent is steep and unrelenting, and plenty of water should be carried, especially on a hot day when the south-facing slopes can really bake. This popular route can be crowded on summer weekends.

PLANNING
When to Walk
Choose fine weather between June and October for this walk and avoid windy days. You should also avoid days when the cloud is down and when there is a chance of electrical storms.

What to Bring
Bring plenty of water as there is none along the route.

Maps
The best map is the CAI 1:25,000 *Parco Nazionale dei Monti Sibillini*.

NEAREST TOWNS & FACILITIES

See Castelsantangelo (p260) and Monte-monaco (p260).

Rifugio degli Alpini

The Rifugio degli Alpini (☎ 0736 80 92 78; dorm beds/half board €10.35/33.55) is well positioned on a hillside overlooking the Forca di Presta at the beginning of the walk.

GETTING TO/FROM THE WALK

There is no public transport to the start of the walk. You will need to read your map carefully if you're approaching by car from Montemonaco. Navigate to Montegallo and then look out for a right turn at a junction that will take you up to the Forca di Presta.

The approach via Castelsantangelo is much more straightforward. Follow the signs for Castelluccio and take a left turn at a junction a few kilometres south of Castelluccio. This road leads up to the Forca di Presta.

The route starts opposite the signpost for the Rifugio delgi Alpini and there is plenty of roadside parking.

THE WALK

Follow the obvious trail onto the grassy slopes above the Forca di Presta. The gradient is moderate at first but soon steepens. In places the trail is littered with loose stones and progress can be tiring. After ascending for 45 minutes to an hour, the gradient eases and the trail sides around the southeastern slopes for a few hundred metres, leading to a small saddle where a rest can be taken.

From this saddle the trail climbs steeply and passes beneath the summit of Monte Vettoretto (2052m) before climbing into a small saddle just to the north of that summit. From here you can walk the short distance (two minutes) out onto the **summit**, which is really no more than a bump on the ridge, but from where there are great views across to the Monti della Laga.

Again the trail steepens as you leave the brief respite of the saddle, climbing diagonally across steep slopes. The **Rifugio T Zilioli** is just visible on the skyline, but you

must negotiate a very steep and eroded section of trail and an awkward outcrop of rock before finally reaching it, 1½ to two hours from the start. The *rifugio* has sleeping platforms but is otherwise a fairly unappealing shelter.

If you have the time and the inclination, from here you can make a worthwhile detour to Cima del Lago (see Side Trip, p266).

Continuing on the main trail, head northeast from the *rifugio*, enjoying the fantastic view down into the Valle Lago di Pilato. After a few hundred metres the slopes steepen and the trail soon begins to make large switchbacks as you near the summit of **Monte Vettore** (2476m), which is reached 2¼ to three hours from the start. From here the great bald summits and ridges of the northern Sibillini are revealed for the first time, and on a clear day you should also be able to make out the Adriatic coast.

Retrace your steps down to the Forca di Presta.

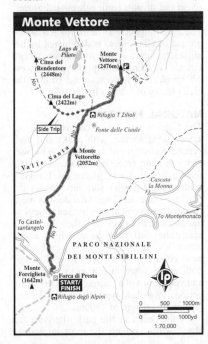

Side Trip: Cima del Lago
40–50 minutes, 1.6km
This fine, rocky and at times narrow ridge gives airy views and adds a little excitement to the main route.

From Rifugio T Zilioli head west on trail 1, eventually swinging around to the northwest and Cima del Lago.

Parco Nazionale del Gran Sasso e Monti della Laga

Although they have been incorporated into one 2030 sq km national park, the regions of Gran Sasso and Monti della Laga are quite distinct in terms of their geology, ecology and the style of walking there. The terrain of Monti della Laga is characterised by deep, wooded valleys, with numerous rivers and streams cutting through the sandstone rock to form spectacular waterfalls. The much higher and more rugged alpine ground of Gran Sasso is dominated by the highest summit in the Apennines, Corno Grande (2912m); an impressive yet accessible peak rising in great splendour from the high plateau of Campo Imperatore.

NATURAL HISTORY
The Gran Sasso Range consists of limestone and dolomite, with peaks and high vertical walls gouged out over time by both water erosion (creating numerous karstic features) and ancient glaciation. Europe's southernmost glacier still survives on the northern slopes of Corno Grande. The more rounded peaks and deeply incised valleys of the Monti della Laga owe their form to a sandstone-marl rock base, which keeps water flowing on the surface. Beech is the most common tree on the lower slopes of both areas, often interspersed with holly and yew (relics of a warmer, wetter climatic period). Woodland typically covers the valleys up to a height of 1800m.

Of the fauna in the park, the Abruzzo chamois has perhaps the most interesting story to tell. A rare species of chamois exclusive to the Apennines, Gran Sasso was once the centre of its territory, until it was hunted to extinction in the area towards the end of the 19th century. Around a century later it was reintroduced, and there are currently around 50 chamois in the region. This is also an important habitat for Orsini's viper, an insect-preying snake that lives in greater numbers here than in any other part of Italy.

PLANNING
Maps & Books
Selca publish a two-map set entitled *Parco Nazionale del Gran Sasso e Monti della Laga*, which covers the park at a scale of 1:50,000. A larger-scale map is not available for Monti della Laga. Much better for walking in the Gran Sasso area is the CAI 1:25,000 *Gran Sasso d'Italia*. For general orientation there's the Kompass 1:50,000 map No 669 *Gran Sasso d'Italia; L'Aquila*

Gran Sasso: Le Più Belle Escursioni, by Alberico Alesi, Maurizio Calibani and Antonio Palermi, details a wide variety of walks within the park. An English supplement is available.

Information Sources
Contact the **park headquarters** (*Ente Parco Nazionale del Gran Sasso e Monti della Laga*, ☎ 0862 40 19 03; ⓦ www.gransassolagapark.it; Via Roma 10–12, 67100 L'Aquila) for information.

ACCESS TOWNS
Acquasanta Terme
On the northern boundary of the park, Acquasanta Terme is a small town whose traditional charm has not been marred by the main road that makes it so accessible today. The town's **visitor centre** (☎ 0736 80 12 91, *Piazza XX Septembre*), is next door to the **park office** (☎ 0736 80 27 97). There are several *alimentari* in town and a **supermarket** just up the road towards Umito, but walking maps of the area can be difficult to obtain.

Places to Stay & Eat The Albergo Roma (☎ 0736 80 13 25; Corso Schiavi 5; doubles €33.55) is very central while **Albergo Terme**

'☎ 0736 80 12 63; Piazza Terme 20; doubles €46.50) is alongside the main road.

Most of the hotels in town have **restaurants**, and the Albergo Terme is a favourite for lunch with the locals. **Il Sole** *(☎ 0335 591 44 28)*, on the main road towards the west of town, is a good pizzeria with a traditional wood-fired oven and rooftop seating.

Getting There & Away Catch **Camelini N & Figli buses** *(☎ 0736 25 90 91)* to travel to and from Rome (three a day). Heading east, **Contravat buses** *(☎ 0736 34 22 43)* run to and from Ascoli Piceno (nine a day), from where there are connections to the east coast and Pescara. By car, Acquasanta Terme is 182km east of Rome along the S4, and 102km northwest of Pescara via the A14 and the S4.

Fonte Cerreto
The main access village on the southern side of Gran Sasso, Fonte Cerreto (1120m) is a small, purpose-built settlement. The village consists mainly of hotels, a camping ground and the cable car that runs to Campo Imperatore. The **park office** *(☎ 0862 60 61 33)* sells maps and guidebooks. Few practical supplies are available in the village, besides the very limited selection of goods (including maps) available at **La Villetta** *(☎ 0862 60 61 71)*, which also has meals and snacks.

Places to Stay & Eat Campers should try **Funivia del Gran Sasso** camping ground *(☎ 0862 60 61 63; 2 people with tent €17.55)*. **La Villetta** *(☎ 0862 60 61 71; doubles €56.80)* is the cheapest of the *alberghi* and includes breakfast. All the **hotels** in the village have **restaurants**.

Getting There & Away Fonte Cerreto is the end of the line for **ARPA buses** *(☎ 0862 41 28 08)* journeying to and from L'Aquila (nine a day). Take bus No 6 leaving from Via Castello in L'Aquila. From L'Aquila, there are frequent bus and train connections to both Rome and Pescara.

By car, Fonte Cerreto is 124km east of Rome via the A24, and around 90km northwest of Pescara via the A14 and the A24.

Cascata del Volpara

Duration	3½–4½ hours
Distance	8km
Difficulty	moderate
Start/Finish	Umito
Nearest Town	Acquasanta Terme (p266)
Transport	private

Summary A small path leads through beautiful beech woodland to the base of the towering Volpara waterfall.

The Cascata del Volpara is among the highest and most spectacular of the many waterfalls in the Monti della Laga Range. On the way to the fall, this route also explores a section of pristine beech woodland, which is as beautiful as any forested slope in the Apennines. The day's ascent is 512m.

PLANNING
When to Walk
The waterfall is at its best in spring or early summer. Avoid walking after rain when the ground can become very slippery.

What to Bring
Although not long, the route, particularly towards the waterfall, is sometimes steep and rough; good boots are essential.

Maps
The northern sheet of Selca's 1:50,000 *Parco Nazionale del Gran Sasso e Monti della Laga* covers the area, though waterfalls are incorrectly positioned and the path isn't marked.

GETTING TO/FROM THE WALK
Take the road to Umito that leads south from the eastern edge of Acquasanta Terme, and continue for 9km. Just before the turning circle at the end of the road in Umito, is a narrow gravel track on the right, signed to Volpara. Follow this for 1km and park beside a footbridge.

THE WALK
Head up the gravel track from the parking area, climbing to a small white building after 2km. The track ends here and a mud

path continues, quickly entering thick beech woodland. The path is immediately attractive, skirting beneath small rock escarpments amidst the trees. The climb is sustained, with switchbacks in places, though the beauty of the plants and flowers of the forest floor, set against the lime green leaves of the beech offers plenty of distraction. At times it is necessary to step over or duck under fallen branches.

Around 1km into the wood the trail passes a grotto beneath a large boulder. Within another few hundred metres there is a second grotto, with entrance wall, doorway, window, and interior oven all virtually intact. These caves served as shelters for local woodsmen until relatively recently. Soon after the grottoes, cross a patch of waist-high vegetation and a stream before reaching the picturesque **Cascata della Prata**.

The route then joins the Volpara stream, and follows up its east bank into more mature beech woodland. The ground underfoot is sometimes rough and steep. An alternative trail joins the main path from the left, and a short climb leads out of the beech trees and into thicker vegetation. You are now close to the Volpara falls, but the path degenerates into something of a maze and it can be difficult to find the way. The best advice is to watch for forks diligently, and keep right at every occasion. Two streams are crossed, and there is a good view of the entire height of the **Cascata del Volpara** from the second. Following this, a steep, rocky section of path leads to a fallen tree. Turn right here (the main path

continues as steep switchbacks into mor beech woodland) to reach the base of rock slab 50m high that forms the lowe falls. This point should be reached two t 2½ hours from the start.

Retrace your steps to the starting point.

Corno Grande

Duration	5–6 hours
Distance	9km
Difficulty	moderate–demanding
Start/Finish	Campo Imperatore (p269)
Nearest Town	Fonte Cerreto (p267)
Transport	cable car
Summary	An impressive and surprisingly

straightforward route to the summit of the highest peak in the Apennines.

As the highest peak in the Apennines Corno Grande (2912m) receives a lot of at tention from walkers, especially since it i so readily accessible from high-altitud starting points at either Campo Imperatore or Prati di Tivo. It even attracts its fair shar of nonwalkers, some of whom find th steep ground more than they bargained for The impressive rock peak has extremely steep faces and from most viewpoints look like the preserve of climbers.

The *via normale* (normal route) provide a relatively straightforward, well-marked out-and-back route. It is graded moderate-demanding because of the steep slopes (the day's ascent is 812m) towards the top. A long as care is taken these should present n problem for most walkers, and the physica demands are really more on a par with walk of a moderate grade.

For a more challenging option see the Al ternative Route: via the West Ridge (p270)

PLANNING
When to Walk

Depending on the previous winter's snow fall, the route should be largely free o snow from early June. The first snows o autumn can be expected in late September or early October, after which the mountain

Cascata del Volpara

Scale 0–500–1000m / 0–500–1000yd 1:65,000

To Acquasanta Terme · ▲ Monte Pozza (1186m) · Umito · START/FINISH · Fiume della Montagna · Parco Nazionale del Gran Sasso e Monti della Laga · Rio Saltarello · Cascata della Prata · Rio Volgara · Cascata del Volpara · Rio della Prata

is best left to alpinists. Even in midsummer conditions can turn nasty, so pick a fine, clear day with light winds. Also consider making an early start to avoid both the crowds and the strong sun, which can reflect quite intensely from the limestone.

What to Bring
There are no reliable water sources on this route, so bring plenty.

Maps
Use the CAI 1:25,000 *Gran Sasso d'Italia*.

NEAREST TOWN & FACILITIES
See Fonte Cerreto (p267).

Campo Imperatore
The small group of buildings where the cable car terminates and the plateau that stems from it, are both known as Campo Imperatore (2135m).

Accommodation options include **Hotel Campo Imperatore** (☎ 0862 40 00 00; B&B/ half board €31/46.50), which also has a bar and restaurant, and **Rifugio Duca Degli Abruzzi** (☎ 0347 623 21 01; half board €25.80), on a ridge a steep 30-minute walk north of the hotel.

There is also a **bar** and **restaurant** at the cable-car station.

Getting There & Away Arrive and depart Campo Imperatore via the **cable car** (☎ 0862 60 61 43), which heads up the mountain from Fonte Cerreto (one way/return €6.20/ 9.30, every 30 minutes from 8.30am to 6pm). Campo Imperatore is also accessible by driving 25km east from Fonte Cerreto.

THE WALK
Leave the Campo Imperatore main parking area and walk north, passing to the left of the observatory. Follow the obvious stony track that zigzags up the steep slope towards the **Rifugio Duca degli Abruzzi** (see Campo Imperatore, above), which is just visible on the skyline. About a third of the way to the *rifugio*, turn right at a signposted junction and follow a narrow path traversing steep slopes to the northeast. The path climbs around a

shoulder, revealing good views of Corno Grande's south face, and then climbs through steep switchbacks to a ridge at the Sella di Monte Aquila (45 minutes to one hour from the start). Turn right along the ridge and then left at a signposted junction a little further along. The right fork leads to the direct route up Corno Grande's south face, which is a challenging scramble, best left to walkers with climbing experience.

Follow the delightful trail across grassy slopes at the head of Valle Maone, continuing straight ahead at a junction. Prominent cliffs and scree rise beneath the west ridge

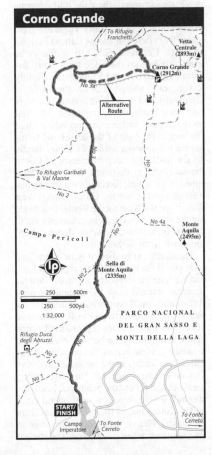

Corno Grande

To Rifugio Franchetti

Vetta Centrale (2893m)

Corno Grande (2912m)

No 3

No 3a

Alternative Route

No 3

To Rifugio Garibaldi & Val Maone

No 2

No 4

No 4a

Monte Aquila (2495m)

Campo Pericoli

Sella di Monte Aquila (2335m)

No 2

0   250   500m
0   250   500yd
1:32,000

Rifugio Duca degli Abruzzi

No 2

No 1

PARCO NACIONAL DEL GRAN SASSO E MONTI DELLA LAGA

START/ FINISH

Campo Imperatore

To Fonte Cerreto

To Fonte Cerreto

Corno Grande

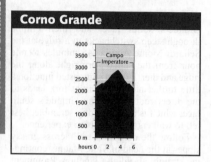

of Corno Grande (snow may persist here into early summer), where the trail steepens and climbs to the foot of the west ridge (1½ to two hours from the start). There are great views from here out across Campo Pericoli to Pizzo Cefalone (2533m). Follow the paint splashes up the ridge for a short distance (be careful not to follow the slightly lower trail signposted to the Rifugio Garibaldi), and then climb around the stony northwest flanks of the mountain. The trail soon steepens and zigzags up into a large flat area at the base of the deep bowl forming the northwestern side of Corno Grande. To the north the steep buttresses of Corno Picolo (2655m) dominate the view. Paint splashes on a rock direct more adventurous walkers right to join the *Cresta Ouest* (West Ridge; see the Alternative Route, this page) but the *via normale* continues across a small depression and onto the scree slopes sweeping down from the summit.

The change in gradient is quite abrupt and soon you'll find yourself picking a way back and forth up the steep, loose ground. Not far from the summit ridge the ground steepens further and you'll need to use your hands for balance in places. After 30 to 40 minutes of effort you should reach a **prominent notch** on the summit ridge, where the rocks frame a fantastic view across the remains of the Calderone Glacier to the pinnacles on Corno Grande's central summit. Turn right along the ridge and follow the paint splashes to the **summit**, where there is a small metal cross and a visitors book (10 or 15 minutes from the notch). The view is spectacular, even in late summer when haze blurs the distant

horizons. All around, the mountain seems to drop away in impossibly steep rock walls, leaving most walkers with a great sense of achievement at having reached the summit of such an apparently improbable peak.

Retrace your steps to return to Campo Imperatore, taking particular care when descending the steep ground from the summit ridge.

Alternative Route: via the West Ridge

45 minutes–1 hour, 1km

The ascent can be spiced up by climbing the *cresta ouest* on the way up, and then descending on the *via normale*. This option requires some scrambling (use of hands for balance) across a moderately exposed rock ridge. Although previous climbing experience would be desirable, the use of ropes is not necessary and the route is suitable for confident walkers with a reasonable head for heights.

Parco Nazionale della Majella

Founded in 1993, the Parco Nazionale della Majella encompasses an 860 sq km area of the Majella mountain chain, an offshoot of the main Apennine Range. There are 30 peaks over 2000m in height clustered within the park's borders. However, the area is renowned for its alpine plateaux and rounded summits rather than for sharp peaks. Monte Amaro (2795m) marks the highest point of the park. Once the mythological home of the goddess Maja, the region became a centre of prayer and retreat for religious hermits during the middle ages. Many of the numerous abbeys and hermitages around the lower mountain slopes date from this time.

NATURAL HISTORY

Below 900m the slopes of the Majella Range are forested with oak and maple, while beech predominates above this. Around and above the tree line, at around

1700m, only stunted mountain pines grow. Almost everywhere is the yellow laburnum, and theory has it that the old local term for this plant, *majo*, is the basis of today's name Majella. The range's location between the two distinct habitats of the Apennines and Adriatic also means that a huge variety of plant life can be found here. In total the park is home to around a third of all Italian plant species, including flora from Mediterranean, alpine, Balkan and arctic species.

The park's wildlife includes wolves, Marsican brown bears, chamois and 130 species of bird, including the dotterel, which nests only here in all of Italy. Also special in the park is the rare apollo butterfly, a large butterfly with black and red spots on otherwise transparent wings. This is the only insect in Abruzzo named by **CITES** *(Convention on International Trade in Endangered Species of Wild Flora & Fauna;* w *www.cites.org)*, which protects species by ensuring trade doesn't threaten their survival.

Beware of the Dogs!

Much of the charm of the Central Apennines revolves around the interaction between the mountains and the people who live and work among them. You'll see herds of cattle, sheep and goats roaming the hillsides, often at very high altitudes, especially in fine weather. Because of predators, such as wolves, bears and lynx, in some areas you'll find the flocks closely attended by a shepherd and several dogs.

On my trip to Monte Acquaviva I was climbing a steep, gravelly section of trail when I heard dogs barking ahead. Without much more warning three large, blonde mastiffs appeared, and charged at me aggressively. They stopped a few metres away, teeth bared savagely. Behind them I saw sheep running through the stunted pines. I reached down and picked up a large rock and a brief standoff ensued while the flock moved off down the hillside. The dogs eventually turned and followed, and I was able to continue up the mountain feeling shaken by the experience.

Gareth McCormack

PLANNING
Maps
The CAI 1:25,000 *Gruppo della Majella* is the best walking map for the area.

Information Sources
For further information contact the **park headquarters** *(Ente Parco Nazionale della Majella;* ☎ *0871 80 07 13;* w *www.parks.it/parco .nazionale.majella; Palazzo di Sciascio, Via Occidentale 6, Guardiagrele)*.

Place Names
There are two commonly found variations with place names in this area. The more frequently used Majella is sometimes seen written as Maiella, while the village of Passolanciano is sometimes referred to as Passo Lanciano.

Monte Acquaviva

Duration	5½–6½ hours
Distance	14km
Difficulty	moderate
Start/Finish	Blockhaus
Nearest Town	Passolanciano (p272)
Transport	private
Summary	Fine ridge walking leads to wild mountain terrain with fantastic views of the Adriatic coast.

The long access road to the ski stations above Passolanciano provides a perfect launching pad for walkers heading into the Majella mountain group. This route has an airy feel to it, heading straight onto a fairly narrow ridge with great views on either side, before climbing up (702m ascent for the day) onto the main spine of the Majella Range. The high starting point offers relatively easy access to the mountains, although the walk is very exposed to bad weather.

There is plenty of scope for extending this route by continuing along the Majella chain, for example, to Monte Amaro (2795m). However, only the fittest walkers will be able to progress much further and still return to Blockhaus in a day.

PLANNING
When to Walk

The terrain on this route is very exposed to high winds. Fine weather during the summer months and early autumn (June to October) would be best. Avoid days when visibilty is poor.

What to Bring

A small spring just south of Monte Cavallo, an hour from the start, offers water; top up supplies here because there is no other water on the route.

Maps

The best map for the walk is the CAI's 1:25,000 *Gruppo della Majella*.

NEAREST TOWN
Passolanciano

This a small ski resort (1318m) in the northern half of the Parco Nazionale della Majella, and has a very off-season feel during the summer months.

The **visitor centre** (☎ *0871 775 55*), in a wooden cabin in the centre of the village, sells local walking maps. Just enough facilities remain open to make it a viable stop, although the nearest **alimentari** and **petrol station** are 11km northeast in Pretoro; make sure to bring all supplies with you.

Places to Stay & Eat On the edge of the village along the road to Pretoro is **Camping Majelletta** (☎ *0871 89 61 32; 2 people with tent €11.35*). Cabins are also available.

Indoor accommodation includes **Albergo Ti Bionda Suisse** (☎ *0871 89 61 11; doubles €56.80*) and for a real mountain feel, the CAI **Rifugio Pomilio** (☎ *0871 33 11 98; dorm beds/half board €18.10/38.75*), 13km west of Passolanciano towards Blockhaus. This is the highest accommodation on the mountain at 1892m.

All the accommodation options have **restaurants**, and the friendly **Bar del Sci** in the centre of Passolanciano offers pasta, panini and salads.

Getting There & Away Public transport to this remote area is somewhat disjointed. The closest bus stop to Passolanciano is in Pretoro, 11km to the northeast. **ARPA** (☎ *085 421 50 99*) buses run to and from Chieti (three a day), from where there are frequent connections to Pescara. By car, Passolanciano is 55km southwest of Pescara via the A25 and S539.

GETTING TO/FROM THE WALK

There is no public transport to the beginning of the walk. By car, from Passolanciano take the road signed to Blockhaus. Follow this for 15km to the large parking area and grotto at the end of the road.

THE WALK

Just to the right of the grotto and information board, a rough trail climbs to the ruins of the **Blockhaus fort**, a small defensive structure built in 1866 by local rebels opposed to the unification of Italy. Descend steeply from this small summit and continue south along trail 1 following a narrow

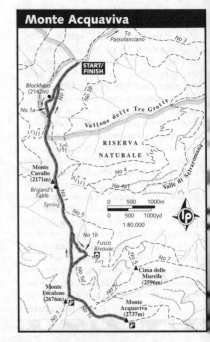

ridge with steep drop-offs on both sides. Views into the deep and rugged Vallone delle Tre Grotte are particularly impressive.

The trail continues across Monte Cavallo, and on the south side of this modest bump on the ridge you should look out for the **Brigand's Table** (*Tavola dei Briganti*) tucked away among the stunted pines. This inscribed slab of rock marked the control of this mountain vastness by the Majella rebel Di Sciascio.

The trail continues past a spring (about one hour from the start) and begins the long and fairly steep climb towards Monte Focalone. Stay to the right at a trail junction, then veer left at a second junction a few hundred metres further up the climb. Follow trail 1b as it climbs diagonally across a steep bowl to bring you onto the northeast spur of Monte Focalone. There is a fantastic view from this point into the wild alpine basin beneath Monte Focalone and Cima delle Murelle. Just a short distance to the east is the **Fusco bivouac**, a tiny yellow shelter, which can sleep four people comfortably.

Follow a line of rock cairns onto the north ridge of Monte Focalone. Continue along this ridge with great views on either side to reach the summit cairn of **Monte Focalone** (two to three hours from the start). This is a good point to assess your energy levels and the weather conditions before continuing. From here the heart of the Majella mountain group is revealed and a broad and stony ridge continues to the east, sweeping around to the plateau-like summit of Monte Acquaviva (2737m). To the southwest a succession of rugged ridges lead to the summit of Monte Amaro (2793m) – a realistic goal for fit walkers.

In clear weather the route finding between Monte Focalone and Monte Acquaviva is straightforward. An unnamed summit at 2727m is crossed without much effort, and you can expect to be at the top of **Monte Acquaviva** about 30 to 45 minutes after leaving Monte Focalone. From this point the views along the Adriatic coast are unrivalled and in clear conditions, views north to the Gran Sasso Range are also stunning. Return to Blockhaus by retracing your steps. Just

before reaching the car park, stay on trail 1 to avoid climbing back up to the ruins.

Parco Nazionale d'Abruzzo

The Parco Nazionale d'Abruzzo was established by royal decree in 1923. Subsequently enlarged several times, the protected area now covers 440 sq km and encompasses 22 towns and villages within its boundaries. The park has always been at the forefront of the conservation movement in Italy (though particularly in the last 35 years), and during this time has frequently encountered hostility from political, bureaucratic and hunting interests. Nonetheless it has managed to successfully initiate a host of campaigns to reintroduce and protect animals such as the Abruzzo chamois, Apennine wolf, lynx, deer and Marsican bear. Thanks perhaps to its longer history, it also receives more visitors (around two million annually) than most of the other parks in the area, and offers better visitor services.

NATURAL HISTORY
The limestone hills and deep valleys of the Parco Nazionale d'Abruzzo are covered by thick forests of beech, blackpine and maple. It is these forests that have offered sanctuary to the recovering populations of protected animals. In 1969 there were an estimated 60 bears, seven wolves, 150 chamois, and no trace of lynx in the park. Today there are thought to be around 100 bears, 60 wolves, 600 chamois and 10 lynx living wild within the park. Numerous other animals have also spread into neighbouring parks and reserves.

PLANNING
Maps & Books
The park-produced 1:25,000 *Carta Turistica: Parco Nazionale D'Abruzzo* is the best walking map for the area.

Stefano Ardito's book *A Piedi Nel Parco D'Abruzzo* (available in Italian only) details over 30 walks of varying difficulty within the park.

Information Sources

Contact the **park headquarters** (*Ente Parco Nazionale d'Abruzzo*; ☎ 0863 91 07 15; **w** *www.pna.it*; *Viale Santa Lucia, 67032 Pescasseroli*) for information.

Regulations

To protect the environment, it is forbidden to leave marked paths within the park. Picking flowers, damaging vegetation, dropping litter or making excessive noise are also forbidden. Camping and campfires are permitted in designated areas only.

Rifugi

The *rifugi* in the park are locked; contact the **park office** (☎ 0863 919 55) to obtain access to park-controlled huts. Facilities are minimal.

The Marsican Brown Bear

The Marsican brown bear is the symbol of the Parco Nazionale d'Abruzzo. Until recently an endangered species, numbers are slowly recovering – thanks to conservation efforts such as those initiated by the park. Marsicans are the only southern European bear species whose numbers are not diminishing. Despite a growing population it remains rare to actually see a bear in the park as they are very shy. Much more common is to find signs of its presence, such as tracks or stones that have been upturned in the search for insects.

Marsican bears are omnivores, eating berries, plants, insects and carrion. An adult male can reach over 200kg in weight, and both males and females have a natural lifespan of 25 to 30 years. Females give birth to one or two cubs in January or February, and keep their young close for about two years. The animals don't hibernate in the same way as many other bear species, but simply reduce their activity levels during the winter months.

A sub-species of the European brown bear, Marsicans demonstrate marked genetic particularities. The Abruzzi population and a smaller population in the Cantabrian mountains of Spain are the only surviving Marsican groups that remain genetically pure.

Rocca Ridge

Duration	6–7 hours
Distance	19.5km
Difficulty	moderate
Start/Finish	Pescasseroli (p274)
Transport	bus

Summary   Pristine beech woodland and a limestone-studded mountain ridge offer a flavour of the typical landscape of this beautiful national park.

Rocca Ridge dominates the skyline as you look west from Pescasseroli, with the summit of La Rocca (1924m) providing the highest point. The ridge is very accessible from the town, and offers one of the most beautiful and convenient walks in the park. This circuit passes through fine beech woodland on its way to the limestone heights (775m ascent), although the descent leads down through ski runs and lacks the same wilderness atmosphere. Views from the ridge are wonderful, and it is worth keeping an eye open for bears in the forested valleys below.

PLANNING
When to Walk

The area should be clear of snow between June and October. The ridge section of the walk is exposed to the elements and has few escape routes; avoid walking in high winds and if lightning is a possibility.

What to Bring

Water is available from the spring below the Rifugio della Difesa, but not anywhere else on the walk; make sure to bring enough.

Maps

Use the park-produced 1:25,000 *Carta Turistica: Parco Nazionale D'Abruzzo*.

NEAREST TOWN
Pescasseroli

A bustling town in the heart of the national park, Pescasseroli (1167m) offers all the amenities of a place used to receiving visitors, while still managing to retain its charm. Staff at the **tourist office** (☎ 0863 91 04 61

Via Piave 2) are friendly and helpful, while the **park office** (☎ 0863 919 55; Viale Gabriele D'Annunzio) is one of the only places in town that sells walking maps. There are plenty of *alimentari* and **general stores** in the town centre, though walking and camping supplies are limited.

Places to Stay & Eat There are five camping grounds within 1km of Pescasseroli. **Campeggio dell'Orso** (☎ 0863 919 55; 2 people with tent €11.35), 1km along the road to Opi, is the cheapest. Someone comes to collect the fees each evening.

Albergo Basel (☎ 0863 918 75; Via Colli Dell'Oro; doubles €31) is one of the cheapest of the numerous hotels in town.

Restaurants in the town are numerous and varied: **Pizzeria San Fransesco** (☎ 0863 91 06 50; Via Isonzo) is recommended locally.

Getting There & Away Pescasseroli is well served by buses. **ARPA** (☎ 0863 265 61) runs to and from Avezzano (seven a day), from where there are frequent bus and train connections to Rome and Pescara. There is a direct bus service to Piazza Tiburtina in Rome (1½ hours, one a day).

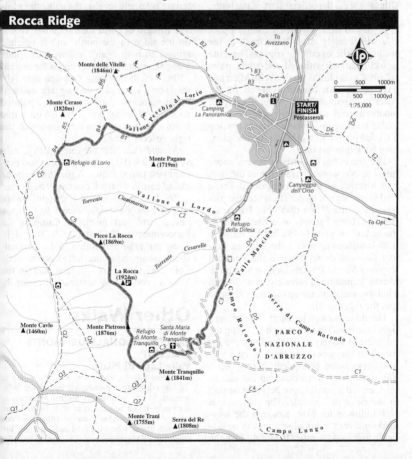

Rocca Ridge

By car, Pescasseroli is 142km from Pescara and 160km from Rome via the A24/A25 and then the S83 south.

THE WALK

From the town hall in the centre of Pescasseroli, walk south along the Viale S Lucia and continue over a crossroads onto the Via Fonte Fracassi. This leads to a fork in the road at a prominent hotel – follow the road to the right. The pavement soon ends and the road becomes a gravel track, leading past large farm buildings to reach a spring below the park-owned **Rifugio della Difesa**. This is the official start of the route, around 3km from the town centre.

A painted sign indicates the start of path C3, which leads left off the track at the spring and climbs past the *rifugio*. The route is well marked with red-and-white paint splashes as it climbs up the Valle Mancina, passing through beautiful **beech forest**. After approximately 45 minutes the path mounts a steep, rocky section and meets the gravel track again. Cross the track, passing a roofed plaque in a clearing, before plunging back into the trees.

The gravel track is crossed several more times before steeper terrain forces the path into a series of tight switchbacks. These lead to the edge of the forest, where the picturesque **Santa Maria di Monte Tranquillo church** (1600m) stands on a bluff. This is the end of the gravel road, but a faint farm track continues up open hillside ahead. Follow this and climb beneath the northern slopes of Monte Tranquillo. Pass **Rifugio di Monte Tranquillo**, a privately owned hut in a hollow, and continue up the rocky slope to join the ridge itself.

The ridge marks a junction of paths; turn right (northeast) to follow path C5 along the ridgeline. A variety of paint colours are apparent on the rocks – a black 'A' on a yellow background prominent among them. The route soon drops down to the east to skirt around a small copse before returning to the ridge at a saddle. The ridgeline is now followed for 5km, although the waymarking over the initial section can be difficult to follow in mist. If you do lose the

path among the limestone outcrops, return to the ridge and continue uphill, and you will soon pick it up.

The first cairn, around 1km onto the ridge, marks the summit of **Monte Pietroso** (1876m) From here the path continues to climb to the large pile of stones at the top of **La Rocca** (1924m), reached around three hours from the start. The views from here are panoramic – craggy ridges and forested valleys fall steeply on either side, with Pescasseroli visible far below to the east.

The ridge narrows to the north of La Rocca but the path is better defined, and the terrain is largely level as the path either follows the ridge top or contours just below it. The **Rifugio di Lorio** soon becomes visible on the ridge to the north, and is reached around an hour from La Rocca. Continue along the ridge past this *rifugio* for around 150m, before dropping down to the right (east) on a stone path that zigzags down to the forest below. Turn right beside a painted rock in a clearing, and a red B4 on a tree trunk will soon confirm that you are on the right descent route.

Around 1km later the forest path joins a vehicle track (B1); turn right here and descend past two ski tows. A gate that may be closed across the track can easily be skirted on the left, and it is then a straightforward (if not overly scenic) descent to join the paved road just north of **Camping La Panoramica** (☎ 0863 91 22 57). Turn right along the road and follow it to a roundabout, taking the second left along the Viale Colli Dell'Oro. This will lead back to the Viale S Lucia and the centre of Pescasseroli.

Other Walks

PARCO NAZIONALE DEI MONTI SIBILLINI
Valle Lago di Pilato

This route follows a long and beautiful valley to the Lago di Pilato, a picturesque lake in the basin beneath Monte Vettore, the highest mountain in the range. It can be walked as a 5½ hour, 12km out-and-back excursion from the village of Foce (the path begins where the road ends, around 7km southwest of Montemonaco). This option involve

995m of ascent but is well worth it. Alternatively the valley walk can be linked with the Monte Vettore walk (p264). Begin at Foce and continue south from the Lago Di Pilato to join up with the Monte Vettore route at Rifugio T Zilioli. This option lends itself to a two-day excursion with an overnight stay at the *rifugio*. Use the CAI's 1:25,000 *Parco Nazionale dei Monti Sibillini*.

PARCO NAZIONALE DEL GRAN SASSO E MONTI DELLA LAGA
Salinello Gorges

In the northeastern corner of the Gran Sasso-Laga national park, the Salinello Gorges are one of its most spectacular areas, and a designated nature reserve. The walk starts and finishes at the enchanting little monastery of Grotte Sant'Angelo, a shrine in a cave that has been used for various religious purposes since prehistoric times. Access the monastery parking area via a signed gravel road from Le Ripe (around 7km southwest of Civitella del Tronto). This is an out-and-back route along a marked path, and you can turn round at any stage. Allow up to four hours to properly explore the canyon and its waterfalls, and make sure you walk as far as the ruins of Castel Manfrino for a wonderful viewpoint over the gorges. The northern sheet of Selca's 1:50,000 *Parco Nazionale del Gran Sasso e Monti della Laga* covers the area, though is not strictly necessary in order to complete the walk.

Vallone delle Cornacchie and Rifugio Franchetti

This route offers two options for walkers of varying abilities. Both begin from Piano del Laghetto, 4km east of Prati di Tivo at the end of the paved road. An easy excursion leads to the spectacularly situated **Rifugio Franchetti** (☎ *0861 95 46 34*). Head south along the ridge-line path, pass the cable car station (closed since 1997 but may reopen in the future), and keep to the left to pass through the rocky Vallone delle Cornacchie (Crow's Valley) to reach the *rifugio*. Allow five hours for the return trip, which involves 800m of ascent. A longer (probably two-day), A-to-B excursion suitable for those with basic scrambling experience is also possible. Continue south from the *rifugio*, keeping left then right at trail junctions, to join up with the path described in the Corno Grande walk (p268). The end of this walk will be Campo Imperatore. Use the CAI's 1:25,000 *Gran Sasso d'Italia*.

PARCO NAZIONALE DELLA MAJELLA
Valle di Santo Spirito Gorge

The most dramatic gorge accessible to walkers in the Majella chain, a trip up the Santo Spirito Valley can also be the first part of an extended mountain circuit. A parking area at the south of Fara San Martino (around 36km south of Pretoro, on the eastern edge of the national park) is the start and finish for both walk options. The gorge features towering vertical walls, with the remains of the San Martino Abbey built into the cliff side. The 8.5km roundtrip from the parking area to the path junction at the top of the gorge involves around 600m of ascent and takes around 2½ hours. A more adventurous alternative to retracing your steps from the top of the gorge is to turn right at the trail junction and climb the ridge to the north, returning along the ridgeline to Fara San Martino (4½ to five hours). Use the CAI's 1:25,000 *Gruppo della Majella*.

Campania

Campania is a big and varied region extending far inland from its long Mediterranean coastline. Midway along the coast Naples (Napoli) its capital, sprawls around the Gulf of Naples. This chapter focuses on Vesuvius (Vesuvio), Italy's most famous volcano; the Sorrento peninsula; facing the southern shore of the Gulf of Naples; and the Amalfi Coast, part of the same peninsula but with its shoreline on the Gulf of Salerno.

Walks on Vesuvius are largely confined to short but exciting routes around the crater, while the 25km-long Sorrento–Amalfi Peninsula, rising to more than 1400m along its crest, has an extensive web of paths. Once the lifelines between rural and coastal settlements, these paths now provide superbly scenic walking through areas where traditional lifestyles are still maintained. Contrasts dominate – between busy coastal towns and peaceful hamlets, isolated mountain farms and intensively cultivated lands, and wild valleys and mountains beyond. The setting is colourfully Mediterranean – vibrant blues and greens, stark white in vast cliffs, bright reds, oranges and pinks in the wildflowers.

CLIMATE

Hot, dry summers and cool, damp winters define Campania's Mediterranean climate, a pattern produced mainly by the movement of Atlantic weather fronts. In summer, the few fronts that approach the western Mediterranean are pushed north and south by a subtropical anti-cyclone anchored near the Azores.

Rainfall between June and September is minimal. Long hours of sunshine are the norm and temperatures are high (25°C upwards). The sirocco, a hot wind from North Africa, can make life uncomfortable by bringing humid and overcast conditions to already very warm days.

From September to November, lurking Atlantic depressions bring changeable and cloudy, though still mild (around 10°C)

Highlights

JON DAVISON

Vesuvius (1281m) looms over a reminder of its destructive ability, the ruins of Pompeii

- Exploring Vesuvius' slopes and a hidden, undisturbed valley on the Vesuvius & Valle del Gigante walk (p283)

- Walking steep, densely wooded mountainsides soaring to precipitous, craggy peaks on the scenic Amalfi Coast (p285)

- Rambling through timeless villages, and olive and citrus groves, among abundant wildflowers on the spectacular Sorrento Peninsula (p294)

- Taking in magnificent views of the Isle of Capri from Punta Penna (p296) and Punta Campanella (p297)

weather. Rainfall comes in short sharp showers. The year's rainfall is confined to about 100 days, with a total fall of 1000mm along the coast and up to 1500mm inland.

INFORMATION
When to Walk

September to mid-May is the ideal time, when the area is least crowded and the weather best suited to walking; from early March until May the displays of wildflowers are superb. Between late May and early September daily temperatures in the high 20°Cs make walking distinctly uncomfortable, unless you're accustomed to a warm climate. From mid-June to the end of August, the area is overflowing with visitors and getting about becomes an endurance test.

What to Bring

Sunscreen and a shady hat are absolutely essential from April onwards. A 1.5L water bottle is indispensable; surface water is virtually non-existent away from the towns and villages, where you'll find fountains and bars. If you're planning to camp, bring plenty of fuel for your stove; there are no reliable local sources.

Maps

Touring Club Italiano's (TCI's) 1:200,000 *Campania - Basilicata* map is ideal for finding your way about. See Planning for each walk for details of specific map requirements.

Emergency

In Campania's mountainous areas contact the **mountain rescue service** (☎ 081 551 59 50). For medical assistance call the **national emergency number** (☎ 118).

GATEWAY
Naples (Napoli)

Naples, the third largest city in Italy, has a little – and often a lot – of everything. The old centre, once the heart of ancient Neapolis, now bristles with countless eateries and cafés, noisy street markets and swarms of people buzzing around on Vespas. The **Jamm Bookshop** (☎ 081 552 63 99, fax 081 552 97 82; w *jammnapoli@libero.it; Via San Giovanni Maggiore Pignatelli 1A*), on the

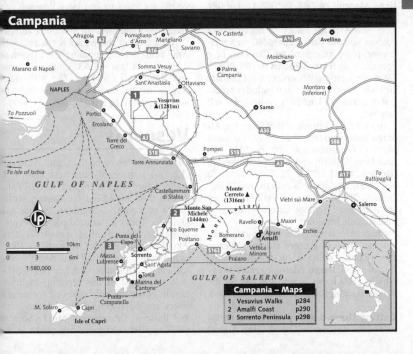

Campania

Campania – Maps	
1 Vesuvius Walks	p284
2 Amalfi Coast	p290
3 Sorrento Peninsula	p298

1:580,000

corner of Piazza San Domenico Maggiore, specialises in maps and travel books. It is among the few places where you can obtain IGM maps covering Vesuvius.

Information Sources Naples has several tourist offices, including the main **EPT office** (☎ 081 40 53 11; Piazza dei Martiri 58; open 8.30am-2.30pm Mon-Fri) and branch offices at the Mergellina train station and the airport. There's a particularly helpful **AAST office** (☎ 081 552 33 28; Piazza del Gesù Nuovo; open 9am-8pm Mon-Sat, 9am-3pm Sun) southeast of Piazza Dante. Also useful is the City of Naples Tourist Board's website (w www.inaples.it).

Places to Stay & Eat Modern **Ostello Mergellina** (☎ 081 761 23 46, fax 081 761 23 91; Salita della Grotta 23; dorm beds/doubles €12.90/15.50) has a 12.30am curfew, and a maximum stay of three nights in July and August. Rates include breakfast. **Hostel Pensione Mancini** (☎ 081 553 67 31, fax 081 554 66 75; w www.hostelpensionemancini .com; Via Mancini 33; dorm beds/singles/ doubles without bath €16/30/40) is a welcoming place near Stazione Centrale, near Spaccanapoli. **6 Small Rooms** (☎ 081 790 13 78; w www.at6smallrooms.com; Via Diodata Lioy 18; dorm beds €15.50) includes breakfast in its rates. A kitchen is available for self caterers.

In charming historical buildings are **Albergo Sansevero** (☎ 081 21 09 07; Via Santa Maria di Costantinopoli 101; doubles with bath from €72.30) and **Albergo Sansevero (Degas)** (☎ 081 551 12 76; Piazza del Gesù Nuovo 53; doubles with bath from €72.30). Because they're protected buildings, they are not signed, so look carefully. Rates at both include breakfast.

Spaccanapoli and Stazione Centrale areas have an array of **grocery stores**, **pizzerias** and a couple of spots for seafood. Santa Lucia offers Borgo Marinaro with many popular **restaurants**, where you pay for the view and ambience as much as for the food.

Getting There & Away About 8km northeast of the city centre **Capodichino Airport** (☎ 081 789 62 59, 848 88 87 77) is southern Italy's main airport, linking Naples with most Italian and some major European cities

Most buses for Italian and some European cities leave from Piazza Garibaldi in front of Stazione Centrale. Check destinations carefully or ask around because there are no signs. The exception is local company **SITA** (☎ 081 552 21 76; w www.sita-on-line.it) You can buy tickets and catch SITA buses at the **main office** (Via Pisanelli), near Piazza Municipio, or Via G Ferraris, near Stazione Centrale. SITA runs buses to Pompeii, Ercolano, Sorrento, other towns on the Amalfi Coast and Salerno (by motorway). See also the boxed text 'Busing it with SITA' (p287).

Many trains originating in the north pass through Rome and terminate in Naples; you can call for **information** (☎ 848 88 08 88) Trains arrive and depart from **Stazione Centrale** (☎ 081 554 31 88) or Stazione Garibaldi (on the lower level). There are up to 30 trains daily to/from Rome. Circumvesuviana trains to Ercolano, Pompeii and Sorrento depart from Corso Garibaldi about 400m southwest of Stazione Centrale

Naples is on the major north to south Autostrada del Sole, numbered A1 (north to Rome and Milan) and A3 (south to Salerno and Reggio di Calabria). The A30 rings Naples to the northeast, while the A16 heads northeast to Bari.

Vesuvius

Of all the volcanoes on the planet, Vesuvius (1281m) is probably the best known. I made history when it erupted in AD 79 and in two days wiped out the Roman settlements of Pompeii, Ercolano, Stabia and Oplontis. Today it sits amid one of the most densely populated urban sprawls in Italy About 600,000 people live within a 10km radius of the crater, and that doesn't even include the population of the city of Naples

In the midst of this teeming Mediterranean chaos the only oases of nature left intact are the slopes of the volcano itself and those of the adjacent Monte Somma (1132m). Between these two peaks is the enchanting Valle del Gigante (Valley of the Giant), where the pioneer vegetation has to recolonise the fertile volcanic ash after every eruption.

In 1995, the Parco Nazionale del Vesuvio was created, partly to protect against illegal building and poaching. Access to the remotest southern parts of the protected area, the Riserva Tirone-Alto Vesuvio, is restricted; for information contact the **Guardia Forestale di Caserta** (☎ 082 336 17 12) or La Porta del Vesuvio (see Guided Walks, p282), which arranges guided visits. Visitors to Vesuvius usually climb to the summit along a trail on the western face. Every day hundreds of people reach the edge of the enormous crater. For the more adventurous, trails link the crater with the crossing of the Valle del Gigante.

HISTORY

Europe was astonished when, by chance, the first traces of the buried city of Pompeii were uncovered. In 1748, the King of Naples, Charles of Bourbon, began the excavations which, even today, continue to yield surprises. The terrible eruption took place on 24 August AD 79, obliterating Pompeii, Ercolano, Stabia and Oplontis under a 5m-thick layer of ash and stone. It is believed that 2000 people died in Pompeii and Ercolano.

The most illustrious victim was Pliny the Elder, commander of the Roman fleet stationed at Porto Miseno. Pliny was a passionate naturalist and it is said that, while carrying out rescue operations along the coast, his curiosity took him too close to the cataclysm.

After a long period of dormancy, another powerful eruption let loose on 16 December 1631. Massa, Somma and Bosco were destroyed. The event reverberated throughout Europe, and Vesuvius, with its smoking peak, became the hallmark of the Neapolitan landscape in prints and paintings of the era. In the second half of the 18th century, Naples, Vesuvius and Pompeii were obligatory destinations on the Italian Grand Tour. From that day to this the list of illustrious visitors has grown. To name a few:

Montesquieu, Casanova, Mozart, Goethe, Shelley, Hans Christian Andersen, Dickens, Mark Twain, Anton Chekhov and Walter Benjamin. The most well-to-do visitors went up with guides and porters on mules or horseback to the Atrio del Cavallo, from where they continued on foot. The laziest were carried up on sedans to the edge of the crater. Those who found the courage climbed down inside the crater, which is no longer permitted. In 1848, King Ferdinand II had the Osservatorio Vesuviano (Vesuvius Observatory), the first vulcanological observatory in the world, built.

NATURAL HISTORY

Vesuvius began to form about 300,000 years ago. The great crater of Monte Somma formed first – ending its activity in ancient times with the collapse of its summit caldera. Inside the depression created by the collapse, Vesuvius began to grow, with its startling crater 500m in diameter and 230m deep. Vesuvius is part of a vast volcanic area that includes the Campi Flegrei (Phlegraean Fields) west of Naples with the adjacent crater lakes of Averno, Fusaro and Miseno, and beyond, the islands of Ischia, Procida and Vivara.

Vesuvius last erupted in 1944, as Naples struggled to recover from the devastation of WWII. A relatively modest eruption generated lava flow in the Atrio del Cavallo, visible from the road that comes up from Ercolano.

Eruptions have exterminated the vegetation on Vesuvius more than once. Regeneration begins immediately after the lava cools with a silvery-grey lichen, which gives colour to the dark, gloomy lava. After a few decades come robust small Mediterranean plants, among them dock and poppies. Then the *ginestre* (broom) arrives, with its brilliant yellow June flowers. Growing in the midst of the broom are artemesia, *elicriso* (helychrisum) and red valerian, and in the late spring they all bloom together in a riotous perfumed technicolour mix.

Reforestation in this century has accelerated the comeback of the wooded areas. There are holm oaks, cluster pines, aleppo

CAMPANIA

pines and, in the Valle del Gigante, clusters of locust trees and silver birch.

Groups of harmless stray dogs hang around the parking area at 1000m. In the park there are foxes, weasels and martens, which probably find food in the outskirts of the towns since only the little dormouse and its relatives the *topo quercino* and *moscardino* remain. Many bird species pass through during migration including buzzards, kestrels, owls, turtledoves, quails, cuckoos, whip-poorwills, golden orioles and many others. A colony of ravens is stationed on Monte Somma where red woodpeckers nest as well, along with tawny owls, wrynecks, tomtits and robin redbreasts.

Among reptiles are two innocuous serpents: the black coluber on the warm slopes of Vesuvius and the robust cervone on Monte Somma. Poisonous vipers may also be encountered in the rocky areas of Valle del Gigante.

PLANNING
When to Walk
The hottest months, July and August, are to be avoided. In spring there is the added spectacle of the wildflowers. In winter Vesuvius is less crowded, offers frequent sunny days; and the special clearness of the winter skies allows great views.

What to Bring
A compass and altimeter are a good idea in case of fog. At the crater (approximately

Warning
Vesuvius is under constant monitoring by seismologists at the **Osservatorio Vesuviano** (Vesuvius Observatory; ☎ 081 610 84 83; w www.ov.ingv.it; Via Diocleziano 328), a few kilometres west of the crater. Sooner or later there will be another memorable eruption. You climb Vesuvius at your own risk, particularly if you plan to go to the crater. Those who wish to be reassured personally by vulcanologists may contact the Osservatorio.

Also watch out for vipers and, on a lighter note, illegal taxi drivers.

1200m), temperatures are lower than at the base of the mountain and there can be strong winds, so bring the appropriate gear. Bring your own supply of water (although a kiosk sells drinks at the summit).

Maps
Vesuvius is covered by two maps in the Istituto Geografico Militare (IGM) 1:25,000 series 25, updated to 1996 – 448 III *Ercolano*, which covers almost the whole walk, and 466 IV *Torre del Greco*. These can be obtained at the Jamm Bookshop in Naples (p279). The information point, on the road leading to the Quota 1000 car park from Ercolano, sells a schematic map of the park at 1:20,000 that shows the main trails.

Information Sources
A good source of park information is the **Ente Parco Nazionale del Vesuvio** (☎ 08 771 09 11, fax 081 771 82 15; w www.park .it/parco.nazionale.vesuvio; Piazza Municip 8, San Sebastiano al Vesuvio; open Mon-Fri). There is also an information point along the road that heads up to the Quota 1000 car park from Ercolano.

Guided Walks
Most people walk Vesuvius independently. However, if you prefer a guided walk consider one of the following operators:

Cooperativa Ossidiana (☎/fax 081 776 44 2; w coop.ossidiana@inwind.it; San Giorgio Cremano) is a group of competent environmental guides that offers large- or small-group walks (€41.30 for four hours, €82.65 for seven hours). For an additional 30% the tour can be in French, Spanish and English; book at least three days in advance.

Guide Vulcanologiche del Vesuvio (☎ 081 77 57 20) monitors tourists along the path to the summit and in the paid tourist area (€6) at the edge of the crater.

La Porta del Vesuvio (☎ 081 27 42 00; w www .laportadelvesuvio.it; Via Cifelli, Loc Casabianca) is on the southern slope of Vesuvius, 2k north of the road from Boscotrecase to Trecas at a traditional farm called Casa Cesaro. The organisation sells local delicacies and organises guided tours, including the nearby restricted area of the Riserva Tirone-Alto Vesuvio.

Museo Vulcanologico (☎ 081 610 84 83; W www
.ov.ingv.it; Via Diocleziano 328; open 10am-
2pm Sat-Sun), at Osservatorio Vesuviano a few
kilometres west of the crater, offers guided visits;
book ahead.

Parco Letterario del Vesuvio (☎/fax 081 563 51
87; W www.parcoletterariovesuvio.it; Via Sotto
ai Camaldoli 9, Torre del Greco; open Mon-Fri
9am-6pm) organises natural history tours (€5.15,
9am to 1pm) for a minimum of 20 people, or
natural history/cultural tours, including reading
and theatre in English (€41.30, 9am to 4pm),
for a minimum of 30 people.

Vesuvius & Valle del Gigante

Duration	3½ hours
Distance	6km
Difficulty	easy–moderate
Start/Finish	Quota 1000 car park
Nearest Town	Naples (p279)
Transport	bus, taxi

Summary Visit Vesuvius' mighty crater and
cross the exquisite and isolated Valle del
Gigante; wide vistas, silence and undisturbed
nature, just around the corner from the tourist
route.

This is a scenic, easy route, with an ascent
of 295m, that crosses the pleasant Valle del
Gigante, reaches the east crest allowing
wide vistas of the Sarno Valley, and ascends
to the east gate ticket booth of the visitors'
area at the edge of the crater.

GETTING TO/FROM THE WALK

The easiest way to get from central Naples
to Vesuvius is by train. **Circumvesuviana**
(☎ 081 772 24 44; W www.vesuviana.it)
runs trains connecting Naples and Sorrento
(every 20 minutes). They leave from the
station on Corso Garibaldi about 400m
southwest of Stazione Centrale (take the underpass from Stazione Centrale). You can
disembark at Ercolano.

Trasporti Vesuviani (☎ 081 559 25 82)
buses leave Ercolano station for the Quota
1000 car park on Vesuvius. (€3.10 return,
five a day). In winter the schedule is reduced. The last bus returns from the Quota

1000 car park at 6pm in summer and at 3pm
in winter.

Another option is a licensed taxi from the
train station at Ercolano. Beware of un-
licensed taxis, which don't have the taxi
sign on the roof – once they've delivered
you, they might demand an exaggerated
fare. The licensed taxis run from 8am to
7pm (€31 return for four people). If you are
only going on the tourist walk to the craters,
the driver will wait until you are ready to
return. **Eurotaxi** (☎ 081 739 36 66) also
rents vans for larger groups.

By car, take the A3 from Naples, exit at Ercolano, and follow the signs to Vesuvio. This
will take you up to the Quota 1000 car park.

THE WALK (see map p284)

From the Quota 1000 car park, go back
downhill to the east along the asphalt road
for 400m until you reach the first curve and
the ruins of a **vulcanological observatory**
(875m). Two unmarked paths leave from
the sides of the ruin. The one to the right
proceeds along the hillside at a constant altitude, the other, to the left of the building,
is narrower and descends into the bush.

Climb over the guard rail where the fenc-
ing is interrupted and descend on the path to
the left, skirting a ruined retaining wall with
iron gratings. The path bypasses the ruined
wall and curves slightly to the right (southeast). Avoid a minor deviation that goes
down to the left, and continue southeast
over massive banks of hardened lava. The
majestic panorama of the **Valle del Gigante**
and the **lava flow of 1944** are on your left.
Watch for huge spiderwebs across the path.

The path curves northeast and descends
sharply into the valley. Flat ground is soon
reached, following the snaking trail across
the peaceful environs of the valley floor, in
a sparse forest of pines and tall broom.

Avoiding deviations, the base of **Monte
Somma** on the other side of the valley is
soon reached – note the strange rock arch.
From here the trail turns to the east and
skirts the rock wall for a few metres before
entering into a natural arena, closed to the
north by a wide scree. Here you may see
kestrels and ravens, and it is good place for

CAMPANIA

a rest. Note the strange blade-like rocks that sprout from the ground and the view of the dark cone of Vesuvius.

Follow the trail (which in some places divides in two to avoid obstacles) heading southeast towards the scree. Passing over it a vegetated pass comes into view, where the crest of Monte Somma begins to drop sharply. The trail takes you to the final short ascent to the pass, where there is a paling fence. From here, to the east, there is a wide vista of the countryside of Sarno, which seems almost a carpet of greenhouse roofs. To the south is the sea with the Sorrento Peninsula and the island of Capri.

The trail heads south, following the crest alongside the barbed wire. On the right, cords of lava come together in strange, beautifully twisted formations. Keep going, up and over the pyramid-like dunes of volcanic slag that make up the crest. Finally, a large clearing with traces of a dismantled building is reached.

Looking southwest towards the valley from the clearing, find the trail to your right (southwest) which, about 30m closer to the mountain, begins a slight ascent into the vegetation. (Another trail descends from the southern corner of the clearing – use it as a point of reference only). Follow the very clear trail up and down little hills of slag which, after an arduous kilometre, turns northwest and soon reaches the dirt road, Strada Matrone, coming from Boscotrecase.

Turn right up this old, winding road that, in some places, retains ancient polished paving stones. Before the 1944 eruption, buses used this road. Where the third hairpin bend turns left, you'll see a dirt road to the right (Point D). This trail leads back to the ruined observatory in 15 pleasant minutes; see the Alternative Route: Backstage Vesuvius (p285).

To go on towards the crater, turn left at Point D and continue to a clearing – the East Clearing (1050m). On the mountain side of the clearing, a faint trail ascends northwest, diagonally. After a few metres, there is a little hairpin bend on the left where another very faint trail continues north (to the right) across the lava slag to Point C. Follow the hairpin bend on your left and continue to ascend sharply along the lava, until you reach the east gate ticket booth of the Guide del Vesuvio (1170m, 30 minutes) at the crater.

To enter the obligatory walkway of the organised visitors' area pay €6. Mingling with the tourists view the impressive chasm of the 230m deep and 550m wide **crater** with its weak fumaroles (vents from which hot gases are emitted). A little road skirts the edge up to the west gate ticket booth, the entrance for those who come up from the Quota 1000 car park. Halfway along is a surreal **kiosk** selling postcards, drinks and traditional fake-lava souvenirs.

On clear days you can glimpse (between the heads of the several hundred tourists) a splendid panorama of the Gulf of Naples. From right to left you can see the islands of Ischia and Procida, Posillipo, Castel dell'Ovo and the port of Naples, the Sorrento Peninsula out to Punta Campanella and the island of Capri on the extreme left.

Vesuvius Walks

Vesuvius – Walks

1 Vesuvius & Valle del Gigante
2 Vesuvius' Crater

Monte Somma

Punta del Nasone (1132m)

To Osservatorio Vesuviano Ercolano & Torre del Greco

Ruined Observatory

Valle del Gigante

START/FINISH

Quota 1000 Car Park

Point B

Point A

Alternative Routes

West Gate Ticket Booth

Vesuvius

1281m
Cratere del 1944
+
951m

Point C

Point D

Bocche del 1906

Valle dell'Inferno

Large Clearing

Cupola del 193?

East Gate Ticket Booth

East Clearing

0   0.5   1km
0   0.25   0.5mi
1:55,000

Strada Matrone

To Boscotrecase, Trecase & Pompeii

After about 1km you reach the west gate ticket booth. Descend on the first part of the tourist trail until you reach a road to the left Point A). There is a wooden bench on the right. Turn left down this road until you reach the third curve, which also turns to the left, and has another bench (Point B). After another curve you are back at the car park.

Vesuvius' Crater

Duration	2 hours
Distance	3km
Difficulty	easy–moderate
Start/Finish	Quota 1000 car park
Nearest Town	Naples (p279)
Transport	bus, taxi

Summary An adventurous loop around the crater's summit slopes with unforgettable views from inner Valle del Gigante to the enchanting Gulf of Naples.

The first part of this route cuts across the steep slope of the great cone over unstable slag. It is a challenging, faint trail over open ground which offers a striking panorama of the Valle del Gigante, but requires good balance and a sure foot. It should be avoided in fog or bad weather. Refer back to the Vesuvius & Valle de Gigante walk (p283) to get your bearings when we refer to Points A, B, C and D, and the East Clearing. The walk contains an ascent of 200m.

GETTING TO/FROM THE WALK
See Getting to/from the Walk (p283).

THE WALK (see map p284)
Ascend in a southwesterly direction from the car park. You'll pass the wooden bench at Point B that marks the start of the Alternative Route: Backstage Vesuvius (this page). Continue along the tourist trail up to the fourth and last curve before the summit, to a wooden bench (Point A), behind which there is a faint trail. Taking this trail cross the slope in an easterly direction. As the trail turns to the south, it comes to Point C, above the East Clearing, where the Strada Matrone ends.

From here, instead of going down to the clearing, keep going up (southwest) on the trail until you come to the east gate ticket booth (30 minutes), where you pay €6 to enter the visitors area. The descent to the car park is from the west gate ticket booth.

Following the crowd of tourists it is impossible to become lost, but you could eventually lose your patience. If you feel like more walking, far from the tourist throng, turn off at Point B for the alternative route.

Alternative Route: Backstage Vesuvius
1 hour, 2km
Behind the bench at Point B take the well-marked trail through vegetation that traverses the slope of the great volcano. The trail breaks up into many tracks about 30m before reaching the East Clearing (30 minutes from Point B), forcing you to find your own way through the thick locust plants.

At the left corner of the clearing, when facing the valley, there is a short cut where, digging your heels into the slag, you descend for 30m, to a turn-off on the Strada Matrone (Point D). You can also descend on the road from the clearing to Point D, where you go left. The wide dirt road leads you in 15 minutes north to the ruined observatory, just below the Quota 1000 car park.

Amalfi Coast

From this slender strip of coast, incredibly steep, densely wooded mountains rise to become the precipitous craggy peaks of the Monti Lattari Range, the spine of the entire peninsula. An extraordinary network of paths climbs high above the coast to religious retreats, isolated and deserted houses, and mountain summits through wild and beautiful valleys. Throughout the Amalfi Coast (Costiera Amalfitana), walking is exceptionally scenic and a fascinating cultural experience. It also requires much energy – long ascents up seemingly endless flights of steps are almost unavoidable.

Any of the coastal towns can serve as a base for the walks described here, as the area

CAMPANIA

is well served by frequent and reliable bus services. Apart from Positano and Amalfi, most of the towns are still largely unspoiled and uncluttered by concessions to modern tourism and have a range of *alberghi* (hotels) and pensiones to suit most budgets.

NATURAL HISTORY

From the coast between Amalfi and Atrani deep valleys cut back towards the spine of the Monti Lattari Range. Here the small Riserva Statale Valle delle Ferriere protects plants usually found in Africa and South America. Everywhere lush woodlands and dense vegetation of the valleys, especially the beautiful, slender Italian cypresses, contrast with the open, sparsely vegetated slopes above. Massed pink and white rock roses are the most colourful of the wildflowers, and orchids are very plentiful.

World Heritage Coast

Category C (ii, iv, v) – what can this bureaucratic tag have to do with walking around Amalfi? Well, it neatly summarises the area's outstanding international importance.

Probably the most rewarding aspect of walking here is the deeply harmonious blend of great natural beauty, superbly preserved buildings in towns and villages and seamlessly interwoven terraces and fields. These characteristics were recognised by UNESCO in 1997 when it declared the Amalfi Coast a World Heritage site – in particular a cultural heritage site. The area fulfils three criteria; it exhibits 'developments in architecture' (ii) in towns such as Amalfi and Ravello; it's an outstanding example of a landscape 'which illustrates ... significant stages in human history' (iv); and also of 'traditional human settlement or land use' (v) where people have adapted to the terrain's diversity with 'terraced vineyards and orchards on the lower slopes (and) wide upland pastures.'

The challenge for the future is to preserve this rural land use by encouraging and enabling people to maintain the higher, less accessible terraces and fields – signs of dereliction are all too obvious.

PLANNING
Maps & Books

The Kompass 1:50,000 map No 682 *Penisola Sorrentina* is helpful for planning purposes only. It includes town maps plus notes about the area's attractions in English, French, German and Italian. The Club Alpino Italiano (CAI) 1:30,000 *Monti Lattari* map is far more useful than the Kompass map, but keep in mind that path numbering differs from what you'll find on the ground.

Julian Tippett's *Landscapes of Sorrento and the Amalfi Coast* describes 20 mostly short walks in the area and is invaluable.

The best local source of maps and books is **Libreria** (*Corso Repubbliche Marinare*), a bookshop in Amalfi, not far from the bus station.

Information Sources

Amalfi's **AAST office** (☎/fax 089 87 11 07; *Corso Roma 19/21; open Mon-Sat*) has only limited facilities – an accommodation guide is of some use. Helpful **Positano AST** (☎ 089 87 50 67, fax 089 87 57 60; *Via del Saracino 4; open Mon-Sat*) issues a local accommodation list and town map. The office is near Santa Maria Assunta, a prominent church on the beach side of town.

Other Information

You can check email at **Il Brigantino** (☎ 089 81 10 55; *Via del Saracino 37*) in Positano, 50m downhill from the AST. The cost is €1.80 per 15 minutes.

GETTING AROUND

A convenient way to get around the region is by bus (see the boxed text 'Busing it with SITA', p287). A less congested but more expensive mode of transport is ferry, worth trying for the views. **Coop Sant'Andrea** (☎ 089 87 31 90; w *www.coopsantandrea.it*) travels between Positano and Amalfi (€3.60, at least seven sailings a day).

ACCESS TOWN
Praiano

Praiano is spread out above and below the coast road, almost midway between Positano and Amalfi. There is no tourist office ere; contact the **APT** (☎ *089 23 04 11; Piazza Vittorio Veneto*) in Salerno for information. Alternatively, w www.praiano.it is a useful source of contacts for local hotels and information.

Places to Stay & Eat On the main coast road (S163), **La Tranquillata** (☎ *089 87 40 84, fax 089 87 47 79; Via Roma 21; camping per person/two people €20.65/38.75*) is an outrageously priced camping ground but it's worth paying for the view across the Gulf of Salerno from the terraced pitches. Facilities are extremely simple. The site is attached to **Hotel Continentale** (*B&B doubles or cabins €87.80*). Doubles have private facilities and a terrace in the main building; the cabins next door are neatly set up. Expect to pay around €18 for dinner in the superb dining room.

A friendly place in Positano, **Ostello Brikette** (☎ *089 87 58 57, fax 089 812 28 14; w www.brikette.com; Via Marconi 358; dorm beds €18.10, doubles with bath €56.80*) is the nearest hostel. It's about 200m west of the Bar Internazionale bus stop and has a fine terrace with sea views.

An excellent *alimentari* (grocery shop) for self catering, **Il Tutto per Tutti** (*Via Umberto I*) is 200 steps up from the coast road opposite Hotel Continentale.

Down by the small beach below Praiano, **Ristorante Il Pirata** (☎ *089 87 43 77; Via Terramare*) is set back a few metres from the rocky shore and overlooked by Torre a Mare, a fortified tower-like building. The restaurant specialises in locally caught seafood. You could eat well and drink local wine here for around €13. In a more public place is **Ristorante Alfonso a Mare** (☎ *089 87 40 91*), where you'll look out through vine-encircled windows to the sea. It also features seafood and pizzas from a wood-fired oven; prices are similar.

Bar Trattoria Armandino, near Ristorante Alfonso a Mare, is a good place to go for coffee and cakes.

Getting There & Away Stopping outside Hotel Continentale are **SITA** (☎ *081 552 21 76*) buses on the Sorrento–Amalfi run

Busing it with SITA

Blue **SITA buses** (☎ *081 552 21 76*; w *www.sita-on-line.it*) provide frequent, inexpensive and reliable links between the coastal towns on the Amalfi Coast and the Sorrento Peninsula and most of those inland.

Tickets must be bought before boarding, at a SITA office, or bar or *tabaccheria* (tobacconist) displaying a SITA sign, usually close to the local bus stop. They must be validated in the machine on the bus. It's a good idea to buy all your tickets for the day's travel in the morning to save being caught out by closed shops later. Zealous inspectors frequently check for tickets and will impose a hefty fine if you don't have one, no matter the reason.

Blue and white *fermate* (bus stop) signs are commonly on one side of the road only; stand opposite the sign when travelling in the other direction.

(Positano/Amalfi €0.95/1.10, 20/25 minutes, at least five a day).

By road Praiano is 54km from Naples via the A3 to the Castellammare di Stabia exit, the S145 to Piano di Sorrento and the S163. From the south and east, exit from the A3 just west of Salerno and follow the S163 (37km from Salerno).

Sentiero degli Dei

Duration	5½–6 hours
Distance	12km
Difficulty	moderate
Start	Positano
Finish	Praiano
Nearest Town	Praiano (p286)
Transport	bus
Summary	One of the classic walks on the entire peninsula: superb paths clinging to near-vertical mountainsides with panoramic views and beautiful groves of Italian cypresses.

The Sentiero degli Dei (Path of the Gods), probably the best-known walk in the area, is the centrepiece of this excursion. Although it's not an unduly strenuous day (with an ascent of 770m), it could be split at the village of Montepertuso by making use of the bus service between there and Positano. The generally excellent paths are occasionally narrow, often rocky, and slightly exposed in places. The most common waymarkers are CAI red-and-white stripes, notably along the spectacular ascent from Positano to Santa Maria. Refreshments are available at three villages en route.

GETTING TO/FROM THE WALK

Positano is on SITA's Amalfi–Sorrento bus route (€1.20, 45 minutes, several a day), get out at the Bar Internazionale stop, at the western end of the town. For transport information for Praiano, at the end of the walk, see Getting There & Away (p287).

Flavio Gioia (☎ 089 81 18 75) operates a frequent bus service between Montepertuso and Positano (€0.75). The Montepertuso bus stop is on the main road opposite the central piazza. The terminus in Positano is on Piazza dei Mulini; there's a stop at the junction of the coast and Montepertuso roads. Purchase tickets on board.

THE WALK (see map pp290–1)

From the coast road at Bar Internazionale, high on the western side of Positano, go up Via Chiesa Nuova; cross the piazza in front of the church and continue along an alley and up steps to a road. Cross it and ascend steps just to the left. About 30 minutes from the start, at a junction, turn sharp left and continue upwards. The superb path takes you to the foot of towering cliffs then up to the edge of the plateau above. Near a small plateau on the right, the path swings left through grass and towards a house. Bear right beside a pylon to a minor road and follow it straight on (following a CAI sign) to a crossroads and turn right. About 200m along you reach a minor road on the right leading to Santa Maria del Castello's large church (1¼ hours from Positano).

Turn left along the main road, soon passing a **bar** on the right. Follow the road for 450m from Santa Maria to a concreted road on the right, with signs to the Sentiero degli Dei, path 29 and CAI's path 00. This short road leads to a path passing above gardens and into beautiful Italian cypress groves, then winding spectacularly around the mountainside to an old stone building – **Caserma Forestale** (an hour from Santa Maria). Facing south in front of the building, head east (to the left) down hundreds of steps through cypresses, across the slope then straight down to the Montepertuso–Nocelle road (45 minutes from Caserma Forestale).

Walk uphill along the road (Via Filippo Mandara), which one day will reach the village of Nocelle, passing **Trattoria La Tagliata**. After 600m, just past a bridge, diverge right down to a path signposted to Nocelle. This takes you to a lane between houses and up to Via Nocelle where you turn left. Soon you reach **Santa Croce** (☎ 089 87 53 19), a bar-trattoria where the view from the light, airy dining room makes a stop worthwhile even before you've taken a sip (30 minutes after reaching the road).

Continue along Via Nocelle to a crossroads and turn left up steps by a small shrine. Take the first right turn along a minor road which soon becomes a path. The **Sentiero degli Dei** stretches ahead, in places defying normal expectations of where a path can go, beneath soaring cliffs. Eventually the route passes through old terraces (where waymarkers are scarce) and goes up past a house on the left to a wider path where there's a tap over a large water barrel (1¼ hours from Nocelle). Colle la Serra is about 100m up to the left.

To reach Praiano, continue downhill from the barrel, soon passing above a terrace, then continuing left across the slope (sparse markers) to long flights of steps. At a large concrete structure follow Via Colle della Serra along the base of the cliffs and across a spur – and there's Praiano below. Continue for another 200m then descend steps on the right, cross a road and descend more steps to a T junction. Take a few steps left and go down Via Oratorio; swing round behind the parish museum to Piazza San Luca, where there's a **bar** (45 minutes from the colle). To reach the coast road, walk away from the church through a short tunnel and continue to steps

The Amalfi Coast from Ravello

ll tales and time to spare

A picturesque town with a Moorish flavour, Amalfi Coast's Positano

e 440-sq-km Parco Nazionale d'Abruzzo is a haven for Marsican bears and Apennine wolves

The smoking crater of Mt Etna (3350m), Europe's largest volcano and one of the world's most active

Relaxing but smelly – Laghetto di Fanghi, Vulcano

Cala Gonone's beach and blue water beckon

Sardinia's spectacular Supramonte near Orgosolo

on the left (Via Antica Seggio) just past a large lookout; descend to Via Umberto I. Follow this to the left, down past the *alimentari* and 20m further on go left down steps (Via San Giovanni) to a T-junction and bear left. Follow this lane around and down to steps on the right almost opposite a small shrine; these steps lead down to the coast road close to Hotel Continentale and a bus stop.

Capo Muro

Duration	6½–7 hours
Distance	14km
Difficulty	demanding
Start	Praiano
Finish	Positano
Nearest Town	Praiano (p286)
Transport	bus
Summary	A superb high-level walk beneath soaring limestone cliffs with panoramic coast and mountain views.

This walk rivals the Sentiero degli Dei walk scenically and in the adrenalin-stimulating capacity of the paths (ascent is 1080m). It can be done in either direction though the best views are gained walking east to west. Paths are generally well marked, except for a stretch west of Capo Muro.

By catching the bus from Montepertuso to Positano (see Getting to/from the Walk, p288) you could knock about an hour off the duration. It's also possible to do the walk based in Amalfi or Atrani, using the daily Agerola bus service to Bomerano and returning by bus from Positano; this would save about 1¾ hours and 600m ascent. You can also reach Bomerano on foot, see Vallone di Praia (p299).

PLANNING
Carry enough water for the duration. Refreshments are available in Bomerano; the next watering place is Montepertuso, a few hours away.

Note that route 41 between Bomerano and Capo Muro now differs from that shown on the CAI 1:30,000 *Monti Lattari* map.

GETTING TO/FROM THE WALK
See Getting to/from the Walk (p288).

THE WALK (see map pp290–1)
From the *alimentari* in Praiano, walk west up Via Umberto I for a few hundred metres; 25m past Hotel Margherita turn right up steps (Via Antica Seggio) and climb to a road. Turn right and continue to Piazza San Luca. Go round behind the large building on the left then bear left up Via Oratorio to a T-junction; take a few steps left then go right, up more steps. Cross a road and climb another flight of steps. At the top, turn left and follow a path (Via Colle della Serra) across a spur, past a large concrete building on the right and start a long haul up flights of steps. At the top, continue uphill in the same direction (this section is poorly way-marked), then along the top of a terrace, past a house to a broad path; turn right at an intersection to reach **Colle la Serra** (about an hour from Praiano).

Follow the path leading north (way-marked 27) past a ruin on the left. The path contours the upper reaches of Vallone di Praia to **Grotta Biscotto**, a huge overhang sheltering disused cliff houses. Continue to a bitumen road and follow it for about 500m to rough concrete steps on the right, almost opposite a two-storey white house. Follow the steps down to a track, cross a bridge and bear left up a path which leads into the piazza in Bomerano (45 minutes from Colle la Serra). Here you'll find a **bar-gelateria** (ice-cream parlour) several *alimentari* and a bus stop for the SITA service to Amalfi.

From the piazza go along the road to the right as you face the church, then turn left along Via Iovieno. Take the first turn left, then go straight through a crossroads (now with route 41) and continue for about 200m. Go right, up steps between gardens and terraces, across a minor road and up rougher steps, with trees on the right, to a road and bear left. About 800m further along this scenic road, immediately before a culvert, faint yellow markers indicate a short cut up rough steps and rocks, across a spur and down a bit to the road. The bitumen ends about 200m further on and a rough vehicle track gains height through chestnut woodland for several hundred metres. The track gives way to a path through trees – follow blue (and some red-and-white) waymarkers up a spur (right) 20m further on. The rough path climbs the open, rosemary-scented spur to **Capo Muro**, a distinct saddle on the spur abutting the towering, tiered cliffs above (about 1¾ hours from Bomerano).

Continue westwards on a better path (No 02) contouring the steep slope above Vallone Grarelle. After about 700m the path swings away from the valley and begins to descend. This section is generously waymarked through the maze of goat and mule tracks. About 500m further on, the path swings into a wide, deep valley and resumes contouring, with superb views across Positano and the awesome cliffs of Sant'Angelo a Tre Pizzi above. In places along here, dense bushes screen the rather long, steep drop to the left. Eventually you reach

Caserma Forestale (forestry barracks), a large stone building (1½ hours from Capo Muro).

Facing south in front of the *caserma*, head east (left) down through cypresses on hundreds of steps, then straight down to the Montepertuso–Nocelle road. Turn right and walk down the road to the village of Montepertuso. In the small piazza on the right, just past the soccer pitch, there are a **bar** and *gelateria* (nearly an hour from the Caserma Forestale).

From the piazza, cross the main road and bear right down a path (Via Pestella), below and to the right of a large church. Follow this down; after several hundred metres, turn right at a T-junction. With houses on both sides, turn right at another T-junction and right again at the next; descend to the coast road on the eastern edge of Positano. Sponda bus stop (on the Amalfi–Sorrento bus route) is about 250m to the left (45 minutes from Montepertuso).

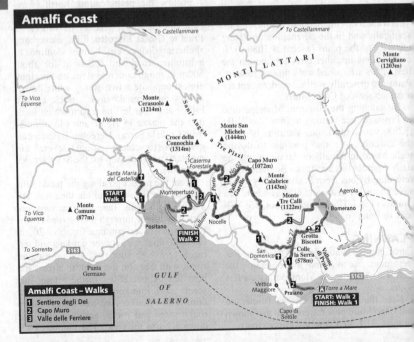

Amalfi Coast

Amalfi Coast – Walks
1 Sentiero degli Dei
2 Capo Muro
3 Valle delle Ferriere

Valle delle Ferriere

Duration	4½–5 hours
Distance	12km
Difficulty	moderate
Start/Finish	Atrani
Nearest Towns	Atrani (p291), Vettica Minore (p292)
Transport	bus

Summary Traditional villages, spectacular limestone cliffs, cool oak and chestnut woodlands, waterfalls, superb coastal views, and an optional side trip to Torre dello Ziro.

This varied walk allows plenty of time for diverging to the incredibly located Torre dello Ziro, perched on a cliff edge above Atrani. It can be done in either direction; it's described clockwise here simply because the author, for no good reason, believes that circular walks are most naturally done clockwise. The total ascent is 500m.

You can avoid the first ascent from Atrani by taking the SITA bus from Amalfi to Pogerola (€0.95, 20 minutes, once an hour). There is a much less frequent bus service from Scala (about 1km north along the road from Minuta, late in the walk) to Amalfi.

Waymarking is sparse where needed in the villages and prolific when much less crucial elsewhere.

NATURAL HISTORY

The 455-hectare **Riserva Statale Valle delle Ferriere** (w *www.parks.it/riserva.statale.valle .ferriere*) contains vegetation and landforms which have adapted to the variations in the local microclimate. The depths of the steep-sided valley shelter a mixed woodland and on the slopes above are typical Mediterranean scrub, adapted to dry conditions and relatively poor soils. Though you'd be lucky to see them, wild boars, hares, wolves and badgers have been recorded in the area.

PLANNING

Although you pass watering places in Pogerola and Pontone and, perhaps, flowing streams in Valle delle Ferriere, it's wise to carry some drinking water.

NEAREST TOWNS
Atrani

The village of Atrani is a 20-minute walk northeast of its famous neighbour Amalfi, and is less frenetic and definitely less blighted by mass tourism. It's a convenient base for walks in the eastern part of the Amalfi Coast.

La Risacca (*Piazza Umberto*), a bar, has Internet access (€3.10 per 15 minutes).

Places to Stay & Eat Something of an institution here is **A'Scalinatella** (☎ 089 87 14 92, fax 089 87 19 30; e *scalinatella@ amalficoast.it; Piazza Umberto 5-6; dorm beds €18.10*). To find reception and friendly English-speaking host Filippo, walk up Via dei Dogi from Piazza Umberto, go under an arch, follow the sign to the hostel for about 150m and then turn right up winding steps. The tariff includes sheets and breakfast. The hostel offers better double rooms with

CAMPANIA

private facilities elsewhere in Atrani for up to €62. In 2002, A'Scalinatella opened a restaurant, **La Piazzetta**, in the piazza.

Also in Piazza Umberto there are three **bars**, a **greengrocer**, a **cake shop** and an excellent *alimentari*.

At the western end of the beach, **Le Arcate** (☎ *089 87 13 67; Via di Benedetto 4; pizzas €6.70*) has mountain views. Dine on seafood, pasta and, in the evenings, more than 30 varieties of pizza. Servings are ample and the fact that it's popular with the locals speaks volumes. Among the pizzas is a local speciality with smoked mozzarella. A less varied menu is available at **Le Palme** (☎ *089 871 17 00; Lungo Vollaro 7*), off Via del Doge. Pasta and a pizza costs around €11.35, and there are only indoor tables.

Getting There & Away Atrani is on the SITA's Amalfi–Salerno bus route (one hour and five minutes, several a day). Buy tickets in Atrani from the newsagent in Piazza Umberto, and in Amalfi from Terminal Sita Bar near the bus terminus on Piazza Flavio Gioia. In Salerno, the SITA bus service to Naples leaves from outside **Bar Cioffi** (*Corso Garibaldi 134*). You can also buy your ticket there.

There are also frequent trains between Salerno and Naples (one hour), departing from Salerno's train station about 400m from the bus station.

Vettica Minore

Perched high above the coast road between Amalfi and Conca dei Marini, this scattered village is the location of an outpost of Atrani's A'Scalinatella empire. **Vettica House** (☎ *089 87 18 14;* e *vetticahousehostel@ amalficoast.it; Via Maestra dei Villaggi 92; quads €62*) has self-contained double and family rooms and a small basic communal kitchen, all with wonderful views. The only catch is that you have to climb 270 steps from the road. It's essential to ring first – there's no-one on site to settle you in.

To reach the local shops, cross the road at the bottom of the steps, bear slightly right then go left down more steps to the road and turn left. It's 50m down to the SITA bus stop, another 50m to an *alimentari* and a bit further down to a good **greengrocer**.

If you walk up the main road from the bottom of the steps and through the tunnel, then go left for 100m you'll come to **Bar Santa Rosa** where you can buy bus tickets; it's a more attractive bar for a drink than that down in Vettica Minore (beyond the *alimentari*).

Getting There & Away Vettica is on the SITA Amalfi–Agerola bus route (€0.95, 20 minutes, several a day Monday to Saturday). The SITA service between Amalfi and Naples (2½ hours, at least seven a day) also passes close to the Vettica House entrance.

THE WALK (see map pp290–1)

From Piazza Umberto I in Atrani, walk along Via Campo, the narrow passage by the red post box. Turn left at a T-junction and head up the steps; turn left at house No 18, then head up more steps between houses and continue generally ahead between and under houses to a scenic path which then winds down to the main road in Amalfi (15 minutes from Atrani). Bear right and then first right, through one small piazza then another, from where a passage in the far left corner leads to Piazza Duomo. Leave this piazza from the left-hand side (with the Banco di Napoli on the right) and walk along Via Lorenzo d'Amalfi for 500m; pass under a long arch beneath houses and go on for 50m, then left up Via Casamare and around a bend. Soon the road ends and steps lead up to the piazza in **Pogerola** (where the bus stops; 40 minutes from Amalfi). Here you'll find a cocktail bar-tea room-*gelateria*, **Bar Sport** – a good place for drinks, and **La Capannina** a *ristorante*-pizzeria.

To continue, go back to the last few metres of the approach to the piazza and turn right along a lane (with La Capannina on the right) and go past **Osteria Rispoli** (a bar) on the left, following route 59 with red-and-white markers. About 150m along, fork left up steps and continue, gaining a little height and ignoring sharp turns to the left. About 10 minutes from Pogerola you merge with a rough path, which leads into woodland; soon there's a longish flight of steps to limb, which brings you to a stream bed (30 minutes from Pogerola). Walk upstream a short distance to more steps; about 150m further on from the steps, the path leads through cultivated terraces then past an old stone building on the right. Swing left here into chestnut woodland, now in the heart of Valle delle Ferriere. About 15 minutes further on, cross a stream near a waterfall. Walk up sloping rocks and back into woodland. Then descend to another stream and, further on, cross the main stream, which, with luck, will be cascading into inviting pools (an hour from Pogerola). You soon pass an old sign marking the boundary of the Valle delle Ferriere reserve and emerge into more open country.

About 45 minutes from the main stream crossing, continue ahead at a prominent path junction, along a path at the base of the cliffs, with fantastic views down to Pogerola and Amalfi. Just 15 minutes from the last junction go through a short tunnel on the far side of which the path is flanked by stone walls. Soon it crosses a spur, descends through terraces then houses and goes steeply down to the right to reach the Minuta–Scala road just below a tight bend. The bus stop is 1km north along the road.

To continue, go down to the right to Minuta's small piazza, continue right, past a fountain, for about 200m then bear left at a fork beneath an archway and go on to the piazza in Pontone where **Bar Luca** is waiting to tempt you (10 minutes from Minuta). Go through the arch left of the church and turn right down a narrow road. Descend to cross a road diagonally in the direction of a sign to Torre dello Ziro and go down past a house. About 150m from the road, turn left down steps (the Side Trip: Torre dello Ziro, below, diverges here). At a T-junction turn left, then cross a bridge, from which steps and paths lead to another junction. Go right and down, then right again on a bend; cross a small piazza in front of **Ristorante Le Palme** to the main road in Atrani – Piazza Umberto is about 250m to the left (50 minutes from Pontone).

Side Trip: Torre dello Ziro
20–30 minutes, 1.5km
From the junction below Pontone, continue ahead along a path, then up concrete steps and on to a partly open area in pines, the site of a curious concrete structure. The path to the left goes out to the end of the spur and the Torre, from where a walled passage continues to the rim with a breathtaking overlook of Amalfi. Other paths around here are worth exploring for even more spectacular views.

Coastal Torri

One of the most eye-catching features of the coastline is the *torri* (fortified tower-like buildings), dotted along the coast on narrow promontories or headlands. Always with an unimpeded strategic outlook, they are squat, plain structures, rounded or angular. There are at least two between Vietri sul Mare and Punta Campanella on the Gulf of Salerno coast, two facing Capri and one at Punta del Capo, just northwest of Sorrento.

All the coast walks from Marina pass close to a *torre*; there's a large one near the camping ground at Praiano – Torre a Mare; a large sign in Italian at the entrance outlines its history.

The *torri* originated in the 16th century when the Ottoman empire had designs on the peninsula, part of the Spanish empire at the time. Following a devastating Ottoman raid on Sorrento and Massa Lubrense in 1558, the local Viceroy ordered the building of *torri*. They were to be fairly closely spaced along the coast, near existing or likely landing places and, in some cases, using sites occupied by fortresses since about the 10th century. An earlier edict by Emperor Charles V required the construction of square or cylindrical towers armed with cannons.

By the 18th century the *torri* had become redundant as defences; some fell into disuse, others were sold and some became state property.

Sorrento Peninsula

The relatively gentle contours of this populous peninsula contrast strikingly with the rugged mountainous profile of the Amalfi Coast. A variety of walks link the peninsula's beautiful coastline with the rural hinterland of villages, terraces and olive groves. Convenient bus services make it easy to enjoy these walks from any one of several possible bases; Marina del Cantone (Marina) on the southern coast is in focus here: it's close to the dramatic headlands at the western end of the peninsula and is as peaceful a place as you'll find in this popular area.

NATURAL HISTORY

A line of cliffs extending southwest from Punta Gradelle on the Gulf of Naples to Punta Germano on the Gulf of Salerno forms a clear divide between the mountains abov The Amalfi Coast and the gentle hills of th Sorrento Peninsula. The highest point on th gently undulating ridge extending southwe to Punta Campanella, the peninsula's spin is Monte Tore (528m) near Sant'Agata. Su face water is sparse, though stream course cut deep into the limestone rock.

On the intensively cultivated peninsul only pockets of the once widespread oak an chestnut woodlands survive. In uncultivate areas maquis thrives, a grouping of sma evergreen trees and shrubs adapted to po rocky soil and the long summer drought. Fo merly cultivated ground eventually reverts t a type of vegetation known as garrigue, wit many colourful dwarf shrubs, among whic the pink and white rock roses stand out.

Wildlife of any kind is, sadly, very scarc on the peninsula – shotgun cartridges sca tered around tell the story. However, i warm weather you are likely to come acros small black snakes, which seem more inter ested in escaping than in investigating yo more closely.

An extensive stretch of this magnificer coast, from Punta del Capo west of Sor rento all the way round to a point just we of Positano is protected, in varying degrees within the Area Marina Protetta di Punt Campanella. A zoning scheme controls fish ing, diving and boat access, guards natura and historical features and ensures tha recreation and fishing can co-exist. Mor information is available in Massa Lubrense from the **Ufficio Turistico** (☎ 081 808 95 7 Viale Filangieri 11) or the **area office** (☎ 08 878 96 88; Viale Filangieri 40).

PLANNING
Maps & Books

An excellent, free brochure is the 1:14,00 Terra del mito di Ulisse dimora delle Siren Passegiate. It has a reliable topographica map showing the numerous waymarke walks in the area as far east as Torca, and great deal of background information. It available in English, German and Italia from the AAST in Sorrento (p295).

Kompass' 1:50,000 map No 682 Penisol Sorrentina is helpful for planning purpose

---

Walking with Sirens

A network of 20 waymarked walks, known as Trails in Siren Land, has been developed throughout the Sorrento Peninsula by local agencies. The network perpetuates the legend of Ulysses and the sirens – they lived on the coast near Massa Lubrense and on the islets nearby (Vetara and li Galli). After hearing their singing, Ulysses built the famous temple of Athena.

These walks are identified by a colour-coding scheme, letters and numbers, and are shown on the first-rate Terra del mito di Ulisse dimora delle Sirene Passegiate map (see Maps & Books, this page). Most of the walks are easy to follow; pairs of small paint stripes in eye-catching places and tiles set into the ground or on rocks at junctions show the direction.

There are also large signs in the piazzas of the towns and villages the routes pass through, titled both Trails in Siren Land and Passegiate nella Terra delle Sirene, with a map and key to the paths. Note that the two CAI routes are shown as CAI1 and CAI2, but the CAI itself calls them both CAI00 on waymarkers and on its own Monti Lattari map (see Maps & Books, this page).

only. The CAI 1:30,000 map *Monti Lattari* usefully supplements the local and Kompass sheets, but paths may be numbered differently on the ground than on the map.

Julian Tippett's *Landscapes of Sorrento and the Amalfi Coast* describes numerous, mainly short walks and is invaluable.

A good source of local maps and guides is La Capsa bookshop in Sorrento.

Place Names

The Kompass map and Tippett's book both use the spelling Marine di Cantone. The local maps and the official village sign use Marina del Cantone, which is the spelling adopted here.

GETTING AROUND

See the boxed text 'Busing it with SITA' (p287). Timetables are available from the AAST office in Sorrento (below).

ACCESS TOWNS
Sorrento

Coming to the area from the north, it's almost impossible to avoid this large, busy town, extremely popular with visitors from Britain in particular. It could serve as your base for the walks described in the Sorrento Peninsula section, and even for those along the Amalfi Coast.

Useful for transport and accommodation details is the **AAST office** (☎ 081 807 40 33, fax 081 877 33 97; w www.sorrentotourism it; Via Luigi de Maio 35; open Mon-Sat). **La Capsa bookshop** (Corso Italia), a short distance east of the side road leading to the train station, has a good stock of local maps and guides.

Places to Stay & Eat Less than 15 minutes' walk from the town centre, beside the road to Massa Lubrense is **Camping Nube d'Argento** (☎ 081 878 13 44, fax 081 807 34 50; w www.nubedargento.com; Via Capo 21; camping per person/tent €9/5, bungalow doubles from €62). It offers camping on terraced pitches with sea views. The site has its own pizzeria and bar.

Ostello Sirene (☎ 081 807 2925; w www hostel.it; Via degli Aranci 160; dorm beds

€16, doubles €25.80) has cramped four- and six-bed dorms, each with a tiny bathroom. The tariff includes sheets and a light breakfast. You can leave luggage here and access the Internet. **Pensione Linda** (☎ 081 878 29 16; Via degli Aranci 125; doubles €41.30) is a clean, friendly place where you can have relative peace and quiet, and some space.

For self-catering, remember that shops are closed on Thursday afternoon. There is a **supermarket** opposite the hostel and a **Standa supermarket** (Corso Italia) between Piazza Tasso and Piazza A Lauro.

The choice of places to eat is vast; look for those with menus predominantly in Italian for food close to genuine Italian cooking. **Ristorante La Lanterna** (☎ 081 807 45 21; Via San Cesareo 23/25; 2 courses €15.50) offers generous servings from an international menu, though pizzas aren't a strong point. The wine list features local vintages. At **Ristorante Giardinello** (☎ 081 877 12 00; Via Accademica 7; open Tues-Sun) you can eat well at garden tables from an extensive menu with seafood for €12.90.

Getting There & Away Sorrento is well served by public transport, land and sea.

Bus There are daily **SITA** (☎ 081 552 21 76) services to Sorrento from Naples (Via Pisanelli) and from Salerno (Piazza della Concordia). In Sorrento, buses depart from outside the Circumvesuviana station and tickets are sold at the adjacent newsagent. **Curreri Viaggi** (☎ 081 801 54 20; w www .curreriviaggi.it) operates a service between Sorrento (Piazza Tasso) and Naples' Capodichino airport (€5.20, one hour, six a day).

Train The privately run **Circumvesuviana** (☎ 081 772 24 44; w www.vesuviana.it) provides a service from the station in Naples at Corso Garibaldi (about 400m southwest of Stazione Centrale) to Sorrento (€2.55, 30 a day). On the state system, reasonably frequent services link Naples Stazione Centrale and Salerno (€7.75).

Car From Naples, take the A3 and leave it at the Castellammare exit near Pompeii and

CAMPANIA

follow the S145 to Sorrento (48km from Naples). From the south and east, take the Vietri sul Mare turn-off from the A3 (just west of Salerno) to join the S163, which snakes along the coast to Colli San Pietro, 8km west of Positano. Here it meets the S145, which leads to Sorrento (50km from Salerno).

Ferry A hydrofoil service run by **Compagnia Linee Marittime Partenopee** *(☎ 081 807 18 12, fax 081 878 18 61)* operates between Naples' Stazione Marittima and Sorrento (€6.70, at least six sailings a day).

Marina del Cantone

This village overlooks a wide, shallow bay on the Gulf of Salerno with Monte San Costanzo towering above and Punta di Montalto guarding the southwestern approach. Its facilities are limited but it has the priceless assets of peace and quiet.

Places to Stay & Eat With shady, level sites, most with a sea view, campers should try the **Villagio Nettuno** *(☎ 081 808 10 51, fax 081 808 17 06; ⓦ www.villaggionettuno .it; camping per person/tent €5.70/7.75)*. The entrance is about 250m uphill from the piazza in the centre of the village. On-site, **Ristorante Nettuno** is open all day for pizza, pasta and fish; €15.50 would see you well fed. There are also a small shop and bar here.

Three hotels front onto the beach and have uninterrupted sea views. **La Certosa** *(☎ 081 808 12 09, fax 081 808 12 45; ⓔ certosa@ syrene.it; doubles €82.65)* offers comfortable doubles; rates include breakfast.

Caputa Alimentari, in Nerano (15 to 20 minutes' walk), is the nearest well-stocked shop.

Ristorante Il Cantuccio *(☎ 081 878 95 49; Piazza Vescovado 8/10; meals €20-50)* at the eastern end of the beach, enjoys an unrivalled location with a magnificent view of Monte San Costanzo. Fish dominates the menu, which also offers pasta, steak, and pizza (lunch only).

Bar Titonno on the beach makes its own superb *gelati* (ice creams) and serves snacks and drinks.

Getting There & Away SITA buses from Sorrento to Marina (called Nerano Cantone on the timetable) go via Sant'Agata and Termini (€1.20, 50 minutes, at least three times a day) or via Massa Lubrense and Termini (€1.20, at least four a day). In Marina, buy tickets from the bar next to the bus terminus.

By road from Sorrento or the Amalfi Coast, reach Sant'Agata, then continue southwest for about 3.5km to the turn-off for Marina, a further 3.4km.

Punta Penna

Duration	3–3½ hours
Distance	7km
Difficulty	easy–moderate
Start/Finish	Marina del Cantone (p296)
Transport	bus

Summary A scenic walk to a spectacular headland with superb views of the Isle of Capri.

This walk provides an excellent introduction to the Sorrento Peninsula, with fine sea and mountain views, typical limestone formations in the sheer cliffs and smaller crags, and extensive remains of olive groves. The Punta Penna headland bounds the eastern side of the beautiful Bay of Ieranto and overlooks the Gulf of Salerno to the east.

The route is easy to follow and is waymarked throughout, with red-and-white and blue-and-green markers from Marina and blue-and-green only from Nerano onwards. The total ascent is about 350m.

When the walk was surveyed, an extensive restoration project was in full swing around Bay of Ieranto, involving stabilisation and some reconstruction of several old buildings including the crumbling Torre d Montalto, stone-wall building and path construction.

The walk starts and finishes in Marina alternatively, you could start and finish a Nerano (on the Sorrento–Marina bus route) thus reducing the distance by 1km and the time by 20 to 30 minutes.

PLANNING

Use the *Terra del mito di Ulisse* map (see Maps & Books, p294). The path to the Torre was temporarily closed, and the east to west path marked on this map linking the Punta Penna path and a path to Bay of Ieranto did not exist in May 2001.

Be sure to carry water for this walk – there are no refreshments available beyond Nerano.

THE WALK (see map p298)

The path up to Nerano starts from the northwestern (uphill) corner of the large car park behind the hotels and bars in Marina. Follow it between houses and gardens and up to the main road. Cross it, and further up bear left along Via Cantone and follow it to the road beside the large church of San Salvatore in Nerano. There are an *alimentari* and two other **shops** close by. Continue left (south) along Via Amerigo Vespucci for about 50m then bear right along Via Ieranto. Further along, the wide path leads through a red archway and passes the flower-decked shrine at the small **Grotta delle Noglie** (Cave of the Cats) where skinny, long-legged cats are fed by the locals. A short distance beyond here a landslide had created some havoc at the time of writing; the 20m of debris can be crossed with great care.

Soon you're out in open grassland with scattered, long-deserted terraces; Capri floats on the horizon ahead. Just past a house and garden on the left is a path junction; bear left for Montalto and Punta Penna. Descend the rocky path; at the entrance to the Riserva Naturale di Ieranto on the right, follow the path beside a superbly built stone wall. At the corner of the wall, about 150m along, you may be able to diverge along a path up to the Torre di Montalto, depending on the progress of stabilisation work.

Continue southwest along the path through olive groves; it angles up slightly to the left to a gap between the two high points of the headland. Follow a path, or make your own way up to the seaward side of the highest point for the best views (one to 1½ hours from Marina).

Retrace your steps up to the path junction near the house and with luck you'll be able to go down the long flight of steps to the shore of Bay of Ieranto, a popular destination with the many yachts and small cruisers that frequent these waters.

Return to Marina by the paths followed on the outward journey.

Punta Campanella

Duration	4–4½ hours
Distance	8km
Difficulty	moderate
Start/Finish	Marina del Cantone (p296)
Transport	bus

Summary Panoramic views from the historic southwest tip of the Sorrento Peninsula and from the chapel on Monte San Costanzo, perched high above Marina del Cantone.

This walk could make a fitting *arrivederci* to the Sorrento Peninsula (and the Amalfi Coast) – the views of Monti Lattari and of Capri and the surrounding waters are inspirational. In early spring the ridge linking Monte San Costanzo and the Punta is enlivened with colourful wildflowers, notably rock roses.

The route between Nerano and Termini is distinguished by blue-and-green markers; from Termini you follow red-and-white, and red-and-green markers. Around 770m of ascent is involved, which could be reduced by simply walking out and back to the Punta from Termini, having arrived there by bus from your base (see Getting There & Away, p296). Another alternative return route (to Termini from near Monte San Costanzo) is outlined in the walk description.

PLANNING

The best map is the local *Terra del mito di Ulisse* (see Maps & Books, p294). Carry plenty of water from Termini.

THE WALK (see map p298)

From Marina, walk up to Nerano as described for the Punta Penna walk (p296). From San Salvatore church cross the road and climb the steps of Via Fontana di Nerano beside the *alimentari* and pass between houses and olive groves. Bear left at a fork and follow the concrete-paved road up to Piazza San Croce in Termini (45 minutes from Marina).

From the imposing church, follow Via Campanella to the left (south) for about 200m then turn right downhill along a minor road. Go round a sharp right-hand bend following a sign to Punta Campanella and continue past the turn-off to Mitigliano. About 400m further on, beyond a small wayside shrine, the minor road leads across the open rocky hillside and becomes a wide track. Punta Campanella (an hour from Termini) makes a spectacular end-point for the peninsula with magnificent views of Capri westwards and across Bay of Ieranto to the mountains beyond. The modern light beacon stands close to the crumbling (and dangerous) ruins of a *torre*.

Walk back along the track to a paved track on the right, distinguished by a red-and-white marker with the figures 00. Follow this path up and across the steep slope to the ridge crest. From here, a well marked, mostly clearly defined path ascends directly along or close to the ridge, through thick, low scrub and rock outcrops. Piles of stones and the remains of small stone shelters are clues to long-gone settlements in this exposed place.

Although the summit of Monte San Costanzo (497m; 1¼ hours from Punta Campanella) is monopolised by a fenced-off military installation, it still provides excellent views. The path skirts the southwestern (right) side of the compound then descends to a minor road; turn right. About 50m along the road at a small car park on the right, turn off with red-and-white waymarkers, keeping to the widest path through a pine grove. From the far (eastern) edge of the pines (the Alternative Route to Termini, below, diverges here), go up steps to the plain white chapel of **San Costanzo**, another superb viewpoint. Retrace your steps from the chapel (200m) and go down to the left with red-and-white markers, through trees. From the edge of the plantation, continue down beside it for 300m then bear left across the grassy slope, and down past a large clump of cactus; about 30m below it, turn left across the slope (level with the top of derelict gardens on the right), to reach the eastern end of the old olive grove below. Contour the slope past a vegetable garden on the right. Then swing left to pass a deep cleft on the right and almost immediately, at the corner of a stone wall, turn diagonally right along a path and descend soon through woodland. Eventually, two flights of steps take you down to the cobbled Punta Penna path; turn left to reach Nerano (an hour from the chapel). Continue down to Marina (15 to 20 minutes).

Alternative Route: San Costanzo to Termini

30–45 minutes, 1km

On the edge of the pine grove 100m west of San Costanzo chapel, an obscure red-and-green marker indicates a turn northwards down through scattered pines to a road. Turn right for only 10m then go left down a path, cross a road and continue downhill to meet

Sorrento Peninsula

Sorrento Peninsula – Walks

1 Punta Penna
2 Punta Campanella

0   1   2km
0   0.5   1mi
1:100,000

Capo di Massa
Sorrento
SS145
134m
Massa Lubrense
To Sant'Agata
Marina Protetta di Punta Campanella
Santa Maria
Monticchio
Schiazzano
Le Tore (380m)
Alternative Route
Termini
Punta di Vaccola
San Costanzo
Nerano
Monte San Costanzo (497m)
Grotta delle Noglie
Marina del Cantone
Recommone Torre
START/ FINISH
Bay of Ieranto
Torre di Montalto
Punta Campanella
Punta Penna
Riserva Naturale di Ieranto
Marina Protetta di Punta Campanella

ne road again. Turn right; 20m along, head left along a path with a stone wall on the right, with red-and-green markers. Then cross the road again and descend a many-stepped path to a road which leads into Termini.

Other Walks

AMALFI COAST

Croce della Conocchia

This is the westernmost peak (1314m) on the long, dramatically rugged chain of huge lumps of limestone called Sant'Angelo a Tre Pizzi – the highest part of the Monti Lattari Range. Unlike the main summits, it's easily accessible from the coast. A path, waymarked with the CAI's red-and-white stripes, ascends north from Caserma Forestale (see the Sentiero degli Dei walk, p287) through woodland and out into open ground with stunning views of cliffs and the coast. The crucifix-topped summit is easily gained, although the waymarked path bypasses it to the left in hazel woodland. The view embraces the sprawling city of Naples, Vesuvius, the isles of Ischia and Capri and mountains to the northwest.

A 8km return walk from the Caserma, allow about two hours uphill (550m ascent) and slightly less down. The CAI 1:30,000 Monti Lattari map shows part of the route, though is now out of date.

Vallone di Praia

This deep, steep-sided valley just northeast of Praiano displays a great array of terraces and some fine high cliffs. It's easily accessible from Praiano. Having traversed the valley, you can then walk up to the small town of Bomerano with several bars and cafés, quite different from the coastal cliff-hanging villages and towns. Return by the same route, or via Colle la Serra (see the Capo Muro walk, p289, for a route description in reverse). Alternatively there's a regular daily SITA bus service to Amalfi.

Allow two hours from Praiano to Bomerano (about 640m ascent) and another 1½ to two hours back to Praiano via Colle la Serra, a total of 9km. The Vallone walk is included in Tippett's book (see Maps & Books, p294). Use the CAI 1:30,000 map Monti Lattari.

Pogerola–San Lazzaro–Vettica Minore

Finishing at the steps to Vettica House (see Vettica Minore, p292) this walk is of particular interest if you're staying there. It passes though a wild and seemingly remote forested valley and leads to a fine viewpoint overlooking the coast.

The 7km walk involves 550m ascent and should take about 3¼ hours.

Pogerola is a walk, or bus ride from Amalfi (see the Valle delle Ferriere walk, p291). San Lazzaro is on the Amalfi–Agerola bus route. The CAI 1:30,000 Monti Lattari map shows the way-marked routes and most of the other paths and tracks followed. The walk is described in Tippett's book (see Maps & Books, p294).

Atrani–Ravello–Maiori

Ravello is a beautiful old town, clustered on a narrow plateau rising steeply between Atrani and the coastal town of Maiori. It can provide the focus for an easy day out from Atrani or can be one of the highlights in a moderate walk from Atrani, up to Ravello, then down to the coast at Minori (the site of an ancient Roman coastal resort) and on to Maiori. The 6km route follows old paths and laneways through olive and citrus groves and quiet villages with extensive coast and mountain vistas.

Allow one to 1½ hours for the walk up to Ravello which includes 300m ascent; from there to Minori via the village of Torello, it's nearly all downhill (40 minutes to an hour). From Minori to Maiori, there's about 260m ascent, for which allow 50 minutes to an hour. You could make a nearly circular walk of it by returning to Minori then following a route back to Atrani via Torello, bypassing Ravello. This involves about 480m of ascent and should take about three hours. The CAI and Kompass maps show the lie of the land; you'll need Tippett's book for precise directions (see Maps & Books, p294).

There are hourly SITA buses between Amalfi and Ravello, and between Amalfi and Salerno via Maiori and Minori.

Monte dell'Avvocata

This prominent peak at the eastern end of the Monti Lattari Range is clearly in view from Atrani and the nearby mountainsides. From its summit (1014m) the magnificent panoramic view takes in Naples, Vesuvius, and mountains to the west and south. A one-time monastery stands just below and southwest of the summit and can be identified from the coast.

The mountain can be approached from the coast road (S163) near the village of Erchie. This involves 940m of ascent, 8km and about six hours of walking, essentially up the western side of a long valley, across its stream to a spur that leads to the main ridge, then along it to the summit. Much of the ascent follows rough paths and flights of steps; the section between the stream crossing and the main ridge had been burnt not very long before the walk was surveyed in May 2001 and the path was very difficult to follow. Elsewhere, either the path is clear, or red-and-white waymarkers indicate the route. From the top, descend the well-used path to Maiori. To reach the start, catch the Amalfi–Salerno SITA bus to the stop above Erchie – ask the driver to let you know when the bus reaches the stop for 'Sentiero all'Avvocata'.

The CAI 1:30,000 *Monti Lattari* map is useful for general orientation only. The walk is described in Tippett's book (see Maps & Book, p294).

SORRENTO PENINSULA
Termini to Massa Lubrense

The highlights of this short walk of 3.4km (an hour) are the views of Capri and Gulf of Naples, views of the towns and villages through which the route passes, and the peaceful, timeless villages themselves. The route links waymarked walks C3 (yellow-and-green markers), C2 (yellow and blue) and C1 (yellow and red) and is downhill (200m descent) almost all the way. The relevant map is the locally produced *Terra del mito di Ulisse* (see Maps & Books, p295). Both the start and finish are on the Sorrento–Marina del Cantone bus route.

Marina to Sorrento via Torca

The CAI's Alta Via dei Lattari (waymarked 00 with the usual red-and-white stripes) is a challenging long-distance route linking Termini and Punta Campanella with Corpo di Cava in the east (6km northwest of Maiori on the Amalfi Coast), a distance of 90km. Sparseness of accommodation would make a full, continuous traverse difficult and camping isn't a realistic option in the absence of adequate water sources. The westernmost section is covered in the Punta Campanella walk (p297).

From Marina, it's not difficult to follow the Alta Via's outstandingly scenic route to Fontanelle, involving about 7km, 5½ to six hours and 550m ascent. From here you can take a moderately amenable route (1¾ hours) down to Sorrento, described in Tippett's book. Between Recommone and Torca is it possible to detour to the ancient settlement of Crapolla. The local map *Terra del Mito di Ulisse* is useful as far east as Monticello. The CAI *Monti Lattari* map covers the whole walk; the route near Malacoccola has changed since it was published. For details of these publications see Maps & Books, p294.

The walk could be spread over two days by breaking off at Torca and following a waymarked route to Sant'Agata on the Sorrento–Marina del Cantone bus route.

Sicily

Sicily (Sicilia) is the essence of Italy, and then some. Isolated by sea, and closer to North Africa and Greece than to many of Italy's own provinces, Sicily is a place of sometimes disturbing contrasts; crumbling antiquity and fast-tracked development, wealth and poverty, great natural beauty and unchecked urban sprawl. Traditional links with the soil and the past are strong. Away from the bustling cities and trendy beach resorts, the island's interior remains sparsely populated and very traditional in character, with small, shuttered villages scattered along valleys amid the isolated grandeur of a predominantly mountainous terrain.

Despite its reputation as an enigmatic and somewhat exotic Mediterranean location, Sicily is relatively undiscovered as a walking destination. Sicilians have not traditionally championed walking as a pastime, and the island's parks lack the basic infrastructure that is taken for granted in northern Italy and Europe. Away from Etna, *rifugi* (mountain huts) and trail markers are sporadic at best, and attempts to develop new areas have often been hampered by bureaucratic and communal divisions, and a lack of clear direction.

This is beginning to change, however, as authorities invest in ecological tourism in a new appreciation of the island's beautiful and surprisingly varied landscapes. For those prepared to tackle the practical challenges, exploring Sicily on foot can be a highly rewarding adventure and an ideal way to experience the island's less visited places.

HISTORY

Paying a sometimes heavy price for its strategic location in the heart of the Mediterranean, Sicily has, since prehistory, been an attractive territorial prize, bringing a succession of colonisers and settlers to its shores. It is believed the earliest settlers were the Sicanians, Elymians and Siculians, arriving from various points around the southern Mediterranean. They were later

Highlights

Rugged Aeolian archipelago – looking across Lipari to the volcanic Vulcano

- Crossing time-worn lava flows on the long walk round the base of Europe's most active volcano, Mt Etna (p303)

- Looking out at the Aeolian Islands from the rim of Vulcano's gently steaming Gran Cratere (p313)

- Staying overnight in an old hunting lodge, surrounded by age-old beech woods on the picturesque Nebrodi Lake Circuit (p318)

DALLAS STRIBLEY

SICILY

followed by the Phoenicians. Greek colonisation began in the 8th century BC with the foundation of Naxos. By 210 BC Sicily was under Roman control, with power eventually passing to the Byzantines and then to the Arabs, who had settled in by AD 903.

Norman conquest of the island began in 1060, when Roger I of Hauteville captured Messina. Mastery of Sicily subsequently passed to the Swabians and the Holy Roman

Emperor Frederick II, known as Stupor Mundi (Wonder of the World). In the 13th century the French Angevins provided a period of misrule that ended in 1282 with the revolt known as the Sicilian Vespers. The island was ceded to the Spanish Aragon family and, in 1503, to the Spanish crown. After short periods of Savoy and Austrian rule in the 18th century, Sicily again came under the control of the Spanish Bourbons of Naples in 1734, who united the island with southern Italy in the Kingdom of the Two Sicilies.

On 11 May 1860 Giuseppe Garibaldi landed at Marsala with his 'One Thousand' and began the conquest that eventually set the seal on the unification of Italy. Life did not greatly improve for the people of Sicily, and between 1871 and 1914 more than one million Sicilians emigrated, mainly to the USA.

In 1943 some 140,000 Allied troops, under General Dwight Eisenhower, landed on southeastern Sicily. Initially blocked by dogged Italian and German resistance, Eisenhower's field commanders entered Messina within six weeks, after heavy fighting had devastated many parts of the island. The Allied occupation lasted until early 1944. In 1948 Sicily became a semi-autonomous region and, unlike other such regions in Italy, it has its own parliament and legislative powers.

NATURAL HISTORY

Extending over 25,708 sq km, triangular-shaped Sicily is the largest island in the Mediterranean. Physically the largely mountainous island (83% of the total surface can be described as either hilly or mountainous) straddles two continental shelves: the northern and eastern half is considered to be an extension of the Calabrian Apennines, while the southern and western half is topographically similar to the Atlas mountains of North Africa.

The topography of the island is a combination of mountain, plateau and fertile coastal

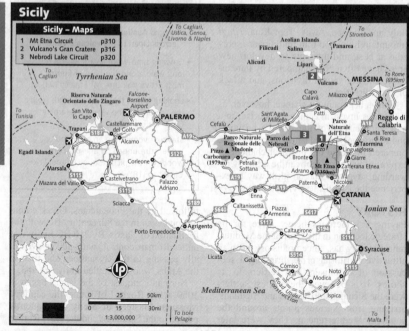

plain. In the northeast, the mountains are made up of three distinct ranges: the Nebrodi and Madonie ranges, which skirt virtually the entire length of the Tyrrhenian coast up to Palermo; and the Peloritani, which rise above the length of the eastern coast. The interior is mostly hills and plateaus, which extend and slope downwards to the southern coast. The coasts are an alternating panorama of rugged cliffs and low, sandy shores, making up some of the island's most beautiful scenery.

Sicily is renowned for its volcanic activity and the eastern half of the island is dominated by the imposing cone of Mt Etna (3350m), Europe's largest active volcano. Sicily's two other active volcanoes are to the north of the island in the Aeolian archipelago: Vulcano and Stromboli.

CLIMATE

Sicily enjoys a temperate Mediterranean climate with mild winters and long, relentlessly hot summers fanned by the *scirocco* (sirocco), blowing from the deserts of northern Africa (see the boxed text 'Windy Italy', p34). During summer, average daily temperatures on the coast are over 30ºC. Mountainous areas remain several degrees cooler. Winter temperatures average between 10ºC and 14ºC. Rainfall is low and occurs almost exclusively during late autumn and winter, when downpours can be sudden and heavy.

INFORMATION
Books

Lonely Planet's *Sicily* guide covers the island in useful yet entertaining detail.

An excellent English-language walking guide to Sicily, with more than 40 short tours to the island's most renowned tourist sites, as well as to some wonderfully undiscovered parts, is the Sunflower Landscapes guide, *Sicily*, by Peter Amann. It concentrates on walks that fit neatly with car tours around the island – a convenient companion for walkers with their own wheels.

Emergency

For search and rescue assistance in the mountains of Sicily, contact **Soccorso Alpino**

(☎ 095 91 41 41). For urgent medical assistance, contact the **national emergency number** (☎ 118). See also Emergency (p307) for local contacts while on Etna.

Mt Etna Circuit

Duration	3 days
Distance	40.5km
Difficulty	easy–medium
Start	Rifugio Brunek (p308)
Finish	Rifugio Sapienza (p308)
Nearest Town	Catania (p307)
Transport	private
Summary	A superbly scenic walk round the base of Europe's most active volcano, crossing lava flows and exploring lava tunnels.

Dominating the landscape in eastern Sicily between Taormina and Catania, the majestic Mt Etna (3350m; known to Sicilians as Mongibello) is Europe's largest live volcano and one of the world's most active. Coated in snow for much of the year, this almost perfectly cone-shaped mountain remains one of Sicily's most enduring and fascinating icons. For volcano lovers, frequent eruptions offer a rare opportunity to glimpse, at a safe distance, something of the massive forces at work beneath the earth's fragile crust.

Since 1987 the volcano and its slopes have been part of a national park covering 590 sq km in a territory that includes 20 communities. The park encompasses a fascinatingly varied natural environment, from the severe, almost surreal summit area, with its breathtaking panoramas, to the deserts of lava encrusting the volcano's sides.

A trail, known as the *altomontana* (high mountain), closed to traffic and well maintained by the Guardia Forestale (forestry department), offers the walker a long, semicircular route from Rifugio Brunek to the Rifugio Sapienza. It is a beautiful route that traverses the wooded slopes of the volcano at altitudes between 1300m and 1800m, and crosses many time-worn lava flows. There are several unstaffed, ranger-maintained *rifugi* (mountain huts) along the way that

SICILY

function similarly to the *bivacchi* (emergency shelters) of the Alps. They are always open and are a good place to spend a night wrapped in a sleeping bag.

The Mt Etna Circuit follows this trail. You can spend three days virtually isolated from the rest of civilisation, but you'll need to carry all your food and water. At the beginning and end of the walk there are comfortable, alpine-style staffed *rifugi* offering food and accommodation. Trips up to the craters can be organised from either end.

HISTORY

In ancient times Etna's summit was frequently lit up by spectacular pyrotechnic displays. The volcano was visible for hundreds of kilometres out to sea and acted as a night beacon for the ancient navigators of the Mediterranean.

Not surprisingly, the spectacularly eruptive Etna features in some very early writings. The classical world saw the volcano in mythological terms as the home of the god Plutone and of the Titans who had rebelled against Zeus. In the 18th century BC, Homer mentioned Etna in the episode of Ulysses and the Cyclops. In the 5th century BC, the historian Thucydides referred to the incredible eruptive activity of Etna. Aeschylus, who was at Syracuse in 472 BC, cited a 16th-century BC legend in his *Prometheus*, in which Etna is described as a 'column holding up the sky', with the giant Tifone (Typhoon) at its base, shaking his 100 heads and making the whole world tremble.

The first documented visitor to Etna was Pietro Bembo in 1493, who wrote the Latin work, *De Aetna*, telling of his adventures. This encouraged an influx of English, German, French, Dutch and Danish travellers. English physicist Patrick Brydone is considered the founder of the Sicilian 'Grand Tour'. In 1773 he published his *Tour Through Sicily & Malta*, which was translated into French and German. His lyrical and dreamy descriptions of the ascent to the crater inspired many aristocrats to visit Etna.

With local guides, it was a two-day mule ride to make the round trip from Nicolosi to see the sunrise at Etna's main crater. Among those who made the trip were Dumas, De Dolomieu and the French landscape painter Jean Hovel. Already in the 19th century, Etna had a strong local economy founded on the presence of these travellers.

NATURAL HISTORY

Triggered by a combination of volcanic and regional tectonic activity more than half a million years ago, a number of eruptive centres appeared off the east coast of Sicily and began to deposit material. Over the next several hundred thousand years, a series of overlapping volcanic cones built up and then collapsed to form giant calderas. The most recent phase of volcanism, about 35,000 years ago, created the present-day stratovolcano, known as Etna.

With a circumference of 165km and covering an area of 1260 sq km, Etna is the largest active volcano in Europe and one of the few large wild areas of Sicily. Rising directly out of the sea, it reaches roughly 3350m, although this figure varies after eruptions and as lava accumulates around the summit craters. Belying the simplicity of its conical shape, the volcano is made up of a complex network of channels and fractures. The central conduit, which leads to the present four summit craters, is surrounded by more than 200 major and secondary cones dotting the volcano's flanks. During an eruption, magma forces its way upwards through any number of these escape valves from a reservoir 20km beneath the surface. Measuring roughly 7km by 5km, the Valle del Bove, a depression on the eastern side of Etna, is a caldera formed after a cone collapsed several thousand years ago.

There is evidence to suggest that volcanic activity was once far more violent than the frequent, relatively low-key eruptions that take place on Etna today. The volcano's most notorious eruption occurred in 1669 and lasted 122 days. A huge river of lava poured down its southern slope, destroying 16 towns and engulfing a good part of Catania, dramatically altering the landscape. Twenty-thousand people were killed by the accompanying earthquake.

ecent eruptions have been restricted to eriodic lava flows which, while newswor- y, generally haven't threatened the local opulation. Flows (at a sizzling 1100°C) rely cover more than 10km, travelling at iywhere between several tens of metres er second (near the source) and a more isurely few metres per hour. The few who ave lost their lives on the volcano were irprised by eruptions while visiting the raters – a risky business at the best of mes. In 1979, nine people died in an ex- losion at the Cratere Sud-Est (southeast rater) and eight years later another two ere killed at the same crater.

lora

nce covered by huge forests, the fertile olcanic soils on the lower flanks of Etna ow support very productive vineyards and roves of olive, almond, pistachio, hazel- it, chestnut and fruit trees. Beyond the gricultural fringe, in steeper terrain and be- een solidified lava flows, patches of holm id deciduous oak survive. Also on the imper eastern slopes, manna ash, horn- eam and maple trees are concentrated. everal species of broom also thrive below e tree line.

Between 1000m and 1800m the larch ne performs an important role as a pioneer ant, recolonising lava flows. Higher up, the cold northwest slopes up to 2000m, pper beech grows – this is the southern- ost point in Europe at which the beech is und. A dwarf version can be found up to 50m in the Punta Lucia area. Etna's birch ows up to 2100m and is considered an en- mic species, like the beech, left over from e last Ice Age.

The most surprising vegetation is found high altitudes beyond the forested areas. iese are surreal, pillow-shaped tussocks milk-vetch, another of Etna's endemic ecies that survives to 2450m. Inside, der its trusty thorns, the sweetly-scented irysanthemum nestles, protected from the ind. Above 2500m even the thorntree dis- pears and the only vegetation are rumex d the odd Sicilian soapwort, with its deli- te pink flowers.

Fauna

Etna's forested slopes were once home to wolves, wild boars, roebucks, otters, mar- tens and griffon. However, unable to adapt to human encroachment on the mountain and hunted to extinction, these larger carni- vores have long since died out. Only three carnivores remain in the Parco dell'Etna: fox, weasels and wild cats. These hunt smaller mammals, such as rabbits, hares, mice and hedgehogs. The porcupine is found along the trail and is the largest wild animal on Etna. There are at least eight species of bat that inhabit the ravines and caves created by the lava, including the rare *molosso del cestoni*.

Among the birds of Etna, the royal eagle has recently returned to nest in the park. You'll also see sparrowhawks, buzzards, kestrels, peregrine falcons and nocturnal predators: the only Sicilian colonies of common owls, tawny owls and barn owls. In the woods and high mountain areas there are many species of woodpecker, as well as ravens, doves, crows, rare rock partridges and an infinite number of small birds.

Etna Roars Again

On 17 July 2001, Etna roared once more, spitting ash into the sky and releasing rivers of molten rock down its southern side. For 24 days the international media camped on the slopes of the volcano, relaying live images around the world as lava flowed from the Cratere Sud-Est and several new fissures. As spectacular eruptions continued, the road leading to the Sapienza ski resort was cut off and several resort buildings were inexorably consumed. While never seriously threatened, residents of the town of Nicolosi, 10km from the lava's source, took to the streets with the best form of spiritual insurance: an effigy of Sant'Agata. A heavy layer of ash covered nearby Catania, forcing its international air- port to close. By the time eruptions had calmed on 15 August, an impressive 50 mil- lion cubic metres of lava and pyroclastic had been spat into the atmosphere.

SICILY

There are numerous innocuous reptiles, but watch out for the viper, a poisonous snake found throughout Italy.

CLIMATE

The climate on Etna varies with altitude. At higher altitudes there is a mountain climate, becoming colder towards the summit area (above 2000m), which is exposed to strong, freezing wind. Snowfall is common from November to April, but can occur year-round. Further down the mountain, the climate becomes gradually more typical of the mild Mediterranean conditions that characterise Sicily – expect cloudless, hot summer days.

PLANNING
When to Walk

The best periods for walking on Etna are spring and autumn, between April and May, and September and October, when the weather is mild and the vegetation puts on a magnificent display of colour. During the height of summer, trekking across lava fields under an unforgiving Mediterranean sun can be an uncomfortably hot experience.

What to Bring

Unlike many of the CAI-run *rifugi* of northern Italy, the huts around Mt Etna are not serviced, although they are clean and stocked with supplies of firewood. Walkers on the circuit will need to bring a sleeping mat to lay out on the stone benches, a sleeping bag, fire-lighting equipment and a torch (flashlight). All food and water for the three days should also be carried, along with cooking gear. The water supplies at the *rifugi* are limited and local advice is that the water is not drinkable.

Solid, comfortable walking shoes are recommended, as the volcanic rock covering Etna's slopes is rough and very abrasive. A hat is essential during the hotter months, while at night, when the temperature drops considerably, you will need warm clothing.

If you are planning on a trip up to the craters, all the trappings of a high-altitude excursion – warm clothes, a wind jacket, warm headgear and gloves – should be taken. It is also advisable to carry a compass, as banks of fog can develop, making orientation difficult.

Mobile phones are an excellent safety precaution, but be aware that they won't work everywhere on the mountain.

Maps

Available free from visitor centres in Catania (p307), the Touring Club Italiano' 1:175,000 map *Province of Catania* is useful tool for planning. If supplies have run out, the same map can also be found in city bookshops. Alternatively, Touring Club Italiano's 1:200,000 map *Sicilia*, covering the whole island, is also perfectly adequate.

For navigational purposes, the best option is the Touring Club Italiano 1:50,000 map *Mt Etna*. There are Istituto Geografic Militare (IGM) maps of the area at 1:25,000. However, these are more than 40 years old and show some trails that no longer exist, while failing to show other, newer trails.

Information Sources

The Office of the Parco Regionale dell'Etna (☎ 095 82 11 11, fax 095 91 47 38; Via Etne 107/a, Nicolosi) is on the southern slopes of Etna above Catania. More convenient for the Mt Etna Circuit, however, is the provincial APT visitor centre in Catania (p307), which has friendly English-speaking staff and numerous useful publications.

If not passing through Catania, on the north side of Etna at Linguaglossa there is a Pro Loco tourist office (☎ 095 64 30 94; w prolocolinguaglossa.it; Piazza Annunziata 5). At Piano Provenzana, 5km west of Rifugio Brunek on the Etna high plain, there is an APT office (☎ 095 64 73 52) and kiosks that sell maps to Etna.

At the end of the walk (Rifugio Sapienza) there's the Etna Sud APT office (☎ 095 9 63 56; open daily).

For up-to-date information on eruptions and weather forecasts, and for a detailed account of the mountain's geology and history, take a look at w www.geo.mtu.edu ~boris/ETNA.html.

Guided Walks

There are several groups that organise tours towards the craters and elsewhere on the mountain, involving both trekking and

WD tours with a volcanologist or alpine uide. Most cater for groups rather than individuals, so unless you can find space on a our, the cost to hire a guide between one or wo people can be prohibitively expensive. Bear in mind that many of the guides do not peak English.

Gruppo Guide Alpine Etna Sud (☎ 095 '91 47 55; Via Etnea 49, Nicolosi) offers a umber of day and multi-day itineraries for £180.75 per day with a guide. Gruppo iuide Alpine Etna Nord (☎ 095 64 78 33; iazza Santa Caterina 24, Linguaglossa) runs similar service from the north side of Etna.

The NeT guides group (☎ 095 91 15 05; 'ia R Quartarano 11, 95125 Catania) is an fficient organisation of motivated, English-peaking guides who run nature walks, as vell as more challenging excursions. Guides re a mine of information on the volcano.

For the more adventurous, Bio Sport Management (☎ 090 640 98 00, 339 233 13 7, fax 090 640 94 97; e biosport@siceas.it; 'ia Garibaldi 110, Messina) delivers every-ling from trekking to cave exploring and orse riding on the mountain. Tour organ-er, Ugo Esposito, speaks excellent English nd is a friendly and knowledgeable guide.

mergency
1 an emergency, ring either Soccorso Alpino tna Nord (☎ 0337 902 82 36) or Soccorso lpino Etna Sud (☎ 0330 36 81 52).

NEAREST TOWN & FACILITIES
Catania
Vith all the edgy chaos, traffic congestion nd general decay you'd expect of Sicily's econd-largest city, Catania sounds like an nsavoury prospect; fortunately someone orgot to tell this to the locals. A glance elow the grit and grime reveals a sophisti-ated and vibrant city, with a rich history nd a rocking summer nightlife.

There's the main APT office (☎ 095 730 2 22, 095 730 62 11; w www.apt.catania.it; ia Cimarosa 10-12; open daily), as well as ranches at the train station (☎ 095 730 62 5) on platform No 1, at the airport (☎ 095 30 62 66) and at the port (☎ 095 730 62 9). The best place to buy maps is Librerie

Cavallotto (Corso Sicilia 91) – an excellent bookshop if you're hunting generally for books on Catania and Sicily. There are a number of bookshops along Via Etnea that also sell Etna maps; try Libreria Editrice (Via Etnea 390) or La Paglia (Via Etnea 393). Luggage can be left at the train station for a flat rate of €3.90 per bag for up to 12 hours.

Places to Stay Close to a beautiful rocky beach is Camping Jonio (☎ 095 49 11 39, fax 095 49 22 77; Via Villini a Mare 2; camping per person/tent €5.40/11.90), about 5km north of the city. To get there, catch bus No 334 from Via Etnea.

In one of the most interesting parts of the old city behind Piazza del Duomo, Agorà youth hostel (☎ 095 723 30 10, fax 178 226 89 79; w agorahostel.hypermart.net; Piazza Curò 6; dorm beds €15.50) is the best option for travellers on a rock-bottom budget. Tucked away in a small courtyard off Via Etnea, the Hotel Rubens (☎ 095 31 70 73, fax 095 715 17 13; Via Etnea 196; singles/doubles €22.20/31, with bath €28.40/40.30) is central, comfortable and well priced. It also has an affable English-speaking owner. Recently renovated Pensione Gresi (☎ 095 32 27 09; Via Pacini 28; singles/doubles €36.15/51.65) is in a quiet street off Via Etnea, just round the corner from Villa Bellini. Possibly the best mid-range hotel in Catania, the Hotel Centrale Europa (☎ 095 31 13 09, fax 095 31 75 31; Via Vittorio Emanuele II 167; singles/doubles with bath €43.90/62) has spotless, elegant rooms, some overlooking Piazza del Duomo.

Places to Eat All manner of fresh produce can be bought from the city's excellent and central markets, open every day except Sunday. La Fiera (Piazza Carlo Alberto) has bread, fresh fruit, cheese and all manner of odds and ends, while La Pescheria (Piazza del Duomo) is the place to buy fish.

Eating out can be pleasant and inexpensive in Catania, with innumerable stalls and bars serving delicious Sicilian snacks and savoury titbits. For a wide selection of delectable sweet and savoury pastries, you can't go past St Moritz bar (Via Etnea), 100m north of Piazza Stesicoro. **I Puritani gelataria** (*Piazza Bellini*) serves up *gelato* (ice cream) to satisfy the fussiest of devotees. **Trattoria de' Fiori** (☎ *095 31 62 83; Via Coppola 24*) isn't much in the glamour stakes but serves as close to authentic Sicilian home cooking as you'll get without an invitation. **Trattoria La Paglia** (☎ *095 34 68 38; Via Pardo 23*), just behind Piazza del Duomo in the heart of the *pescheria* (fish market), is one of Catania's best traditional seafood restaurants. Freshness is guaranteed.

Getting There & Away Catania's airport, Fontanarossa, is 7km southwest of the city centre and services domestic and European flights (the latter via Rome or Milan). In summer you may be able to dig up the odd direct charter flight to London or Paris. Take the special Alibus (No 457; €0.70) from outside the train station or in Via Etnea.

Intercity buses terminate in the area around Piazza Giovanni XXIII, in front of the train station. **SAIS** (☎ *095 53 61 68; Via d'Amico 185*) serves Syracuse, Palermo (€11.60, 2½ hours), Agrigento and Messina (€6.20, 1½ hours). It also has services to Naples (€29.95, 8¾ hours) and Rome (€38.75, 10½ hours).

AST (☎ *095 746 10 96, 095 53 17 56; Via Luigi Sturzo 232*) also services these destinations and many smaller provincial towns around Catania, including Nicolosi, the cable car on Mt Etna and Noto. **Interbus-Etna Trasporti** (☎ *095 53 27 16, 095 746 13 33; Via d'Amico 185*) runs buses to Piazza Armerina, Taormina, Messina, Enna, Ragusa, Gela, Syracuse and Rome.

Frequent trains connect Catania with Messina and Syracuse (both 1½ hours) and there are less frequent services to Palermo (€11, 3¼ hours), Enna (€4.5, 1¾ hours) and Agrigento (€11). The private Ferrovie Circumetnea Catania (FCE) railway line circles Mt Etna, stopping at the towns and villages around the volcano's base (see Rifugio Brunek, this page, for details).

Catania is easily reached from Messina on the A18 and from Palermo on the A19. From the A18, signs for the centre of Catania will bring you to Via Etnea.

Rifugio Brunek

In the tranquil setting of the lovely Pinet Ragabo pine forest on the eastern slopes c Etna, Rifugio Brunek (☎ *095 64 30 15, 36 85 98 26; B&B/half board €20.65/31)* i light years from the chaos of Catania. Th chalet-style *rifugio* has very pleasant room and a dedicated host. There is fresh loca produce on the menu.

Getting There & Away Public transpo only gets you as far as Linguaglossa, 10k east of Rifugio Bruneck.

Departing Catania, **Ferrovie Circumetne Catania** (*FCE;* ☎ *095 54 12 50, 095 54 12 5* runs a bus service to Linguaglossa (€3.3! from Monday to Saturday. It departs ju outside the Piazza Giovanni XXIII bus te minal, opposite the central train station. Yo can buy a ticket on the bus (destinatic Randazzo). Get off at the train station i Linguaglossa.

For a more scenic alternative, you ca catch the private FCE train from Catania Linguaglossa (€3.60), which leaves regu larly from the train station about 500i north of Piazza Cavour, off Via Caronda Ask at the train station **ticket office** (☎ *09 37 48 82)* for timetable details.

If arriving from Messina, you can eith catch a train from Messina to Giarre, to con nect with the Circumetnea train to Lingu glossa (€1.55, several a day), or catch train to Fiumefreddo, from where there ai **SAIS** (☎ *095 53 61 68)* and FCE buses (th last leaving at 7.30pm) to Linguaglos every day except Sunday.

From Linguaglossa, if you arrange it in a vance, the manager of Rifugio Brunek wi pick you up from the train station. Be warne however, that he doesn't speak much Englis

Rifugio Sapienza & Around

Closed at the time of writing, this CAI-ru *rifugio* (☎ *095 91 63 56)*, on the south side c Etna, is scheduled to reopen in March 200.

Another option, 100m west of the *rifugi* is **Hotel Corsaro** (☎ *095 780 99 02; B& singles/doubles €50/70)*, which offers yea round accommodation in a stark enviro ment of rock and hardened lava flows.

Getting There & Away An AST (☎ 095 746 10 96) bus service operates between Sapienza and Catania (€2.85, once a day at 4.30pm), leaving from the piazza below the cable car station. Buy tickets on the bus.

GETTING TO/FROM THE WALK

For information on getting to and from the walk, see Getting There & Away for Rifugio Brunek (p308) and Rifugio Sapienza (above).

If leaving the walk early via Randazzo (Day 1) or Maletto (Day 2), you can catch a FCE train back to Catania. The last train leaves Randazzo at 7.21pm (€3.10, two hours) and Maletto at 7.38pm (€3.10, 1½ hours). FCE buses do the same trip between Randazzo (2¼ hours, once a day at 2.45pm) and Maletto (once a day at 2.50pm).

THE WALK
Day 1: Rifugio Brunek to Rifugio Saletti
4–5 hours, 14km

From Rifugio Brunek (1380m) take the dirt road that heads northwest through the Pineta Ragabo pine forest. After roughly 1km you'll pass a Corpo Linguaglossa forestry hut (Caserma Pitarrone) on the right. Stay on the dirt road, following it to the left, and climb over a boom gate. The trail crosses a series of old lava flows – visible evidence of eruptions in 1923, 1911 and 1879. The first of these flows provides magnificent views north to Taormina and Monti Peloritani.

Shortly after crossing the 1879 lava flow, you'll pass signed routes to the right for Grotta delle Palombe and Grotta delle Femmine (20m from the track). Continue along the main trail, crossing the 1947 lava flow, to a trail junction at Passo dei Dammusi (1709m), 1½ to two hours from Rifugio Brunek.

The trail heading uphill to the left leads to the unusable Rifugio Timparossa (1838m), about 3km from the turn-off. A sign for the 'Grotta del Gelo e dei Lamponi' points south to a faint trail leading uphill across lava cordate (lava shaped like huge coils of rope). Grotta del Gelo is a 4km walk over lava on a trail that is at times difficult to follow. However, **Grotta dei Lamponi** (Cave of the

Raspberries) is only a short detour from the main track and is well worth visiting (see Side Trip: Grotta dei Lamponi, below).

Continue west on the dirt road in the direction of Monte Spagnolo, descending among beech trees and through coil-like lava flows until you reach **Rifugio di Monte Santa Maria** (1620m), 20 minutes later. The *rifugio* has a fireplace but is otherwise bare and without a water supply. The cosy Rifugio Saletti, another 4.5km downhill, is a much better option for the night. Skirt the base of Monte Santa Maria, avoiding a deviation to the right for the Cisternazza (you can exit from the walk here; see Alternative Finish: Randazzo, p311). After 2.5km from Rifugio di Monte Santa Maria you'll pass a very small *bivacco* (shelter) at 1493m.

Continue the descent over an old lava flow dating from 1614. After a double curve, the road turns sharply to the right and descends northeast. At this point, note the dirt road heading off to the west (tomorrow's short cut), which follows the route of the original *altomontana*, covered by lava in 1981. Another 1km along the dirt road you have been walking on is **Rifugio Saletti** (1373m). Set in a quiet and shady spot, with views to the north over the town of Randazzo, this small, unstaffed *rifugio* is well looked after and stocked with firewood. Tank water is piped to a water fountain on the road's edge.

Side Trip: Grotta dei Lamponi
15 minutes, 500m

To find the cave entrance, follow the cairned trail to the south across the lava. After 50m you'll come to an opening – where you'll later exit the cave. The entrance is another 100m along the cairned trail to the left of the opening. Once inside the cave, head south along the tunnel for about 100m – you'll pass two lovely pools of light framed by delicate grasses at points where the roof of the cave has collapsed. At the end of the cave is a tongue-shaped strip of lava.

Go back the way you came. Just before the cave entrance, you'll find a small tunnel on the left. A bit narrow at first, it then widens and opens onto the main tunnel. Go in and descend for about 300m, passing

SICILY

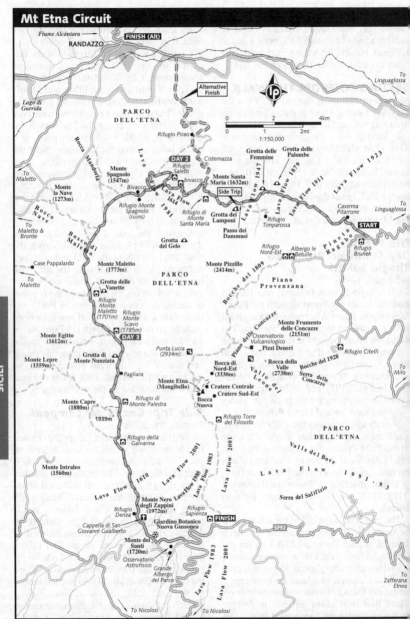

Mt Etna Circuit

Fiume Alcántara →

FINISH (Alt)

RANDAZZO

Lago di Gurrida

PARCO DELL'ETNA

Alternative Finish

To Linguaglossa

Rifugio Pirao

Cisternazza

Grotta delle Femmine

Grotta delle Palombe

Rocca Mandorla

DAY 2

Rifugio Saletti

bivacco

Monte Santa Maria (1632m)

Lava Flow 1947

Lava Flow 1879

Lava Flow 1911

Lava Flow 1923

Monte Spagnolo (1547m)

Bivacco

Lava Flow 1614

Side Trip

To Maletto

Monte la Nave (1273m)

Rifugio Monte Spagnolo (ruins)

Lava Flow 1981

Rifugio di Monte Santa Maria

Grotta dei Lamponi

Rifugio Timparossa

Caserma Pitarrone

To Linguaglossa

Bosco Nave

To Maletto & Bronte

Bosco di Maletto

Passo dei Dammusi

Rifugio Nord-Est

Albergo le Betulle

START

Rifugio Brunek

Pineta Ragabo

Case Pappalardo

Grotta del Gelo

Monte Pizzillo (2414m)

Piano Provenzana

Bocche del 1809

To Maletto

Monte Maletto (1773m)

Grotta delle Vanette

PARCO DELL'ETNA

Rifugio Monte Maletto (1701m)

Rifugio Monte Scavo (1785m)

DAY 3

Monte Egitto (1612m)

Grotta di Monte Nunziata

Punta Lucia (2934m)

Piano delle Concazze

Monte Frumento delle Concazze (2151m)

Osservatorio Vulcanologico

Pizzi Deneri

Rifugio Citelli

To Milo

Monte Lepre (1559m)

Pagliara

Bocca di Nord-Est (3330m)

Rocca della Valle (2738m)

Bocche del 1928

Serra delle Concazze

Monte Capre (1880m)

Rifugio di Monte Palestra

Monte Etna (Mongibello)

Cratere Centrale

Cratere Sud-Est

Valle del Leone

1939m

Bocca Nuova

Rifugio Torre del Filosofo

PARCO DELL'ETNA

Rifugio della Galvarina

Lava Flow 2001

Lava Flow 2001

Valle del Bove

Monte Intraleo (1560m)

Lava Flow 1610

Lava Flow 2001

Lava Flow 1985

Lava Flow 1983

Lava Flow 1991-93

Serra del Salifizio

Monte Nero degli Zappini (1972m)

Rifugio Denza

Rifugio Sapienza

FINISH

SP92

Cappella di San Giovanni Gualberto

Giardino Botanico Nuova Gussonea

Monte dei Santi (1720m)

Osservatorio Astrofisico

Grande Albergo del Parco

Lava Flow 1983

Lava Flow 2001

To Nicolosi

To Nicolosi

To Zafferana Etnea

SICILY

1:150,000

0   2   4km

0   1   2mi

carefully over a large landslide, to reach the cave exit. The tunnel actually continues its descent underground to the north, but there is a danger of cave-ins and continuing is not recommended.

Alternative Finish: Randazzo
2 hours, 7.5km

From the base of Monte Santa Maria, turn right onto the dirt road that descends for less than 1km to the Cisternazza, a quaint cistern covered by a round building. From here the road continues to Rifugio Pirao (not open to the public). The town of Randazzo is 6km away along a paved road.

Randazzo is a pleasant if quiet town on the FCE railway line. It has only one hotel, the **Hotel Scrivano** (☎ *095 92 11 26; Via G Bonaventura; singles/doubles €36.15/62)* with smart rooms. Nearby, **Ristorante-Pizzeria da Antonio** (☎ *0957 99 20 56; Via Pietro Nenni 8; open Wed-Mon)* has local, wild mushrooms on the menu.

For transport options from Randazzo, see Getting to/from the Walk (p309).

Day 2: Rifugio Saletti to Rifugio Monte Scavo
3–4 hours, 12km

From Rifugio Saletti there are two route options. You can either continue west along the road, following the sign to 'Nicolosi-Monte Spagnolo', or retrace your steps to the beginning of the short cut mentioned at the end of Day 1.

The first option is longer but may be more navigable in foggy weather. If you choose this option, avoid the turn-off to the right for Rifugio Pirao and Randazzo, 1km from Rifugio Saletti. After the turn-off, the road ascends across the 1981 lava flow, past the startling vents thrown up by that eruption. The short cut joins the road 2km from Rifugio Saletti.

To take the short cut, retrace your steps to the sharp curve described in Day 1. Turn right (west) along the dirt road that heads off through the forest to the beginning of a lava flow edged with long-dead beech trees. In 1981 the lava flow that erupted from this break reached Randazzo, destroying houses,

roads and the railway line, eventually flowing into the Fiume Alcántara.

Traverse the slope of the lava, still going west. Try to maintain a constant altitude and keep to the trail. Once past the lava flow you'll find the old *altomontana* dirt road, which continues for about 200m through a lovely forest to join up with the new dirt road, 1km from the beginning of the short cut. At this point the two routes rejoin.

Walk on to the ruined Rifugio Monte Spagnolo (1440m). Opposite is a small, badly maintained *bivacco*, which is useful only as an emergency shelter. The road continues west, through an area reafforested with cedar pines, to the south of the little Monte Spagnolo volcano (1547m). You'll pass two turn-offs to the right, one immediately after the mountain and another about 1km from Rifugio Monte Spagnolo (both lead to Rocca Mandorla and Randazzo, about 8km away). After 2km you'll pass another turn-off to the right, this time for Bosco Nave and then west to Maletto, about 8km away. Ignore this and continue on the dirt road, which now ascends to the south.

Walking for another 3km, you'll pass through Bosco di Maletto and under the volcanic cone of Monte Maletto (1773m), before passing a track to the left for **Rifugio Monte Maletto** (1701m). Immersed in a thick and isolated forest a little more than 1km from the turn-off, this charming *rifugio* is among the least frequented on Mt Etna. Stocked with firewood and with a good supply of water, this could be an alternative point at which to end the day, although the next *rifugio* at Monte Scavo is only 3.5km away.

If you prefer to continue to Rifugio Monte Scavo, ignore the turn-off for Rifugio Monte Maletto and continue the ascent south on the dirt road. After 200m there is a deviation to the right for Case Pappalardo, from where, if you wish to end the walk early, you can reach Maletto.

After walking for just under 2.5km, you'll reach the spacious **Rifugio Monte Scavo** (1785m). At the halfway point on the Etna circuit, the hut is among the most frequented of the volcano's *rifugi*, especially on weekends and often by boy scouts. Like other *rifugi* on the mountain, Monte Scavo has firewood and water (across the track from the hut).

If you still have some energy, you can make the two-hour return walk to **Monte Egitto** through an immense, dramatic desert of lava formations. The path leaves from next to the water pump and is signed with yellow trail markers. Be careful of vipers in this area.

Day 3: Rifugio Monte Scavo to Rifugio Sapienza
4–5 hours, 14.5km

Walk south on the dirt road again. Avoid a deviation on the left that peters out on the slopes of the volcano. Slightly more than 1km from the *rifugio*, on the right side of the road, is a depression known as the Grotta di Monte Nunziata. In the past, the people of Bronte filled this depression with snow in winter, so they could have ice in summer.

After another 900m, in a forest of birch trees, you'll come to a *pagliara*, a typical conical shelter for workers producing charcoal, built of branches and earth. Less than 2km further on is the small and gracious **Rifugio di Monte Palestra** (1917m). Pass a turn-off to the right for the lava-covered areas around the volcanic cones of Monte Capre, Monte Lepre and Monte Intraleo.

You will soon reach **Rifugio della Galvarina**, the last of the *rifugi* on the circuit. To the right of the *rifugio* is another trail, which connects with the trail for the volcanic cones mentioned previously.

Continue on the dirt road for 4km, across large fields of lava. Ignore the minor, lateral roads and keep going until you reach the sealed road near Rifugio Denza (1740m; uninhabitable and always closed), 45 minutes from Rifugio della Galvarina. Turn right along the road, which almost immediately veers left and soon passes the Cappella di San Giovanni Gualberto on the left. Continue for about 1.5km to a little bridge, beyond which you will see the entrance to the **Giardino Botanico Nuova Gussonea** (botanical garden) on the left. If open, the garden (admission free) is worth a brief stopover as it recreates on a small scale the main environments and botanical species found on Etna.

Keep going straight and you'll soon find a turn-off to the left, onto a smaller sealed road, closed by a green bar. A sign indicates the Osservatorio Astrofisico (Astrophysics Observatory). Monte dei Santi (1720m) is on the right – a little volcanic cone, covered with larch trees, rising out of the lava.

This road is a shorter alternative to the longer main route to Rifugio Sapienza. The

Summit Dangers

The ever-present danger of eruption, combined with highly changeable weather conditions at the summit, means that Etna should be approached with great caution. Officially, the summit area of Etna is out of bounds, although there is nothing but a rope barrier and good sense to prevent walkers from going to the craters. Those considering the extra trek should bear in mind that the eruptive activity of the craters, although usually relatively moderate, can intensify suddenly and without warning, with potentially catastrophic results. Lava bombs and overpowering fumes are among the many hazards awaiting the unwary near the crater's rim.

As a general rule, never go alone to the summit area, never go unless weather conditions are extremely stable, and let someone in a position of responsibility know where you are going and when you expect to return. Follow the advice of the local guides, who will be able to provide information about the volcano's current behaviour and weather forecasts. If rescuers do have to carry you off the mountain, you will not be covered by insurance.

It is also very important to consider the high altitude at the summit, with frequent thunderstorms, strong winds, low temperatures and fog. Once the clouds close in, it is very easy to become disoriented and risk falling. Since 1999 three people have been killed by lightning strikes.

short cut heads east, corresponding to a section of the Monte Nero degli Zappini nature trail. Pass the observatory, which is some distance off to your right, and avoid all subsequent deviations. After about 1.5km the road joins provincial road 92, which connects Nicolosi, Rifugio Sapienza and Zafferana Etnea. You can either end the walk here, waiting at the junction of SP92 and the road to the Grande Albergo del Parco for the bus descending from the resort (you'll need to flag it down), or tackle the 3km climb up to **Rifugio Sapienza** (p308). You can eat a hot meal and spend the night at the staffed *rifugio*, operated by the CAI.

If you haven't yet visited the craters, consider taking the **Funivia dell'Etna** (☎ 095 91 42 09) service from Sapienza up to 2900m. Operating between 9am and 5.30pm, the 4WD trip with a guide costs €37.20 and takes roughly two hours. Some walkers choose to catch the 4WD to 2500m (€10.35) and walk the rest of the way to the craters, although officially this area is out of bounds and you will be doing so at your own risk (see the boxed text 'Summit Dangers', p312). The guides will only take you as far as they consider safe (which was 2900m at the time of writing).

Vulcano's Gran Cratere

Duration	2½–3 hours
Distance	11km
Difficulty	easy
Start/Finish	Porto di Levante
Nearest Towns	Porto di Levante (p315), Milazzo (p315)
Transport	ferry

Summary A short but steep climb up to the steaming rim of a still-active island crater, with magnificent views across to the other islands in the Aeolian archipelago.

A world away from Italy's urban chaos, Vulcano is in the starkly beautiful volcanic Aeolian archipelago (Isole Eolie). Visible from the mainland of northeastern Sicily, the seven islands appear adrift on the sea haze.

Approaching Vulcano by boat, the mythological grandeur of the landscape is even more striking – a rugged volcanic cone rising abruptly out of the sea, smoking fissures and steaming sulphur-yellow rocks. This is a land where, according to legend, the gods of wind and fire once conjured up the elements, and where, amid the rotten-egg stench of volcanic fumes, the medieval popes decreed the mouth of hell lay. While today the island attracts a somewhat more prosaic crowd of summer tourists, the Vulcano experience has lost little of its primal appeal.

One of two still-active volcanic islands in the archipelago, the 21-sq-km Vulcano is formed by the vast high plain of Vulcano Piano. The island is dominated to the south by Monte Aria (500m); to the north by the promontory of Vulcanello (123m), with its three, small inactive craters; and by the large active central cone called the Fossa, which looms over Porto di Levante. Although steep, Fossa is a relatively small volcano, measuring 391m at its highest point. Its lower slopes are covered by a mantle of shrubbery that, when flowering in late spring, sweetens the landscape with beautiful yellow flowers and an intense perfume. From the rim of the Gran Cratere, as Fossa's crater is called, are superb panoramic views of the island, the Sicilian mainland and the rest of the archipelago.

The Gran Cratere is an easy half-day excursion, suitable for the whole family. The walk provides a rare (and safe) opportunity to get a close look at a still active, if geriatric, volcano and the classic 'Vulcanian' landforms it has created. With only the gentle seeping of gases from fumaroles on the cone's rim to remind visitors there is life in the old girl yet, it is hard to imagine that only a century ago the volcano's last explosion wiped out a settlement and the burgeoning alum extraction business of a Scottish tycoon.

The more adventurous volcano enthusiasts may like to continue on to the nearby island of Stromboli, where eruptions are continuous and an immense expanse of volcanic waste, the Sciara del Fuoco, edges its way down to the sea.

SICILY

HISTORY

The Aeolian Islands were already inhabited in the 4th millennium BC by people who prospered from mining and trading obsidian, a sharp, black, lustrous and valuable volcanic glass that can still be found on Lipari. In the Bronze Age, around the 18th century BC, the islands were colonized by people of Mycenaean Greece who gave the archipelago its name, linking it with the myth of the wind god, Aeolus (Eolo). Thucydides, in the 5th century BC, reported a tremendous eruption on Vulcano.

With their strategic position in the Mediterranean, the Aeolian Islands were coveted by the Sicilian city-states of Magna Grecia, and later by Carthage and Rome. Since ancient times, the caves of Vulcano have yielded alum, a mineral salt used as a powerful caustic, and in the days of the Roman Empire, Cicero praised the island's excellent thermal waters. In the Middle Ages, the Fossa crater was believed to be the mouth of hell.

In 1083 the Aeolians were conquered by the Normans. In 1544 the islands' population was decimated when Lipari, less than 1km from Vulcano, was sacked by the Moslem pirate Ariadeno Barbarossa and all the inhabitants were taken into slavery. In the 1550s, Lipari was repopulated by Charles V of Spain, and from that time on the history of the archipelago has followed that of Sicily and the Kingdom of Naples. During the years of economic hardship before and after World War II, many of the islands' residents were forced to emigrate. Most went to Australia, which is often referred to as the eighth Aeolian island.

NATURAL HISTORY

The Aeolian archipelago is found in the lower Tyrrhenian Sea, from 20km to 40km north of Sicily, and is made up of seven originally volcanic islands. During the Pliocene Age, as tectonic plate movements created the shelves of the Tyrrhenian Sea, magma escaped through fissures up to 1000m deep in the sea floor, gradually creating an underwater mountain chain. Emerging from the sea at different times during the last 300,000 years, the visible tips of these mountains form the islands. Wind and rain erosion have consumed and compacted the exposed landscape, leaving it low and flattened.

The youngest of the islands, Vulcano and Stromboli (100,000 and 40,000 years old respectively), are the only ones still active today. Vulcanello (123m), a small, inactive peninsula on Vulcano, was created suddenly in an underwater eruption in 183 BC recorded in eyewitness accounts of the time.

After a century of only minor 'secondary' activity, limited to gas emissions from fumaroles, there is evidence that pressure may again be building up within the volcano. It may be comforting (or not) to know that the area has been placed under observation by the Ministry of Civil Protection.

CLIMATE

Mild temperatures in winter and not-too high temperatures in summer, combined with scarce rain, make for a very pleasant climate year-round in the Aeolian Islands. Average temperatures vary from 13°C in January to 27°C in July. Only 500mm to 600mm of rain falls annually, with the wettest months in January and December. Summers are dry. Winds are predominantly from the northwest (the *maestrale*) or from the southeast (the *scirocco*).

PLANNING
When to Walk

The warm season is from April to October. The best months to walk are April and May (when the wildflowers are blooming), and September and October (when it is still possible to swim in the warm sea). Dawn and sunset are the optimum times to head towards the crater, escaping the worst of the heat and avoiding any crowds. Prices are lower from November to March (not including Easter), but during this time most of the hotels and restaurants close, transport to the island is irregular and Porto di Levante reverts to being a sleepy island village.

What to Bring

There is absolutely no shade around the crater of Vulcano and the sun becomes searingly hot as the day progresses, so bring adequate su protection and plenty of water. If you find the sulphurous smell that seeps out of the crater offensive (although for brief periods of exposure the fumes are not dangerous), it's not a bad idea to take along a cotton scarf to filter out the worst emissions. Running shoes (trainers) are quite adequate if you don't have good walking shoes.

Maps

The path up to Fossa's Gran Cratere is self-evident and few people bother to take a map along with them, although it would be useful for identifying the surrounding islands and Vulcano landmarks visible from the crater's rim.

There are several widely available maps that use an old IGM 1:25,000 map as their base, covering all the islands of the archipelago. If intending only to visit Vulcano, pick up a copy of the easy-to-read Rebus Edizioni 1:25,000 map *Vulcano* (€1.55), sold in shops around the island.

Emergency

For medical assistance contact the **Guardia Medica** (☎ 090 985 22 20).

NEAREST TOWNS
Milazzo

The industrial sea port of Milazzo is not one of Sicily's stand-out tourist destinations, and is usually only glimpsed en route to the islands. However, if you find yourself staying overnight, a stroll around the streets of the Old City can be a pleasant way to pass the evening.

The **APT office** (☎ 090 922 28 65; *Piazza C Duilio 10*) is behind Via Crispi. All of the ticket offices for travel to the islands are virtually next door to each other on the quayside.

Places to Stay & Eat On the pretty Capo di Milazzo promontory, **Riva Smeralda camping ground** (☎ 090 928 29 80; *Strada Panoramica; camping per person/tent €5.95/ 2.85, 2-person bungalows €54.25; open May-Sept*) is roughly 6km north of the centre. Catch a bus to Cirucco and ask to get off at the camping ground.

Basic but friendly, **Hotel Capitol** (☎ 090 928 32 89; *Via Giogio Rizzo 91; singles/ doubles €25.80/41.30, with bath €31/51.65*) is only a block from the port and a convenient standby. A smarter alternative is **Hotel La Bussola** (☎ 090 922 12 44, fax 090 928 29 55; *Via XX Luglio 29; singles/doubles €49.05/72.30*).

La Vecchia Cucina (☎ 090 922 30 70; *Via Nino Ryolo 17*) serves tasty Sicilian delicacies. It's worth staying in Milazzo just for the treat of a meal here.

Getting There & Away Numerous trains connect Milazzo with Messina (€2.30, daily), Catania and Palermo. Milazzo's train station is a 10-minute bus trip from the town centre (€0.80).

Giunta (☎ 090 67 37 82) runs an hourly bus service between Messina train station and Milazzo (€2.85), stopping on Lungomare Garibaldi, opposite Via Garibaldi; buy a ticket on the bus. There's also a daily Giunta bus between Catania's Fontanarossa airport and Milazzo (€10.35), leaving Milazzo at 8.30am and returning from the airport at 4pm, connecting with boat services to the Aeolian Islands.

If you want to leave your car at Milazzo, there are several supervised car parks, including the **Mylarum 2 garage** (☎ 090 928 11 45; *Via XX Luglio 18*), where covered parking costs €7.75 for 24 hours (€5.15 for motorcycles). Leaving your car or motorcycle parked in the open for several days could be risky.

If travelling under your own steam, turn off the A20 onto the S113.

Porto di Levante & Around

Boats bring you into Porto di Levante at the northern end of the island. Resort facilities are concentrated on the narrow strip of land between Porto di Levante and Porto di Ponente, which boasts the Spiaggia Sabbia Nera (Black Sand Beach), the only sandy – if soot-black – beach on the islands.

The summer-only **visitor centre** (☎ 090 985 20 28; *open 8am-2pm June-Oct*) is housed in a dome-like building on the main street, 50m from the boat dock. The centre

SICILY

provides basic information on the island's accommodation and tourist services. Many of the shops lining the main street in the port sell maps and books on the archipelago, along with the usual collection of tourist paraphernalia.

A number of companies on the main street offer day trips to the volcanic island of Stromboli. Boats take tourists to the base of the Sciara del Fuoco, an immense expanse of volcanic waste that descends towards the sea. Alternatively, you can take a guided walk up 918m to a vantage point above the crater, with sunset views of the eruptions below.

Places to Stay & Eat On the black sand beach of Porto di Ponente is **Club Togo Togo** (☎ 090 985 23 03; camp sites/bungalows per person €7.75/12.90; open Apr-Sept).

Hostel accommodation is available at **L'Isola Magica** (☎ 090 985 21 05; **w** www .lisolamagicavulcano.it; dorm beds €15.50).

Dorms have four beds (sheets cost an extra €2.60). L'Isola Magica also rents out holiday villas.

A pleasantly low-key place on the way to the crater is **Pensione La Giara** (☎ 090 985 22 29, 330 437 08 02; Via Provinciale 18; B&B/half board €43.90/59.40; open Apr-mid-Oct), offering rooms with bathroom and air-con. Beachside accommodation is available at **Rojas Bahia Hotel** (☎ 090 985 20 80; B&B singles/doubles €80.05/142.05, half board €87.80), across the road from the infamous (read smelly) mud baths of Laghetto di Fanghi.

There is a **supermarket** and **bakery** on the road to Vulcano Piano, Via Provinciale. **Ristorante da Maurizio** (☎ 090 985 24 26; Via Porto di Levante) is one of the smartest, if overpriced, restaurants in Porto di Levante. Otherwise, there are a number of **restaurants**, **cafés** and **pizzerias** along Porto di Levante's main street.

Getting There & Away Vulcano is served regularly by hydrofoil and ferry. There are around 20 hydrofoils daily from Milazzo to Vulcano (€10.35, 30 minutes) and on to the other islands, run by **Siremar** (☎ 090 928 32 42) and **SNAV** (☎ 090 928 78 21; **w** www .snavali.com).

SNAV also has hydrofoils to/from Reggio di Calabria (€17, once a day) and Messina (€16, several a day), as well as summer-only services to Cefalù (€24.30, three a week on Wednesday, Thursday and Friday), Naples (€74.90, once a day) and Palermo (€36.15, once a day).

Siremar car ferries to Vulcano are slower and less frequent than the hydrofoils but cost about half the price (€5.70). There is an overnight service between the island and Naples (€62/46.50 cabin/seat, three a week)

Less frequent, **Navigazione Generale Italiano** (NGI; ☎ 090 928 40 91) car ferries travel between Milazzo and Vulcano for around the same rates.

THE WALK

From the waterfront in Porto di Levante, follow the narrow, sealed road that leads southwest towards Vulcano Piano, past the

SICILY

Vulcano's Gran Cratere

Bocche di Vulcano

Punta Samossà

To Isola di Lipari

Punta

•Vulcanello (123m)

Porto di Ponente

To Milazzo (Sicily)

Capo Grosso

Laghetto di Fanghi

Spiaggia Sabbia Nera

Porto di Levante

Punta del Monaco

START/ FINISH

Punta Lùccia

Boat Storage Facility

Testa Grossa

208m

Fossa di Vulcano (391m)

Gran Cratere

TYRRHENIAN SEA

Monte Sareceno (481m)

Monte Rosso (328m)

Cappo Secco

Vulcano Piano

0   1   2km
0   0.5   1mi
1:100,000

Punta del Mortaro

oftop terrace restaurant of **Al Cratere**, on
e right. The massive body of the crater
ses before you.

After a 10-minute walk along the road,
d 50m beyond a boat storage facility on
e left, take an unmarked trail that heads
eeply uphill to the left through stands of
ushwood; this is a short cut that, in two
inutes, links up with the main trail. (The
ain path begins on the left, another 200m
the road.) When you reach the main trail,
ntinue left (east) until you come to a sharp
rve to the right, where a sign in four lan-
uages announces the dangers of the crater.
you proceed (which everyone does) you
on't have any problems with officialdom,
t you do need to be aware that Fossa is
ly sleeping and is an active volcano.

Several minutes later, the trail turns left
gain. The soil underfoot, which until now
s been made up of a small, dark volcanic
avel, changes to a sandy colour. The trail
kes on the impressive look of a deep ero-
on furrow where the path has been worn
to a grooved shelf cutting obliquely
ross the slope. At the end of this shelf you
ach a wide, flat clearing of lava pebbles.
scend again to the left (southeast), fol-
wing the main trail. In three minutes
u'll arrive at the lowest point of the
ater's edge (290m, 45 minutes to an hour
m the start).

To your left, the inside wall of the crater
full of countless fissures, covered in
lendid yellow-orange crystals, that let off
lumns of sulphurous gases. The bottom of
e volcano is clearly visible less than 50m
low, formed by two 'cold' (inactive)
lderas – two perfectly circular and level
tersecting spaces covered by a layer of
lid, sun-dried mud. A steep trail descends
the bottom in three minutes. Many go
wn for an unconventional walk along the
rd crater floor (see the boxed text 'At the
oor to Hades', this page).

Once on the crater's rim, walk clockwise
und the crest of the crater, with stunning
0-degree views of the Aeolian Islands
ed up to the north. From left to right they
e Alicudi, Filicudi, Salina peeking out
om behind Lipari (beyond the little crater

At the Door to Hades

It must be remembered that, although this
volcano is sleeping, it is still carrying out its
mysterious work. The great quantity of gas
that it emits creates large and small underground voids, especially among the fumaroles.
While walking among the fumaroles on the interior slope, searching out incredible sulphurous colours to photograph, the ground
gave way and I sank a good 10cm. 'Big deal!'
you'll say. But I immediately thought of all
those films where the first 10cm are only the
beginning of the end. Here we are, inside –
actually *inside* – a real volcano.

The mud floor looks like it gets softer in
places and it is not difficult to imagine scenes
of a sudden cave-in, where you drop directly
into the inferno below. The ancients believed
Vulcano was the entrance to Hades, the kingdom of the dead. In the Middle Ages, Chris-
tians also believed that the volcano was the
entrance to hell and inhabited by demons.
Even Dante mentions it. However, there is no
record of anyone ever being swallowed up by
the volcano, which, in the last century, was
frequented daily by prisoners who were
forced by armed guards to mine sulphur as
part of their punishment.

As with all of the volcano walks in this book,
we point you in the right direction, but you
must be aware of the potential danger of
climbing an active volcano and, particularly, of
descending into the crater. It's your decision!

Stefano Cavedoni

of Vulcanello), then to the northeast Panarea, and the dark and distant smoking cone
of Stromboli. To the south, from east to
west, you can see the province of Calabria
with its Aspromonte (1437m) and, on clear
days, a long piece of the Sicilian coast dominated by the imposing bulk of Etna. Depending on the direction of the wind, fumes
from the fumaroles will be wafting over
some sections of the trail; it is a good idea
to pass these sections quickly, avoid walking
too close to any of the vents as the temperature of the escaping gas can be searing.

SICILY

It's the changing panorama that makes this part of the walk interesting. You can get to the highest point of the crest (391m) in about 20 to 25 minutes, from where you can see to the Sicilian coast and over the part of the island called Vulcano Piano. To the west you will note that the crest of the cliff is no more than a section of the great ancient volcano, eroded by the millennia, inside which the present crater was formed.

Returning back down the volcano, take the same trail. Deviations are not recommended down the very steep slope, with its unstable, crumbly soil. In any case, it is best to keep to the main trail to avoid damaging the rare plants that are attempting to grow in this inhospitable land of lava.

Nebrodi Lake Circuit

Duration	4–4½ hours
Distance	18km
Difficulty	easy–moderate
Start/Finish	Villa Miraglia (p320)
Nearest Town	Sant'Agata di Militello (p319)
Transport	bus

Summary A circuit walk into the heart of the Nebrodi, climbing to near the summit of Monte Soro, before descending along shady tracks to Lago di Biviere, a wetland haven for migrating birds.

A short detour inland from Sicily's crowded north coast resorts takes you up into Parco dei Nebrodi and the cool, leafy respite of the largest beech forest in Europe. The soft, rolling peaks of Nebrodi form part of the Sicilian extension of the Apennines. With Nebrodi's highest point (Monte Soro) a modest 1847m, the thickly wooded slopes and green meadows are a far cry from the harsh, scorched landscape characteristic of much of the island. This is not a pristine natural environment (there is very little of that left in Sicily) but since its creation in 1993, the 850-sq-km park has become a valuable ecological haven – an island within an island. Around 25% of Sicily's forest lies inside the park's boundaries and,

despite the ever-present human factor, shelters a rich array of animal and plant life.

The described walk is a full-day circuit into the central Nebrodi area, climbing the flank of Monte Soro and then descending through beech wood to skirt the edge of the Lago di Biviere. Set against a serene natural backdrop of forest and open meadows, the lake is the jewel in the Nebrodi crown, considered Sicily's most ecologically valuable mountain wet area.

The return route along an unsealed road used by grazing livestock provides a delightful rural idyll, passing stone farmhouses on the northern edge of the Contrada Sollazzo Verde forest and skirting Lago di Maulazzo. Herds of wild Sanfrettelan horses, introduced by the Normans during the Middle Ages, keep a watchful eye on the passing human traffic.

It's good to remember before setting off that recreational walking has never been part of the Sicilian tradition and the park's foray into the world of ecotourism is only a very recent phenomenon. Trails are poorly marked, if marked at all, and there is little or no walking infrastructure. If you stray off the trail, you may well end up on private property.

CLIMATE

Nebrodi's climate varies considerably across the region, influenced by altitude and coastal proximity. Near the coast, average annual temperatures range from 17°C to 18°C; further inland and up into the hills, the thermometer drops to between 10°C and 13°C. The coldest days are in January and February, with minimum average temperatures of around -1°C. Autumn and winter are the wettest months. Snow begins to fall in November and can remain until well into March.

PLANNING
What to Bring

There is only one reliable water source along the trail, so bring supplies with you.

When to Walk

Like elsewhere on the island, spring and autumn are the best times for exploring the mountains. In spring (March to May) wild-flowers turn the mountain pastures into a heady riot of colour, while the woods in autumn (September to November) are transformed into blazing orange. Do not rule out walking in summer, however, when the cool mountain breezes provide a welcome relief from the sweltering heat on the coast below.

Maps

The only map with sufficient detail on the park is the Touring Club Italiano 1:50,000 map *Parco dei Nebrodi*, produced in cooperation with the park's administration. Be warned, however, that tracks have been marked inaccurately in a number of places and the map leaves out quite a few of the smaller forestry tracks found on the ground – potentially confusing. For the section of the walk described here between Monte Soro and Lago di Biviere, refer closely to the walk description and use the 1:50,000 map in conjunction with the one in this book.

Books

The park's administration has produced a number of Italian-language publications on the region, including *Parco dei Nebrodi*, by Francesco Alaimo, which describes in detail a number of possible (read 'unmarked') walk itineraries in the park.

Information Sources

Tracking down information on Parco dei Nebrodi is frustratingly difficult. Few of Sicily's general tourist offices keep tourist material on the area, while the park's visitor centres are relatively inaccessible for walkers dependent on public transport. The most useful centre, if you can get there, is the **Cesarò park office** (☎ 095 69 60 08; *Strada Nazionale, 98033*), which has very enthusiastic staff and publications for sale, including the Touring Club Italiano *Parco dei Nebrodi* map. There is another **office** (☎ 0941 9 39 04; *Via Ugo Foscolo 1*) in Alcara li Fusi, in Nebrodi's northern foothills.

For a list of publications and other information, see the Parco dei Nebrodi website at www.parks.it/parco.nebrodi).

NEAREST TOWN & FACILITIES
Sant'Agata di Militello

This business-like seaside town is the easiest base on the north coast from which to access the Parco dei Nebrodi. Worth a quick browse before heading up into the hills is **Museo Etno-Antropologico dei Nebrodi** *(Via Cosenz, also called Via Lungomare)*, near the train station. The *comune* (town council) **tourist office** (☎ 0941 722 02; *open 8.30am-12.30pm*), in the Castello dei Gallego, is a fairly basic outfit.

Places to Stay & Eat There are only two hotels in town: **Roma Palace Hotel** (☎ 0941 70 35 16, fax 0941 70 35 19; e *hotelroma@tiscalinet.it; Via Medici 443; singles/doubles €25.80/41.30*) and **Hotel Parimar** (☎ 0941 70 18 88, 0941 70 14 97; Via Medici 1; singles/doubles €46.50/77.80). Both offer reasonable, if unexceptional, accommodation.

There are several **restaurants** and **pizzerias** to be found along Via Cosenz, just below Castello dei Gallego. **Ristorante Carletto** (☎ 0941 70 31 57) is where diners can choose from a sumptuous array of Sicilian *antipasti* (appetisers).

Getting There & Away Sant'Agata di Militello is on the main railway line between Messina and Palermo, with frequent services daily.

An **ISEA** (☎ 095 53 68 94) bus service operates between Piazza della Repubblica in Catania (€10.35, once a day at 2pm) and and Sant'Agata di Militello (once a day at 5am). The bus stops along the way at Villa Miraglia (the beginning of the walk). The bus stop in Sant'Agata can be hard to find. From the tourist office walk up Via Medici from the eastern edge of the piazza. When the street veers left, continue ahead up Via Generale Aurelio Iotta for 100m before turning right into Via Cernaia. The bus stop is another 50m on the left in a parking bay.

Sant'Agata di Militello is on the A20 connecting towns along the north coast. At the time of writing, the autostrada was yet to be completed all the way to Palermo, and the section between Sant'Agata di Militello and Cefalù was serviced by the S113.

Villa Miraglia

This lovely old, stone albergo (☎ 095 773 21 33; rooms with half/full board €46.50/62), once a hunting lodge, is set in the middle of the Nebrodi beech wood beneath Portella Femmina Morta. Now owned and managed by the province of Messina, it is stuffed full of fabulous collectibles: quirky ceramics, colourfully painted cart panels, old paintings and an absorbing collection of Italian detective novels. With good, simple food, this is a rural retreat to savour. You will need to book ahead on weekends and in the height of summer.

Getting There & Away Villa Miraglia lies between Sant'Agata di Militello (33km north) and Cesarò (18km south) on the S289, one of three main routes traversing the park. Cesarò is easily accessible from Enna (100km), towns around the base of Mt Etna and from Taormina (75km) on the east coast.

The only public transport link is the ISE (☎ 095 53 68 94) bus between Catani (€3.35, 2½ hours) and St Agata di Militell (€2.85, one hour). See Getting There Away (p319) for Sant'Agata di Militello.

THE WALK

Head north along the road (S289) from Villa Miraglia to Portella Femmina Mort (1524m), 300m away. Just before the pass turn right onto an unsealed forestry trac that heads east. (Note that this is not th main road into Monte Soro.) The trac winds through wood and meadow, with tan talising glimpses of Mt Etna smoking in th distance, climbing gently to meet the mai road at Portella Calacudera (1562m), a li tle over 1km later.

Here the main road divides. The unseale left fork heads down towards Lag Maulazzo (the afternoon's route). Follo instead, the sign to 'Monte Soro' along th sealed road (right fork), which climbs it

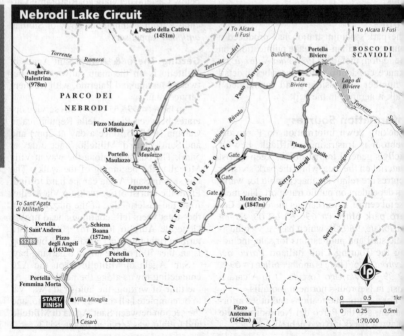

Nebrodi Lake Circuit

Map showing: To Alcara li Fusi, Poggio della Cattiva (1451m), Torrente Ramosa, Anghera Balestrina (978m), PARCO DEI NEBRODI, Pizzo Maulazzo (1498m), Portello Maulazzo, Lago di Maulazzo, Torrente Inganno, Torrente Cuderi, To Sant'Agata di Militello, Portella Sant'Andrea, Schiena Boana, Pizzo degli Angeli (1632m), S5289, Portella Calacudera, Portella Femmina Morta, START/FINISH, Villa Miraglia, To Cesarò, Torrente Cuderi, Passo Rivolo, Vallone Rivolo, Contrada Sollazzo Verde, Gate, Gate, Gate, Monte Soro (1847m), Taverna, Building, Portella Biviere, BOSCO DI SCAVIOLI, Casa Biviere, Lago di Biviere, Torrente Spanedo, Piano Basile, Serra Intagli, Vallone Castagnera, Serra Lupo, To Alcara li Fusi, Pizzo Antenna (1642m), 0 0.5 1km, 0 0.25 0.5mi, 1:70,000

SICILY

ay up through a hunting reserve. Higher p are long views back to the hilltop towns f Troina and Enna.

About 1km before the summit (one hour rom the start of the walk), just as the road egins a tight curve to the south, turn off eft along a leafy track. The summit, ristling with telecommunications equipment, doesn't really warrant a detour. The rack passes through a wooden gate (50m rom the turn-off), then a second, five mintes later, as it descends steadily north then ast through the beech trees. Stay on the nain track as it crosses two streams in uick succession and then negotiates a third ate. The trail switches to the north again as he wood opens out into a small, green neadow, then swings back east to cross another stream with a paved crossing. Shortly fterwards (40 to 45 minutes from the road) he trail forks. Take the left, descending rack, which opens out onto another magificent view of Mt Etna. Five minutes later ou arrive at the meadow of the Piano Basile. To the north on a fine day you can ee the distinctive outline of Rocche del Crasto, standing sentinel over the village of Alcara li Fusi.

Continue to the end of the meadow and a -intersection with a north-south cart track. ollow this track left (north), descending teeply through more woodland for 2km to he shores of Lago di Biviere. As it nears the ake, the trail opens out onto a grassy slope nd swings left to meet a track running parllel to the shore's edge. Go left to pass a mall tile-roofed building, then turn almost mmediately right along a track that leads to he lake's edge (2½ hours from the beginning of the walk). This is a perfect spot to ick off your shoes and crack open the *panini* (bread rolls). A bank of trees lines the hore to the south, while to the north the ake is bounded by a gentle, grassy slope. Before beginning the walk back to Villa Miaglia, you could continue on the trail that eads southeast along the water's edge (a ull circuit takes 20 minutes).

From the western end of the lake, cross he fence next to the lake track and walk cross the small field to the glorified cart track that follows the northern edge of Lago di Biviere. Turn left for Lago Maulazzo (5km, one hour). This is probably the least attractive, but still very enjoyable, section of the walk, sticking to the stony road as it negotiates several small streams and winds its way west through farming country along the woodland border. The Rocche del Crasto dominates views to the north.

Roughly 30 minutes from the Lago di Biviere, the road reaches a junction at Passo Taverna. A sign pointing north indicates the way to Alcara li Fusi (20km). To the left, the road climbs gently up the Torrente Cuderi valley to Lago di Maulazza. Just before the lower dam wall of the artificial lake is a fountain with deliciously drinkable water. At a road junction on the near edge of the lake, a sign indicates the road back to 'Portella Femmina Morta' (4.1km) curving round the western shore of the lake. Ignore a right turn to Militello Rosamarino and cross the upper dam wall. From here, the road rises steadily back to Portella Calacudera, an easy climb of 100 vertical metres. Retrace your steps to the beginning of the walk (20 minutes away).

Other Walks

PARCO DELL'ETNA

Parco dell'Etna offers some wonderful walking opportunities against the scenic backdrop of Etna's summit craters. Walkers can either base themselves at **Rifugio Sapienza** (p308), on the southern side of the volcano, or on the less-visited northern slopes, at **Rifugio Brunek** (p308). The Touring Club Italiano 1:50,000 map *Mt Etna* is the best available for navigation.

Summit Walks

There are several possible routes going up to or close to the summit craters, although the summit area is officially out of bounds. If conditions are favourable (always check with mountain guides first; see the boxed text 'Summit Dangers', p312), it is possible to walk right across the mountain from Piano Provenzana, in the north, to Sapienza, in the south (seven to eight hours, 22.5km). Although the route, along 4WD tracks used by vehicles ferrying visitors to the summit, is not hard to follow, it is long and tiring, graded moderate–hard, with almost 1500m of climbing involved.

An alternative finish to the walk is **Rifugio Citelli** (☎ 095 93 00 00), to the east of the summit, where walkers can overnight in comfort. This is a longer option (9½ to 11½ hours), graded hard, and walkers need to be aware that the long, very steep descent from the summit (1515m) is over loose, bouldery ground. There are no paths or markers and the walk should not be undertaken except in fine weather (navigation without good visibility is potentially dangerous). You'll need a pair of sturdy walking boots.

VULCANO

The north coast of Vulcanello, the little volcanic promontory to the north of the island, offers short walks to admire the splendid panorama over the *faraglioni* (rock stacks) of Lipari. You can also visit the little craters of Vulcanello (one hour).

If you want to spend another half day exploring the island, go back to the sealed road at the beginning of the trail to Vulcano's crater. Go to the left towards Vulcano Piano and get lost in the countless little country roads beneath Monte Aria (500m), the highest point on the island. And to top it all off, follow the road that descends from the Piano to the extreme south of the island to reach the lighthouse at Gelso, from where there are views across to Sicily (three to four hours). There are frequent buses back to Portro di Levante from here.

PARCO NATURALE REGIONALE DELLE MADONIE

Established in 1989, Parco Naturale Regionale delle Madonie covers 400 sq km of the Madonie mountains, west of the Nebrodi range in northern Sicily. Thickly wooded and crowned with limestone cliffs, the park is botanically the richest region in the Mediterranean; half of Sicily's plant species grow here. Like Nebrodi, this is not an

untouched wilderness, but a glimpse of traditiona rural Sicily, complete with hamlets, farms an grazing livestock. Walkers will find trails are sti in the process of being marked, while publi transport access is limited. The 1:50,000 *Madoni Carta dei Sentieri e del Paesaggio* map can b obtained from the **Palermo Tourist Office** (P. azza Castelnuovo). For more information, contac the **park headquarters** (☎ 0921 68 02 01; Pe tralia Sottana).

RISERVA NATURALE ORIENTATO DELLO ZINGARO

After a successful grass roots protest against th construction of a coastal road, a large tract of th Zingaro region in the north-west of Sicily was de clared a nature reserve in 1980; the island's firs This stunning coastal landscape of limesto mountains overlooking the turquoise-blue Gu of Castellamare lies within easy distance of eith Palermo or Trapani, and makes for an ideal da trip by car. There is public transport as far as th small town of Scopello (with accommodation 2km south of the park. A visitor centre at th park's southern entrance has copies of th 1:25,000 park map.

Gulf of Castellamare

Starting from the southern park entrance, th 15km circuit climbs inland and north along a wel maintained nature trail, passing between the peak of Pizzo del Corvo (403m) and Pizzo Passo de Lupo (615m), and eventually reaching the isolate hamlet of the Baglio Cosenza. The return rou curves back south along a cliffside path that pro vides superb views over the gulf, with some eas detours down to sheltered, sandy coves. Grade moderate, with 600m of ascent, the whole circu takes between four and five hours. There is litt shade along the route, so take plenty of water.

Sardinia

The second-largest island in the Mediterranean, Sardinia (Sardegna) has always been considered an isolated, faraway land. Even today, its people and culture maintain a separate identity from the Italian mainland, which they call *il continente* (the continent). The landscape of the island ranges from the 'savage, dark-bushed, sky-exposed land' described by DH Lawrence, with incredibly beautiful gorges and mountains, to the 1900km of unspoiled coastline with clear waters, lovely sandy beaches and dramatic rocky stretches.

Finding yourself immersed in this picturesque solitude, in a primordial silence disturbed only by the wind, you are catapulted back in time. The fascinating mountainous area of Barbagia in the central eastern part of the island (see the boxed text 'Nuoro Province', p325) offers walkers vast and spectacularly well-preserved areas, for centuries the domain of shepherds who lived there with their flocks in almost complete isolation. The people of these mountains live in little towns, connected by a few roads and served by infrequent buses. A network of trails, which are rarely marked, crosses the rocky limestone terrain of the high plains. In some areas sheep have created a network of trails and it is extremely easy to become disoriented. For first-time visitors not expert in navigation with map and compass, it would be a good idea to first explore Barbagia with a local guide.

Although this area is now protected by the proposed Parco Nazionale del Gennargentu e Golfo di Orosei, *rifugi* (mountain huts) are few and far between. Walking here means bringing along all the necessities.

The two walks described in this chapter are both in Barbagia. One is through the Valle del Lanaittu and includes visits to the ancient Nuraghic villages and the spectacular Gola di Gorropu (Gorropu Gorge). The other is along the coast, where navigational problems might arise only along a short section of the walk. The two walks can connect

Highlights

The isolated beach of Cala Goloritzè, one of many on the spectacular Gulf of Orosei

- Visiting the ancient Nuraghic villages of Sos Carros and Tiscali (p330)
- Exploring the mountainous area of Barbagia, with Gola di Gorropu (p330)
- Wandering along the secluded and scenic coastline of the Golfo di Orosei (p335)

at Dorgali to make one of the best walking circuits in Sardinia.

Sardinia is ideal for walking, but it is important that you take some time to first learn a bit about the island and its people. Both can be indifferent and hostile if you come on too strong – but the people are ready to respond with great generosity when approached with respect.

HISTORY

Sardinia is dotted with thousands of *nuraghi*, cone-shaped megalithic fortresses, that are the only remnants of the island's first inhabitants,

Sardinia

1:1,650,000

he Nuraghic people (see the boxed text Homes Made of Stone', p326). These people lived in separate communities led by warrior-king shepherds, and their culture flourished from around 1800 BC. Sardinia's coast was often visited by Greeks and Phoenicians, who came first as traders and later as invaders, before the island was eventually colonised by the Romans.

The Romans, in turn, were followed by the Pisans, Genovese, Spanish, Austrians and, finally, the Savoy royal family, whose possessions became the Kingdom of Sardinia and were eventually incorporated into the newly united Kingdom of Italy in 1861. The countryside offers imposing Nuraghic royal fortresses (such as at Barumini), Carthaginian towns (such as Nora and Tharros on the west coast) and isolated Pisan-style Romanesque churches (in the province of Sassari).

NATURAL HISTORY

Sardinia is in the middle of the western Mediterranean, 190km from the coast of Africa and 180km from the Italian peninsula.

The island is separated from Corsica, to the north, by an 11km stretch of sea, known as the Straight of Bonifacio. The island has a population of about 1.7 million, which equals an average of 68 people per sq km – making it a very sparsely inhabited region compared with the Italian average (190 per sq km). The island is 68% mountainous, with plains making up only 18% of the territory. The Gennargentu, in Barbagia, is the highest area, reaching 1834m at Punta La Marmora. On the east coast there are long, sandy beaches between San Teodoro and Capo Comino, between Santa Maria Navarrese and Arbatax, and at Poetto beach at Cagliari. The rest of the eastern Sardinian coastline is mainly rocky. The west and south coasts of Sardinia retain a rich heritage of brackish lagoons – ideal habitat for many birds, including the pink flamingo, and a strategic point for migratory species using the island as a stopover between Africa and northern Europe.

Millions of years ago Sardinia and Corsica broke off the southern coast of France, leaving behind the Côte d'Azur. Ancient volcanic

Nuoro Province

This province, about halfway up the east coast of Sardinia, encompasses the area known as Barbagia. The Romans were prompted to call the island's central-eastern mountains Barbagia (from the Latin for barbarian) based on their views of the lifestyle of the warrior/shepherds who wouldn't give up Nuraghic practices. Even today the central-eastern Sardinians speak a very ancient Latin-based dialect and are proud of their traditional social behaviour, which is based on belonging, firstly, to one's family and then to the village community.

Probably more than in any other part of Sardinia, where traditions which have been swept aside by tourism, you will be able to get a sense of the island's traditional culture and isolation. It is common to see older women in the traditional black, ankle-length dresses, their heads covered by Spanish-style black, fringed shawls. Shepherds still tend their flocks in remote areas of the province, although they usually return to the village at night in their 4WDs. Consequently, the *pinnettas* (cone-shaped huts of stone and juniper wood), which most shepherds used to live in for long periods until 20 years ago, are now in danger of being destroyed. Walkers occasionally use *pinnettas* illegally for shelter and several have been accidentally burned down.

If you venture into the interior, you will find the people incredibly gracious and hospitable, although contact can be difficult at first. If you want to try what little Italian you might know, the locals will respond with enthusiasm and hospitality – usually in the form of a first drink, then a second...

This is also an area long associated with *banditismo* (banditry) and the unfortunate practice of kidnapping. It is important to note, though, that Sardinians have recently been turning out en masse at public demonstrations against the kidnapping of people from wealthy families, whereas 30 years ago they would have maintained a conspiratorial silence.

SARDINIA

activity, extinct for centuries, has left distinct traces in Monte Ferru, Meilogu and Monte Arci along the west coast; in the evocative granite formations of the Gallura to the north; and in flat, basalt high plains such as the Giara di Gesturi, inland from the Gulf of Oristano. The vast central-east limestone high plains that form the Supramonte of Orgosolo and Oliena are, on the other hand, originally sedimentary and contain numerous grottoes, underground streams and deep gorges.

Sardinia's rich flora is shaped by the Mediterranean climate, and the generally arid and rocky terrain. Numerous species endemic to Sardinia and Corsica have evolved in this hard, dry environment, restricted at times to particular areas – such as filigree centaury on the coast of Baunei, morigian rushes on the Gennargentu, and the Sardinian currant of the Supramonte.

There are three prevalent landscape types: coastal, plain-hillside and mountain. On the east coast the typical low Mediterranean scrub of cistus (rockrose), myrtle and gum trees, often found together, make a splendid, multi-coloured and perfumed floral spectacle in spring and summer. Also found here, heather, euphorbia, rosemary and broom are often associated with trees such as the holm oak, juniper, oleander and tamarisk. In the grassy vegetation you'll see many flowers including the violet, the blue of the periwinkle and lavender, and the colourful mix of irises and many species of orchid. On the Supramonte, the elegant rose-pink bloom of the peonies is justifiably famous.

Although hunters and poachers have traditionally been active in Sardinia, some wildlife remains. The list includes the everpresent wild boar, the mouflon with its great curved horns, the endemic Sardinian wild cat and the Sardinian deer. Fox, weasel, marten, hare and dormouse complete the list of wild terrestrial animals. The Mediterranean monk seal was recently declared extinct in the area.

Sardinia is a paradise for birdwatchers. There are many species, some of which are really spectacular – such as the flamingos in the salt ponds near Cagliari and Oristano and the colony of griffon vultures on the west coast near Bosa. Among birds of prey, the golden eagle is easy to find throughout Barbagia, while the smaller Bonelli's eagle nests in the coastal area of the Supramonte and Eleanora's falcon along the rocky shores of the Golgo area.

You can see kestrels, peregrine and swamp falcons, buzzards, goshawks, sparrowhawks and Sardinian owls. Besides the Barbary partridge, crow, jay, hoopoe and wood pigeon, there are many species to be found in the ponds. These include the rare purple gallinule and waders such as the grey heron, white egret, purple heron, night heron, water rail, little egret, curlew, avocet and other migratory species of duck and goose.

Sardinia is the only region of Italy where there are no poisonous vipers. You might meet harmless species of snake like the natrix viper (similar in appearance to the poisonous adder), the Sardinian coluber and the endemic Sardinian lizard. Interesting among amphibians is the cave-dwelling Sardinian newt.

CLIMATE

High average temperatures and little rain mean that Sardinia has at least seven months of good weather each year. Average daily maximum temperatures along the coast are 19°C in autumn, 10°C in winter, 12°C in spring and 22°C in summer. On the east coast, winds from the north create clear

Homes Made of Stone

Among the most dominant features of Sardinia's landscape are the 7000 or so *nuraghi* dotted around the island. Dating from 1800 to 400 BC, these truncated conical structures were made out of huge basalt blocks taken from extinct volcanoes. The towers were used for shelter and for guarding the surrounding territory. The name *nuraghe* derives from the Sardinian word *nurra*, which means 'heap' or 'mound'. Very little is known about the identity of the Nuraghic people. Judging by their buildings, they were well organised and possessed remarkable engineering skills, but they appear to have left no written word.

skies and a cool airflow, while winds from the south or east bring occasional rain, which rarely lasts long. However, there can be strong winds which last for several days.

INFORMATION
When to Walk

The best period for walking is from March to June, when the days are beginning to lengthen and the wildflowers are in bloom. In addition there are frequent patron saint feast days in the local towns and villages. On these occasions, the young women and men dress in their traditional costumes with beautiful, coloured embroidery and perform traditional folk dances. Autumn is also a pleasant time to walk. Winter is too cold, and summer is far too hot for walking, with the beaches packed with tourists.

What to Bring

To complete both of the walks described, you'll need the full complement of camping equipment: tent, sleeping bag, cooking equipment including a portable stove, fuel and food (see also the equipment Check List, p58). Boots suitable for rocky terrain are essential; long pants would provide protection when walking through dense, spiny vegetation. Don't forget insect repellent and a large water bottle (at least 2L capacity) as fresh springs are rare.

Maps

Ente Sardo Industrie Turistiche (ESIT; see Cagliari, p328) produces and distributes a good 1:300,000 road map of the island, which has maps of the major cities and some useful tourist itineraries. It's available from most local tourist offices. You can also find other regional maps at newsstands and in bookshops.

The Touring Club Italiano's 1:200,000 map Sardegna (available outside the island) is ideal for route planning and general orientation.

Books

DH Lawrence (1885–1930), the English novelist and poet, wrote about Sardinia after he visited the island on a one-week

Sardinian Cooking

The island's cuisine is as varied as its history. Along the coast most dishes feature seafood and there are many variations of *zuppa di pesce* (fish soup) and pasta. Inland you will find *porcheddu* (roast suckling pig), kid goat with olives and lamb trotters in garlic sauce. The Sardi eat *pecorino* (sheep's milk cheese) and the preferred bread throughout the island is the paper-thin *carta musica*, also called *pane carasau*, often served sprinkled with oil and salt.

winter excursion from Sicily in the early 1920s. The Penguin Travel Library edition *DH Lawrence and Italy* includes his interesting *Sea and Sardinia*.

Rother Guides' *Sardinia* (in English) describes 50 walks throughout the island. The Sunflower guide, *Landscapes of Sardinia*, by Andreas Steiglitz, covers 37 long- and short-day walks; both are useful if you would like to explore more of Sardinia.

Permits

If you plan an overnight stop in a *pinnetta* (see the boxed text 'Nuoro Province', p325), bear in mind that they are private property and you should ask for permission in the nearest village. It's very easy to set fire to these huts if you don't know which kind of wood is suitable for the inside fire.

Place Names

Place names on the IGM maps and on signs throughout the island are sometimes in local dialects, and may differ slightly from those used in this book.

Guided Walks

The **Società Gorropu** (☎ 0782 64 92 82, 333 850 71 57; ⓦ web.tiscali.it/gorropu; Via Sapreda Lada 2, Urzulei) is an organisation of young, competent and environmentally motivated guides. There is a variety of one-, five- and six-day walks, including the descent of the Codula di Luna to the sea, climbing from the depths of the Gola di Gorropu, and the six-day 'Selvaggio Blu'

SARDINIA

climbing-walk from Pedra Longa (Baunei) to Cala Luna. Guides can also take you to explore fascinating caves crossed by underground rivers.

Cooperativa Goloritzè *(☎/fax 0782 61 05 99, 368 702 89 80; e goloritze@tiscalinet.it)* has a base in the Golgo high plain, 8km north of Baunei, and offers guided treks in the area – on foot, horseback or, if you prefer, donkey. The programme includes a day on horseback exploring the Golgo high plain, a two-day walk from Golgo to Cala Sisine and a one-week walk along the spectacular Golfo di Orosei. The company also organize a six-day 'Selvaggio Blu' climbing-walk from Pedra Longa (Baunei) to Cala Luna.

The **Cooperativa Ghivine** *(☎ 338 834 16 18, fax 0784 967 21; w www.ghivine.com; Via La Marmora 69E, Dorgali)* organises nature walks, and archaeological, caving and scuba excursions in the Dorgali area.

The **Barbagia Insolita** *(☎ 0784 28 60 05; w www.barbagiainsolita.it; Corso Vittorio Emanuele 48, Oliena)* has guided tours to out-of-the-way areas by 4WD and on foot. You can choose between demanding treks and relaxing walks to places including Tiscali, the Gola di Gorropu and Monte Corrasi.

Levamus Viaggi travel agency *(☎/fax 0784 28 60 88; Corso Vittorio Emanuele 33, Oliena)* offers guided tours and can organise transport for groups between Nuoro and the start and finish of the walks.

Emergency

For urgent assistance while walking in Sardinia, contact the **mountain rescue service** *(☎ 070 28 62 00)* or the **national emergency number** *(☎ 118)*.

GATEWAYS
Cagliari

The capital city has a Roman amphitheatre, an interesting medieval centre and an important archaeological museum. See Lonely Planet's *Sardinia* for more information.

Information The **ESIT office** *(☎ 800 01 31 53; w www.esit.net; Via Goffredo Mameli 97; open 8am-8pm daily, May-Sept, reduced hours the rest of the year)* has information about all of Sardinia. The **AAST office** *(☎ 070 66 92 55; e aastinfo@tiscalinet.it; Piazza Matteotti; open 8am-8pm daily during summer, 8am-7.30pm the rest of the year)* has a reasonable amount of information about the town and will advise on accommodation. There is a **provincial tourist information booth** *(☎ 070 66 83 52)* at the port.

Supplies & Equipment If you want to buy supplies, head for Via Sardegna, where there are several good **grocery shops** as well as a **bakery**.

Georock *(☎ 070 66 66 80, e artrek@ libero.it, Corso Vittorio Emanuele 64)* has a good range of walking equipment, including fuel for portable stoves. **Azimut** *(☎/fax 070 348 10 98; e sardegnaazimut@libero.it; Via della Pineta 201/a)* has the full range of the IGM 1:25,000 and 1:50,000 maps of Sardinia, and a good selection of outdoor books. Take bus No 5 from the port area.

Places to Stay & Eat There are numerous budget hotels in the old city near the station. Try the basic **Albergo La Perla** *(☎/fax 070 66 94 46; e la-perla-ca@yahoo.it; Via Sardegna 18; singles/doubles without bath €31/ 38.75)*, the very pleasant **Pensione Vittoria** *(☎ 070 65 79 70, fax 070 66 79 70; Via Roma 75; singles/doubles with bath €41.30/62)* or the comfortable **Hotel Italia** *(☎ 070 66 05 10, fax 070 65 02 40; Via Sardegna 31; singles/ doubles €64.55/92.95)*, where breakfast is included.

There are several reasonably priced **trattorias** in the area behind Via Roma, particularly around Via Cavour and Via Sardegna. **Trattoria Lillicu** *(☎ 070 65 29 70; Via Sardegna 78; full meal around €20.65)* is favoured by locals and specialises in typical Sardinian seafood. **Trattoria Gennargentu** *(☎ 070 65 82 47; Via Sardegna 60; full meal €23.25)* has excellent pasta and seafood. **Corsaro** *(☎ 070 66 43 18; Viale Regina Margherita 28; full meal with wine from €49.05)* is one of the city's top restaurants. During summer it opens a branch at the Marina Piccola at Poetto beach, including cheaper pizzeria section.

Getting There & Away Cagliari is linked by air with major Italian and European cities. The airport is 8km northwest of the city at Elmas and has a **tourist office** (☎ *070 24 02 00).* ARST buses leave regularly from Piazza Matteotti, linking with flights.

ARST (☎ *070 409 83 24, 800 86 50 42;* W *www.arst.sardegna.it)* buses leave for nearby towns from the **bus station** *(Piazza Matteotti)* in front of the FS railway station, northwest of the port. **Pani** (☎ *070 65 23 26)* buses leave from the port, in front of the Stazione Marittima, where you can buy tickets at the bar inside. **Turmotravel** (☎ *079 214 87;* W *www.gruppoturmotravel.com)* buses leave twice a day for Olbia and Santa Teresa di Gallura (€17.55, 4½ hours), from Piazza Matteotti (5.30am) or from inside the ARST bus station (2.30pm, except Sunday).

The main **FS** (☎ *8488 880 88, 199 166 17)* train lines link Cagliari with Oristano, Sassari and Olbia (four hours, twice a day). The private railways that link smaller towns throughout the island can be slow. However, the **Trenino Verde** *(Green Train;* ☎ *800 46 02 20;* W *www.treninoverde.com)*, which runs from Cagliari to Arbatax through Barbagia, is a relaxing way to see part of the scenic interior.

The main ferry company, **Tirrenia** (☎ *199 12 31 99, 081 317 29 99;* W *www.tirrenia.it)*, connects Cagliari with Palermo (€39.90, 13½ hours), Trapani, Naples (€46.10, 6½ hours), Civitavecchia (€42, 16½ hours) and Genoa (€55.05, 20 hours). Bookings can also be made at **Stazione Marittima** (☎ *070 66 60 65)* in the port area.

Sardinia Ferries (☎ *019 21 55 11;* W *www.sardiniaferries.com)* runs services between Cagliari and Civitavecchia.

Olbia

The major port for ferries from Civitavecchia, Genoa and Livorno and a busy industrial centre, Olbia is not particularly pleasant but is convenient as a first port of call in Sardinia.

Information The **AAST office** (☎ *0789 214 53;* W *www.esit.net; Via Catello Piro 1; open 8am-8pm daily in summer)* is off Corso Umberto. The staff speak English, and are very keen to help and advise on places to stay and eat. They can also provide information about accommodation and places to visit elsewhere on the island.

Supplies & Equipment As well as selling outdoor equipment (including fuel for portable stoves), **Mediterraneo** *(*☎*/fax 0789 217 59;* W *www.miditerraneosport.com; Centro Martini, Via D'Annunzio 45)* organizes guided tours and walks.

Places to Stay & Eat The best deal in town, **Hotel Gallura** (☎ *0789 246 48; Corso Umberto 145; singles/doubles with bath €56.80/82.65)* is a pleasant place. Its **restaurant** *(full meal around €67.15)*, run by Miss Rita, is considered one of the best in Sardinia and is really something special.

You could also try **Hotel Centrale** (☎ *0789 230 17; Corso Umberto 85; singles/doubles €61.95/82.65)* or **Terranova** (☎ *0789 223 95;* e *htlterranova@tiscalinet.it; Via Garibaldi 6; singles/doubles €67.15/98.15).*

Getting There & Away The majority of flights between Olbia and other major cities in Italy and Europe are operated by **Meridiana** (W *www.meridiana.it)*. City bus No 2 heads to the airport. Call the **airport**

Warning

As you'll be walking in some very isolated areas, it's a good idea to notify someone of your route and destination before setting out. A mobile telephone could solve a lot of problems.

Never underestimate the difficulty of navigation in Sardinia's wilderness areas! You might also encounter problems crossing the limestone terrain of the Supramonte – it is full of deep holes and channels covered by vegetation, and therefore it is not a good idea to leave the trail. If you do lose the trail, the best idea is to retrace your steps to find it. If you would like to explore the area but doubt your orienteering abilities, hire a local guide for an initial exploration of the area.

information office (☎ 0789 56 34 44) for detailed information in English.

See Getting There & Away (p329) under Cagliari for bus and train details.

Tirrenia (☎ 199 12 31 99, 081 317 29 99; ⓦ www.tirrenia.it) ferries connect the port of Olbia (Isola Bianca) with Genoa (€47.05, 13 hours) and Civitavecchia (€26.25, eight hours). Tirrenia also runs a fast, summer-only service between Olbia and Genoa (€78, six hours) or Civitavecchia (€48.70, four hours); and between Golfo Aranci (18km north of Olbia) and Fiumicino (20km west of Rome) or La Spezia (105km south-east of Genoa).

Moby Lines (☎ 0565 93 61; ⓦ www .mobylines.it) runs ferries between Olbia and Genoa, Livorno or Civitavecchia, and offers special fares for daytime passages in low season. At the time of writing, this fare was around €144.60 return (Livorno–Olbia or Civitavecchia–Olbia) for a car and two people. **Sardinia Ferries** (☎ 019 21 55 11) runs ferries between Golfo Aranci and Livorno or Civitavecchia. Both Moby Lines and Sardinia Ferries also run services between Sardinia and Corsica. **Grandi Navi Veloci** (ⓦ www.grimaldi.it) runs ferries, summer only, between Olbia and Genova.

Tiscali-Gorropu

Duration	3 days
Difficulty	easy
Start	Oliena (p330)
Finish	Dorgali (p330)
Transport	bus

Summary This walk links the Nuraghic villages of Sos Carros and Tiscali with the imposing natural monument of the Gola di Gorropu.

Sardinia's past, human and natural, is jealously guarded in the remote Valle del Lanaittu. This walk provides a unique opportunity to explore these secrets, marvelling at the abilities of ancient civilisations (see the boxed text 'Homes Made of Stone', p326) and mother nature. Make sure you allow plenty of time to explore the ruins of Sos Carros and Tiscali, and to admire the spectacular chasm of Gola di Gorropu.

If you arrive in Oliena with half a day to spare before starting the walk, you can head up to Scala è Pradu (p341) to admire the panoramic and enchanting view. Note you can continue from Scala è Pradu to Rifugio Lanaittu (the end of Day 1), however, this route presents serious navigational difficulties and is suitable for experts only. The route is not marked and is basically only a faint trail over rocky ground. Occasional fog can cause further difficulties higher up. This route involves nearly 900m of ascent and over 1000m of descent, and takes at least six hours. Walkers who fancy this option are advised to employ a local guide (see Guided Walks, p327).

If you want to shorten the described walk, you can cut the first 6km of road walking by catching a local bus (every two hours in summer) from Oliena to the Su Gologone junction on the Dorgali road.

Although Day 1 ends at a *rifugio*, it is not possible to stay here and you will need to come prepared for camping.

To extend this walk, it can be linked with the three-day coastal Golfo di Orosei walk (p335), which starts in Cala Gonone (9km from Dorgali).

PLANNING
Maps

This walk is mainly covered by two IGM 1:25,000 maps, Nos 500 III *Oliena* and 500 II *Dorgali*. Unfortunately, the southernmost section of the route, the entrance to the Gola di Gorropu, lies on the border between Nos 517 IV *Funtana Bona* and 517 I *Cantoniera Genna Silana*. It isn't worth buying them just for this section as it presents no serious navigational problems.

NEAREST TOWNS & FACILITIES
Oliena & Around

In the centre of town is the **tourist office** (☎ 0784 28 60 78; ⓔ galaveras@tiscalinet.it Via Grazia Deledda 32).

Places to Stay & Eat In the centre of Oliena, **Hotel Ci Kappa** (☎ 0784 28 87 33

)784 28 80 24; Via Martin Luther King 2; singles/doubles €31/43.90) is simple but comfortable and the restaurant/pizzeria is very friendly.

Albergo Monte Maccione (☎ 0784 28 83 53; e coopenis@tiscalinet.it; doubles in low/high season €41.30/62, half board from €46.68), run by the Cooperativa Turistica Enis, on the way up to Scala è Pradu (p341). From the hotel, a 4WD ride up to Scala è Pradu costs around €8.25 per person for a minimum of five people.

Luxurious **Hotel Su Gologone** (☎ 0784 28 75 12; w www.sugologone.it; singles/doubles €87.80/129.10, half board in low season up to €113.60) is on the way to Valle del Lanaittu, on Day 1 of the walk. In a lovely setting, this elegant hotel is a good option for people wanting to enjoy easy exploration of the area; the hotel organises guided tours and walks. The restaurant is justifiably renowned throughout the island.

Getting There & Away Connecting Olbia port with Oliena via Siniscola, **ARST** (☎ 070 409 83 24, 800 86 50 42) buses leave after the landing of the Tirrenia ferry from Civitavecchia at about 7am.

You can also get to Oliena via Nuoro. From Cagliari, **Pani** (☎ 070 65 23 26) buses leave from in front of Stazione Marittima (where you can buy tickets at the bar inside) for Nuoro (€11.30, 3½ hours, four times a day). There's a daily ARST bus from Cagliari to Nuoro (€14, three hours), which leaves Cagliari at 3.30pm. From Olbia, there's a direct ARST service to Nuoro (€8.55, 2½ hours, five times a day); and **Fratelli De Planu** (☎ 0784 29 50 30) buses run to Nuoro from Olbia airport (€5.85, 1¾ hours, four times a day). Once in Nuoro, there's a bus service from the ARST station to Dorgali and Cala Gonone via Oliena. This operates six times a day Monday to Saturday (6.53 and 7.50am, and 1.10, 2, 3.50 and 7pm) and three times on Sundays (6.53am, and 2 and 7pm). There are two additional runs during July and August (8am and 12.15pm).

From Arbatax there is one daily bus to Dorgali at 7.10am, with a connection to Oliena (7.30am) and on to Nuoro.

Dorgali & Around
At the **Pro Loco tourist office** (☎ 0784 962 43; Via la Marmora, Dorgali) you can pick up information about accommodation and trails in the area. The bookshop **La Scolastica** (☎ 0784 948 01; Via la Marmora 69) sells local IGM maps.

Places to Stay & Eat In Dorgali itself, **Hotel San Pietro** (☎ 0784 961 42; Via la Marmora; singles/doubles €15.50/33.55) is a basic place. **Hotel Sant'Elene** (☎ 0784 945 72; singles/doubles €31/56.80), on Day 3 of the walk, is set in a panoramic position 3km south of Dorgali at Monte Sant'Elene. It has an excellent restaurant with a reasonably priced tourist menu.

Favoured by climbers, **Rifugio Gorropu** (☎ 0784 948 97; e johnnygrem@hotmail .com; open Easter–mid-November; dorms or rooms €15.49-18.08), is 300m south from the junction for the Hotel Sant'Elene. Accommodation is very basic. There is also a **camping ground** (with own tent/tent hire €7.75/12.90).

Getting There & Away Travelling along the S125, **ARST** (☎ 070 409 83 24, 800 86 50 42) buses connect the port of Olbia (leaving at 8.15am) with Lanusei via Dorgali (€6.75, arriving 10.20am).

You can also get to Dorgali via Nuoro (see Getting There & Away, this page, for Oliena & Around). The most direct way from Cagliari is to take the 3.30pm ARST bus to Nuoro, then change for Dorgali (€15, arriving 7.50pm).

There is one bus a day from Arbatax to Dorgali (via Tortolì), leaving the port following the arrival of the ferry, at approximately 5.05am (Monday to Saturday). The bus arrives in Dorgali at 7.10am, then continues to Oliena and Nuoro.

THE WALK
Day 1: Oliena to Rifugio Lanaittu
4–5 hours, 18km, 103m ascent, 268m descent

Take the asphalt road from Oliena heading towards Dorgali and, after about 6km, turn off to the right onto another minor asphalt road with a signpost to Su Gologone. This junction is served by a local bus (every two hours during summer). After another 2km you'll reach the **Hotel Su Gologone** (see Oliena & Around, p330). Go past the entrance ramp of the hotel and, shortly afterwards, turn right onto the road that climbs a little valley. It may be worth taking the 300m detour straight ahead here to reach a pure, icy underground spring, called **Sorgenti di Su Gologone**, which gushes out in a strong jet from the mountain, then flows into Fiume Cedrino. On the rock above the striking fissure is the little church of **Nostra Signora della Pietà**.

Back on the paved road, which climbs the little valley, you will gain altitude and round a rocky shoulder to enter the fresh green **Valle del Lanaittu**, crowned by imposing limestone peaks as high as 1400m.

The road then descends towards Rio Sa Oche and runs alongside it until the road divides into two, one straight and to the left crossing a plateau of abandoned fields, and

one to the right at mid-slope cutting through the vegetation. Both reach the speleologists' shelter of Rifugio Lanaittu (145m). Follow the road to the left, which follows a level section and a wide curve to the left, arriving at a fork. Here you turn right to get to the *rifugio* and the imposing entrance to **Grotta Sa Oche** (Cave of the Voice), which is named after the sound made by the large amounts of water which pour out of it when flooded. The *rifugio* is closed to walkers but it's usually possible to **camp** out in the fenced courtyard (beware there are wild pigs in the area).

Side Trip: Sos Carros
30 minutes, 600m

Three hundred metres north of Rifugio Lanaittu, on the wooded slope overlooking the bridge, is an important archaeological site with the remains of the Nuraghic village of Sos Carros *(entry €2.60; open 9.30am – 6.30pm)*. The area is fenced in but you can ask the guard, who is also the shepherd of

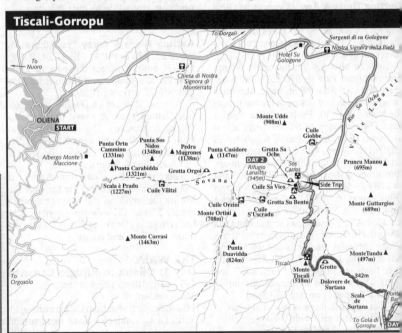

he adjacent sheepfold, to let you in. You
an see the remains of a small area where a
amily would have gathered together at an
nusual circular stone seat, perhaps to per-
orm some ancient ritual.

Day 2: Rifugio Lanaittu to Ponte Sa Barva, via Gola di Gorropu

5–6 hours, 460m ascent, 262m descent

Head south on the dirt road, which, after a
few curves, reaches a junction. Follow the
dirt road to the right until you reach a curve
.7km from the *rifugio*, at a small clearing
on the right. Continue north on the dirt road
and 20m after the curve, at another clearing,
take the rambling, steep dirt road to the
right, which heads southwest. After about 20
minutes of hard climbing, you'll come to a
boulder with a painted arrow and a marker
for Tiscali. Here you leave the dirt road and
climb uphill to the left (east) into the forest,
climbing the very steep slope until you come

to the base of a rockface. To your left (north)
is an obvious and quite impressive **split in
the mountain**, which you climb into, one at
a time, thankful that Sardinia isn't subject to
earthquakes. After another short climb,
you'll come out of the fissure onto a wide
ledge. The end of the ledge is high on the
western edge of the enormous *dolina* (sinkhole) where the village of Tiscali is (labelled
'Sa Curtiga de Tiscali' on the IGM map), although you're unable to see the village at
this point. To enter the dolina and reach the
village, you need to go round to the east –
head north and to the right – where you'll
find a passage down through the rocks to the
renowned Nuraghic village of **Tiscali** *(admission €2.60; open 8am-sunset)*, 1½ hours
from the *rifugio*. Count on spending an hour
exploring the village.

The natural karst environment of the
enormous *dolina*, formed by a collapse of
the limestone rock on a mountain crest, appears to have been utilised by the Nuraghic

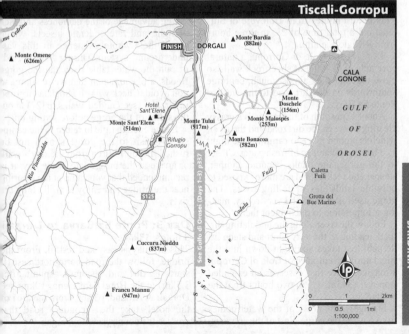

inhabitants of Sos Carros as a hiding place from invading enemies. Sited on a crest, Tiscali offered various possibilities for escape and received a constant supply of water, which dripped from the roof of the cave overhanging the settlement.

After visiting Tiscali, return to the main track via the passage through the rocks. After a few metres, when you see a cairn, head right (southeast) into the scrub on a track, which leads steeply downhill. At a junction 20 minutes from Tiscali, shortly after passing a small *nuraghe*, the track joins another trail. Go left (northeast) and, passing the foot of a huge grotto, descend for a short distance to a grassy area (250m). From here you go up to the right (southeast) into the shady gorge of the Dolovere di Surtana, continuing until you reach a pass (342m), 25 minutes from the junction. From here, go downhill along the steep, narrow, rocky gorge of **Scala de Surtana** and, once at the bottom, go right (south) on the dirt road, along the true left side of the Rio Flumineddu, to reach Ponte Sa Barva (190m). This is 30 minutes from Dolovere di Surtana and a total time of 2½ to three hours from Rifugio Lanaittu.

To reach the Gola di Gorropu, a natural spectacle with 400m of sheer rock walls so close together they almost touch, continue southwards on the dirt road to the west of Ponte Sa Barva.

About 1km south of the bridge is a grassy clearing between the dirt road and the river, which is a good place to **camp** for the night as it has the advantage of fresh water. Closer to the gorge, the banks become damper, steeper and rockier, and are more exposed to possible landslides or falling rocks. The gorge itself is narrow and very rocky, making it impossible to pitch a tent there.

Follow the river along the undulating dirt road, leading to the very short and steep little path that takes you right down into the silent northern entrance of **Gola di Gorropu**, a magical place that deserves an extended stopover (343m, 1½ to two hours from the bridge).

Strangely, the noise of the water comes from outside the gorge. East of the entrance,

beyond the enormous boulders and a lovely, little limestone clearing, the Rio Flumineddu gushes back out into the open after a journey of several kilometres underground. The clearing is an ideal place to enjoy the sun and a snack, alongside the gurgling, crystal-clear water. To the right of the clearing, looking downhill, you can see the start of a tough trail that ascends to the Genna Silana pass on the S125 (650m uphill, two to three hours).

A visit to the gorge is not complete without a walk through the narrow passageway overhung by high walls that are clogged with giant blocks of fallen rock shaped by water erosion. It's an exciting and humbling experience to climb among the deep channels of a river that isn't there, among huge rocks in perennial shadow, being hit now and then by mysterious drips. Those who are able to get through the tricky (mountaineering grade three) passages can ascend the gorge as far as an impassable 20m gap.

Very few plants survive under these conditions; however, there are ferns and mosses taking advantage of the dampness and lack of light, and rare endemic insects, which spend their whole existence in this vast underground system. During long periods of rain the water table rises and the gorge floods, a phenomenon that we recommend you avoid. Check with the Società Gorropu in Urzulei (see Guided Walks, p327) about the status of the gorge before setting out.

Leave enough time to return to the campsite. A visit to the gorge should not be rushed. If you're tired from the day's walk or arrive at the bridge late in the day, it is recommended that you camp at the clearing near the bridge and enjoy a stroll along the river.

Day 3: Ponte Sa Barva to Dorgali
3 hours, 13km

This last day is easy and restful. From the bridge, follow the road north-northeast (it starts as dirt and becomes asphalt after 3.5km) to the **Hotel Sant'Elene** (10km; see Dorgali & Around, p331). From the area of the hotel, take the secondary road that crosses the countryside to Dorgali.

Golfo di Orosei

Duration	4 days
Difficulty	moderate
Start	Cala Gonone
Finish	Baunei
Nearest Towns	Cala Gonone (p335),
	Baunei & Santa Maria (p335),
	Arbatax (p336)
Transport	bus

Summary A varied coastal walk from the fascinating beach of Cala Luna to spectacular sections of secluded coastline.

Wandering along this stretch of Mediterranean coast, considered among the most scenic in Sardinia, you will encounter both beautiful and demanding sections. It is a largely self-sufficient route, although the recently restored Rifugio Golgo at the end of Day 3 is a great place to spend an extra day or two while exploring the area.

The walk starts and ends with 4km and 8km of road walking respectively. These can be eliminated by using local ferry services or organising 4WD transport (see Getting to/from the Walk, p336). There are also some alternative finish options, Urzulei via Codula di Luna and Santa Maria Navarrese via Pedra Longa. For more information and assistance with these demanding options, contact Società Gorropu or Cooperativa Goloritzè (see Guided Walks, p327).

The coastal walk can also be linked with the three-day Tiscali-Gorropu walk (p330), which ends in Dorgali (9km from Cala Gonone).

PLANNING
Maps

This walk is covered by four IGM 1:25,000 maps, Nos 500 II *Dorgali*, 517 I *Cantoniera Genna Silana*, 518 III *Capo di Monte Santu* and 518 IV *Punta è Lattone*.

NEAREST TOWNS
Cala Gonone

Set on the coast 9km from Dorgali, the resort village of Cala Gonone is a popular base for divers, climbers and walkers. Information on the area is available at the **tourist office** (☎ 0784 933 87; Viale del Bue Marino; open Easter-Sept).

Accommodation options include **Camping Cala Gonone** (☎ 0784 931 65, fax 0784 932 55; Via Collodi 1; camping per person €14.45). Behind the busy harbour is **Pop Hotel** (☎ 0784 931 85; e ifancel@box1.tin.it; half board €36.15-74.90). Rates vary depending on the season. It also has a reasonably priced restaurant.

Due Chiacchiere (☎ 0784 933 86; Via Acquadolce 13; full meal around €18.10) is a *spaghetteria*/pizzeria overlooking the sea.

Getting There & Away See Getting There & Away (p331) for transport to/from Dorgali. Cala Gonone is served by buses from Dorgali.

Baunei & Santa Maria Navarrese

There are no hotels or camping grounds in Baunei itself. In the quiet resort of Santa Maria Navarrese, ask at the **tourist office** (☎ 0782 61 53 30; e turinforma@tiscalinet.it) for information.

For somewhere to stay, try the comfortable **Albergo Santa Maria** (☎ 0782 61 53 15, fax 0782 61 53 96; e albergosantamaria@ tiscalinet.it; Via Plammas 30; half board in June & late Sept €43.90, in Aug €82.65; open March-Oct). The staff are particularly helpful and offer van and boat service to shuttle guests to the beginning and from the end of walks (see Side Trip: Cala Goloritzè, p340), or to the more secluded beaches in the area. They also have bikes for hire.

Getting There & Away Travelling along the S125, **ARST** (☎ 070 409 83 24, 800 86 50 42) buses connect the port of Olbia (leaving at 8.15am) with Lanusei, via Baunei (€9.50, arriving 11.40am) and Santa Maria Navarrese (€9.50, arriving noon).

See Getting There & Away (p331) under Oliena & Around for transport to/from Nuoro. Only the 2pm bus (Monday to Saturday) from the Nuoro ARST station, which goes to Dorgali and Cala Gonone via Oliena, continues along the S125 to Arbatax via Baunei and Tortolì.

SARDINIA

There are frequent buses from Baunei south to Santa Maria Navarrese, Tortolì and Lanusei. A daily direct bus runs to Cagliari (€8.55, four hours, 4.45am), and a few go north to Dorgali (5.55am, Monday to Saturday, change for Oliena and Nuoro; and 4pm daily, continuing to Siniscola and Olbia).

Arbatax

This small port town, 13km south of Santa Maria Navarrese, is probably the most convenient place for access by ferry to the southern end of the walk. For cheap accommodation, try **Il Gabbiano** (☎ *0782 62 35 12; singles/doubles with bath €46.50/51.65*) in the Porto Frailis area, 2km south.

Getting There & Away Twice every week **Tirrenia** (☎ *199 12 31 99, 081 317 29 99;* W *www.tirrenia.it*) ferries dock here from Civitavecchia, as do the fast ferries from Fiumicino in summer (16 July to 5 September). If you're heading north to Baunei, Cala Gonone, Dorgali or Nuoro, you will need to catch an ARST bus or walk 4km to Tortolì, where you can catch the direct daily ARST bus for Nuoro (via Lanusei). It's best to check at the tourist offices in Dorgali or Nuoro for up-to-date information. Buses leave from Arbatax for Cagliari two or three times a day, not necessarily coinciding with ferry arrivals.

Another, more expensive option would be to catch the **Trenino Verde** (*Green Train;* ☎ *800 46 02 20;* W *www.treninoverde.com*), which runs from Arbatax to Cagliari through Barbagia, a relaxing way to see part of the scenic interior.

GETTING TO/FROM THE WALK

This walk can be shortened at both ends. From Cala Gonone, **Nuova Consorzio Trasporti Marittimi** (☎ *0784 933 05*) operates large boats along the coast, several times a day from the end of March to mid-November. The boats go to the Grotto del Bue Marino (€12.90 return), which includes a guided visit to the caves where a colony of the now extinct monk seal once lived, Cala Luna (€13.95 return), Cala Sisine (€14.45 return) and Cala Mariolu (€21.70 return). The first boat from Cala Gonone to Cala

Luna (the overnight stop on Day 1 of the walk) departs at 9am (11am low season) and the last boat from Cala Luna to Cala Gonone leaves at 5.30 or 3.30pm, depending on the season; the one way trip is €8.25.

At the other end, you can organise transport between Rifugio Golgo and Baunei (8km). Cooperativa Goloritzè (see Guided Walks, p327), which operates the *rifugio*, offers car transfers for €7.75 per person. You could also use the coop's transport to get from Cala Sisine to Baunei, thus shortening the route by 23km.

Another option is, from the *rifugio*, walk to Cala Goloritzè (see Side Trip: Cala Goloritzè, p340) and catch a boat to Santa Maria Navarrese. Organise this through Albergo Santa Maria (see Baunei & Santa Maria Navarrese, p335).

THE WALK
Day 1: Cala Gonone to Cala Luna
3 hours, 274m ascent/descent

Head south for about 4km along Viale del Bue Marino, following the asphalt coast road. You could consider asking your hotel for a lift along this section. You'll reach the deep fissure of the **Codula Fuili**, where the road ends at a parking area, after one hour. The stepped trail descends to cross the *codula*, a long gorge formed by water erosion. From here you can spend some time exploring the gorge (see Side Trip: Codula Fuili, p337) and a few metres to your left (east) is the nice beach of Cala Fuili.

The main trail continues south, climbing the opposite side of the gorge to reach a junction. Here a trail descends to the east to a dangerous cliff where there is a closed access to the Grotta del Bue Marino. This cave is only accessible from the sea on the boat service from Cala Gonone. At the junction, stay on the well-marked trail heading south and continue to the highest point of the day (131m), one hour from Codula Fuili. The trail then begins to descend, reaching the rocky entrance of the Oddoana cave and passing **Codula Oddoana** a short distance from the beach.

From the gorge, the trail ascends again to the south and passes the hill known as

runcu Nieddu (120m), crossing its eastern
lope at about 100m altitude with a great
iew of the sea. The trail then begins a steep
escent, with sharp turns, to the gravel
iverbed of the magically beautiful **Codula di
una** (see Side Trip: Codula di Luna, this
age). Follow this canyon to the left (east),
ross the riverbed and reach the low building
f **Ristorante Su Neulagi** (☎ 0784 933 92;
pen April-Oct), one hour from the high
oint. A caretaker lives here all year round,
ut out of season he only sells mineral water.
he free **camping ground** is open year-round.

You are now separated from the sea by
nly a narrow strip of oleanders, full of
olourful flowers in summer, and the low
unes of the beach, which sometimes hold
he water of the *codula* to form lovely little
reshwater ponds. The beach stretches be-
ond the cliffs and rocky outcrops to the
orth towards a series of strange caves that
ook like great garages for resting whales.

In July and August the beach is crowded
vith day-trippers from Cala Gonone. Most
•f them will leave with the last boat, so you
ould consider spending a romantic night
earby under the stars.

Side Trip: Codula Fuili
¹ hours

from the bottom of **Codula Fuili** on Day 1,
ollow the easy, dry riverbed of the gorge
nland (west). You'll enter a quiet and fas-
inating, secluded world, inhabited by wild
•igeons and some solitary climbers. When
ou're tired of the solitude, retrace your
teps to the beach.

Side Trip: Codula di Luna
² hours

from the Cala Luna beach, follow the dry
iverbed of the gorge inland (west). This is
real riverbed made up of large, rounded
iver stones, so the walking can be difficult.
Enjoy a short walk along this majestic lime-
tone canyon and then return to the beach.

Day 2: Cala Luna to Cala Sisine
4–5 hours, 630m ascent/descent

t is advisable to set out early, since you will
eed to do some careful navigating in order

not to lose the trail. It is essential that you have the proper map.

From behind the restaurant, where the toilets are, ascend south along easy curves on a 2m-wide dirt track. After 20 minutes you come to a level section, at about 100m altitude. Here you'll find an unpleasant bottle dump, where there's a marvellous panorama of the coast to the south. From here, the track descends into the striking gorge called Badde de Lupiru and then ascends again in a south-southwesterly direction. Continue to ascend along the wide, sunbeaten track, passing an imposing rock arch called S'Architieddu Lupiru (365m), after one hour.

You'll soon reach a section where the track veers south. It develops into a level track at mid-slope along the eastern face of Punta Onamarra until it crosses over the bare ridge (600m) and leads along the western rocky face of Punta Onamarra – where there are exciting views inland (west) and over the deep incision of the Codula di Luna. You will have to be vigilant along here as you approach an important turn-off to the left, which is quite difficult to see. The track now descends gradually for a short distance, ascends, descends again and finally ascends in a wooded area with a curve to the left, immediately followed by another curve to the left and then one to the right. Ascend another 20m after the last curve, looking out for an isolated, 2.5m-high fillirea (similar to a holm oak) on the right (west) side of the trail, with a 4m-high juniper on the left (east) side. Two metres after these two trees, note a cairn on the left (east), at about 630m elevation, one hour from S'Architieddu Lupiru. From this point, a faint trail goes off to the left into the vegetation, occasionally marked by faded red-and-white markers.

You now leave the easy track behind and venture into the fascinating wilds of Sardinia. Once on the trail, which ascends easily to the left (east-northeast) among the bush-covered, rocky terrain, walk about 30m until you reach the flat area of the ridge where, on a stone on the left, you can see a red-and-white trail marker. If you can't find this marker within the first 30m, go back to the tree and check your directions.

Continuing, you should find an old, leaning juniper with a red marker, followed by other red-and-white markers on rocks, then you veer right and descend steeply in a little rocky valley to a circular, grassy coal merchant's clearing surrounded by stones. Here the track passes a rocky shoulder and turns southeast, descends steeply northeast, then heads east into the bush to reach a peculiar, circular threshing-floor made of flat stones. Pass along the right of the circle to a junction close by, turn left, and in few metres you'll reach the distinctive Cuile Sacedderano (531m), an abandoned, cone-shaped shed made of juniper logs, with a goat pen alongside. This takes 30 minutes from the turn-off. Baunei's shepherds call this Cuile Girove Longu.

Descend to the right (south), pass a juniper tree leaning south, then zigzag down a short steep scree slope towards the bottom of the valley (called Girove Longu on the IGM map), where a dense wood begins. Note a triangular, white mountain face in front of you. Enter the wood and zigzag east down the sporadically marked trail along a dry riverbed. Walk for about 30 minutes and you'll pass the base of a big, white rock. Five minutes later, the trail begins to veer right along the rocky shoulder to the southeast. The trail then leaves the valley floor, rising gradually until it emerges from the woods with breathtaking views of the northern coast and Cala Gonone. Continuing on, cross over the rocky shoulder to reveal a view to the south of the imposing cliff of Cala Sisine.

Now the more obvious trail re-enters a forest, descending in sharp curves among invasive vegetation. Open sections across rocks alternate with sections through woods. The trail descends diagonally towards the inside of Codula Sisine, then at a junction it curves sharply to the left towards the beach (1½ hours from Cuile Saccederano), which you can reach by a steep descent near a small ruin.

Following the gravel riverbed for about 600m, you reach Ristorante Su Coile (☎ 0784 932 71; open May-Sept) on the left (south).

You can **camp** here (free) all year, but there is no fresh water. When the restaurant is open, it is advisable to camp on the south side of the beach, which is secluded and often downwind. During the rest of the year, when the restaurant is closed, it is possible to set up your bivouac overnight on its external cement skirting block, which is protected from the wind and the wild cows that live in the *codula*.

Day 3: Cala Sisine to Golgo
4–5 hours, 15km, 450m ascent

From the restaurant ascend into the *codula* keeping to the trail on the left (south) side. This soon curves left at a junction with another *codula* (Bacu Arala) and leads south into Codula Sisine. After 30 minutes, you'll reach a dirt clearing where 4WDs stop in front of a large, tormented-looking rock. A dirt road that goes up into the *codula*, often washed out by floods, starts here. Meander through the *codula* past a collection of bizarre rock formations modelled by the wind. These structures, sheltered by thick vegetation, are inhabited by many species of small birds.

One hour from the start of the dirt road you will reach another dirt road ascending steeply to the right. This road was built in 1996 and is not always marked on maps. Ignore it and continue on the main dirt road within the *codula*. After another 30 minutes of walking, leave the *codula* and ascend to the left following the steep, sharp curves to reach a junction (270m) on the high plain where a road leads to the left (north) towards Cuile Ololbizzi. Ignore this and continue south on the dirt road that, after a while, starts to descend, passing a turn-off to the right (which you shouldn't take) and then begins a long uphill climb. You will pass another turn-off to the right where there's a signpost to a *nuraghe*, soon followed on the left by a turn-off to Ispuligi, ½ hours from the road to Cuile Ololbizzi.

Go straight on. You will know that you are nearing your destination when you pass the interesting **Chiesa Campestre di San Pietro** (385m), above and to the right of the track, 30 minutes after the Ispuligi turn-off.

Slightly further on, you'll find the little road that leads to the right to the enclosed churchyard, which is dominated by an enormous, centuries-old tree. In front of the church entrance is an ancient Nuraghic *betile*, a monolith of dark stone with the outlines of female attributes – a symbol of fertility. The wall that encircles the church contains shelters used by pilgrims who have been gathering here for centuries for the annual feast of San Pietro on 28 and 29 June.

Follow the church road south and soon you will reach a crossroads with a deviation to the right (west) for the low, fenced buildings of the recently restored **Cooperativa Goloritzè – Rifugio Golgo** (*☎/fax 0782 61 05 99, 368 702 89 80; *e* goloritze@tisca linet.it; B&B in single/double with bath €25.80/41.30, half board €41.30*). It is worth spending a couple of nights here, allowing time to explore this fascinating area, including a walk to the magnificent beach of Cala Goloritzè (see Side Trip, p340).

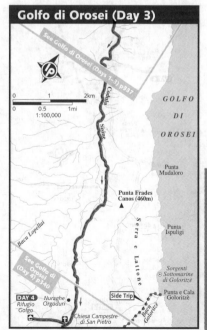

Golfo di Orosei (Day 3)

See Golfo di Orosei (Days 1–2) p337

0   1   2km
0   0.5   1mi
1:100,000

GOLFO
DI
OROSEI

Punta Mudaloro

Punta Frades Canos (460m) ▲

Punta Ispuligi

See Golfo di Orosei (Day 4) p340

Sorgenti Sottomarine di Goloritzè

Punta e Cala Goloritzè

DAY 4 Nuraghe Orgoduri
Rifugio Golgo

Side Trip

Chiesa Campestre di San Pietro

SARDINIA

Staff at the *rifugio* can also organise short guided walks in the area, including horse riding or a dinner at a shepherd's *pinnetta*.

Continuing south along the church road you soon reach a crossroads with signs pointing to the left (east) for Su Sterru and *piscinas*, and to the right (west) for Il Golgo restaurant. About 300m away, on the hilltop (430m), **Il Golgo restaurant** (☎ *337 81 18 28;* e *efisio.incollu@tiscalinet.it; full meal, drinks excluded, around €25.80)* is renowned for its local dishes. You can arrange to pitch a tent outside the restaurant in the **camping ground** *(camping per person €5.15; open March-Nov)* with full use of the facilities.

Side Trip: Cala Goloritzè
3½ hours, 521m ascent/descent
About 300m east of the crossroads, downhill from Il Golgo restaurant, is the impressive natural chasm of **Su Sterru**, a huge opening covered over with a net. It's a 280m sheer drop. A short distance to the south of the

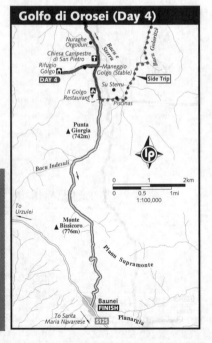

chasm are the **piscinas**, atmospheric archaic tubs, where animals come to drink.

To get to the beach from the crossroads take the dirt road heading east towards and beyond the *piscinas* and, after crossing the dry Bacu e Sterru riverbed, continue north-east until you come to a parking area near a sheep pen. From here take the trail that ascends diagonally to the left among the rocks up to a level saddle (471m). Crossing over the saddle, you then enter the evocative **Bacu Goloritzè** gorge, which descends rapidly to the sea. The atmosphere is truly fairytale-like, with centuries-old oaks and rocky ravines where shepherds have built their unusual huts, evoking images of Homer's *Odyssey*. Still descending, you arrive at the beach with its imposing, 143m-high rocky spire, well-known among free-climbers. There are no springs here so you will need to bring drinking water with you.

Day 4: Golgo to Baunei
2 hours, 8km, 430m descent
Since the road to Baunei was paved, it has lost much of its charm. Staff at the *rifugio* can arrange 4WD transport to Baunei which gives you the option of finishing the walk in the high plain and avoiding a long walk on the road. They can also organise a guided walk to Pedra Longa (three hours) where you can be picked up by 4WD and taken to Santa Maria Navarrese. This is an excellent way to end the walk, but is recommended for walkers with mountaineering experience only. It has an exposed section along a spectacular, high ledge.

Other Walks

Capo Testa
The seaside resort of Santa Teresa di Gallura on the north coast is a very pleasant spot for a relaxing walk, particularly if the magnificent granite rock pools of Capo Testa, 5km west of Santa Teresa, appeal to you. The best time to walk is March to October, apart from August when the area becomes extremely crowded. The **AAST tourist office** (☎ *0789 75 41 27;* w *www.regione.sardegna .it/aaststg; Piazza Vittorio Emanuele 24)*, in the town centre, distributes a rough walking map. At Capo Testa is the basic hotel **Bocche di Bonifacio**

(☎ 0789 75 42 02, fax 0789 75 90 09; half board €62). From the lighthouse, at the end of the asphalt road, turn left (southwest) following the coast, through easy passages, to enchanting coves. Follow the coast until you reach a wide valley, called Valle della Luna, from where you ascend to the left (south) until you reach the road. During the tourist season, frequent local buses depart for Capo Testa from Via Eleonora d'Arborea in Santa Teresa di Gallura.

Scala è Pradu

This is a good option for anyone who arrives in Oliena with half a day to spare before starting the Tiscali-Gorropu walk (p330). Although only about 3km, it takes about three hours to climb to the pass with a tough 877m of ascent. However, the view from Scala è Pradu is panoramic and enchanting. From the centre of Oliena, follow the signs for Orgosolo, but before leaving the town take the road that ascends to the left at a sign that reads 'Coop Turistica ENIS – Monte Maccione'. The

road ascends and turns left again, then, at an intersection, continues to the right, climbing in narrow switchbacks along the slope of the mountain under the majestic limestone face of Punta Carabidda, up to Albergo Monte Maccione (one hour). From the turn-off for the hotel, continue at mid-slope on the now unsealed road to the right, which begins a very demanding ascent. Avoid the deviation to the right for Fonte Daddana and keep going up the dirt road that climbs the practically vertical wall along horrible, scalloped curves that become narrower and narrower. You will leave the forest behind to arrive at Scala è Pradu (1227m, two hours from Albergo Monte Maccione). To the southeast of the pass you can take in the immense wilderness of the Supramonte, separating you from the sea; and to the northwest is Nuoro, with its ugly, spaceship-like hospital right in the worst possible spot. A bit further south, the summit of Monte Corrasi (1463m), the highest point of the Supramonte, should be visible. Use the IGM 1:25,000 map No 500 III *Oliena*.

Travel Facts

TOURIST OFFICES
Local Tourist Offices

There are three tiers of tourist office in Italy: regional, provincial and local. Regional offices, which focus on promotion, budget and other esoteric concerns, are of no use to the average visitor.

Provincial offices are called either the Ente Provinciale per il Turismo (EPT) or, more commonly, Azienda di Promozione Turistica (APT). They usually have information about their province and the town in which they're located, especially accommodation, and can be particularly helpful with details of transport between the province and major cities; many have an exchange office.

Local offices have two common names, Informazioni e Assistenza ai Turisti (IAT) and Azienda Autonoma di Soggiorno e Turismo (AAST), and you'll occasionally come across a Pro Loco office. These concentrate on their town. You can obtain information about local accommodation options (including *rifugi* or mountain huts), transport, walking routes, organised walks and mountain guides. Some also sell maps and guidebooks, particularly those places where walking is popular – the Alps and Tuscany (Toscana).

English is usually spoken at offices in larger towns and major tourist areas, but isn't widely spoken in small towns and villages. It's much more likely that staff will speak French and/or German in addition to Italian. Printed information is generally provided in several languages. Tourist offices are generally open from 9am to 12.30 or 1pm, and from 3 to around 7pm Monday to Friday, and on Saturday morning. During summer many offices open daily, or at least extend to all day Saturday and part of Sunday.

Small information offices at most major train stations keep similar hours, but some only open during summer. Many will help you find a hotel.

Tourist Offices Abroad

The Ente Nazionale Italiano per il Turismo (ENIT) – Italian State Tourist Board – has offices in a number of countries. Some of these include:

Australia (☎ 02-9262 1666, fax 02-9262 1677, ℮ lenitour@ihug.com.au) Level 26, 44 Market St, Sydney 2000
Canada (☎ 416-925 4882, fax 416-925 4799, ℮ enit.canada@on.aibn.com) Suite 907 South Tower, 17 Bloor St East, M4W3R8 Toronto
UK (☎ 020-7355 1557, fax 020-7493 6695, ℮ enitlond@globalnet.co.uk) 1 Princess St, London W1R 9AY 1
USA (☎ 212-245 5095, fax 212-586 9249, ℮ enitny@italiantourism.com) Suite 1565, 630 Fifth Ave, New York 10111

VISAS & DOCUMENTS

Citizens of the EU member states, Iceland and Norway can travel to Italy with their ID cards alone; people from those countries that do not issue ID cards, including the UK, must carry a valid passport. Nationals from all other countries must also have a valid passport.

Citizens of EU member states, Iceland and Norway do not need visas to visit Italy. Citizens of several other countries, including Canada, the US, New Zealand and Australia, do not need visas for tourist visits of up to 90 days.

Several walks in this book briefly pass through neighbouring countries, including France, Austria and Slovenia, but there are no border-crossing formalities.

Travel Insurance

Buy a policy that generously covers you for medical expenses, theft or loss of luggage and tickets, and for cancellation of and delays in your travel arrangements. It may be worth taking out cover for mountaineering activities and the cost of rescue. Check your policy doesn't exclude walking, particularly on *vie ferrate* (iron ways), as a dangerous activity.

Buy travel insurance as early as possible
ensure you'll be compensated for any
nforseen accidents or delays. If items are
st or stolen get a police report immediately
otherwise your insurer might not pay up.

Driving Licence & Documents

you want to drive a car or motorcycle in
aly, you will need your national driving li-
ence. All EU member states' driving li-
ences are fully recognised throughout
urope. However, if you are coming from
he UK and hold an old-style green driving
cence, you will need to obtain an Inter-
ational Driving Permit (IDP). Non-EU li-
ence holders are also supposed to obtain an
DP to accompany their national licence. In
ractice you will probably be OK with na-
onal licences from countries such as Aus-
alia, Canada and the USA. The IDP is
vailable from your national automobile as-
ociation and is valid for 12 months; it must
e kept with your national licence.

To drive your own vehicle in Italy, third-
arty motor insurance is a minimum re-
uirement and, as proof of this, you must
arry an International Insurance Certificate,
lso known as a Carta Verde (Green Card).
hese are available from your insurer. Also
sk your insurer for a European Accident
tatement form (it can simplify matters in
he event of an accident). You should also
arry proof of ownership of a private ve-
icle (a Vehicle Registration Document for
JK-registered cars).

If you are a member of an automobile as-
ociation in your home country, it is worth-
hile bringing proof of this. The Automobile
lub Italiano (ACI) will provide free emer-
ency roadside assistance once only to
embers of foreign automobile associ-
ions – but only to get you and the car to
he nearest ACI-registered mechanic
which is not always convenient). If you are
ot entitled to free assistance you must pay
minimum fee of €82.70.

Discount Cards

Hostel Card A valid **Hostelling Inter-**
national (HI; w www.iyhf.org) card is re-
uired to stay in any of the hostels run by

the **Associazione Italiana Alberghi per la**
Gioventù (AIG; ☎ 06 487 11 52, fax 06 488
04 92; w www.ostellionline.org; Via Cavour
44, 00184 Rome). Obtain this in your home
country by becoming a member of your national Youth Hostel Association (YHA).
You can also join in Italy – on each of the
first six nights you stay in a hostel, you collect a stamp for €2.58 (on top of the hostel
fee); once you have six stamps on your
membership card, you are a full international member. Membership entitles you
to various discounts in Italy, including on
train travel and car hire, and at some bookshops. Check out the AIG website for more
discounts.

Student, Teacher & Youth Cards The
International Student Identity Card (ISIC)
for full-time students, and the International
Teacher Identity Card (ITIC) for full-time
teachers and professors, entitle you to a
range of discounts, including cheap air
fares. For more information see w www
.istc.org.

The Euro<26 (Carta Giovani) is for anyone aged under 26 and gives similar discounts to the ISIC card. For more information
see w www.cartagiovani.it.

These cards are issued by student unions,
hostelling organisations and some youth
travel agencies. In Italy, **Centro Turistico**
Studentesco e Giovanile (CTS; ☎ 06 462 04
31; w www.cts.it; Via Genova 16, Rome)
can issue ISIC, ITIC and Euro<26 cards,
but you have to join CTS first, which costs
around €16.

EMBASSIES
Italian Embassies
Some Italian embassies abroad are:

Australia (☎ 02-6273 3333, fax 02-6273 3198,
  e embassy@ambitalia.org.au) 12 Grey St,
  Deakin, Canberra 2600
Canada (☎ 613-232 2401, fax 613-233 1484,
  e ambital@italyincanada.com) 21st Floor, 275
  Slater St, Ottawa, Ontario KIP 5H9
France (☎ 01 49 54 03 00, fax 01 45 49 38 51,
  e ambasciata@ambi-italie/fr) 47–51 rue de
  Varenne, Paris 75343
Germany (☎ 049-30 25 4400, fax 049-25 44
  0169, e ambitalia.segr@t-online.ie) Dessauer
  Str 28–29, 10963 Berlin
Ireland (☎ 01-660 1744, fax 01-668 2759,
  e italianembassy@eircom.net) 63–65
  Northumberland Rd, Dublin 4
Netherlands (☎ 070-302 1030, fax 070-361
  4932, e italemb@worldonline.nl) Alexander-
  straat 12, The Hague 2514 JL
New Zealand (☎ 04-473 5339, fax 04-472
  7255, e ambwell@xtra.co.nz) 34 Grant Rd,
  Thorndon, Wellington
Spain (☎ 914 2333 00, fax 915 75 7776,
  e ambital@cempresarial.com) Calle Lagasca
  98, Madrid 28006
UK (☎ 020-7312 2200, fax 020-7499 2283,
  e emblondon@embitaly.org.uk) 14 Three
  Kings Yard, London W1Y 2EH
USA (☎ 202-612 4400, fax 202-518 2154,
  e stampa@itwash.org) 3000 Whitehaven St
  NW, Washington, DC 20008

Embassies in Italy
Some embassies in Rome are:

Australia (☎ 06 85 27 21, fax 06 85 27 23 00,
  e consular-rome@dfat.gov.au) 250 Corso
  Trieste
Canada (☎ 06 44 59 81, fax 06 44 59 89 12,
  e rome@dfait-maeci.gc.ca) Via Zara 30, 00198
France (☎ 06 68 60 11, fax 06 68 60 13 60,
  e france-italia@france-italia.it) Piazza Farnese 67
Germany (☎ 06 49 21 31, fax 06 445 26 72,
  e germanembassy.roma@pronet.it) Via San
  Martino della Battaglia 4
Ireland (☎ 06 678 25 41) Largo Nazareno 3
Netherlands (☎ 06 322 11 41, fax 06 321 91
  43) Via Michele Mercati 8
Spain (☎ 06 580 01 44) Via Garibaldi 35
UK (☎ 06 42 20 00 01, e consularenquiries@
  rome.mail.fco.gov.uk) Via XX Settembre 80a
USA (☎ 06 467 41, fax 06 488 26 72) Via
  Veneto 119/A

CUSTOMS
Goods purchased in one EU country and
taken from there to another incur no add
itional taxes, provided duty has been pai
somewhere within the EU and the good
are for personal consumption.

Travellers coming into Italy from out
side the EU can import, duty free, 200 cig
arettes or 100 small cigars, 50 cigars o
250g of tobacco, 2L of spirits, 2L of wine
500mL of perfume and 500g of coffee
Anything over this limit must be declare
on arrival and the appropriate duty paid
carry all receipts.

MONEY
Currency
The euro (€) is now the currency of cas
transactions in Italy, along with 11 other EU
countries. The euro comprises 100 cents
Coin denominations are one, two, five, 10
20 and 50 cents, €1 and €2. The notes ar
€5, €10, €20, €50, €100, €200 an
€500. For more information check out th
euro section of the EU website at **w** www
.europa.eu.int/euro.

Exchange Rates
A good currency converter is **w** www.oand
.com. At the time of going to print, ex
change rates were:

country	unit		euro
Australia	A$1	=	€0.55
Canada	C$1	=	€0.65
Japan	¥100	=	€0.83
New Zealand	NZ$1	=	€0.48
United Kingdom	£1	=	€1.59
USA	US$1	=	€1.03

Exchanging Money
At airports and train stations in large citie
and at tourist offices, exchange office
(look for the 'Cambio' sign) are muc
faster, open longer hours and easier to dea
with than banks. However, banks are gen
erally more reliable and tend to offer th
best rates. You can also exchange money a
post offices. Keep a close eye on the com
mission charged and, if it seems absurdl
high, ask for your money back.

Travellers Cheques Banks, post offices and exchange offices may give a better rate for travellers cheques than for cash, but banks exact a charge of at least €1.55 and up to €3.90. The post office charges a flat rate of €2.60.

Credit & Debit Cards For withdrawing cash and for general purchases, Visa and MasterCard are accepted in most places in large towns and cities, but much less commonly in small towns and rarely in villages. American Express cards aren't widely recognised.

ATMs The quickest and most flexible source of cash are ATMs (Automatic Teller Machines). Look for the sign 'Bancomat'. You'll find them in the wall of most banks and at major train stations. It's not uncommon for Italian ATMs to reject foreign cards – if that happens try a few more ATMs at major banks (where your card's logo is displayed) before assuming that your card is the problem and not the local system.

On the Walk

Generally the safest way to travel is with a moderate amount of cash, to be topped up regularly via a credit card, supplemented by some travellers cheques. On longer walks when you won't be passing through any towns, ensure that you have enough cash to last several days.

Costs

Apart from transport costs, you should be able to live comfortably on €36 to €52 per day. Public transport isn't expensive in Italy, although USA and Canadian visitors might regard car fuel as expensive.

A typical daily budget might include:

Item	cost
camping ground	€15.50
rifugio (B&B)	€20.70
pensione (B&B)	€20.70
filled bread roll	€2.10
dinner at a pizzeria	€12.90
small bottle of beer	€0.80
espresso	€1.10

Tipping & Bargaining

You are not expected to tip on top of restaurant service charges but it is common practice to leave a small amount. In the absence of a service charge, you might consider leaving a 10% tip, but this certainly isn't obligatory. In bars, Italians often leave any small change as a tip, even only €0.05 or €0.10.

Bargaining in shops is not acceptable, though you might wangle small discounts on large purchases or if you're staying in a pensione for more than a few days.

Receipts

Laws to tighten controls on payment of taxes place the onus on the buyer to ask for and keep receipts for *all* goods and services. Although it rarely happens, you could be asked by an officer of the Guardia di Finanza (fiscal police) to produce the receipt immediately after you leave a shop or restaurant. If you don't have it, you may have to pay a very hefty fine.

POST & COMMUNICATIONS
Post

Italy's postal service is notoriously slow, unreliable and expensive.

Post offices and authorised *tabaccherie* (tobacconists) – look for a big white 'T' on black – sell *francobolli* (stamps).

An air-mail letter can take up to two weeks to reach the UK or the USA and up to three weeks to Australia. Postcards take much longer. Within Italy, local letters take from three to seven days to arrive at another city.

Postal Rates Letters (up to 20g) sent *posta prioritaria* (air mail) cost €0.60 to EU countries, and €0.75 to the USA, Australia and New Zealand. Postcards cost €0.40 within Europe and €0.70 air mail to Australia and New Zealand. Aerograms cost €0.15 plus the appropriate *priorita* (priority) surcharge.

Raccomandata (registered mail) or *assicurata* (insured mail) may be quicker than normal mail. A standard *raccomandata* envelope to European countries costs an additional €2.60, and for *assicurata* the surcharge is €5.15.

Receiving Mail Letters marked *fermo posta* (poste restante) will be held at that counter in the main post office in the relevant town. You need to pick up your letters personally and you must present your passport as ID.

Amex card or travellers cheque holders can use the free client mail-holding service at Amex offices.

Telephone

Telecom Italia's public payphones are plentiful. The older orange models, some of which are very temperamental if you ask them to make too many toll-free or international calls, are slowly being replaced by sleek grey models, which are infinitely more friendly and efficient. Although the oldest machines accept coins and *carte/schede telefoniche* (phonecards), coin machines are in the minority.

Peak times for domestic calls are from 8am to 6.30pm Monday to Friday and from 8am to 1pm Saturday. Cheap rates apply outside these times and public holidays. Different times apply for international calls. You can make cheap calls to the UK from 10pm to 8am Monday to Saturday and all day Sunday, to the USA and Canada from 7pm to 2pm Monday to Friday and all weekend, and to Australia from 11pm to 8am Monday to Saturday and all day Sunday.

A *comunicazione urbana* (local call) from a public phone costs €0.10 for three/six minutes during peak/off-peak. Rates for a *comunicazione interurbana* (long-distance call within Italy) depend on the time of day and distance involved. At the most, one minute costs about €0.20 in the peak period. A five-minute call to Australia at 11pm will cost around €6.20 from a public phone. Calls to most of Europe cost around €0.65 for the first minute and €0.40 thereafter.

Phonecards These are available at post offices, *tabaccherie*, newspaper stands and from vending machines in Telecom offices in three stated values: €2.60, €5.15 and €7.75. They can be used for both local and long-distance/international calls.

Telecom Italia also issues international call cards for €5.15, €7.75 and €25.80 (for either Europe, USA and Canada, or for other parts of the world), which give up to three hours' call time – provided you're ringing off-peak and to a nearby country.

Lonely Planet's eKno Communication Card, specifically aimed at travellers, provides competitive international calls (avoid using it for local calls), messaging services and free email. Visit **w** www.ekno.lonely planet.com for information on joining and accessing the service.

Mobile Phones Italy has very good mobile phone coverage, although reception can be variable in the mountains and in more isolated areas such as the Supramonte in Sardinia. Mobiles will usually receive at open, high points, but might not receive in isolated mountain valleys.

Italy uses the GSM cellular phone system, compatible with phones sold in the UK, Australia and most of Asia, but not those from North America or Japan. Check with your service provider before you leave home that they have a roaming agreement with a local counterpart.

Country & Area Codes Area codes of up to four digits are an integral part of the phone number for all calls – even if calling within a single zone. Mobile phone numbers in Italy begin with a three digit prefix, such as ☎ 330, ☎ 335 or ☎ 347. *Numeri verdi* (freephone or toll-free numbers) begin with ☎ 800. The prefix ☎ 147 indicates that a national number is charged at a local rate.

The country code for Italy is ☎ 39; you must always include the initial 0 in area codes.

Direct international calls can be made from most public telephones by using a phonecard. Dial ☎ 00 to get out of Italy then the relevant country and area codes followed by the telephone number.

Fax

A useful means of making accommodation arrangements at many small places and obtaining information from tourist offices i

Useful Numbers

Emergency	☎ 118
Reverse-charge (collect)	☎ 170
Local directory inquiries	☎ 12
International directory inquiries	☎ 176

by fax. There are plenty of places where you can do this and some Telecom Italia phones have fax facilities; however, it is expensive to send faxes within Italy.

Email

You'll find Internet cafés and public libraries with Internet access in the cities and in some larger towns. Telecom Italia operates an Internet Corner in some of its major offices (such as on Roma Termini, Rome's main train station). For a fairly comprehensive list of Internet cafés throughout Italy, see **w** www.netcafeguide.com. Some conveniently located cafés are listed in the walks chapters.

Expect to pay up to €5.15 per 30 minutes; Telecom Italia charges €1.30 per 15 minutes.

TIME

Italy generally operates on the 24-hour clock, although the 12-hour system is also used. The country is one hour ahead of GMT/UTC and in the same time zone as neighbouring countries. When it's noon in Rome, it's 3am in San Francisco, 6am in New York and Toronto, 11am in London, 9pm in Sydney and 11pm in Auckland.

Daylight-saving time starts on the last Sunday in March, when clocks are put forward one hour. Clocks are put back an hour on the last Sunday in October.

ELECTRICITY

The electric current in Italy is 220V, 50Hz. Power points (outlets) have two or three round holes. Electrical and hardware stores sell adapter plugs that cater for every conceivable local combination. International plug adaptors are virtually impossible to buy in Italy. Travellers from North America need a voltage converter.

WEIGHTS & MEASURES

Italy uses the metric system (see the conversion table on the inside-back cover of this book). Like other Continental Europeans, Italians use commas in decimals, and points to indicate thousands.

BUSINESS HOURS

Business hours vary across the country, but follow the general pattern:

Alimentari (grocery shops) Open 9am–1pm and 3.30–7.30pm (or 5–9pm in summer) Monday to Saturday; may close on Saturday afternoon and Monday or Thursday afternoon.

Banks Open 8.30am–1.30pm and 3.30–4.30pm Monday to Friday (on weekends some exchange offices in larger cities and major tourist towns will be open – try the local tourist information office).

Bars & Cafés Open 7.30am–8pm, sometimes later.

Medical Clinics Open 8am–12.30pm Monday to Friday; some open for a few hours in the afternoon and on Saturday morning.

Pharmacies Open 9am–12.30pm and 3.30–7.30pm; closed Sunday and usually Saturday afternoon (when closed, must display a list of pharmacies in the area that are open).

Post Offices (big) Open 8.30am–5 or 6pm Monday to Friday, and 8.30am–1 or 2pm Saturday.

Post Offices (small) Usually closed afternoons; closed weekends.

Restaurants Open noon–3pm and 7.30–11pm (later in summer and in the south).

Shops Open 9am–1pm and 3.30–7.30pm (or 4–8pm) Monday to Saturday.

Supermarkets Many open 9am (or earlier)–7.30pm Monday to Saturday and 9am–1pm Sunday; some for a day/half day on Monday or Thursday.

Tourist offices In summer, open 9am–12.30 or 1pm and 3–7pm Monday to Saturday, and sometimes Sunday; closed Saturday afternoon and Sunday outside summer.

Restaurants and bars are required to close for one day each week, which varies between establishments.

PUBLIC HOLIDAYS

Many businesses and shops close for at least part of August, when most Italians take their annual holidays, particularly during the week around Ferragosto (Feast of the Assumption) on 15 August.

National public holidays include:

date	holiday
6 January	Epiphany
March/April	Easter Monday
25 April	Liberation Day
1 May	Labour Day
15 August	Feast of the Assumption
1 November	All Saints' Day
8 December	Feast of the Immaculate Conception
25 December	Christmas Day
26 December	Feast of Santo Stefano

Individual towns have public holidays to celebrate the feasts of their patron saints. Religious festivals are particularly numerous in Sicily and Sardinia.

Getting There & Away

For travel between Italy and other parts of Europe, including the UK, buses are the cheapest but most tiring type of transport, although discount rail tickets are competitive and budget flights can be good value.

Warning

The information in this section is particularly vulnerable to change: prices for international travel are volatile, routes are introduced and cancelled, schedules change, special deals come and go, and rules and visa requirements are amended. You should check directly with the airline or a travel agent to make sure you understand how a fare (and ticket you may buy) works.

The upshot of this is that you should get opinions, quotes and advice from as many airlines and travel agents as possible before you part with your hard-earned cash. The details given in this section should be regarded as pointers and are not a substitute for your own careful, up-to-date research.

AIR
Airports & Airlines

Italy's main intercontinental gateway is Rome's **Leonardo da Vinci airport** (☎ 06 65 95 36 40), also known as Fiumicino. International flights also operate in and out of many other airports including Milan's **Malpensa** (☎ 02 748 52 20) and **Naples** (☎ 081 789 62 59). The major airports are linked to their nearby cities by regular bus (and in some cases train) services.

Airlines operating to Italy include:

Air France (☎ 0820 820 820,
 W www.airfrance.com) 119 ave des Champs Elysées, 75008 Paris, France
Alitalia (☎ 0807-544 8259,
 W www.alitalia.co.uk) 2A Cains Lane, Bedfont, Middlesex TW14 9RL, UK
British Airways (☎ 0845-773 3377,
 W www.britishairways.com) Waterside, PO Box 365, Harmondsworth UB7 OGB, UK
British Midland (☎ 0870-607 0555, 1332 854854, W www.flybmi.com) Donington Hall, Castle Donington, Derby DE74 2SB, UK
Delta Air Lines (☎ 800-241 4141,
 W www.delta.com) 1600 Cumberland Mall, Atlanta, GA 30339, USA
easyJet (☎ 0870-600 0000,
 W www.easyjet.com) London Luton Airport, Bedfordshire LU2 9LS, UK
Lufthansa (☎ 01803 803 803,
 W www.lufthansa.com) Von Gablenz Strasse 2–6, 50679 Köln, Germany
Qantas (☎ 02-9691 3636, W www.qantas.com) Qantas Centre, 203 Coward St, Mascot, NSW 2020, Australia
Ryanair (☎ 0818-30 30 30,
 W www.ryanair.com) 28 Conyngham Rd, Dublin 8, Ireland
United Airlines (☎ 1800-241 6522,
 W www.ual.com) PO Box 66100, Chicago, IL 60666, USA
Virgin Express (☎ 02-752 0551,
 W www.virgin-express.com) Brussels Airport, Bldg 116, B-1820, Melsbroek, Belgium

Departure Tax

The departure tax, payable when you leave Italy by air, is included in your airline ticket.

The UK

Direct flights to Italy go from London Heathrow, Gatwick and Stansted and some regional airports. Italian regional airports served direct include Milan, Verona, Florence and Naples. The main carriers are British Airways, British Midland, easyJet, Ryanair and Alitalia.

Continental Europe

Air travel between Italy and other places in continental Europe is worth considering if you are pushed for time. Short hops can be expensive but good deals are available from some major hubs. Alitalia and Air France offer cut-rate fares between cities on the European legs of long-haul flights. These are usually cheap but often involve flying at night or early in the morning.

The USA & Canada

The North Atlantic is the world's busiest long-haul air corridor and the flight options are bewildering. Several airlines fly direct to Italy, landing at either Rome or Milan. These include Alitalia, Lufthansa, Air France and Delta Air Lines. If your trip will not be confined to Italy, check for cheaper flights to other European cities.

Australia & New Zealand

Cheap flights from Australia and New Zealand to Europe generally go via South-East Asian capitals, involving a stopover at Kuala Lumpur, Bangkok or Singapore. If a long stopover between connections is

---

Best-Value Air Tickets

For short-term travel, it's usually cheaper to travel midweek and to take advantage of short-lived promotional offers. Return tickets usually work out cheaper than two one-ways or even less than a single ticket.

Booking through a travel agent or via airlines' websites is generally the cheapest way to get tickets. However, while on-line ticket sales are fine for a simple one-way or return trip on specified dates, they're no substitute for a travel agent who is familiar with special deals and can offer all kinds of advice.

Buying tickets with a credit card should mean you get a refund if you don't get what you paid for, or go through a licensed travel agent covered by an industry guarantee scheme.

Whatever your choice, make sure you take out travel insurance (p342).

---

necessary, transit accommodation is sometimes included in the price of a ticket. If the transit accommodation is at your own expense, it may be worth considering a more expensive but direct ticket.

Qantas and Alitalia offer the only direct flights from Australia; if you are looking for a bargain airfare you will probably end up with another airline.

Another option is a Round-the-World (RTW) ticket – it is often cheaper to go right round the world on an RTW ticket than to do a U-turn on a return ticket. On an RTW, you will most likely fly into Rome or Milan.

LAND

Not quite all roads lead to Rome, but there's a good choice of routes into Italy by train, bus or car. Bus travel is generally cheaper, but with less frequent and much less comfortable services than those offered by trains.

If you're travelling to Italy overland, check whether you need visas to the countries you'll pass through en route.

Bus

The main long-distance bus company in Europe is **Eurolines** (☎ 0870-514 3219,

---

Baggage Restrictions

The 2001 terrorist attacks on the USA mean airlines worldwide now impose tight restrictions on carry-on baggage. No sharp implements of any kind are allowed onto the plane – this means you need to pack items such as pocket knives, camping cutlery and first-aid kits into your checked luggage.

If you're carrying a camping stove you should remember that airlines also ban fuels (unleaded gasoline, white spirits or any flammable liquid) and gas cartridges from all baggage, both check through and carry on. Empty all fuel bottles and buy what you need at your destination.

1582-404 511; **W** *www.eurolines.com; 52 Grosvenor Gardens, London SW1W 0AU, UK).* The Eurolines Pass is good for those planning to do a lot of bus travel. It's valid for unlimited travel to 46 cities in 26 countries for 30 or 60 days. Italian cities on the network include Milan, Florence, Venice, Rome and Naples.

Busabout *(☎ 0207-950 1661, fax 0207-950 1662;* **W** *www.busabout.com; 258 Vauxhall Bridge Rd, London SW1V 1BS, UK)* operates a Europe-wide network of services. The Consecutive pass is for continuous travel and the Flexi pass is for a specified number of days' travel during a given number of months. Single, point-to-point fares are not available. Italian cities on Busabout routes include La Spezia, Como, Verona, Florence, Rome and Sorrento.

Train

If coming from the UK, **Eurostar** *(☎ 0870-518 6186, 0207-928 5163;* **W** *www.eurostar .com; Eurostar House, Waterloo Station, London SE1 8SE)* passenger train service links London Waterloo and Paris Nord via the Channel Tunnel. Alternatively you could buy a train ticket that includes the Channel crossing by ferry, SeaCat or hovercraft, to Calais and other ports, then onwards by train.

Regular EuroCity (EC) services connect European countries with Italy along eight lines: from southern France you can reach Genoa; other lines go from Paris and Barcelona to Turin and beyond; there are trains to Milan from Swiss, German and French stations; and from Eastern Europe, Austria and Germany services go to Rome via Verona. High-speed Cisalpino trains operate between Milan and Switzerland and southern Germany.

Several discount passes and cards are available for train travel to/from Italy, including:

Eurail Pass This is for people who live outside Europe and should be purchased before arriving in Europe. The passes are good for travel in 17 European countries (not including the UK) and are valid for 15 or 21 days or for one, two or three months. Eurail passes are expensive (you need to cover more than 2400km within two weeks to get value for money), so look at the options before committing yourself. For more information on this and other Eurail options check out the website at **W** www.eurail.com.

InterRail Pass This pass is designed for people who have lived in Europe for six months or more and are aged under 26, but there is a more expensive version for older folk, the InterRail 26+. The InterRail map of Europe is divided into eight zones, one of which comprises Italy, Greece, Slovenia and Turkey. You can purchase passes for one, two, three or all zones, covering 12 or 22 days, or one month. A two-zone ticket covers travel from the UK to Italy.

For more information on European train travel and passes contact **Wasteels** *(☎ 0207 834 7066; Victoria Station, London, UK),* the **Rail Europe Travel Centre** *(☎ 0870-58 8848;* **W** *www.raileurope.co.uk; 178 Piccadilly, London W1, UK)* or **Freedom Rail** *(☎ 01252-728 506, fax 728 504;* **W** *www .freedomrail.com; Runwick Lane, Farnham, GU10 5EF, UK).*

Car & Motorcycle

You can take your car or motorcycle from the UK to France by ferry or via the Channel Tunnel on the **Eurotunnel** *(☎ 0870-535 3535;* **W** *www.eurotunnel.com)* car train. Operating between Folkestone and Calais, trains run around the clock with up to four crossings (35 minutes) per hour in July and August. You only pay for the vehicle, and fares vary according to season and time of day. The most expensive fares are between May and September; it costs more if you depart during the day Friday to Sunday. Motorcyclists rarely have to book ahead for ferries.

The main points of entry to Italy are the Mont Blanc tunnel from Chamonix in France, which leads to the A5 for Turin and Milan; the Grand St Bernard tunnel from Switzerland, which also connects with the A5; and the Brenner pass from Austria, which links with the A22 to Bologna. Other routes via high-altitude mountain passes, such as Grand St Bernard and Little St Bernard into Valle d'Aosta, are generally open only from mid-June to mid-September but do provide a much more scenic approach.

SEA

Ferry services link several Baltic ports, Greece and Spain to Italy. The most expensive time to travel is from June to August. Prices for cars, camper vans and motorcycles vary according to the size of the vehicle; bicycles can sometimes be carried free of charge.

From Barcelona, **Grandi Navi Veloci** (☎ 010 58 93 31; W www.gnv.it; Via Fieschi 17, 16100 Genoa) operates ferries to Genoa (18 hours, three sailings a week).

Getting Around

Very few of the walks described in this book cannot be reached by public transport. Given the excellent network of relatively cheap bus and train services in Italy, this is a great, stress-free way of seeing the country between walking destinations – and of being part of the great Italian travelling public.

Bus travel is the less expensive of the two, but as there are many different operators it is less straightforward than train travel. Your own wheels give you the most potential freedom and flexibility, although bear in mind that many walks in this book start and finish at widely separated places, and both fuel and *autostrada* (motorway) tolls are rather expensive. Domestic air travel can be costly and is probably worth it only if you are really short of time.

AIR

The main airports are in Rome, Pisa, Milan, Naples, Palermo and Cagliari; the many smaller airports include Aosta, Florence, Trieste, Venice, Verona and Turin.

The domestic airlines are:

Air One (☎ 848 84 88 80, 06 48 88 00;
 W www.flyairone.it)
Alitalia (☎ 848 86 56 41, W www.alitalia.it)
Meridiana (☎ 199 111 333,
 W www.meridiana.it)

Domestic flights can be booked through any travel agency, including Sestante CIT and Centro Turistico Studentesco e Giovanile (CTS).

Domestic air passes are unknown in Italy. Alitalia offers discounts for young people, families, seniors and weekend travellers, as well as occasional promotional fares and advance-purchase deals. Barring special deals, a one-way fare is generally half the cost of the return fare.

BUS

Within Italy, bus services are provided by numerous companies and range from local routes linking small villages to fast, reliable intercity connections, making it possible to reach just about any location throughout the country. Buses can be a cheaper and faster way to get around if your destination is not on a main train line. Buses almost always leave on time.

Bus timetables for the provincial and intercity services are usually available from local tourist offices. In larger cities, most of the main intercity bus companies have ticket offices or operate through agencies. In some smaller towns and villages, tickets are sold in bars – ask for *biglietti per il pullman* – or on the bus.

It is not usually necessary to reserve a seat, although it is advisable in July and August for longer journeys.

TRAIN

The great majority of train services are operated by Ferrovie dello Stato (FS), the partially privatised state train system. There are also several private train lines, some duplicating FS services, others in areas outside the FS network.

For train information throughout Italy, ring ☎ 1478 880 88 from 7am to 9pm (in Italian only) or go to the information office at any train station; in larger cities you're sure to find staff who speak English. You can also check timetables and book some tickets online at W www.fs-on-line.com. If you are doing a fair amount of travelling, it's worth buying a train timetable (available from newsagents in or near train stations).

There are several types of trains. *Regionale* (Reg) and *interregionale* (IR) travel within and between regions respectively. There is also the fast Espresso (Ex), semi-express *diretto* (direct) and stop-every-station *locale* (local), which is being phased out, services. The faster InterCity (IC) and EuroCity (EC) services, and the super-fast Cisalpino (CIS or Pendolino ETR 470) and Eurostar Italia (ES) trains stop only in major towns and cities, and usually require a supplementary payment.

All tickets (except those purchased outside Italy) must be validated *before* boarding your train by punching them in the yellow machines at the entrance to all train platforms. If you don't, you risk a large fine.

Rail Passes

It is not worth buying a Eurail or InterRail pass if you are going to travel only in Italy, since train fares are reasonably cheap. The FS offers its own discount passes for travel within the country. Discount cards and tickets include:

Biglietto Chilometrico (Kilometric Ticket) This allows one to five people to split up to 3000km of travel across Italy within two months.

Carta d'Argento This card entitles those 60 years old and over to a 20% discount on 1st- and 2nd-class travel for one year.

Carta Verde This is for 12- to 26-year-olds, is valid for one year and gives 20% discount on all train travel, but you need to do a fair bit of travelling to get your money's worth.

Children Those aged between four and 12 years are automatically entitled to a 50% discount, and those under four years travel free.

Foreigners are also eligible for several Italy-only passes, which may require supplementary payments for some services. These passes include:

EuroDomino This is available for as few as three and up to eight days' travel during one month.

Italy Flexi Rail Card This pass is valid for four, eight or 12 days' travel within one month.

Italy Railcard Valid for eight, 15, 21 or 30 consecutive days, this card is available for 1st or 2nd class.

For more information on these passes contact the **Rail Europe Travel Centre** (☎ *0870-584 8848;* ⓦ *www.raileurope.co.uk; 178 Piccadilly, London W1, UK*) or **Freedom Rail**

(☎ *01252 728 506, fax 728 504;* ⓦ *www.fre domrail.com; Runwick Lane, Farnham GU10 5EF, UK).*

Classes

There are 1st- and 2nd-class sections on nearly all Italian trains; on Eurostar trains 2nd class is about as good as 1st class on other trains. A 1st-class ticket costs a bit less than double the price of a 2nd-class one.

Reservations

It's worth reserving a seat on a long train trip – particularly if you're travelling at the weekend or during holiday periods. Reservations are obligatory for Eurostar and other fast trains. There are special booking offices for Eurostar trains at the relevant stations. Allow plenty of time as long queues are the norm.

Costs

To travel on InterCity, EuroCity and Eurostar Italia trains you have to pay a *supplemento* (supplement), an additional charge determined by the distance you are travelling. Always check what type of train you are about to catch and pay the appropriate supplement before you get on (otherwise you pay extra on the train). CIS trains have their own ticketing system.

On overnight trips within Italy it can be worth paying extra for a *cuccetta* – a sleeping berth (commonly known as a couchette) in a four-bed compartment.

CAR & MOTORCYCLE

Italian roads are generally good and there is an excellent network of *autostrade*, for which tolls apply. Contact **Società Autostrade** (☎ *06 436 31;* ⓦ *www.autostrade.it*, for details.

Strade statali (state roads) can be multilane dual carriageways (divided roads) and are toll free. They are represented on maps and road signs as 'S' or 'SS'. The *strade regionali* (regional roads) and *strade provinciali* (provincial roads) are sometimes little more than country lanes, linking the many small towns and villages. They are represented as 'SR' and 'SP' on maps and signs.

See Driving Licence & Documents (p343) for details of paperwork needed when driving in Italy.

Road Rules

In Italy, drive on the right side of the road and overtake on the left. Unless otherwise indicated, you must always give way to cars coming from the right. Random breath tests now take place across the country; the blood-alcohol limit is 0.08%. Speed limits, unless otherwise indicated, are 130km/h on *autostrade* (the speed limit is reduced for small cars and motorcycles, cars towing caravans or trailers, and on weekends and holiday periods); 110km/h on all main, non-urban highways; 90km/h on secondary, non-urban highways; and 50km/h in built-up areas.

It is compulsory to wear seat belts if fitted to the car. If you are caught not wearing a seat belt, you will be required to pay an on-the-spot fine. To ride a motorcycle or scooter up to 125cc, you must be aged 16 or over and be licensed (a car licence will do). For motorcycles over 125cc you do need a motorcycle licence. Helmets are compulsory for everyone riding a motorcycle bigger than 50cc.

To get roadside assistance call ☎ 116. *Motoring in Europe*, published in the UK by the RAC, summarises road regulations in each European country, including parking rules. Motoring organisations in other countries have similar publications.

Rental

It is cheaper to arrange car rental before leaving your own country, ideally through a fly/drive deal offered by one of the major car-hire firms. In Italy, most tourist offices can provide information about car or motorcycle rental; otherwise, look in the local Pagine Gialle (Yellow Pages) under *autonoleggio*.

You have to be aged 21 or over (23 or over for some companies) to hire a car in Italy and you have to have a credit card. Most firms will accept your standard licence, sometimes with an Italian translation which can usually be provided by the agencies themselves).

You'll have no trouble hiring a small motorcycle such as a scooter (Vespa) or moped. There are numerous rental agencies in cities and tourist destinations, where you'll also usually be able to hire larger motorcycles for touring. Most agencies will not rent motorcycles to people aged under 18. Many places require a sizable deposit; you could be responsible for reimbursing part of the cost of the bike if it is stolen.

BICYCLE

Cycling is a national pastime in Italy. There are no special road rules for cyclists. Helmets and lights are not obligatory, but you would be wise to equip yourself with both. You cannot take bikes onto the *autostrade*.

Bikes can be taken very cheaply on trains, although only certain trains will actually carry them. If bikes cannot be accommodated, they may be sent as registered luggage, which can take a few days. Bikes can be transported free on ferries to Sicily and Sardinia.

You can hire bikes in most Italian towns, and many places have both city and mountain bikes available.

Look out for Lonely Planet's *Cycling Italy*, packed with cyclist-friendly information and tours throughout the country.

HITCHING

Hitching is never safe in any country and we don't recommend it. Women travelling alone should be extremely cautious about hitching anywhere. Hitchhiking is not a major pastime in Italy, but Italians are friendly people and you will generally find a lift.

It is illegal to hitchhike on Italy's *autostrade*, but quite acceptable to stand near the entrance to the toll booths. It is sometimes possible to arrange lifts in advance – ask at youth hostels. The **International Lift Centre** (☎ 055 28 06 26) in Florence may be able to help.

BOAT

Navi (large ferries) service the islands of Sicily and Sardinia; all vessels carry vehicles. Ferries and hydrofoils ply the waters of the three big lakes in the Lake District, and offer a relaxing alternative to buses or cars as you move around the area.

LOCAL TRANSPORT

All major cities have good transport systems, with frequent and reliable buses and trams. There are also good underground train systems in Rome (Metropolitana), Milan (MM) and Naples (Metropolitana).

Tickets can be bought at most *tabaccherie* (tobacconists), at many newspaper stands, and at ticket booths or dispensing machines at bus stations and in underground stations. They are valid for buses, trams and the underground systems. Most cities offer 24-hour or daily tourist tickets, which can represent big savings. You must always buy tickets before you board and

you must validate them. If you get caught with an unvalidated ticket, you will be fined on the spot.

Taxi

Taxis are expensive and it is better to catch a bus.

You can usually find a taxi in ranks at train and bus stations – the only realistic place from which to catch one. Taxis will rarely stop when hailed on the street as, strictly speaking, it's illegal for them to do so and, generally, they will not respond to telephone bookings if you are calling from a public phone.

Watch out also for taxi drivers who take advantage of new arrivals and stretch out the length of the trip, and consequently the size of the fare.

Language

Italian is a Romance language related to French, Spanish, Portuguese and Romanian, all directly descended from Latin. The Romance languages belong to the large Indo-European group of languages, which includes English. As English and Italian have common roots in Latin, you'll recognise many Italian words.

If you have more than the most fundamental grasp of Italian, remember that many older Italians still expect to be addressed in the third person formal (*lei* instead of *tu*). What's more, it's not considered polite to use the greeting *ciao* when addressing strangers, unless they use it first; it's better to say *buongiorno* (or *buona sera* as the case may be) and *arrivederci* (or the more polite form, *arrivederla*). We have used the formal address for most of the phrases in this chapter; use of the informal address is indicated by 'inf' in brackets. Italian has both masculine and feminine forms, usually ending in 'o' and 'a' respectively. Where both forms are included, they are separated by a slash, with the masculine first.

For a more comprehensive guide to the language, get a copy of Lonely Planet's *Italian phrasebook*.

Pronunciation

Italian isn't difficult to pronounce once you learn a few basic rules. Some of the more clipped vowels and stress on double letters require a bit of practice for English-speakers.

Vowels

- as in 'art'
- as in 'tell'
- as in 'pit'
- as in 'dot', eg, *donna* (woman); as in 'port', eg, *dormire* (to sleep)
- as in 'put'

Consonants

The pronunciation of many Italian consonants is similar to that of their English counterparts, but depends on certain rules.

c	as 'k' before **a**, **o** and **u**; as the 'ch' in 'choose' before **e** and **i**
ch	as the 'k' in 'kit'
g	as in 'get' before **a**, **o**, **u** and **h**; as the 'j' in 'job' before **e** and **i**
gli	as the 'lli' in 'million'
gn	as the 'ny' in 'canyon'
h	always silent
r	a rolled 'rr' sound
sc	as 'sk' before **a**, **o**, **u** and **h**; as the 'sh' in 'sheep' before **e** and **i**
z	as the 'ts' in 'lights', except at the beginning of a word, when it's like the 'ds' in 'beds'

Note that when **ci**, **gi** and **sci** are followed by **a**, **o** or **u**, the 'i' is not pronounced unless the accent falls on the 'i'. Thus the name 'Giovanni' is pronounced 'joh-**vahn**-nee'.

Double consonants are pronounced as a longer, often more forceful sound than a single consonant.

Word Stress

Stress often falls on the second-last syllable, as in *spa*-**ghet**-*ti*. When a word has an accent, the stress falls on that syllable, as in *cit*-**tà** (city).

Greetings & Civilities

Hello.	*Buongiorno.*
	Ciao/Salve. (inf)
Goodbye.	*Arrivederci.*
	Ciao. (inf)
Yes.	*Sì.*
No.	*No.*
Please.	*Per favore/Per piacere.*
Thank you.	*Grazie.*
That's fine, You're welcome.	*Prego.*
Excuse me.	*Mi scusi/Scusami.*
Sorry (forgive me).	*Mi scusi/Mi perdoni.*
What's your name?	*Come si chiama?*
	Come ti chiami? (inf)
My name is ...	*Mi chiamo ...*
Where are you from?	*Di dov'è?*
	Di dove sei? (inf)

I'm from ...	Sono di ...
How are you?	Come sta?
	Come stai? (inf)

Language Difficulties

I understand.	Capisco.
I don't understand.	Non capisco.
Do you speak English?	Parla inglese?
Please write it down.	Può scriverlo, per favore.

Getting Around

What time does ... leave/arrive?	A che ora parte/ arriva ...?
bus (city)	l'autobus
bus (intercity)	il pullman
ferry	il traghetto, la nave
plane	l'aereo
train	il treno

| I want to go to ... | Voglio andare a ... |

I'd like a ... ticket.	Vorrei un biglietto ...
one-way	di solo andata
return	di andata e ritorno
1st-class	di prima classe
2nd-class	di seconda classe

| Do I have to change trains/platforms? | Devo cambiare treno/binario? |
| The train has been cancelled/delayed. | Il treno è soppresso/in ritardo. |

the first	il primo
the last	l'ultimo
platform number	binario numero
station	stazione
ticket office	biglietteria
timetable	orario
left luggage office	deposito bagagli

I'd like to hire ...	Vorrei noleggiare ...
a bicycle	una bicicletta
a car	una macchina

Directions

Where is ... ?	Dov'è?
Go straight ahead.	Si va sempre diritto.
Turn left.	Gira a sinistra.

Signs

Entrata	Entrance
Uscita	Exit
Completo	No Vacancies
Informazioni	Information
Aperto/Chiuso	Open/Closed
Vietato	Prohibited
Camere Libere	Rooms Available
Gabinetti	Toilets
Uomini	Men
Donne	Women

Turn right.	Gira a destra.
at the next corner	al prossimo angolo
at the traffic lights	al semaforo
behind	dietro
in front of	davanti
opposite	di fronte a

Around Town

I'm looking for ...	Cerco ...
a bank	un banco
the police station	la questura
the post office	la posta
a public toilet	un gabinetto/bagno pubblico
the tourist office	l'ufficio di turismo

| What is the address? | Cos'è l'indirizzo? |
| I'd like to make a telephone call. | Vorrei telefonare. |

I want to change ...	Voglio cambiare ...
money	denaro
travellers cheques	degli assegni per viaggiatori

Accommodation

I'm looking for ...	Cerco ...
a camping ground	un campeggio
a guesthouse	una pensione
a hotel	un albergo
a youth hostel	un ostello per la gioventù

| Do you have any rooms available? | Ha camere libere/C'è una camera libera |

I'd like ...	Vorrei ...
a bed	un letto
a single room	una camera singola
a double room	una camera matrimoniale
a room with two beds	una camera doppia
a room with a bathroom	una camera con bagno
to share a dorm	un letto in dormitorio

How much is it ... ?	Quanto costa ... ?
per night	per la notte
per person	per ciascuno?

| May I see it? | Posso vederla? |

Do you accept ...?	Accettate ...?
credit cards	carte di credito
travellers cheques	assegni per viaggiatori

I'm staying for ...	Resto per ...
one day	un giorno
two days	due giorni

Shopping

bookshop	libreria
chemist/pharmacy	farmacia
newsstand	edicola
stationers	cartolaio
supermarket	supermercato

I'd like to buy ...	Vorrei comprare ...
How much is it?	Quanto costa?
I'm just looking.	Sto solo guardando.
I'll take it.	Lo/La compro.
more/less	più/meno

Health

I'm ill.	Mi sento male.
It hurts here.	Mi fa male qui.
I need a doctor.	Ho bisogno di un dottore/medico.
I'm pregnant.	Sono incinta.

I'm ...	Sono ...
asthmatic	asmatico/a
diabetic	diabetico/a
epileptic	epilettico/a

Emergencies

Help!	Aiuto!
Call a doctor!	Chiami un medico!
Call the police!	Chiami la polizia!
Careful!	Attenzione!
I'm lost	Mi sono perso/a
Go away!	Va' via!/Lasciami in pace!

I'm allergic ...	Sono allergico/a ...
to antibiotics	agli antibiotici
to penicillin	alla penicillina

antiseptic	antisettico
aspirin	aspirina
blister	vescica
condoms	preservativi
contraceptive	anticoncezionale
diarrhoea	diarrea
medicine	medicina
nausea	nausea
sunblock cream	crema/latte solare (per protezione)
tampons	tamponi

Time & Dates

What time is it?	Che ora è?/ Che ore sono?
It's (8 o'clock).	Sono (le otto).
When?	Quando?

in the morning	di mattina
in the afternoon	di pomeriggio
in the evening	di sera
today	oggi
tomorrow	domani
yesterday	ieri

Monday	lunedì
Tuesday	martedì
Wednesday	mercoledì
Thursday	giovedì
Friday	venerdì
Saturday	sabato
Sunday	domenica

January	gennaio
February	febbraio

March	*marzo*
April	*aprile*
May	*maggio*
June	*guigno*
July	*luglio*
August	*agosto*
September	*settembre*
October	*ottobre*
November	*novembre*
December	*dicembre*

Numbers

0	*zero*
1	*uno*
2	*due*
3	*tre*
4	*quattro*
5	*cinque*
6	*sei*
7	*sette*
8	*otto*
9	*nove*
10	*dieci*
11	*undici*
12	*dodici*
13	*tredici*
14	*quattordici*
15	*quindici*
16	*sedici*
17	*diciasette*
18	*diciotto*
19	*diciannove*
20	*venti*
21	*ventuno*
22	*ventidue*
30	*trenta*
40	*quaranta*
50	*cinquanta*
60	*sessanta*
70	*settanta*
80	*ottanta*
90	*novanta*
100	*cento*
1000	*mille*
2000	*due mila*

one million	*un milione*
quarter	*un quarto*
half	*un mezzo*

FOOD
Basics

breakfast	*prima colazione*
lunch	*pranzo*
dinner	*cena*

What is this?	*(Che) cos'è?*
I'm a vegetarian.	*Sono vegetariano/a.*
I'd like the set menu.	*Vorrei il menù turistico.*
bill/cheque	*il conto*
cover charge	*coperto*
service charge	*servizio*

bottle	*bottiglia*
cup	*tazza*
fork	*forchetta*
glass	*bicchiere*
knife	*coltello*
plate	*piatto*
spoon	*cucchiaio*
teaspoon	*cucchiaino*

Common Food & Drink

bread	*pane*
butter	*burro*
cheese	*formaggio*
coffee	*caffè*
eggs	*uova*
fruit juice	*succo di frutta*
jam	*marmellata*
milk	*latte*
mineral water	*acqua minerale*
oil	*olio*
pepper	*pepe*
rice	*riso*
salt	*sale*
sugar	*zucchero*
tea	*tè*
vinegar	*aceto*
wine	*vino*

Self Catering

baker	*fornaio/panetteria*
delicatessen	*salumeria*
greengrocer	*fruttivendolo*
grocer	*alimentari*
pastry shop	*pasticceria*
supermarket	*supermercato*

a portion of ...	*un etto di ...* (100g)
a slice of ...	*una fetta di...*

Menu Decoder
Fish & Seafood
acciughe	anchovies
calamari	squid
cozze	mussels
gamberi	prawns
pesce spada	swordfish
sarde	sardines
tonno	tuna
vongole	clams

Fruit & Nuts
albicocce	apricots
arachide	peanuts
arance	oranges
banane	bananas
castagne	chestnuts
ciliegie	cherries
fragole	strawberries
mandorle	almonds
mele	apples
noci	walnuts
noccioli	hazelnuts
pere	pears
pesche	peaches
pompelmi	grapefruit
uva	grapes

Meat & Poultry
agnello	lamb
bistecca	steak
maiale	pork
manzo	beef
pollo	chicken
prosciutto	ham
cotto/crudo	cooked/cured
salsiccia	sausage
vitello	veal

Vegetables
aglio	garlic
cipolle	onions
fagiolini	string beans
finocchio	fennel
funghi	mushrooms
melanzane	aubergines (eggplant)
patate	potatoes
pomodori	tomatoes

ON THE WALK
Clothing & Equipment
backpack	*zaino*
battery	*pila*
(walking) boots	*scarpone*
camera	*macchina fotografica*
compass	*bussola*
crampons	*ramponi/grappette*
film	*pellicola*
fleece jacket	*giubotto di pile* (as in English 'pile')
gloves	*guanti*
ice axe	*piccozza da alpinisti*
lighter	*accendino*
(walking) map	*carta*
matches	*fiammiferi*
pocket knife	*temperino*
rainjacket	*impermeabile*
sleeping bag	*sacco a pelo*
socks	*calzini*
sunglasses	*occhiali da sole*
tent	*tenda*
toilet paper	*carta igienica*
torch/flashlight	*torcia elettrica*
walking pole	*bastone da passeggio*
warm hat	*cappello di stoffa calda*
water bottle	*borraccia*

Directions & Trail Terms
How many more hours to ...?
: *Restano quante ore a ...?*

We're walking from ... to ...
: *Andiamo da ... a ...*

Does this path go to ...?
: *Questo sentiero arriva a ...?*

Can you show me on the map?
: *Può mostrarmi sulla carta?*

Where have you come from?
: *Da dove è venuto/a?*

How long does it take?
: *Ci vuole quanto tempo?*

How much snow is there on the pass?
: *Quanta neve c'è sul passo?*

Can the river be crossed?
: *Si può attraversare il fiume?*

Go straight ahead.	*Si va sempre diritto.*
Turn left.	*Gira a sinistra.*
Turn right.	*Gira a destra.*
the first left.	*il primo a sinistra*
the first right.	*il primo a destra*
direction	*direzione*
round trip	*(viaggio di) andata e ritorno*
turnoff	*bivio*
ahead	*avanti/avanti*
behind	*dietro*

in front of	davanti
opposite	di fronte a
above	sopra
below	sotto
before	prima di/davanti a
after	dopo
beginning	inizio
end	fine
downstream	a valle
upstream	a monte
flat	piatto
steep	ripido
high	alto
low	basso
near	vicino
far	lontano
beside	accanto a
between	tra
level with	alla pari di
opposite	di fronte
north	nord
south	sud
east	est
west	ovest

Weather

What's the forecast?
  Come sono le previsioni?
Tomorrow it will be ...
  Domani sarà ...

good weather	bel tempo
bad weather	brutto tempo
cold	freddo
hot	caldo
flood	alluvione
fog/mist	nebbia
ice (it's icy)	ghiaccio (è ghiacciato)
lightning	fulmine
rain (it's raining)	pioggia (piove)
snow (it's snowing)	neve (nevica)
storm	tempesta
thunderstorm	temporale
wind (it's windy)	vento (c'è vento)

Features

bend (in road)	curva
bridge	ponte
cable car	funivia
cairn	tumolo (di peitre)
farm	fattoria
fence	recinto
footbridge	passerella
ford	guado

forest	foresta/bosco
house, building	casa, edificio
hut	rifugio
path	sentiero
quarry	cava
road	strada
shelter	bivacco
signpost	cartello indicatore
spring (of water)	sorgente
town	città
tree	albero
village	frazione/paese/villagio
way marker	segnale

Landforms

avalanche	valanga
bay	baia
bog/swamp	palude
cape/headland	capo
cave	caverna/grotta
cliff	scogliera scoscesa, rupe
coast	costa
crater	cratere
gap	passo/valico
glacier	ghiacciaio
gorge	gorge
hill	collina/colle
island	isola
junction (in river or stream)	confluenza
lake	lago
landslide	frana
moraine	morena
mountain	montagna
mud	fango
pass	passo/forcella
peninsula	peninsola
plateau	altipiano
ridge	cresta
river	fiume/rio/torrente
riverbank	riva
rockfall	caduta di pietra/ caduta massi
saddle	sella
scree/talus	ghiaione
slope	versanto
snowfield	nevaio
stream	ruscello/torrente
summit/peak	cima/sommità
valley	valle/val/vallone
volcano	vulcano
waterfall	cascata

Speak a Little German

In South Tyrol and the Carnic Alps the first language of many locals is German and you're more likely to be greeted in (Austrian) German than Italian. While Italian will suffice, it certainly won't hurt to know a few greetings and trail words in German, and it may help with map references.

Basics

Hello.
Grüss Gott.
Bye.
Wiedersehn/Tschss.
Yes.
Ja.
No.
Nein.
Please.
Bitte.
Thank you (very much).
Danke (schön).
What is your name?
Wie heissen Sie?
My name is ...
Ich heisse ...
Where are you from?
Woher kommen Sie?
I'm from ...
Ich komme aus ...
I have a reservation for the rifugio/inn.
Ich habe eine Reservierung für die Hütte/ Gusthof.
How much is it per night?
Wieviel kostet es pro Nach?

Walking Talk

Is this the trail/road to ...?
Ist das der Weg/die Strasse nach ...?
Which trail goes to ...?
Welcher Weg führt nach ...?
How many kilometres to ...?
Wieviele Kilometer sind es bis ...?
Where are you going?
Wohin gehen Sie?
Is the trail safe?
Ist der Weg sicher?
Can you show me (on the map)?
Können Sie mir (auf der Karte) zeigen?
I'm looking for ...
Ich suche ...
Go straight ahead.
Gehen Sie geradeaus.

Turn left.
Biegen Sie links ab.
Turn right.
Biegen Sie rechts ab.
near/far
nahe/weit

alp hut	*Alphütte*
alp track	*Alpweg*
avalanche	*Lawine*
backpack	*Rucksack*
bridge	*Brücke*
cable car	*Luftseilbahn*
cairn	*Steinmännchen*
crampons	*Steigeisen*
crossing	*Übergang*
direction	*Richtung*
east	*Ost*
food/meal	*Speise*
gap	*Furgge/Scharte*
glacier	*Gletscher*
gorge/ravine	*Schlucht*
hut	*Hütte*
lake	*See*
map	*Landkarte*
mountain guide	*Bergführer*
north	*Nord*
path/trail	*Pfad/Wanderweg*
peak/summit	*Gipfel*
reservoir	*Stausee*
ridge	*Grat*
river	*Ufer*
rockfall	*Steinschlag*
saddle	*Joch/Sattel*
scree/talus	*Geröll*
signpost	*Wegweiser*
snow	*Schnee*
snowfield	*Firn*
south	*Süd*
stream	*Bach*
thunderstorm	*Gewitter*
valley	*Tal*
walking map	*Wanderkarte*
waterfall	*Wasserfall*
west	*West*

Glossary

AAST – Azienda Automona di Soggiorno e Turismo; local tourist office
agriturismo – farmstay, tourist accommodation on a working farm
AIG – Associazione Italiana Alberghi per la Gioventù; Italy's youth hostel association
albergo (s), **alberghi** (pl) – hotel, guesthouse
alimentari – all-purpose shop for groceries and fresh food
alluvione – flood
alm – summer grazing pastures and associated buildings
alp, alpe, alpeggio – summer base in mountain pastures for making dairy products
alpinismo – mountaineering, requiring technical skills
alta via – high level walking route
APT – Azienda di Promozione Turistica; tourist office (usually regional)
AST – Azienda Soggiorno e Turismo; local tourist office

bach – stream
baia – bay (maritime)
baita – building providing shelter, open to all, usually not at high altitudes
becca – mountain peak with pointed profile
berg – mountain
berghütte – mountain hut (see *rifugio*)
bivacco (s), **bivacchi** (pl) – remote, high mountain shelter, which may or may not be locked
bocca – mouth, entrance
bocchetta – pass, saddle, low point on a ridge
borgo (s), **borghi** (pl) – ancient town or village
bosco – woodland, forest
bussola – compass

caccia – hunting (of animals)
caduta massi – falling rocks (a common sign beside roads and some paths)
CAI – Club Alpino Italiano; Italian Alpine Club

cairn – mound of stones
cala – bay
campeggio (s), **campeggi** (pl) – camping ground with facilities
campo – field
canale, canalone – rocky Alpine gorge, valley
capo – cape (coastal)
cappella – chapel
carabinieri – police with military and civil duties
carreggiabile – accessible by vehicle
carta, cartina – map
caserma – barracks
cascata – waterfall
castello – castle
cattivo – bad (as in bad weather)
caverna – cave
chiesa – church
cima – mountain peak, summit
codula – geo or gorge (Sardinia)
colle – hill, pass
comune – town council; the local government area for which it is responsible
conca – hollow, valley
corno – mountain peak, usually steep sided
cresta, crinale – mountain ridge, the divide between streams
curva di livello – contour line

discesa – descent
dislivello – gradient; difference in altitude between two places
divieto d'accesso – keep out
divieto di sosta – no parking or stopping
doccia – shower (bathing)
dora – river (similar to a *fiume*)
dosso – rise

ENIT – Ente Nazionale Italiano per il Turismo; Italian state tourist office
EPT – Ente Provinciale per il Turismo; provincial tourist office
escursione – walk, hike, tramp
est – east

fermata – bus stop
ferrovia – train station
finestra – narrow gap or pass on a mountain ridge
fiore selvatico – wildflower
fiume – major river (larger than a *torrente*)
fonte – spring (water source)
forcella – col, saddle, low point on a ridge
frana – landslide
frazione – village
FS – Ferrovie dello Stato; Italian state railway
fulmine – lightning
fumarole – vent in a volcano from which hot gases are emitted
funivia – cable car

galleria – tunnel
GEA – Grande Escursione Appenninica; long distance route in the Apennines
gestore – manager of a *rifugio*
gettone – token, occasionally needed to operate shower at a *campeggio* or *rifugio*
ghiacciaio – glacier
gias – herders' camp (Maritime Alps)
golfo – gulf
grotta – cave
GTA – Grande Traversata delli Alpi; long distance route through foothills of the Alps
guardia forestale – forest ranger

IAT – Informazioni e Assistenza ai Turisti; local tourist office
itinerario – route rather than a formed path

joch – mountain ridge, pass from one valley to another
jôf – peak (Julian Alps)

laghetto – small lake
lago – lake
lama – very narrow mountain ridge
letto – bed
LIPU – Lega Italiana Protezione Uccelli; Italian League for the Protection of Birds
locanda – country inn, smaller than a *pensione*

malga (s), **malghe** (pl) – herders' summer hut
marcellaria – butcher's shop

meridione – south
mezza pensione – half pension, half board (dinner, bed and breakfast)
montagna – mountain
monte – mount
mouflon – mountain sheep
mulattiera – path originally used by mules, along which mules were led

nebbia – fog, mist
névé – mass of porous ice, formed from snow, that has not yet become a glacier
nord – north
nuraghi (s), **nuraghe** (pl) – cone-shaped megalithic stone fortresses (Sardinia)
nuvoloso – cloudy (weather)

occidentale – western
oratorio – wayside shrine
oriente – east
ospizi – hospices, inns
ostello per la gioventù – youth hostel
ovest – west

paese – village, small town
panetteria, pasticceria – baker, cake shop
parco naturale regionale – regional natural (nature) park
parco nazionale – national park
parete (di rocccia) – rockface
passerella – footbridge
passo – pass, crossing between two valleys
pensione – small hotel
percorso – route
pericolosissimo – very dangerous
pericoloso – dangerous
pian, piano – plain, fairly level area
piazza – town square
pieve – parish church
pineta – pine forest
pioggia – rain
piovoso – wet (weather)
ponte – bridge
posto tappa – place to stay at the end of a day's walk, especially on a long-distance path
prato – meadow, flat grassy area
previsioni del tempo – weather forecast
Pro Loco – small local tourist office
proprietà privata – private property
punta – mountain peak

quota – altitude, height above sea level

ramponi – crampons, spiked metal frames strapped to boots for walking or climbing on ice or snow

ricovero – fairly basic shelter in mountain areas

rifugio (s), **rifugi** (pl) – mountain hut, similar to a simple hotel, often with bunkrooms

rio – river (smaller than a *fiume*, similar to a *torrente*)

riva – river bank

rovina, rudere – ruin(s) of a building

salita – climb, ascent

scarpone – walking/hiking/mountain boots

scharte – gap, low point on ridge

scorciatoia – shortcut

scree – accumulated rock fragments at the foot of a cliff or across a mountainside

seggiovia – chair lift

segnale, segnaletica – signposting

sentiero (s), **sentieri** (pl) – footpath or defined walking route on formed path

settentrionale – northern

SI – Sentiero Italia; long-distance route through Italy

soccorso – help, assistance

soccorso alpino – mountain rescue

sopra – upper

sorgente – spring, often of mineral water

sotto – lower

spitze – mountain peak with pointed profile

strada – street, road

sud – south

tabaccheria – tobacconist, all-purpose shop where bus tickets are sold

TCI – Touring Club Italiano

tempesta – storm

tempo – weather

tempo di percorrenza – time needed to complete a walk

temporale – thunderstorm

terme – thermal baths

testa – mountain resembling a head in shape or position

tetti – small group of houses, hamlet

torre – tower, fortified tower-like building

torrente – small river, stream

trattoria – cheap restaurant

UIT – Ufficio Informazioni Turistiche

Unesco – United Nations Educational, Scientific & Cultural Organisation

val, valle – valley

valanga – avalanche

Valdostane – particular to Valle d'Aosta

vallone – deep or large valley

vedretta – hanging glacier

vento – wind

vetta – mountain peak

via – street, road

via ferrata (s), **vie ferrate** (pl) – very steep route over rock equipped with fixed cables, ladders, bridges and/or metal rungs

via normale – normal route

wald – forest

zaino – rucksack

LONELY PLANET

You already know that Lonely Planet produces more than this one guidebook, but you might not be aware of the other products we have on this region. Here is a selection of titles that you may want to check out as well:

Italy
ISBN 1 86450 352 1
US$24.99 • UK£14.99

World Food Italy
ISBN 1 86450 022 0
US$12.95 • UK£7.99

French phrasebook
ISBN 1 86450 152 9
US$7.99 • UK£3.99

Sicily
ISBN 1 74059 031 7
US$16.99 • UK£10.99

Tuscanny
ISBN 1 86450 357 2
US$11.99 • UK£5.99

Cycling Italy
ISBN 1 74059 315 4
US$21.99 • UK£14.99

Rome Condensed
ISBN 1 86450 360 2
US$29.99 • UK£17.99

Walking in France
ISBN 0 86442 601 1
US$19.99 • UK£12.99

Walking in Swtizerland
ISBN 0 86442 737 9
US$19.99 • UK£12.99

Western Europe
ISBN 1 74059 313 8
US$27.99 • UK£16.99

Mediterranean Europe
ISBN 1 74059 302 2
US$27.99 • UK£16.99

Read This First: Europe
ISBN 1 86450 136 7
US$14.99 • UK£8.99

Available wherever books are sold

Lonely Planet Guides by Region

onely Planet is known worldwide for publishing practical, reliable and no-nonsense travel information in our guides and on our Web site. The Lonely Planet list covers just about every accessible part of the world. Currently there are 16 series: Travel guides, Shoestring guides, Condensed guides, Phrasebooks, Read This First, Healthy Travel, Walking guides, Cycling guides, Watching Wildlife guides, Pisces Diving & Snorkeling guides, City Maps, Road Atlases, Out to Eat, World Food, Journeys travel literature and Pictorials.

AFRICA Africa on a shoestring • Botswana • Cairo • Cairo City Map • Cape Town • Cape Town City Map • East Africa • Egypt • Egyptian Arabic phrasebook • Ethiopia, Eritrea & Djibouti • Ethiopian Amharic phrasebook • The Gambia & Senegal • Healthy Travel Africa • Kenya • Malawi • Morocco • Moroccan Arabic phrasebook • Mozambique • Namibia • Read This First: Africa • South Africa, Lesotho & Swaziland • Southern Africa • Southern Africa Road Atlas • Swahili phrasebook • Tanzania, Zanzibar & Pemba • Trekking in East Africa • Tunisia • Watching Wildlife East Africa • Watching Wildlife Southern Africa • West Africa • World Food Morocco • Zambia • Zimbabwe, Botswana & Namibia
Travel Literature: Mali Blues: Traveling to an African Beat • The Rainbird: A Central African Journey • Songs to an African Sunset: A Zimbabwean Story

AUSTRALIA & THE PACIFIC Aboriginal Australia & the Torres Strait Islands •Auckland • Australia • Australian phrasebook • Australia Road Atlas • Cycling Australia • Cycling New Zealand • Fiji • Fijian phrasebook • Healthy Travel Australia, NZ & the Pacific • Islands of Australia's Great Barrier Reef • Melbourne • Melbourne City Map • Micronesia • New Caledonia • New South Wales • New Zealand • Northern Territory • Outback Australia • Out to Eat – Melbourne • Out to Eat – Sydney • Papua New Guinea • Pidgin phrasebook • Queensland • Rarotonga & the Cook Islands • Samoa • Solomon Islands • South Australia • South Pacific • South Pacific phrasebook • Sydney • Sydney City Map • Sydney Condensed • Tahiti & French Polynesia • Tasmania • Tonga • Tramping in New Zealand • Vanuatu • Victoria • Walking in Australia • Watching Wildlife Australia • Western Australia
Travel Literature: Islands in the Clouds: Travels in the Highlands of New Guinea • Kiwi Tracks: A New Zealand Journey • Sean & David's Long Drive

CENTRAL AMERICA & THE CARIBBEAN Bahamas, Turks & Caicos • Baja California • Belize, Guatemala & Yucatán • Bermuda • Central America on a shoestring • Costa Rica • Costa Rica Spanish phrasebook • Cuba • Cycling Cuba • Dominican Republic & Haiti • Eastern Caribbean • Guatemala • Havana • Healthy Travel Central & South America • Jamaica • Mexico • Mexico City • Panama • Puerto Rico • Read This First: Central & South America • Virgin Islands • World Food Caribbean • World Food Mexico • Yucatán
Travel Literature: Green Dreams: Travels in Central America

EUROPE Amsterdam • Amsterdam City Map • Amsterdam Condensed • Andalucía • Athens • Austria • Baltic States phrasebook • Barcelona • Barcelona City Map • Belgium & Luxembourg • Berlin • Berlin City Map • Britain • British phrasebook • Brussels, Bruges & Antwerp • Brussels City Map • Budapest • Budapest City Map • Canary Islands • Catalunya & the Costa Brava • Central Europe • Central Europe phrasebook • Copenhagen • Corfu & the Ionians • Corsica • Crete • Crete Condensed • Croatia • Cycling Britain • Cycling France • Cyprus • Czech & Slovak Republics • Czech phrasebook • Denmark • Dublin • Dublin City Map • Dublin Condensed • Eastern Europe • Eastern Europe phrasebook • Edinburgh • Edinburgh City Map • England • Estonia, Latvia & Lithuania • Europe on a shoestring • Europe phrasebook • Finland • Florence • Florence City Map • France • Frankfurt City Map • Frankfurt Condensed • French phrasebook • Georgia, Armenia & Azerbaijan • Germany • German phrasebook • Greece • Greek Islands • Greek phrasebook • Hungary • Iceland, Greenland & the Faroe Islands • Ireland • Italian phrasebook • Italy • Kraków • Lisbon • The Loire • London • London City Map • London Condensed • Madrid • Madrid City Map • Malta • Mediterranean Europe • Milan, Turin & Genoa • Moscow • Munich • Netherlands • Normandy • Norway • Out to Eat – London • Out to Eat – Paris • Paris • Paris City Map • Paris Condensed • Poland • Polish phrasebook • Portugal • Portuguese phrasebook • Prague • Prague City Map • Provence & the Côte d'Azur • Read This First: Europe • Rhodes & the Dodecanese • Romania & Moldova • Rome • Rome City Map • Rome Condensed • Russia, Ukraine & Belarus • Russian phrasebook • Scandinavian & Baltic Europe • Scandinavian phrasebook • Scotland • Sicily • Slovenia • South-West France • Spain • Spanish phrasebook • Stockholm • St Petersburg • St Petersburg City Map • Sweden • Switzerland • Tuscany • Ukrainian phrasebook • Venice • Vienna • Wales • Walking in Britain • Walking in France • Walking in Ireland • Walking in Italy • Walking in Scotland • Walking in Spain • Walking in Switzerland • Western Europe • World Food France • World Food Greece • World Food Ireland • World Food Italy • World Food Spain **Travel Literature:** After Yugoslavia • Love and War in the Apennines • The Olive Grove: Travels in Greece • On the Shores of the Mediterranean • Round Ireland in Low Gear • A Small Place in Italy

Lonely Planet Mail Order

onely Planet products are distributed worldwide. They are also available by mail order from Lonely Planet, so if you have difficulty finding a title please write to us. North and South American residents should write to 150 Linden St, Oakland, CA 94607, USA; European and African residents should write to 10a Spring Place, London NW5 3BH, UK; and residents of other countries to Locked Bag 1, Footscray, Victoria 3011, Australia.

INDIAN SUBCONTINENT & THE INDIAN OCEAN Bangladesh • Bengali phrasebook • Bhutan • Delhi • Goa • Healthy Travel Asia & India • Hindi & Urdu phrasebook • India • India & Bangladesh City Map • Indian Himalaya • Karakoram Highway • Kathmandu City Map • Kerala • Madagascar • Maldives • Mauritius, Réunion & Seychelles • Mumbai (Bombay) • Nepal • Nepali phrasebook • North India • Pakistan • Rajasthan • Read This First: Asia & India • South India • Sri Lanka • Sri Lanka phrasebook • Tibet • Tibetan phrasebook • Trekking in the Indian Himalaya • Trekking in the Karakoram & Hindukush • Trekking in the Nepal Himalaya • World Food India **Travel Literature:** The Age of Kali: Indian Travels and Encounters • Hello Goodnight: A Life of Goa • In Rajasthan • Maverick in Madagascar • A Season in Heaven: True Tales from the Road to Kathmandu • Shopping for Buddhas • A Short Walk in the Hindu Kush • Slowly Down the Ganges

MIDDLE EAST & CENTRAL ASIA Bahrain, Kuwait & Qatar • Central Asia • Central Asia phrasebook • Dubai • Farsi (Persian) phrasebook • Hebrew phrasebook • Iran • Israel & the Palestinian Territories • Istanbul • Istanbul City Map • Istanbul to Cairo • Istanbul to Kathmandu • Jerusalem • Jerusalem City Map • Jordan • Lebanon • Middle East • Oman & the United Arab Emirates • Syria • Turkey • Turkish phrasebook • World Food Turkey • Yemen **Travel Literature:** Black on Black: Iran Revisited • Breaking Ranks: Turbulent Travels in the Promised Land • The Gates of Damascus • Kingdom of the Film Stars: Journey into Jordan

NORTH AMERICA Alaska • Boston • Boston City Map • Boston Condensed • British Columbia • California & Nevada • California Condensed • Canada • Chicago • Chicago City Map • Chicago Condensed • Florida • Georgia & the Carolinas • Great Lakes • Hawaii • Hiking in Alaska • Hiking in the USA • Honolulu & Oahu City Map • Las Vegas • Los Angeles • Los Angeles City Map • Louisiana & the Deep South • Miami • Miami City Map • Montreal • New England • New Orleans • New Orleans City Map • New York City • New York City Map • New York City Condensed • New York, New Jersey & Pennsylvania • Oahu • Out to Eat – San Francisco • Pacific Northwest • Rocky Mountains • San Diego & Tijuana • San Francisco • San Francisco City Map • Seattle • Seattle City Map • Southwest • Texas • Toronto • USA • USA phrasebook • Vancouver • Vancouver City Map • Virginia & the Capital Region • Washington, DC • Washington, DC City Map • World Food New Orleans **Travel Literature:** Caught Inside: A Surfer's Year on the California Coast • Drive Thru America

NORTH-EAST ASIA Beijing • Beijing City Map • Cantonese phrasebook • China • Hiking in Japan • Hong Kong & Macau • Hong Kong City Map • Hong Kong Condensed • Japan • Japanese phrasebook • Korea • Korean phrasebook • Kyoto • Mandarin phrasebook • Mongolia • Mongolian phrasebook • Seoul • Shanghai • South-West China • Taiwan • Tokyo • Tokyo Condensed • World Food Hong Kong • World Food Japan **Travel Literature:** In Xanadu: A Quest • Lost Japan

SOUTH AMERICA Argentina, Uruguay & Paraguay • Bolivia • Brazil • Brazilian phrasebook • Buenos Aires • Buenos Aires City Map • Chile & Easter Island • Colombia • Ecuador & the Galapagos Islands • Healthy Travel Central & South America • Latin American Spanish phrasebook • Peru • Quechua phrasebook • Read This First: Central & South America • Rio de Janeiro • Rio de Janeiro City Map • Santiago de Chile • South America on a shoestring • Trekking in the Patagonian Andes • Venezuela **Travel Literature:** Full Circle: A South American Journey

SOUTH-EAST ASIA Bali & Lombok • Bangkok • Bangkok City Map • Burmese phrasebook • Cambodia • Cycling Vietnam, Laos & Cambodia • East Timor phrasebook • Hanoi • Healthy Travel Asia & India • Hill Tribes phrasebook • Ho Chi Minh City (Saigon) • Indonesia • Indonesian phrasebook • Indonesia's Eastern Islands • Java • Lao phrasebook • Laos • Malay phrasebook • Malaysia, Singapore & Brunei • Myanmar (Burma) • Philippines • Pilipino (Tagalog) phrasebook • Read This First: Asia & India • Singapore • Singapore City Map • South-East Asia on a shoestring • South-East Asia phrasebook • Thailand • Thailand's Islands & Beaches • Thailand, Vietnam, Laos & Cambodia Road Atlas • Thai phrasebook • Vietnam • Vietnamese phrasebook • World Food Indonesia • World Food Thailand • World Food Vietnam

ALSO AVAILABLE: Antarctica • The Arctic • The Blue Man: Tales of Travel, Love and Coffee • Brief Encounters: Stories of Love, Sex & Travel • Buddhist Stupas in Asia: The Shape of Perfection • Chasing Rickshaws • The Last Grain Race • Lonely Planet ... On the Edge: Adventurous Escapades from Around the World • Lonely Planet Unpacked • Lonely Planet Unpacked Again • Not the Only Planet: Science Fiction Travel Stories • Ports of Call: A Journey by Sea • Sacred India • Travel Photography: A Guide to Taking Better Pictures • Travel with Children • Tuvalu: Portrait of an Island Nation

Index

Bold indicates maps.
or a full list of maps, see the
  map index (p8).
or a full list of walks, see the
  walks table (pp4-7).

LONELY PLANET OFFICES

Australia
Locked Bag 1, Footscray, Victoria 3011
☎ 03-8379 8000 fax 03-8379 8111
✉ talk2us@lonelyplanet.com.au

USA
150 Linden St, Oakland, CA 94607
☎ 510-893-8555 or ☎ 800-275-8555 (toll free)
fax 510-893-8572
✉ info@lonelyplanet.com

UK
10a Spring Place, London NW5 3BH
☎ 020-7428 4800 fax 020-7428 4828
✉ go@lonelyplanet.co.uk

France
1 rue du Dahomey, 75011 Paris
☎ 01 55 25 33 00 fax 01 55 25 33 01
✉ bip@lonelyplanet.fr
w www.lonelyplanet.fr

World Wide Web: w www.lonelyplanet.com or AOL keyword: lp
Lonely Planet Images: ✉ lpi@lonelyplanet.com.au